Ninth Edition

D0211827

Accounting Information Systems:
A Practitioner Emphasis

Cynthia D. Heagy
University of Houston-Clear Lake

Constance M. Lehmann
University of Houston-Clear Lake

 TEXTBOOK\MEDIA

The Quality Instructors Expect.
At Prices Students Can Afford.

Replacing Oligarch Textbooks since 2004

Accounting Information Systems:
A Practitioner Emphasis/9e
Cynthia D. Heagy
Constance M. Lehmann

Copyright © 2017 Textbook Media Press

ISBN: 978-0-9969962-5-9

All rights reserved.
No part of this work covered by the copyright hereon may be reproduced or used in any form or by any means—graphic, electronic, or mechanical, including photocopying, recording, taping, Web distribution, or information storage and retrieval systems—without the prior written permission of the publisher.

For more information, contact:
Textbook Media Press
1808 Dayton Avenue
Saint Paul, MN 55104

Or you can visit our Internet site at
http://www.textbookmedia.com or write info@textbookmedia.com

For permission to use material from this text or product, submit a request online at
info@textbookmedia.com

Textbook Media Press is a Minnesota-based educational publisher. We deliver textbooks and supplements with the quality instructors expect, while providing students with unique media options at uniquely affordable prices.

Brief Contents

Contents

Batch versus Real-Time Posting 81

4 Data Flows, Activities, and Structure of Accounting Systems 87

5 Reporting Process, Coding Methods, and Audit Trails 131

6 Internal Control and Risk Assessment 159

14 Big Data and Data Analytics

Preface

A Message to Students

Students, this accounting information systems course is unlike any other accounting course you have taken. Accounting Information Systems (AIS) has become an integral part of business operations, and your knowledge of how systems work and interact with business processes, combined with your expertise of internal controls, gives you an advantage over other business majors—and even some accounting majors! The IT audit/security professions are booming, salaries are skyrocketing, and this course will give you an introduction into this exciting and growing area.

Our goal in writing this book includes providing you with an understanding of business processes (i.e., revenue, procurement, inventory, and financial processes), risk identification and internal controls, and the use of information from accounting information systems. We write this book to you, assuming that you have had little or no exposure to AIS. What makes this course unique is that you step away from debits and credits, which are the focus of many accounting courses. We focus on how accounting events are processed and how the information from those events is used in decision making. As an accountant, auditor, or security professional, your knowledge of AIS will take your accounting knowledge to the next level by allowing you to be a consultant to management in areas such as operational efficiencies, reporting, and compliance with regulations.

If you are interested in certifications, AIS topics are included on several certification exams. This includes the Certified Public Accountant (CPA) exam, where the percentage of the exam requiring knowledge of systems has increased as the exam has changed in recent years. Knowledge of systems is essential to passing the Certified Information Systems Auditor (CISA) exam, an internationally recognized certification that is often more valued in the IT audit profession than the CPA certification! Other certifications, such as the Certified Internal Auditor (CIA), also require knowledge of systems and controls. Public accounting firms (e.g., external auditors and consultants) and industry employers (e.g., internal auditors and accountants) expect employees with accounting degrees to be fluent in the language of systems (note: this does *not* mean you will be programming code!). As an auditor or accountant, you can bridge the communications gap between IT and management with knowledge of AIS. An understanding of risk assessment and internal controls gives the accounting major expertise valued by management in the monitoring of system and information security.

We start each chapter with an introductory scenario related to the chapter topics. These scenarios are meant to help you get a sense of how the topic areas in the chapter relate to "real life" situations. The thought questions included with the scenarios help you consider the issues described in the scenario so you get an idea of how to apply the chapter material.

Ralph Waldo Emerson said, "The man [or woman] who can make hard things easy is the educator." In writing this book, we tried our best to be educators.

A Message to Instructors

This textbook is intended to meet the needs of a first course in accounting information systems at either the undergraduate or graduate level. It may also be used as a review text in second or subsequent courses in this area. Instructor resources include a solutions manual, PowerPoint slides, and a test bank for each chapter. The test items are available in two formats, Word files or on a test CD (Diploma software by Blackboard).

This ninth edition continues a primary objective of all previous editions, which is to present the accounting information systems knowledge students need to make them more marketable in the accounting profession. We recognize that most accounting systems are licensed from third party software vendors rather than developed internally. So instead of devoting several chapters to systems analysis and design, as many traditional accounting systems textbook do, we focus on helping students understand the fundamentals of an accounting system to make them better users, auditors, and consultants.

We give the students an understanding of events-based accounting, what the business processes are, how an accounting system integrates all the data from the business processes, the reports and financial statements that should be produced by the system for managing an organization and for meeting its external reporting requirements, the internal controls essential to a good accounting system, how systems based on databases work, and the issue of big data and data analytics.

Another objective in writing this edition was to make the material student friendly. Therefore, we took great care in directing our words to the students. Recognizing this is their first introduction to accounting systems, we included clear definitions of terms (and included a glossary) and incorporated numerous examples and illustrations to explain the material.

The book consists of fourteen chapters. With each edition we try to incorporate the most essential accounting systems material so students can benefit from covering the entire book in one semester. Each chapter begins with an Introductory Scenario to help students understand the relevance of the material they are about to study to the real world. Interspersed throughout several of the chapters are vignettes to again bring in real-world relevance of particular topics.

Because students learn best by doing, we have included several hands-on learning activities at the end of many chapters. These activities require students to apply the theoretical knowledge from the chapter to solve practical problems. We realize the importance of using cases in the course. The introductory scenarios and vignettes can be assigned as cases. We have included "thought questions" at the end of the scenarios and vignettes for the benefit of instructors wishing to make use of cases in their classes. (Suggested answers to the questions are included in the instructor materials.)

A common difficulty in teaching the AIS course is that students are unfamiliar with the documents, reports, and activities associated with an accounting system. Although students were exposed to these in other accounting courses, these were not the main focus and may have been only partially retained. Therefore, we thought it was important to do something early in the course that would (a) provide students with a familiar context in which to understand the issues of computerized accounting systems and (b) bring all students up to the same level before adding on more layers of knowledge. We wrote Chapter 3 for these purposes. It reviews the essential elements and basic activities of paper-based accounting systems, introduces the essential elements and basic activities of computerized accounting systems, and compares the two. Students have responded to this chapter with gratitude for reviewing issues that they had not previously considered as "accounting systems" related, and non-accounting students have expressed appreciation for reviewing accounting issues that they must know to fully understand accounting information systems.

The first chapter captures the interest of the students by stressing the importance of this course to a successful career in accounting regardless of the accounting specialty students may choose. Chapter 2 gives students the knowledge they need to enable them to read and prepare systems documentation. Chapter 3, as previously discussed, gives students a context in which to anchor what they will be learning in the course. It gives instructors comfort that we have covered some basics so that we will then be dealing with a fairly homogenous group of students. After giving students an understanding of the data flows, functions, and structure of an accounting system in Chapter 4, the general reporting principles and coding methods that form a foundation for effective reporting and audit trails are covered in

Chapter 5. A comprehensive coverage of internal control is included in Chapters 6 and 7. These chapters are built around the concepts reflected in the COSO 2013 Internal Control–Integrated Framework, the Institute of Internal Auditors Research Foundation's *Systems Auditability and Control Report*, the Information Systems Audit and Control Foundation's *Control Objectives for Information and Related Technology* (COBIT), and several standards issued by the American Institute of Certified Public Accountants. These include *Statement on Standards for Attestation Engagements (SSAE) 16: Reporting on Controls at a Service Organization, Service Organization Control Reports (SOC-1, SOC-2, SOC-3), SAS 94, SAS 99, and SAS 109*. These chapters stress compliance with the Sarbanes-Oxley Act. IT auditing, IT governance, and cybersecurity are integral parts of these chapters.

The financial, revenue, procurement, and inventory processes are covered in Chapters 8–11. These chapters introduce students to the activities, data flows, functions, coding systems, reporting, special accounting requirements, and internal controls peculiar to each process. Because most accounting systems are based on database management systems, Chapters 12 and 13 discuss how accounting data are stored and retrieved using database technology.

Chapter 14 is a new chapter that introduces the topics of "big data" and data analytics. The need for professionals with the skills to analyze large data sets is growing rapidly. Big data is changing the way we think about who is using the data we generate through our use of technology and how that data are being used. The massive quantities of data being generated, coupled with advances in the services offered by cloud computing providers, suggests that accounting professionals need to be aware of these important topics. This includes an understanding of the impacts and benefits of utilizing big data, as well as risks and controls that should be considered when collecting and analyzing big data.

About the Authors

Cynthia D. Heagy, DBA, CPA, CMA, CNA. She earned her doctoral and masters degrees from the University of Memphis. Dr. Heagy entered higher education after working as a wealth management officer at a large national bank and later as a systems analyst. Dr. Heagy has published in several professional and academic journals, including *Journal of Information Systems, Advances in Accounting Education, Journal of the Academy of Business Education, Compendium of Classroom Cases and Tools for AIS Applications, The Journal of Accountancy, Issues in Accounting Education, International Journal of Accounting, Journal of Cost Management, Journal of Accounting Education, Accounting Educators' Journal, EDP Auditing, Data Security Management, The Journal of Accounting Case Research, The CPA Journal, Journal of Accounting and Computers,* and *The Accounting Systems Journal.* She is coauthor of *Principles of Bank Accounting and Reporting,* published by the American Bankers Association.

Constance M. Lehmann, PhD, CISA, is an associate professor of accounting at the University of Houston–Clear Lake. She earned her PhD from Texas A&M University and her MBA from University of Texas at San Antonio. Dr. Lehmann entered higher education after working as an internal auditor and branch manager for financial institutions including the Federal Reserve Bank (San Antonio branch) and various savings and loans in the San Antonio area. Dr. Lehmann has published in several professional and academic journals, including *Behavioral Research in Accounting, Journal of Information Systems, Advances in Accounting Education, Journal of Education for Business, Journal of Accounting Education, Internal Auditing Journal, Issues in Accounting Education, AIS Educator Journal, Journal of Forensic and Investigative Accounting,* and *Journal of Financial Education.* Dr. Lehmann is an active member of the Greater Houston ISACA chapter, and has been a faculty advisor for the University of Houston–Clear Lake ISACA/ACFE Student Group.

C.D.H.
C.M.L.

Significance of Accounting Information Systems and the Accountant's Role

Source: Zadorozhnyi Viktor/Shutterstock.

Learning Objectives

After studying this chapter, you should be able to:

- Explain the nature of accounting data, who needs it, and why.
- Describe the nature, scope, and importance of accounting information systems.
- Explain why accounting information systems should be studied regardless of the accounting specialty you may choose.

Source: GaudiLab/Shutterstock.

"So you see, Jennifer, I feel really good about the growth of the business over the last 4 years. Since I bought the three restaurants, sales and profits have completely turned around. Two of the managers have worked very hard, putting in 60- to 70-hour weeks, and the manager who replaced Barker has also put his back into the job. They have all responded to the new leadership and like our new image. From 'breakfast any time' joints frequented mostly by truck drivers, we have upgraded the facilities to attract families eating out because both parents work. The 'come for seconds' buffet lines we set up in the evenings have proved to be a great success. We were able to cut back on staff requirements as well as let people see the food they are going to eat. Yes, a few folks abuse the privilege, but waste has been quite a bit lower than we expected.

"When I bought out the Sabatino sisters, they were $55,000 in debt and losing $3,500 a month. The first year, I paid off most of the debt, spent $180,000 to spruce up the restaurants, and almost broke even. We had a setback when we found that Barker was letting his friends eat for free— and there were a few other things he did that I never told you about, but since he left, we haven't had many problems. And I really appreciate what you have done for us. The Sabatinos kept their own books and, as you know, made a real mess of them. I still don't know how you managed to prepare that first P and L—uh, income statement. But I knew that we had to bring in an accountant, and I'm pleased with the work you've done for us.

"But all this leads up to what I wanted to ask you. So far you've done our taxes and prepared those financials for the bank. But we badly need a new accounting system here in the restaurants. I write the checks and take the cash deposits to the bank, but I really don't know what's going on until the end of the year. We carry a substantial inventory of canned and packaged foods and soft drinks. We always have a bunch of bills outstanding. And there is that depreciation on the new kitchen equipment, serving counters, and furniture—not to mention the two vans we bought for deliveries. I know I could ask you for quarterly statements, but that still wouldn't solve my problem. I need to be able to see how we are doing on a week-by-week basis.

"I've thought about putting a computer in the office. My staff could punch in the food and drinks when they are received and when they are used. At the end of the day, they could key in the day's receipts from the cash-register tapes. Perhaps we could use it to run the payroll. The computer might even help you because I could give you more than just our check stubs and an old shoe box full of receipts. A couple of weeks ago, I looked at some computers in an electronics store and they weren't expensive. But someone said that I would need software as well. Could we use Excel, Quickbooks, or Visual Basic for that? So much software is out there, and I don't know what we need. Can you take care of this sort of thing?"

"Sure, Marshall, I'm glad you brought this up. The important thing is to get an accounting software package for your kind of business—the restaurant business. You don't want to see stuff on the screen like 'Enter your factory overhead rate' but you must be able to account for tips for the IRS. I think I can hook your cash registers up to the computer. Then, your daily sales data would be entered automatically. This would save us the job of keying in all the data and prevent mistakes too. First, we'll need to spend 2 to 3 hours discussing exactly what you want the new system to do for you. Then, I'll research accounting systems software and make some recommendations to you. After we decide on the software, I'll work on a timetable for implementing the system."

Introductory Scenario Thought Questions:

1. What are some examples of non-accounting data that Marshall might need to appropriately monitor the day-to-day activities in his restaurants?
2. If you were Marshall, what types of concerns would you want to be sure to bring up with the accountant?
3. If you were the accountant, what information would you want to know about Marshall's situation?
4. What is the primary reason that the owner of the restaurant wants a new accounting system?

Accounting Information

What Are Accounting Data?

Review the information below. These items are all examples of **accounting information**.

LEARNING OBJECTIVE 1
Explain the nature of accounting data, who needs it, and why.

Net income for the year is $24,965,831.

Gross pay: $593.80 Deductions: $185.29 Net pay: $408.51

It costs $50,000 a year just to have our staff standing in line to use the copying machine.

Direct materials	$10.45
Direct labor	$2.85
Manufacturing overhead	$18.20
Total manufacturing cost per unit	$31.50

Accounting information
Information that meets the legitimate needs of external users, communicates among parties transacting business with one another, and provides a basis for informed management decisions. It can be expressed in monetary terms as well as ratios, percentages, or units and includes any data that are either directly or indirectly reflected in the financial statements whether in this or in future periods.

Next year's sales budget is $105,560,000.

Delivery equipment	$1,268,800	
Less accumulated depreciation	$ 284,700	$984,100

Joe worked 42 hours this week.

If we close the Bridgeton plant, we will save $5,500,000 in avoidable operating costs but will lose $7,200,000 in company-wide revenue.

Total current assets: $3,599,704

$25,000 was transferred to the special assessment fund.

We turn our inventory over 3.2 times per year, compared with an industry average of 4 times.

Pay this amount: $804,525.10

The new product will break even at a volume of 2,700 units per week.

Total direct labor hours this month	32,482
Total indirect labor hours this month	8,836
Total base rate hours this month	30,883
Total overtime hours this month	10,435

A new computer-controlled milling machine will provide a tax shield of $245,000 in its first year.

Unfilled sales orders: $285,095

Corporate overhead is applied at a rate of 15 percent of segment margin.

Over the last 2 years, our manufacturing reject rate has decreased from 2 percent of total output to less than 0.2 percent.

Accounts receivable	$33,050	
Allowance for uncollectible accounts	$ 661	$32,389

Costs are applied at a rate of $42.75 per customer service inquiry.

Two hundred bushels of apples were ordered for the produce department.

While most of the information is expressed in traditional monetary terms, some is expressed as ratios, percentages, or units. Traditionally, accountants have limited their concern to monetary amounts. This was understandable for the era of manual accounting systems because the cost of capturing and processing data was far more expensive than is the case today. But a contemporary view of accounting must expand to include any data that are either directly or indirectly reflected in the financial statements whether in this or in future accounting periods. Thus, hours worked, units processed or even planned, employee vacation days earned, and customer telephone numbers are all data that are captured, processed, stored, and reported by the accounting system, and represent information used for decision making by managers.

Who Needs Accounting Information?

Accounting information meets the legitimate needs of external users, communicates among parties transacting business with one another, and provides a basis for informed management decision making. The external financial statements—presently consisting of the balance sheet, the income statement, the statement of changes in ownership equity, and the cash flow statement—are prepared for investors, creditors, labor unions, suppliers, customers, and other outside parties. Financial statements are routinely read and analyzed by stockbrokers and financial analysts. In the United States, corporations with securities listed on national exchanges are required to file 10K reports annually with the Securities and Exchange Commission (SEC). Also, organizations in certain industries, such as insurance, are required to file routine reports with government regulatory bodies. Tax returns must be filed with federal, state, and, in some cases, local revenue authorities.

Accounting information of a different nature provides a basis for an organization's transactions with its vendors, customers, and employees. An organization purchases goods and services from vendors (suppliers) and purchases services from employees. The organization may then sell goods and/or services to customers. Accounting information communicates the need for these goods and services, requests payment, and facilitates the transfer of cash. Checks serve a dual purpose—providing accounting information and also disbursing cash. In addition to their paychecks, employees routinely receive statements on tax withholdings and may also receive reports on sick leave, insurance, and retirement account information.

The advent of e-commerce has led many companies to reduce the number of suppliers and/or customers with whom they do business. On the other hand, closer relationships have developed between companies and outside parties. Thus, many companies grant their suppliers and customers significant access to their computerized accounting systems. For example, sellers may interrogate their customers' records, ascertain that certain inventory items are low, and then ship goods, notifying the customer of the expected arrival date. These relationships are clearly defined in written contracts, with customers and suppliers often referred to as **trading partners** (Vignette 1.1).

Trading partners Two or more participants in a business relationship.

Contemporary accounting information systems include data that could not be economically collected before the current level of computerization. For example, a hospital system may input pollen readings in order to schedule the hours of allergy physicians in the outpatient clinic; such scheduling feeds into the daily/weekly cash budgeting (both revenues and expenses). When there is a significant delay between order receipt and fulfillment, the manager of a manufacturer's sales force will find a weekly report of sales orders by salesperson to be more useful than sales reports. The sales order report will indicate what each salesperson accomplished last week, while a report of shipped sales may indicate what they did three months ago. Sales reports are more accurate, but sales orders are more relevant. Accounting systems should support statistical accounts so that physical data such as barrels, tons, or hours worked can be accumulated and reported. To properly serve management, accounting system designers must remove the blinders that restrict our vision to only dollar-denominated data representing only consummated transactions. Rather, accounting systems should be designed to collect, process, and report any physical or dollar-denominated data that are useful for enterprise management.

The largest volume of accounting information is prepared for managers at all levels in an organization. Some first-level managers require detailed accounting data on day-to-day operations. Middle managers require somewhat broader data for control and performance evaluation responsibilities, and upper managers require accounting data with the broadest

---

Vignette 1.1

Trading Partner Relationships

GenMart, a nationwide retailer of general merchandise, has numerous domestic and international suppliers. Ten years ago GenMart had approximately 4,600 suppliers, with many providing competitive goods. Purchasing and scheduling delivery of merchandise required about 100 employees, and competitive bids were taken for each significant order. As a cost reduction, the number of suppliers was reduced to 1,700 and all were required, with GenMart's assistance, to implement electronic data interchange (EDI) as a means of automating sales to GenMart. Today, EDI has been implemented between GenMart and 99 percent of its suppliers and represents all except 0.3 percent of purchasing dollar volume.

Unit sales by product and store are collected by GenMart's corporate headquarters daily and placed in computer files accessible to most suppliers' computers each morning between 2 and 6 A.M. Thus, these suppliers maintain a record of GenMart inventory and sales by item and by store and are responsible for inventory replenishment at each store. The supplier is held responsible for stockouts and, in the extreme, business with that supplier may be discontinued. When significant overstocking occurs, a formula

agreed upon by GenMart and the supplier may result in penalty charge-backs to the supplier. Long-term negotiated contracts with suppliers have largely displaced competitive bidding. In spite of a fourfold increase in volume, the number of employees in purchasing and merchandise logistics has been cut by 50 percent. Suppliers no longer invoice GenMart. Rather, payments for purchases are based on quantities of merchandise received. Approval of payments to suppliers is entered in GenMart's computer, which then dials their bank's computer system, and directs cash transfers to the suppliers. Such electronic funds transfer (EFT) ordinarily occurs within 48 hours after merchandise is received. Because the receipt of merchandise is entered into GenMart's computer systems on the receiving dock, no paperwork exists for the purchasing function.

THOUGHT QUESTIONS

1. What are some of the benefits of reducing the number of suppliers?

2. What are some of the advantages of having electronic data interchanges (EDI) and electronic funds transfer (EFT) systems?

---

perspective for strategic management. Accounting data include historical data and estimates, budgets, and projections.

The role of accountants and accounting data in support of continuing operations and performance evaluation are widely recognized. However, the notion that accounting information can or should play a role in strategic management is comparatively new. An increasing number of large organizations recognize that financial—and particularly cost—information concerning the organization's product and its competitors' products are essential for the development of successful strategies. An organization's strategies are attainable only if goods and services can be produced at costs comparable to or less than those of its competitors. Accountants can provide valuable estimates of the effects of a strategy, such as diversification, and can then monitor the actual effects over time. For this purpose, accountants must extend the accumulation and analysis of cost data beyond the limits of the immediate organizational boundaries. In addition, accounting information is one of the organization's most important strategic resources, which is discussed later in this chapter.

Managers receive routine and non-routine paper reports of historical and budgeted data. Accountants are often called on to make oral and visual presentations of accounting data at management meetings. Increasingly, managers also have access to networked computer systems that permit both downloading of accounting data to desktop and portable computers and further analysis of the data using spreadsheets and reporting software.

The content and format of external reports are regulated by accounting rule-making bodies and by government agencies. Purchase orders, invoices, and checks are constrained somewhat by industry practices. Internal accounting information is determined by management's needs. But rules and requirements are not enough to explain the flow of information and certainly not enough to make it happen. From where does the information come? How is it processed? How is it communicated to the various types of users? The answer to these questions is the accounting information system.

Accounting Information Systems

What Is an Accounting Information System?

LEARNING OBJECTIVE 2
Describe the nature, scope, and importance of accounting information systems.

Accounting information system A system that delivers accounting information. Its purposes are. to meet an organization's statutory reporting requirements- to provide relevant and accurate accounting information to those who need it and when they need it- to conduct or at least enable most business processes ranging from the recording of sales orders to the reconciliation of bank accounts after liabilities have been paid- and to protect the organization from possible risks stemming from abuse of accounting data or of the system itself.

A system is a framework that exists for the benefit of one or more defined objectives. Systems ordinarily use resources and are subject to constraints. They operate within an environment requiring the specification of the boundaries between the system and the environment. Most systems have both inputs and outputs. Except for the most rudimentary instances, systems are composed of subsystems that perform tasks contributing to the operation and goals of the greater system.

An automobile can be thought of as a system. The objective is to convey people and goods from one location to another. Automobiles consume gasoline, lubricants, oxygen, and they require the driver's commands. Automobiles are constrained both physically and legally. They function on land (not on water or in the air), must be operated on legal roadways, and are subject to traffic regulations and customs. An automobile is composed of various subsystems such as the ignition system, the steering system, and the braking system.

An **accounting information system** is a delivery system for accounting information. Its purposes are:

- To meet an organization's statutory reporting requirements.
- To provide relevant and accurate accounting information to those who need it when they need it.
- To conduct or at least enable most business processes ranging from the recording of sales orders to the reconciliation of bank accounts after liabilities have been paid.

- To protect the organization from possible risks stemming from abuse of accounting data or of the system itself.

The accounting system captures, stores, processes, and communicates information in accordance with applicable professional, industry, and government standards and also meets the organization's own requirements. A well-designed accounting system enables an organization to manage one of its most valuable resources—information.

Accounting systems deal primarily with **economic events** that affect an organization's accounting equation, that is, ASSETS = LIABILITIES + OWNERSHIP EQUITY. Economic events fitting this definition are called **accounting transactions**. Some **accounting events** will have matured into accounting transactions while others may not have yet done so. Those that are accounting transactions require a conventional journal entry with at least one account debited and at least one account credited. Other events, such as the ordering of apples mentioned in the table at the beginning of the chapter, are events that have not matured into accounting transactions, but are nevertheless accounting events that must be captured and reported by the accounting system. These events provide useful information to managers tracking the activity of their apple purchase order agents. This information might be used to determine how quickly orders are filled, and how active the agents are.

The apple order, for example, requires an entry into the purchase order system. Thus, in addition to events qualifying as accounting transactions, other quantitatively measured events will likely mature into accounting transactions and therefore qualify as accounting data. This view of accounting systems is often referred to as **events accounting**. Many attributes of accounting events are captured by events accounting systems. The issuance of a sales order may require that the following be recorded: (1) time and place the order is received, (2) company and person placing the order, (3) salesperson responsible for the order, (4) when, where, and how the order is to be shipped, and (5) detailed description of the items being ordered, quantities, and the sales price.

Most accounting transactions result from an organization's day-to-day operations, such as charging materials, labor, and overhead to production; selling goods or providing services to customers; receiving payments from customers; purchasing materials for inventory; and paying employees and vendors. Transactions can be divided into two main types: external transactions and internal transactions. **External transactions** arise from exchanges with outsiders, such as purchasing or selling goods and services. **Internal transactions** arise largely from the accumulation of cost data and the assignment of costs to products, business units, or activities.

Manual accounting systems included very little data beyond the basic elements. For example, a customer account included only the customer name, account identifier, and perhaps the customer address along with transaction data of the current period. The same data were usually stored in many departments. A customer's address might be maintained by credit and collections, billing, shipping, and accounts receivable. Errors and inconsistencies were common because an address change would have to be made in several different records. In contrast, well-designed computerized systems maintain such data in only one location that is available to all users. Thus, all relatively permanent data related to a customer, for example, name, address, telephone number, sales by month, credit limit, contact person, and perhaps even birthdays of key customer personnel, would be stored in one place. Human resource systems encompassing payroll ordinarily include all personnel data such as employee age, skill sets, vacation days earned, and accumulated sick leave.

In the past, accounting systems were designed primarily to process data for the financial statements and reports to external agencies, such as the Securities and Exchange Commission and the Internal Revenue Service. To the extent that the data also might be of interest to managers, the accounting system played a secondary role of decision support. Now, the emphasis is reversed. Accounting information systems still provide needed external information, but most systems are more heavily oriented toward supporting

Economic events Events of an organization that may not necessarily affect its accounting equation.

Accounting transaction Economic events that affect an organization's accounting equation.

Accounting events are economic events that have or may become accounting transactions. For example, a completed sale is an accounting event that has become an accounting transaction; a sales order is an accounting event that may or may not become an accounting transaction.

Events accounting An accounting system that captures accounting events and other events that are relevant to the operating of the organization.

External transaction A transaction that arises from an exchange with an outsider, such as the purchase or sale of goods and services.

Internal transaction A transaction that arises largely from the accumulation of cost data and the assignment of costs to products, business units, or activities.

Vignette 1.2

Volume of Accounting Reports

Weller Corporation prepares quarterly and annual financial statements for its stockholders and annual 10K reports for the Securities and Exchange Commission. It files estimated corporate income tax returns each quarter and files its annual tax returns to the Internal Revenue Service and the state revenue agency on March 15 of each year. In addition, the corporation reports and pays payroll and withholding taxes after each semimonthly pay period and files a quarterly report of payroll tax withholdings.

Each month, Weller Corporation prepares 85 separate accounting reports required by managers in the organization. Some of these reports contain monetary values, some contain physical units, and some contain both. Examples are the daily cash receipts and disbursements reports ($), the weekly report of materials and labor usage ($ and units), the weekly production backorder report (units), the weekly schedule of aged accounts receivable ($), the monthly inventory

status ($ and units) and reorder reports (units), and the monthly trial balance ($). These reports vary in length from 1 page to more than 100 pages and vary in distribution from 1 copy to 20 copies.

Each month, the corporation also issues an average of 675 purchase orders and 2,600 invoices. It writes more than 13,000 checks to vendors and employees and processes about 2,500 cash remittances from customers. At year-end, Weller issues roughly 23,000 W-2 forms to present and former employees.

THOUGHT QUESTIONS

1. Which type of information (dollars, units, or both) do you think a manufacturing manager would find most useful when making staffing decisions and why?

2. Give some examples of the information the manager would want collected to help him/her with staffing decisions.

management decision making and operations (Vignette 1.2). Because of management's need for information beyond just what is essential for external financial reporting, many systems are events-based. These systems can capture and store full information about each accounting event, making it available to authorized users in the organization. Accounting events other than transactions include sales orders and purchase orders.

External reporting Reporting by an organization to parties outside of the organization.

The information used for **external reporting** and the information supporting management decision making and operations come from the same primary source: accounting events measured in monetary terms. Payroll, cost accounting, and accounts receivable data flow into the external financial statements. The same payroll data may form the basis of a decision regarding personnel levels. The same cost accounting data may provide input to a decision to add a new product or to discontinue an existing one. And the same accounts receivable data may support a decision concerning credit policy. Among their accounting data, many organizations have found strategically valuable information to increase their market share and competitive position (Vignette 1.3). On the other hand, meeting management's demands for decision-making information may require data from other internal and external sources and data measured in nonmonetary terms. Data expressed in labor hours, units of production, manufacturing reject rates, and customer satisfaction indices may be needed. Furthermore, more sophisticated analysis may be necessary before the information is delivered to management.

The expanding role of accounting and the increasing presence of computerized data processing have led to difficulties in properly defining the boundaries of both accounting and accounting information systems. Several activities, including decision support, operations research, modeling, information management,

Source: EKKAPON BOONYOUNG/Shutterstock.

Vignette 1.3

Strategic Use of Accounting Information

Green Acres, Inc. is a leading supplier of yard and garden products. It distributes seed, fertilizers, gardening gloves, small tools, mulchers, yard tractors, and 2,417 other products needed by homeowners, nursery owners, and small farmers. Service support for its equipment is provided through local dealers.

Three years ago, a senior manager recognized that a gold mine of information lay in the company's accounting records. Now, each month, Green Acres' sales records are analyzed to identify customers who have bought products in each of several categories. Marketing personnel use the monthly list to target those customers who are most likely to buy additional products. For example, a customer who has recently bought a lawn mower is also likely to need grass seed, lawn care products, and equipment such as edgers and leaf blowers. Over time, complete profiles have been drawn up of customers and their needs.

Lists of customers may also be sold to firms in the industry that are not in direct competition. For example, names of customers who have bought garden equipment may be sold to nurseries. Green Acres has no immediate plans to sell live plants, but it can bring in additional revenue from firms that do not enjoy its large accounting database. Management has even contacted lawn service companies with similar propositions. Its reasoning is that some people who have purchased lawn mowers may have become tired of using them.

THOUGHT QUESTIONS

1. What are some of the issues Green Acres should consider when analyzing or sharing information from its accounting information system?

2. Give some examples of information that could be extracted from the accounting information system for use in future planning.

and the planning and implementation of information systems, are "gray areas" in which the responsibilities of accountants may overlap those of other professionals.

For many years, leaders of the accounting profession have taken a broad view of the function of accounting. As far back as 1969, a committee of the American Accounting Association encouraged accounting involvement in such decision support areas as modeling and forecasting. And in 1971, another committee of the Association included the design and management of accounting systems in a list of an accountant's principal and "traditional" responsibilities. The 1971 committee also expressed the following opinion:

> The Committee believes that accounting in the broad sense of the term can and should rise to the challenge and opportunities of the developing information technologies and take the lead in the information management. In the narrowest sense of the term, the accountant is only a part of the organization's formal information system and hence is both a user of information and a part of the operating and design group concerned with information as a whole.[1]

Accounting Systems Technology

At one time, accounting data were captured and stored on paper documents and processed and reported manually. Accounting clerks transcribed data from paper source documents, such as time cards and customer purchase orders, to paper journals. The transaction data were then posted to paper ledgers. Checks, invoices, and other output documents were prepared by hand, and financial statements were typed from handwritten drafts. Manual accounting systems were slow, were prone to error, and severely limited in the volume of data that could be processed. With the rapid development of computers, the manual processing of accounting data has become rare. Today, most accounting systems—even in very small organizations—are computerized. Computerized accounting systems are faster, more accurate, and more reliable, and they can easily handle large volumes of data. They are also less expensive to operate than manual systems. More importantly, certain types of information processing and ways of communicating accounting information are only possible with the use of computers. For example, managing large databases, moving data rapidly to and from remote locations, and obtaining immediate feedback on the effects of transactions would be impossible without computer technology.

Computerized accounting systems include a number of key components. The first and most visible component is the computer equipment, or hardware. **Computer hardware** performs the essential functions of input, processing, storage, transmission, and output of data. The second component is the accounting activities that are used to process data. Most of these processes are embodied in **accounting software**, the sets of instructions that tell the hardware what to do. Such software includes general ledger, customer, and human resource accounting. Accounting procedures not automated include control of pre-numbered documents (checks, for example) and operation of the accounting software.

The third component is people. Computers do certain things much better than people and complement those tasks at which people excel, such as making judgments and being creative. People no longer carry out routine processing tasks, but they continue to provide input data, monitor processing of that data, and interpret the output. Also, people are needed to manufacture the hardware, write the software, install the systems, and maintain the systems in working order. Finally, people are required to supervise and control the accounting function to ensure that it does its proper job. It is not an exaggeration to say that people remain the most important element of the accounting system, and they must be sold on the merits of any system for it to succeed (Vignette 1.4).

Computer hardware The most visible component of computerized accounting systems. It performs the essential functions of input, processing, storage, transmission, and output of data.

Accounting software Sets of instructions that tell hardware what to do in order to process data. Such software includes general ledger, customer, and human resource accounting.

Vignette 1.4

Importance of People in Accounting Systems

Angus Associates' new controller, Ryan Lehmann, soon set about replacing the firm's obsolete computer equipment. He supervised the installation of a system of networked desktop and laptop computers and printers. After sifting through 2 years' copies of a weekly microcomputer magazine and reading articles in The Journal of Accountancy, Lehmann ordered a complete line of highly recommended accounting software that would meet the firm's information needs. Everything seemed to be going smoothly. Then Lehmann was seriously injured in a car accident on the way to work and was forced to take early retirement.

His replacement, Monica Kluger, had been with the company for a long time. From the start, she had been suspicious of her predecessor's plans for a new accounting system. She liked the old minicomputer even though it was slow, particularly when all the terminals were in use. And she felt comfortable with the old accounting software even though significant manual processing was required to provide needed information. The new software looked good on paper, but she did not have the time to figure out how to operate it.

Kluger was stuck with the new system, but she decided to ignore it as best she could. She delegated all the computer operations to Jack Thompson, an eager but inept young man. He set about installing the new software and made a complete mess of it. Several of the packages were never installed, two because the CDs were damaged. Kluger and Thompson made no arrangements for training users to operate

Source: Antonio Guillem/Shutterstock.com.

the network, so everybody treated the computers as stand-alone units.

Also, Kluger canceled the maintenance contract on the computers, and when hardware problems—however trivial—arose, the inoperable machines were simply moved to a storage room to gather dust. Within a year, one-half of the equipment Lehmann had bought was out of commission.

When executive managers asked Kluger how the new accounting system was working out, she made disparaging remarks about the choice of hardware and software and about Lehmann's wisdom in acquiring "such a complicated and unmaintainable system."

THOUGHT QUESTIONS

1. How could this situation been avoided?
2. What should Angus Associates do now?

Organizations use computers to do more than just process accounting data. Computers are used in engineering departments to help design products and in manufacturing plants to control the machinery that makes the products. They are used in finance, marketing, and administrative departments. Computers are used by all levels of management. Computers form part of management information systems, decision support systems, administrative support systems, and executive support systems.

Importance of Accounting Systems

The accounting system touches most or all of an organization's activities. It touches the organization's external activities through the transaction documents sent to customers, vendors, and employees, through the financial statements prepared for the stockholders and creditors, and through the tax and regulatory reports sent to government agencies. The accounting system touches the internal activities through product costing, reflecting the conversion of raw materials into finished products. It also touches internal activities through budgets and budget tracking. Budgets are established to provide performance targets and to set limits on authorized expenses. Accounting data measure actual performance—at least in its financial aspects—and monitor compliance with the performance targets. However, the measurement system influences the activities being measured. People are aware that they are being monitored by accounting measurements and adjust their behavior accordingly.

Because of the pervasive influence of an accounting system, the quality of accounting information and the performance of the accounting system are of great concern to management. The accounting system is the organization's "nervous system." System outages have become more common in recent years primarily due to cybercrimes and human error. According to a recent study by Ponemon Institute, the average cost of an outage rose to $740,357 in 2015—an increase of 38 percent since 2010. The increase in the maximum downtime cost ($2,409,991) was even greater, climbing 81 percent over that same time period. The most expensive cost was business disruption, followed by lost revenue and end-user productivity.[2]

While a good accounting system may not guarantee an organization's success, a bad one can destroy an organization. Untrustworthy accounting information, unreliable computer equipment, and incompetent or dishonest people carrying out accounting functions can also drive an organization into bankruptcy. The difference between good and bad systems lies in the way they are developed, operated, and controlled. An accounting system is expected to carry out its tasks without the need for upper management's day-to-day intervention. It should operate so reliably that top management can safely forget about the system and devote its energy and attention to more pressing issues. Management should be confident, for example, that the payroll will be processed, customers will be billed, production will be controlled, and information will be readily available as needed for decision making.

The mode of acquiring accounting software systems has changed dramatically. In the past, many large companies maintained a large IT department and developed their own accounting systems software in-house. But today most new systems are licensed from companies specializing in the development, licensing, and support of accounting systems software. (See **Exhibit 1.1** regarding the licensing of software.)

Selecting, acquiring, and installing a suitable accounting system is costly and time-consuming. The acquisition of a new accounting system should be undertaken with much care to ensure that the system does its job, not just when it first goes into operation but over an extended useful life. The system's job is to meet the accounting information needs of the organization and the users. Determining what these needs are requires much data gathering before the system can be selected and implemented. Control features (which minimize the opportunity for an individual to perpetrate and hide fraudulent activity) should be integrated into the accounting system to protect the accounting information and to ensure that the system cannot be abused. Before acquiring a new system, you

In everyday parlance, we speak of "buying" software. But anything a person buys is owned and can be copied, sold, and given away. Clearly, in purchasing a word processing program, you do not have the right to make copies and sell them. Therefore, licensing a word processing program gives you only the right to personally install and use the program on one computer. The medium on which the program is recorded is your property, but the program is not. Usually, you do not acquire the right to install the program on replacement computers and cannot sell it with your computer. While there is certainly an illegal market in used software by individuals, businesses must be diligent in observing license agreements because punitive damages often result from license infringement lawsuits. A single disgruntled employee can notify a software vendor that the employer is not complying with software licensing agreements, resulting in significant financial and legal penalties being imposed on the business.

The Software Alliance (BSA) is an association of global software companies. It serves as the world's leading antipiracy organization to promote technology innovation and protect intellectual property. Through government relations, intellectual property enforcement and educational activities around the world, BSA protects intellectual property and fosters innovation. Its anti-piracy and compliance programs cover the areas of investigations and enforcement, fighting Internet-based piracy, software asset management, and education.

Source: Dukes/Shutterstock.

EXHIBIT 1.1 Licensing Software

The Software Alliance (BSA) is an association of global software companies that serves as the world's leading antipiracy organization.

should be assured that its developer has and will be able to provide continuing support. Moreover, employees who will operate and use the system must receive proper training.

Finding the best accounting system software package for a particular business can be daunting given the large number of packages available. The Internet is a good start. Three helpful resources are Accounting Software Library (accountinglibrary.com), CTS Guides (ctsguides.com) and Find Accounting Software (findaccountingsoftware.com). Accounting Software Library allows you to answer some questions about the requirements for a system and then gives you names of software that meets those requirements. The site can also connect you with a systems consultant in your area or a reseller if you know the product you want to purchase. CTS Guides provides a software selection kit you can download. The kit includes software reviews and collects information so a consultant can recommend packages. Find Accounting Software asks some questions online and then has a consultant contact you.

Since the advent of the microcomputer in 1977, accounting software has become far more sophisticated and diverse. Just a handful of packages were available for microcomputers when the IBM PC appeared in 1981. The widespread use of microcomputers and the Internet, and the software development environment have resulted in a deluge of accounting software.

Accounting programs can be categorized in many ways. One is by the size of company the software can accommodate. Hence we have entry-level, low cost accounting programs and complex programs for **small to medium-size businesses (SMB)** and large companies. Some programs are specific to particular industries such as auto dealerships, banking, churches, construction, healthcare, legal, oil and gas, and retail. Some programs are cloud-based while others reside on the premises. The demand for increased functionality has grown along with the growth of global sales, multiple currencies, and domestic and international locations of divisions. To meet these needs, **Enterprise Resource Planning (EPR) software** has evolved. This software groups an organization's accounting functions

SMB is a small to medium-size business.

Enterprise Resource Planning (ERP) software Software that groups an organization's accounting function with finance, sales, manufacturing, and human resources into a coherent, integrated system making financial and operational data available to personnel throughout the organization.

with finance, sales, manufacturing, and human resources into a coherent, integrated system making financial and operational data available to personnel throughout the organization. ERP software is available for large, global companies and even for small to midsize businesses (**SME-small to midsize enterprise businesses**).

Accounting software includes various modules for specific areas of accounting. The core modules include sales order, invoicing, accounts receivable, purchase order, accounts payable, inventory, and general ledger. Additional modules can be added such as payroll, human resources, customer relationship management, report generation, job costing, and taxation.

A single software company may offer several accounting programs so it can meet the needs of many users. Some may have been developed by the company and some acquired through mergers and consolidations with other companies in the industry. As the result of a merger, the acquiring company may end up with some programs it really wants and some it is not so interested in. The latter may be shelved while the company decides what to do with them. The desirable programs will be rebranded under the acquiring company's name. The end result is that one company will offer several versions of its software. For example, a company called The Sage Group offers approximately ten different programs including Sage One, Sage 50, Sage 100, Sage 300, and Sage X3. The programs differ in scalability and functionality ranging from entry level (one to ten users) to complex (20 – 1,000+ users).

SME is a small to midsize enterprise business.

Why Study Accounting Information Systems?

During its useful life, the accounting system must be given adequate care to ensure that the accounting system continues to operate satisfactorily. Software corrections and updates should be installed and monitored on a controlled basis. Computer equipment must be maintained properly, new people must be trained, and existing people must be supervised. Control features should be monitored to ensure their continued performance and, where necessary, they should be strengthened. Periodically, the system should be evaluated to determine whether it continues to provide the required service. From time to time, the system may need to be upgraded or enhanced to improve its performance.

As an accountant, you need to be, at a minimum, a capable user of an accounting system. You may also be an auditor or perhaps a consultant. The most recent edition of the *Occupational Outlook Handbook* of the U.S. Department of Labor says that "Employment of accountants and auditors is expected to grow 11 percent between 2014 and 2024, which is faster than the average for all occupations. Globalization, a growing overall economy, and an increasingly complex tax and regulatory environment are expected to lead to strong demand for accountants and auditors."[3]

LEARNING OBJECTIVE 3
Explain why accounting information systems should be studied regardless of the accounting specialty you may choose.

Accountants as Users of Accounting Systems

Users of accounting systems include financial, managerial, governmental, and tax accountants. As users, accountants depend on accounting systems to provide information in a timely manner. First and foremost, accountants need to understand how an accounting system works so as to be able to determine that the outputs are trustworthy. In addition, because accountants' duties encompass business analysis, they need to know what, how, and where data are stored so that they can retrieve and evaluate appropriate data.

Often, end users are asked to participate as project team members in the evaluation of an existing accounting information system, the acceptability of a new system, and the implementation of a new system (Vignette 1.5). Their primary role in such projects is to offer advice on matters of concern to users, such as:

- How easy is the system to operate?
- How are data entered?
- How is access limited to authorized users?
- What interaction is possible between the user and the system?

Accounting User Concerns in AIS Design

Charles Hardin is the manager of a software division of Conglomerates, Inc., a manufacturer of marine pumps and motors. Some years ago the software division was acquired along with several recreational boat dealerships. While the dealerships were subsequently sold, the software division was retained by Conglomerates. The division has an accounting system—Boat Accounting Software System (BASS)—developed specifically for boat dealers and marine docking facilities. BASS is sold to recreational boat dealers and operators of boat docking facilities and is supported by five employees staffing a help desk. Charles is heading up a team to update the program. His development team includes three programmers from the parent company, a programmer from Charles' division who is learning new software tools, and an accountant who previously worked for both boat dealers and docking/storage companies. Charles has an accounting degree, picked up some programming skills early in his career, and participated heavily in the design (not programming) of BASS in recent years.

Considerable tension has arisen in Charles' team concerning redesign of the product. The decision has been made to use the Oracle database to manage data for the accounting system. Charles knows how the current product works and has always felt comfortable with the audit trail produced and with built-in software controls. He believes he represents the users of the software and feels that audit trails and controls are essential and must be built into the software at the design phase and before any programming begins. This concern has been expressed to the lead programmer from corporate who only responds that Charles should only tell her what outputs are desired and leave the question of "how to do it" up to the programmers.

THOUGHT QUESTION

1. As a representative of the users of the software, how can Charles improve the redesign process to help ensure its success?

- What outputs are generated?
- Is "on demand" reporting available?
- Is the output reliable?
- Can the data be lost or contaminated?
- What should be done if the system crashes?
- Can the system be abused and in what ways?
- What controls are necessary?

To provide such advice, accountants need to have systems skills as well as a sufficient understanding of the activities of the users whom they represent. Tax specialists need sufficient knowledge of computerized accounting systems to extract required information for tax returns and to understand what has happened to data in processing to ensure that extracted information is presented according to tax requirements. Most controllers and chief financial officers are responsible for operation of the accounting system and thus must possess sufficient knowledge of computerized accounting systems to judge the accuracy of statements about the system made to them by their employees and peers, particularly if they are required to attest to the controls over the generation of financial statement information in their Sarbanes-Oxley Section 404 report.

Accountants as Auditors of Accounting Systems

External auditor An auditor who performs a public service by expressing an opinion about the "fairness" of a client's financial statements. The auditor's opinion gives stockholders, creditors, and others confidence that an organization's financial statements provide a basis for investment decisions.

External, internal, and governmental auditors also require a high level of accounting systems expertise to perform their jobs. **External auditors** perform a public service by expressing an opinion about the "fairness" of a client's financial statements, to include their assessment of management's attestation of the control system based on their own testing. The auditor's opinion gives stockholders, creditors, and others confidence that an organization's financial statements provide a basis for investment decisions. External auditors are independent of the client organizations, working individually or for accounting firms, and are regulated by the Public Company Accounting Oversight Board (PCAOB). The auditors are part of the quality assurance program that organizations and the accounting profession mutually seek to establish for financial information.

An auditor who performs a financial statement audit is required by professional standards to gain an understanding of a client's accounting information system before expressing an opinion. The auditor's concern is to determine whether the processing of accounting data conforms to generally accepted accounting principles and whether the system's control features are adequate to reduce the likelihood of errors in the financial statements to an acceptable level. If an auditor finds the controls to be adequate, he or she may be able to reduce the amount of testing of transactions and account balances necessary to support an opinion on the fairness of the financial statements.

External auditors must adhere to standards issued by the Auditing Standards Board of the American Institute of Certified Public Accountants, as well as standards issued by the Public Company Accounting Oversight Board. The Auditing Standards Board of the AICPA has issued several SASs (e.g., Nos. 55, 78, 94, 95) relating to the need for external auditors to understand a client's internal controls and assess the likelihood of fraudulent financial information (SAS 99). SAS 94 states that in obtaining this understanding of internal controls, the auditor must consider how an entity's use of information technology may affect controls relevant to a financial statement audit.[4] The Public Company Accounting Oversight Board (PCAOB) has also issued several standards for auditors related to identifying controls and planning the audit of an organization's accounting system. As a result, external auditors need substantial technical knowledge about accounting systems to be able to carry out their responsibilities.

Internal auditors are employed by business organizations to perform auditing work for corporate management, and **governmental auditors** are employed by government agencies to report to government officials and the public. Internal auditors perform compliance and operational audits, as well as participate in special projects to aid management's quality assurance program. They ensure that accounting systems are properly designed to meet the organization's present and future needs, they monitor the effectiveness of internal controls, and they provide advice on operational efficiency within the organization.

Obviously, auditors need to have a good understanding of an accounting system and its technology. To address the complexity of today's advanced technology, a highly specialized group of auditors has emerged, called "IT auditors." These auditors can work as external, internal, or governmental auditors. The job market for IT auditors has exploded in the past few years due to documentation requirements demanded for compliance with the Sarbanes-Oxley Act of 2002, and companies' heavy reliance on information technology. In the near future, all types of auditors will be called on to work more closely with technology.

Several professional organizations provide support to auditors by offering certifications, education, research, and technological guidance. These organizations include the American Institute of Certified Public Accountants (AICPA), the Institute of Internal Auditors (IIA), ISACA (formerly known as the Information Systems Audit and Control Association), and the Association of Certified Fraud Examiners (ACFE). The certifications sponsored by these organizations are outlined later in this chapter.

Accountants as Consultants for Accounting Systems

The addition of systems **consulting services** to the typical services of audit and tax was a natural progression for public accounting firms. Indeed, the accountant already had a wealth of knowledge about the client's operations. When a company had a question about implementing or updating its accounting system, the company turned to its trusted CPA for informed, objective advice, as described in the Introductory Scenario. Accounting firms quickly recognized systems consulting as an attractive way to enhance revenues. During the 1990s, systems consulting grew at a rapid rate. This growth was primarily

Internal auditor An auditor who is employed by a business firm to perform auditing for corporate management. An internal auditor lacks the necessary independence to express opinions about the financial statements of the organization for which he/she works, but is nevertheless part of the same quality assurance program.

Governmental auditor An auditor who is employed by a government agency to report to government officials and the public.

Consulting services A wide range of services, such as systems implementation, business valuations, litigation support, estate planning, employee benefits, strategic planning, health care, forensics (fraud) and financing arrangements.

attributable to the implementation of ERP systems to avoid the Y2K problem (the bug that was supposed to crash all the computers when the year changed to 2000). With the passage of the Sarbanes-Oxley Act of 2002, external auditors were no longer permitted to perform consulting services for their audit clients. Consequently, many of the public accounting firms sold off their consulting branches. For example, before the collapse of Arthur Andersen, it spun off Andersen Consulting, which is now called Accenture. Ernst and Young's consulting arm became Ernst and Young Consulting, was acquired by Cap Gemini, and became Cap Gemini Ernst and Young. The name was changed to Capgemini. Deloitte formed Deloitte Consulting, changed its name to Braxton, and then back to Deloitte Consulting. PriceWaterhouseCoopers spun off PWC Consulting, which was bought by IBM in 2002 to create IBM Global Business Services. The KPMG spin-off of KPMG Consulting changed its name in 2002 to BearingPoint to further differentiate itself from its former parent. Consulting firms often form alliances with vendors to provide full coverage, fill in technology gaps, improve positioning, and strengthen capabilities. (See **Exhibit 1.2**.)

We work in partnership with all major technology suppliers, developing solutions and strategies to suit our clients' requirements.

This reduces your costs through the efficient use of our suppliers' resources. It also helps us to maintain outstanding quality through our exceptional industrial and project experience with these major technological players.

Our solutions are put in place by well-functioning teams and supported by a co-ordinated service portfolio. You will enjoy lower risk because of our central project management of all partners involved.

Our technology partners include IBM, Microsoft, Oracle and SAP.

EXHIBIT 1.2 BearingPoint's Statement on Technology Partners

Source: www.bearingpoint.com.

Despite the Sarbanes-Oxley Act of 2002 that bans accounting firms to do consulting work for their audit clients, accounting firms soon realized that they can still do consulting work for many companies as long as these companies are not their audit clients. Today, business consulting ranging from management and risk consulting to financial and tax advisory remains a significant service provided by public accounting firms, small or large. Many accounting professionals enjoy working with their consulting clients to help them solve problems and improve business operation.

Other services prohibited by Sarbanes-Oxley for audit clients include bookkeeping functions, internal audit outsourcing, and information systems design/implementation. This Act does not directly apply to nonpublic companies. Consulting firms outside of public accounting also provide systems consulting, and other services previously provided by public accounting firms; many accounting graduates follow career paths with these firms.

The extent of implementation engagements varies widely depending on the size of the client company, the way the client company is organized, and the scope of the engagement. Implementations of the SAP ERP system average about 2 years, while a typical implementation of Sage 50 might be 4 to 6 weeks and require a smaller staffing effort than SAP. Accountants taking part in systems evaluation must be able to assess different approaches to the capture, storage, processing, transmission, and output of data, and they must be able to estimate the level of assurance provided by different types of controls.

Professional Certifications and AIS Knowledge

Accountants frequently acquire professional certification, either as a requirement for their particular area of practice or to enhance their professional status and career prospects. Generally, certification requires passing an examination, meeting specified experience

Certification Designation	Sponsoring Organization	Comments
Certified Public Accountant	American Institute of CPAs and State Boards of Public Accountancy	Only certification awarded by state agencies; necessary to express opinions on financial statements.
Certified Information Technology Professional	American Institute of CPAs	Acknowledges additional training in the areas of emerging trends, security and privacy, business solutions, IT assurance and risk and data analytics.
Certified Management Accountant	Institute of Management Accountants	Designed for accountants employed in the corporate world.
Certified Internal Auditor	Institute of Internal Auditors	Designed for those working as internal auditors in corporations and non-profit organizations.
Certified Information Systems Auditor	ISACA (formerly Information Systems Audit and Control Association)	Designed for those who audit, control, monitor and assess an organization's information technology and business systems.
Certified Information Security Manager	ISACA (formerly Information Systems Audit and Control Association)	Designed for individuals who design, build and manage enterprise information security programs.
Certified Fraud Examiner	Association of Certified Fraud Examiners	Emphasizes investigation and deterrence of fraud.
Certified Information Systems Security Professional	International Information Systems Security Certification Consortium	Designed for those who design and manage an information security program to protect organizations from sophisticated attacks.

EXHIBIT 1.3 Professional Certifications Requiring AIS Knowledge

and educational requirements, and agreeing to be bound in their professional conduct by a code of ethics established by the respective certifying body. In addition, certifications require holders to complete a minimum number of hours of continuing education in approved fields to maintain certification.

Exhibit 1.3 lists professional certifications in the US that require knowledge of accounting information systems, the sponsoring organizations, and a brief statement of their purposes. However, this list is not all-inclusive as the professional organizations continually add new certifications to meet new areas of expertise needed in the accounting profession.

Summary

Accounting information is needed to transact business, support management decision making and operations, and meet statutory requirements for external reporting. While most accounting data are expressed in monetary terms, significant other accounting data necessary for effective reporting include units of product, ratios, percentages, or other terms.

Accounting systems are the delivery systems that provide accounting information to users within an organization and to stockholders, creditors, government agencies, labor unions, and others outside the organization. They process transactions, provide routine and non-routine reports, and support an accounting database from which information can be retrieved when needed for decision-making purposes.

Accountants in all branches of the profession must have a basic understanding of accounting systems to do their jobs. But an increasing number of accountants, in public practice as well as in industry and government, are systems professionals who require a more detailed knowledge of accounting systems topics. CPAs offer auditing services to their clients, providing an independent assessment of the controls and reliability of the financial statements. Consulting services, internal auditing, and many management and government accounting positions require special technical competence to carry out their ongoing responsibilities. This type of competence is provided by AIS courses, by textbooks, by practical experience, and by continuing professional education.

Several professional certifications, such as the Certified Public Accountant designation in the U.S. and the Certified Information Systems Auditor (international), are available to entrants to the accounting profession. These certifications provide evidence that the holders have met certain minimum standards of competence in their areas of accounting or accounting-related practice. Success in passing the qualifying examinations for all of the professional certifications requires a significant level of competence in accounting information systems.

Key Terms

Accounting events   7
Accounting information   3
Accounting information system   6
Accounting software   10
Accounting transaction   7
Computer hardware   10
Consulting services   15
Economic events   7
Enterprise Resource Planning (ERP) software   12
Events accounting   7

External auditor   14
External reporting   8
External transaction   7
Governmental auditor   15
Internal auditor   15
Internal transaction   7
SMB   12
SME   13
The Software Alliance (BSA)   12
Trading partners   5

Discussion Questions and Problems

1. Arnold Finkelstein and Associates owns a shopping mall in a city of 50,000 people. The mall, containing 240,000 square feet of retail space, was built more than 10 years ago and is in need of repairs and decoration. However, Finkelstein is considering a larger project to upgrade the mall's image and install a "food court." The project might also include a 40-percent expansion to bring in more specialty shops and another big-name retail store. At present, 65 small and 2 major retailers lease space in the mall. The owner is responsible for the mall's upkeep and promotion and for all janitorial and security services.

Required:

What types of accounting information does Finkelstein need to make a decision on the proposed project? How much of this information can be extracted from the owner's accounting records? What additional accounting and non-accounting information is needed?

2. Vignette 1.3 illustrates the potential strategic value of accounting information in increasing an organization's market share and profitability.

Required:

a. Suggest possible strategic uses of the types of accounting data listed below:
   Purchasing data
   Perpetual inventory records

   Manufacturing cost data
   Customer credit and accounts receivable data
   Personnel and payroll records

b. Are any legal or ethical issues involved in the use of accounting data for such purposes?

3. Both external auditors and accountants engaged in implementing or updating systems need a basic understanding of accounting information systems.

Required:

Compare the needs of the two groups, identifying the areas where both need the same kind of understanding and the areas where one group has essentially different needs.

4. Explain the impact the Sarbanes-Oxley Act of 2002 has on the ability of public accounting firms to provide systems consulting services.

5. The chapter indicates that users may be represented on project teams organized to find and select new accounting information systems.

Required:

Do users belong on systems projects? Recognizing the complexity and sophistication of today's accounting systems, is it not better to leave systems selection and implementation to professionals, such as consulting specialists or computer scientists?

6. "All those certifications like the CMA and CIA are a waste of time, effort, and money. Every accounting student should sit for the CPA examination, regardless of where he or she intends to finish up, because the CPA license is the only one that's recognized. Getting some other certification is like going to a school that's not accredited."

Required:

Discuss this statement.

7. Classroom Activity:

You are the controller for Aspen Ski Equipment Co. Snowmass Ski Village has sent you their purchase order for 50 ski poles. Assume you have the ski poles in stock and assume a manual accounting system. Make a list of all the processes, documents, and journal entries necessary for the sale transactionto work its way through the accounting system and appear on the financial statements. It is not necessary for you to include amounts. One team will be selected randomly to present its solution to the class.

Notes

1. American Accounting Association, "Report of the Committee on Accounting and Information Systems," *The Accounting Review* 46 (supplement) (1971): 344.
2. Hickey, Kathleen, "What's Behind Most Data Center Outages?" February 9, 2016, GCN Magazine online.
3. Bureau of Labor Statistics, U.S. Department of Labor, *Occupational Outlook Handbook, 2016-17 Edition*, Accountants and Auditors. www.bls.gov/ooh/business-and-financial/accountants-and-auditors.htm
4. Auditing Standards Board, *Statement on Auditing Standards No. 94* (New York: American Institute of Certified Public Accountants, May 2001).

Accounting Systems Documentation

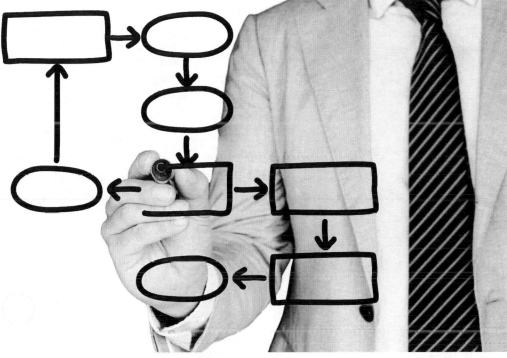

Source: BeeBright./Shutterstock.

CHAPTER 2

Chapter Outline

Documentation of Accounting Systems

Documentation Standards

Types of System Documentation

Computer-Assisted System Documentation Tools

Learning Objectives

After studying this chapter, you should be able to:

- Understand what documentation is and why it is needed.
- Explain the importance of documentation standards.
- Recognize the appropriate use of the various types of system documentation.
- Describe, read, and prepare a system narrative description.
- Describe, read, and prepare a block diagram.
- Describe, read, and prepare a data flow diagram.
- Describe, read, and prepare a system flowchart.
- Discuss business process modeling and how business processes are mapped using the Unified Modeling Language (UML).
- Appreciate the advantages of computer-assisted systems documentation tools.

Source: Pressmaster/Shutterstock.

Introductory Scenario

An American subsidiary of a large international oil company had undertaken a project to consolidate its computer operations in the United States. A major part of the consolidation was the transfer of the company's personnel systems, all of which resided on the computers in Houston, Texas, to its computers in Anchorage, Alaska. The company hired a consultant, Jon Tran, to be responsible for this transfer.

Within the first few days of the engagement, Tran developed a plan to ensure a successful relocation of all personnel systems to Anchorage and presented his plan to the oil company's representative, Victoria McNichols. The plan consisted of the following tasks:

- Identify all supporting software products driving the personnel systems, such as operating systems, compilers, file and database management systems, telecommunications systems, and general purpose utility packages.

- Identify all personnel systems; the users; all components, including computer programs, screens, files and databases, reports; along with documentation on how to use the systems, what the systems do, and how the systems operate.

- Understand three types of relationships: (a) between each personnel system and its users, that is, how to use each system; (b) among components of each system (e.g., computer programs, screens, files, and databases, reports); and (c) among all the personnel systems.

- Transmit electronically, using a satellite transmission program, computer programs, screens, and test data from Houston to Anchorage.

- Test each personnel system on Anchorage's computer system.

- Transfer all production data in Houston onto storage media on a Friday night, fly them to Anchorage on Saturday, load them in files and databases residing on Anchorage's computers on Saturday night, and test them on Sunday. On Monday, users of all personnel systems throughout the nation should not notice the massive relocation of their systems undertaken during the weekend.

The above tasks were carried out by Tran and another consultant, Nina Merchant. Of the six tasks, the easiest ones were Tasks 1, 2, 4, and 6, which consumed one person-month. The most difficult ones were Tasks 3 and 5, which consumed eleven person-months due to a severe lack of documentation.

The identification of supporting software products was accomplished quickly by interviewing personnel in the Houston information center who were very familiar with all supporting software products. A list of all personnel systems and their users was quickly provided by McNichols. The systems included a personnel recordkeeping system, an employee skills inventory system, a personnel training-scheduling system, and a series of personnel reporting systems including Equal Employment Opportunity Commission, salary administration, employee performance evaluation, and employee performance tracking. The identification of computer programs, screens, files, and databases was also simple because the Houston information center adhered rigidly to a naming convention for these components. Their names typically started with "PER," standing for "personnel." With the use of their utility program, lists of 1,000+ program names, 100+ screen names, and 300+ file and database names were developed within 2 weeks.

Documentation on how to use the personnel systems was available and adequate. However, documentation describing what the systems did and how they operated did not exist, creating a very difficult situation for Tran and Merchant in understanding the relationships among the components of each personnel system and among all the personnel systems. The two consultants conducted lengthy and exhausting user interviews to obtain a general understanding of these systems. Furthermore, they had to trace the flows of data through each system and document them by creating flowcharts and diagrams. This effort cost about nine person-months. If documentation had been available and adequate, this task would have taken only one person-month, saving the client $60,000.

The satellite transmission of computer programs, screens, and test data was a simple task with the use of an in-house-developed satellite transmission program. This task cost the company $20,000. The testing of all personnel systems on Anchorage's computer took two person-months. McNichols was very surprised at the high cost of documenting the personnel systems to assist in understanding them. Her comment was:

"It cost us $60,000 for you two consultants to gain an understanding of our personnel systems. Over the years, it has probably cost the company hundreds of thousands of dollars for all our company accountants and auditors and our external auditors to obtain a working knowledge of these systems. Adequate documentation would have saved us a lot of money. What a waste!"

Introductory Scenario Thought Questions:

1. Why would proper documentation have been helpful in this systems consolidation project?
2. Why do you suppose documentation describing what the systems did and how they operated did not exist?
3. What measures do you think organizations can take to ensure that systems are adequately documented?
4. What types of documentation of the personnel systems would have been helpful to the consultants and what knowledge about the systems would the consultants have gained from each type?

Documentation of Accounting Systems

Documentation as it relates to accounting systems is a communication device that describes in pictures, words, or both how to use the system, what the system does, and how the system operates. Without documentation, a system is nothing but a "black box" with inner workings and relationships between inputs and outputs, which may be only partially understood. When adequately prepared, documentation provides a rich source of information to help people in doing their jobs.

LEARNING OBJECTIVE 1 Understand what documentation is and why it is needed.

Documentation is a critical business activity today because of the Sarbanes-Oxley Act of 2002. This Act requires that a company's internal control be documented in detail for use by both management and the external auditors in their review of the control system. In addition, internal auditors performing operational audits also require documentation of business processes to perform their reviews. Examples of the items that should be documented include:

- The design of controls on which management financial reporting assertions and disclosures will be based; this provides a basis for management's testing of the controls
- Descriptions of how transactions significant to financial reporting are initiated, authorized, recorded, processed, and reported to document proper authorization
- Establishment and continued assessment/testing of fraud prevention controls

- Controls over the financial reporting process that provide management with confidence that the information in the financial statements can be relied upon

- Controls over the safeguarding of assets, whether obvious (e.g., locked warehouses for inventory) or not (e.g., security for information assets)

- Controls over the information technology environment (e.g., access security, program changes)[1]

Therefore, it is more important than ever that accounting students understand how to document accounting systems.

The documentation of an accounting information system can be divided into two types according to its intended recipients. One, addressed to the system's operators, is appropriately referred to as **user documentation**. The second, addressed to technical personnel involved with the system, is referred to as **system documentation**. User documentation describes the system "from the outside, looking in." Different classes of users have different capabilities and needs and require different types of user documentation. Instructions in interpretation may be all that is necessary for users who simply receive output from the system. Documentation addressed to end users emphasizes how to operate the system and includes instructions for executing the various programs and instructions for handling data (e.g., to create reports). Typically, end-user documentation would include the following:

- Brief narrative description covering the objectives of the system, the overall mode of operation, and the structure of the major subsystems

- Graphical descriptions showing information flows among the subsystems

- List of programs with operating instructions

- Description of principal files used by programs

- Sample input illustrating what is required by each program

- Sample output showing what is produced by each program

- Control procedures

- Error recovery procedures

- Crash recovery procedures

In contrast, system documentation offers an inside view of the accounting system and is written in precise technical language. It is prepared by and for the benefit of system implementers, auditors, accountants, programmers, systems analysts, and other systems professionals and is needed to help:

- Understand complex accounting systems.

- Understand what internal controls are in place and how effectively they are working.

- Identify and solve problems in existing accounting systems.

- Implement successful new accounting systems.

- Train new personnel in both accounting and systems environments.

- Meet the ongoing need to keep existing accounting systems current.

- Communicate system design decisions.

Documentation Standards

LEARNING OBJECTIVE 2
Explain the importance of documentation standards.

Good documentation is not generated by accident. Rather, it is produced as a result of careful planning by an organization that takes seriously the need for good documentation. The preparation of documentation should be governed by appropriate standards. **Documentation standards** are written policies and procedures that govern the

---

User documentation Documentation that describes a system "from the outside looking in."

System documentation Documentation that provides an inside view of the accounting system and is written in precise technical language.

Documentation standards Written policies and procedures that govern the preparation, use, and maintenance of documentation.

preparation, use, and maintenance of documentation. The standards should include (at a minimum) the following:

- Identification of the preparer
- Information included and omitted
- The manner in which the material is to be presented
- Authorizations required for each type of documentation
- Instructions for preparation of the documentation
- Distribution and use of the documentation
- Review and maintenance procedures for the various types of documentation

People who prepare documentation should conform to applicable industry, national, or international documentation conventions to improve clarity and consistency in interpretation. Each item of documentation should be dated and bear the name of the person who prepared it so that, if possible, future questions can be directed to that individual. The documentation should also bear the name of the person who checked it and the person who authorized it for use. Any unauthorized/informal documentation circulating in an organization should be reviewed to determine whether it should be formalized or destroyed.

Reproduction and distribution methods should reflect the environment in which the documentation is to be used. Traditionally, documentation has been on paper, but the trend today is to store documentation in machine-readable form for retrieval and editing on personal computers or interactive workstations. Distribution of or access to documentation should be on a "need to know" basis. The purpose of documentation is to inform, but security should be provided to ensure that this purpose is not abused by unauthorized access. Documentation should not be the means by which individuals gain information—particularly about the workings of internal controls—to perpetrate irregularities.

Designated persons should be responsible for ensuring that documentation is properly maintained to reflect updates, additions, or deletions. These individuals should receive copies of all authorizations for system modifications so they can verify that system documentation has been updated. As new documentation is made available, old versions should be destroyed or taken out of circulation and archived. This process is aided by electronic methods of preparing and indexing documentation. Persons responsible for documentation should also conduct periodic reviews of system documentation to ensure that it is up to date (see Vignette 2.1). These periodic reviews should be documented to provide evidence that the review was performed as required.

Vignette 2.1

Documentation or Archeology?

The auditor spent several days reviewing the documentation of the organization's purchase-order processing subsystem. The documentation was extensive, complete, and properly authorized by management. It was stored in carefully labeled file boxes in the information services library and was duly signed out to the auditor. The documentation appeared to provide much of the information needed by the auditor to evaluate the existing subsystem.

However, something puzzled the auditor. He noticed a small discrepancy between an actual purchase requisition form and the description of the form as it appeared in the documentation. Further investigation revealed discrepancies in other forms and then in computer program listings. Eventually, it emerged that substantial changes had been made to the subsystem two years after it went into operation. None of these changes had been documented.

Inquiries revealed that a new controller had taken over between development of the original subsystem and the subsequent

Source: pathdoc/Shutterstock.

modifications. The former controller had insisted on careful preparation and maintenance of accounting system documentation. But her successor had been under pressure to reduce costs and to correct the problems in the purchase-order processing subsystem by making some changes. He had delayed documenting the changes. Then other problems had arisen that needed correcting; five years later, the documentation had still not been corrected. Unfortunately, the cost of the audit increased by 20 percent because the auditor had to create correct documentation for the existing system—documentation that should have been available when the audit started.

THOUGHT QUESTIONS

1. What should the auditor recommend to the client with regard to documentation?

2. How could the auditor have approached the problem in a way that might have encouraged cooperation from the client as well as reduced the cost of the audit?

Types of System Documentation

LEARNING OBJECTIVE 3
Recognize the appropriate use of the various types of system documentation.

System documentation can range from information that provides a broad overview of the entire system, or a subsystem, to information that provides the details of a computerized process, such as the computation of net income or the calculation of gross pay. Documentation of the details of computerized processes can take the following forms:

- Task description
- HIPO (hierarchy plus input/processing/output) chart
- Pseudocode
- Program flowchart
- Decision table
- Program source code

Because these types of documentation are used primarily by systems analysts and computer programmers, as opposed to accountants, they are not included in this discussion of the types of system documentation. Instead, this section focuses on those types of documentation that are used most frequently by accountants.

System documentation can take one or more of the following forms:

- Narrative description
- Block diagram
- Data flow diagram
- System flowchart (not to be confused with "program" flowchart in the above list)
- Business process modeling

System narrative description The highest level and broadest form of systems documentation. This description is the basic source of information regarding the system's goals and objectives and helps accountants quickly understand the system without being involved with the details of each file or database table and each program.

These forms of documentation are arranged from the least amount of detail provided to the most amount of detail. A narrative description provides the most general overview and correspondingly shows the fewest details. At the other end of the spectrum, a system flowchart provides the most detail and less of an overview. Business process modeling is meant to focus management's attention on an entire process, so as to be able evaluate and improve processes that are often interdependent. Depending on how it is prepared, each type of documentation can cover a range of detail creating considerable overlap between neighboring types and their flexibility in accommodating users' needs. In the following discussion of the various types of systems documentation, the appropriate use of each will become evident.

System Narrative Description

LEARNING OBJECTIVE 4
Describe, read, and prepare a system narrative description.

A **system narrative description** provides the highest level and broadest form of system documentation.

This description is the basic source of information regarding the system's goals and objectives and helps accountants and others quickly understand the system without being involved with the details of each file or database table and each program. A system narrative description should cover the following:

- Reasons for having the accounting system, including the background, the objectives of the system, and the scope of the system
- System specifications describing the major tasks performed by the system
- Evidence of the users' approval of the accounting system
- Staffing requirements for operating and maintaining the system with an explanation of the different roles and responsibilities of those involved

The appropriate use of a narrative description would be as a companion to a graphical representation that explains the system in greater detail. Notwithstanding, a narrative description is sometimes used to describe the details of a system. However, if used to show details of a complex system, a narrative description can be cumbersome and ambiguous and packed with technical jargon.

System Graphical Representation

Graphical representations are the dominant choice for showing details because most people are visually oriented. Pictures, diagrams, and other visual aids can communicate concepts that are difficult or inefficient to convey by other means. Thus, providing a diagram or "picture" of an accounting system helps people understand the accounting system better. Four types of graphical representation are the block diagram, data flow diagram, system flowchart, and business process modeling.

Block Diagram

A **block diagram** is commonly used to provide an overview of an accounting system in terms of its major subsystems. Thus, a block diagram helps a person understand the system being depicted without being presented with needless details. A block diagram is easy to draw and easy to understand.

Two types of block diagrams are noteworthy. One is the **horizontal block diagram** that shows the subsystems of an accounting system and the direction of the information flows among the subsystems. The blocks represent the various subsystems and the connecting lines represent the major information flows. **Exhibit 2.1** illustrates this type of block diagram.

A second type of block diagram is the **hierarchical block diagram** that typically shows the analysis of an accounting system into successive levels of subsystems or, alternatively, the synthesis of subsystems into a complete system. The connecting lines in hierarchical block diagrams represent not the flow of information but the associations among the levels, which take the form of "parent-child" relationships. Hierarchical block diagrams, often referred to as structure charts, are commonly used to provide a general view of accounting systems and their subsystems.

An example of a hierarchical block diagram is shown in **Exhibit 2.2**. It shows the division of the revenue process (one of the several processes in an accounting system) for a sales-supported organization into the sales order processing, shipping, and accounts receivable subsystems. In turn, accounts receivable is divided into customer invoicing and cash receipts.

Both horizontal and hierarchical block diagrams are useful documents to explain how subsystems relate to one another. However, they only show a few aspects of the system and do not contain enough detail to be used as system blueprints. Therefore, block diagrams are used typically in conjunction with other documents that show complementary aspects of the system. A block diagram frequently is drawn as a preliminary step in the preparation of a data flow diagram or a system flowchart.

LEARNING OBJECTIVE 5
Describe, read, and prepare a block diagram.

Block diagram A type of graphical systems documentation that provides an overview of an accounting system in terms of its major subsystems.

Horizontal block diagram A type of block diagram that shows the subsystems of an accounting system and the direction of the information flows among the subsystems.

Heirarchical block diagram A type of block diagram that shows the analysis of an accounting system into successive levels of subsystems or, alternatively, the synthesis of subsystems into a complete system.

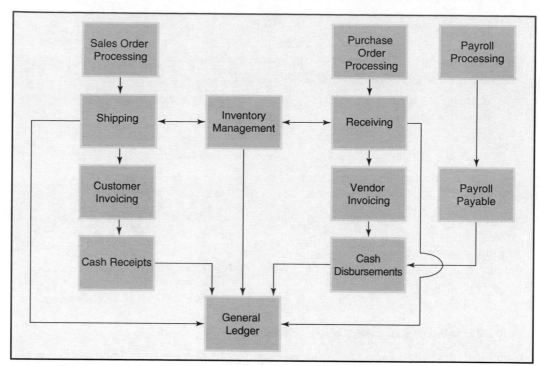

EXHIBIT 2.1 Horizontal Block Diagram of an Entire Accounting System

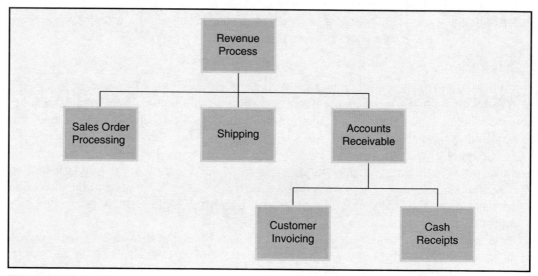

EXHIBIT 2.2 Hierarchical Block Diagram of the Revenue Process

Data Flow Diagram

LEARNING OBJECTIVE 6
Describe, read, and prepare a data flow diagram.

Data flow diagram A type of graphical system documentation that provides a more detailed representation of an accounting system than a block diagram, but fewer technical details than a system flowchart.

A logical **data flow diagram** (also called DFD or bubble chart) provides a more detailed representation of an accounting system than a block diagram can provide, but it has fewer technical details than does a system flowchart. A data flow diagram only shows what an accounting system is doing, whereas a flowchart shows what an accounting system is doing and how the system is doing it. Because a data flow diagram shows few technical details, it may be used to obtain an overall understanding of the system and as a first step in developing a system flowchart. The symbols in a data flow diagram are used to depict the flow of data from the origination of transactions and other events, through various stages of processing and refinement, to the distribution of processed or captured data. No attention is given to how the individual processing activities are performed.

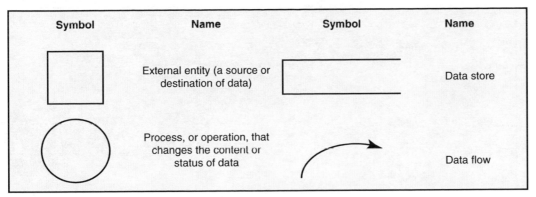

EXHIBIT 2.3 Data Flow Diagram Symbols

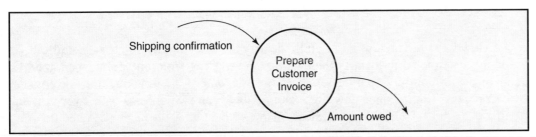

EXHIBIT 2.4 Example of Process Symbol in Data Flow Diagram

A data flow diagram uses four basic symbols (see **Exhibit 2.3**). A square represents an external entity with an entity being a person, place, or thing and is involved with at least one data flow. The "thing" is usually another subsystem. An external entity is a source, or originator, of data going into the system being modeled in the data flow diagram. Or an external entity may be the destination, or receiver, of data coming out of the system being modeled. The criterion for being an "external" entity is not whether the entity is outside the organization. Rather, an entity is external if it resides outside of the system being modeled. The name of the external entity, for example, customer, vendor, accounts receivable subsystem, is written inside the entity symbol.

A circle represents a process, or operation, which typically has at least one data flow in and one data flow out of the process. In other words, a process identifies the activities, procedures, or both that change the data coming into it. The process may change the content (what the data consists of) or the status (condition, state, classification) of the data. An example is data that confirms the shipment of a customer's order is changed into the amount owed by the customer by the activity—prepare customer invoice. Another example is a check that is changed into an endorsed check by the activity—endorse check.

An active verb and an object, such as "prepare customer invoice," is written inside the process symbol. This process with the inflow and outflow of data might appear as shown in **Exhibit 2.4**. If more than one process symbol is used in a data flow diagram, a unique identification number, such as 1.0, is written inside the process symbol along with the verb and object. The circle is used as the process symbol whether the process is computerized or manual because a data flow diagram illustrates what an accounting system is doing, but not how the processing activities are performed.

An open-ended rectangle is a data store where data resides and is involved with at least one data flow. For example, data about customers, such as name, address, credit limit, and outstanding balance, are stored in a customer master file. Data about inventory, such as description, selling price, quantity on hand, and reorder point, are stored in an inventory master file. Data can be stored in a paper file or a file on magnetic medium, but this aspect is not important in a data flow diagram. A label should be written inside the symbol to identify the file.

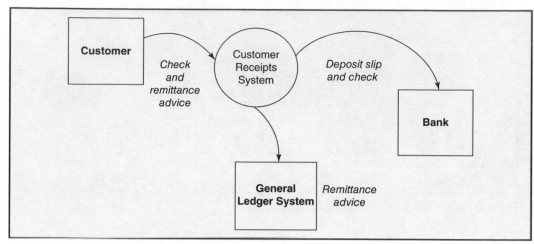

EXHIBIT 2.5 Context Diagram for Cash Receipts System

A flow line with an arrow is used to identify the direction in which the data flow. Each flow line is labeled to identify the data that are moving from one point to another. Data must flow into or out of a process. Therefore, one end of the flow line must be connected to a process. Data cannot flow, for example, between two entities or between an entity and a data store. Data can be physical, such as a customer invoice or a schedule of aged accounts receivable. Data can take other forms, however, such as a customer's inquiry, a verbal message, or an electronic message.

For a complex accounting system, multiple data flow diagrams may be needed to represent the entire system. An initial diagram, called a **context diagram**, shows a high-level overview of the system in which only the system being diagrammed and its relevant environment are displayed. An example of a context diagram for a cash receipts system is shown in **Exhibit 2.5**. This diagram shows that the system of interest is the cash receipts system. The relevant aspects of the system's environment are the customer, the general ledger system, and the bank. Note that a context diagram has only one process. The name of the system of interest is printed inside the process symbol.

The next diagram is the **level 0 data flow diagram**. It describes the entire system on a single sheet of paper. All major processes, data stores, data flows, and external entities are shown. Subsequently, each process in the level 0 diagram can be further detailed by another data flow diagram. This process is called "explosion." Each broad process can be exploded further into subprocesses using additional data flow diagrams. A level 0 data flow diagram is shown in **Exhibit 2.6**.

Please note the introduction of several processes and data stores that were not shown in the related context diagram. This level 0 diagram shows that data originate with the customer; are changed by five processes; and finally reach their destinations—the general ledger system and the bank. The level 0 data flow diagram can be read and interpreted as follows:

- Compare customer check and remittance advice (1.0). A customer sends a check and a remittance advice. A **remittance advice** is a document that shows the invoice or invoices to which a customer's payment is to be applied. Generally, a remittance advice is attached to the customer's invoice or statement so it can be conveniently torn off and sent back to the organization with a check, such as the bill you receive for your cell phone and utility statements. In the first process, the check and remittance advice are compared to ascertain whether they match. If not, the check and remittance advice are filed away to be investigated later. If a match occurs, that information flows to the next process.

- Compare check and remittance advice (1.0) to Separate check and remittance advice (2.0). The status of the check and the remittance advice are changed in process 2.0 from being attached to being separated with the check taking one path and the remittance advice taking another.

Context diagram A type of graphical system documentation that shows a high-level overview of the system. Only the system being diagrammed and its relevant environment are displayed.

Level 0 data flow diagram A type of graphical systems documentation that describes the entire accounting system on a single sheet of paper. All major processes, data stores, data flows, and external entities are shown.

Remittance advice A document that shows the invoice or invoices to which a customer's payment is to be applied.

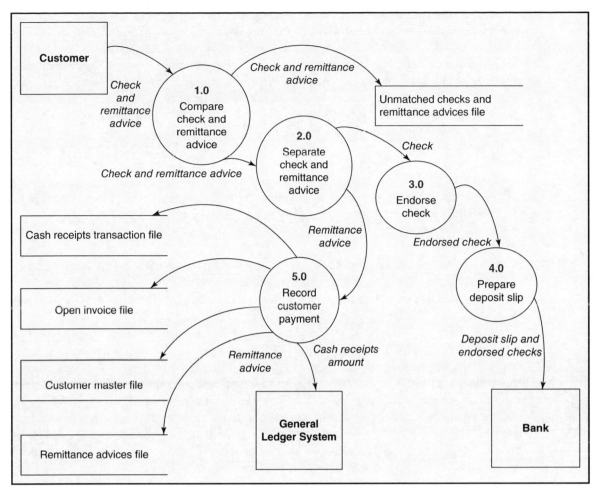

EXHIBIT 2.6 Level 0 Data Flow Diagram for Cash Receipts System

We will first follow the path of the check.

■ Separate check and remittance advice (2.0) to Endorse check (3.0). The status of the check is changed in process 3.0 from being an unendorsed check to being an endorsed check.

■ Endorse check (3.0) to Prepare deposit slip (4.0). The information on the endorsed check is transcribed onto a deposit slip.

■ Prepare deposit slip (4.0) to Bank. The check reaches its final destination—the bank.

We continue reading the data flow diagram by going back to process 2.0, where the check and the remittance advice are separated, and follow the path of the remittance advice.

■ Separate check and remittance advice (2.0) to Record customer payment (5.0). The information on the remittance advice is changed into information that is stored in the cash receipts transaction file, the open invoice file (a file that holds unpaid invoice information), and customer master file. The remittance advice itself is stored in the remittance advice file.

■ Record customer payment (5.0) to General ledger system. Finally, the information from the remittance advice reaches its final destination—the general ledger system.

As discussed earlier, processes can often be further detailed by another data flow diagram—one for process 1.0, another for process 2.0, and so on. For example, if we were going to provide more detail with regard to process 4.0, the next level diagram would be 4.1 (a level 1 data flow diagram). However, exploding this process to a lower level would require you to think about how you are going to implement the process. That is, if we were to explode 4.0—Prepare deposit slip, we would be getting into the details of how to prepare the deposit slip. Consequently, this is the point where you probably would decide not explode this particular data flow diagram further.

Data flow diagrams tend to be easy for even nontechnical people to understand, and thus serve as an excellent communication tool. Most accountants prefer to convert data flow diagrams into system flowcharts; however, a small but increasing number regard data flow diagrams as permanent documentation. The main disadvantage of data flow diagrams lies in the difficulty or inability to represent points of detail.

System Flowchart

LEARNING OBJECTIVE 7
Describe, read, and prepare a
system flowchart.

System flowchart A
type of graphical system
documentation that shows what
a system does and how the
system does it. It documents
complex activities and details
the sources of information, the
processes involved, and the
disposition of the information.

A **system flowchart** is a graphic that shows what a system does and how the system does it. It is the type of documentation most frequently used by accountants. System flowcharts document complex activities and detail the sources of information, the processes involved, and the disposition of the information. Flowcharts make processes and interrelationships easy to grasp. A flowchart has more of an "if-then" format, allowing you to see what happens if something else happens. It allows you to see very clearly what a process really is, versus what it should be, and to see where the problems or weaknesses are in the process. Because of the amount of detail that can be shown in a system flowchart, it is used extensively throughout this textbook to clarify many explanations.

The symbols in a flowchart represent the sources of data, the processes to move data through the system, and the disposition of the data. Lines connecting these symbols provide the paths. You can think of a flowchart as a map that outlines the processes necessary to achieve a goal. Although our interest is in flowcharts of accounting systems, you can flowchart almost any activity, for example, an internal control review, audit, accounting system installation, inventory count, manufacturing process, or bidding process.

Although a system flowchart emphasizes the flow of data elements through the system and the role of computer programs and human beings in the processing of accounting data, it may also show which functional areas are responsible for the various processes. The inclusion of this additional information, however, makes a flowchart more complex and difficult to understand.

Internal control flowchart
A system flowchart that
also shows the functional
areas to permit identification
of the authorization of the
transactions, the custody
of assets, and the recording
functions. In addition, an
internal control flowchart
identifies all existing control
procedures for preventing
or detecting errors and
irregularities.

A variation of the system flowchart is the **internal control flowchart**. The difference between the two is that an internal control flowchart shows the functional areas to permit identification of the authorization of transactions and other events, the custody of assets, and the recording functions—the functions that need to be segregated for good internal control to prevent irregularities from occurring. In addition, an internal control flowchart identifies all existing control procedures for preventing or detecting errors and irregularities.

In contrast to other types of graphical representation, system flowcharting is governed by national and international standards. The purpose of these standards is to provide uniformity in order to minimize misinterpretation among users of system flowcharts throughout the world. The national standards are accredited by the American National Standards Institute (ANSI). International standards are set by the International Organization for Standardization (ISO). Adherence to standards helps reduce ambiguities and makes system flowcharts more useful and easier to interpret.

The common system flowcharting symbols are shown in **Exhibit 2.7a**. Examples of various ways to use some of the symbols in Exhibit 2.7a are illustrated in Exhibit 2.7b–f. For example, the first symbol in Exhibit 2.7a is the process, or operation, symbol. Exhibit 2.7b illustrates eight ways that this symbol can be used. Another example is the paper file

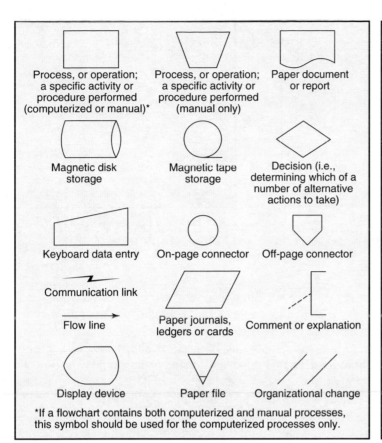

EXHIBIT 2.7a System Flowcharting Symbols

- Process, or operation; a specific activity or procedure performed (computerized or manual)*
- Process, or operation; a specific activity or procedure performed (manual only)
- Paper document or report
- Magnetic disk storage
- Magnetic tape storage
- Decision (i.e., determining which of a number of alternative actions to take)
- Keyboard data entry
- On-page connector
- Off-page connector
- Communication link
- Flow line
- Paper journals, ledgers or cards
- Comment or explanation
- Display device
- Paper file
- Organizational change

*If a flowchart contains both computerized and manual processes, this symbol should be used for the computerized processes only.

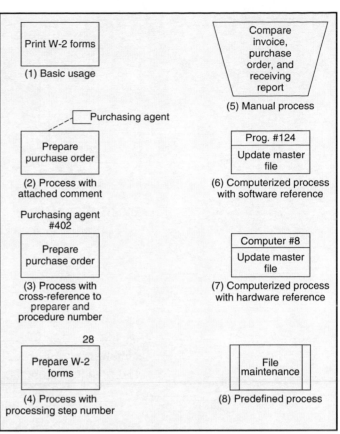

EXHIBIT 2.7b Examples of Process, or Operation, Symbol Usage

- Print W-2 forms — (1) Basic usage
- Prepare purchase order / Purchasing agent — (2) Process with attached comment
- Prepare purchase order / Purchasing agent #402 — (3) Process with cross-reference to preparer and procedure number
- Prepare W-2 forms / 28 — (4) Process with processing step number
- Compare invoice, purchase order, and receiving report — (5) Manual process
- Update master file / Prog. #124 — (6) Computerized process with software reference
- Update master file / Computer #8 — (7) Computerized process with hardware reference
- File maintenance — (8) Predefined process

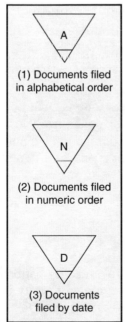

EXHIBIT 2.7c Examples of Paper File Symbol Usage

- A — (1) Documents filed in alphabetical order
- N — (2) Documents filed in numeric order
- D — (3) Documents filed by date

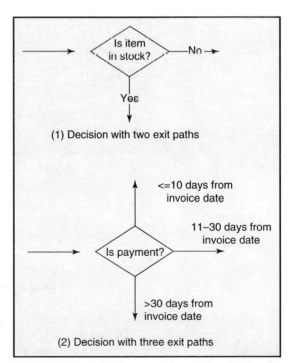

EXHIBIT 2.7d Examples of Decision Symbol Usage

- Is item in stock? — No / Yes — (1) Decision with two exit paths
- Is payment? — <=10 days from invoice date / 11–30 days from invoice date / >30 days from invoice date — (2) Decision with three exit paths

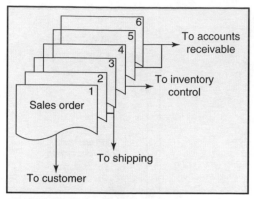

EXHIBIT 2.7e Example of Document Symbol Usage

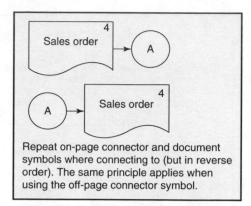

Repeat on-page connector and document symbols where connecting to (but in reverse order). The same principle applies when using the off-page connector symbol.

EXHIBIT 2.7f Example of On-page Connector Symbol Usage

symbol in Exhibit 7.2a; Exhibit 2.7c shows three different ways that this symbol can be used. You will notice in Exhibit 2.7b that example (8) is the predefined operation symbol. The example is for a predefined file maintenance process, which would actually require several symbols to describe. This one symbol can be used as shorthand for a group of symbols for a process that may be repeated at several different locations in a flowchart. The predefined operation symbol must be defined—that is, exploded into its constituent symbols—elsewhere in the flowchart, possibly on a separate page.

The decision symbol, illustrated in Exhibit 2.7a, is further illustrated in Exhibit 2.7d. Notices the first decision has two exit paths, and the second decision has three exit paths. The important thing to remember with the decision symbol is to be certain all possible results of the decision have an exit path. An example of the use of the document symbol in Exhibit 2.7a is shown in Exhibit 2.7e, where six copies of the sales order are distributed. The use of the on-page connector symbol in Exhibit 2.7a is illustrated in Exhibit 2.7f. Notice the connector symbol and the document it refers to are both repeated on the page to reduce confusion.

As simple as it is, flowcharting is not always easy to do. Adhering to the following four steps prior to actually creating a flowchart can help produce an accurate, usable flowchart:

- Determine the system to be flowcharted, for example, sales order processing, purchase order processing, or payroll processing.

- Determine the level of detail required; in other words, determine the purpose of the flowchart.

- Gain an understanding of the inputs, processes, outputs, files or database tables, and controls in the system by interviewing personnel involved in the system, observing the activities of these personnel, examining the inputs and outputs of the system, and tracing transactions and other events of different types through the system.

- List the steps in the processes.

Some useful guidelines for drawing a system flowchart are listed in **Exhibit 2.8**. They are not hard-and-fast rules, but they will help preparers represent systems more clearly and make the flowcharts easier to understand.

As mentioned earlier, system flowcharting is governed by national and international standards. The purpose of these standards is to provide uniformity in order to minimize misinterpretation among users of system flowcharts throughout the world. Flowcharting is by no means a science; individual style, particularly as it helps achieve a clear, orderly, and pleasing layout, is most welcome. But adherence to the accepted rules helps reduce ambiguities and makes system flowcharts more useful.

1. Start with the entry of data into the system you are flowcharting.
2. Show all working files or database tables.
3. Show the source and disposition of all major documents and reports. This does not apply to paper journals and ledgers because they do not flow anywhere.
4. Use arrowheads on all flow lines to indicate the direction of the flow.
5. Make the direction of the flow lines primarily from left to right and top to bottom. Occasionally, these directions can be reversed when it makes the flowchart more concise, but this should be done sparingly.
6. Avoid crossing flow lines to the extent possible.
7. Put the entire system on one page unless it is impractical to do so.
8. Use on-page and off-page connectors sparingly. An overuse of connectors indicates poor layout and makes the flowchart hard to follow.
9. Use telegraphic, keyword active style in the words on the flowchart, leaving out nonessential words, such as "a," "an," and "the".
10. When abbreviating is necessary, use standard abbreviations only, or use a footnote or legend to explain nonstandard abbreviations.
11. Include written comments whenever it helps make a flowchart more complete or easier to understand. Comments can be included within the flowchart using the comment symbol, or they can be included as footnotes at the bottom or on one side.
12. If showing segregation of duties, use vertical columns, horizontal rows, or the organizational change symbol.
13. Do not leave dangling branches. A dangling branch occurs when a process suddenly stops on the flowchart, but obviously needs other activities to complete the process. Explain what happens with a note or show data going into another system.
14. Place a title, the preparer's name, and the date on all pages of the flowchart. Number pages as "page x of n," for example, "page 1 of 3," so the reader will know when the flowchart is complete.

EXHIBIT 2.8 Guidelines for Effective System Flowcharting

Exhibit 2.9 shows a system flowchart of a cash receipts system. A first step that will help you in reading this and any flowchart is to look for the first activity, which will be a process symbol or a decision symbol. Next, observe the input symbol(s) shown for this activity. Next, observe the output symbol(s) of this same activity. Then proceed to the next symbol, the next, and so on. An interpretation of the flowchart in Exhibit 2.9 is given. It is too early in this course for you to be able to understand all the terms (particularly the file names) used in the following interpretation. Do not be concerned; you will learn them later. The purpose of this exercise is to give you some guidance and practice in reading a flowchart.

- The first activity is a decision as to whether documents match. According to the input symbols for this decision, the documents in question are the customer's check and the remittance advice that were submitted by the customer.

- The possible exit paths from this decision are yes and no. If the conclusion is no, the documents do not match, then both documents are sent to the individual who will resolve the discrepancy.

- If the conclusion is yes, the documents do match, and the check and the remittance advice are separated.

We will follow the path for the customer's check first and then will come back to follow the path for the remittance advice.

- The customer's check is endorsed and a deposit slip is prepared for it as well as all other checks that have reached this point in the system.

- The endorsed checks and deposit slip are taken to the bank.

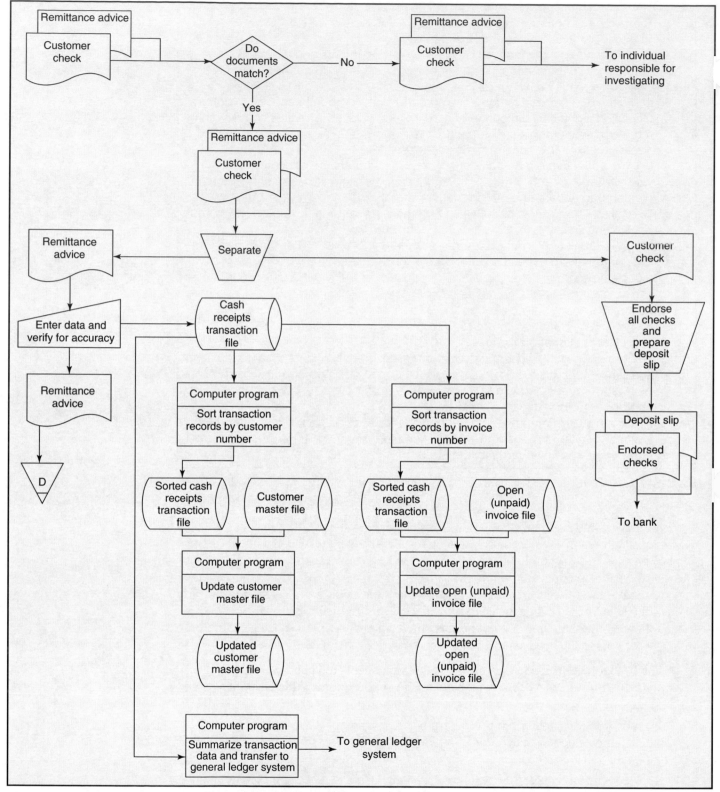

EXHIBIT 2.9 Flowchart of Cash Receipts System

We now can go back to the point in the flowchart where the customer's check and remittance advice were separated and follow the path for the remittance advice.

■ Data from the remittance advice are entered into the cash receipts transaction file in the computerized system, and the data are verified for accuracy.

Two paths flow from this last process. We can either follow what happens to the remittance advice or to the cash receipts transaction file. We will follow the remittance advice first.

- The remittance advice whose data have now been captured in the computerized system are filed away by date.

Now, we can follow what happens with the cash receipts transaction file. As you can see, three paths flow from this file.

- A computer program sorts the records in the cash receipts transaction file by customer number and then uses the sorted file to update (makes changes to) the customer master file.

- A computer program sorts the records in the cash receipts transaction file by invoice number and then uses the sorted file to update (make changes to) the open (unpaid) invoice file.

- A computer program summarizes the data in the cash receipts transaction file and transfers the summarized data to the general ledger system.

When comparing this flowchart to the level 0 data flow diagram in Exhibit 2.6, you can observe the differences in the two graphical representations since they are for the same system. The system flowchart depicts a greater level of detail and could be presented at an even greater level of detail by using more symbols to show the cash receipts transaction file is archived, to show the various reports that are generated in the system, and to show how the data that have been entered into the system are verified for accuracy. It could also show who performs the matching of the documents, who endorses the checks, who prepares the deposit slips, and who takes the deposits to the bank. Comment symbols could also be included to explain the decision procedures, to explain what happens to customer checks and remittance advices that do not match, to explain document and archive file retention policies, and to indicate how frequently the updating of files takes place and how frequently deposits are made. Alternatively, these explanations could be provided in footnotes.

System flowcharts can be as simple or as complicated as is necessary to convey the intended description of the accounting system. An overview presentation may be all that is needed as a visual aid for presentation to upper management. Its purpose may be to show how the system cuts across organizational boundaries, how it affects management responsibilities, and what coordination is required. On the other hand, a detailed representation may be necessary, for example, for an auditor to evaluate the internal controls in a system to determine whether data are being processed error-free. In addition, the detailed representation also provides a means for management and auditors to review the control system of a process. Frequently, a set of related flowcharts is prepared, each providing a different view of the system and incorporating a different level of detail. An overview flowchart may be expanded by providing several charts with more details of the system. System flowcharting provides considerable flexibility in representing systems for multiple purposes (Vignette 2.2).

Business process modeling Another form of graphical representation. Common languages used to illustrate the business process include the Business Process Modeling Notation (BPMN) and the Unified Modeling Language (UML). Business process modeling has the advantage of allowing communication to stakeholders and others regarding how the process operates.

Business Process Modeling

Business process modeling is another form of graphical representation. Common languages used to illustrate the business process include the Business Process Modeling Notation (BPMN) and the Unified Modeling Language (UML). Business process modeling has the advantage of allowing communication to stakeholders and others regarding how the process operates and some tools offer the ability to run simulations (e.g., Provision, TIBCO).

One of the benefits of process modeling is to steer organizations away from a function or procedure focus and encourage organizations to evaluate their operations in terms of the total process (e.g., the revenue process in a sales-supported organization begins with a call to a customer by a sales representative and ends with collection of cash from the customer and the sales analysis function). Process orientation allows management to

LEARNING OBJECTIVE 8
Discuss business process modeling and how business processes are mapped using the Unified Modeling Language (UML).

Vignette 2.2

Evaluation of Internal Control

While reviewing a client's system documentation, an auditor noticed a reference to a programmed control procedure in a system flowchart. The control was supposed to screen transaction dates and to accept transactions and other events only if they were dated in the current month. The flowchart indicated that transactions and other events with past or future dates would be rejected and listed on an exception report. The auditor examined the source code for the input program and saw that it contained a subroutine to segregate offending transactions and other events and generate the exception report. She made a note to test the control later and then continued to review the documentation.

A test run failed to verify the existence of the control. When transactions and other events were entered with past or future dates—or even ones with invalid dates such as 13/35/2018—they were all processed, and no exception report was generated. Inquiries revealed that the control had indeed been built into the system, but it never worked successfully and was removed so that the system could be implemented on schedule. The developers intended to go back later to fix the control, but they never had time. Also, they forgot that the control was still referred to in the system flowchart.

The auditor concluded not only that the control was missing, but also that the client's organization was lax in its systems development and documentation

Source: thodonal88/Shutterstock.

procedures. In the letter addressed to management at the end of the audit engagement, the accounting firm recommended that both weaknesses be remedied. In particular, the accounting firm recommended that the client establish documentation standards to guide the future preparation and maintenance of system documentation.

THOUGHT QUESTIONS

1. What recommendations would you list in your report?

2. What actions should the firm take to avoid documentation problems in the future?

---

focus on measurements and improvement solutions that take into account interdependencies among activities within a process. Examples of interdependencies among processes includes the interaction of the revenue process with the procurement and inventory processes (**Exhibit 2.10**)

A business process model describes more than just the flow of information or activities. It can also include descriptions of other aspects of the business such as infrastructure, trading practices, and operational policies and procedures. Business processes can be (1) operational (such as those illustrated in Exhibit 2.10), (2) governance/strategic (such as IT governance), or (3) sustaining/support (such as technical support or hiring practices). A business process can have several subprocesses (or subsystems). Review of Exhibit 2.10 illustrates the subprocesses in the revenue process that include Sales Order Processing, Shipping, Customer Invoicing, and Cash Receipts. All business processes and subprocesses should be structured to allow the organization to meet its business objectives.

Business process mapping is a form of business process modeling that can be described as an enhanced flowchart—a graphical representation of a business process that includes (1) descriptions of exactly what the process does to promote the organization's strategy, (2) who is responsible for what, (3) standards to be maintained in the process, and (4) performance indicators or other measures of process success. Business process mapping can help an organization comply with standards such as ISO 9001, which requires the organization to use a process-focused approach in managing the business. The purpose of standards such as ISO 9001 is to provide assurance that the process(es) is (are) in

Business process mapping A form of business process modeling that can be described as an enhanced flowchart—a graphical representation that includes 1) descriptions of exactly what the process does to promote the organization's strategy, 2) who is responsible for what, 3) standards to be maintained in the process, and 4) performance indicator's or other measures of process success.

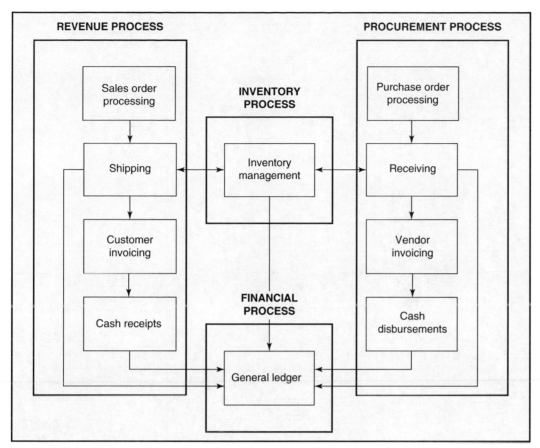

EXHIBIT 2.10 Interdependencies of the Processes in a Sales-Supported Organization

compliance with the related standard and that the process(es) are consistently performing procedures, using resources efficiently. Business process maps can include drivers and triggers for activities within a process, as well embedded key performance indicators to evaluate operations. Consequently, business process mapping can assist the organization in reaching multi-dimensional goals such as improved service level agreement (SLA) transparency, achievement of business process reengineering, compliance with laws and regulations, and activity analysis.

A simple example of a business process map using Unified Modeling Language (UML) can be found in **Exhibit 2.11**. The narrative for this business process map is as follows: our customers send us purchase orders for the items they need. This information enters our sales order process through an interface with the sales order process subsystem, which converts the customer's purchase order information to a sales order in a format our system can translate/understand. If the items ordered are available, the sales order is processed and the information is sent to the warehouse personnel for processing of the shipment of items. If the items ordered are not available, the customer has the option to agree to wait for the items to come in or can cancel the order. If the customer agrees to wait, a sales order is processed as a backorder. If the customer wants to cancel the order, a sales representative notifies the customer by phone that the order will be cancelled; the call includes recommendations for other items that might be substituted for the originally ordered items. Once the sales order is processed, the open sales order repository is updated and relevant reports (such as aging reports) are generated and sent to the Sales Manager. Information from the processed sales orders is used to prepare an invoice, which is processed in the Billing department. Note that the Sales Order Aging Report is a performance measure of the effectiveness/efficiency of the inventory management system and the sales order processing system. The notification of order cancellation and options for alternative

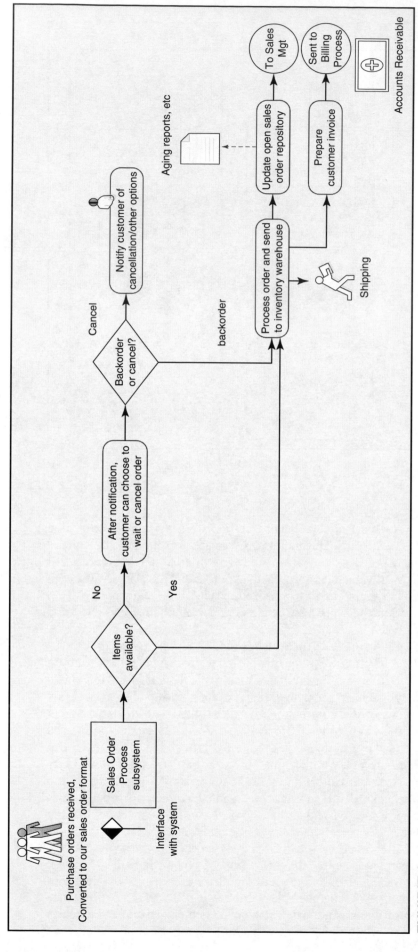

EXHIBIT 2.11 Business Process Map of Sales Order Process Subsystem

items communicated by a phone call to the customer is an example of how follow-up to maintain customer relationships is accomplished.

The Sarbanes-Oxley Act (SOX) has encouraged a process-oriented approach to auditing and managing the controls affecting financial statement disclosure. The identification of key financial reporting controls required by SOX demands an understanding of business processes so that the auditor and management can focus on the true key controls when developing, maintaining, and testing a business unit's control system.[2]

Computer-Assisted System Documentation Tools

Flowcharting software programs offer a major breakthrough in productivity by significantly reducing the time and effort needed to create and maintain system documentation. Microsoft's Visio is a popular program for microcomputers. Flowcharting software programs come with many standardized flowchart and diagram symbols. The symbols are categorized into templates that are shown on the computer screen in the same way as toolbars. Symbols are easily placed on a drawing page on the screen by using a "drag and drop" process to move the symbol in the template to the flowchart worksheet area. They can be moved from one part of the drawing page to another and can be enlarged or reduced. Straight or curved flow lines connecting symbols are added using a pointer tool that allows the user to draw the flow lines between symbols. Titles, legends, footnotes, and other textual material can be added as needed. Completed charts or diagrams are stored in electronic files and can be retrieved quickly for future use.

Once a chart or diagram is created and stored, it can be edited quickly and efficiently without redrawing the chart. Frequently used components of charts—such as a data input routine or a file maintenance routine, for example, changing a customer's address—can be stored for insertion into a number of charts. The charts or diagrams can be printed using a high-quality printer. The low cost of editing and printing graphical documentation is an important advantage of the use of these software programs.

Software programs for preparing charts and diagrams are rudimentary forms of CASE software. **CASE**, which stands for Computer Aided Software Engineering, consists of a number of software tools that assist in the development of information systems. Among these tools are aids for the preparation of various types of system documentation, including block diagrams, data flow diagrams, and system and program flowcharts. CASE software automatically indexes and cross-references documentation to facilitate retrieval and exchange of information (Vignette 2.3).

LEARNING OBJECTIVE 9
Appreciate the advantages of computer-assisted systems documentation tools.

CASE Software that consists of a number of tools that assist in the development of information systems. Among these tools are aids to preparation of various types of systems documentation, including block diagrams, data flow diagrams, and systems and program flowcharts.

Vignette 2.3

Electronic Documentation Speeds Evaluation

Charles Meyer Associates was a leading producer of high-quality accounting software. It marketed a full range of prepackaged software and also developed accounting software to customers' specifications. The use of a CASE system greatly accelerated the development of software. Systems developers prepared documentation using interactive workstations. As soon as one designer released a document into the common database, it was available for others to use. The CASE system made possible the review and evaluation of systems designs as soon as they were produced.

During the development of a payroll package, Dan Geiger pulled up the specifications for the payroll transaction file. Dan was trained as an auditor, and his job was to review the control effectiveness of the programs sold by the company. He immediately noticed that the transaction type code would fail to distinguish between hourly and piecework employees.

Dan entered a message through his terminal, alerting the designer of the file about his concern. A few minutes later, a message flashed up on Dan's screen:

Thanks for the tip. I had forgotten the problem of employee crossover. By the way, you auditors are really on the ball. I only designed that file 20 minutes ago!

Cheers, Ruth

THOUGHT QUESTION

1. Why would it be important to distinguish between hourly and piecework employees?

Documentation stored in machine-readable form—whether using simple flowcharting programs or sophisticated CASE software—can also be distributed electronically to others. Documentation files can be shared or transferred to other computers over a common network.

Narrative descriptions are easily prepared and maintained using word-processing software. All of the word-processing programs available for use on PCs are suitable for this task and permit the importation of graphics material prepared in other software programs. CASE software often includes word-processing functions that can be interfaced with graphics functions and canned functions for preparing specific types of documentation such as file and database specifications.

Summary

This chapter has presented the concepts, types, and uses of graphical and narrative techniques in documenting accounting systems. The Sarbanes-Oxley Act of 2002 requires companies to document their internal control in detail.

System narrative descriptions, block diagrams, data flow diagrams, and system flowcharts are used frequently by accountants. Flowcharts and other types of system documentation are essential tools for accountants, whether they are system implementers, auditors, end users, systems designers, managers, or others who are involved with accounting systems in performing their work. To be effective, accountants should acquire the basic skills necessary to read and prepare system flowcharts and other types of diagrams.

Business process modeling is an extended form of system flowcharting, as it shows what the process does to promote the organization's strategy, who is responsible for what, and indicates standards and key performance measure for process success.

Software packages have made creating and maintaining graphical documentation considerably easier and less expensive. These packages also make updating and changing flowcharts much easier. Available tools range from simple flowcharting packages for personal computers to elaborate CASE software operated on large computers with interactive workstations.

Key Terms

Block diagram (horizontal and hierarchical)   27
Business process mapping   38
Business process modeling   37
CASE (computer-aided software engineering)   41
Context diagram   30
Data flow diagram   28
Documentation standards   24
Hierarchal block diagram   27

Horizontal block diagram   27
Internal control flowchart   32
Level 0 data flow diagram   30
Remittance advice   30
System documentation   24
System flowchart   32
System narrative description   26
User documentation   24

Discussion Questions and Problems

1. What symbol would be used in a data flow diagram to represent the processing of employees' time cards?

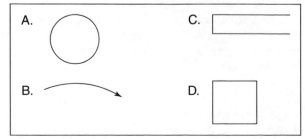

2. What symbol would be used in a data flow diagram to represent employees' payroll data stored on magnetic disk?

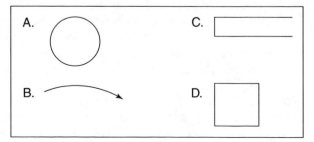

3. Flowcharting as a prelude to internal control evaluation provides what advantage over the use of narrative descriptions?
   a. Ease of preparation.
   b. Comprehensive coverage of controls.
   c. Cost effective.
   d. Ease in following information flow.
   [CIA adapted]

4. The flowchart of a client's accounting system is a diagrammatic representation that depicts the:
   a. way the system should be.
   b. way the system currently is.
   c. the types of irregularities that are probable, given the present system.
   d. key controls of the business process represented.

5. Exhibit 2.8 lists some recommended guidelines for effective system flowcharting. Which of the following describes the normal flow of documents and operations on a well-prepared systems flowchart?
   a. Top to bottom and left to right.
   b. Bottom to top and left to right.
   c. Top to bottom and right to left.
   d. Bottom to top and right to left.

6. What does the diamond-shaped symbol commonly used in flowcharting show or represent?
   a. Process or single step in a procedure or program.
   b. Display device.
   c. Decision point.
   d. Predefined process.
   [CIA adapted]

7. Which of the statements below properly describes the section of the flowchart illustrated below?

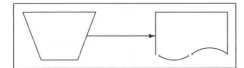

   a. A master file has been created by a manual operation.
   b. A master file has been created by a computer operation.
   c. A document has been generated by a computer operation.
   d. A document has been generated by a manual operation.

8. What is the correct labeling, in order, for the following flowchart symbols?

   a. Document, display device, magnetic disk storage, and manual process.
   b. Manual process, processing, paper file, and paper journal.

   c. Display device, document, magnetic disk storage, and computerized process.
   d. Manual process, document, magnetic disk storage, and computerized process.
   [CMA adapted]

9. What is the symbol that would be used for determination of whether an employee's wages are above or below the maximum limit for FICA taxes?

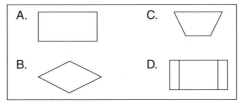

   [CMA adapted]

10. In a system flowchart, what symbol would be used to represent the printing of the employees' paychecks by the computer?

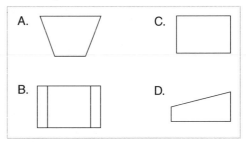

   [CMA adapted]

11. In a system flowchart, what symbol would be employed to represent that the employees' checks have been printed by the computer?

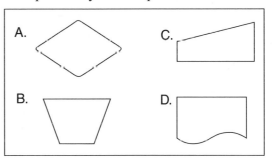

   [CMA adapted]

12. In a systems flowchart, the symbol that would be used to represent the physical act of collecting employees' time cards for processing is:

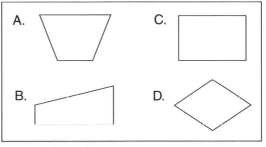

   [CMA adapted]

13. In a systems flowchart, the symbol that would be used to represent the employees' payroll records stored on magnetic disk is:

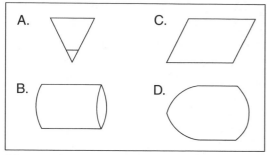

[CMA adapted]

14. In a systems flowchart, the symbol that would be used to represent the weekly payroll register generated by the computer is:

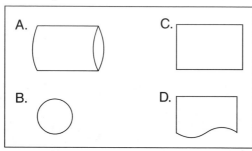

[CMA adapted]

15. Which of the following flowcharts indicates that new sales transactions and the customer master file have been used to prepare sales orders, a sales journal has been printed, and the customer master file has been updated?

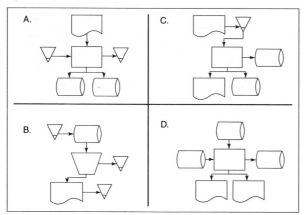

16. Which of the representations below illustrates that a sales invoice has been filed?

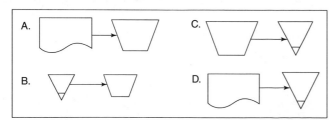

The following flowchart applies to questions 17 and 18.

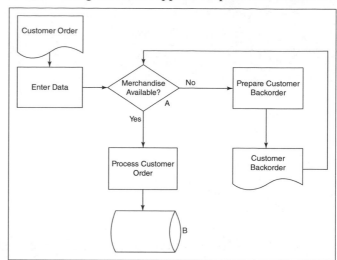

17. The symbol at Point **A** represents:
   a. input or output processing.
   b. a decision.
   c. operations.
   d. a computer program.
   [CMA adapted]

18. The symbol at Point **B** represents a:
   a. magnetic storage device.
   b. connector.
   c. floppy disk drive.
   d. display device.
   [CMA adapted]

19. Draw the correct flowcharting symbol for each of the following decision situations:
   a. Does the account have a zero balance?
   b. Is the quantity on hand less than or equal to the reorder point?
   c. Is the age of the account less than or equal to 30 days old, 31 to 60 days old, or over 60 days old?

20. Draw the correct flowcharting symbols for the following storage activities:
   a. A paper purchase order going into a file arranged by date.
   b. A sales transaction file stored on magnetic disk.

21. Draw the correct flowcharting symbol for each of the following processing activities. If a legend is noted in parentheses beside a process, include the legend in some suitable manner.

Manual processes:

   a. Prepare invoice.
   b. Make bank deposit (First National Bank).
   c. Verify transaction entries (assistant controller).
   d. Post transactions to the ledger (reference E9).

Computerized processes:

   e. Sort customer file alphabetically.
   f. Retrieve all open accounts (program #RTVOPN).

g. Copy the sales transaction file (Computer #20).

h. Perform file maintenance on inventory file (operator #J-2).

22. Draw the correct symbol for each of the following documents:

    a. A monthly open order report

    b. Four copies of a materials requisition form, all of which go to the stores clerk

    c. Five copies of a customer invoice distributed as follows: Copies 1 and 2 to the customer, Copy 3 to accounting, Copy 4 to sales, and Copy 5 to shipping

23. Aquamarine Company, a manufacturer of heavy machinery, uses materials requisition forms to control the release of raw materials into production. Four copies of a materials requisition form are prepared by personnel in the production department. The supervisor in the production department must authorize each materials requisition before it can be used to withdraw materials from the stores department. If the supervisor does not authorize the requisition, all four copies are marked "not authorized" and filed in a paper file by number. If the supervisor authorizes the requisition, all four copies are taken to the stores department.

    Required:

    Prepare a detailed systems flowchart of the portion of the production system described. Show who does what by making one column for the production department and one column for the stores department.

24. Adam Company uses a job costing system to keep track of the 2,000 jobs that typically are in the factory at any one time. The direct materials, direct labor, manufacturing overhead costs are stored in a production cost transaction file on magnetic disk. A computer program sorts this transaction file by job number and then uses the sorted file to update the open (unfinished) job file, which is also maintained on magnetic disk. An unfinished jobs report is prepared from the open job file and is delivered to the production manager.

Required:

Prepare a detailed systems flowchart of the portion of the production system described.

25. Mason Company uses a purchase order processing system to handle its purchase orders. The broad perspective of the system is that an authorized purchase requisition comes into the system from the warehouse. A purchase order flows out of the system and goes to the vendor.

Required:

Prepare a context diagram to show the high-level overview of this system as described.

26. Mason Company's purchase order processing system can be described in more detail than it was in the previous question. When an authorized purchase requisition comes into the system, it is checked to see that it has been authorized. Furthermore, the budget master file is accessed to ensure the purchase is covered by the authorizer's budget. After the purchase requisition has been validated, a vendor is selected from those in the vendor master file. At this time, a purchase order is prepared and the purchase requisition is filed away in the purchase requisition file.

All the departments in the organization that will be affected by this purchase are notified. These departments are the warehouse, receiving department, and accounts payable department.

The purchase order is submitted to the vendor. The purchase order data are recorded in the open purchase order file, which is a file that stores unfilled purchase orders. The vendor sends back an acknowledgment that the order will be filled. That information is also entered into the open purchase order file.

Required:

Prepare a level 0 data flow diagram for Mason Company's purchase order processing system.

27. What are some of the advantages of business process mapping over system flowcharts?

Notes

1. Adapted from the PWC University for Faculty, 2004.

2. For more information about business process mapping, refer totalk.bmc.com/blogs/blog-wiles/van-wiles/ PROCESSDOC1

Essential Elements and Basic Activities of Accounting Systems

Source: Ribah/Shutterstock.

Chapter Outline

Why Review Paper-Based Accounting Systems?

Similarities Between Paper-Based and Computerized Accounting Systems

Batch versus Real-Time Posting

Learning Objectives

After studying this chapter, you should be able to:

- Discuss the significant similarities between paper-based accounting systems and computerized accounting systems.
- Identify the essential elements of a paper-based accounting system.
- Understand the basic activities of a paper-based accounting system.
- Identify the essential elements of a computerized accounting system.
- Understand the basic activities of a computerized accounting system.
- Compare batch posting in a computerized accounting system to real-time posting.

Source: Stephen Coburn/Shutterstock.

Introductory Scenario

"Frank, I know you've built a fine accounting system that does everything it's supposed to. But computerized systems are just 'black boxes' to me." Alice DuBois, chief executive officer of Carmen Enterprises, was chatting to her controller during an airport layover.

"In college," she continued, "I took accounting principles and even the two intermediate accounting courses. We learned about the general journal, special journals, the general and subsidiary ledgers, trial balances, and financial statements. And we had to do a comprehensive practice set. I can still remember trying to make all the required reversing and closing entries. By the end of my junior year I was pretty good at accounting—or so I thought at the time. But real accounting systems don't seem to have journals, ledgers, and all that stuff."

"Cheri Petit [Carmen's information systems manager] has tried to explain what the computer does, but I get lost in the files, disk drives, object code, printer drivers, and so forth. And what people see on the computer screens doesn't look anything like the exhibits in the intermediate accounting textbooks."

"I suppose I can do my job without ever knowing what goes on inside the computer. But, for curiosity's sake, I would like someone to explain to me just how the millions of transactions and other events Carmen records every month are processed to generate the accounting reports and screen displays we receive."

"I'm pleased that you asked, Ms. DuBois." Frank Beecham was gratified that his CEO was interested in the accounting function, but he was more than a little nervous about trying to explain how the system worked. The CEO would soon lose interest if he sounded too technical. On the other hand, she was too smart to be content with superficial answers.

"It's really not that complicated," he began after a moment's thought. "The computerized accounting system carries out virtually the same sequence of operations as you did in your college practice set. You just can't see the intermediate results. In large companies it's best to store processed data in computer files rather than printing out paper journals or ledgers. Because we process millions of transactions and other events, paper journals would be expensive to produce and cumbersome to use. Instead, any authorized user can retrieve records from a computer terminal and look at them. The user can also summarize or analyze sets of records to meet specific information needs.

"Even though we can't see the transactions and other events being processed," Beecham continued, "we know they are processed correctly because the system has been exhaustively tested. And, because of the controls built into the system, we are confident that it will always provide reliable output—at least so long as we're careful to screen input data for authorization, reasonableness, and the like."

The controller paused to catch his breath. What else would Ms. DuBois want to know? He had only started his explanation, but already he was finding it hard to describe the accounting system in simple terms without sacrificing accuracy.

Introductory Scenario Thought Questions:

1. How would you explain the concept of a master file to Alice DuBois?
2. How would you explain the concept of a transaction file to Alice DuBois?
3. How would you explain the concept of an open file to Alice DuBois?
4. Frank Beecham was perplexed about adequately explaining to Alice DuBois how the accounting system worked. What was his explanation? Do you think any additional information would have been helpful? If so, what?

Why Review Paper-Based Accounting Systems?

At the beginning of a course in accounting information systems, we can benefit from spending time to review paper-based accounting systems. As accounting students, you have, at least to some extent, been exposed to paper-based accounting systems. For example, financial accounting textbooks explain the flow of transactions through a paper-based accounting system by describing the recording of transactions in a paper journal, the posting of amounts to a paper ledger, and the preparation of trial balances and financial statements. Paper-based accounting systems provide a simple and familiar context in which to understand the issues of computerized accounting systems.

Source: gopixa/Shutterstock.

The first section of this chapter points out the similarities between paper-based and computerized accounting systems. The next section reviews the essential elements and basic activities of paper-based accounting systems. The next section of this chapter introduces the essential elements and basic activities of computerized accounting systems and compares them to paper-based systems. The final section explains the effects of processing data in a computerized accounting system using the real-time mode versus the batch mode.

Similarities Between Paper-Based and Computerized Accounting Systems

An accounting system, whether paper-based or computerized, consists of two broad categories: (1) essential elements, that is, *where* data are captured, recorded, processed, stored, and reported, and (2) basic activities, that is, *how* data are captured, recorded, processed, stored, and recorded in the essential elements. Essential elements and basic activities are discussed in the next two sections for both paper-based and computerized accounting systems.

LEARNING OBJECTIVE 1
Discuss the significant similarities between paper-based accounting systems and computerized accounting systems.

Paper-Based Accounting Systems

Essential Elements of a Paper-Based Accounting System

The essential elements of a paper-based accounting system are:

- Source documents
- Accounts
- Chart of accounts
- Journals (special and general)
- Ledgers (subsidiary and general)
- Outputs

LEARNING OBJECTIVE 2
Identify the essential elements of a paper-based accounting system.

Source document A document that captures data about transactions and other events and about file maintenance for entry into an accounting system. Examples of internally generated source documents are employee time cards, purchase requisitions, receiving reports, and production orders. Externally generated source documents include purchase orders from customers, remittance advices and checks from customers, and debit or credit memos from banks.

Source Documents

In a paper-based system, the data that describe transactions and other events are captured on paper **source documents**. Source documents, sometimes called input documents, may be generated internally or externally. Examples of internally generated source documents are employee time cards, purchase requisitions, receiving reports, and production orders. Externally generated source documents include purchase orders from customers, remittance advices and checks from customers, and debit or credit memos from banks. Data on source documents must be extracted, processed, and eventually summarized and presented on various output documents and reports to be provided to managers, investors, creditors, employees, and regulatory authorities. Source documents include:

Authorization for file maintenance	Debit and credit memos
Authorization for inventory adjustment	Expenditure request
Authorization for payroll adjustment	Labor ticket
Bill of lading	Materials requisition
Cash receipts prelist	Move ticket
Customer allowance claim	Overhead application work sheet
Customer purchase order	Production order
Customer remittance advice	Purchase requisition
Sales order	Time card
Scrap ticket	Vendor invoice

Examples of some source documents are presented in this chapter. For the purpose of illustrating documents, assume we are employed by a company named Aca Pool Co., an incorporated organization that sells merchandise for pools and patios. Our customers are as follows:

Aberdeen Park

Allen, G. H.

Purchase order A document that a customer issues to request goods or services. The essential data elements in a purchase order are the customer's and vendor's names and addresses, the goods or services being ordered, and the expected delivery or performance date.

Exhibit 3.1 shows a **purchase order** that Aca Pool Co. has received from Aberdeen Park for the purchase of 600 pounds of chemical pool treatment and 12 pool divider ropes. As you review this purchase order, it is important to note the data elements that are necessary for the purchase order to capture. The essential elements are the customer's and the vendor's names and addresses, the goods or services being ordered, and the expected delivery or performance date. This purchase order serves as a source document for Aca Pool Co. because we will prepare a sales order from Aberdeen Park's purchase order. (S.K.U. stands for stock keeping unit.)

Another source document is a bill of lading and is shown in **Exhibit 3.2**. This bill of lading is for the goods that Aca Pool Co. is shipping to our customer, Aberdeen Park. A bill of lading is considered a source document because it captures some of the information that Aca Pool Co. needs to record the sale to Aberdeen. You will recall that a sale is recognized when the merchandise is delivered.

Bill of lading A written contract between the shipper (also known as consignor) of goods and a carrier engaged in the business of transporting goods. This document evidences receipt of the goods for shipment.

A **bill of lading** is a written contract between the shipper, who is also known as the consignor, and a carrier engaged in the business of transporting goods. Aca Pool Co. is the shipper in our case. The carrier is Rao Freight Co. The carrier quotes a rate (per 100 pounds) to be charged for the shipment. The person to whom the goods are being shipped is the consignee who, in our case, is Aberdeen Park. If Aca Pool Co. had its own fleet of trucks to make deliveries, a shipping document, or packing slip, similar to the bill of lading but without the contract terms would be prepared. Note in the bill of lading in Exhibit 3.2 that 50 pounds of pool chemical are shipped in one box and 24 pounds of rope are shipped in one box.

Purchase Order

Aberdeen Park
1903 Dwire Street
San Antonio, TX 78202
Tel: (210) 555-1000
Fax: (210) 555-2000

Date: June 24, 2018

P. O. Number: PO3310
This number must appear on all invoices, packages, and correspondence.

Our P.R. No.: R999

Vendor:

Aca Pool Co.
2700 Bay Area Boulevard
Clear Lake City, TX 77058-1098

Ship to above address.

Please inform us immediately if unable to fill this order **now**.

VENDOR CODE	PLACED BY	DATE EXPECTED	SHIP VIA	F.O.B.	TERMS
60938	J. Hammond	7/1/18	Rao Freight Co.	Clear Lake City	2/10, Net 30

PRODUCT NO.	QUAN-TITY	S.K.U.	DESCRIPTION	UNIT PRICE	DIS-COUNT	EXTENDED AMOUNT
P1050	600	lb.	Chemical Pool Treatment	$ 1.60		$960.00
P1080	12	ea.	Pool Divider Rope - 20'	$60.00		$720.00
			SUBTOTAL			$1,680.00
			SALES TAX RATE %			exempt
			SALES TAX			
			SHIPPING & HANDLING			COD
			TOTAL DUE			**$1,680.00**

IMPORTANT INSTRUCTIONS & TERMS OF THIS PURCHASE ORDER
1. Enclose invoice copy or packing list in all shipments.
2. Incomplete or partial shipments will be accepted. Place shorts on back order and notify immediately of anticipated in-stock date. Purchaser reserves the right to cancel unfilled items at any time prior to receipt by notifying vendor.
3. Vendor will be responsible for extra freight cost on partial shipment unless prior permission is obtained.

Kevin Call   PURCHASING AGENT

EXHIBIT 3.1 Purchase Order

STRAIGHT BILL OF LADING

Aca Pool Co.
2700 Bay Area Blvd.
Clear Lake City, TX 77058-1098

DOCUMENT No. BL021

TO:
Consignee   Aberdeen Park
Street   1903 Dwire St.
City/State/Zip   San Antonio, T X 78202
Route: Clear Lake City - San Antonio - Direct
Vehicle #:   TX-8880

Date   June 30, 2018
Shipper No.   S6118
Carrier No.   F3696

Carrier Name: Rao Freight Co.

QUAN-TITY SHIPPED	PROD. NO.	KIND OF PACKAG-ING	DESCRIPTION OF ARTICLES	SPECIAL MARKS & EXCEP-TIONS	WEIGHT (SUBJECT TO CORREC-TION)	RATE	CHARGES (FOR CARRIER USE ONLY)
12	P1050	Boxes	Pool Chemicals	None	600 lbs	$33.22	$199.32
1	P1080	Boxes	Pool Rope	None	24 lbs	28.11	6.75
				FUEL CHARGE		2%	4.12

FREIGHT CHARGES (CHECK ONE):
___Prepaid   ___Bill to Shipper   X_Collect

TOTAL: $210.19

SHIPPER: Aca Pool Co.   CARRIER: RAO FREIGHT CO.

BY: *Ron Ying*   BY: *Val Mason*   DATE: June 30, 2018

Note - Where the rate is dependent on value, shippers are required to state specifically in writing the agreed or declared value of the property.
  The agreed or declared value of the property is hereby specifically stated by the shipper to be not exceeding.
$_____per_____

Subject to Section 7 of the conditions, if this shipment is to be delivered to the consignee without recourse on the consignor, the consignor will sign the following statement:
  The carrier will not make delivery of this shipment without payment of freight and all other lawful charges.

_____
(Signature of Consignor)

  Received subject to the classifications and tariffs in effect on the date of the issue of this Bill of Lading, the property described above is in apparent good order, except as noted (contents and condition of contents of packages unknown), marked, consigned, and destined as indicated above which said carrier (the word carrier being understood throughout this contract as meaning any person or corporation in possession of the property under the contract) agrees to carry to its usual place of delivery at said destination, if on its route, otherwise to deliver to another carrier on the route to said destination. It is mutually agreed as to each carrier of all or any of, said property over all or any portion of said route to destination and as to each party at any time interested in all or any said property, that every service to be performed hereunder will be to all the bill of lading terms and conditions in the governing classification on the date or shipment.

  Shipper hereby certifies that he is familiar with all the bill of lading terms and conditions in the governing classification and the said terms and conditions are hereby agreed to by the shipper and accepted for himself and his assigns.

EXHIBIT 3.2 Bill of Lading

Cash receipts prelist A record, maintained by date, of each cash receipt.

Time card A document for recording the time an employee started and stopped working each day and the number of hours worked.

A **cash receipts prelist** for Aca Pool Co. is shown in **Exhibit 3.3**. This document is a record, maintained by date, of each cash receipt. This particular prelist shows that Aca Pool Co. received payment from Aberdeen Park in payment of its outstanding invoice. This prelist is considered a source document because it captures most of the information necessary to record a cash receipts transaction.

The final source document illustrated (**Exhibit 3.4**) is a **time card**. This document indicates the employee's name, the pay period, the time the employee started and stopped

CASH RECEIPTS PRELIST

ACA POOL CO.
2700 BAY AREA BLVD.
CLEAR LAKE CITY, TX 77058-1098

Document No. CR564
Month July
Prepared By *J. Rowland*

	DATE	RECEIVED FROM	CASH SALE	A/R COLLECTION INVOICE NO.	A/R COLLECTION INVOICE AMT.	OTHER	CHECK NO.	AMOUNT RECEIVED
1	7/29/18	Aberdeen Park		I00022	$1,680		2345	$1,680
2								
3								
4								
5								
6								
7								
8								
9								
10								

EXHIBIT 3.3 Cash Receipts Prelist

TIME CARD—Aca Pool Co.

Pay Period Ending July 15, 2018
Name Lauren Sutton

DATE	TIME IN	TIME OUT	REG. TIME HOURS	OVERTIME HOURS
7/11	8.00	12.50	4.50	
7/11	13.25	18.25	3.50	1.50
7/12	8.00	11.25	3.25	
7/12	12.25	18.75	4.75	1.75
7/13	8.00	12.50	4.50	
7/13	13.25	17.00	3.50	.25
7/14	8.00	12.50	4.50	
7/14	13.00	16.50	3.50	0
7/15	8.00	13.50	5.50	
7/15	14.50	18.50	2.50	1.50
TOTALS			40.00	5.00

APPROVAL OF SUPERVISOR *Ed Altemus*

EXHIBIT 3.4 Time Card

working each day, and the number of hours worked. Note that the times are recorded in hours and hundredths of an hour, as opposed to hours and minutes, to simplify the calculations of the numbers of hours worked. This particular time card captures some of the data necessary to record a payroll transaction for Aca Pool Co.'s employee Lauren Sutton. Other information such as the rate of regular and overtime pay and authorized deductions would be retrieved from Personnel records.

Accounts

An **account** is an element in an accounting system that is used to classify and summarize monetary measurements of business activity of a similar nature. An account is established whenever it is necessary to provide useful information about a particular type of economic event. For example, every organization has a "cash" account in its accounting system. The number of accounts in an accounting system depends on the information needs of the organization.

Chart of Accounts

A **chart of accounts** is a listing of all account names, along with their codes, used by an organization. The accounts are classified into assets, liabilities, ownership equity, revenues, and expenses and are aligned with their related blocks of codes, which typically are as follows:

1000–1999 - Assets

2000–2999 - Liabilities

3000–3999 - Ownership Equity

4000–4999 - Revenues

5000–5999 - Expenses

Accounts can be subdivided within these major categories as necessary. For example, current assets could be assigned the numbers 1000–1499 and noncurrent assets the numbers 1500–1999. Current liabilities could be assigned the numbers 2000–2499 and noncurrent liabilities the numbers 2500–2999. A chart of accounts for Aca Pool Co. is shown in **Exhibit 3.5**.[1]

Journals

A **journal** lists transactions in chronological order and is considered the "book of original entry." The two types of journals are special and general. A *special* journal is created to record a particular type of transaction. For example, if an organization makes many sales it may create a sales journal. If the organization frequently receives cash, it may create a cash receipts journal. An advantage of special journals is that they save time in journalizing transactions and in posting the transaction amounts to the individual accounts. When posting from a special journal, one total amount for several transactions can be posted to an account instead of an amount for each individual transaction. The *general* journal, on the other hand, is used to record all transactions that are not recorded in special journals.

To understand the difference between special and general journals, consider two credit sale transactions—one to Aberdeen Park for $1,680 and one to G. H. Allen for $1,050. For purposes of illustration, we will assume that Aca Pool Co. is not required to collect sales tax from Aberdeen Park but does collect sales tax from the individual G. H. Allen. We will also assume for our paper-based system that a perpetual inventory system, average cost, is in effect. The sale transactions could be recorded in either a special sales journal or a general journal as illustrated in **Exhibit 3.6**. Note from this exhibit that the amount of time it takes to record the transactions in the sales journal is substantially less than the amount of time to record the transactions in the general journal.

As Exhibit 3.6 shows, the pertinent data elements in a journal, whether special or general, consist of, at a minimum, the transaction date, the account name and number, and the amount by which each account is debited or credited. The recording of these data elements ensures that transactions will be reported in the correct accounting period, in the correct account, and for the correct amount. Other data elements that are captured depend

Account An element in an accounting system that is used to classify and summarize monetary measurements of business activity of a similar nature. An account is established whenever it is necessary to provide useful information about a particular type of economic event.

Chart of accounts A listing of all account names along with their numbers, or codes, used by an organization.

Journal A listing of transactions in chronological order that is considered the "book of original entry." A special journal is created to record a particular type of transaction such as sale transactions. The general journal is used to record all transactions that are not recorded in special journals.

	Assets		**Stockholders' Equity**
1110	Cash on hand	3100	Common stock
1120	Cash in bank	3400	Additional paid-in capital
1200	Foreign currency holdings	3500	Retained earnings
1220	Marketable securities	3600	Current earnings
1230	Accounts receivable		
1240	Allowance for bad debts		**Revenues**
1300	Merchandise inventory	4100	Sales of goods
1370	Merchandise returns and allowances	4130	Sales discounts
1380	Allowance to reduce inventory to lower	4160	Sales returns and allowances
	of cost or market	4200	Sales of services
1400	Supplies inventory	4510	Other income
1410	Prepaid expenses		
1550	Long-term investments—bonds		**Expenses**
1560	Long-term investments—stocks	5010	Cost of goods sold
1600	Equipment	5020	Cost of services sold
1650	Accumulated depreciation on equipment	5130	Wages and salaries expense
1700	Buildings	5160	Employee fringe benefits expense
1750	Accumulated depreciation on buildings	5190	Social security tax expense
1800	Vehicles	5220	Medicare tax expense
1850	Accumulated depreciation on vehicles	5250	Federal unemployment tax expense
1900	Land	5280	State unemployment tax expense
1950	Intangibles	5310	Corporate income tax expense
1960	Deferred charges	5340	Depreciation expense
1980	Other assets	5370	Amortization expense
		5400	Interest expense
	Liabilities	5430	Bad debt expense
2110	Accounts payable	5460	Entertainment expense
2130	Wages and salaries payable	5490	Transportation expense
2160	Social security tax payable	5520	Travel expense
2190	Medicare tax payable	5550	Advertising expense
2220	Federal income tax (employees') payable	5580	Packing expense
2250	Federal unemployment tax payable	5610	Shipping expense
2280	State unemployment tax payable	5640	Supplies expense
2340	Corporate income tax payable	5670	Telephone and fax expense
2370	Accrued expenses payable	5700	Rent expense
2400	Current portion of long-term bonds payable	5730	Utilities expense
2430	Current portion of long-term notes payable	5760	Miscellaneous expense
2460	Sales tax payable		
2600	Bonds payable		
2650	Premium or discount on bonds payable		
2700	Deferred income taxes		
2800	Notes payable		

EXHIBIT 3.5 Chart of Accounts

on the nature of the transactions and what information the organization wants to retain about these transactions. For example, a credit sale transaction, as in Exhibit 3.6, also includes the customer name and invoice number. In the case of a cash sale, the customer name may or may not be captured.

To repeat, a journal is a listing of transactions in chronological order. But listing transactions in order of their occurrence is only one way of storing transaction data. For preparing many of the outputs of an accounting system, it is necessary to have data for the same transactions stored by account name, and this is the subject of the next section.

SALES JOURNAL Page 1						
Date	Customer Name	Invoice No.	Accounts Receivable, Dr. 1230	Sales of Goods, Cr. 4100	Sales Tax Payable, Cr. 2370	Cost of Goods Sold, Dr. 5010 Mdse. Inventory, Cr. 1300
2018						
June 30	Aberdeen Park	I00022	1,680	1,680	0	840
30	G. H. Allen	I00023	1,134	1,050	84	525
TOTAL			2,814	2,730	84	1,365

GENERAL JOURNAL			Page 1	
Date	Account Name and Explanation	Account No.	Debit	Credit
2018				
June 30	Accounts receivable	1230	1,680	
	Cost of goods sold	5010	840	
	Merchandise inventory	1300		840
	Sales of goods	4100		1,680
	To record sale of merchandise to Aberdeen Park, invoice #I00022, terms 2/10, net 30			
June 30	Accounts receivable	1230	1,134	
	Cost of goods sold	5010	525	
	Merchandise inventory	1300		525
	Sales tax payable	2370		84
	Sales of goods	4100		1,050
	To record sale of merchandise to G. H. Allen, invoice #I00023, terms 2/10, net 30			

EXHIBIT 3.6 Special and General Journals in a Paper-Based Accounting System

General Ledger

General ledger A collection of all the asset, liability, ownership equity, revenue, and expense accounts used by an organization. Each account in the general ledger has an account number, an account name, and the amounts (debits and credits) of the transactions that affect the account's balance.

Transaction data are *classified by account* by copying selected *details* of the transactions from the journals to the general ledger. The **general ledger** is a collection of all the asset, liability, ownership equity, revenue, and expense accounts used by an organization (and listed in its chart of accounts). Each account in the general ledger has its own separate sheet that shows at a minimum an account name, an account number, and the amounts (debits or credits) of the transactions that affect the account's balance. For example, the sheet for the Accounts Receivable account in the General Ledger for the posting from the sales journal in Exhibit 3.6 would appear as follows:

GENERAL LEDGER

Accounts Receivable Account No. 1230			
Date	Debit Amount	Credit Amount	Current Balance
6/30/18	2,814		2,814 Dr.*

*This current balance assumes a zero beginning balance.

Some accounts in the general ledger may be **control accounts**. These accounts are defined in the next section.

Subsidiary Ledger

When a large number of accounts of one type are required, it may be more efficient to remove the accounts from the general ledger and substitute a single account in the general ledger to represent the removed accounts. The removed accounts, however, are still maintained but in a different ledger—a **subsidiary ledger**. The new general ledger account is called a *control account* to indicate that it has a subsidiary ledger. For example, an organization may have many customers to whom credit has been extended. Instead of maintaining an account in the general ledger for each customer, a control account called Accounts Receivable is created in the general ledger, and a subsidiary ledger (Accounts Receivable Subsidiary Ledger) is created to store one account for each customer. **Exhibit 3.7** shows how these particular accounts would appear before and after establishing a control account and a subsidiary ledger.

Each control account in the general ledger has one subsidiary ledger that contains several accounts. To restate this last sentence to fit our example, the Accounts Receivable control account in the general ledger has an Accounts Receivable subsidiary ledger that contains two accounts, one for Aberdeen Park and one for G. H. Allen. The amount in the control account equals the sum of the control account's subsidiary ledger account balances. In our example, the $2,814 balance in the Accounts Receivable account equals the $2,814 sum of the customer Aberdeen Park ($1,680) and the customer G. H. Allen ($1,134).

Detailed data are maintained for each customer in the Accounts Receivable Subsidiary Ledger. For example, each account would include, at a minimum, the customer's name, address, credit limit, and current balance. These subsidiary ledger accounts are used for many operating purposes such as gathering sales data to be analyzed and answering customer inquiries. To accommodate these particular information requirements, additional data for each customer would have to be maintained.

As the need-to-know details in general ledger accounts grows, the number of subsidiary ledgers increases. Potentially, each account in the general ledger could have a

Control account One master general ledger account that represents several related subsidiary ledger accounts. The amount in the control account equals the sum of the control account's subsidiary ledger account balances.

Subsidiary ledger A collection of individual accounts that comprise the details for a related control account in the general ledger. The sum of the individual account balances equals the amount of the related control account.

BEFORE CREATING CONTROL ACCOUNT AND SUBSIDIARY LEDGER:

General Ledger	
Account Name	**Current Bal.**
Receivable-Aberdeen Park*	1,680
Receivable-G. H. Allen*	1,134

*These accounts would be on separate sheets in an accounting system. However, to clarify the comparison, they are presented in this manner.

AFTER CREATING CONTROL ACCOUNT AND SUBSIDIARY LEDGER:

General Ledger		Accounts Receivable Subsidiary Ledger	
Account Name	**Current Bal.**	**Account Name**	**Current Bal.**
Accounts Receivable (control account)*	2,814	Aberdeen Park*	1,680
		G. H. Allen*	1,134

*These accounts would be on separate sheets in an accounting system. However, to clarify the comparison, they are presented in this manner.

EXHIBIT 3.7 A Control Account with a Subsidiary Ledger in a Paper-Based Accounting System

subsidiary ledger. **Exhibit 3.8** shows the difference between the general ledger accounts and the subsidiary ledger accounts.

GENERAL LEDGER ACCOUNTS*		SUBSIDIARY LEDGER ACCOUNTS†
General Ledger Control Accounts	**Other General Ledger Accounts‡**	
Accounts Receivable		Accounts Receivable Subsidiary Ledger (one account for each customer)
Merchandise Inventory		Inventory Subsidiary Ledger (one account for each item)
Accounts Payable		Accounts Payable Subsidiary Ledger (one account for each vendor)
	Cash in Bank Accrued Expenses Payable Sales of Goods Advertising Expense	

*Accounts in the general ledger are included in the chart of accounts, and their balances are used in preparing the financial statements and other reports.

†Accounts in subsidiary ledgers are NOT included in the chart of accounts. Their balances are used in preparing many operational reports.

‡If it was necessary to maintain details about these accounts, they could be made into control accounts with related subsidiary ledger accounts. For example, it might be necessary to have subsidiary ledger accounts for various types of advertising expenses. Conceivably, each general ledger account could be a control account with a related subsidiary ledger.

EXHIBIT 3.8 Difference Between General Ledger and Subsidiary Ledger Accounts in a Paper-Based Accounting System

Outputs

Output Various documents and reports needed by managers and employees within an organization to facilitate day-to-day operations and decision making, as well as documents and reports needed by people outside the organization. Examples of output are a sales journal, sales order, general journal, tax return, and budget variance report.

The **outputs** of an accounting system consist of various documents and reports needed by managers and employees within the organization to facilitate day-to-day operations and decision making, as well as documents and reports needed by people outside the organization. Output documents include:

Cash disbursements journal	Paycheck
Cash receipts journal	Payroll and deductions journal
Closed job report	Production/construction status report
Employee earnings record	Receiving report
General journal	Sales (customer) invoice
Income tax return	Sales journal
Inventory reorder report	Sales order
Inventory status report	Schedule of aged accounts payable
Machine utilization report	Schedule of aged accounts receivable
Materials and labor usage report	Scrap and lost-time report
Open job report	Shipment journal
Open purchase order report	Trial balance
Open sales order report	W-2 form

Sales order A document created internally to facilitate the delivery of goods or services. The essential data elements in a sales order are the customer's name and address, the goods or services being ordered, and the expected delivery or performance date.

Examples of several output documents and reports are presented in this chapter. A **sales order** that would be created by Aca Pool Co. for the sale to Aberdeen Park of chemical pool treatment and pool divider ropes is illustrated in **Exhibit 3.9**. You will recall that Aca Pool Co. uses the information on Aberdeen Park's purchase order (Aca Pool Co.'s source document) to create its sales order (an output document). Sales orders are especially useful for keeping up with which orders need to be filled in those situations where there is a time delay between receipt of the customer's purchase order and delivery of the goods or services.

Upon delivering or shipping the merchandise to its customer, Aca Pool Co. generates a **sales invoice**. This document is used to bill a customer and indicates the dollar amount of

Sales invoice A document used to bill a customer that indicates the dollar amount of a sale and the date the amount is due.

Sales Order

Date: June 24, 2018

S. O. Number: SO585

Aca Pool Co.
2700 Bay Area Blvd.
Clear Lake City, TX 77058-1098
Tel: (713) 555-1234
Fax: (713) 555-1235

Sold To and Bill:

Aberdeen Park
1903 Dwire Street
San Antonio, TX 78202

Ship to (if different address):

Customer No.	Customer P. O. No.	Customer P. O. Date	Promised Shipment Date	F.O.B.	TERMS
C100	PO3310	June 24, 2018	June 30, 2018	Clear Lake City	2/10, Net 30

PRODUCT NO.	QUAN-TITY	S.K.U.	DESCRIPTION	UNIT PRICE	DIS-COUNT	EXTENDED AMOUNT
P1050	600	lb.	Chemical Pool Treatment	$ 1.60		$ 960.00
P1080	12	ea.	Pool Divider Rope - 20'	60.00		720.00
				SUBTOTAL		$1,680.00
				SALES TAX RATE %		exempt
				SALES TAX		
				SHIPPING & HANDLING		COD
				TOTAL DUE		**$1,680.00**

Sold By   Ted Marks

Renee Sweeney
Authorized Signature

EXHIBIT 3.9 Sales Order

a sale and the date the amount is due. An example of the sales invoice for Aberdeen Park is shown in **Exhibit 3.10**. Sales invoices are useful for keeping up with the cash Aca Pool Co. is entitled to receive.

An output that is extremely helpful to management in controlling its cash inflows is a **schedule of aged accounts receivable**, sometimes called customer aged detail, which is shown in **Exhibit 3.11**. Note that this report lists the unpaid sales (customer) invoices by whether they are current, which is typically 0–30 days from the date of the invoice, or whether they are delinquent and, if so, by the number of days. This report helps management determine which customers it needs to contact for payment. In some cases,

---

Invoice

Aca Pool Co.
2700 Bay Area Blvd.
Clear Lake City, TX 77058-1098
Tel: (713) 555-1234
Fax: (713) 555-1235

Invoice Number: I00022

Date: June 30, 2018

Customer No.: C100

Customer Service Hotline:
(800) 555-1236

Bill to:

Aberdeen Park
1903 Dwire Street
San Antonio, TX 78202

Ship to (if different address):

SALES REPRESENT-ATIVE	CUSTOMER P.O. NO.	OUR S.O. NO.	S.O. DATE	DATE SHIPPED	SHIPPED VIA	F.O.B.	TERMS
Ted Marks	PO3310	SO585	6/24/18	6/30/18	Rao Freight Co.	Clear Lake City	2/10, net 30

PRODUCT NO.	QUAN-TITY	S.K.U.	DESCRIPTION	UNIT PRICE	DIS-COUNT	EXTENDED AMOUNT
P1050	600	lb.	Chemical Pool Treatment	$ 1.60		$ 960.00
P1080	12	ea.	Pool Divider Rope - 20'	60.00		720.00
					SUBTOTAL	1,680.00
					SALES TAX RATE %	exempt
					SALES TAX	
					SHIPPING & HANDLING	COD
					TOTAL DUE	$1,680.00

THANK YOU FOR YOUR ORDER!

EXHIBIT 3.10 Sales (Customer) Invoice

management may decide to suspend sales to customers who are overdue. A repeated record of late payments may cause Aca Pool Co. to increase its finance charge for a particular customer who does not pay within 30 days, reduce the customer's credit limit, or, in more serious cases, cease making sales to the customer.

An output that helps management in planning its cash outflows is a **schedule of aged accounts payable**, sometimes called vendor aged detail, which is shown in **Exhibit 3.12**. This report lists the purchase (vendor) invoices that are coming due. Management can use

Schedule of aged accounts payable (also known as vendor aged detail) A report that lists the unpaid vendor invoices by whether they are current, which is typically 0–30 days from the date of the invoice, or whether they are delinquent and, if so, by the number of days.

				Aca Pool Co. Schedule of Aged Accounts Receivable As of 7/15/18				
	Invoice Date	Total	Current	01–30 Days Past Due	31–60 Days Past Due	61–90 Days Past Due	91+ Days Past Due
Aberdeen Park I00022	6/30/18	1,680	1,680	0	0	0	0
Allen, G. H. I00023	6/30/18	1,134	1,134	0	0	0	0
Totals		2,814	2,814	0	0	0	0

EXHIBIT 3.11 Schedule of Aged Accounts Receivable

				Aca Pool Co. Schedule of Aged Accounts Payable As of 7/15/18				
	Invoice Date	Total	Current	01–30 Days Past Due	31–60 Days Past Due	61–90 Days Past Due	91+ Days Past Due
Coventry Auto Co. 1572	4/20/18	3,300			3,300		
1798	6/24/18	3,100	3,100				
		6,400		0		0	0
Deakin Pool Supplies 1094	6/21/18	5,100	5,100	0	0	0	0
Fennell Chemical Co. 15440	6/21/18	2,600	2,600				
15463	6/22/18	1,800	1,800				
		4,400	4,400	0	0	0	0
Chan Pool Supplies 060	5/20/18	1,600		1,600			
190	6/21/18	400	400				
260	6/22/18	3,400	3,400				
		5,400	3,800		0	0	0
Major Pool Supplies 1097	6/23/18	5,200	5,200				
1099	6/25/18	3,800	3,800				
		9,000	9,000	0	0	0	0
Totals		30,300	25,400	1,600	3,300	0	0

EXHIBIT 3.12 Schedule of Aged Accounts Payable

this report to make sure that cash will be available on the due date of the invoice, generally 30 days from the date of the invoice, for paying the invoice. Also, management can use this report to determine whether it wants to take advantage of a cash discount that some vendors offer for payment made before the due date of the invoice.

A **receiving report** is shown in **Exhibit 3.13**. This report is prepared to document the receipt of goods that were purchased. The essential data elements on a receiving report are a description of the goods, the quantity received, the date received, and the condition of the goods. Suppose that our company, Aca Pool Co., had sent a purchase order to Chan Pool Supplies for the purchase of ten vinyl liners: 24' x 20' x 10'. Aca Pool Co.'s receiving department would be aware of the outstanding purchase order. Upon receipt of the merchandise, the receiving department would examine the merchandise and compare the merchandise received to the merchandise described on the purchase order. If the merchandise is acceptable, the receiving department prepares a receiving report.

Receiving report A report that documents the receipt of goods that were purchased. The essential data elements are a description of the goods, the quantity received, the quality, or condition, of the goods, and the date received.

RECEIVING REPORT				
ACA POOL CO. 2700 Bay Area Blvd. Clear Lake City, TX 77058-1098			**Report No.** R21 **Date** 7/29/18	
Purchase Order No. Or Return Request No. PO6543				
Received From Chan Pool Supplies				
Address Houston, TX				
Freight Carrier Rao Freight Co.			**Freight Bill No.** BL909	
	ITEM NO.	QUANTITY		DESCRIPTION
1	P1120	10		Vinyl liners 24' × 20' × 10'
2				
3				
4				
5				
6				
7				
8				
9				
10				
11				
12				
REMARKS: CONDITION OF ITEMS, ETC.				
Good				
RECEIVED BY: *J. Dedmon*				

EXHIBIT 3.13 Receiving Report

Chapter 3 Essential Elements and Basic Activities of Accounting Systems

Several journals are outputs of an accounting system. Examples of the sales journal (a special journal) and the general journal were shown earlier in this chapter in Exhibit 3.6. Another type of special journal is the cash receipts journal, which is shown in **Exhibit 3.14**.

CASH RECEIPTS JOURNAL					
Page 1					
Date	**Customer Name**	**Invoice No.**	**Customer Check No.**	**Cash in Bank, Accounts Receivable,**	**Dr. 1120 Cr. 1230**
2018					
July 29	Aberdeen Park	I00022	2345		1,680
TOTAL					1,680

EXHIBIT 3.14 Cash Receipts Journal

The four financial statements—Balance Sheet, Statement of Income, Statement of Changes in Ownership Equity, and Statement of Cash Flows—are examples of outputs needed by people outside the organization.

The **Balance Sheet** presents the overall financial position of the organization at a given moment. The **Statement of Income**, sometimes called a Statement of Earnings, reports the profitability of an organization for a stated period of time such as a month or a year. A **Statement of Changes in Ownership Equity** is a summary of the transactions affecting the accounts in the Ownership Equity section of the Balance Sheet for a stated period of time. The **Statement of Cash Flows** reports the cash receipts and cash payments of an organization during a stated period of time. Each financial statement contains a list of unique accounts and their respective balances. The format and data items on financial statements are dictated by generally accepted accounting principles, industry standards, and the organization's accounting policies.

Balance sheet The financial statement that presents the overall financial position of an organization at a given moment.

Statement of income The financial statement that reports the profitability of an organization for a stated period of time such as a month or a year.

Statement of changes in ownership equity The financial statement that summarizes the transactions affecting the accounts in the Ownership Equity section of the Balance Sheet for a stated period of time.

Statement of cash flows The financial statement that reports the cash receipts and cash payments of an organization during a stated period of time.

Basic Activities of a Paper-Based Accounting System

The basic activities of a paper-based accounting system are as follows:

- Completing source documents
- Recording transactions in the appropriate journals
- Posting (copying) data from the journals to the appropriate accounts in the subsidiary ledgers and the general ledger
- Preparing output documents and reports

LEARNING OBJECTIVE 3
Understand the basic activities of a paper-based accounting system.

Completing Source Documents

When transactions occur, source documents are prepared to capture the appropriate information about the transactions. For example, when the goods that had been ordered by Aberdeen Park were shipped by Aca Pool Co., an invoice was prepared indicating the consummation of the sale.

Recording Transactions in Appropriate Journals

Transactions are recorded in either special journals or a general journal. Recording two sale transactions for Aca Pool Co. was illustrated earlier in this chapter when explaining the difference in these journals.

Posting (Copying) Data from Journals to Accounts in Subsidiary Ledgers and General Ledger

Debits and credits from the journals are posted to the subsidiary ledger accounts and general ledger accounts also in the form of debits and credits. If a general ledger account, such as Accounts Receivable, has related subsidiary ledger accounts, such as Aberdeen Park and G. H. Allen, posting from the journal to the subsidiary ledger accounts may be done often. But posting from the journal to the general ledger control account may be done only occasionally. It is important to keep subsidiary ledger accounts sufficiently current to support operating activities. For example, before making a sale to a customer, the salesperson needs to make certain the sale will not cause the customer to exceed the approved credit limit. Also, the salesperson needs to know the quantity of inventory available. On the other hand, it is necessary to post to the general ledger accounts only before financial statements are prepared.

An illustration of posting to subsidiary ledger accounts and general ledger control accounts is given in **Exhibit 3.15**. Consider the same two sale transactions that were recorded in the journals in Exhibit 3.6. Regardless of whether the transactions originally were recorded in a special journal or a general journal, the posting procedure is the same. In this illustration, a special journal, that is, the sales journal, is used as the book of original entry.

SALES JOURNAL						Page 1
Date		Customer Name	Invoice No.	Accounts Receivable, Dr. 1230	Sales of Goods, Cr. 4100	Sales Tax Payable, Cr. 2370	Cost of Goods Sold, Dr. 5010 Mdse. Inventory, Cr. 1300
2018							
June	30	Aberdeen Park	I00022	1,680	1,680	0	840
	30	G. H. Allen	I00023	1,134	1,050	84	525
TOTAL				2,814	2,730	84	1,365

The following postings from the sales journal to two subsidiary ledgers are done as often as is necessary to keep the subsidiary ledger accounts sufficiently current:

ACCOUNTS RECEIVABLE SUBSIDIARY LEDGER

Aberdeen Park*
1903 Dwire Street
San Antonio, TX 78202
Contact Person: Kevin Call

Beginning Balance	Invoice, Check, Debit/Credit Memo No.	Date	Debit Amount	Credit Amount	Amount Owing
0	I00022	6/30/18	1,680		1,680

Allen, G. H.*
200 Scarsdale Drive
Dallas, TX 76033

Beginning Balance	Invoice, Check, Debit/Credit Memo No.	Date	Debit Amount	Credit Amount	Amount Owing
0	I00023	6/30/18	1,134		1,134

* A subsidiary ledger account.
Notes:
   Other data maintained for each customer would be, for example, credit limit.
   Other customers of Aca Pool Co. are omitted to simplify the illustration, but a record for each one also would be included in this ledger.

EXHIBIT 3.15 Posting Process in Paper-Based Accounting System (page 1 of 2)

MERCHANDISE INVENTORY SUBSIDIARY LEDGER

Chemical Pool Treatment*   Product No. P1050

Unit	Selling Price Per Unit	Quantity Beginning Balance	Increase + Decrease −	Quantity Current Balance	Cost Per Unit	Total Cost
lb	1.60	25,000	600−	24,400	.80	19,520

Pool Divider Rope-20'*   Product No. P1080

Unit	Selling Price Per Unit	Quantity Beginning Balance	Increase + Decrease −	Quantity Current Balance	Cost Per Unit	Total Cost
each	60.00	65	12−	53	30.00	1,590

Table with Umbrella*   Product No. P1100

Unit	Selling Price Per Unit	Quantity Beginning Balance	Increase + Decrease −	Quantity Current Balance	Cost Per Unit	Total Cost
each	1,050.00	4	1−	3	525.00	1,575

*A subsidiary ledger account.
Notes:
  Other data maintained for each inventory item would be, for example, the profit margin.
  Other inventory items owned by Aca Pool Co. are omitted to simplify the illustration, but a record for each one also would be included in this ledger.

The following postings from the sales journal to the general ledger are done only occasionally but at least before the financial statements are prepared:

GENERAL LEDGER

Accounts Receivable*   Account No. 1230

Date	Debit Amount	Credit Amount	Current Balance
6/30/18	2,814		2,814 Dr.

Sales   Account No. 4100

Date	Debit Amount	Credit Amount	Current Balance
6/30/18		2,730	2,730 Cr.

Sales Tax Payable   Account No. 2460

Date	Debit Amount	Credit Amount	Current Balance
6/30/18		84	84 Cr.

Cost of Goods Sold   Account No. 5010

Date	Debit Amount	Credit Amount	Current Balance
6/30/18	1,365		1,365 Dr.

Merchandise Inventory   Account No. 1300**

Date	Debit Amount	Credit Amount	Current Balance
6/30/18		1,365	35,339 Dr.

**A general ledger control account.

EXHIBIT 3.15 Posting Process in Paper-Based Accounting System (page 2 of 2)

Exhibit 3.16 summarizes some of the posting processes of a paper-based accounting system that are key for making correlations later in this chapter with computerized accounting systems. For this summary, assume a merchandising organization such as Aca Pool Co. maintains a perpetual inventory system. For recording transactions, the organization uses four special journals—sales, cash receipts, purchases, and cash disbursements—and one general journal. The organization maintains three general ledger control accounts—accounts receivable, merchandise inventory, and accounts payable.

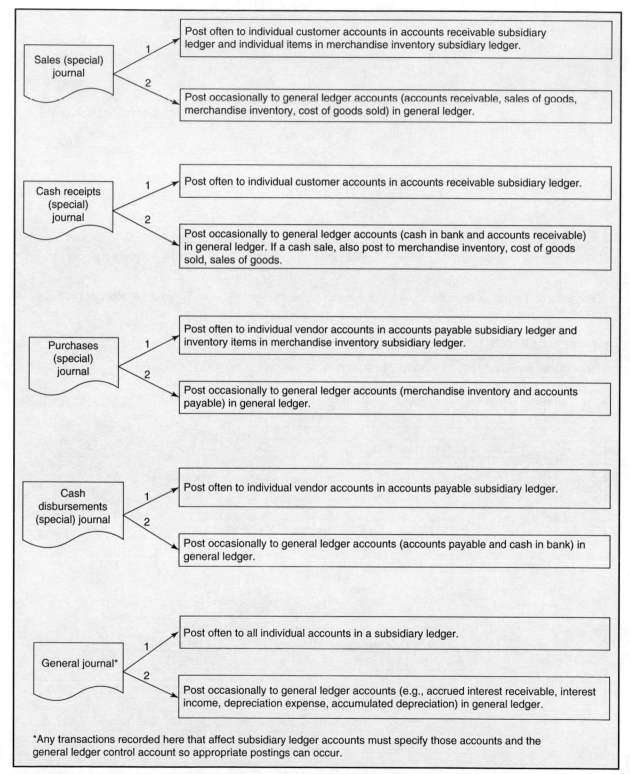

Sales (special) journal
1. Post often to individual customer accounts in accounts receivable subsidiary ledger and individual items in merchandise inventory subsidiary ledger.
2. Post occasionally to general ledger accounts (accounts receivable, sales of goods, merchandise inventory, cost of goods sold) in general ledger.

Cash receipts (special) journal
1. Post often to individual customer accounts in accounts receivable subsidiary ledger.
2. Post occasionally to general ledger accounts (cash in bank and accounts receivable) in general ledger. If a cash sale, also post to merchandise inventory, cost of goods sold, sales of goods.

Purchases (special) journal
1. Post often to individual vendor accounts in accounts payable subsidiary ledger and inventory items in merchandise inventory subsidiary ledger.
2. Post occasionally to general ledger accounts (merchandise inventory and accounts payable) in general ledger.

Cash disbursements (special) journal
1. Post often to individual vendor accounts in accounts payable subsidiary ledger.
2. Post occasionally to general ledger accounts (accounts payable and cash in bank) in general ledger.

General journal*
1. Post often to all individual accounts in a subsidiary ledger.
2. Post occasionally to general ledger accounts (e.g., accrued interest receivable, interest income, depreciation expense, accumulated depreciation) in general ledger.

*Any transactions recorded here that affect subsidiary ledger accounts must specify those accounts and the general ledger control account so appropriate postings can occur.

EXHIBIT 3.16 Summary of Posting Processes in a Paper-Based Accounting System

Preparing Output Documents and Reports

Documents and reports, such as those already described in this chapter, can be prepared after the completion of any of the activities. For example, customer invoices would be prepared after goods have been shipped; the schedule of aged accounts receivable and a forecast of cash inflows would be prepared after customer invoices have been prepared; financial statements would be prepared after the general journal has been posted to the general ledger.

Computerized Accounting Systems

Many of the essential elements that are on paper medium in a paper-based system are on electronic medium in a computerized accounting system. In computerized systems, related data elements, or fields, are grouped into a record, and related records are grouped into a file. In many accounting systems, related files are stored in the database of a database management system. Files must be designed carefully to provide efficient storage and quick access to data. Moreover, files should be designed in such a way that data redundancy and inconsistency are reduced to a minimum.

As accountants, we are generally concerned with the user's perception of a file, or collection of records. In other words, we are interested in how a file is organized in a logical, or conceptual, sense as opposed to how the file is organized physically on the electronic medium. Files can be viewed logically as tables where the rows are the records and the columns are the fields, or data elements. References made to files in this textbook are to the logical organization unless noted otherwise. Sometimes when we discuss files it is not important to know whether the files are stored as separate, isolated entities, as they are in accounting systems based on an older technology called file-processing systems, or whether the files are stored in a single facility as tables that can be combined, as they are in accounting systems based on the newer database technology. Therefore, the distinction between files used in file-processing systems or files used in database-processing systems is made in this textbook only when the distinction is important to the discussion at hand.

Essential Elements of a Computerized Accounting System

The essential elements of a computerized accounting system include source documents, reference files, open files, transaction files, master files, and outputs. **Exhibit 3.17** compares the elements of a computerized system to those of a paper-based system.

The source documents and outputs are very similar in paper-based and computerized accounting systems. But because computerized systems can process and store more data than would be feasible in paper-based systems, computerized systems can provide a much wider array of useful information, provided the necessary inputs are captured.

LEARNING OBJECTIVE 4
Identify the essential elements of a computerized accounting system.

Elements of Paper-Based Systems		Elements of Computerized Systems	
Type	Medium	Type	Medium
Source documents	Paper	Source documents	Paper
Accounts/chart of accounts	Paper	Reference files	Electronic
Documents awaiting further processing	Paper	Open files	Electronic
Journals	Paper	Transaction files	Electronic
Ledgers	Paper	Master files	Electronic
Outputs	Paper	Outputs	Paper and screen

EXHIBIT 3.17 Comparison of Elements of Paper-Based and Computerized Accounting Systems

Source: Karuka/Shutterstock.

As in a paper-based accounting system, a computerized accounting system also contains accounts that are organized into a chart of accounts, documents awaiting further processing (such as a sales order), journals, and ledgers. But because this information is stored electronically in files, how these files function and how they are related become very important issues. The same data elements that are stored in the paper chart of accounts, in paper documents awaiting further processing, in paper journals, and in paper ledgers in a paper-based accounting system are stored in files in a computerized system. These files that store the data elements are conveniently called data files. The four types of data files, as ordered in Exhibit 3.17, are:

- Reference file
- Open file
- Transaction file
- Master file

In the following discussion about the elements (documents, files, outputs), the files appear in an order different from that in Exhibit 3.17 to facilitate the discussion.

Source Documents

The contents, or data elements, of source documents are basically the same in both paper-based and computerized accounting systems. However, in computerized environments, a current trend is to design paper source documents so they can be electronically scanned into the system. Another trend in computerized accounting systems is to capture data electronically at the time and place the transactions originate thereby eliminating many paper source documents. For example, an electronic time clock located in an operating facility, a point-of-sale (POS) terminal in a sales department, or an automated teller machine (ATM) in a bank all accept transactions at their point of origin. Electronic data capture is called **source document automation** (SDA). The advantages of SDA are speed and a reduction in errors because the manual keying of data has been eliminated. The disadvantage is that the transaction data may be lost as a result of a power failure or equipment malfunction before they can be stored and processed. Suitable internal controls must be incorporated to overcome this problem. One possibility is to write the transactions immediately upon capture to a failure-resistant storage medium such as magnetic tape or paper.

Source document automation The electronic capture of data.

Reference Files

A **reference file** stores data that are used repeatedly for processing transactions. For example, tax tables are necessary for processing payroll transactions so these tables would be stored in a tax table reference file and updated only when tax rates change. Another reference file, a chart of accounts, is necessary for processing all transactions.

A chart of accounts reference file corresponds to the paper chart of accounts. Each account is represented by one record. For example, one record in the chart of accounts reference file would be 1230-Accounts Receivable. Another record would be 4100-Sales of Goods. In a computerized system, the chart of accounts is a reference file that contains, at a minimum, the account number, or code; account name; and account classification, that is, asset, liability, ownership equity, revenue, or expense. For example, the records for the Accounts Receivable and Sales of Goods accounts would be as follows:

Reference file A file that stores data that are used repeatedly for processing transactions. An example is a tax table reference file that is used for processing payroll transactions.

Account No.	Account Name	Account Type
1230	Accounts Receivable	Asset
4100	Sales of Goods	Revenue

This chart of accounts reference file is used to validate account numbers, or codes, when transactions are entered in a transaction file. For example, when the account #4100 (Sales of Goods) is entered to record that part of the sale transaction, the chart of accounts reference file will be examined to determine whether 4100 is a valid account number.

General Ledger Master File

The **general ledger master file** is an extension of the chart of accounts reference file and corresponds to the general ledger in a paper-based accounting system. The main purpose of a general ledger master file is to store account balances to be presented in reports.

Although the general ledger master file is viewed logically as one file, it actually is comprised of two files that are linked to one another on the account number field. The second file is necessary because more than one transaction may affect the current balance, and it is desirable to maintain a record of each change in the balance for audit evidence.

Each account in the general ledger, such as the accounts receivable account, is represented by one record in the first file. Each account in the second file will have as many records as there are transactions that affect the account. The first field of the record contains the account number, or code. Other fields in the record contain financial data for the account. The records for the Accounts Receivable account in the general ledger master file for Aca Pool Co. would be as follows:

General ledger master file A file that stores detailed data about the general ledger accounts in an accounting system.

File 1:

Account No.	Beginning Balance	Current Balance*
1230	0	2,814

*A positive number denotes a debit balance, and a negative number denotes a credit balance.

File 2:

Account No.	Debit/Credit Activity*	Transaction No.	Transaction Date	Explanation
1230	2,814	SA444	6/30/18	Credit sales

*Positive numbers are debits, and negative numbers are credits.

Note that the account name is not included in either file. When the account name is needed for a report, a match on the account number in a record in the first file and the account number in a record in the chart of accounts reference file can be made to produce the account name. Suppose, for example, you want to generate a Trial Balance that includes the account number, account name, and current balance for every account. The software program that produces the Trial Balance will retrieve the account number and current balance from the general ledger master file and the account name from the chart of accounts reference file so that the row for accounts receivable will be presented as follows:

Account No.	Account Name	Current Balance
1230	Accounts Receivable	2,814

The account number could be suppressed and not appear in the Trial Balance.

Because of the concern with information privacy, the general ledger master file and the chart of accounts reference file should be maintained as two separate files. If they are combined into one file, financial data can be read by users who need access to only chart of accounts data. In many computerized accounting systems, the data elements in the chart of accounts reference file are included in the general ledger master file, and this is the approach we take in this textbook. Therefore, the record above would also include the account name and type.

Subsidiary Ledger Master Files

Subsidiary ledger master file A file that stores detailed data about the subsidiary ledger accounts in an accounting system.

As with subsidiary ledgers in a paper-based system, the main purpose of **subsidiary ledger master files** in a computerized system is to store detailed information about general ledger *control* accounts. This detailed information supports many operating activities.

The first field of the record for a subsidiary ledger master file contains the account number, or code. Other fields in the record vary depending on the nature of the file. For example, the subsidiary ledger master file that supports the accounts receivable control account would include necessary information on each *customer* such as name, address, credit limit, credit terms, sales tax code, and amount owing. Two of the records for Aca Pool Co. would be as shown below:

Customer Code	Name	Address	Credit Limit	Credit Terms	Sales Tax Code	Amount Owing
C100	Aberdeen Park	San Antonio, TX	50,000	2/10, net 30	E	1,680
C200	G. H. Allen	Dallas, TX	50,000	2/10, net 30	T1	1,134

Subsidiary ledger master files and their records are analogous to subsidiary ledgers and their accounts in a paper-based accounting system. When we refer to a *specific* subsidiary ledger master file, we generally use a more descriptive term for the file. For example, the subsidiary ledger master file that supports the Accounts Receivable control account stores records about individual customers. Therefore, we refer to this file as the Customer Master File. The subsidiary ledger master file that supports the Inventory control account stores records about individual items of inventory. Therefore, we refer to this file as the Inventory Master File or the Product Master File. The subsidiary ledger master file that supports the Accounts Payable control account stores records about individual vendors so we call this file the Vendor Master File. The subsidiary ledger master file that supports Payroll is called the Employee Master File.

Using our earlier example of the accounts receivable control account and the two customers Aberdeen Park and G. H. Allen, the general ledger master file and the customer master file (a specific type of subsidiary ledger master file) would be as shown in **Exhibit 3.18**. This figure corresponds to the right-hand side (the "After" columns) of Exhibit 3.7 for a paper-based system.

General Ledger Master File

Account No.	...	Current Balance
1120		23,590
1230*		2,814
1410		1,650
(All other accounts in the file would be included, as well as these three.)		
*Accounts Receivable		

Customer Master File

Customer Code	...	Amount Owing
C100		1,680
C200		1,134
Total		2,814

EXHIBIT 3.18 General Ledger and Customer Master Files in a Computerized Accounting System

Exhibit 3.19 summarizes the difference between the General Ledger Master File and the various Subsidiary Ledger Master Files for a computerized accounting system and correlates to the illustration in Exhibit 3.8 for a paper-based system.

GENERAL LEDGER MASTER FILE*		SUBSIDIARY LEDGER MASTER FILES
General Ledger Control Account Records	**Other General Ledger Account Records†**	
Accounts receivable		Customer master file (one record for each customer)
Merchandise inventory		Inventory master file (one record for each item)
Accounts payable		Vendor master file (one record for each vendor)
	Cash in bank Accrued expenses Payable sales of goods Advertising expense	

*Account numbers, or codes, in the general ledger master file are the same as those included in the chart of accounts reference file (unless the two files are combined). Their balances are used in preparing the financial statements and other reports.

†If it was necessary to maintain details about these accounts, they could be made into control accounts with related subsidiary ledger master files. For example, it might be necessary to have an advertising expense master file for various types of advertising expenses. Conceivably, each account in the general ledger master file could be a control account with a related subsidiary ledger master file.

EXHIBIT 3.19 Difference Between General Ledger Master File and Subsidiary Ledger Master Files in a Computerized Accounting System

Subsidiary ledger master files store information that supports both accounting and operating activities while the general ledger master file stores information that mainly supports accounting activities such as financial reporting, auditing, and budgeting. **Exhibit 3.20** lists some subsidiary ledger master files typically used in a computerized accounting system and some of the data elements that are captured and stored in these files.

Open Files

An **open file** contains the data about transactions that have been started but cannot be fully processed until a subsequent event occurs. They are similar to paper documents pending further action. For example, a sales order open file contains the same data as would be on a paper sales order retained in a paper file pending shipment of the goods ordered or provision of the services requested. In addition, the file would have fields to be completed to denote, for example, when the shipment was made and the number of units that were shipped.

Although an open file is viewed logically as one file, it is actually comprised of two or more files that are linked to one another. An example of the records in the sales order open file for the order received by Aca Pool Co. from Aberdeen Park for the chemical pool treatment and the pool divider ropes would be as follows:

Open file A file that stores the data about transactions that have been started but cannot be fully processed until a subsequent event occurs. An example is a sales order open file pending shipment of ordered goods or completion of services.

File 1:

Sales Order No.	Sales Order Date	Customer Code	Customer P.O. No.
SO585	6/24/18	C100	3310

File 2:

Sales Order No.	Product No.	Quantity Ordered
SO585	P1050	600
SO585	P1080	12

Name	Essential Data Elements*
Customer (sometimes called Accounts Receivable Master File)	Customer code, name, address, customer type (retail, wholesale), credit limit, credit terms, account balance beginning of year, YTD sales, YTD payments, amount owing
Vendor (sometimes called Accounts Payable Master File)	Vendor code, name, address, credit limit, credit terms, account balance beginning of year, YTD purchases, YTD payments, amount owing
Employee (sometimes called Payroll Master File)	Employee code, name, address, spouse/dependent(s), job skills, pay rate, birth date, insurance, deductions code, withholding code, YTD earnings, YTD deduction amounts, YTD withholding amounts
Fixed Asset	Asset code, name, cost, estimated life, depreciation method, accumulated depreciation current balance
Investment Securities	Security code, name, number of shares/units, purchase date, cost, YTD interest/dividends received
Shareholder	Shareholder code, name, address, tax identification number, number of shares held, purchase date, YTD dividends paid
Raw Materials†	Material code, name, warehouse location, unit cost, reorder point, quantity on hand
Work in Process	Job code, name, raw material cost, labor cost, overhead cost
Inventory (sometimes called Product Master File)‡	Inventory code (or product number), description, warehouse location, unit cost, unit sales price, reorder point, reorder quantity, quantity on order, quantity on hand
Expense	Expense code, name, YTD amount incurred

*Other data elements could be added to accommodate users' reporting needs.

†This master file is necessary if the accounting system is for a manufacturing organization.

‡In a system for a manufacturing organization, this file is called Finished Goods Inventory Master File.

EXHIBIT 3.20 Typical Subsidiary Ledger Master Files in a Computerized Accounting System

The second file is necessary because more than one inventory item can be involved in a single order. The two files are linked to one another on the common field, which is sales order number. For our example, the above records indicate the single order from Aberdeen Park involves two products. To complete the sales order, information about customer C100, such as the customer's name and address, credit terms, shipping instructions, discount terms, and sales tax rate, needs to be extracted from the customer master. Also, information about products P1050 and P1080, such as description, S.K.U., and selling price, needs to be extracted from the inventory master file. Instead of using valuable storage space for the dollar amount of the order, it may be calculated when needed.

Exhibit 3.21 lists some typical open files in a computerized accounting system, their purpose, and their data elements. Note that these open files are critical for tracking the status of unfilled sales orders and purchase orders and unpaid customer and vendor invoices. These files are also important for maintaining sales history and purchases history.

Transaction Files

Transaction file A file that stores records pertaining to a group of like transactions occurring during a short period of time. Examples are sales, cash receipts, and purchases transaction files. A transaction file corresponds to a paper journal.

The special and general journals in paper-based accounting systems are replaced by transaction files in computerized accounting systems. A **transaction file** stores records pertaining to a group of like transactions occurring during a short period of time. For

Name	Purpose	Essential Data Elements*
Sales order	To store sales order data pending delivery of goods or services	Sales order number, sales order date, customer code, customer purchase order number and date, product number, quantity ordered, promised shipment date, quantity shipped, date shipped, shipping document number. Data elements retrieved from the inventory and customer master files are the product's description, S.K.U., unit sales price, customer's name, address, credit terms, shipping instructions, discount terms, sales tax rate.[†] *When "quantity ordered" and "quantity shipped" are equal, the record is closed and moved to sales history file.*
Customer invoice	To store customer invoice data pending receipt of cash for the invoice	Invoice number, invoice date, customer code, salesperson, sales order number, sales order date, customer purchase order number, product number, quantity purchased, quantity shipped, date shipped, shipping document number, date invoice paid, amount paid, customer check number. Data elements retrieved from the inventory and customer master files are the product's description, S.K.U., unit sales price, customer's name, address, credit terms, shipping instructions, discount terms, sales tax rate.[†] *When "invoice amount" and "amount paid" are equal, the record is closed and moved to sales history file.*
Purchase order	To store purchase order data pending receipt of goods or services	Purchase order number, purchase order date, vendor code, purchase requisition number, expected date of receipt, product number, quantity ordered, quantity received, date order received. Data elements retrieved from the inventory and vendor master files are the product's description, S.K.U., unit purchase price, vendor's name, address, credit terms, shipping instructions, discount terms, sales tax rate.[†] *When "quantity ordered" and "quantity received" are equal, the record is closed and moved to purchases history file.*
Vendor invoice	To store vendor invoice data pending disbursement of cash for the invoice	Voucher number, invoice date, vendor code, purchase order number, receiving document number, invoice due date, discount date, product number, date invoice paid, amount paid, check number. Data elements retrieved from the inventory and vendor master files are the product's description, S.K.U., unit purchase price, vendor's name, address, credit terms, discount terms, sales tax rate.[†] *When "invoice amount" and "amount paid" are equal, the record is closed and moved to purchases history file.*

*Other data elements could be added to accommodate user's reporting needs.
[†]The extended amounts and total amount may be stored or derived as needed by multiplying the quantities by prices, calculating any discounts and sales taxes, and then totaling.

EXHIBIT 3.21 Typical Open Files in a Computerized Accounting System

example, all sales transactions that are captured in one day are stored in a sales transaction file. Although each transaction file is viewed logically as one file, it may actually be comprised of two or more files that are linked together.

An example of the records in the sales transaction file for the sale to Aberdeen Park of the chemical pool treatment and the pool divider ropes would be as follows. In the field labeled "Cash/Credit Sale" in file 1, the number "0" denotes a cash sale, and the number "1" denotes a credit sale.

File 1:

Invoice No.	Invoice Date	Customer Code	Cash/Credit Sale	Sales Order No.
I00022	6/30/18	C100	1	S0585

File 2:

Invoice No.	Product No.	Quantity Shipped/ Delivered
I00022	P1050	600
I00022	P1080	12

The second file is necessary because more than one inventory item can be involved in a single sale. One record in the first file is linked to one or more records in the second file on the common field, which is invoice number.

For our example, the above records indicate our single sale to Aberdeen Park involved two products. Two elements that are essential for a sales transaction are (1) the amount of the sale, because this is the amount by which accounts receivable and sales will be increased, and (2) the cost of the inventory items sold, because this is the amount by which cost of goods sold will be increased and inventory will be decreased. The selling price per unit and the cost per unit, which are needed to calculate the amount of a sale and the cost of the inventory items sold, are stored for each item in inventory master file. A record in the inventory master file is linked to a record in the sales transaction file on the product number. The sales tax rate and the discount terms, also needed to calculate the amount of a sale and sales tax payable, are stored in the customer master file. A record in the customer master file is linked to a record in the sales transaction file on the customer code. Instead of using valuable storage space for the total amount of the sale and the cost of the inventory items sold, they may be calculated when needed.

Exhibit 3.22 lists some typical transaction files in a computerized accounting system, their purpose, and their data elements. You will notice that for transactions where an internal document is generated, the document number serves as the transaction number. However, for those transactions where no internal document is generated, a transaction number must be assigned.

Other Files in Computerized Accounting System

Four types of files in a computerized accounting system that have not yet been mentioned are:

- Scratch file
- Backup file
- Archive file
- Program file

Scratch file A file that is set up during a processing operation to aid in the processing and is purged when the operation is completed.

A **scratch file** is set up during a processing operation and is purged when the operation is completed. It is a very temporary file, aiding the operation with which it is associated but having no lasting importance. Sometimes a scratch file is used to collect data before insertion into a master file or a transaction file. A scratch file may also be a copy of a file sorted in another way, perhaps for the preparation of a report. For example, if a vendor master file is normally maintained in vendor code order but a report is

Name	Purpose	Essential Data Elements
Sales	To record sales transactions	(Customer) invoice number, invoice date, customer code, sales order number, product number, quantity shipped/delivered. Data elements retrieved from the inventory and customer master files are selling price per unit, cost per unit, sales tax rate, and discount terms.*
Shipping	This file is necessary for recording sales transactions only if sales require more than one shipment. Otherwise, sales are recorded in the sales transaction file.	Same as for sales transaction file
Cash receipts	To record cash receipts transactions	Transaction number or remittance advice number, cash receipt date, customer code, customer's check number, invoice number, receipt amount
Purchases	To record purchases transactions	Transaction number, purchase order number, vendor code, product number, date received, quantity received, receiving report number. Data elements retrieved from the inventory and vendor master files are cost per unit, sales tax rate, and discount terms.
Receiving	This file is necessary for recording purchases transactions only if purchases require the receipt of more than one shipment. Otherwise, purchases are recorded in the purchases transaction file.	Same as for purchases transaction file
Cash disbursements	To record cash disbursements transactions	Check number, cash disbursement date, vendor code, (vendor) invoice number, disbursement amount
Inventory adjustments	This file is necessary for recording only changes in inventory discovered from taking a physical inventory or to reduce inventory to its lower of cost or market valuation.	Transaction date, debit amount, credit amount, explanation
General journal	To record summarized transaction data from the above transaction files and to record transactions that do not fit in the above transaction files.	Transaction number, transaction date, account number, transaction amount, explanation

*Amounts may be stored or calculated as needed from other data elements.

EXHIBIT 3.22 Typical Transaction Files in a Computerized Accounting System

required in order of increasing dollar purchases, a scratch file may be set up for sorting and analysis.

A **backup file** is a duplicate copy of a file that is made for security reasons. It is placed in some safe location, such as a vault, for use in case the original file is damaged or lost. A backup file can be stored on a less expensive medium than the original file.

An **archive file** is a file or copy of a file that provides a *permanent* record of the *transactions* captured during an accounting period. In most cases, an archive file is accessed only infrequently, when the history of the accounting period becomes of

Backup file A duplicate copy of a file that is made for security reasons in case the original file becomes damaged or lost.

Archive file A file, or copy of a file, that provides a permanent record.

interest. An auditor may retrieve and analyze the records in the file as part of an audit procedure.

Program file A file that contains instructions to tell the computer how to process the data stored in the accounting system.

A **program file** contains instructions to tell the computer how to process the data stored in the accounting system. Accountants need to understand whether a program file is processing the data correctly.

Outputs

The major difference in outputs from a computerized system and a paper-based system is in the number and speed with which outputs from a computerized system can be generated. If the files have been designed properly to capture all the necessary information and to enable the building of relationships among the files, many different types of documents and reports that will help management in making decisions can be generated when and as needed. In addition, the standard reports such as financial statements can be automatically produced. The format and data items on output documents and reports are typically not affected by the type of accounting system used by an organization. Thus, the outputs themselves would be almost identical to those illustrated earlier in this chapter for a paper-based system.

Basic Activities of a Computerized Accounting System

LEARNING OBJECTIVE 5
Understand the basic activities of a computerized accounting system.

The basic activities of a computerized accounting system generally are as follows:

- Preclassifying transactions according to type (such as sales, cash receipts, purchases, cash disbursements)
- Creating a transaction file for each class of like transactions for each data-capturing period
- Updating, or posting to, the subsidiary ledger master files and open files
- Summarizing transaction files and transferring the summarized data to a general journal transaction file
- Updating, or posting to, the general ledger master file
- Preparing documents and reports

These activities occur in the order listed with a couple of exceptions. One exception is that documents and reports are prepared after each of the activities, not as a final activity. Another exception arises if the system uses real-time posting instead of batch posting. In real-time posting, the system could conceivably update all the subsidiary ledger master files and open files at the same time that it creates the transaction files and could, therefore, eliminate the step of summarizing transaction files and transferring the summarized data to a general journal transaction file. Although the technology for real-time posting is available today, in reality, the multi-user accounting system packages on the market use batch posting while only the packages for very small accounting systems use real-time posting. A more complete discussion of batch and real-time posting is at the end of this chapter. To provide you with the most comprehensive understanding of an accounting system, this discussion will continue under the assumption of batch posting so that all the activities listed above take place.

Preclassifying Transactions

In a computerized environment, transactions must be preclassified according to type to facilitate the data-capturing activity. Preclassifying occurs naturally within an organization because source documents originate in different locations. For example, receiving reports that indicate a purchase transaction has been completed are created in the receiving department, and shipping documents that indicate a sales transaction has been completed are created in the shipping department. Transaction data that are captured electronically can be preclassified by a software program based on an account code.

Creating a Transaction File

A separate transaction file is maintained for each class of transaction, such as sales, cash receipts, purchases, cash disbursements, occurring within a data-capturing period. Entering data in separate transaction files is comparable to recording transactions in a special journal, for example a sales journal, in a paper-based accounting system. Transactions, such as adjusting entries, which do not fit into one of the separate transactions files are captured in the general journal transaction file. This procedure corresponds to recording transactions in the general journal in a paper-based system. Transaction files are created regardless of whether the accounting system uses batch posting or real-time posting. The files are necessary to provide audit evidence.

A transaction file can be created using the following three methods:

■ Keying in or scanning data found on source documents

■ Transmitting data electronically

■ Extracting data from master files or open files (for adjusting entries only)

In early computerized accounting systems, a transaction file was created by extracting data from like source documents and keying in the data. This is an expensive technique for creating a transaction file because it involves the laborious task of entering and editing the entered data. As mentioned earlier in this chapter, many organizations have redesigned internally generated paper source documents to make them machine readable thereby eliminating the need to key in the data. The data are *scanned* into a transaction file.

Another method of creating a transaction file is electronic, or real-time, data capture. This method involves the electronic transmission of transaction data over telecommunications links between the place where the transaction occurs (such as in a retail store or on the factory floor) and the organization's computer that houses the accounting system. Both machine-readable source documents and electronic data capture help organizations reduce the cost of creating transaction files because the resources required to enter and edit data are reduced dramatically.

A transaction file also can be created by extracting data from subsidiary ledger master files and from open files. However, this method is limited to recording only some of the adjusting entries that are made periodically to bring accounting records up to date so that correct financial statements can be prepared. For example, one of the master files that is described in Exhibit 3.20 is the fixed asset master file, which includes each fixed asset's code, name, cost, estimated life, depreciation method, and accumulated depreciation current balance. The data necessary to make an adjusting entry to record the increase in depreciation expense and accumulated depreciation can be extracted from this file. Another example has to do with an adjusting entry for recognizing accrued interest. One of the open files described in Exhibit 3.21 is the vendor invoice file, which stores the invoice due date and the amount due. One of the master files in Exhibit 3.20 is the vendor master file, which stores the credit terms. If any of the invoices are overdue and the vendor imposes a finance charge, the invoice due date, amount due, the credit terms, and the accounting period's ending date are the data necessary to make an adjusting entry to record the increase in interest expense and accrued interest payable. **Exhibit 3.23** illustrates these three methods of creating a transaction file.

Updating, or Posting to, Subsidiary Ledger Master Files and Open Files

Subsidiary ledger master files and open files are updated by transaction files. This updating, or posting, process is similar to the paper-based posting process shown in Exhibit 3.15. A transaction file can be sorted on various keys and used to update multiple

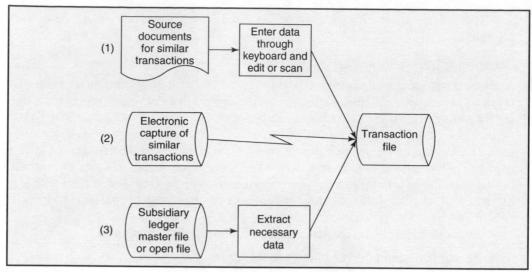

EXHIBIT 3.23 Three Methods for Creating a Transaction File of Like Transactions in a Computerized Accounting System

subsidiary ledger master and open files. For example, in the case of a sales transaction file, the files to be updated are:

- Customer master file (increase amount due from customers)
- Inventory master file (decrease quantities for individual inventory items sold)
- Sales order open file (close records for open sales orders that have been filled)
- Customer invoice open file (create records for new invoices to be submitted to customers). **Exhibit 3.24** illustrates the updating of these master and open files with the sales transaction file.

Because subsidiary ledger master files and open files support an organization's daily operating activities, these files are updated soon after the transaction data are entered. This updating process corresponds to the posting process in a paper-based system coded "1" in Exhibit 3.16. Transaction files are *summarized* and used at a later time (before financial statements are prepared) to update the general ledger master file. This updating process corresponds to the posting process in a paper-based system coded "2" in Exhibit 3.16.

One record in a transaction file will modify or create at least one record in at least one related master file or open file. For example, the sale to Aberdeen Park of $1,680 on 6/30/18 is one record in the Sales Transaction File. This record will update the record for Aberdeen Park in the Customer Master File by increasing its amount owing from 0 to $1,680. This same record in the Sales Transaction File will also update two records in the Inventory Master File (one for chemical pool treatment and one for pool divider rope-20') by decreasing the quantity of the inventory items by the number of units sold in the transaction. Also, this same record in the sales transaction file will update one record in the Sales Order Open File by closing out (or marking) the record for the sales order that this sale filled. Finally, this same record in the sales transaction file will create one new record in the Customer Invoice Open File for a new invoice so that Aca Pool Co. can bill Aberdeen Park and track receipt of its payment of the invoice.

Summarizing Transaction Files and Transferring to General Journal Transaction File

Data in the separate transaction files (e.g., sales, cash receipts, purchases, cash disbursements) are summarized into appropriate pairs of debit-credit journal entries for the general ledger accounts that will be affected by the transactions. Then these summarized

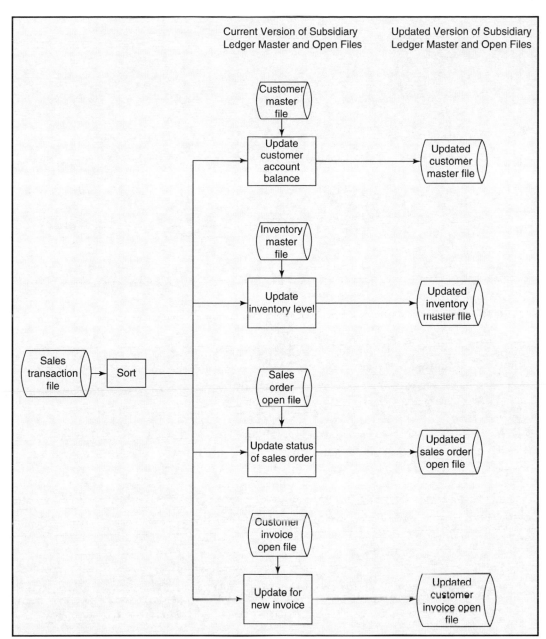

EXHIBIT 3.24 Subsidiary Ledger Master and Open File Updates from a Sales Transaction File in a Computerized Accounting System

journal entries are transferred into the general journal transaction file. For example, the sales transaction file is summarized into a debit entry to Accounts Receivable, a credit to Sales, a debit to Cost of Goods Sold, and a credit to Inventory. This process of summarizing and transferring transaction data is depicted in **Exhibit 3.25**.

An alternative to transferring data into the general journal transaction file is to maintain a "transfer" transaction file for the transaction data transferred from other transaction files so that the general journal transaction file can be used solely for transactions that do not fit in other transaction files.

Transferring summarized data from the original transaction files enables more efficient data storage. As mentioned before, subsidiary ledger master files and open files are updated immediately, or at least daily, and general ledger master files are updated periodically, at least before the financial statements are prepared. Therefore, after the subsidiary

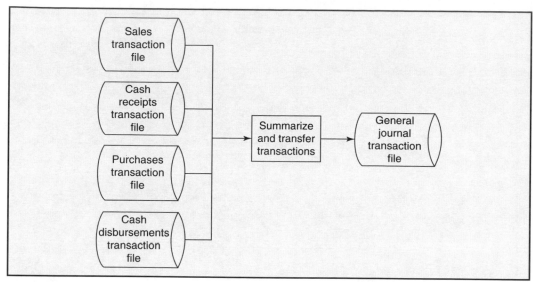

EXHIBIT 3.25 Process of Summarizing Transaction Data in a Computerized Accounting System

ledger master files and open files have been updated, and summarized data transferred to the general journal transaction file, the original transaction file can be archived so a new one can be created for the next day's transactions.

Updating, or Posting to, the General Ledger Master File

Exhibit 3.26 illustrates how the general ledger master file is updated from the general journal transaction file. Again, this process corresponds to the posting process in a paper-based system coded "2" in Exhibit 3.16.

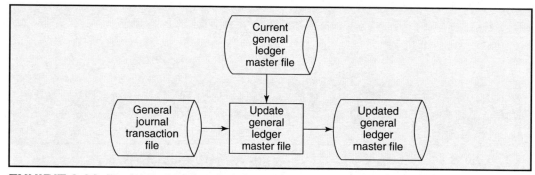

EXHIBIT 3.26 Periodic Update of General Ledger Master File from General Journal Transaction File in a Computerized Accounting System

Preparing Output Documents and Reports

Various documents and reports are prepared from the files, for example, the sales journal from the sales transaction file and the schedule of aged accounts receivable from the customer invoice open file.

The financial statements are prepared from the General Ledger Master File. But first, the account balances in the General Ledger Master File must be totaled to verify that the total debit balances equal the total credit balances and that the balances for each control account in the General Ledger Master File equals the sum of the account balances in the related subsidiary ledger master file. For example, the balance in the Accounts Receivable account in the General Ledger Master File should equal the sum of the balances in the Customer Master File. If there is an out-of-balance situation, adjusting entries and/or correcting entries are made to bring the General Ledger Master File accounts and any related subsidiary ledger master file accounts back into balance.

Revenue and expense account balances are used for the Statement of Income. Ownership equity account balances and net income are used for the Statement of Changes in Ownership Equity. Asset, liability, ownership equity, revenue, and expense account balances are used to create the Statement of Cash Flows. Asset, liability, and ownership equity account balances are used for the Balance Sheet.

Batch versus Real-Time Posting

Batch Posting

Most computerized accounting systems today still emulate paper-based accounting systems. One similarity is that transaction files are created to represent paper journals so that each transaction file represents a batch of like transactions. At a designated time, preferably at least at the end of each day, the data from transaction files are used to update master and open files—similar to posting in a paper-based system. These systems use what is called batch posting because all posting, or updating, is done in a batch.

LEARNING OBJECTIVE 6
Compare batch posting in a computerized accounting system to real-time posting.

Optimally, batch posting occurs when there is no conflicting activity on the system. A conflicting activity is one that accesses the same record in a master or open file that is being updated by the posting activity. To avoid this situation, batch posting is often scheduled to be done after the close of business. Alternatively, batch posting can be programmed as a background task. This means that upon being instructed to post transactions, the system posts to only those records not requested by other users. Thus, if a large number of users are on the system, posting takes a back seat and proceeds more slowly.

An effect of batch posting is that master and open file records are only up to date immediately after posting has occurred. To overcome this limitation, most prepackaged accounting systems permit posting on demand so that master and open files can be as current as is necessary. An accounts receivable department might, for example, post to the customer master file several times a day. For some accounting operations, such as payroll, frequent posting is not essential.

A valuable feature of batch posting is that a user can print a proof list of a transaction file *before* posting. This list is reviewed to detect errors that can be corrected before posting occurs. As a result, the accounting records should be error-free.

Real-Time Posting

Today, we have the technology that permits real-time posting. The impact of real-time posting is that as the data are captured for each transaction, they can immediately update the appropriate master and open files. Continuing with our example of a sale transaction, when the data are captured for a sale, the data could be simultaneously (a) sent to a transaction file to be stored in debit and credit format and (b) used to update the following files:

- Customer master file (increase amount owing for customer)
- Inventory master file (decrease balance for individual inventory items sold)
- Sales order open file (close record for open sales order that has been filled)
- Customer invoice open file (create record for new invoice)
- General ledger master file (increase Accounts Receivable, decrease Inventory, increase Cost of Goods Sold, increase Sales)

Even today, however, real-time posting ordinarily is used only on an as-needed basis. For example, if a company accepts orders over the telephone, inventory balances must be current at all times. In this case, the inventory master file would be posted in real time to keep the balances on hand current. All the other files would be posted in batches using data from the transaction files. Real-time posting is also important to the airline industry to keep its inventory of available seats up to date. Most of the prepackaged accounting systems for large organizations (i.e., high-end and mid-market accounting packages) use batch posting while the systems written for very small "mom and pop" organizations (called low-end accounting packages) use real time. Even when posting is performed in real time, transaction files may be created to provide a record of transaction activity for audit evidence.

The frequently touted advantage of real-time posting is the availability of up-to-the-minute information. Managers of organizations are often impressed by the fact that, for example, a current Statement of Income can be produced at any moment in a real-time system. Several warnings, however, need to be heeded. Whereas the balance in the sales revenue account may be increased immediately when a sale is made, some expenses that should be matched against these sales revenues may not have been entered in the system. Also, if transaction data are keyed in or scanned into the system, the system can be up to date only if all the transactions have been entered. Thus, a system is not truly real time unless it has both real-time data capture, provided by input devices such as point-of-sale terminals, ATM machines, or electronic time clocks, *and* real-time posting.

A significant disadvantage of real-time posting is that it requires more computer and personnel resources than does a well-organized batch posting operation. Besides writing entered data to a transaction file, real-time requires that the system look up the appropriate accounts in any affected master and open files and update them. Other users may have to wait (a) because of slow computer speed or (b) because other users are accessing the record being updated.

Another disadvantage of real-time posting is that when erroneous data are entered, the errors are propagated throughout the system. For example, a *single* error, such as recording the incorrect number of units of inventory sold and delivered, may result in the numerous errors itemized below.

- In the accounts receivable subsystem:
  - Error in the invoice generated for the customer
  - Error in the shipping document (bill of lading)
  - Error in the sales transaction file
  - Error in the customer master file
  - Error in the monthly statement sent to the customer
- In the inventory subsystem:
  - Error in the cost of sales journal entry (both debit and credit)
  - Error in the inventory balance on hand
  - Possibly an error in the inventory order recommendations report, with items being ordered that are not needed
  - If the quantity recorded is less than the quantity delivered, orders may be accepted for units that are not in stock. If the quantity recorded is more than the quantity delivered, orders may be rejected for units that are in stock.
  - Error in the monthly statement sent to the customer
- In the payroll subsystem (if salespeople are paid commissions on sales):
  - Error in sales commissions earned
  - Error in commissions paid
  - Error in payroll withholdings and payroll deposits
  - Error in payroll reports to the Internal Revenue Service
- In the general ledger subsystem:
  - Error in general ledger journal file to which data are transferred from the sales transaction file and payroll transaction file
  - Errors in the related general ledger accounts, which are accounts receivable, sales, cost of goods sold, inventory, sales commissions, payroll taxes payable, and payroll tax expense

All reports to management that are based on the above data will be incorrect. Later chapters in the text cover several internal controls that can be used to ensure that recorded data are correct before posting occurs. But many of these controls assume that batch-posting is being used rather than real time. The use of batch posting combined with good internal controls results in a much cleaner set of records by eliminating both errors and journal entries needed to correct the errors.

Best Uses of Batch and Real-Time Posting

Real-time posting should be used only when up-to-date information is critical. Batch posting should be used at all other times to minimize costs and to ensure that the maximum number of data-entry errors have been eliminated from transaction files before posting occurs. The most time-critical data are usually related to inventory (either physical quantities of merchandise or quantities of services such as the number of seats on an airplane). The next most time-critical data often are accounts receivables. Accounts payable should be updated as often as reports are run or cash disbursements are made. In large organizations this will be daily while two times a month may be sufficient for small organizations. Payroll can usually be posted any time between pay periods. Because some of the information needed for end-of-the-month general ledger closings is usually not available until a few days after the end of each month, real-time posting in this subsystem is a waste of resources.

Summary

A review of a paper-based accounting system is a good starting point for understanding computerized accounting systems. Accounting students have become familiar with the essential elements and basic activities in a paper-based system from previous accounting courses. Paper-based accounting systems provide a simple and familiar context in which to understand the issues of computerized accounting systems.

The essential elements of a paper-based accounting system are source documents, accounts, chart of accounts, journals (special and general), ledgers (subsidiary and general), and outputs. It is necessary to understand the purpose of each of these elements and to know how each is used in an accounting system. Several examples of each element are presented in the chapter.

The basic activities of a paper-based accounting system are completing source documents, recording transactions in the appropriate journals, posting (copying) data from the journals to the appropriate accounts in the subsidiary ledgers and the general ledger, and preparing output documents and reports during each activity.

In a computerized accounting system, many of the essential elements are on electronic medium instead of paper medium. Therefore, an understanding of files becomes critical to understanding these systems. Accounts and the chart of accounts are stored in a reference file. Internally generated documents awaiting further processing are stored in open files. Transactions are stored in transaction files, and detailed information about accounts is stored in master files.

The basic activities of a computerized accounting system are preclassifying transactions, creating a transaction file for each class of like transactions, updating subsidiary ledger master files and open files, summarizing transaction files and transferring the data to a general journal transaction file, updating the general ledger master file, and preparing documents and reports in each activity.

Many accounting systems today have the capability of real-time posting. The impact of real-time posting is that as the data are captured for each transaction, they immediately update the appropriate master and open files, thus leading to the impression that the data in the accounting system are up to the minute. In fact, the data are truly current only if the system also uses real-time data capture.

Key Terms

Discussion Questions and Problems

1. Where does the information that is reported in an organization's accounting system come from?
2. Identify the essential elements of a paper-based accounting system.
3. Identify the data elements contained in the following documents:

Bill of lading	Receiving report
Cash receipts prelist	Sales order
Customer invoice	Time card
Purchase order	

4. What are the five major categories in a Chart of Accounts?
5. Aca Pool Co. owes Deakin Pool Supplies $5,100 and Major Pool Supplies $9,000. Instead of having these two payable accounts in its general ledger, Aca Pool Co. wants to move the accounts to a subsidiary ledger and substitute a single control account in the general ledger to represent the removed accounts.

Required:

Illustrate what the general ledger would look like before establishing a control account and a subsidiary ledger. Also show what the general ledger and subsidiary ledger would look like after the control account and subsidiary ledger have been created.

6. Identify one difference between general ledger and subsidiary ledger accounts in a paper-based accounting system.
7. What is the substitute in a computerized accounting system for paper medium in a paper-based accounting system?
8. What file in a computerized accounting system corresponds to the paper journal in a paper-based system?
9. Discuss the purpose and ways of preclassifying transactions.
10. In Exhibit 3.6, you see a credit sale to G. H. Allen that is recorded in a paper-based accounting system. On July 28, 2018, Aca Pool Co. received check number 6311 from G. H. Allen in payment of his outstanding invoice.

Required:

a. Record the receipt of Allen's check on the cash receipts prelist, document number CR645. Your instructor will provide you a blank form.
b. Use the prelist as your source document to record this cash receipts transaction in the appropriate special journal. Your instructor will provide you a blank journal.
c. What are the two ledgers that need to be posted because of this cash receipt and what are the effects of the postings?

11. Refer to the data in question 10.

Required:

Post the special journal to the appropriate ledgers. Use the chart of accounts in the chapter to locate the appropriate account numbers and omit any "current balance" amounts. Your instructor will provide you the blank ledgers.

12. Refer to the data in question 10 but assume Aca Pool Co. has a computerized accounting system.

Required:

a. What is the name of the file that contains a record that stores the data regarding G. H. Allen's unpaid invoice?
b. What is the name of the transaction file where the receipt of the check will be entered?
c. What are the names of the three files that need to be updated as a result of the receipt of the check from G. H. Allen?

13. Aca Pool Co. needs to order the following goods from Deakin Pool Supplies, vendor code V15, Kansas City, MO, and receive them on July 11, 2018, in accordance with purchase requisition number 8686:

Number	Description	Quantity	Cost Per Unit
P1060	Diving board-8'	10 each	$98.00
P1140	Water volleyball sets	30 each	18.75

Aca Pool Co. wants to instruct Deakin to ship the goods via Rao Freight Co., FOB Kansas City, freight charges COD. B. Wang is the purchasing agent handling the order.

Required:

Prepare purchase order number 2121 for Aca Pool Co. to send to Deakin. Date your purchase order June 27, 2018. Your instructor will provide you a blank purchase order.

14. Refer to the data in question 13.

Required:

In a computerized accounting system, what is the name of the file that will contain a record to store the data regarding unfilled purchase order number 2121?

15. Refer to the data in question number 13. Rao Freight Co. (carrier #F3696), vehicle number TX-8880, has arrived at Deakin Pool Supplies to pick up the goods to deliver to Aca Pool Co. The shipment will take two days to get to Aca Pool Co. The diving boards weigh 120 pounds each, and the volleyball sets weigh 5 pounds each. The freight rate is $30 per 100 pounds for both items, and the freight charges are COD. Deakin's shipper number is S4455. Mary Chen signs all shipping documents for Deakin Pool Supplies. Val Mason signs for Rao Freight Co.

Required:

Complete bill of lading number BL062 for the shipment. Your instructor will provide you a blank form.

16. Refer to the data in questions 13 and 15. Aca Pool Co. has received the 10 - 8' diving boards and the 30 water volleyball sets from Deakin Pool Supplies. J. Dedmon receives the shipment for Aca Pool Co.

Required:

Prepare a receiving report, document #R46, for Aca Pool Co. Your instructor will provide you a blank form.

17. Aca Pool Co. has received invoice #1207, dated July 8, 2018, from Deakin Pool Supplies for 10 - 8' diving boards and 30 water volleyball sets.

Required:

In a computerized accounting system, what is the name of the file in Aca Pool Co.'s accounting system that contains a record to store the data regarding the unpaid invoice?

18. Aca Pool Co. has sent check number 4444, dated August 1, 2018, to Deakin Pool Supplies in payment of invoice #1207, for $1,542.50. Assume a paper-based accounting system.

Required:

Prepare the appropriate journal entry in the cash disbursements journal and post to the appropriate subsidiary ledger and the general ledger. Use the chart of accounts in Exhibit 3.5 to locate the appropriate account numbers. Your instructor will provide you a blank journal and ledgers.

19. Refer to the data in question 18. Assume a computerized accounting system.

Required:

a. What is the name of the file where the cash disbursement will be entered?

b. What are the names of the two files that need to be updated as a result of the cash disbursement?

20. Aca Pool Co. has the following four invoices that are due from customers:

Customer	Invoice No.	Date of Invoice	Amount of Invoice
Bath YWCA	I20021	6/06/2018	$6,900
Franklin Resorts	I20003	3/28/2018	2,200
Franklin Resorts	I20016	4/25/2018	3,937
Leeds Hotel	I20020	5/12/2018	3,700

Invoices are due 30 days after the date of the invoice.

Required:

Prepare a Schedule of Aged Accounts Receivable for Aca Pool Company as of July 1, 2018. Make your schedule similar to the one in the chapter.

21. Aca Pool Co. has the following five invoices that are due to its vendors:

Vendor	Invoice No.	Date of Invoice	Amount of Invoice
Coventry Auto Co.	2002	6/06/2018	$6,900
Deakin Pool Supplies	1986	5/12/2018	3,700
Fennell Chemical Co.	17622	3/28/2018	2,200
Chan Pool Supplies	984	4/25/2018	3,900
Major Pool Supplies	2030	6/30/2018	1,300

Invoices are due 30 days after the date of the invoice.

Required:

Prepare a Schedule of Aged Accounts Payable for Aca Pool Co. as of July 1, 2018. Make your schedule similar to the one in the chapter.

22. Ingram's Shoe Store, located in Watertown, NY, has a paper-based accounting system. The store faxed its purchase order, dated November 1, 2018, to Black Shoe Company, vendor code V32, located in Syracuse, NY, for the following shoes:

Product No.	Quantity	S.K.U.	Description	Unit Price
L4445	200	Pair	Light Spirit-Encore	$30.00
L4446	200	Pair	Light Spirit-Pleasure	34.00
M2221	150	Pair	Exeter-Sport	40.00
M2222	150	Pair	Exeter-Executive	60.00

Ingram's will resell the shoes in its retail stores in the Midwest. This is the first order that Ingram's has placed with Black Shoe Company. Ingram's wants to have the shoes by January 5, 2019, and requests that they be shipped by Splash Trucking Company, a common carrier, FOB Syracuse, NY. Ingram's will pay for the shipping costs upon receipt of the goods. Black Shoe Company will sell the shoes to Ingram's on credit. The order was placed by Sue Connor, the purchasing agent, from purchase requisition number 623.

Required:

Complete a purchase order, document number PO6521, for Ingram's Shoe Store. Your instructor will provide you a blank form.

23. Refer to the data in question 22.

Required:

Prepare the sales order that would be prepared by Black Shoe Company. Number the sales order SO777, and date it November 1, 2018. The customer code that Black Shoe Company has given to Ingram's Shoe Store is C800. The shipment will take one day to reach Ingram's and will arrive on the date requested. Steve Hite authorizes all sales and is the sales representative for Ingram's. Your instructor will provide you a blank form.

24. Refer to the data in question number 22 and your sales order created in question number 23. Black Shoe Company is ready to ship all of the items ordered by Ingram's Shoe Store. The shoes are shipped 50 pairs to a box, and each box weighs 75 pounds. The freight rate is $30 per 100 pounds and will be paid COD. The shipper number is S3002, and Maria Garcia signs the bill of lading for Black Shoe Company. The carrier number is F2003, and Ruth Adams signs for the carrier. The route will be direct from Syracuse to Watertown on vehicle number NY-7777.

Required:

Prepare a bill of lading, document number BL999, for Black Shoe Company. Your instructor will provide you a blank form.

25. Refer to the data in question number 22 and the documents you completed in question numbers 23 and 24. Because Black Shoe Company has shipped the goods, it needs to record the sales transaction. Additional information for Black is as follows:

Product No.	Cost per Unit	Quantity on Hand Before Sale
L4445	$15.00	8,200
L4446	17.00	8,200
M2221	20.00	7,150
M2222	30.00	7,150

Required:

a. Record the sale transaction in the sales journal. Assume that the number of the invoice that Black would have sent to Ingram's Shoe Store is I8899. Your instructor will provide you a blank journal.
b. Post from the sales journal to the appropriate subsidiary ledgers. Your instructor will provide you the blank ledgers.

26. Refer to the data in question numbers 22 and 25 and the documents you completed in question numbers 25 and 26. For answering this question, assume Black Shoe Company has a computerized accounting system.

Required:

What would the record look like after the sale has been captured in the sales transaction file?

27. Refer to the data in question number 22. Assume that Black Shoe Company has a computerized accounting system instead of a paper-based accounting system.

Required:

a. What would the record for Ingram's Shoe Store in the Customer Master file look like after the credit sale has been made, but before Ingram's has paid for the goods? Assume Ingram's has a credit limit of $100,000, credit terms are 2/10, net 30, and its sales tax exemption number is NY4000.
b. What would the record for Ingram's Shoe Store in the Customer Master file look like after Ingram's has paid for the goods?

Note

1. A more detailed discussion of the Chart of Accounts is presented in Chapter 8.

Data Flows, Activities, and Structure of Accounting Systems

Source: rangizzz/Shutterstock.

Chapter Outline

Data Flows in an Accounting System

Activities of an Accounting Information System

Structure of an Accounting Information System

Learning Objectives

After studying this chapter, you should be able to:

- Explain the flow of transaction and other event data through an accounting system.
- Identify and explain the major activities of an accounting system: input, process, store, and output data.
- Divide the accounting system into four business processes and identify typical accounting subsystems, or modules, in each process.
- Understand how integration of the subsystems is achieved through the sharing of data files and the movement of data from one subsystem to another.

Source: Syda Productions/Shutterstock.

Introductory Scenario

Blake felt really good about himself. This was his first week on the job with a public accounting firm, and as he sat at his desk in his conservative gray suit, he reflected on how he had gotten where he was today. It had been a tough decision for Blake to declare an accounting major in college. He had embraced no definite goals beyond getting a degree in business and had never thought seriously about an accounting degree until his accounting principles instructor had persuaded him to pursue that route. He had been a little embarrassed about telling his friends he had decided to become a "bean counter." His friends had responded by giving him a green eyeshade and a sleeve garter.

Today Blake was proud that he had gotten an accounting degree. Many of his friends in other disciplines who had graduated when he did were still looking for jobs. Blake had gotten three job offers. Although it took a lot of agonizing to decide which offer to accept, he had to admit he had kind of liked being courted by the firms. It was nice being wanted.

"Blake, I need to talk to you about a financial statement audit we are starting next month," said Shari. Shari was the supervisor in charge of the audit of a big client. "I have a lot of planning to do before the audit. We are going to need several people for this one, and I think you will get some good experience from it." Blake was excited that he would be getting his feet wet so soon on the job.

"Here are some materials on the company. Also, you need to review the working papers from last year's audit within the next few days. You're going to be working on an evaluation of the application controls in this company, which requires an understanding of how transaction data flow through the accounting system." Blake started feeling a small knot in his stomach. He had been a good student at the university and had graduated with honors. However, Blake had taken only one auditing course and now he was getting ready to work on a real live audit! He wanted to impress Shari. He had heard she was a good supervisor to work with—very competent and professional.

Thank goodness he had a couple of weeks to do some homework. That night, Blake dug out his old auditing textbook. The topics started coming into focus. He reviewed the audit objectives that apply to the account balances on the financial statements— validity, completeness, ownership, valuation, classification, cutoff, accuracy, and disclosure. He had memorized these objectives, and each sounded pretty clear at the time. But he was still stuck on Shari's comment on "the flow of transaction data." Then he remembered his accounting information system textbook. Aha! There it was! He dug his heels into the pages on general and application controls and the flow of transaction data.

Introductory Scenario Thought Questions:

1. How do updates affect the master, transaction, and open files (i.e., the number of records or field data)?
2. Identify the accounting subsystems that might be included in the revenue process in each of the following types of organizations:
   a. A large manufacturing firm that produces cars and trucks
   b. A large insurance company offering life, health, accident, and liability policies
   c. A federal government agency

3. Blake was concerned about whether he understood the flow transactions through an accounting system. What is meant by the "flow of transactions"?

Data Flows in an Accounting System

In the previous chapter, you became familiar with the essential elements and basic processes that are found in computerized accounting systems. In this section, you will see how the elements and processes work together to move transaction data through the system.

LEARNING OBJECTIVE 1
Explain the flow of transactions and other event data through an accounting system.

Life Cycle of Transactions and Other Events

Some transactions and other events are initiated by personnel within the organization who are acting within the framework of authority established by management.[1] Examples of these transactions and other events are the purchase of raw materials by purchasing agents, the introduction of raw materials into production by production managers, and the sale of finished goods by salespersons. Transactions and other events may also be initiated by programmed instructions in a computer program, for example, the purchase of an item of merchandise inventory when its balance drops to a specific level. Other transactions and events are initiated by outside bodies, for example, a liability for federal income tax. Still others are associated with the passage of time, such as depreciation or accrual of interest.

A transaction must first be recognized through observation, notification, agreement, or judgment. Upon recognition, the data that reflect the transaction must be captured and input into the accounting system. Transaction data are coded to relate them to accounts that serve as a classification scheme for subsequent processing and reporting.[2] Thus, a transaction involving cash is related to the cash account, which is a record in the general ledger master file,[3] and a transaction involving a particular customer is related to that customer's record in the customer master file. The accounts in the chart of accounts and the accounts in the various subsidiary ledger master files provide the primary bases for classifying transaction data.

A transaction or other event may be reported individually or as part of aggregate, or summary, information, such as an account balance. Individual transactions and other events may be reported to customers, vendors, or employees. For example, an invoice reports a given sale to a particular customer. Aggregate transaction data provide the basis for preparing the financial statements and reports addressed to groups such as managers, stockholders, or government agencies. Most reporting is in summary form. The final resting place for transaction and other event data ordinarily is an archive file. In such a file, the transaction awaits its eventual destruction at a time governed by the company's record retention policies or by applicable legal requirements.

The flow of transactions and other events from their point of origin to their final destination must be understood clearly by the users and implementers of the accounting information system and by internal and external auditors whose job is to ensure that the system is performing satisfactorily.

Illustration of Data Flows

To explain how transaction and other event data flow through an accounting system, a narrative and graphic illustration of transactions and other events for a small *service* organization for the month of January is presented. We are using a service organization to simplify the illustration. Our system contains only sales processing, customer invoicing, cash receipts, and general ledger subsystems, or modules. Each month, the system processes sales, prepares customer invoices, and collects cash. Then the sales and cash receipts data are transferred to the general ledger, where other transaction data, such as purchases, are entered in our accounting system. Finally, a general ledger account activity report and external financial statements are prepared. Other types of organizations, for example, a merchandising organization, would include the shipping and merchandise inventory aspects of sales transactions. A systems flowchart of the flow of information in our service organization is presented in **Exhibit 4.1**, which is separated into the four subsystems, or modules, as follows:

a. Sales Processing
b. Customer Invoicing
c. Cash Receipts
d. General Ledger

You may want to read the narrative descriptions that follow for each subsystem before reading the flowcharts for the subsystems. As you read, you will notice that subsystems denote activities and, in general, the activities of one subsystem are completed before the activities of another take place. However, there are exceptions to these timing differences. For example, the activity of entering billable hours, which occurs only one time, initiates both the sales processing and the customer invoicing processes.

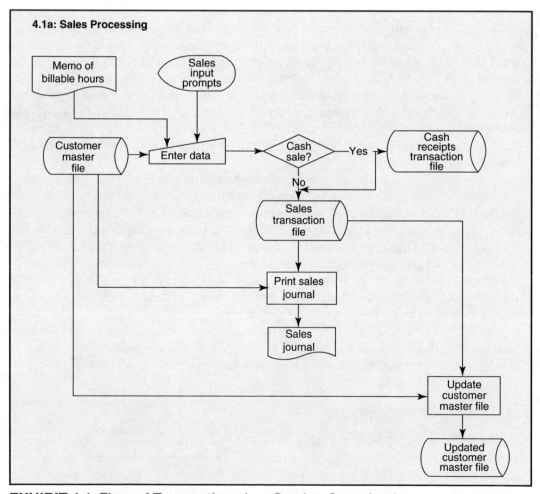

EXHIBIT 4.1 Flow of Transactions in a Service Organization

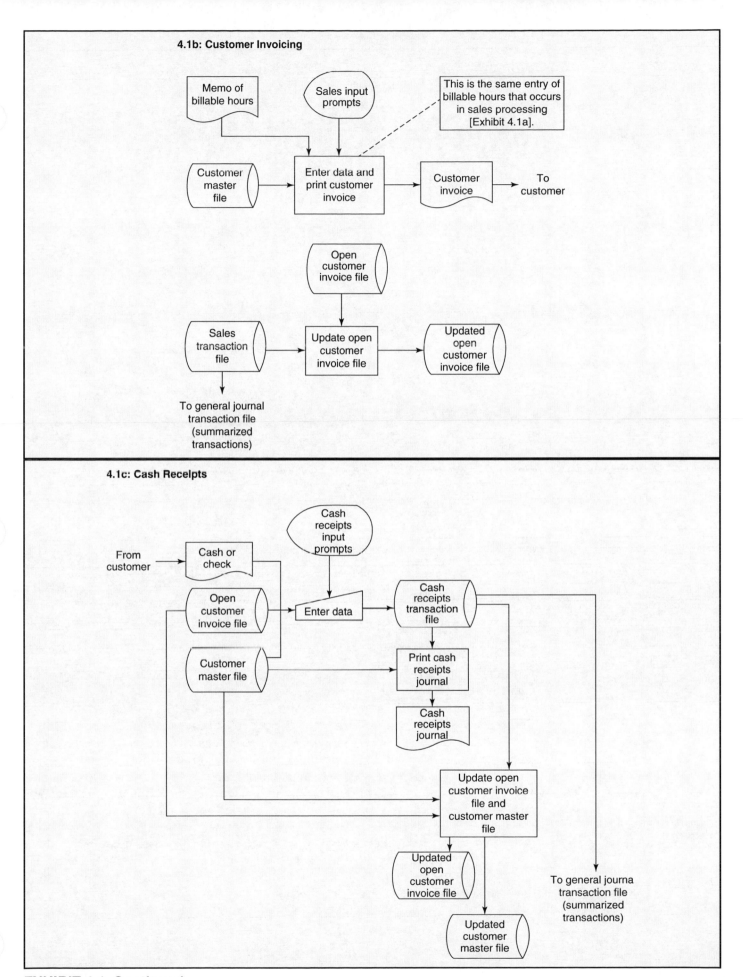

4.1b: Customer Invoicing

Memo of billable hours

Sales input prompts

This is the same entry of billable hours that occurs in sales processing [Exhibit 4.1a].

Customer master file

Enter data and print customer invoice

Customer invoice

To customer

Open customer invoice file

Sales transaction file

Update open customer invoice file

Updated open customer invoice file

To general journal transaction file (summarized transactions)

4.1c: Cash Receipts

Cash receipts input prompts

From customer

Cash or check

Open customer invoice file

Enter data

Cash receipts transaction file

Customer master file

Print cash receipts journal

Cash receipts journal

Update open customer invoice file and customer master file

Updated open customer invoice file

Updated customer master file

To general journal transaction file (summarized transactions)

EXHIBIT 4.1 Continued

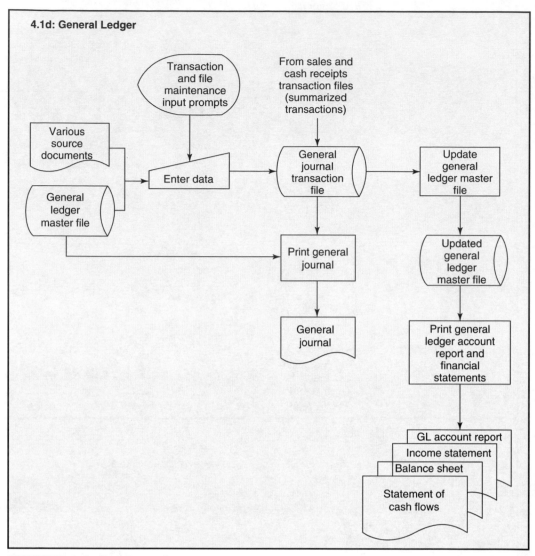

4.1d: General Ledger

EXHIBIT 4.1 Continued

Inputting Sales Transaction Data

Exhibit 4.2 shows some rather ordinary-looking computer screen forms for entry of sales data into the computerized accounting system. Accounting system software packages embellish the forms by adding color and making them look much like a printed invoice. The areas with heavy borders denote where data must be keyed into the entry form. The data regarding the sales of services could have been captured on memos prepared by the employees who rendered the services. Two of the sales in our illustration are cash sales (invoice numbers 1001 and 1005) and the other four are credit sales (invoice numbers 1002, 1003, 1004, and 1006). The accounting system automatically assigns the invoice numbers. The system also displays the customer code upon entry of a customer name to provide a check on the customer data. If a user sees a wrong customer code on the screen, he or she can verify that the correct customer name has been entered. Customer codes are retrieved from the customer master file by the input program (**Exhibit 4.3**). On the sales transaction entry screen (Exhibit 4.2), commands appear giving the user options to edit the entry, get online help, or process the entry.

SALES TRANSACTION ENTRY

EDIT   HELP   SUBMIT

Invoice No.	1001	
Invoice Date	01/03/18	
Customer Name	Green Brothers	202
Cash/Credit	Cash	
Billable Hours	Billable Rate	Total Amount
6	$100	$600

SALES TRANSACTION ENTRY

EDIT   HELP   SUBMIT

Invoice No.	1002	
Invoice Date	01/04/18	
Customer Name	Black Corp.	201
Cash/Credit	Credit	
Billable Hours	Billable Rate	Total Amount
42	$100	$4,200

SALES TRANSACTION ENTRY

EDIT   HELP   SUBMIT

Invoice No.	1003	
Invoice Date	01/07/18	
Customer Name	Brown Company	204
Cash/Credit	Credit	
Billable Hours	Billable Rate	Total Amount
27	$100	$2,700

SALES TRANSACTION ENTRY

EDIT   HELP   SUBMIT

Invoice No.	1004	
Invoice Date	01/10/18	
Customer Name	Green Brothers	202
Cash/Credit	Credit	
Billable Hours	Billable Rate	Total Amount
30	$100	$3,000

SALES TRANSACTION ENTRY

EDIT   HELP   SUBMIT

Invoice No.	1005	
Invoice Date	01/21/18	
Customer Name	Red flag Sales	206
Cash/Credit	Cash	
Billable Hours	Billable Rate	Total Amount
15	$100	$1,500

SALES TRANSACTION ENTRY

EDIT   HELP   SUBMIT

Invoice No.	1006	
Invoice Date	01/28/18	
Customer Name	Cherry Gardens	203
Cash/Credit	Credit	
Billable Hours	Billable Rate	Total Amount
60	$100	$6,000

EXHIBIT 4.2 Inputting Sales Transaction Data into Computerized Accounting System

Customer Code	Customer Name	Year-To-Date Sales	Current Balance
201	Black Corp.	0	0
202	Green Brothers	0	0
203	Cherry Gardens	0	2,400
204	Brown Company	0	4,300
206	Red Flag Sales	0	3,600

EXHIBIT 4.3 Retrieving Customer Names from the Customer Master File

The system writes the transaction data for all sales (whether cash or credit) to the sales transaction file (**Exhibit 4.4**). Notc that customers are identified only by customer code. Customer names are omitted from the transaction file to save file space. You will recall from Chapter 3 that the sales transaction file, although viewed logically as one file, is actually comprised of two files.

File 1 (0 for cash sale, and 1 for credit sale):

Invoice No.	Invoice Date	Customer Code	Cash/Credit Sale
1001	01/03/18	202	0
1002	01/04/18	201	1
1003	01/07/18	204	1
1004	01/10/18	202	1
1005	01/21/18	206	0
1006	01/28/18	203	1

File 2:

Invoice No.	Billable Hours	Billable Rate
1001	6	100
1002	42	100
1003	27	100
1004	30	100
1005	15	100
1006	60	100

EXHIBIT 4.4 Writing Sale Transactions to the Sales Transaction File

The system also writes cash receipts from the *cash* sale transactions to the cash receipts transaction file (**Exhibit 4.5**) and automatically assigns transaction numbers. You will notice a gap in the transaction numbers because other cash receipts transactions are occurring in other subsystems. These other transactions are discussed later in this illustration.

Chapter 4 Data Flows, Activities, and Structure of Accounting Systems

Transaction No.	Cash Receipt Date	Customer Code	Invoice No.	Cash Sale	Collection on Account	Customer Check No.
CR.550	01/03/18	202	1001	600		99102
..	..	..	..	..		..
CR554	01/21/18	206	1005	1,500		63340

EXHIBIT 4.5 Writing Cash Receipts from Cash Sales to the Cash Receipts Transaction File

(Other cash receipts occur between the dates of these sales and are discussed later in this illustration.)

SALES JOURNAL Month Ending 01/31/18					
	Customer		Cash Sales	Credit Sales	Invoice No.
Date	Code	Name	Cash Sales	Credit Sales	Invoice No.
01/03/18	202	Green Brothers	$600		1001
01/04/18	201	Black Corp.		$4,200	1002
01/07/18	204	Brown Company		2,700	1003
01/10/18	202	Green Brothers		3,000	1004
01/21/18	206	Red Flag Sales	1,500		1005
01/28/18	203	Cherry Gardens		6,000	1006
Totals			$2,100	$15,900	
Totals for Customer Codes:					
		201		$4,200	
		202	$600	3,000	
		203		6,000	
		204		2,700	
		206	1,500		

EXHIBIT 4.6 Printing the Sales Journal

Printing the Sales Journal

Data from the sales transaction file are listed in journal format to provide the sales journal (**Exhibit 4.6**). Customer names, retrieved from the customer master file, are included to help users interpret the printed information.

Updating the Customer Master File

Data from the sales transaction file are used to update (or post to) the customer master file. Records for the customers to whom sales were made are changed to reflect the increase in the customer's year-to-date sales amount and, if a *credit* sale, the customer's current balance. Note in **Exhibit 4.7** that the year-to-date sales amounts for all five customers have increased from what they were in Exhibit 4.3, and the current balances have increased for the four customers to whom credit sales were made.

a. File Before Posting (as it was in Exhibit 4.3)

Customer Code	Customer Name	Year-To-Date Sales	Current Balance
201	Black Corp.	0	0
202	Green Brothers	0	0
203	Cherry Gardens	0	2,400
204	Brown Company	0	4,300
206	Red Flag Sales	0	3,600

b. File After Posting

Customer Code	Customer Name	Year-To-Date Sales	Current Balance
201	Black Corp.	4,200	4,200
202	Green Brothers	3,600	3,000
203	Cherry Gardens	6,000	8,400
204	Brown Company	2,700	7,000
206	Red Flag Sales	1,500	3,600

EXHIBIT 4.7 Updating the Customer Master File with the Sales Transaction File

Reading the Flowchart of Sales Processing

Now that you have read text on how the sales data flow through the three processes—inputting sales transaction data, printing the sales journal, and updating the customer master file—you can follow the flow of transaction data by turning back to and reading the flowchart in Exhibit 4.1. As noted in the previous chapter, begin reading the flowchart by focusing on the first activity, which in this case is "Enter Data." Then observe what flows into this activity and then what flows out of this activity. Next, proceed through the flowchart one symbol at a time. The entire narrative description is captured in this one picture.

Printing Customer Invoices

The system prints customer invoices following the entry of sales transaction data into the system. The data needed for the invoices come from data keyed into the system, and some data, such as customer name and address, come from the customer master file. Abbreviated printed invoices are shown in **Exhibit 4.8**.

Updating the Open Customer Invoice File

Four of the January sales in our service organization are credit sales. Therefore, the accounting system has to provide means for keeping up with the cash that is due the organization, and this is accomplished by maintaining data about unpaid customer invoices. The sales transaction file updates the open (unpaid) customer invoice file by inserting a new

CUSTOMER INVOICE

Green Brothers		Invoice No.	1001
		Invoice Date	01/03/18

Cash X Credit

Billable Hours	Billable Rate	Total Amount Due
6	$100	$600

CUSTOMER INVOICE

Black Corp.		Invoice No.	1002
		Invoice Date	01/04/18

Cash ___ Credit X

Billable Hours	Billable Rate	Total Amount Due
42	$100	$4,200

CUSTOMER INVOICE

Brown Company		Invoice No.	1003
		Invoice Date	01/07/18

Cash ___ Credit X

Billable Hours	Billable Rate	Total Amount Due
27	$100	$2,700

CUSTOMER INVOICE

Green Brothers		Invoice No.	1004
		Invoice Date	01/10/18

Cash ___ Credit X

Billable Hours	Billable Rate	Total Amount Due
30	$100	$3,000

CUSTOMER INVOICE

Red Flag Sales		Invoice No.	1005
		Invoice Date	01/21/18

Cash X Credit

Billable Hours	Billable Rate	Total Amount Due
15	$100	$1,500

CUSTOMER INVOICE

Cherry Gardens		Invoice No.	1006
		Invoice Date	01/28/18

Cash ___ Credit X

Billable Hours	Billable Rate	Total Amount Due
60	$100	$6,000

EXHIBIT 4.8 Printing Customer Invoices

record for each new invoice. See **Exhibit 4.9**. You will notice that invoices for the cash sales are also entered in the open invoice file but are shown as having been paid at the time of the sale. The reason that invoices for cash sales as well as credit sales are stored in this file is that it is a major source of sales history.

a. File Before Posting

Invoice No.	Invoice Date	Customer Code	Invoice Amount	Date Invoice Paid	Amount Paid
0998	12/06/17	206	3,600		
0999	12/16/17	203	2,400		
1000	12/17/17	204	4,300		

b. File After Posting

Invoice No.	Invoice Date	Customer Code	Invoice Amount	Date Invoice Paid	Amount Paid
0998	12/06/17	206	3,600		
0999	12/16/17	203	2,400		
1000	12/17/17	204	4,300		
1001	01/03/18	202	600	01/03/18	600
1002	01/04/18	201	4,200		
1003	01/07/18	204	2,700		
1004	01/10/18	202	3,000		
1005	01/21/18	206	1,500	01/21/18	1,500
1006	01/28/18	203	6,000		

EXHIBIT 4.9 Updating the Open Customer Invoice File with the Sales Transaction File

Reading the Flowchart of Customer Invoicing

Now that you have read text on how the sales data flow through the two processes—printing customer invoices and updating the open customer invoice file—you can follow the flow of transaction data by turning back to and reading the flowchart in Exhibit 4.1.

Inputting Cash Receipts Transaction Data

During the month of January, cash is received from the two cash sales and is entered in the computerized system as was shown in Exhibit 4.2 (invoice numbers 1001 and 1005). These cash receipts are stored in the cash receipts transaction file as was shown in Exhibit 4.5. Cash is also received in January in payment of four invoices—two of which had been issued in December of the previous year and another two that were issued in January of the current year. **Exhibit 4.10** shows computer screen forms for entry of these four cash receipts into the accounting system. The areas with heavy borders denote that data must be keyed into the entry form. The system assigns transaction numbers automatically and retrieves customer codes from the customer master file upon entry of the customer names so the user can verify that the correct customer name has been entered. The system also automatically retrieves all unpaid invoices for the customer whose name was entered so the receipt can be applied to a particular invoice or invoices.

Chapter 4 Data Flows, Activities, and Structure of Accounting Systems

CASH RECEIPTS TRANSACTION ENTRY		
EDIT HELP PROCESS		
Transaction No.	CR551	
Date of Receipt	01/05/18	
Customer Name	Red Flag Sales	206
Invoice No.	0998	
Amount	$3,600	
Check No.	9666	

CASH RECEIPTS TRANSACTION ENTRY		
EDIT HELP PROCESS		
Transaction No.	CR552	
Date of Receipt	01/14/18	
Customer Name	Black Corp.	201
Invoice No.	1002	
Amount	$4,200	
Check No.	3116	

CASH RECEIPTS TRANSACTION ENTRY		
EDIT HELP PROCESS		
Transaction No.	CR553	
Date of Receipt	01/14/18	
Customer Name	Cherry Gardens	203
Invoice No.	0999	
Amount	$2,400	
Check No.	54445	

CASH RECEIPTS TRANSACTION ENTRY		
EDIT HELP PROCESS		
Transaction No.	CR555	
Date of Receipt	01/31/18	
Customer Name	Brown Company	204
Invoice No.	1003	
Amount	$2,700	
Check No.	22221	

EXHIBIT 4.10 Inputting Cash Receipts Transactions Data into Computerized Accounting System

The system writes the cash receipts, which are from both cash sales and the payment of invoices, to the cash receipts transaction file (**Exhibit 4.11**). As before, customer names are omitted from the transaction file.

Transaction No.	Cash Receipt Date	Customer Code	Invoice No. Paid	Cash Sale	Collection on Account	Customer Check No.
CR550	01/03/18	202	1001	$600		99102
CR551	01/05/18	206	0998		$3,600	9666
CR552	01/14/18	201	1002		$4,200	3116
CR553	01/14/18	203	0999		$2,400	54445
CR554	01/21/18	206	1005	$1,500		63340
CR555	01/31/18	204	1003		$2,700	22221

EXHIBIT 4.11 Writing Cash Receipts Transactions to the Cash Receipts Transaction File

Printing the Cash Receipts Journal

Data from the cash receipts transaction file are also used to prepare the cash receipts journal (**Exhibit 4.12**). Customer names are retrieved from the customer master file.

CASH RECEIPTS JOURNAL
Month Ending 1/31/18

Transaction No.	Cash Receipt Date	Customer Code	Customer Name	Cash Sale	Collection on Account	Invoice No.
CR550	01/03/18	202	Green Brothers	$600		1001
CR551	01/05/18	206	Red Flag Sales		$3,600	0998
CR552	01/14/18	201	Black Corp.		$4,200	1002
CR553	01/14/18	203	Cherry Gardens		$2,400	0999
CR554	01/21/18	206	Red Flag Sales	$1,500		1005
CR555	01/31/18	204	Brown Company		$2,700	1003
Totals				2,100	$12,900	
Totals for Customer Codes:		201			$4,200	
		202		$600		
		203			$2,400	
		204			$2,700	
		206		$1,500	$3,600	

EXHIBIT 4.12 Printing the Cash Receipts Journal

Updating the Open Customer Invoice File and the Customer Master File

Data from the cash receipts transaction file are used to update (or post to) the open customer invoice file in order to reflect that certain invoices have been paid (**Exhibit 4.13**).

a. File Before Posting [as it was in Exhibit 4.9(b)]

Invoice No.	Invoice Date	Customer Code	Invoice Amount	Date Invoice Paid	Amount Paid
0998	12/06/17	206	3,600		
0999	12/16/17	203	2,400		
1000	12/17/17	204	4,300		
1001	01/03/18	202	600	01/03/18	600
1002	01/04/18	201	4,200		
1003	01/07/18	204	2,700		
1004	01/10/18	202	3,000		
1005	01/21/18	206	1,500	01/21/18	1,500
1006	01/28/18	203	6,000		

b. File After Posting

Invoice No.	Invoice Date	Customer Code	Invoice Amount	Date Invoice Paid	Amount Paid
0998	12/06/17	206	3,600	01/05/18	3,600
0999	12/16/17	203	2,400	01/14/18	2,400
1000	12/17/17	204	4,300		
1001	01/03/18	202	600	01/03/18	600
1002	01/04/18	201	4,200	01/13/18	4,200
1003	01/07/18	204	2,700	01/31/18	2,700
1004	01/10/18	202	3,000		
1005	01/21/18	206	1,500	01/21/18	1,500
1006	01/28/18	203	6,000		

EXHIBIT 4.13 Updating the Open Customer Invoice File with the Cash Receipts Transaction File

The same cash receipts transaction file is also used to update the customer master file. Records for the customers who remitted cash in payment of outstanding invoices are changed to reflect the decrease in the customer's current balance (**Exhibit 4.14**).

a. File Before Posting [as it was in Exhibit 4.7(b)]

Customer Code	Customer Name	Year-To-Date Sales	Current Balance
201	Black Corp.	4,200	4,200
202	Green Brothers	3,600	3,000
203	Cherry Gardens	6,000	8,400
204	Brown Company	2,700	7,000
206	Red Flag Sales	1,500	3,600

b. File After Posting

Customer Code	Customer Name	Year-To-Date Sales	Current Balance
201	Black Corp.	4,200	0
202	Green Brothers	3,600	3,000
203	Cherry Gardens	6,000	6,000
204	Brown Company	2,700	4,300
206	Red Flag Sales	1,500	0

EXHIBIT 4.14 Updating the Customer Master File with the Cash Receipts Transaction File

Reading the Flowchart of Cash Receipts

Now that you have read text on how cash receipts data flow through the three processes—inputting cash receipts transaction data, printing the cash receipts journal, updating the open customer invoice file and the customer master file—you can follow the flow of transaction data by going back to and reading the flowchart in Exhibit 4.1.

Performing File Maintenance on the General Ledger Master File

During January, an event occurs that requires the addition of a new account to the chart of accounts. The accountant who is responsible for maintaining the chart of accounts determines that the account should be assigned the name "Repair Expense" and the number 5690. The new account is added by interactive file maintenance in the general ledger master file (**Exhibit 4.15**).[4] The account number and related information are entered into the

FILE MAINTENANCE ENTRY	
EDIT HELP SUBMIT	
Account No.	5690
Account Type	Expense
Account Name	Repair expense
Current Balance	0
Authorization Code	R111

EXHIBIT 4.15 Adding a New Account to the General Ledger Master File

computerized system. If the system determines that this account number is already in use, the system so indicates.

Exhibit 4.16 shows the general ledger master file before and after the file maintenance. Our new record was added within the body of the file to preserve the order of the

(a) File Before File Maintenance

Account No.	Account Name	Beginning Balance*	Current Balance*
1120	Cash in bank	4,100	4,100
1230	Accounts receivable	10,300	10,300
1600	Equipment	15,000	15,000
1650	Accumulated depreciation	(1,800)	(1,800)
2110	Accounts payable	(2,800)	(2,800)
3100	Owner's equity	(24,800)	(24,800)
4200	Sales of services	0	0
5130	Salary expense	0	0
5340	Depreciation expense	0	0
5700	Rent expense	0	0

(b) File After File Maintenance

Account No.	Account Name	Beginning Balance*	Current Balance*
1120	Cash in bank	4,100	4,100
1230	Accounts receivable	10,300	10,300
1600	Equipment	15,000	15,000
1650	Accumulated depreciation	(1,800)	(1,800)
2110	Accounts payable	(2,800)	(2,800)
3100	Owner's equity	(24,800)	(24,800)
4200	Sales of services	0	0
5130	Salary expense	0	0
5340	Depreciation expense	0	0
5690	Repair expense	0	0
5700	Rent expense	0	0

EXHIBIT 4.16 Effect of File Maintenance on the General Ledger Master File

*A positive number denotes a debit balance; a negative number denotes a credit balance.

accounts. You will recall from Chapter 3 that the general ledger master file is actually split into two files that are linked. Because the second file stores account debit and credit activity, it is not affected by file maintenance and so is not included in Exhibit 4.16.

Inputting of Transaction and Other Event Data into the General Ledger Subsystem

As mentioned, the simple accounting system described here has only sales processing, customer invoicing, cash receipts, and general ledger subsystems, or modules. Therefore, purchases, payroll, and other transactions and events have to be entered through the general ledger subsystem. Some examples of these transactions and other events are shown in **Exhibit 4.17**. Transaction numbers are assigned automatically, and account names are displayed automatically upon entry of account numbers. The account names are retrieved from the general ledger master file. The areas with heavy borders denote that data must be keyed into the entry form.

Note that a brief explanation of a transaction can be entered. This feature is helpful because of the wide variety of transactions that can be entered in the general ledger

GENERAL JOURNAL TRANSACTION ENTRY

EDIT   HELP   SUBMIT

Transaction No. GJ850

Transaction Date 01/10/18

Acct. No.	Account Name	Debit	Credit
5700	Rent expense	3,300	
1120	Cash in bank		3,300
Explanation:	Office rent		

GENERAL JOURNAL TRANSACTION ENTRY

EDIT   HELP   SUBMIT

Transaction No. GJ851

Transaction Date 01/14/18

Acct. No.	Account Name	Debit	Credit
5690	Repair expense	1,800	
2110	Accounts Payable		1,800
Explanation:	Repairs to vehicles		

GENERAL JOURNAL TRANSACTION ENTRY

EDIT   HELP   SUBMIT

Transaction No. GJ852

Transaction Date 01/31/18

Acct. No.	Account Name	Debit	Credit
5130	Salary expense	6,300	
1120	Cash in bank		6,300
Explanation:	Monthly payroll		

GENERAL JOURNAL TRANSACTION ENTRY

EDIT   HELP   SUBMIT

Transaction No. GJ853

Transaction Date 01/31/18

Acct. No.	Account Name	Debit	Credit
5340	Depre. expense	300	
1650	Accum. depre.		300
Explanation:	Depreciation of equipment		

EXHIBIT 4.17 Inputting Other Transaction Data into Computerized Accounting System

subsystem. The system writes the transactions, including the explanations, to the general journal transaction file. These transactions are the first eight records, that is, transaction numbers GJ850–GJ853, in **Exhibit 4.18**.

Transaction No.	Transaction Date	Account No.	Amount*	Explanation
GJ850	01/10/18	5700	3,300	Office rent
GJ850	01/10/18	1120	(3,300)	Office rent
GJ851	01/14/18	5690	1,800	Repairs to vehicles
GJ851	01/14/18	2110	(1,800)	Repairs to vehicles
GJ852	01/31/18	5130	6,300	Monthly payroll
GJ852	01/31/18	1120	(6,300)	Monthly payroll
GJ853	01/31/18	5340	300	Depreciation on equipment
GJ853	01/31/18	1650	(300)	Depreciation on equipment
SA854	01/31/18	1120	2,100	Cash sales
SA854	01/31/18	4200	(2,100)	Cash sales
SA855	01/31/18	1230	15,900	Credit sales
SA855	01/31/18	4200	(15,900)	Credit sales
CA856	01/31/18	1120	12,900	Collections on account
CA856	01/31/18	1230	(12,900)	Collections on account

EXHIBIT 4.18 Writing Other Transaction Data to the General Journal Transaction File

*Positive numbers are debits; negative numbers are credits.

Transferring Data from the Sales Processing and Cash Receipts Subsystems

Periodically, usually at the end of the month, data in the sales and cash receipts transaction files are summarized and transferred to the general journal transaction file that is in the general ledger subsystem. This would be done automatically, upon selection of an appropriate function from a menu or command button displayed on the screen. Our illustration shows the summarized transaction data written to the general journal transaction file in Exhibit 4.18.[5] These summarized transactions are the last six records, that is, transaction numbers SA854–CA856, in the exhibit. SA denotes that the transactions were transferred from the sales transaction file, and CA denotes that the transactions were transferred from the cash receipts transaction file.

Printing the General Journal

Data in the general journal transaction file are listed to provide the general journal (**Exhibit 4.19**). Account names retrieved from the general ledger master file are included in the report.

		Account				
GENERAL JOURNAL **Month Ending 1/31/18**						
Transaction No.	**Transaction Date**	**No.**	**Name**	**Debit**	**Credit**	**Explanation**
GJ850	01/10/18	5700	Rent expense	3,300		Office rent
GJ850	01/10/18	1120	Cash in bank		3,300	Office rent
GJ851	01/14/18	5690	Repair expense	1,800		Repairs to vehicles
GJ851	01/14/18	2110	Accts. payable		1,800	Repairs to vehicles
GJ852	01/31/18	5130	Salary expense	6,300		Monthly payroll
GJ852	01/31/18	1120	Cash in bank		6,300	Monthly payroll
GJ853	01/31/18	5340	Depre. expense	300		Depre. on equipment
GJ853	01/31/18	1650	Accumulated depre.		300	Depre. on equipment
SA854	01/31/18	1120	Cash in bank	2,100		Cash sales
SA854	01/31/18	4200	Sales of services		2,100	Cash sales
SA855	01/31/18	1230	Accounts receivable	15,900		Credit sales
SA855	01/31/18	4200	Sales of services		15,900	Credit sales
CA856	01/31/18	1120	Cash in bank	12,900		Collections on account
CA856	01/31/18	1230	Accounts receivable		12,900	Collections on account
				$42,600	$42,600	

EXHIBIT 4.19 Printing the General Journal

Updating the General Ledger Master File

The transaction data in the general journal transaction file are used to update (or post to) the general ledger master file. First, the general journal transaction file is sorted by account number (**Exhibit 4.20**). This operation brings together all transactions affecting each particular account. Then the net debit and credit transaction activity for each account can be readily computed.

Exhibit 4.21 shows the effect of posting January's transaction data to the general ledger master file. The "current balances" in the file, before posting, are as of the last day of December. After posting, the current balances correspond to January 31. Note that beginning and current balances and debit and credit activities are included in the master file. The debit and credit activities could be omitted, but they provide information that supports the ending balances and helps establish audit evidence.

a. File in Original Chronological Order (as it was in Exhibit 4.18)

Transaction No.	Transaction Date	Account No.	Amount*	Explanation
GJ850	01/10/18	5700	3,300	Office rent
GJ850	01/10/18	1120	(3,300)	Office rent
GJ851	01/14/18	5690	1,800	Repairs to vehicles
GJ851	01/14/18	2110	(1,800)	Repairs to vehicles
GJ852	01/31/18	5130	6,300	Monthly payroll
GJ852	01/31/18	1120	(6,300)	Monthly payroll
GJ853	01/31/18	5340	300	Depreciation on equipment
GJ853	01/31/18	1650	(300)	Depreciation on equipment
SA854	01/31/18	1120	2,100	Cash sales
SA854	01/31/18	4200	(2,100)	Cash sales
SA855	01/3118	1230	15,900	Credit sales
SA855	01/31/18	4200	(15,900)	Credit sales
CA856	01/31/18	1120	12,900	Collections on account
CA856	01/31/18	1230	(12,900)	Collections on account

*Positive numbers are debits; negative numbers are credits.

b. File Sorted by Account Number

Transaction No.	Transaction Date	Account No.	Amount	Explanation
GJ850	01/10/18	1120	(3,300)	Office rent
GJ852	01/31/18	1120	(6,300)	Monthly payroll
SA854	01/31/18	1120	2,100	Cash sales
CA856	01/31/18	1120	12,900	Collections on account
SA855	01/31/18	1230	15,900	Credit sales
CA856	01/31/18	1230	(12,900)	Collections on account
GJ853	01/31/18	1650	(300)	Depreciation on equipment
GJ851	01/14/18	2110	(1,800)	Repairs to vehicles
SA854	01/31/18	4200	(2,100)	Cash sales
SA855	01/31/18	4200	(15,900)	Credit sales
GJ852	01/31/18	5130	6,300	Monthly payroll
GJ853	01/31/18	5340	300	Depreciation on equipment
GJ851	01/14/18	5690	1,800	Repairs to vehicles
GJ850	01/10/18	5700	3,300	Office rent

EXHIBIT 4.20 Sorting the General Journal Transaction File by Account Number

a. File Before Posting [as it was in Exhibit 4.16(b)]

Account Number	Account Name	Beginning Balance	Current Balance
1120	Cash in bank	4,100	4,100
1230	Accounts receivable	10,300	10,300
1600	Equipment	15,000	15,000
1650	Accumulated depreciation	(1,800)	(1,800)
2110	Accounts payable	(2,800)	(2,800)
3100	Owner's equity	(24,800)	(24,800)
4200	Sales of services	0	0
5130	Salary expense	0	0
5340	Depreciation expense	0	0
5690	Repair expense	0	0
5700	Rent expense	0	0

b. Files After Posting

File 1:

Account Number	Account Name	Beginning Balance	Current Balance
1120	Cash in bank	4,100	9,500
1230	Accounts receivable	10,300	13,300
1600	Equipment	15,000	15,000
1650	Accumulated depreciation	(1,800)	(2,100)
2110	Accounts payable	(2,800)	(4,600)
3100	Owner's equity	(24,800)	(24,800)
4200	Sales of services	0	(18,000)
5130	Salary expense	0	6,300
5340	Depreciation expense	0	300
5690	Repair expense	0	1,800
5700	Rent expense	0	3,300

EXHIBIT 4.21 Updating the General Ledger Master File with the General Journal Transaction File

File 2:

Account No.	Debit/Credit Activity	Transaction No.	Transaction Date	Explanation
1120	(3,300)	GJ850	01/10/18	Office rent
1120	(6,300)	GJ852	01/31/18	Monthly payroll
1120	2,100	SA854	01/31/18	Cash sales
1120	12,900	CA856	01/31/18	Collections on account
1230	15,900	SA855	01/31/18	Credit sales
1230	(12,900)	CA856	01/31/18	Collections on account
1650	(300)	GJ853	01/31/18	Depreciation on equipment
2110	(1,800)	GJ851	01/14/18	Repairs to vehicles
4200	(2,100)	SA854	01/31/18	Cash sales
4200	(15,900)	SA855	01/31/18	Credit sales
5130	6,300	GJ852	01/31/18	Monthly payroll
5340	300	GJ853	01/31/18	Depreciation on equipment
5690	1,800	GJ851	01/14/18	Repairs to vehicles
5700	3,300	GJ850	01/10/18	Office rent

EXHIBIT 4.21 Continued

Printing the General Ledger Account Activity Report

Accounting system packages provide a general ledger account activity report that shows the beginning and the current balances and the intervening transaction activity for each account. This report, shown in **Exhibit 4.22**, provides a very clear explanation of why the balances changed as they did.

The accounting system also computes net income for the period and automatically updates the owner's equity account. In other words, the system automatically processes closing entries. Alternatively, owner's equity could be updated only at year-end, and net income could be posted to a separate "current earnings" account for inclusion in interim statements.

Transaction No.	Transaction Date	Debit	Credit	Explanation
Account No. 1120 Cash in bank				
Beginning balance		$ 4,100		
GJ850	01/10/18		$ 3,300	Office rent
GJ852	01/31/18		6,300	Monthly payroll
SA854	01/31/18	2,100		Cash sales
CA856	01/31/18	12,900		Collections on account
		19,100	9,600	
		9,600		
Current balance		$ 9,500		
Account No. 1230 Accounts receivable				
Beginning balance		$ 10,300		
SA855	01/31/18	15,900		Credit sales
CA856	01/31/18		12,900	Collections on account
		$ 26,200	12,900	
			12,900	
Current balance		$ 13,300		
Account No. 1600 Equipment				
Beginning balance		$ 15,000		
		15,000	0	
		0		
Current balance		$ 15,000		
Account No. 1650 Accumulated depreciation				
Beginning balance			$ 1,800	
GJ853	01/31/18	0	300	Depreciation on equipment
			2,100	
			0	
Current balance			$ 2,100	

EXHIBIT 4.22 Printing the General Ledger Account Activity Report

Transaction No.	Transaction Date	Debit	Credit	Explanation
Account No. 2110 Accounts payable				
Beginning balance			$ 2,800	
GJ851	01/14/18		1,800	Repairs to vehicles
		0	4,600	
			0	
Current balance			$ 4,600	
Account No. 3100 Owner's equity				
Beginning balance			$ 24,800	
Net income for period			6,300	
		0	31,100	
			0	
Current balance			$ 31,100	
Account No. 4200 Sales of services				
Beginning balance			0	
SA854	01/31/18		2,100	Cash sales
SA855	01/31/18		15,900	Credit sales
		0	18,000	
			0	
Current balance			$ 18,000	
Account No. 5130 Salary expense				
Beginning balance		$ 0		
GJ852	01/31/18	6,300		Monthly payroll
		6,300	0	
		0		
Current balance		$ 6,300		

EXHIBIT 4.22 Continued

Transaction No.	Transaction Date	Debit	Credit	Explanation
Account No. 5340 Depreciation expense				
Beginning balance		$ 0		
GJ853	01/31/18	300		Depreciation on equipment
		300	0	
		0		
Current balance		$ 300		
Account No. 5690 Repair expense				
Beginning balance		$ 0		
GJ851	01/14/18	1,800		Repairs to vehicles
		$ 1,800	0	
		0		
Current balance		$ 1,800		
Account No. 5700 Rent expense				
Beginning balance		$ 0		
GJ850	01/10/18	3,300		Office rent
		3,300	0	
		0		
Current balance		$ 3,300		
Control totals		$ 49,500	$49,500*	

EXHIBIT 4.22 Continued

*This exhibit excludes the $6,300 added to Owner's Equity to prevent double counting of the revenues and expenses.

Preparing the Financial Statements

Exhibit 4.23 shows the income statement and balance sheet for January. The statements are prepared from data in the general ledger master file, and the balances are the same as those listed on the general ledger account activity report.

Reading the Flowchart of the General Ledger

As before, now that you have read text on how data flow through the general ledger subsystem, you can follow the flow of transaction data by turning back to and reading the flowchart in Exhibit 4.1.

Income Statement 1/01/18 to 1/31/18		
REVENUE		
Sales of services	$ 18,000	
TOTAL REVENUE		$ 18,000
EXPENSES		
Salary expense	6,300	
Depreciation expense	300	
Repair expense	1,800	
Rent expense	3,300	
TOTAL EXPENSES		11,700
NET INCOME		$ 6,300

Balance Sheet As of 1/31/18		
ASSETS		
Cash		$ 9,500
Accounts receivable		13,300
Equipment	$ 15,000	
Accumulated depre.	−2,100	12,900
TOTAL ASSETS		$ 35,700
LIABILITIES AND OWNER'S EQUITY		
Accounts payable	$ 4,600	
Owner's equity	31,100	
TOTAL LIABILITIES & OWNER'S EQUITY		$ 35,700

EXHIBIT 4.23 Preparing the Financial Statements

Data Flows in a Complex Accounting System

The accounting system described in the previous illustration was simplified so specific points could be made. Accounting systems would include, at a minimum, purchase order processing, payroll, vendor invoicing, and cash disbursements subsystems. These subsystems would include their own transaction files, master files, and open files. Data would flow from these subsystems to the general ledger subsystem in the same way they did in the illustration. Also, master file records usually have fifty or more data fields rather than the four fields in our illustration.

Activities of an Accounting Information System

LEARNING OBJECTIVE 2
Identify and explain the major activities of an accounting system: input, process, store, and output data.

An accounting system is a collection of activities that are designed to produce and deliver information. As you were studying the illustration of the data flows in a simple accounting system, you probably noticed that the system was performing the following major activities: input (capture) data, process data, store data, and output (communicate) data. These activities were also discussed in Chapter 3. In addition to these *major* activities, an accounting system has *support* activities that improve the quality of the major activities. The support activities are manage people, manage technology, and manage internal control. **Exhibit 4.24** shows the activities of an accounting information system. The major activities are discussed in this section.

Input (Capture) Data

Input data An information processing activity that captures and feeds transaction and other data into the accounting system for processing.

Input data is an information processing activity that captures and feeds transaction and other data into the accounting system for processing. Input is an interface between the users and the accounting system. Frequently, transaction data are captured on *input*, or *source, documents*, and then are keyed into the computerized accounting system. A discussion of source documents and several examples were given in Chapter 3. Keying the input data is vulnerable to errors. One of the most common errors is a transposition error in which two digits in a number are inadvertently interchanged; thus, 12345 might be

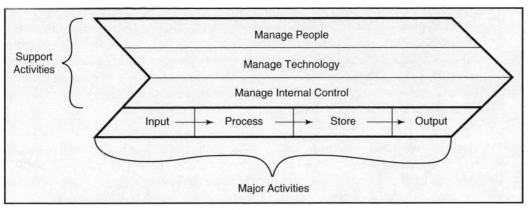

EXHIBIT 4.24 Activities of an Accounting Information System

keyed as 12435. Accordingly, the keyed data must be verified to ensure, to the extent possible, that erroneous data will not be processed into erroneous output. The verification may be performed by programmed error controls, by visual checking, or by a combination of both. Programmed controls examine each data element as it is entered and reject the element and display a diagnostic message if the data element fails to "pass" certain tests of acceptability. Correction and re-entry can be done at once. As mentioned in Chapter 3, keying errors can be avoided by scanning source documents or capturing transaction data electronically at the point of origin.

Process Data

Process data is an information processing activity that transforms data according to a prescribed set of instructions. An accounting system processes data in a variety of ways. Some of the most basic types of processing are listed below. More complex forms of processing may be built from combinations of these basic forms.

- **Classification.** Data may be classified, or placed into categories. All transaction data are classified by the account they affect. For example, when inventory is received, the cost of the purchase goes into the inventory account. Inventory transaction data may be further classified into receipts, issuances, and back orders. General ledger accounts are classified into balance sheet and income statement accounts. Classification usually is accomplished by transaction coding.

- **Calculation, or Computation.** Data may be manipulated mathematically. A very simple example is the multiplication of a unit cost by a quantity to produce the extended cost. More complex examples are the determination of payroll withholdings, purchase or sales discounts, and sales commissions. Some quantitative models that are used for decision support involve large numbers of complex calculations.

- **Comparison.** Data elements may be compared to determine whether they are similar. For example, a comparison is made when the name of a customer is checked against a list of individuals or organizations to whom credit terms have been extended. A comparison also is made to determine whether an employee's year-to-date earnings have reached the FICA tax ceiling.

- **Sorting.** Sorting consists of rearranging the records in a file into some meaningful sequence, usually in either ascending or descending order of a data element within the record. For example, vendor files may be sorted in alphabetical order by vendor name, or in ascending order by vendor number. As noted in our illustration of data flows in an accounting system, a transaction file is sorted by account number before updating the general ledger master file to bring together all transactions affecting the same account.

- **Updating, or Posting.** The updating, or posting, of master files and open files by transaction files was discussed not only in our illustration of data flows in

Process data An information processing activity that transforms data according to a prescribed set of instructions.

Classification A processing activity in which data are classified, or divided, into categories.

Calculation (computation) A processing activity in which data are manipulated mathematically.

Comparison A processing activity in which data are compared to determine whether they are similar.

Sorting A file processing activity that consists of rearranging the records in a file into some meaningful sequence, usually in either ascending or descending order of an appropriate data attribute, or key.

Updating/Posting An information processing activity that updates the balances in master files to reflect transaction activity.

an accounting system at the beginning of this chapter but also in Chapter 3. An example is the updating of a customer master file (using the sales transaction file) to show the increase in a customer's current balance for the amount of a credit sale to the customer. Another example is the updating of the customer open invoice file (using the cash receipts transaction file) to reflect the payment of an invoice. Updating is one of the most common processing activities, playing a central role in most of the accounting subsystems.

■ **Summarization, or Aggregation**. Data may be added to produce a summary total. As discussed in Chapter 3, data in the transaction files (sales, cash receipts, purchases, cash disbursements) are summarized into appropriate pairs of debit-credit journal entries before being transferred to the general journal transaction file.

■ **Merging**. Merging consists of combining two or more files into a single new file. Usually, the separate files are already ordered on the same data element, and the resulting file is similarly ordered. For example, inventory reorder files prepared by regional warehouses, each sorted by part number, may be combined into a single company-wide reorder file also sorted by part number.

■ **File maintenance**. File maintenance is a nonroutine process in which changes are made to a master file by direct intervention by a user. Typical file maintenance includes adding new records to a file (as was done in our illustration of data flows in an accounting system), deleting unwanted ones, and changing the content of existing records. For example, a new vendor may be added to a vendor master file, or an existing vendor's address may be changed. Account balances, which are updated by routine transaction posting, should not normally be changed by file maintenance because audit evidence would be incomplete.

Store Data

Store data is an information processing activity that provides for the storage of data to accommodate the timing differences between the input, process, and output of the data. Data that have been entered and processed at different times can be accumulated and combined to produce types of output that otherwise would not be possible if it were not for the storage activity. Data can then be retrieved from storage as needed to satisfy the requirements of the system's users.

The stored data must be able to support an organization's operations, mandatory external reporting requirements, and management decision making. Data find their way into storage as a result of the entry of transaction and other data. Data routinely needed for the organization's day-to-day operations and the form in which they must be delivered are known in advance and can be planned. On the other hand, requests for information to support management's decision-making function may be nonroutine, and their specific nature may be difficult or impossible to plan. The requests depend on what management needs at a given moment. Thus, the stored data must be maintained in a state of readiness, and the accounting system must be able to respond to requests as they arrive.

To provide for the various kinds of requests for information, the data are stored in meaningful structures. A popular data structure is the database management system that includes one system wide "super-file" containing all the individual files in an accounting system. Data files store sets of related records, such as inventory or sales records. An elaborate system of linkages among the files enables information to be retrieved on demand. Database management systems provide for the organization's routine reporting needs. But the most impressive capability of a database management system is that it can respond to managers' unexpected requests for information. Database management systems are discussed in more detail in Chapters 12 and 13.

Accountants and other users typically view data as being stored in "files."[6] Files provide logical models of the stored data as opposed to the actual physical arrangement on the storage medium. Accounting subsystems require several data files (as well as program files to instruct the computer in how to input, process, store, and output the data). The

---

Summarization (aggregation) A processing activity in which data are added to produce a summary total.

Merging A file processing activity that consists of combining two or more files into a single composite file.

File maintenance A nonroutine process in which changes are made to a master file through direct intervention by a user.

Store data An information processing activity that provides for the storage of data to accommodate the timing differences between the input, process, and output of the data.

data files in accounting systems are primarily of four main types: reference files, open files, transaction files, and master files. Explanations and examples of these files were presented in Chapter 3. The major subsystems and the data files accountants and others use are discussed later in this chapter.

Output (Communicate) Data

Output data is an information processing activity that retrieves, formats, and distributes data to users. Output is the second main interface between the users and the accounting system. The output may be a financial statement, a management report, a document, such as a customer invoice or paycheck, or a graph. The output medium may be paper, microfilm, a video screen display, or possibly voice synthesis. Sometimes the "output" from the system is in a machine-readable medium, forming the input to another computer, and the interface with an end user is deferred to some later processing stage. The broad range of available media enables an accounting system to meet a correspondingly wide variety of user needs.

The financial statements and many of the management reports are examples of status reports. **Status reports** focus on the balances recorded in the master and open files after updating from transaction files has been completed. Thus, the balance sheet lists the asset, liability, and ownership equity accounts in the general ledger master file and their associated balances. The income statement presents the equivalent information for the revenue and expense accounts. A status report may compare balances in a master file that result after being updated by transaction files and after undergoing file maintenance. For example, a customer master file may contain fields in which sales by month are retained for each of the 12 months of the previous year and each of the 12 months of the current year and the budgeted sales for the customer for each of the 12 months of the current year.[7] Some status reports list only a small subset of the total number of records in a file. An example is an inventory reorder report that identifies only those items whose on-hand balances have fallen below prescribed minimum levels. In contrast to status reports, which are produced from data in the master files, activity reports are produced from data in the transaction files. An **activity report** is a listing of the transaction file showing the transaction activities that have occurred over a period of time. An example is a sales journal.

More than one status or activity report may be produced from a single file, each formatted to meet a different need. The contents of a report may be sorted differently from the records in the file. A sales transaction file normally would be ordered chronologically, whereas an inventory issuance report prepared from the same file might be sorted by inventory item.

Frequently, a report may contain information that is not contained in the principal file from which it is produced. This additional information may be retrieved from another file or derived from a calculation. For example, a purchase activity report may show both the vendor number and the vendor name; the report is essentially a listing of the purchase transaction file, but the vendor names may have to be retrieved from the vendor master file because they are not recorded in the transaction file. In other situations, data may be derived from calculations either based on historical data or originating from some other sources. Reports may include estimates or projections of what might happen if a certain course of action were followed.

An important element of the output activity is the formatting of the information for communication to the user. Information formats are referred to as *forms* regardless of the medium, such as a document, report, or screen display. The way the form is designed depends on the medium, but in all cases the principal objective is to provide for the effective and efficient transfer of information to the human user. Paper reports containing tables of figures have been the traditional medium of communication for accounting data. Screen displays also often present data in tabular form. Tabular presentation apparently will continue as the principal output format for the foreseeable future. However, other media and formats, such as the graphical representation of data, are gaining in popularity. Graphics do not provide the quantitative detail of tables of figures but offer improved qualitative comprehension and "feel" for the underlying meaning of the data. Accordingly,

Output data An information processing activity that retrieves, formats, and distributes data to users.

Status report A listing of the balances in the master and open files as of a specific point in time.

Activity report A listing of the transaction file showing the transaction activities that have occurred over a period of time.

information specialists increasingly are turning to multimedia (and multiformat) communications in which the same data may be communicated to the users in more than one form. For example, a table of figures may be supplemented by a graph; or a screen display may be supplemented by synthesized voice output.

The output from the accounting system must meet the organization's and users' information requirements. Meeting their requirements is the chief justification for the investment in implementing, maintaining, operating, and controlling the accounting information system. To this end, an accounting system should not only provide useful information but also provide it in a timely, effective, and easy-to-understand manner. Ultimately, the information should provoke action of some kind or influence someone's behavior. If it fails to do either, the value of the output and the justification for the accounting system are in doubt.

Structure of an Accounting Information System

LEARNING OBJECTIVE 3
Divide the accounting system into four business processes and identify typical accounting subsystems, or modules, in each process.

Types of accounting systems are as numerous as types of organizations. This lack of uniformity complicates a person's ability to understand accounting systems. Systems are customarily divided into component subsystems, or modules, but there is more than one way to do this. Also, a subsystem that exists in one organization's accounting system may not have a counterpart in another organization's accounting system. For example, service organizations have no merchandise inventory for resale; merchandising organizations have no production operations; and nonprofit institutions have no ownership equity. Even the accounting systems for two merchandising organizations will differ.

Business Processes and Subsystems

Business process A group of interrelated business events. The business processes comprise the first, or most general, level of subsystems in an accounting information system and are defined according to the types of events they capture, process, store, and communicate.

In the face of this complexity and diversity, several attempts have been made to simplify the understanding of accounting systems and to establish a framework to unify the elements and processes that are common to all accounting systems. One of the most successful attempts produced the notion of business processes. A **business process** is a group of interrelated business events. The business processes comprise the first, or most general, level of subsystems in an accounting information system and are defined according to the types of events they capture, process, store, and communicate.

Four business processes that comprise an accounting information system are listed below and are also identified in the block diagram in **Exhibit 4.25**.

- Revenue Process
- Procurement Process
- Inventory Process
- Financial Process

Source: Syda Productions/Shutterstock.

Each business process can be further divided into one or more subsystems that have their own unique responsibilities, so to speak, to input (capture), process, store, and output (communicate) information about business events. The nature, purpose, and even the existence of each of the subsystems in this second level depend on the nature of the organization. These subsystems are generally referred to as modules in accounting software packages. Whereas the business processes are defined in general terms so they have the broadest possible relevance, accounting subsystems are defined more narrowly and may have relevance only in certain types of organizations. The subsystems perform well-defined activities, which are explained in the following sections. The principal subsystems within each business process are shown in **Exhibit 4.26**.

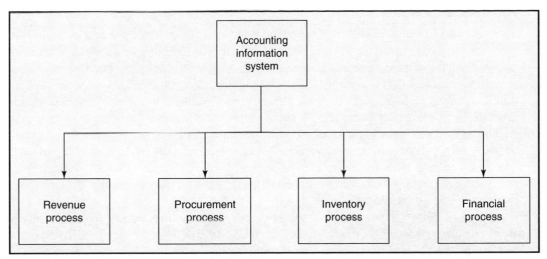

EXHIBIT 4.25 Business Processes of an Accounting Information System

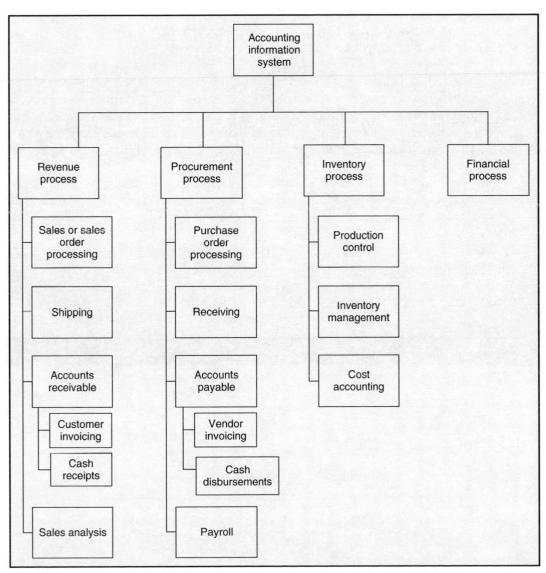

EXHIBIT 4.26 Subsystems of Business Processes in an Accounting Information System

Revenue Process[8]

Revenue process (also selling or selling and collection process) One of the business processes in an accounting system. It pertains to the distribution of resources to customers and others and the collection of earned revenues.

Sales subsystem A subsystem in the revenue process that is concerned with the sale of goods or the provision of services for immediate delivery.

Sales order processing subsystem A subsystem in the revenue process that is concerned with processing orders received from customers for the subsequent delivery of goods or provision of services.

Shipping subsystem A subsystem in the revenue process that is concerned with the retrieval of goods from the warehouse, the preparation of goods for shipment, the preparation of the paperwork to accompany shipped goods, and the recording of the shipments.

Accounts receivable subsystem A subsystem in the revenue process that is concerned with receiving payment for goods and services sold to customers.

Sales analysis subsystem A subsystem in the revenue process. It is a decision support activity that is concerned with the analysis of historical sales data to provide management with information for marketing and similar purposes.

The **revenue process**, sometimes referred to as the selling or selling and collection process, encompasses activities related to the distribution of goods and services to customers and the receipt of money in exchange for these goods and services. The revenue process is typically broken down into its subsystems—sales, sales order processing, shipping, accounts receivable, and sales analysis. Accounts receivable can be further subdivided into customer invoicing and cash receipts subsystems.

The **sales subsystem** is concerned with the sale of goods or services for *immediate* delivery of goods or provision of services. This subsystem may include establishing credit terms, recording sales tax data, and determining sales commissions. Any organization that provides goods or services on demand, such as a retail store or a health-care facility, requires a sales subsystem.

The **sales order processing subsystem** deals with the processing of orders received from customers for *subsequent* delivery of goods or provision of services. This is an extension of the sales subsystem in that it includes the same activities; however, an added activity here is the management of unfilled sales orders.

The **shipping subsystem** handles the retrieval of goods from the warehouse as well as the preparation of the goods for shipment and the accompanying paperwork. It includes recording the shipment of the goods. Shipping may extend to identifying appropriate modes of shipment and negotiating with common carriers. All organizations that ship significant amounts of goods require a shipping subsystem.

The **accounts receivable subsystem** is concerned with receiving payment for goods and services sold to customers. It involves preparing customer invoices and periodic customer statements, maintaining records of customer balances and total receivables, and collecting cash. Accounts receivable sometimes is divided into two subsystems: customer invoicing and cash receipts. All organizations that extend credit to customers or who bill third parties, such as credit card companies or health-care facilities, need an accounts receivable subsystem.

The **sales analysis subsystem** is a decision support activity dealing with the analysis of historical sales data to provide management with information for marketing and similar purposes. Organizations selling multiple products may benefit from having a sales analysis subsystem.

The data files that are used by the subsystems in the revenue process are shown in the following table:

Revenue Process Subsystems	Data Files Used
Sales order processing	Customer master file Open Sales order file
Shipping	Sales transaction file Open sales order file
Customer invoicing	Sales transaction file Customer master file Open customer invoice file
Cash receipts	Cash receipts transaction file Open customer invoice file Customer master file
Sales analysis	Sales history file

Procurement Process[9]

The **procurement process**, sometimes called the purchasing, expenditure, or acquisition process, encompasses activities related to the acquisition of goods and services and the disbursement of money in exchange for these goods and services. The procurement process (Exhibit 4.26) is typically broken down into its subsystems—purchase order processing, receiving, and accounts payable. In turn, accounts payable can be further subdivided into vendor invoicing and cash disbursements subsystems. Payroll may be considered a part of the procurement process. However, it is common to treat payroll as a separate business process because its complexity makes it somewhat different from the usual purchase of, for example, merchandise inventory for resale. Payroll includes the payroll processing, payroll payable, and cash disbursements subsystems.

The **purchase order processing subsystem** deals with the issuance and tracking of purchase orders to vendors, or suppliers. Purchase orders may be for goods or services. The purchase order processing subsystem may extend to the negotiation and monitoring of agreements with subcontractors. Virtually all organizations, from General Motors to the Salvation Army to local governments, need an ordering subsystem.

The **receiving subsystem** refers to the receipt, inspection, and acceptance of goods delivered to the organization by vendors. It includes recording the receipt of goods and distributing the goods within the organization. Any organization purchasing significant amounts of inventories or supplies requires a receiving subsystem.

The **accounts payable subsystem** is concerned with paying for goods and services purchased from vendors. It involves processing invoices received from vendors, maintaining records of vendor balances and total liabilities, and disbursing cash. Accounts payable sometimes is divided into two subsystems: vendor invoicing and cash disbursements. Virtually all organizations require an accounts payable subsystem.

The **payroll subsystem** provides for the payment of wages, salaries, and sales commissions to employees and the related withholding of taxes and other deductions. It includes the custody and disposition of liabilities arising from amounts withheld from employee earnings. It also includes depositing tax withholdings and reporting withholding data to the appropriate federal, state, and local taxing authorities. Except for those staffed solely by volunteers, all organizations require payroll subsystems.

The data files that are used by the subsystems in the procurement process are as follows:

Purchasing Process Subsystems	Data Files Used
Purchase order processing	Vendor master file Open purchase order file
Receiving	Purchases transaction file Open purchase order file
Vendor invoicing	Purchases transaction file Vendor master file Open vendor invoice file
Cash disbursements	Cash disbursements transaction file Open vendor invoice file Vendor master file
Payroll	Payroll transaction file Cash disbursements transaction file Employee master file Tax table reference file Taxing authority master file

Procurement process (purchasing, expenditure, or acquisition process) A business process that encompasses activities related to the acquisition of goods and services and the disbursement of money in exchange for these goods and services.

Purchase order processing subsystem A subsystem in the procurement process that is concerned with the issuance and tracking of purchase orders to vendors, or suppliers.

Receiving subsystem A subsystem in the procurement process that is concerned with the receipt, inspection, and acceptance of goods and the distribution of the goods within the organization.

Accounts payable subsystem A subsystem in the procurement process that is concerned with paying for goods and services purchased from vendors.

Payroll subsystem The business process that is concerned with the payment of wages, salaries, and sales commissions to employees and the related withholding of taxes and other deductions.ç

Inventory Process[10]

Inventory process One of the business processes in an accounting system. The scope of the inventory process depends on the nature of an organization. In manufacturing and construction organizations, the inventory process encompasses events related to the transformation of raw materials into finished goods, the accumulation of product costs, and the management of inventories.

The scope of the **inventory process** depends on the nature of an organization. In manufacturing and construction organizations, the inventory process encompasses activities related to the transformation of raw materials into finished goods, the accumulation of product costs, and the management of inventories. In the manufacturing environment, this process may be referred to as the production business process. In a merchandising organization, the inventory process encompasses activities related to the accumulation of product costs and the management of merchandise inventories. In a service organization, the inventory process encompasses activities related to the accumulation of the cost of services and the management of parts and supplies inventory.

The inventory process (Exhibit 4.26) is broken down into its subsystems depending on the nature of the organization. For example, in a manufacturing organization the subsystems would be production control, inventory management, and cost accounting. In a service organization the subsystems would be inventory management (for parts and supplies inventory) and cost accounting.

Production control subsystem A subsystem in the inventory process of a manufacturing organization that is concerned with production orders and control of production operations.

The **production control subsystem** is used in a manufacturing organization. It handles the initiation of production orders in the factory and the tracking and control of production operations. In addition, the preparation of bills of materials, labor and machine schedules, and product routing through the factory are all part of this subsystem.

Inventory management subsystem A subsystem in the inventory process that is concerned with accounting for raw materials, finished goods, merchandise, and supplies inventories.

The **inventory management subsystem** refers to accounting for raw materials, finished goods, merchandise, and supplies inventories. Inventory management extends to the regulation of inventory levels to satisfy demand while avoiding the extremes of stockouts or excessive inventory levels. All organizations that have inventory require an inventory management function.

Cost accounting subsystem A subsystem in the inventory process that is concerned with the accumulation of product costs.

The **cost accounting subsystem** is concerned with the accumulation of product costs in manufacturing and merchandising organizations or with the accumulation of the costs of providing services. All manufacturing and most merchandising and service organizations need cost accounting subsystems. The data files that are used by the subsystems in the inventory process are shown in the following table:

Inventory Process Subsystems	Data Files Used
Production control	Open production order file
Inventroy management	Raw materials inventory master file Finished goods inventory master file Merchandise inventory master file Supplies inventory master file Inventory transaction file
Cost accounting	Production cost transaction file Work-in-process inventory master file (also called open job master file)

Financial Process[11]

Financial process One of the business processes in an accounting system. It provides for the following types of transactions. (1) data captured in and transferred from other processes to the financial process, (2) transactions originally recorded in the financial process, and (3) end-of-period adjustments required in the financial process.

The financial process is commonly referred to as the general ledger. Three types of entries are found in the **financial process**:

1. Data captured in and transferred from other processes to the financial process. Because reports (such as the financial statements, tax and governmental regulatory reports, and internal management reports) that are generated from this process require information from all the subsystems, this process receives essential information, usually in summarized form, from the revenue, procurement, and inventory processes.
2. Transactions originally recorded in the financial process. Some events that occur in an organization and need to be recorded in the accounting system do not fall within

the revenue, procurement, or inventory process. Examples of these events are the issuance of stocks and bonds and the payment of stock dividends and bond interest.

3. End-of-period adjustments required in the financial process. The recognition of pre-paid income and expenses, and the recognition of accrued assets, liabilities, and contra accounts are recorded in the financial process.

The data files that are used in the financial process are as follows:

- General journal transaction file
- Chart of accounts reference file
- General ledger master file

Integration of the Subsystems

The accounting subsystems are not stand-alone subsystems. Rather, they are integrated with one another, sharing data files and transferring data from one subsystem to another. These interrelationships exist among subsystems within a business process and among subsystems in different processes. **Exhibit 4.27** shows the relationships among the accounting subsystems and provides a very broad overview of a simple accounting information system. This block diagram shows only ten subsystems; payroll, for example, is omitted. This diagram is for a *merchandising* organization; therefore, as opposed to a service organization, this exhibit includes inventory management; as opposed to a manufacturing organization, this exhibit excludes the production subsystems. As mentioned earlier, accounting systems are not uniform, and they are certainly not as simple as this diagram implies. Each block represents a different subsystem, and you can view each block as consisting of the elements (source documents, transaction files, master files, open files, reference files, and outputs) and the computer programs related to that subsystem. The computer programs would consist of at least one program for entering data and one or more programs to process, store, retrieve, and output data.

LEARNING OBJECTIVE 4
Understand how integration of the subsystems is achieved through the sharing of data files and the movement of data from one subsystem to another.

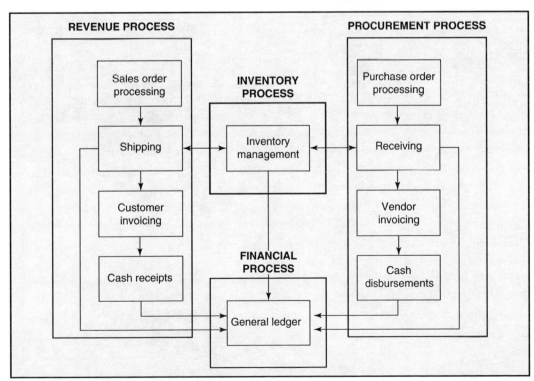

EXHIBIT 4.27 Integration of Accounting Subsystems and Overview of Accounting Information System

The sale of goods and services originates in the sales or sales order processing subsystem (depending on whether the goods or services are to be delivered immediately or at some future date). Sales data subsequently flow into shipping, inventory management, customer invoicing, and cash receipts. The purchase of goods and services originates in the purchase order processing subsystem, and purchase data subsequently flow into receiving, inventory management, vendor invoicing, and cash disbursements. Sales, cash receipts, inventory, purchases, and cash disbursements provide input data into the financial business process. The relationship between the general ledger subsystem and the other accounting subsystems is a strong one. Note that all transaction data eventually flow into the general ledger. This is because the financial statements and many other essential reports are generated by this subsystem.

Exhibit 4.28 presents more detail than does Exhibit 4.27 by including data files to show that data are shared and transferred to achieve integration. The files in Exhibit 4.28 are the minimum ones required by an accounting system. As before, each rectangle represents a different subsystem. But now that the relevant data files are shown, you can view each block as consisting of only the source documents, outputs, and computer programs related to that subsystem.

A few comments of explanation may help you understand Exhibit 4.28. A user can enter data directly into an appropriate subsystem. For example, data about a purchase would be entered in the purchase order processing subsystem; data about the receipt of ordered goods would be entered in the receiving subsystem. You can begin reading this flowchart

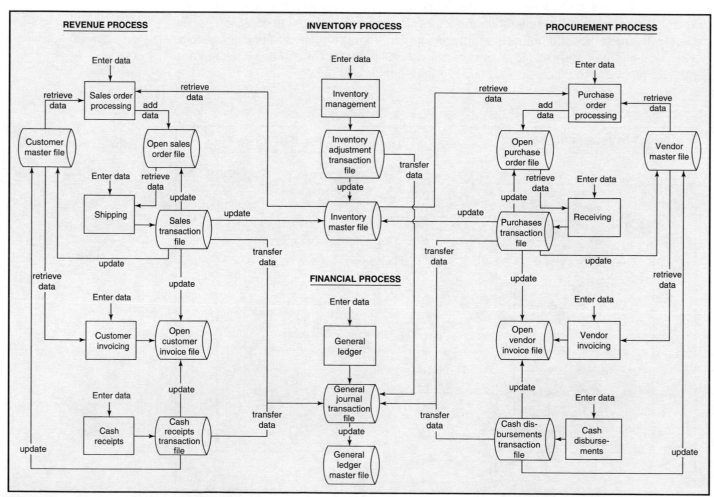

EXHIBIT 4.28 Integration of Accounting Subsystems Through Files and Overview of an Accounting Information System

at the point where data are entered into the sales order processing subsystem or at the point where data are entered into the purchase order processing subsystem. We will start your reading of this flowchart by going through the revenue business process with you.

Sales Order Processing

Data about a sale are entered in the sales order processing subsystem and are stored in the open sales order file pending shipment of the goods. Data, such as customer name, that are relevant to the entering of a sales order are retrieved from the customer master file. Data such as the description of an item of merchandise inventory are retrieved from the inventory master file.

Shipping

Data about the shipment of goods to fill the outstanding sales order are entered in the shipping subsystem and are stored in the sales transaction file. The sales transaction file is used to:

1. update the open sales order file to show that the sales order has been filled,
2. update the customer master file to show the increase in the customer's current balance, and
3. update the inventory master file to show the decrease in the number of units on hand.

Data from sales transaction file are summarized and transferred to the general journal transaction file, which resides in the general ledger subsystem.

Customer Invoicing and Cash Receipts

The sales transaction file is also used to update the open invoice file to insert a new record about the new invoice for the goods that were shipped. Data necessary for preparing invoices, such as customer name and address, are retrieved from the customer master file. When cash is received for the payment of this invoice, data are entered in the cash receipts subsystem and stored in the cash receipts transaction file. The cash receipts transaction file is used to:

1. update the open customer invoice file to show that the invoice has been paid, and
2. update the customer master file to show the decrease in the customer's current balance.

Data from the cash receipts transaction file are summarized and transferred to the general journal transaction file, which resides in the general ledger subsystem. You should now be able to read through the procurement business process in Exhibit 4.28. You can refer to the appendix at the end of the chapter for assistance. Note that sales and purchases of inventory items flow into the inventory master file from the appropriate processes. Therefore, the only time a user needs to enter data directly into the inventory business process is when inventory balances need to be adjusted because of shrinkage or obsolescence.

Summary

Much can be learned about the accounting information system by tracing the flow of transaction and other event data through the system. The accounting system's major activities of input, process, store, and output are necessary to move data through the system. The input and output activities form the two main interfaces with the users in which data are fed into the system for processing and subsequently returned to the users in processed form. Inputting data is vulnerable to errors, so verification is necessary to reduce the risk that contaminated data will be processed further. Data storage supports both the routine operational and the nonroutine decision support aspects of the accounting system. The output must effectively and efficiently communicate information to the users. The success of the accounting system can be measured by its ability to supply users with the right outputs, at the right time, and in the right form. A wide range of media is available to help achieve this objective.

Business processes provide a framework for understanding systems that is sufficiently general to transcend the differences among accounting systems in various types of organizations. Accounting systems are comprised of four business processes: revenue, procurement, inventory, and financial. These business processes comprise the first, or most general, level of subsystems in an accounting information system and can be further divided into subsystems. The nature, purpose, and even the existence of each of the subsystems in the second level depend on the nature of the organization. The subsystems at the second level may include, for example, sales order processing, shipping, customer invoicing, cash receipts, purchase order processing, receiving, vendor invoicing, cash disbursements, and inventory management. The subsystems incorporated into any given accounting system are highly integrated, sharing common data and transferring data from one subsystem to another.

Key Terms

Accounts payable subsystem   119
Accounts receivable subsystem   118
Activity report   115
Business process   116
Calculation (computation)   113
Classification   113
Comparison   113
Cost accounting subsystem   120
File maintenance   114
Financial process   120
Input data   112
Inventory management subsystem   120
Inventory process   120
Merging   114
Output data   115
Payroll subsystem   119

Process data   113
Procurement process   119
Production control subsystem   120
Purchase order processing subsystem   119
Receiving subsystem   119
Revenue process   118
Sales analysis subsystem   118
Sales order processing subsystem   118
Sales subsystem   118
Shipping subsystem   118
Sorting   113
Status report   115
Store data   114
Summarization (aggregation)   114
Updating/Posting   113

Appendix – Chapter 4

Interpretation of Procurement Process in Exhibit 4.28

1. When the data for the purchase order are input into the accounting system, the data are stored in an open purchase order file pending receipt of the goods. The vendor address is retrieved from the vendor master file, and the inventory description is retrieved from the inventory master file.
2. When the merchandise inventory is received, data regarding this event are entered in the purchases transaction file.
3. The purchases transaction file is used to update the open purchase order file to show that the items of inventory have been received. The purchase order now is closed, and the associated record will be purged.
4. Data from the purchases transaction file are used to update the inventory master file.

5. The purchases transaction file is used to update the vendor master file for the amount owed to the vendor.
6. Data from the purchases transaction file flow into the general journal transaction file.
7. A record for a vendor invoice is created in the open vendor invoice file upon receipt of the invoice from the vendor.
8. When payment is made for the invoice, data are entered in the cash disbursements transaction file.
9. The cash disbursements transaction file is used to update the open vendor invoice file. The invoice record is now closed and will be purged.
10. The cash disbursements transaction file is used to update the vendor master file for the amount paid to the vendor.
11. Data from the cash disbursements transaction file flow into the general journal transaction file.

1. An accounting information system
   a. can only exist with computers.
   b. primarily processes data and produces reports.
   c. supports the operations, management, and decision-making functions in an organization.
   d. is a single large system in an organization. [CIA adapted]
2. What are the **major** activities of an accounting information system?
   a. Input, process, output, and manage people
   b. Process, store, output, and manage technology
   c. Input, process, store, and output
   d. Input, process, output, and manage internal control
3. Under which business process would each of the following accounting subsystems fall?
   a. Production control
   b. Shipping
   c. Accounts payable
   d. Accounts receivable
   e. Inventory management
   f. Cost accounting
   g. Receiving
4. Identify the accounting subsystems that might be included in the revenue process in each of the following types of organizations:
   a. A large manufacturing firm that produces automobiles and trucks
   b. A large insurance company offering life, accident, health, and liability policies
   c. A federal government agency
   d. A charitable organization involved in Third World famine relief

5. Describe in words, as opposed to creating a flowchart, the flow of the transaction data originating from a check received from a customer through an accounting information system. Identify the files, documents, and reports encountered on the transaction path.
6. Identify at least ten different kinds of data files. For each file you identify, indicate whether it would be found in the accounting system for the following organizations:
   a. service organization
   b. merchandising organization
   c. manufacturing organization
   d. nonprofit institution
7. In how many different ways might an inventory master file be sequenced? Identify those that might be useful in an accounting information system.
8. The raw materials purchase transaction file shown below records the receipt of raw materials to be used in a manufacturing process. The raw materials issuance transaction file shown below records raw materials issued to production. The raw materials inventory master file shown below shows only one record, and it is for Part No. A12. The quantity on hand is as of June 30, 2018.

Required:

Update the record in the inventory master file for Part No. A12 for the month of July. Determine the quantity on hand and the total dollar value for Part No. A12 by day and at the end the month.

Data for Problem 8			
Raw Materials Purchase Transaction File			
Receiving Report No.	Receiving Report Date	Part No.	Quantity Received
R123	7/1/18	A12	100
R126	7/4/18	B06	150
R131	7/8/18	A24	20
R135	7/13/18	A12	100
R136	7/14/18	C36	50
R142	7/20/18	A12	200
R148	7/26/18	A12	100

Data for Problem 8

Raw Materials Issuance Transaction File

Requisition No.	Requisition Date	Part No.	Department	Job No.	Quantity
RQ100	7/1/18	B06	22	122-G	30
RQ110	7/4/18	C12	24	108-P	25
RQ166	7/5/18	A12	16	124-J	120
RQ221	7/12/18	B06	08	121-G	1,000
RQ245	7/19/18	A12	22	98-B	70
RQ304	7/22/18	C36	18	130-A	5
RQ339	7/26/18	A12	16	124-K	20
RQ479	7/29/18	A12	02	116-A	160

Data for Problem 8

Raw Materials Inventory Master File

Part No.	Description	Reorder Point	Economic Order Quantity	Vendor Number	Quantity on Hand	Unit Cost
A12	Right-hand widget	150	1001	V256	150	2.00

9 and 10. Use the following cash disbursements file for problems 9 and 10. This file records the disbursements made to vendors. The file is stored in order of check number. The company (Clark Service Industries) in problems 9 and 10 wants to match payments to specific invoices. One way to do this and have a clear trail of events, is to separate the cash disbursements file into the following two files.

Data for Problems 9 and 10

Cash Disbursements Transaction File (File 1)

Check No.	Check Date	Vendor No.
146	3/31/2018	301
147	3/31/2018	302
148	3/31/2018	310
149	3/31/2018	312
150	3/31/2018	305

Data for Problems 9 and 10

Cash Disbursements Transaction File (File 2)

Check No.	Voucher No.	Amount Paid
146	962	105.00
146	966	325.00
146	969	100.00
147	964	50.00
147	967	140.00
148	963	225.00
149	965	85.00
150	961	275.00

9. The cash disbursements transaction file is used to update the open vendor invoice file and the vendor master file in an accounting system that uses batch posting. In this problem, you are required to update the open vendor invoice file with the cash disbursements file.

The following open vendor invoice file 1 stores the invoices that Clark Service Industries (CSI) owes its vendors. Note that CSI assigns a sequential voucher number to each vendor's invoice to uniquely identify each record in the file. The company cannot use the vendors' invoice numbers as identifiers because those numbers would not be in sequential order and may not be unique. Also, please be aware that the company wants to be able to match its payments to specific invoices. Occasionally, one check may be in payment of more than one invoice, and one invoice may be paid by more than one check. One way to maintain a clear trail of events is to maintain a second file 2 for payments made on invoices.

Data for Problem 9				
Open Vendor Invoice File (File 1)				
Voucher No.	**Vendor No.**	**Invoice Date**	**Invoice Amount**	**Vendor Invoice No.**
961	305	3/2/2018	275.00	135
962	301	3/2/2018	105.00	22
963	310	3/4/2018	260.00	A8
964	302	3/7/2018	50.00	P267
965	312	3/9/2018	85.00	98
966	301	3/11/2018	325.00	4
967	302	3/14/2018	140.00	67S
968	304	3/14/2018	400.00	Y48
969	301	3/14/2018	130.00	5555
970	311	3/25/2018	45.00	GG33
971	303	3/28/2018	92.00	RYX

Data for Problem 9			
Open Vendor Invoice File (File 2)			
Voucher No.	**Date Invoice Paid**	**Amount Paid**	**Check No.**
(Rows are added as needed.)			

Required:

Update the open invoice file by the payments made by CSI and purge the invoices that have been paid in full. This requirement is presented in more detail in parts a through d. CSI uses a batch posting process.

a. In an accounting system that uses a batch posting process, the cash disbursements transaction file is sorted in voucher number order before being posted to the open invoice file. Sorting the records in the same order as the records in the open invoice file speeds up the posting process. Illustrate this activity by creating a sorted cash disbursements transaction file. Because the voucher number is stored in file 2, only this part of the file needs to be sorted. However, in your solution, recreate file 1 as it is so you will have the entire cash disbursements transaction file together and can use it for the next step in the posting process.

b. The open invoice file is updated by posting the sorted cash disbursements file to the open invoice file. Illustrate this activity by using the data in the cash disbursements transaction file to create new records in file 2 of the open invoice file. File 1 does not need to be changed, but recreate it as it is in this question so you will have the entire open invoice file for the next step.

c. The records in the open invoice file where the invoice amount in file 1 equals the amount paid in file 2 can be purged. Illustrate this activity by modifying the open invoice file (1 and 2) to eliminate the invoices that have been paid in full.

d. Does the total amount still owed equal the difference between the total dollar amount of invoices before posting, minus the total cash disbursements? Show your reconciliation of these amounts.

10. The cash disbursements transaction file (also used in question 9) is used to update the open vendor invoice file and the vendor master file in an accounting system that uses batch posting. In this problem, you are required to update the vendor master file by the payments made by Clark Service Industries (CSI). This requirement is presented in more detail in parts a through d. CSI uses a batch posting process.

The following vendor master file shows the current balances owed to each vendor. This file is stored in order of vendor number. The total of the invoice amounts in the open invoice file in problem 9 equals the total of the current balances owed to vendors.

Data for Problem 10		
Vendor Master File		
Vendor No.	Name	Current Balance
300	Elm Company	0
301	Apple, Inc.	560.00
302	Yew & Sons	190.00
303	Pine Associates	92.00
304	Oak Company	400.00
305	Cedar, Inc.	275.00
306	Peach Bros.	0
307	Maple Enterprises	0
308	Fir, Inc.	0
309	Cyprus Company	0
310	Fig Bros.	260.00
311	Pear Associates	45.00
312	Plum Company	85.00

a. Sort the cash disbursements transaction file by vendor number. Sorting the records in the same order as the records in the vendor master file speeds up the posting process. Illustrate this activity by creating a sorted cash disbursements transaction file. Because the vendor number is stored in file 1, only this part of the file needs to be sorted. However, in your solution, recreate file 2 as it is so you will have the entire cash disbursements transaction file together and can use it for the next step in the posting process.

b. The vendor master file is updated by posting the sorted cash disbursements file to the vendor master file. Illustrate this activity by using the data in the cash disbursements transaction file to change records in the vendor master file.

c. Under what circumstances would you purge records from the vendor master file?

d. Does the total amount still owed equal the difference between the total dollar amount of the current balances before posting, minus the total cash disbursements? Show your reconciliation of these amounts.

11. An inventory application calls for the weekly updating, or posting, of the merchandise inventory master file from the purchases transaction file and the sale transaction file. This updating process is performed every Friday just before the close of business. Sales of Item No. #12345 are stable at a rate of 5 units a day, 5 days a week. Purchases are made every 3 weeks in quantities of 75 units, and the purchased goods are received first thing Monday morning. On Friday

evening, January 28, the inventory level of Item No. 12345 in the warehouse was 10 units, and the balance for the item in the inventory master file was verified as being correct. The receipt of purchased goods was scheduled for the following Monday.

Required:

Perform a simulation for the month of February to determine the maximum discrepancy between the actual quantity of Item No. 12345 on hand and the balance shown in the inventory master file. (Set up a table with a line for each day in the month and calculate the quantity on hand corresponding to the stated pattern of purchases and sales. Also calculate the net transaction activity used to update the inventory master file on each updating date and the resulting balance in the inventory master file.)

Notes

1. Transactions and other events initiated without this authority are considered inappropriate acts, or irregularities. Inappropriate acts are prevented and detected through internal controls, which are discussed in later chapters.
2. Coding is discussed in greater detail later in Chapters 5 and 8.
3. You will recall from Chapter 3 that this file stores the chart of accounts.
4. You will recall from Chapter 3 that instead of maintaining a separate chart of accounts reference file and general ledger master file, we take the position in this textbook that the files are combined into the general ledger master file.
5. Data can be transferred to the general ledger subsystem by means other than writing transaction summaries to the general journal transaction file. However, this is a convenient method, and it provides better audit evidence than does other methods.
6. Files in a database management system are technically called tables, or tuples. In this textbook, database tables are frequently referred to as files when the logical view of stored data is relevant.
7. Note that storing these sales data requires thirty-six fields in the customer master file.
8. The revenue process is discussed in detail in Chapter 9.
9. The procurement process is discussed in detail in Chapter 10.
10. The inventory process is discussed in detail in Chapter 11.
11. The financial process is discussed in detail in Chapter 8.

Reporting Process, Coding Methods, and Audit Trails

Source: create jobs 51/Shutterstock.

Learning Objectives

After studying this chapter, you should be able to:

- List, describe, and illustrate principles that form a foundation for effective reporting.
- Understand XBRL reporting and the basics of preparing an instance document.
- Describe the objectives and methods of common coding systems.
- Design coding systems for various accounting entities and events.
- Describe the concept and dimensions of an audit trail.
- Design a coding system to support audit trails.

Introductory Scenario

Source: Zern Liew/Shutterstock.

Albert Davis founded Yellow Box Movies several years ago. The stand-alone vending machines for DVD and Blu-ray movies are located in convenience stores throughout the metropolitan San Francisco area. Each convenience store has a full-time manager who hires students and others to work on a part-time basis. Every week Albert forwards advance notices of forthcoming movies (usually first-run movies currently showing at the dollar cinemas and on cable TV as well as updated classics) to each convenience store manager. Customers who make requests for movies not available in the Yellow Box listing of movies can request that they be ordered by filling out a special order form and submitting it to the convenience store manager. Store managers submit these requests to Albert, who consolidates them and places orders if additional copies are needed. As managers perceive the desirability of adding to the existing inventory of particularly popular films, these are added to the weekly purchase requests and Albert places a consolidated purchase order. Every week, the convenience store manager generates a report of the rentals by title and sends it to Albert. Albert pays monthly commission checks to each manager based on the number of movie rentals at his/her store.

Currently, Albert only receives a monthly income statement from his CPA around the 10th of each month that shows total sales broken down by type and a detailed balance sheet. Although these reports are useful to gauge the progress of the Yellow Box Movies concept and Albert has no criticism of the accounting reports, he has a feeling that he is unable to monitor individual store sales and inventory as well as he could. Also, store managers are having difficulty monitoring their inventory, and Albert is considering setting up a way to transfer inventory between stores when one store has few rentals of a particular movie, while another store has many requests for that movie. For example, having seven copies of "The Fast and the Furious: Tokyo Drift" at a convenience store next to a retirement community might not be necessary. However, one copy of "The Fast and the Furious: Tokyo Drift" at a convenience store next to local high school might not meet the demand for the movie in that location.[1]

Introductory Scenario Thought Questions:

1. What reports would be useful for the convenience store managers to monitor sales and for Albert to monitor his rentals and manage his inventory? How often should the reports be generated, and in what format should the reports be (e.g., by cost center, function, etc.)? In addition, what is the purpose of each report? You might want to set up a chart that has the following headings:

Report Name   Report Frequency   Report Format   Report Purpose

2. What types of exception reports would allow Albert to manage the inventory at the various locations?
3. What type of coding system would you recommend for the inventory of movies (e.g., block, group)?

Reporting Principles

LEARNING OBJECTIVE 1
List, describe, and illustrate principles that form a foundation for effective reporting.

Certain basic principles underlie all information reporting, and these apply particularly to the reporting of accounting data. This section discusses these principles and illustrates their use with examples from a variety of accounting processes, such as revenue, procurement, and financial reporting.

To fully understand the function of reporting in accounting systems, you must first consider the information needed by managers to plan and control operations and where they get that information. Recent research suggests that conventional accounting reports—such as balance sheets, income statements, and departmental cost reports—play a significant but limited role in the total information picture required by managers. Although there are many other sources for this position, the most comprehensive is that set forth in an empirical study published as *The Information Mosaic* by accounting professors McKinnon and Bruns of Harvard and Northeastern University, respectively. Their broad view of management information is illustrated by the following example given about a sales executive:

> His first activity is interacting with his sales representatives and their customers, frequently going along on a customer visit. Before going, he gets a verbal briefing from the rep about who the customer is, who the decision makers are, what their account history is, and any special problems that exist. Some of this is quantifiable, but much is social information....[His] second activity is interacting with marketing in bidding on tenders [formal supply bids] to customers. He needs a competitive history, which he gets from his files, and he talks to his sales reps to discuss their sales tactics. With this information in hand, he talks with his counterparts in marketing to give them the sales department viewpoint on pricing strategy for the particular potential order.... [His] third activity is dealing with the plants about customer orders.[2]

Data used by this sales executive range from monthly shipping reports to purchase orders received, but also include considerable "social" data. While some of the data are numerical, they vary greatly in nature, in source, and in the frequency with which they are obtained.

Sam Walton, the founder of Walmart, related how he selected new store sites by counting automobiles in the parking lots of K-Mart stores and by counting traffic at street intersections. Thus, direct observation is a significant means of acquiring data for decision making.

In the following sections, general principles that underlie reporting will be explained. These principles are:

- Necessity for concise reports
- Emphasis on both physical and monetary measures
- Frequency of reporting
- Responsibility reporting
- Reporting by function
- Comparative reporting
- Exception reporting

Necessity for Concise Reports

Concise reports contain only the data that are essential to the performance of the recipient's duties. In most business processes there are only a few factors that largely determine its success or failure. Not surprisingly, managers concentrate on those factors and pay little or only periodic attention to items of lesser importance. These critical success factors vary greatly, depending on the nature of a business and the responsibilities of the manager. For departmental managers, only a couple of items of information may be of overriding importance. Concise reports are important for two reasons. First, most operations have relatively few critical success factors, and a manager's attention should be focused on these factors. Second, peoples' ability to simultaneously process multiple data elements is limited, and report contents should not exceed these limitations. Thus, reports to managers should contain only data that are vital to the performance of their responsibilities.

In some manufacturing processes the number of direct labor hours used and the number of units produced may be the only information that a production manager needs on a day-to-day basis. In these cases materials cost, labor rates, and overhead costs are either controlled by direct observation or are uncontrollable by the production manager. **Exhibit 5.1** illustrates reporting under such conditions. Note that the production manager receiving this report has weekly data only for labor hours and costs. By focusing only on critical success factors, effective management reports tend to be relatively concise.

Concise reports Reports that contain only the data that are essential to the performance of the recipient's duties.

FURNITURE FACTORY PERFORMANCE REPORT Framing Department			
Date: Week Ending Friday, October 19, 2018			
	Units Produced	Std. Labor Hrs. Allowed	Std. Labor Cost Allowed
Chairs	213	426	$ 5,112
Sofas	78	234	2,808
Total		660	7,920
Actual Labor Hours Used		662	
Actual Labor Hours @ Standard Rates			7,944
TOTAL EFFICIENCY VARIANCE–Unfavorable		2	$ 24

EXHIBIT 5.1 Concise Report for a Furniture Factory Production Manager

Emphasis on Both Physical and Monetary Measures

A large portion of the information used by managers is nonfinancial. McKinnon and Bruns found that production managers have a compelling preference for the use of physical measures of performance rather than monetary (financial) measures in reports covering short reporting periods. A report reflecting the number of units processed last week in each department may be the most valuable report to a factory superintendent. When the accounting information system does not provide such data, managers often make informal attempts to record it using their own time and resources. For example, if the factory manager referred to in Exhibit 5.1 does not receive the report depicted, she may personally accumulate daily labor hours and production units. Other frequently desired physical measures are units spoiled, downtime hours, and number of new customers. Managers can both observe and influence these tangible measures, while related monetary measures will often be influenced by other factors over which the same managers have little or no control. Consequently, all operating managers find physical data to be an essential element of reporting.

While purchasing managers must be cognizant of costs, maintenance of an adequate quantity of both expensive and inexpensive parts may be essential to avoid production interruptions that would be catastrophic. It should be no surprise that physical measures are primary management data in the purchasing function.

Marketing and sales managers seem to prefer a mixture of both physical and monetary data. Much of the information necessary for marketing and sales management is obtained from external sources. One product manager in the McKinnon and Bruns study required customer buying patterns, specifications, credit rating, and the customer's status in the industry.[3] **Exhibit 5.2** illustrates the data that might be needed by the marketing manager of a cable TV company. Note that this report is purely physical data with no monetary values. Assume that Columbus Cable TV mounted a campaign in September and October to increase the total number of subscribers and to induce present subscribers to upgrade their service. Analyze the report and draw any possible conclusions as to the success of the fall drive.

Frequency of Reporting

Often it is assumed that the more frequently data are reported, the better. Such a practice does ensure that data are available earlier than might otherwise be the case. However,

Service Level	Beginning of Month (1)	New (2)	Lost (3)	Service Level Changes (4)	End of Month (5)*
Basic	45,932	839	441	−147 (a)	46,183
Super	12,971	110	579	−26 (b)	12,476
Premium	13,847	605	285	173 (c)	14,340
Total	72,750	1,554	1,305	0	72,999

Service Level Change		Basic	Super	Premium	
(From) To		−312	213	99	
(From) To		75	−294	219	
(From) To		90	55	−145	
		−147 (a)	−26 (b)	173 (c)	

*(1) + (2)−(3) + (4)

EXHIBIT 5.2 Physical Data Report

if you critically examine various environments and reporting practices, this assumption does not correspond with reality even when early reporting is feasible. Among the factors influencing the frequency of reporting are the significance of the data, the nature of the activity being reported on, and the type of data reported (physical vs. monetary).

Significance of the Data

Only when data are important (1) to the detection of an out-of-control situation or (2) to make a specific decision should reporting be issued on a daily or even a weekly basis. As an example, Ed Jones' insurance agency does $1 million annually in premium volume. His office equipment repair expense varies from zero to $2,000 annually. Ed wants a report on repair expense only when it exceeds $500 on any single transaction or $2,000 for the year. He believes more frequent expense reports would be a waste of his time.

Nature of the Activity

The nature of the activity affects the behavior of related data. Some data may be expected to conform closely to predicted values while other data vary considerably in the normal course of events. Processors of natural resources (e.g., pulp timber) experience significant and, to some extent, uncontrollable variation in the quality of raw materials from batch to batch, resulting in processing costs that vary widely. Conversely, manufacturers using processed raw materials (e.g., plastic pellets) that are very homogeneous can exert tighter controls over manufacturing variances.

Examples of large variations in data over short periods that are more predictable over longer periods are:

- An oil drilling rig manufacturer experiences a typical time lapse of 6 months between initial customer contact and the receipt of a firm purchase order. A good salesperson is expected to sell about ten rigs a year. The sales vice president might find a quarterly report of sales by salesperson to be more useful than either monthly or weekly reports. (Nonquantitative information about the status of prospective sales probably should be reported monthly.) In contrast, the reporting cycle for a department store shoe salesperson would likely be weekly.

■ The expected yield (percentage of good product) from the manufacture of computer central processing unit (CPU) chips is 90 percent. Because daily volume of output is typically 100 CPU chips on each production station, 90 good CPUs are expected per day per station. If the yield is between 85 and 95 units on a given day, the process is considered to be "in control." If fewer than 5 units are bad, the quality of inspection is suspect. Attempts were made by a company to monitor the yield rate hourly. But upon investigation, it was found that a great deal of time was wasted investigating spoilage that was normal and within acceptable limits.

As demonstrated by these examples, the length of the reporting period should vary with the degree of normal fluctuation in costs associated with given phenomena. A reporting period should be sufficiently long that it will include representative data, and sufficiently short that management can take timely action.

Type of Data Reported

Earlier in this chapter, we said that physical measures of performance are often preferred to monetary measures. However, the reporting measure used is strongly associated with the optimal length of the reporting period. Production managers consider physical measures essential in reports that cover a short period of time, but consider financial measures useful in reporting that covers a longer period of time. For example, a manufacturing department supervisor may receive daily reports on physical production volume, weekly reports on spoilage rates, and monthly cost reports showing unit production cost and spoilage cost. After some exposure to the reporting system, the supervisor will have formed a mental association between physical performance measures and monetary performance measures. Based on her interpretation of interim physical reports, she will then have a good idea of what to expect in the monthly financial reports. The financial reports will, by placing monetary value on the physical data, give greater depth to her understanding. Both types of reports are useful so long as the monthly financial reports confirm her impressions of operations indicated by the more frequent physical reports. Inconsistencies may occur because either (1) one or more reports contain errors or (2) previously understood relationships between physical and monetary data have changed. In the latter case, an investigation should reveal the relationship changes and provide operating management with a mental structure for interpreting the significance of physical and monetary data reported.

These concepts are illustrated by **Exhibit 5.3** that shows a daily report for the framing department supervisor who receives the weekly report shown in Exhibit 5.1. Notice the use of physical data in the daily reports and then turn back to Exhibit 5.1 and compare the relationships between the daily and weekly reports. Note that the sums of the daily physical data are equal to the amounts shown on the weekly report.

While much physical data should be reported daily, some financial data also have daily significance. Daily sales of a traveling snack stand at the Oregon State Fair can be meaningful information. Given the vagaries of weather and fair attendance, weekly sales might be even more useful. But profit calculations must include setup, dismantling, transportation, and other costs that are not incurred on a daily or even weekly basis. Consequently, profits for each fair and for the entire season are the best overall measures of success. Most companies find that the convention of preparing financial statements (balance sheet, income statement, and cash flow statement) on a monthly basis is sufficient and that financial statements prepared more frequently cover such short periods as to be largely devoid of meaningful information. Banking is the only industry noted for daily financial statement preparation because regulatory authorities impose this requirement.

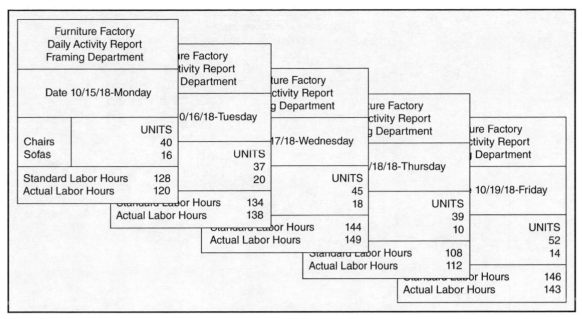

EXHIBIT 5.3 Daily Report Showing Use of Physical Units

Responsibility Reporting

Responsibility reporting is the process of reporting data to a manager that measure activities over which the manager has some authority and for which the manager is held responsible. A small business having only five employees might be effectively managed and controlled by the owner through visual observation. As the business and the number of employees grow, the ability of a single person to supervise all employees and operations begins to be spread too thinly. When organizations reach a size of several hundred employees and operations must be divided into, for example, functional areas, such as purchasing, sales, and accounting, then considerable subdivision in supervisory responsibility must occur. The reporting capability of the accounting system must also grow to accommodate the requisite functional and hierarchical supervisory positions.

Responsibility reporting
The process of reporting to a manager data that measure activities over which the manager has some authority and for which activities the manager is held responsible.

Exhibit 5.4 depicts such an organizational structure. At the top level are the corporate officers. Reports for these officers must reflect the overall operations of the company and the subsidiaries of the company, mining and retailing. Financial statements would include a (1) consolidated balance sheet, (2) consolidated income statement, and (3) consolidated cash flow statement. In addition, these top officers would likely want to review the same three statements for each subsidiary company. Management of each subsidiary company should receive these same statements for its respective company plus statements for each major location. Location managers should receive statements related to their assigned location with detailed breakdowns of the various expense and revenue categories.

Because the consolidated entity has assets and liabilities, as well as revenues and expenses, it is considered to be an investment center, and consequently is judged on return on investment (ROI). Because the two corporate subsidiaries also have their own assets and liabilities, they are also investment centers. Each department store in the retail subsidiary is responsible for sales and expenses but not for assets and liabilities so is a profit center as are departments within stores. The mining subsidiary, in contrast, handles the sales function at the division level, and no sales are attributed to the mines. Consequently, each of the mines is a cost center, and reports given to each mine's general manager reflect only cost and production figures.

Because the size of a business unit that can be supervised by direct observation is limited, growth beyond that size requires the delegation of authority to lower levels of management. With the delegation of authority comes the necessity to hold these lower levels accountable for results achieved. Providing financial statements and other reports supporting such accountability is an essential element of the accounting information system.

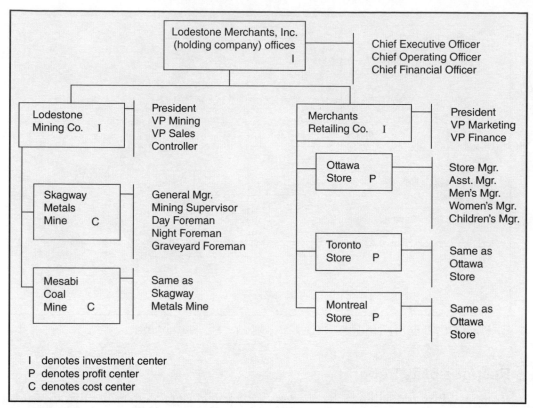

EXHIBIT 5.4 Hypothetical Organizational Structure

Exhibit 5.4 depicts four levels of operations. Two examples of the four levels are:

Mining Operations	Retail Operations
Lodestone Merchants	Lodestone Merchants
Lodestone Mining	Merchants Retailing
Skagway Metals	Ottawa Store
Night Foreman	Children's Manager

Reporting that might be appropriate for this organization is described in **Exhibit 5.5**. Each of the two subsidiaries composing Lodestone Merchants (the consolidated holding company) has an income statement. Each mine composing Lodestone Mining has only cost reports because the sales function is located at the company level. Each mine has reports for shift foremen. These shift reports do not show equipment costs because the shift foremen do not make decisions on equipment acquisition. A balance sheet is made for the mining company, but not for the mines because they are cost centers. In contrast to the mining company, the retailing company prepares income statements for each store because store managers are responsible for both sales and costs. Department managers within stores are provided income statements showing sales for their departments and those costs over which the department managers have significant influence. A conventional balance sheet (not shown) will be made for Merchants Retailing; however, balance sheets (not shown) for stores will reflect only assets at those stores and only liabilities clearly attributable to the specific store.

Reporting by Function

Another way of viewing the reporting mosaic is by the functional duties of managers—functional reporting. While the relative preference for physical or monetary data will vary

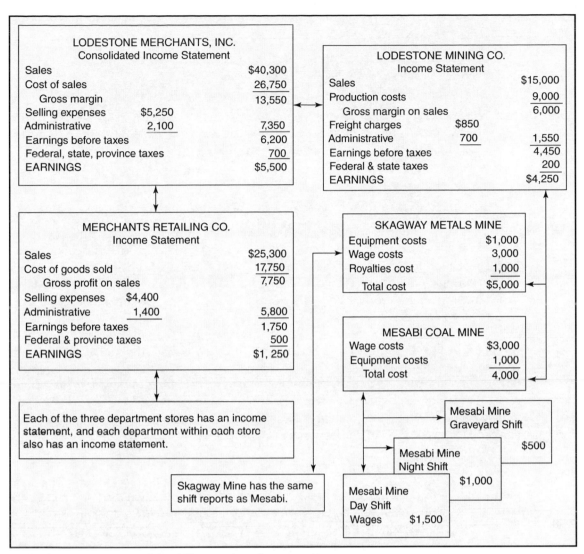

EXHIBIT 5.5 Hierarchical Reporting Structure

somewhat randomly for general managers, a clear pattern of preferences to which we have previously alluded can be observed when dealing with functional managers.

Much accounting data is of a physical nature—product units, production cycles (number of heats of a blast furnace or of vats of pulpwood cooked), or hours worked. Production personnel find this information to be invaluable in judging the efficiency of their efforts. On the other hand, marketing and sales personnel make more limited use of physical data, finding that dollar-denominated data (such as sales dollars by customer, by salesperson, or by geographic area) are perhaps of equal value. Financial managers, in contrast, use almost exclusively financial data for evaluating operations. A large part of the job for many financial managers is discovering operating problems as reflected in financial reports and pointing these out to operating management. McKinnon and Bruns found that general managers made only modest use of financial statements; they relied on their chief financial officer to interpret for them the significance of financial reports.[4]

In Exhibit 5.5 you saw reporting at all levels for the mining operation, but only at the top level for the department store operation (Merchants Retailing Co.). Holding company officers (Lodestone Merchants) receive the consolidated earnings statement for the holding company that is prepared by the chief financial officer (CFO) using holding company data and financial statements received from the two subsidiary companies. The holding company officers most likely will rely on the CFO for interpretation of the statements.

The Lodestone Mining controller prepares the following statements for the use of personnel specified below:

- Lodestone Mining income statement for the president, forwarding a copy to the CFO of Lodestone Merchants. (Refer to Exhibit 5.4.)
- Cost statements for general managers of each of the two mines.
- Wage/cost reports for each shift foreman. Note that reports (Exhibit 5.5) used by shift foremen contain only wage costs because they do not control the equipment cost and, therefore, cannot be held responsible for it.
- Report of sales by product, by geographic area, and by salesperson for the vice-president of sales.
- Statement of their sales by customer for each salesperson.

Reporting in the retailing company is a real contrast to that in the mining operation because every level of the organization has significant influence over the magnitude of both sales and most costs. Income statements can be prepared down to the store department levels such as cosmetics, shoes, and children's clothing. Consequently, the women's department manager receives an income statement, while the general manager of a mine receives a cost report.

Exhibit 5.6 shows the possible mixes of physical and monetary data and a general representation of the importance attached to these mixes by various functional managers. The relationships depicted should not be interpreted in a rigid manner because they represent only a general pattern. Certainly some financial managers use physical data and desire it on a relatively frequent schedule.

The range of personal preferences and the nature of the industry often have a significant impact on the type of data reported.

Comparative Reporting

Comparative reporting The arranging together of actual data for a current period with either budget data for the current period or actual data for the prior period, thereby facilitating comparison of the data.

Comparative reporting is the arrangement together of actual data for a current period with either budget data for the current period or actual data for a prior period, thereby facilitating comparison of the data (e.g., income statements). Such arrangements may include data at fixed points in time as well (balance sheets).

No single stroke of an artist's paintbrush has any meaning—it could be the beginning of a landscape or a futuristic automobile. In a like manner, no single piece of data has

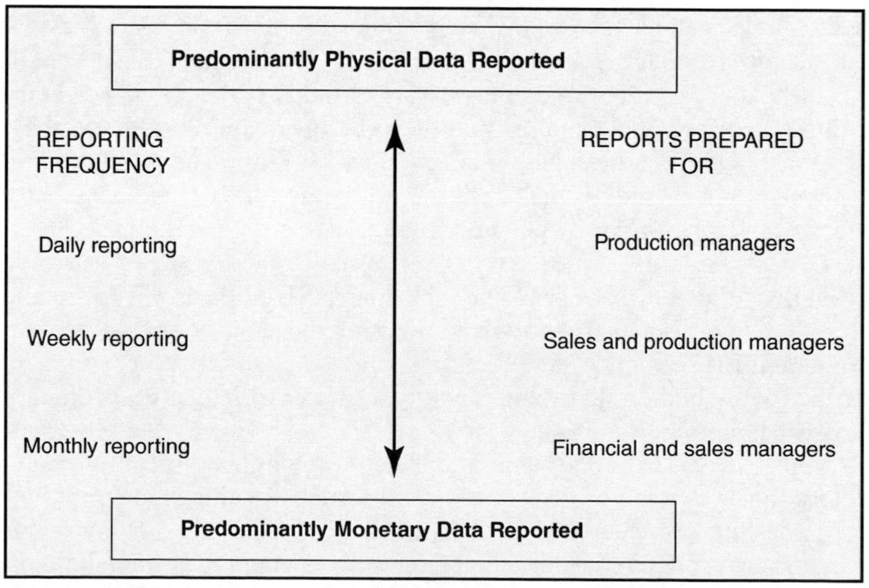

EXHIBIT 5.6 Relationships among Type of Data Reported, Reporting Frequency, and Functional Responsibilities

meaning. A profit of $2 million might be incredible for a small restaurant, but a disaster for General Motors Corporation. Many pieces of financial data must be presented in a meaningful format in financial statements for any one item to assume meaning. Comparative data—both historical and budget— add to the picture from which you may draw conclusions regarding the financial health and prospects of an organization. Furthermore, even financial data are not sufficient. To arrive at any firm conclusions, you must have some knowledge of the history of the organization and its environment—including customers, suppliers, competitors, taxing bodies, and regulators.

Accordingly, an accounting information system must provide reports that place current data in a context that gives them meaning. To observe from a single period's balance sheet that inventory is $300,000 at the fiscal year-end permits you to make only tentative conclusions as to the desirability of that level of stock. But if the balance sheet compares the current year's actual amounts with the prior year's amounts and with the current year's budgeted amounts, your ability to judge the appropriateness of the inventory level is enhanced considerably. Showing variances between current year and prior year's amounts as well as current year and budgeted amounts further increases the informational content of a report. (See **Exhibit 5.7**.)

Exhibit 5.7 lists sales to customers, comparing the current year's actual sales to the prior year's and the budgeted amounts. Such analysis permits sales executives to select

NORTHWEST SALES REPS, INC. SALES BY CUSTOMER FOURTH QUARTER 2018					
Customer	This Year	Last Year	Variance	Budget	Variance
Able Company	$32,000	$26,000	$6,000 I	$30,000	$2,000+
Baker, Inc.	43,000	43,300	300−	43,200	200−
Calloway Bros.	83,000	95,000	12,000−	90,000	7,000−
Dunn Partnership	17,000	16,500	500+	17,800	800−
•					
•					
•					
Page 1 of 12					
NORTHWEST SALES REPS, INC. SALES BY CUSTOMER FOURTH QUARTER 2018					
Customer	This Year	Last Year	Variance	Budget	Variance
•					
•					
•					
Tsay Industries	27,000	26,000	1,000+	21,000	6,000+
Young Insurance	45,000	44,000	1,000+	45,100	100−
Zaidi Imports	37,000	82,000	45,000−	90,000	53,000−
Page 12 of 12					

EXHIBIT 5.7 Comparative Reporting Illustrated

customers to whom sales increased or exceeded budget and to analyze why such good results were obtained. Likewise, reasons for sales declines or sub-budget performance can be investigated and remedial actions taken.

Exception Reporting

Exception reporting The reporting of data reflecting a significant deviance from expected, budgeted, or normal that should be reported to managers.

The meaning of **exception reporting** is that only data reflecting a significant deviation from expected, budgeted, or normal should be reported to managers. Managers should be given reports covering only those aspects of operations that are likely to require their attention. Managers should not waste time scanning large sets of data when only a few data sets suggest problems that may require remedial action. The periodic aging of accounts receivable report is an excellent example. If the report includes all accounts, then the user will have to spend a great deal of time finding the problem accounts. An effective report to be used by a credit manager for contacting delinquent customers would include only those customer accounts with one or more overdue amounts having a sum that is material.

Selection of Records

Most accounting information systems permit the user to invoke selection criteria that determine which records to include in reports. But these criteria are usually limited to account classifications embedded in the account identifier or to the amount of an account balance. Although this does permit some selection of records, it is usually not sufficient for effective exception reporting. Effective exception reporting requires the ability to select records based on the difference between an account's current balance and its prior year's balance, or between an account's actual balance and a budgeted amount.

Some examples are:

■ **Sales to customers—actual this quarter compared with budget.** While we might want a report of all customers having sales exceeding $30,000, a more useful report may be one comparing actual sales with budgeted sales and including *only* those customers in the report whose sales fell short of budget by perhaps 10 percent. Consequently, the ability to select customers based on the difference between actual and budgeted sales and based on percentage changes is necessary.

■ **Supplies expense by location—this year compared with last year.** Rather than getting a report of all 200 locations, a manager should receive a report showing only those locations exceeding last year by more than some specified percentage or monetary amount.

■ **Number of workdays lost due to work-related injuries.** This report would reflect on crew leader performance. Timber cutting and hauling, for example, is an inherently dangerous occupation and some injuries are inevitable. A report comparing the current period's actual workdays lost with the budgeted days lost and with the prior period's actual workdays lost is useful. In an organization with a large number of crews, the safety manager must focus on problem crew leaders. Therefore, this manager should be provided a report including only the problem crew leaders and excluding leaders whose crews have low accident rates.

The "sales by customer" report you saw in Exhibit 5.7 has twelve pages. The sales vice-president of Northwest Sales must look through the entire list although many of the changes in sales to customers are inconsequential. A threshold of "significance" should be set, and only the customer accounts exceeding the threshold should be included in the report. **Exhibit 5.8** is a report that includes customer sales having actual or budget differences that exceed $1,000. This report directs management's attention to unusual customer results.

Sequencing of Records

In spite of an exception reporting being more concise, it still may cover several pages. Frequently, a busy manager will only complete an investigation of some items on the first page. The back-page problems will not receive adequate attention unless they emerge in

NORTHWEST SALES REPS, INC.					
SALES BY CUSTOMER					
FOURTH QUARTER 2018					
Customer	This Year	Last Year	Variance	Budget	Variance
Able Company	$32,000	$26,000	$6,000+	$30,000	$2,000+
Calloway Bros.	83,000	95,000	12,000−	90,000	7,000−
Everman Coaches	62,000	59,000	3,000+	68,000	6,000−
Hall Enterprises	97,000	84,000	13,000+	100,000	3,000−
Tsay Industries	27,000	26,000	1,000+	21,000	6,000+
Zaidi Imports	37,000	82,000	45,000−	90,000	53,000−
Page 1 of 1					

EXHIBIT 5.8 Exception Reporting—Selection of Records

future reporting periods. Even in those periods, the same problems may appear on the back pages of the report. Thus, the most severe problems may continually appear on the report's back pages and never be resolved. But if the records are arranged in order by severity of the problem, with the most severe at the beginning of the report, the probability that the most serious problems will be addressed is significantly enhanced. **Record sequencing** is the process of placing data in a specified order.

Although the record sequencing may be based on the balance of an account, you should be able to sequence records based on the difference between current actual account balances and prior period actual account balances, and between current actual account balance and budget for those accounts. Only when an accounting information system has the ability to do the following can we assert that the system is effective for exception reporting:

■ Select records for inclusion in a report based on differences between current year actual and prior period actual, and between actual and budget

■ Sequence the selected records based on the magnitude of the differences

Exhibit 5.9 shows the effect of both selecting and sequencing records in descending order based on these criteria. The accounts are sequenced first by the larger (absolute)

Record sequencing The process of placing data in a specified order.

NORTHWEST SALES REPS, INC.					
SALES BY CUSTOMER					
FOURTH QUARTER 2018					
Customer	This Year	Last Year	Variance	Budget	Variance
Zaidi Imports	$37,000	$82,000	$45,000−	$90,000	$53,000−
Hall Enterprises	97,000	84,000	13,000+	100,000	3,000−
Calloway Bros.	83,000	95,000	12,000+	90,000	7,000−
Everman Coaches	62,000	59,000	3,000+	68,000	6,000−
Able Company	32,000	26,000	6,000+	30,000	2,000+
Tsay Industries	27,000	26,000	1,000+	21,000	6,000+
Page 1 of 1					

EXHIBIT 5.9 Exception Reporting—Sequencing of Selected Records

differences, either actual or budget, and second by the size of the other differences. The report is an improvement over Exhibit 5.8 because selected accounts appear in the order of deviation from either prior period actual or budget. Thus, Zaidi Imports is listed first because the budget variance of $53,000 is largest. Hall Enterprises with an actual variance of $13,000 is next followed by Calloway Bros. with an actual variance of $12,000. The last three customers have the same largest variance, $6,000, so they are listed in order by the second largest variance. Thus, Everman Coaches based on an actual variance of $3,000 is next followed by Able Company with a budget variance of $2,000 and Tsay Industries with an actual variance of $1,000. The particular method of sequencing will vary depending on management preferences, but the idea is that more significant problems appear at the beginning of reports. A manager using this report would ordinarily address the most significant items first.

XBRL

LEARNING OBJECTIVE 2
Understand XBRL reporting and the basics of preparing an instance document.

An innovation in the reporting process is XBRL (eXtensible Business Reporting Language), which greatly enhances the usefulness of accounting information. XBRL is becoming the primary format for financial reporting over the Internet and has been mandated by the Securities and Exchange Commission (SEC) for public companies' filings of financial statements. As a result, accountants must understand XBRL.

Benefits of XBRL

Traditionally, words and figures have been standalone blocks of data. If, for example, you want to use the net income from an income statement in the calculation of return on investment (ROI), you would copy and paste or rekey that amount into your spreadsheet or financial analysis software. You know the number you copied is net income because you are a human being who has accounting knowledge to understand the meaning of net income. You looked at the income statement, and you know the numerator of the ROI ratio is net income. But what if that number had its own identity that belonged solely to it and no other? If you use software with an XBRL reader, you could electronically search for that number and transmit it from one accounting system to another or one accounting system to a database or spreadsheet program and it always retains its identity as net income for a particular company for a particular period. XBRL attaches an identity to words and numbers. Data can be searched and retrieved and seamlessly imported and exported by different software systems thereby eliminating time-consuming and error-prone manual data entry. Analysts can automatically populate spreadsheet valuation models with the proper data from financial reports instead of having to identify and key in this information manually. Suppose you are consolidating data from several business units within an organization. Data are submitted in different currencies and from different accounting systems. If the data are in XBRL, you can quickly and easily combine the data into a consolidated report.

XBRL Background

But before focusing on just XBRL, let's look at a bigger picture of Web-enabled markup languages. You've probably heard of a couple of these so they need to be put in perspective. All these languages involve marking up, or tagging, data. It's these tags that describe the data and enable not only human beings to read the data but also a large number of different software applications. A tag looks like this <netincome>350000</netincome>. Note the tag is always in angle brackets, also called diamond brackets or

Source: ScandinavianStock/Shutterstock.

chevrons. They are always in pairs of an opening tag and a closing tag (preceded by a forward slash) to markup or define the number. Additional tags could be added to further describe this number.

All these Web-enabled markup languages are originated from Standard Generalized Markup Language (SGML). SGML was originally designed to enable the sharing of machine-readable documents in large projects in government, law and industry that needed to remain readable for several decades. Had these documents not been stored in a markup language, they could have been lost forever. A subset of SGML is **XML** (e**X**tensible **M**arkup **L**anguage). This term may be more familiar to you. Extensible simply means users can extend the basic language by defining markup elements themselves thereby making XML much more flexible than SGML. XML is used specifically for Web applications. The files for this textbook are XML tagged so they can be posted on a website for you to read, print, search, and extract sections you are interested in. Because it is tagged, this book can be put on a website, Kindle™, or any other e-reader that comes along. Think of water versus ice. It's easy to pour water into any shape of container, but not so easy with a block of ice.

Don't confuse XML with **HTML** (HyperText Markup Language), another subset of SGML, and one you're probably somewhat familiar with. HTML is used to create Web pages. HTML also uses tags, but they are primarily formatting tags such as the data are italicized, for example, <i>AIS</i>, or the data are in boldface type, such as AIS. HTML tags identify the elements of a page so a browser such as Internet Explorer can display that page on your computer screen. The tags in HTML don't say anything about the meaning of the data. XML tags, on the other hand, describe the content, for example <course_name>AIS</course_name> and are used for data exchange over the Web. Content is separated from presentation. An XML document contains only data (no formatting).

Explanation of XBRL

XBRL is a markup language derived from XML used for the electronic communication of specifically business and financial data. It uses features of XML but adds more to make XBRL a fully automated business reporting language. XBRL was being developed by an international non-profit consortium of approximately 450 major companies, government agencies, and organizations, one of which is the American Institute of Certified Public Accountants (AICPA). The XBRL websites www.xbrl.org and www.xbrl.us contain a wealth of information. After the SEC's mandate of XBRL financial reporting, its website xbrl.sec.gov became the official source for regulations on XBRL filings and other XBRL related technical issues.

As you saw from the examples in the first paragraph of this section, XBRL benefits the preparers of financial information as well as the users of financial information. Accountants, auditors, managers, investors, analysts, financial institutions, and regulatory agencies can send, receive, find, compare, and analyze data much more rapidly and efficiently if they are in XBRL format.

The SEC coined the phrase "interactive data" for XBRL and named its new system for financial filings Interactive Data Electronic Applications (IDEA). IDEA is replacing the SEC's electronic data gathering and retrieval (EDGAR) database.

Tags

Unique identifying **tags**, or labels, are applied to items of financial data, such as "net profit." However, these are more than simple identifiers. They provide a range of information about the item. Several tags can be appended to one data item to fully explain its content, such as whether it is a monetary item, the type of currency, and/or whether it is a percentage or a fraction. XBRL can even show how items are related to one another. Therefore, it can represent how data are calculated. It can also identify whether data fall into particular groupings for organizational or presentational purposes. The tags stay with the data and are computer readable. XBRL allows tags in any language to be applied to

XML (eXtensible Markup Language) A markup language used specifically for Web applications. Extensible simply means users can extend the basic language by defining markup elements themselves.

HTML HyperText Markup Language is a markup language that is used to create Web pages.

XBRL (eXtensible Business Reporting Language) A markup language derived from XML used for the electronic communication of specifically business and financial data. XBRL attaches an identity to words and numbers.

Tag (or label) In XRL, a unique identifier applied to an item of financial data, such as "net profit." However, a tag is more than a simple identifier. It provides a range of information about the item.

items, as well as accounting references or other subsidiary information. Specific rules for how the tags are worded and punctuated must be followed.

Fortunately, we have software tools to help us in preparing tagged XBRL documents. One popular program is Rivet Software's Dragon Tag (a clever play on "drag and tag"). Dragon Tag is a Microsoft Office add-in that simplifies the process of tagging existing Excel and Word documents into XBRL format. This particular program is for smaller organizations that prepare their financial statements from smaller accounting packages and export them into Word or Excel. The program doesn't come bundled with Microsoft Office; companies need to purchase it separately. There are also many other software programs commercially available for companies to tag their financial statements and file them with the SEC.

The user has to have some understanding of XBRL to use tagging software. Very large accounting information system vendors are embedding XBRL capabilities in their financial reporting modules. For example, SAP's XBRL tool gathers data directly from the SAP databases and converts the data directly into XBRL. It can create single financial statements or consolidated statements. Another option, regardless of company size, is to outsource the conversion of documents to XBRL. Many companies offer this service. One example is Workiva, which offers a variety of XBRL related tagging and filing solutions.

Taxonomy

Taxonomy In XBRL, a dictionary of element names that represent financial reporting concepts (e.g., cash and cash equivalents, accounts receivable, net income) and are established by the XBRL consortium. These taxonomies are used to tag data.

XBRL has standardized **taxonomies**, which are dictionaries of items that represent financial reporting concepts (e.g., cash and cash equivalents, accounts receivable, net income) and were established by the XBRL consortium. These taxonomies are used to tag data. After the SEC's XBRL mandate, the SEC has been periodically releasing taxonomies to reflect new needs in the financial reporting process. The SEC taxonomies are developed based on consortium established taxonomies, and they continue to work together to update these taxonomies. The SEC's taxonomy for financial reporting is called US GAAP. Below are some United States taxonomies for specific industries:

- US GAAP Commercial and Industrial
- US GAAP Banking and Savings
- US GAAP Insurance
- US GAAP Investment Banking

The XBRL GL (general ledger) taxonomy is available for internal reporting and consolidations within organizations only. It collects general ledger detail from various internal accounting systems, processes the data, and presents it in a standard, useful, and integrated platform. In addition, IFRS-GP (International Financial Reporting Standards, General Purpose) is for financial statements using international financial reporting standards.

Instance Document

Instance document An XBRL document that has been tagged according to the rules of XBRL making it available for analysis and processing.

An XBRL **instance document** is a document that has been tagged according to the rules of XBRL thus making it available for analysis and processing. In other words, the document is an instance of one that follows the rules of XBRL. An instance document includes coding that comes from an appropriate taxonomy. Four basic steps go into the creation of an instance document:

1. Select a standard taxonomy and download this taxonomy into the XBRL software product. Taxonomies are available at no cost at xbrl.sec.gov.
2. Mark up the data. Assign a specific XBRL tag from the standard taxonomy to each data item in the financial report. If an appropriate tag is not available from the standard taxonomy, the preparer can create a new customized XBRL tag.
3. Edit the tagging to detect any errors. The XBRL software does this.
4. Generate the instance document. The XBRL software does this.

Exhibit 5.10 presents an example of a portion of a balance sheet in human-readable form.

Exhibit 5.11 presents the same portion of a balance sheet as an instance document, which is in computer-readable form.

Current Assets	
Assets Held for Sale	100,000
Construction in Progress, Current	100,000
Inventories	100,000
Other Financial Assets, Current	100,000
Hedging Instruments, Current [Asset]	100,000
Current Tax Receivables	100,000
Trade and Other Receivables, Net, Current	100,000
Prepayments, Current	100,000
Cash and Cash Equivalents	100,000
Other Assets, Current	100,000
Current Assets, Total	1,000,000

EXHIBIT 5.10 Portion of Balance Sheet (human-readable form)

Source: www.xbrl.org.

```
<ifrs-gp:AssetsHeldSale contextRef="Current_AsOf" unitRef="U-Euros"
   decimals="0">100000</;ifrs-gp:AssetsHeldSale>
<ifrs-gp:ConstructionProgressCurrent contextRef="Current_AsOf"
   unitRef="U-Euros" decimals="0">100000</ifrs-gp:ConstructionProgressCurrent>
<ifrs-gp:Inventories contextRef="Current_AsOf" unitRef="U-Euros"
   decimals="0">100000</ifrs-gp:Inventories>
<ifrs-gp:OtherFinancialAssetsCurrent contextRef="Current_AsOf"
   unitRef="U-Euros" decimals="0">100000</ifrs-gp:OtherFinancialAssetsCurrent>
<ifrs-gp:HedgingInstumentsCurrentAsset contextRef="Current_AsOf"
   unitRef="U-Euros" decimals="0">100000</ifrs-gp:HedgingInstrumentsCurrentAsset>
<ifrs-gp:CurrerrtTaxReceivables contextRef="Current_AsOf" unitRef="U-Euros"
   decimals="0">100000</ifrs-gp:CurrentTaxReceivables>
<ifrs-gp:TradeOtherReceivablesNetCurrent contextRef="Current_AsOf" unitRef="U-Euros"
   decimals="0">100000</ifrs-gp:TradeOtherReceivablesNetCurrent>
<ifrs-gp:PrepaymentsCurrent contextRef="Current_AsOf" unitRef="U-Euros"
   decimals="0">100000</ifrs-gp:PrepaymentsCurrent>
<ifrs-gp:CashCashEquivalents contextRef="Current_AsOf" unitRef="U-Euros"
   decimals="0">100000</ifrs-gp:CashCashEquivalents>
<ifrs-gp:OtherAssetsCurrent contextRef="Current_AsOf" unitRef="U-Euros"
   decimals="0">100000</ifrs-gp:OtherAssetsCurrent>
<ifrs-gp:AssetsCurrentTotal contextRef="Current_AsOf" unitRef="U-Euros"
   decimals="0">1000000</ifrs-gp:AssetsCurrentTotal>
```

EXHIBIT 5.11 Instance Document for Portion of Balance Sheet (computer-readable form)

Source: www.xbrl.org.

Coding Methods

Now that we have covered the general principles of reporting, we can begin a discussion of coding. Until the desired outputs from a system are known, the desired inputs and required processing cannot be identified. Coding is an essential element enabling processing to occur.

Coding Objectives

LEARNING OBJECTIVE 3
Describe the objectives and methods of common coding systems.

Codes are used for identification and classification. A valid social security number uniquely identifies some person, either living or deceased. The letters M and F can be used to classify the person by gender. Some of the digits composing a social security number also have meaning depending on their position. Various symbols may be used for codes, although in accounting information systems the most common symbols are the set of numeric and alphabetic characters used by a given society.

Types of Codes

Sequence code Typically, the most simple coding system used by accountants—a numerical code.

Probably the simplest coding system used by accountants is a numerical **sequence code**. For example, sales invoices and payroll checks are preprinted, used, and recorded in a numerical sequence. While a sequential code uniquely identifies an object, the particular number used on an object, such as a paycheck, has no meaning other than that each check number is increased by one.

Block coding A complex coding system that assigns meaning to various positions within a code.

Block coding assigns meaning to various positions in a code. A block code you are no doubt familiar with is the universal product code, which is commonly used in retail sales. One block of five numbers of the code represents the vendor and another block of five numbers represents the product. These numbers are human readable. Vertical black bars and white spaces above the numbers represent the vendor and product numbers making the code machine readable. A scanner identifies the sequence of numbers and retrieves the product's information on a computer, tablet or smartphone using barcode software. The UPC code simply identifies the product. When the UPC is scanned at a store, the retailer's point-of-sale (POS) system retrieves the selling price for that item and captures the sale transaction. The selling price is determined by the retailer and stored in its POS system.

Group code A code that can be used to express significant amounts of information. Most often it is used in a hierarchical structure so that the largest category is identified by the first symbols, followed by increasingly detailed subcategories as you move to the right.

A **group code** can be used to express the significance of amounts of information. Most often it is used in a hierarchical structure so the largest category is identified by the first (leftmost) symbols, followed by increasingly detailed subcategories as you move to the right. Postal ZIP codes are an excellent example. The first digit represents an area of the country starting with 0 on the East Coast and ending with 9 on the West Coast. Moving to the right through the code you find identifiers of smaller and smaller geographic subdivisions with some (albeit, not strict) east to west logical association. Group codes are often used for the chart of accounts with the leftmost number or numbers representing a category such as assets and the next number or numbers representing a subcategory such as short term.

Mnemonic code A code that expresses some logical association between the characters forming the code and the item being identified.

Mnemonic codes express some logical association between the characters forming the code and the item being identified. Codes identifying states, such as IL and OH, are easily remembered. A disadvantage is the lack of flexibility. The code for Alabama (AL) is easily mistaken or substituted for Alaska (AK). The word processing package "Microsoft Word" uses B for bold, C for copy, F for find, N for new, P for print, and U for underline, but must use o for Format because the F has been previously assigned.

Entity coding Coding that identifies master file records (such as general ledger, customer, vendor, employee, and inventory) using account numbers or alphabetic characters.

Application of Coding to Accounting Systems

LEARNING OBJECTIVE 4
Design coding systems for various accounting entities and events.

The most significant use of coding in accounting information systems is to identify entities and events. **Entity coding** identifies master file records (such as general ledger, customer, vendor, employee, and inventory) using account numbers or alphabetic characters. The type of code used differs by the nature of the entity due to various reporting requirements. For example, alphabetic characters are often used for identifying inventory items.

Event coding is used to uniquely identify events recorded in an accounting information system. An event may be a transaction event, such as a sale, or a nontransaction event, such as the receipt and acceptance of a sales order.

Reporting requirements heavily influence the choice and use of codes in accounting information systems. Accounting data are classified according to reporting needs and until someone specifies those needs, any coding system adopted will likely prove to be inadequate. Consequently, some of the following general reporting principles described earlier in this chapter and listed below will, at least in part, prescribe the coding systems used.

1. Necessity for concise reports
2. Emphasis on both physical and monetary measures
3. Frequency of reporting
4. Responsibility reporting
5. Reporting by function
6. Comparative reporting
7. Exception reporting

The principle of concise reports (principle 1 above) requires the coding system be designed so detailed accounts may be summed to provide an appropriate level of aggregation in reports. Furthermore, responsibility reporting requires the accounts be sufficiently detailed (in the master file) to enable reporting to all levels of management (principle 4). As an example, consider the following advertising expense accounts that might be required for a department store.

Product-related advertising expense accounts:

- Shoes, Ladies', Newspaper advertisement space
- Shoes, Ladies', Newspaper advertisement layout
- Shoes, Ladies', Television broadcast time
- Shoes, Ladies', Television film production
- Shoes, Men's, Newspaper advertisement space
- Shoes, Men's, Newspaper advertisement layout
- Shoes, Men's, Television broadcast time
- Shoes, Men's, Television film production
- Shoes, Children's, Newspaper advertisement space
- Shoes, Children's, Newspaper advertisement layout
- Shoes, Children's, Television broadcast time
- Shoes, Children's, Television film production

(Replicated for all departments, such as ladies'/men's/children's clothing, cosmetics, linens, housewares, furniture, appliances, and electronics.)

With a separate account for each of the above expenses, a few of the possible ways the balances of these accounts can be selected for inclusion in a report are:

- Men's products (shoes and clothing, etc.) advertising expense
- All clothing advertising expense
- All advertising (newspaper and television) expense
- Total newspaper advertising (space and layout) expense
- Total television advertising (broadcast time and film production) expense

While the most common reporting of physical units is for inventory items, other applications include hours billed, administrative hours, and unassigned hours in CPA firms; number of customers and orders received; number and percent of damaged units received from suppliers; and employee turnover rate. Special coding requirements for accumulating physical information will be covered in the business process chapters later in the text.

Event coding Coding that is used to uniquely identify events recorded in an accounting information system. An event may be a transaction event, such as a sale, or a non-transaction event, such as the receipt and acceptance of a sales order.

Exception and functional reporting principles require no additional coding to be implemented. The business process chapters that follow will give numerous applications of all the reporting principles.

Audit Trails

Audit trails are referenced in many accounting works, but they are seldom rigorously defined. As a consequence, an audit trail is frequently and falsely assumed to exist even though no explicit effort has been expended to create one. Accounting software packages almost universally claim to provide an audit trail, with the delivery on this promise ranging from:

- the provision of a clear audit trail that is automatic to
- the enabling of a knowledgeable and diligent computer operator to create an audit trail to
- the inability of a knowledgeable and diligent computer operator to create an audit trail.

Unfortunately, a significant number of packages fall into the last two categories.

Concept of an Audit Trail

LEARNING OBJECTIVE 5
Describe the concept and dimensions of an audit trail.

Audit trail A set of processing references that enables the tracing of an event from its source to its designation or, alternatively, from its designation back to its source. It consists of codes (or references) attached to data as they flow through the accounting system so they can be traced from originating documents, to transaction and open files, and to their inclusion in output reports and documents and vice versa.

An **audit trail** is a set of processing references that enables the tracing of an event from its source to its destination or, alternatively, from its destination back to its source. In other words, an audit trail consists of codes (or references) attached to data as they flow through the accounting system so they can be traced from originating documents, to transaction and open files, to master and open files, and to their inclusion on output reports and documents. This tracing should also be possible starting with the data on output reports or documents and working back to the original entries in the transaction or open files and then to any supporting documents.

An adequate audit trail requires that these codes be unique, thereby permitting direct tracing from one point to another in the audit trail and making a random search of the files unnecessary. For example, an accountant or auditor should be able to look at a printout of a sales journal and select one credit-sale entry from that journal. The accountant or auditor should then be able trace the entry to a printout or screen display of the customer master file and to the open invoice file, observing that the transaction increased the customer's outstanding balance and appears as a new record in the open invoice file. If the journal entries are batched before posting, you may trace from the entry to the batch and use the batch identifier for tracing to the customer account. This particular transaction should also be easily traceable from the sales transaction file to its location in the general journal transaction file; from the general journal transaction file to accounts that it increased and/or decreased in the general ledger master file; and, finally, from the general ledger master file to the proper accounts on the financial statements. Conversely, the accountant or auditor should be able to select any amount on a financial statement or other report and trace the transactions that compose a report amount back to their original entries in the transaction files and then to any supporting documents.

A second aspect of the audit trail is that you should be able to easily trace from the beginning balance of an account to the ending balance for an accounting period, and back from the ending balance to the beginning balance. This tracing is required for all accounts whether they are general ledger, customer, inventory, or other accounts. Thus, an adequate audit trail is both bi-directional and multi-dimensional as illustrated in **Exhibit 5.12**.

Source: Ollyy/Shutterstock.

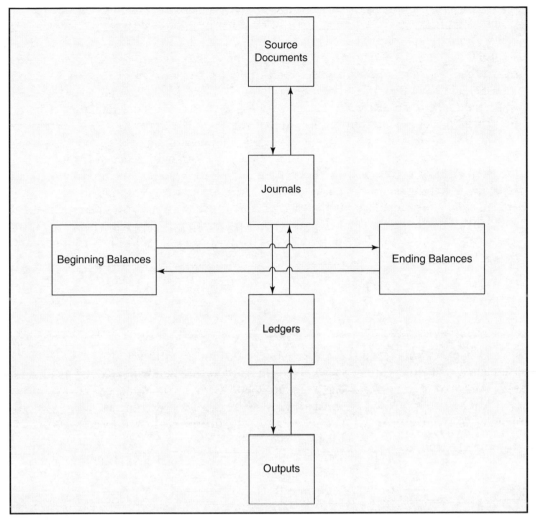

EXHIBIT 5.12 Illustration of Bi-directional and Multi-dimensional Aspects of Audit Trails

Coding for Audit Trails

A **reference identifier** leads an accountant or auditor from a data item's specific location in the accounting information system to its preceding or successor location. These identifiers have an ordinal value permitting you to easily locate a particular identifier when they are in order. Such identifiers are unique to each event, account, and document. For those events for which the accounting system generates prenumbered documents evidencing completed transactions, such as customer invoices or checks issued, the document numbers are ordinarily used as the unique identifier.

For example, each of the sales transactions in our example accounting system at the beginning of Chapter 4 has a unique invoice number (1001–1006). Therefore, when looking at the open customer invoice file and seeing invoice number 1001, you can use this number to refer to the sales transaction file and find the original entry. You can trace the increases in a customer's balance in the customer master file by matching the invoices in the open customer invoice file to the customer code. For those events that are not evidenced by internally generated, prenumbered documents, the transactions should be coded with sequential numbers for each transaction file. For example, each of the general journal transactions in our example accounting system in Chapter 4 has a unique number.

Numbers that should not be used for unique reference identifiers include (1) numbers of internally generated, prenumbered documents that represent the initiation (as opposed to the completion) of a transaction and (2) numbers of any externally generated

LEARNING OBJECTIVE 6
Design a coding system to support audit trails.

Reference identifier An identifier that leads an accountant or auditor from a data item's specific location in the accounting information system to its preceding or successor location.

documents. The numbers on internally generated, prenumbered documents, such as sales orders and purchase orders, should not be used because they do not evidence completed transactions. Therefore, these numbers will not be in the same order as the completed transactions, and some may never materialize into completed transactions. The numbers of externally generated documents, such as invoices received from vendors, should not be used as unique identifiers because they vary in form (alphabetic and numeric). More importantly, because externally generated documents are in no particular order, they do not permit direct tracing from ledgers to journals.

Batch code A sequential identifying number for a specific batch of data which can be used for tracing between journals and the ledger accounts.

If journal entries are batched before posting, then each batch is assigned a sequential identifying number (**batch code**) that may be used for tracing between the journals and the ledger accounts (master file records). An audit trail includes any information that assists you in tracing data from place to place in the accounting system. Consequently, reference identifiers include entity codes, event codes, batch codes, dates, and even account names. Just as "trails" in the wilderness vary in your ability to follow them, audit trails likewise vary in quality. The preceding discussion is an attempt to specify the requirements for clear and efficient audit trails.

Summary

One of the principal functions of accounting information systems is reporting. As a consequence, principles of reporting underlie all accounting information reporting. Seven principles are:

1. Necessity for concise reports
2. Emphasis on both physical and monetary measures
3. Frequency of reporting
4. Responsibility reporting
5. Reporting by function
6. Comparative reporting
7. Exception reporting

An innovation in the reporting process is XBRL (extensible business reporting language). XBRL is a markup language for the electronic communication of specifically business and financial data. For an accounting information system to support the reporting principles, adequate coding systems for events and entities must be present. To provide adequate audit trails, reference identifiers must be used that permit users and auditors to easily trace the flow of events through the system.

Key Terms

Discussion Questions and Problems

1. FasComm, Inc. manufactures high-performance communication chips for a modem manufacturer. Jill Roberts, the production manager, was "called on the carpet" this morning by Ray Ashburne, the plant superintendent, and asked to explain the following report that both Jill and Ray received upon arriving at work on Tuesday, March 16:

PRODUCTION COST REPORT				
Week Ending March 12				
		Materials	**Labor**	**Overhead**
Costs incurred		$36,439	$29,674	$14,578
Units produced	2582			
Units not passing inspection	−277			
Good units produced		2305	2305	2305
Cost per unit		$15.81	$12.87	$6.32
Total unit cost	$35.00			

Jill uses the cost report to judge the performance of her employees for the prior week, and Ray uses it to monitor overall costs. The purchasing department is responsible for the cost of material purchases, and Jill has no control over the overhead incurred. Jill immediately saw that the spoilage was far above the expected 5 percent rate. After spending from 8–10 A.M. on Tuesday investigating, she discovered that a new machine (one of five in use) that had been installed the preceding Tuesday was not calibrated correctly and was responsible for most of the defective output. It was recalibrated around noon, and the Tuesday afternoon production by that machine appeared to result in a normal yield of good chips.

Required:

Assuming that the above report is the only one received by Jill and Ray, what suggestions do you have to improve reporting? Be specific, sketching the report. Indicate the frequency of the report and to whom it should be directed.

2. Hans Burgstaller, marketing and sales manager of Columbus Cable TV, Inc. (Exhibit 5.2) retained a new consultant in 2019 to plan and monitor the annual fall advertising campaign that was designed to increase the number of subscribers and persuade subscribers to move to higher priced services. While the numbers and service profiles in Exhibit 5.2 show improvements for October 2018, this might be typical of such campaigns. Mr. Burgstaller wonders how the results for October 2019 compare with last year. New subscribers for October 2019 for basic, super, and premium service were 1,234, 296, and 599, respectively, and lost subscribers were 450, 563, and

257, respectively. Net changes in level of service were (120), (15), and 135.

Required:

a. Prepare a report for Mr. Burgstaller comparing October 2019 with October 2018 using the layout shown below.

COLUMBUS CABLE TV, INC.				
For October 2019 and 2018				
	Service Level	2019	2018	Incr. (Decr.)
New Subscribers:				
	Basic			
	Super			
	Premium			
Subscribers Lost:				
	Basic			
	Super			
	Premium			

b. Evaluate the effect of the fall advertising campaign on the acquisition of new subscribers, loss of subscribers, and changes in the service level. What conclusions would you suggest to Mr. Burgstaller?

c. Which principles of reporting do your answers illustrate? Explain.

3. What general relationship exists between:
   a. the type of data reported and the frequency of reporting?
   b. the type of data reported and the job function of the report recipient?
4. Discuss the four basic steps that go into the creation of an instance document.
5. Define an instance document.
6. Name some XBRL taxonomies.
7. Explain the difference in extensible markup language (XML) and hypertext markup language (HTML).
8. Refer to the example in the chapter regarding advertising expense accounts required for a department store. Assume that the store's accounting software permits a general ledger account number with the following attributes:
   - The first field consisting of three digits uniquely identifies the account, distinguishing it from other general ledger accounts and places it in the correct location in the chart of accounts.
   - The second field has four digits, each of which may be used as individual fields or used in combination.
   - The report writer for the software package permits you to use the question mark (?) as a wildcard symbol when specifying which accounts to include in a report. For example, the specification 330.?4?? includes in a report all accounts having the first field equal to 330 and the second digit in the second field equal to 4.

Required:

Assuming that 640 is the number assigned for the first field of the advertising expense account, design and describe a system that uses the four digits of the second field for classifying various advertising accounts so you could design reports showing any of the twelve advertising expense accounts in the first list in the section, "Application of Coding to Accounting Systems."

9. A vendor account on the books of Pannell Partnerships is reproduced below:

Required:

Comment on your ability to trace the different types of entries in the Wichita Suppliers account to source entries in Pannell's journals using the reference identifiers given. Which of the reference identifiers are for documents prepared by Pannell? By Wichita Suppliers? What suggestions do you have to improve the quality of the audit trail?

10. Some accounting transactions have source documents whose preprinted numbers can be used effectively as audit trail reference identifiers. The preprinted number on other source documents evidencing transactions cannot be so used.

Required:

   a. Identify those document identifiers that are useful components of an audit trail.
   b. Identify other common document identifiers that are not.
   c. What two characteristics do useful reference identifiers possess?

11. One transaction in the "Illustration of Data Flows" section of Chapter 4 is a credit sale to Cherry Gardens for $6,000, invoice number 1006.

Required:

Document the audit trail for this transaction from the time it appears in the sales transaction file until it appears in the sales of services account on the income statement and accounts receivable on the balance sheet. Your documentation should include the names of the reports and files where the transaction appears and the reference identifier that identifies the transaction. Because this is a "textbook" assignment, include the exhibit numbers of the reports and files.

Wichita Suppliers					
			6/01/18	Beginning bal.	$351
6/03/18	Check #874	$111	6/06/18	PO 451	75
6/19/18	Cr. Memo 994	35	6/10/18	PO 410	227
6/25/18	Check #888	250	6/16/18	PO 470	544
			6/27/18	Invoice 1910	86
			6/27/18	PO 475	101
6/30/18	Balance forward	988			
			7/01/18	Beginning bal.	$988

12. Kenbart Company decided increased emphasis had to be placed on profit planning and the analysis of results as compared to its plans. A new computerized profit planning system has been implemented to help in this objective.

The company employs contribution margin reporting for internal reporting purposes and applies the concept of flexible budgeting for estimating variable costs. The following terms are used by Kenbart's executive management when reviewing and analyzing actual results and the profit plan:

- Original Plan—Profit plan approved and adopted by management for the year.
- Revised Plan—Original plan modified as a consequence of action taken during the year (usually quarterly) by executive management.
- Flexed Revised Plan—The most current plan (i.e., either original plan or revised plan, if one has been prepared) adjusted for changes in volume and variable expense rates.
- YTD Actual Results—The actual results of operations for the year.
- Current Outlook—The summation of the actual year-to-date results of operations plus the flexed revised plan for the remaining months of the year.

Executive management meets monthly to review the actual results as compared to the profit plan. Any assumptions or major changes in the profit plan usually are incorporated on a quarterly basis once the first quarter is completed.

KENBART COMPANY PROFIT PLAN REPORT MONTH, YEAR						
	Month Over/(Under)			Year-to-Date Over/(Under)		
Sales	Actual Plan	$	%	Actual Plan	$	%
Variable Manufacturing costs						
Raw materials						
Direct labor						
Variable overhead						
Total Variable manufacturing costs						
Manufacturing margin						
Variable selling expenses						
Contribution margin						
Fixed Costs						
Manufacturing						
Sales						
General administration						
Income before taxes						
Income taxes						
Net income						

An outline of the basic Profit Plan Report is reproduced below. This report is prepared at the end of each month. In addition, this report is generated whenever executive management initiates a change or modification in its plans. Consequently, many different versions of a company profit plan exist, which make analysis difficult and confusing.

Several members of executive management have voiced the disapproval of the Profit Plan Report because the "plan column" is not well defined and varies in meaning from one report to another. Furthermore, no "current outlook" column is included in the report. Therefore, the Accounting Department has been asked to modify the report so users can understand better the information being conveyed and the reference points for comparison of results.

Required:

a. What are the advantages to Kenbart Company's having its profit plan system computerized?

b. Redesign the layout of the Profit Plan Report so it will be more useful to Kenbart's executive management in its task of reviewing results and planning operations. Explain the reason for each modification you make in the report.

c. What types of data would Kenbart Company be required to capture in its computer-based files in order to generate the plans and results that executive management reviews and analyzes? [CMA adapted]

13. Universal Floor Covering is a manufacturer and distributor of three floor covering products—carpet, vinyl, and padding. The home office is located in Charlotte, North Carolina. Carpet mills (i.e., manufacturing plants) are located in Dalton, Georgia, and Greenville, South Carolina. A vinyl floor covering manufacturing plant is in High Point, North Carolina. Total sales last year were just over $250 million.

The company manufactures over 200 different varieties of carpet. The carpet is classified as being for commercial or residential purposes and is sold under five brand names with up to five lines under each brand. The lines indicate the different grades of quality; grades are measured by type of tufts per square inch. Each line of carpet can have up to 15 different color styles.

The company manufactures just under 200 varieties of vinyl floor covering This product is also classified as

being for commercial or residential use. The company has four separate brand names (largely distinguished by the type of finish), up to eight different patterns for each brand, and up to eight color styles for each pattern.

The company manufactures ten different grades of padding.. The padding is usually differentiated by intended use (commercial or residential) in addition to thickness and composition of materials.

Universal serves over 2,000 wholesale customers. Retail showrooms are the primary customers. Many major corporations are direct buyers of Universal's products. Large construction companies have contracts with Universal to purchase floor covering products at reduced rates for use in newly constructed homes and commercial buildings. In addition, Universal produces a line of residential carpet for a large national retail chain. Sales to these customers range from $10,000 to $1,000,000 annually.

Each plant has a company-owned retail outlet store. The outlets carry overruns, seconds, and discontinued items. This is Universal's only retail sales function.

The company has divided the sales market into seven territories, with the major concentration on the East Coast. The market segments are New England, New York, Mid-Atlantic, Carolinas, South, Midwest, and West. Each sales territory is divided into five to ten districts with a salesperson assigned to each district.

The current accounting system has been adequate for monitoring the sales by product. However, there are limitations to the system because specific information is sometimes not available. A detailed analysis of operations is necessary for planning and control purposes and would be valuable for decision-making purposes.

Required:

Account coding systems are based on various coding concepts.

a. Briefly define and give an example of the following coding concepts:
Sequence coding
Block coding
Group coding

b. Identify and describe factors which must be considered before a coding system can be designed and implemented for an organization.

c. Design a code to assign to each sales transaction that would permit Universal to prepare sales analyses that reflect the characteristics of the company's business. For each portion of the code:

A partial solution is provided to get you started.

Explain the meaning and purpose of the position.

Identify and justify the number of digits required.

[CMA adapted]

Partial Solution for part c to get you started:

Item	No. of Digits	Explanation
Product	1	Three product lines—carpet, vinyl floor covering, padding. One digit is sufficient.
Product Use	1	Commercial and residential. One digit is sufficient.

Notes

1. Constance Lehmann and Cynthia Heagy (2014). "Organizing Information into Useful Management Reports: Short Cases to Illustrate Reporting Principles and Coding", *Journal of Accounting Education Special Issue on AIS Education* 32 (2): 130-145.

2. Sharon M. McKinnon and William J. Bruns, *The Information Mosaic* (Harvard Business School Press Boston, 1992): 48

3. McKinnon and Bruns, 57.

4. McKinnon and Bruns, 151.

Internal Control and Risk Assessment

Source: Phonton photo/Shutterstock.

Learning Objectives

After studying this chapter, you should be able to:

- Define internal control and explain its importance.
- Explain why stakeholders are interested in internal control.
- Explain the control implications of the Foreign Corrupt Practices and Sarbanes-Oxley Acts.
- Explain why external auditors are interested in a client's internal control.
- Explain what positions several professional organizations have taken regarding internal control.
- Describe the relationship among organizational objectives and components of the COSO 2013 framework.
- Explain the nature of organizational objectives.
- Recognize how internal control components are integrated.
- Discuss the factors of the control environment.
- Understand the importance of risk assessment (to include an evaluation of the potential for fraud), and discuss how changes in the identified risks can change the risk profile of an organization.
- Understand how a cost/benefit model is used in risk assessment.

Introductory Scenario

Jérôme Kerviel almost brought down the second largest bank (in market capitalization) in France. Société Générale hired Mr. Kerviel as a back office worker, working a desk that monitors traders. Seven years later, he was an apprentice trader on the futures desk investing the bank's money by hedging on European equity indices using near-term futures. Mr. Kerviel took huge bullish positions on indices such as the Dow Jones Eurostoxx 50 Index and the German DAX. His trades took place over the course of a year with no red flags noted by supervisors or internal auditors during that period. He was investigated for breach of trust, computer abuse, and falsification/forgery. The results of his actions were believed to have resulted in €4.9 billion (US$7.7 billion) in losses. He was arrested in late January 2008, released two months later, and in 2010, was found guilty of falsifying documentation, abusing the trust of his employer, and entering false computer data. He was given a 5-year sentence (2 years suspended), banned from working in the financial services industry for life, and ordered to pay restitution ($6.7 billion). His initial appeal in 2012 resulted in the court upholding the 3-year sentence and the restitution. France's Court of Cassation in 2014 ruled that Mr. Kerviel should not have to repay Société Générale for the full €4.9 billion loss. It argued that the lower courts had failed to take proper account of the weaknesses in the bank's own risk-management procedures at the time. A new trial has been ordered to determine how much Mr. Kerviel should pay in retribution.

Interestingly, on June 7, 2016, a labor court ordered the Société Générale to pay Mr. Kerviel €450,000 in back wages, unpaid vacation, and a performance bonus from 2007 (which represents €300,000 of the award). According to the New York Times, the tribunal ruled that Mr. Kerviel's illegal actions presented "no real and serious cause" for his dismissal, in effect, backing Mr. Kerviel's defense that his managers at the bank knew what he was doing. Needless to say, Société Générale plans to appeal the ruling.

How did Mr. Kerviel's legendary exploits occur? According to reports in Reuters and abc.com, Kerviel appears to have hacked into the computer system to steal passwords and to falsify documents. He knew how to bypass security because of his background in the back office. Although he was not considered a "computer genius" by some, he still managed to have unusually high levels of cash flow, high brokerage expenses, was able to avoid taking vacation (never allowing anyone to work his desk), and exceeded the desk's market risk limit for a single position. In addition, his bosses missed over one thousand false trades, failed to note his huge increase in earnings (approximately €1.4 billion in 2007 alone), and failed to follow up on questions about his trades from the Eurex Exchange. Allegedly, he acted alone and, unlike other fraudsters in the financial markets, appeared to be trying to increase profits for Société Générale, which would in turn increase his earnings (i.e., he was not embezzling funds). Preliminary charges were brought against Mr. Kerviel after Société Générale "unwound" (i.e., sold) the futures contracts he had purchased. Because the futures market was falling, Société Générale had met margin calls of €2.5 billion prior to its launching an investigation into Mr. Kerviel's actions on January 18, 2008.

France's Central Bank assessed fines of US$6.3 million for "serious shortcomings" in internal control at several levels at Société Générale. Their report noted "significant weaknesses" in computer security systems and in the monitoring of traders by supervisors. In addition, there were allegations that warnings about Kerviel's activities were ignored, and that there was a culture of risk-taking at the bank. Société Générale claims that this was an "isolated incident." Kerviel claims that his supervisors were aware of what he was doing and did not monitor him as long as he was making money for the bank (he made approximately €1.4 billion for Société Générale in 2007). He insists that the "mechanisms of control and assistance didn't function at all."

Source: Alex Bonney/Shutterstock.

How different things would have been had the futures market been rising and Kerviel's actions had resulted in a US$7 billion (or more) profit! Ironically, in April of 2008, Kerviel started a new job with Lamaire Consultants and Associates, a computer security and system development company while awaiting trial (he has since resigned from that position to focus on his appeals).

Introductory Scenario Thought Questions:

1. What were some of the things that management could have done to prevent the fraudulent activity perpetrated by Kerviel?
2. Why do you think the warnings about potential problems were ignored?

Where Was Internal Control?

The media have covered several instances of a lack of internal controls over financial reporting in corporations in various industries. Ponzi schemes such as those allegedly perpetrated by Stanford Financial and Bernie Madoff, coupled with allegations of misappropriation of assets in companies such as American International Group (AIG) have infuriated the public, who relied on the financial disclosures made by representatives of the organizations. Management collusion and falsification of financial statements drove Enron into bankruptcy. In all of these cases, investors lost money because of their reliance on financial information provided by the organization's representatives. The incidents occurred because of poor internal control or management override of internal control.

What Is Internal Control?

Internal control is a *process* designed to provide *reasonable assurance* that organizational objectives related to the reliability of both internal and external reporting, the effectiveness and efficiency of operations, and compliance with applicable laws and regulations will be achieved. Absolute assurance that management and organizational objectives will be met would be ideal; however, it is only practical to admit that reasonable assurance is the more realistic expectation, since it is impossible to guarantee that fraud will not occur (e.g., in the situation of collusion among several employees). The internal control process is continuously being developed, maintained, and improved by an organization's board of directors, executive management, business process owners, internal auditors, and other personnel. In fact, all employees should be involved in maintaining and improving the internal control process. Inevitably, the responsibility for internal control rests with the chief executive officer of the organization.

LEARNING OBJECTIVE 1
Define internal control and explain its importance.

Internal control A process designed to provide reasonable assurance that management objectives related to the quality of data, the effectiveness and efficiency of operations, and compliance with applicable laws and regulations will be achieved.

While internal control is an ongoing process, its effectiveness is a state or condition at a point in time. The effectiveness of internal control depends on its being built into the very fabric of an organization's culture and activities. In addition, the effectiveness depends on an understanding by employees of their roles and the vital contributions they make. When internal control is "built in," it supports an organization's achievement of its objectives.

As demonstrated in the Introductory Scenario, the management of Société Générale was not in control of the activities going on in its trading unit. This weakness in internal control gave an unscrupulous trader uncontrolled access, allowing him to make reckless trades which led to enormous losses when he "bet the wrong way." But weaknesses in internal control do not just open windows for deliberate fraud; they also open opportunities for unintentional mistakes (Vignette 6.1).

Erroneous Record Keeping

"This is it, Max—either you get our account straightened out, or we're taking our business to Sudential!" This was the fourth customer in one week that had threatened Max. The large health insurance company Max worked for received hundreds of checks each day from its customers in payment of insurance premiums. Because of the routine nature of the job of keying in payments, the cash data entry clerk often got bored. His mind would wander to more scintillating topics. In the middle of the afternoon, the clerk had to really struggle just to stay awake. As a result, the clerk made many errors in entering the payments. He would transpose numbers and key in the customer codes incorrectly causing credits to go into the wrong customer accounts.

Max and other sales reps complained to top management about the mistakes in their customers' accounts. As a result, management brought in two employees from other departments to review the customer accounts and correct the errors. However, the organization would have been much better off if management had instituted some internal controls to prevent the errors from ever happening in the first place.

Source: Blend Images/Shutterstock.

THOUGHT QUESTIONS

1. What types of controls could be implemented to reduce the number of clerical errors in this situation?
2. What are some things that the company can do to alleviate the monotonous nature of data entry?

The next section of this chapter discusses the strong interest in internal control shown by parties outside an organization—stakeholders, legislators, auditors, and professional organizations. Later sections explain the relationships among the objectives of the organization and the components of internal control. Two of the components of an integrated control framework—the control environment and risk assessment—are discussed in detail in this chapter.[1]

Outside Interest in Internal Control

Concern for internal control within an organization has always been keen. Management wants to ensure that the organization's activities are "in control" so that, at least internally, management is doing what it can to achieve its objectives. Management of publicly held companies is required to establish, test, and maintain the organization's internal control. Internal and external auditors perform reviews of the adequacy and effectiveness of internal control. Internal control is also of considerable interest to parties outside the organization because it provides a measure of protection against erroneous or fraudulent financial reporting. A number of public, private, and professional bodies (including the U.S. Congress, the Securities and Exchange Commission, the Public Company Accounting Oversight Board, and the National Commission on Fraudulent Financial Reporting) play active roles in the area of internal control.

Stakeholders' Interest in Internal Control

LEARNING OBJECTIVE 2
Explain why stakeholders are interested in internal control.

Stakeholders' (i.e., shareholders, customers, suppliers, employees, creditors) interest in an organization's internal control is high because of their dependence on the accuracy of issued financial information for decision-making. Furthermore, stakeholders are concerned about the failure of external auditors to detect management wrongdoing. The collapse of Enron through internal fraud caused by failure to adhere to the internal controls in place is probably the best known financial failure of our era. Not only were billions of dollars in stakeholder assets lost, but Arthur Andersen, one of the then Big-Five public accounting firms, was forced to close as a result of complicity in aiding the unethical practices at Enron.

LEARNING OBJECTIVE 3
Explain the control implications of the Foreign Corrupt Practices and Sarbanes-Oxley Acts.

Legislators' Interest in Internal Control

All publicly traded companies are required by law to have internal control. The management of companies registered with the Securities and Exchange Commission (SEC) may be fined or imprisoned if the company intentionally fails to comply with the requirement to have adequate internal control. This legal liability stems from the **Foreign Corrupt Practices Act (FCPA)** of 1977, amended in 1998.

The FCPA was enacted in response to allegations of corporate wrongdoing that happened during the 1970's. From the testimony of corporate executives, the SEC learned of (1) money "laundering," often involving foreign banks, for the purpose of making illegal domestic political contributions and (2) the payment of bribes to foreign officials to secure export sales. To deter these kinds of activities, the FCPA did two things: (1) it established criminal liability for bribery of foreign officials by any U.S. company (with an amendment to include "foreign firms and persons who cause, directly or through agents, an act in furtherance of such a corrupt payment to take place within the territory of the United States")[2] and (2) it established provisions for record keeping and internal control for all companies registered with the SEC. Essentially, this meant keeping accurate records and devising and maintaining adequate internal control to protect company assets. Internal controls also provide reasonable assurance that transactions are executed with management's authorization and are recorded completely for the accurate preparation of financial statements. Good controls imply that access to assets is permitted only with management's authorization, and recorded assets are compared with existing assets at reasonable intervals to check for inconsistencies.

The **Sarbanes-Oxley Act of 2002 (SOX)** was passed in 2002 to protect investors by improving the "transparency" (i.e., accuracy and reliability) of corporate disclosures issued by publicly-held companies after financial disasters such as the Enron debacle. In addition to establishing the **Public Company Accounting Oversight Board (PCAOB)** to issue auditing standards, oversee quality control, and set independence standards, there are several sections of this act that directly address internal control issues, but the most important is section 404, which has two major subsections:

Source: Ellen McKnight/Shutterstock.

Foreign Corrupt Practices Act (FCPA) An act that (1) established criminal liability for bribery of foreign officials by any U.S. company and (2) established provisions for record keeping and internal control for all companies registered with the Securities and Exchange Commission.

Sarbanes-Oxley Act of 2002 (SOX) Passed in 2002 to protect investors by improving the "transparency" (i.e., accuracy and reliability) of corporate disclosures issued by publicly-held companies after financial disasters such as the Enron debacle.

Public Company Accounting Oversight Board (PCAOB) An organization created by the Sarbanes-Oxley Act of 2002 to issue auditing standards, oversee quality control, and set independence standards for auditors of public companies.

- Section 404(a) discusses management's responsibilities with regard to the establishment, maintenance, and assessment of the internal control system, focusing on the "key" controls over the management objective related to the reliability of financial reporting. The internal control system must be attested to by executive management and a report must be issued with the annual (audited) financial statements. This report includes certification of management's responsibility for establishing, maintaining, and testing the internal controls, and must identify the framework on which the system is evaluated (e.g., COSO 2013, described below).

- Section 404(b) addresses the independent auditor's issuance of an opinion on management's report of the internal controls of the company. This opinion is separate from the general audit opinion issued traditionally with regard to the fairness of the financial statements. In addition, the type of opinion regarding management's assessment of the internal control system can be different than the opinion on the fairness of the financial statements (e.g., a qualification on the internal controls opinion, but an unqualified opinion on the fairness of the financial statements).

Another piece of legislation, The Federal Deposit Insurance Corporation Improvement Act (effective 1993), requires the management of banks and thrifts with assets of

$150 million or more to assess and report annually on the effectiveness of the institution's internal control. The Federal Deposit Insurance Corporation Improvement Act also requires that the financial institution's external auditors report on management's assertions about internal control.[3]

External Auditors' Interest in Internal Control

LEARNING OBJECTIVE 4
Explain why external auditors are interested in a client's internal control.

External auditors are interested in internal control as they perform financial statement audits so they can express an opinion on how fairly a company's financial statements present its financial position, results of operations, and cash flows in conformity with generally accepted accounting principles. This opinion has a direct bearing on the credibility of the financial statements produced by the accounting system. In the past, auditors were subject only to the Statements on Auditing Standards (SAS), but with the passage of SOX and the establishment of the Public Company Accounting Oversight Board (PCAOB), auditors now must comply with both SAS and PCAOB Auditing Standards. An important definition of the auditor's responsibility can be found in the Statement on Auditing Standard No. 94, which addresses the role of external auditors. SAS No. 94 requires that the auditor obtain an understanding of internal control sufficient to plan the audit by performing procedures to understand the design of controls relevant to an audit of financial statements. SAS Nos. 104-111 expand this responsibility by requiring auditors to have an understanding of the IT environment as it relates to the financial information stored, processed, and used in reporting.

If internal control is ineffective, the entire burden of the auditors' opinion must be borne by testing the accounting records. On the other hand, if control is found to be effective, the auditors can place some degree of reliance on it and correspondingly reduce the level of required testing. The Public Company Accounting Oversight Board (PCAOB) has issued a series of auditing standards related to the testing of internal controls for SOX-compliance purposes. The standards have recently been reorganized (refer to https://pcaobus.org/Standards/Auditing/Pages/ReorgStandards.aspx) and are intended to encourage auditors to focus on detecting material misstatement of the financial statements and any related material disclosures. According to the PCAOB AS 2201, which addresses the auditor's responsibility to determine any material misstatements, examples of entity-level controls relevant to analyzing the proper presentation and disclosure of financial statements include controls over:

- The internal control environment (e.g., as defined in the COSO 2013 framework)
- Management override
- Risk assessment performed by the organization
- Centralized processing
- The monitoring of operations' results
- Other monitoring functions, such as internal auditing, the audit committee, and self-assessment programs
- Period-end reporting processes resulting in financial reports (e.g., procedures for journal entries and adjustments)
- Policies addressing significant business risks/risk management processes

Professional Organizations' Interest in Internal Control

LEARNING OBJECTIVE 5
Explain what positions several professional organizations have taken regarding internal control.

From the 1990s to the present, several professional organizations have addressed the concept of internal control. While specific to the needs of their different audiences, the following documents all provide similar views about the nature and purpose of internal control and the methods to audit and achieve effective internal control:

- The Committee of Sponsoring Organizations of the Treadway Commission's *Internal Control—Integrated Framework* (IC)[4]

- The Committee of Sponsoring Organizations of the Treadway Commission's *Enterprise Risk Management—Integrated Framework (ERM),* first issued in 2004 and currently under revision[5]
- The Institute of Internal Auditors Research Foundation's *Systems Auditability and Control Report (SAC)*
- The Information Systems Audit and Control Foundation's *Control Objectives for Information and Related Technology* (currently COBIT 5)
- The American Institute of Certified Public Accountants' Statement on Standards for Attestation Engagements (SSAE) 16: Reporting on Controls at a Service Organization (superseding the American Institute of Certified Public Accountants' Statement of Auditing Standard (SAS) No. 70—Service Organizations)
- The American Institute of Certified Public Accountants' Service Organization Control Reports (SOC-1, SOC-2, SOC-3)
- The American Institute of Certified Public Accountants' Statement of Auditing Standard (SAS) No. 94—The Effect of Information Technology on the Auditor's Consideration of Internal Control in a Financial Statement Audit: An Amendment to SAS No. 55
- The American Institute of Certified Public Accountants' Statement of Auditing Standard (SAS) No. 99—Consideration of Fraud in a Financial Statement Audit.
- The American Institute of Certified Public Accountants' Statement of Auditing Standard (SAS) No. 109—Understanding the Entity and Its Environment and Assessing the Risks of Material Misstatement[6]

The first Committee of Sponsoring Organizations (COSO) internal control report was a result of the efforts of the National Commission on Fraudulent Financial Reporting (known as the Treadway Commission). This committee was organized in response to the rash of fraudulent financial reporting of the late 1970s and 1980s.[7] The Committee of Sponsoring Organizations developed a common definition and framework of internal control that culminated with the issuance of *Internal Control—Integrated Framework* in 1992. This report establishes a common definition serving the needs of different parties and provides a standard against which organizations assess their internal control and determine how to improve it. COSO defines internal control as a process, affected by an entity's board of directors, management, and other personnel, designed to provide reasonable assurance regarding the achievement of objectives related to the effectiveness and efficiency of operations, the reliability of financial reporting and compliance with applicable laws and regulations. Designed primarily for management, the COSO report makes recommendations on evaluating, reporting, and improving internal control. This *Internal Control—Integrated Framework* has become a widely accepted authority on internal control; an updated version was released in May 2013 and is now the internal control framework required for publicly-traded companies in the US (illustrated in **Exhibit 6.1**). While the five components of the framework did not change, the 2013 version of the integrated framework (referred to as COSO 2013) includes 17 principles to further define and explain the components while considering the effects of changes in the organizational environment. The discussion of internal control in this and the next chapter will be organized to reflect the **COSO 2013** framework.

Since AS 2201 focuses on the top-down approach to identifying entity-level controls, the focus of both management and external auditors is risk-focused.[8] In addition, internal auditors and management have become much more conscious of the role of risk in strategy setting and control development.

The Institute of Internal Auditors Research Foundation's Systems Auditability and Control Report (SAC Report 1991, revised 1994) provides guidance for internal auditors on the audit and control of information systems and technology. SAC defines internal control as a system consisting of a set of processes, functions, activities, subsystems,

COSO 2013 An internal control framework developed by The Committee of Sponsoring Organizations that is required for publicly-traded companies in the U.S.

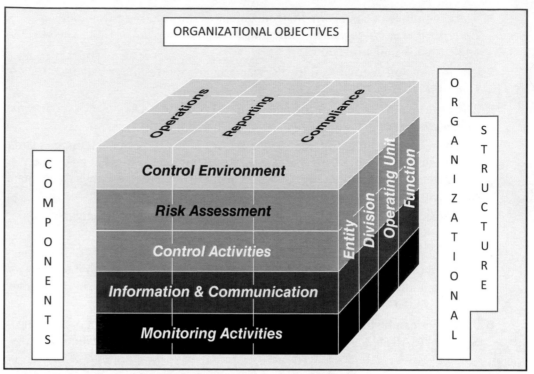

EXHIBIT 6.1 Internal Control Framework

Source: The Committee of Sponsoring Organizations of the Treadway Commission, Internal Control—
Integrated Framework, Executive Summary, May 2013 Also available at:
www.coso.org/documents/coso 2013 icfr executive_summary.pdf

and people who are grouped together or deliberately segregated to ensure the effective achievement of organizational objectives.

The ISACA (formerly the Information Systems Audit and Control Association) COBIT 5 framework, is a standard for information technology (IT) governance. This framework combines three frameworks previously developed to provide: (1) IT governance guidance (COBIT 4.1), (2) value delivery for IT (ValIT), and (3) IT risk management (RiskIT). COBIT 5 provides:

- A comprehensive framework to assist organizations in achieving strategic goals and deliver value through effective governance and management of IT.

- Guidance to organizations in maintaining a balance between benefits and risks of IT

- A holistic approach to management of IT, taking into consideration interests of internal and external stakeholders.

- A framework that is useful in all commercial, not-for-profit, and public sector businesses regardless of size of organization.[9]

The AICPA's Statement on Standards for Attestation Engagements (SSAE) 16: *Reporting on Controls at a Service Organization* (effective June 2011) supersedes the SAS 70 recommendations. SAS No. 70 (effective April 1992) was developed to provide guidance to auditors in attesting to the effectiveness of internal controls of third-party service providers (TPSP) engaged by their audit clients. The new standard in many ways is simply an expansion of the SAS 70 requirements to be more in line with regulatory requirements (e.g., International Financial Reporting Standards, SOX 2002), although the auditor's work is considered an attestation and not an audit. SSAE 16 requires a report similar to the Type II SAS 70 report.[10] In addition to a review and a report of the internal controls over financial statement reporting, SSAE 16 includes a "management assertion" section. In this section, the management of the TPSP provides a written assertion as to the fairness of the description of the third-party service provider's (TPSP) system, as well as the suitability and effectiveness of the financial reporting controls.

The AICPA Service Organization Control (SOC) reports provide guidance for evaluating TPSP controls as follows:

- SOC-1: Internal controls over financial reporting (guidance for evaluating the internal controls over financial reporting of a TPSP for use by user management, TPSP management, and the auditor).

- SOC-2: Controls over security/systems and privacy (guidance for the evaluation of privacy, confidentiality, and security of data of the TPSP).

- SOC-3: Technical practice aid for SOC-2 (similar to SOC-2, but the resulting report can be used by the public or as a marketing tool by the TPSP).

The AICPA's SAS No. 94 (effective June 1, 2001) emphasizes reliable financial reporting and external auditing and incorporates COSO's definition and description of internal control. This standard describes how information technology may affect internal control, the auditor's understanding of internal control, and the assessment of control risk.

The AICPA's SAS No. 99 provides guidance for external auditors to analyze the potential for fraudulent activity. This standard includes requirements for documented audit team brainstorming sessions regarding the possibility of misstatement of the financial statements due to fraud.

As a group, the AICPA's SAS Nos. 104-111 (effective December 15, 2006) require the auditor to use a risk-based approach to auditing high-risk areas. This includes the IT environment, which produces the financial information. This implies that auditors must have a thorough understanding of the IT environment. Specifically, SAS No. 109 requires the external auditor to gain an understanding of the risks associated with their clients with regard to their regulatory, legal, and political environment. This guidance is related to the COSO framework component requiring an assessment of risk of material misstatement of the financial statements.

The discussion in this chapter and Chapter 7 is based on the concepts reflected by COSO, ERM, SAC, COBIT, SOX, SSAE No. 16, the SOC reports, SAS No. 94, SAS No. 99 and SAS Nos. 104-111. The following discussion of the integrated control framework follows the COSO 2013 model illustrated in Exhibit 6.1.

Integrated Control Framework

To understand how management and other groups within an organization develop, maintain, and continuously improve internal control, we begin by discussing the framework in Exhibit 6.1.

The framework illustrates the relationships among three types of organizational objectives. Organizational (or entity) objectives, which are desired results, are directly related to internal control components because these components must be present for an organization to achieve the objectives.

The three categories of objectives in the framework are:

- Effectiveness and efficiency of operations
- Reliability of both internal and external reporting
- Compliance with applicable laws and regulations

The framework also illustrates that entity objectives and the COSO 2013 framework components can be viewed in the context of their relationship with any of the following:

- The entire organization/entity-level
- A division
- An operating unit
- A function

LEARNING OBJECTIVE 6
Describe the relationship among organizational objectives and components of the COSO 2013 framework.

Organizational Objectives

Organizational objectives The critical results that management must achieve to increase the organization's probability of being successful. The three categories of organizational objectives are effectiveness and efficiency of operations, reliability of both internal and external reporting, and compliance with applicable laws and regulations.

Organizational objectives are the critical results that management must achieve to increase the organization's probability of being successful. As mentioned before, the three categories of organizational objectives are as follows:

- Effectiveness and efficiency of operations
- Reliability of both internal and external reporting
- Compliance with applicable laws and regulations

Before management can identify events that may have positive or negative impacts on the organization's operations, objectives must first be developed. The COSO 2013 framework provides a process for management to set objectives related to the efficiency of operations, the reliability of internal and external reporting, and compliance with related laws and regulations. These categories are not mutually exclusive; management and the board of directors should focus on the separate aspects of their risk management, as well as identify who is responsible for maintaining the objectives. The safeguarding of resources is an objective which overlaps with several categories of objectives. The safeguarding of resources is not only a compliance and strategic objective (e.g., prevent fines from non-compliance with SOX and financial losses from losing a competitive advantage), but also ties into the reporting objective (e.g., the detection of unauthorized use of an asset) and the operations objective (e.g., preventing the sale of a product at too low a price). Discussion of the three categories of objectives are discussed next.

Effectiveness and Efficiency of Operations Objective

The objective of effective and efficient operations pertains to the operations that are fundamental to an organization's existence, such as the development of new products, the manufacture of products, the marketing of products, and the provision of services. The effectiveness and efficiency of these operations are critical to an organization's success. An implicit message in this objective is the need for an organization to be responsive to competitive pressures and technological changes.

The safeguarding of assets, such as cash, inventory, investments, accounting data, and the accounting system, is also part of the operations objective. Assets need to be safeguarded against unauthorized acquisition, use, or disposition. Measures for safeguarding assets range from simply locking up cash to bonding employees who handle negotiable securities.[11] Another way to safeguard assets is to protect computer hardware, software, and data from unauthorized access and use. If data can be altered by individuals who stand to gain personally, enormous problems can arise (Vignette 6.2). Physical safeguards to protect accounting information systems from failure or destruction include fire prevention, insurance, preventive maintenance, and backup files.

Reliability of Reporting Objective

Reliable information is accurate, current, complete, relevant, accessible, and, when necessary, confidential. Some information is confidential (e.g., payroll data and competitive strategy information) and access to that information should be limited. Reliable information also requires adherence to generally accepted accounting principles for the preparation of financial statements. In addition, the COSO 2013 framework also focuses on the reliability of information used for internal reporting. This includes both financial and non-financial information used for decision-making. This objective is important because stakeholders, management, and others rely on reliable information for making critical decisions.

Compliance Objective

An organization must comply with applicable laws and regulations. These laws and regulations relate to, for example, taxes, the environment, international trade, and employment

Vignette 6.2

Unauthorized Access to Data

At a motel furnishings retailer with $300 million in annual sales, quarterly bonuses for product managers depended primarily on sales contracts signed. A product manager was responsible for credenzas, for example, and might carry as many as two dozen styles that were available from six different manufacturers. The retailer's primary customer was a major motel chain. Sales contracts with the motel chain called for supplying most of the more than 500 different items of furniture and equipment needed to open a new or remodeled motel.

The typical sales contract ran about one year from the signing of the contract to the delivery of the furnishings in the last 30 days before the opening of a motel. The timing of deliveries was critical because it was most efficient to unload directly from the trucks into the motel. However, most motel projects ran into some delays, causing deliveries to be made to temporary warehouses in the city where the motel was located.

The retailer also maintained inventory at warehouses in its headquarters' city. Although most furnishings were drop-shipped from the manufacturer to the motel site, some inventory wound up in possession of the retailer because of mistakes in style, timing errors, and closeouts of particular manufacturers.

Product managers would buy as many as 1,000 units of the most popular product styles. Upon completion of production, the manufacturer would ship any items needed at motel sites and store the remainder until the retailer needed to have the items delivered to other motel sites. All inventory, whether located in a warehouse at the motel site or at headquarters or held by the manufacturer for later delivery, was the property of the motel furnishings retailer.

The accounting system that handled the very complex mix of products and contracts was programmed to refuse a sales order for any product unless the product was in inventory or was on order for availability before the proposed delivery date on the particular sales contract. Management felt this refusal feature would

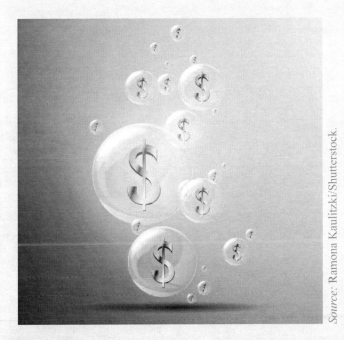

Source: Ramona Kaulitzki/Shutterstock.

force product managers to better manage their product line inventories.

During the physical inventory count at close of the fiscal year, an $11,000,000 inventory shortage was identified. After substantial and costly rechecking, it was found that product managers had discovered that no internal controls were in place to prevent them from entering data that indicated products were on order when, in fact, they were not. By entering "phantom inventory," with availability dates to match immediate needs, the system would accept sales contracts and increase the product managers' bonuses.

THOUGHT QUESTIONS

1. How could the problem with the "phantom inventories" have been avoided?

2. What kind of incentives would have discouraged the activities discussed in this vignette?

---

issues. All organizations must obey the law of the land, but certain industries, such as financial institutions and health-care facilities, must also comply with specific regulations prescribed by government agencies. An organization's compliance or noncompliance with laws and regulations can have a significant impact on its reputation.

Components of Internal Control

The COSO 2013 framework includes several internal control components that are needed to achieve the organizational objectives in the framework, which were discussed in the previous section. The achievement of any category of organizational objectives, for

LEARNING OBJECTIVE 8
Recognize how internal control components are integrated.

Components of internal control The elements that enable an organization to achieve management objectives. The internal control components are the control environment, risk assessment, control activities, information and communication, and monitoring.

example, reliability of reporting, depends on whether the five internal control components are present and functioning effectively. These interrelated **components of internal control** in the COSO 2013 framework include the following:

- Control environment
- Risk assessment
- Control activities
- Information and communication
- Monitoring

You will recall these five internal control components are depicted in Exhibit 6.1 and are shown again in **Exhibit 6.2**.

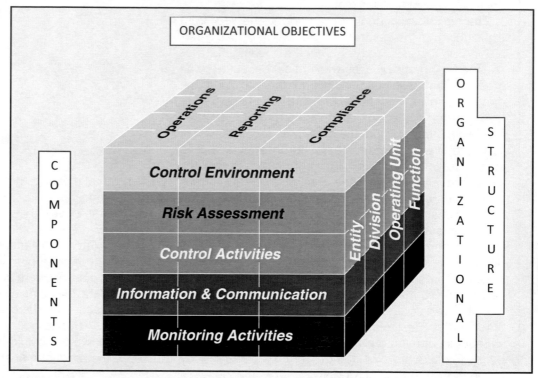

EXHIBIT 6.2 COSO 2013—Integrated Framework

The control environment is the basis for the framework because it serves as the foundation for the other components and influences the entire system. Once objectives are set, an assessment of risk can be completed. Assessment of risk has recently received considerable attention, as compliance with section 404 of the Sarbanes-Oxley Act and several PCAOB Auditing Standards require the identification of risk exposures and an assessment of the effectiveness of "key" controls. Monitoring relates to management's scrutiny of the effectiveness of the other framework components and, therefore, is the last component in the cube. Information and communication support the other components, which in turn, support the information system.

The control environment and risk assessment components are discussed in depth in this chapter. Control activities (some of which address assurance of the quality of information) and monitoring are discussed in Chapter 7. This entire textbook addresses accounting information systems, which include the activities of capturing, processing, storing, and communicating data. The information and communication component of the COSO 2013 framework includes three related principles: principle 13 (the importance of relevant information to support functioning of the internal controls), principle 14 (the importance of communicating information to support internal control), and principle 15 (communication of information to external parties about the internal control system). These principles are addressed in Chapter 5.

Therefore, to avoid repetition, information and communication (and related principles) will not be discussed as a separate component of internal control.

Control Environment

The **control environment** is the organizational infrastructure that supports internal control. The control environment establishes the tone of an organization and influences the control consciousness of an organization's board of directors, management, internal auditors, and other personnel. It also provides discipline and structure by influencing how strategy and objectives are set, as well as how risks are assessed and addressed. In addition, the control environment affects how control activities are designed and monitored. The control environment in COSO 2013 includes five principles that address the following:

1. Integrity and ethical values
2. Board of directors and the audit committee that are independent of management and oversee the internal control process (to include IT governance)
3. Organizational structure, to include the assignment of authority and responsibilities
4. Human resource policies and practices that relate to hiring and development of competent personnel
5. Individuals are accountable to uphold and maintain internal control responsibilities

LEARNING OBJECTIVE 9
Discuss the factors of the control environment.

Control environment The foundation for the other components of internal control. It establishes the tone of an organization and influences the control consciousness of the organization.

All of these factors are important, but the extent to which each needs to be emphasized varies from organization to organization. For example, a small organization may have a strong control environment in spite of not having a formal organizational structure.

Factors such as the board of directors and human resource policies and practices may seem a long way from the accounting system. However, accounting information systems are not simply software packages or sets of procedures for printing paychecks and invoices and preparing reports. Nor do they operate in an organizational vacuum. Accounting systems operate at the heart of the organization, affecting the way it conducts its business, influencing the way that most business decisions are made, and exposing the whole range of resources at the organization's disposal to proper use or abuse. To ensure that the organizational objectives are achieved and the accounting system does its job, organizations should take whatever steps are necessary to establish and maintain a favorable control environment.

Principle 1: *Integrity and ethical values* are important principles of the control environment. Because an organization's good reputation can determine its success, standards for the behavior of employees should extend far beyond those required to be in compliance with the law. Sarbanes-Oxley Act section 404 requires that management disclose the presence of an ethics code for employees. Most organizations' codes of ethics include expected ethical principles such as honesty, fairness, objectivity, due diligence, and responsibility.[12]

Management should implement an ethics program that includes a code of conduct, training and awareness programs, and policies for resolving ethical dilemmas. Management can also encourage honest and ethical conduct by setting a good example, reminding employees of its commitment to integrity and ethics, and reducing temptation and opportunity for dishonest, illegal, or unethical acts. An organization's integrity and ethical values affect the design, administration, and monitoring of the other factors of the control environment.

Principle 2: *The independence of board of directors and the audit committee* are essential to the success of the control environment. The **board of directors** is a committee

Board of directors
A committee that primarily represents stockholders but may also represent employees, communities, and environmental interests. The board is responsible for overseeing operations, evaluating management's performance, and assuring that the organization is in compliance with applicable laws and regulations.

that represents the organization's shareholders whose interests generally are considered paramount. Increasingly, boards also are charged with representing employees, communities, and environmental interests. The board is responsible for overseeing operations, evaluating management's performance, and assuring that the organization is in compliance with applicable laws and regulations. Boards set broad policies and see that they are carried out. They typically choose the chief executive and participate in selecting other senior officers. More specific responsibilities vary, depending on the organization's charter and the nature of the business.

The board of directors should be independent from management. An independent board of directors is one in which its members are outside directors, that is, without financial or other ties to the organization. Board members who are also executives or are financially dependent on management's decisions (i.e., not independent) may not be as objective in evaluating management's activities as are board members who are independent. Also, if the board's chairperson is independent from management, the chairperson will be in a better position to facilitate a discussion of management's performance (Vignette 6.3). A chairperson who is also an executive of the company

---

Vignette 6.3

Should the Board Chairperson Be an Executive?

Burrin Corporation's sales and profits had slipped from their highs of 3 years ago. Everyone knew that the company faced increasing pressure from foreign competition and general maturing of the industry. However, some directors wondered whether Jay Kelly, CEO and chairman of the board, was the man to turn the company around. Kelly was a "numbers man" who had come up through corporate finance. He had an exceptionally good feel for the bottom line but had demonstrated little ability to sense technological and market trends.

Prior to the June bimonthly board meeting, venture capitalist Linda Lopez and another independent board member requested a full discussion of Kelly's performance. Kelly had no option but to comply. However, he manufactured twelve other agenda issues, guaranteed to generate extensive discussion, and put them ahead of Lopez's item.

By the time Lopez's agenda item was reached, it was late in the evening and some of the directors had already left. One of Kelly's cohorts on the board proposed deferring discussion of the CEO's performance until the next meeting "because of its obvious importance to all of us." Lopez had little choice but to concur. After the meeting, several board members expressed support for Lopez's position and shared their own impatience with Kelly's stalling tactics.

However, when Lopez received the agenda for the August meeting, she was surprised to see several items still ahead of her requested discussion. Fortunately for her cause—although not so fortunately for the company—two days before the meeting, Kelly was bound over to a grand jury on a fraud charge. With the

Source: mariakraynova/Shutterstock.

board shaken by that event and some other suspicions of high-level fraud, Lopez was able to convince the directors to appoint a nonexecutive chairperson.

Kelly remained as CEO pending the outcome of the grand jury's deliberations. Meanwhile, the board instructed the audit committee to conduct its own investigations into possible fraud and to report to the October meeting.

THOUGHT QUESTIONS

1. What are the conflicting incentives that Jay Kelly was facing (e.g., shareholder incentives vs. management incentives)?

2. What are some things that the board could have done to more effectively address the issues brought up by Linda Lopez and the other independent board member?

(frequently the chief executive officer) may be unwilling to expose information that is critical of upper management.

The **audit committee** is a standing subcommittee of independent board members (discussed in SOX section 301) whose main objectives are to protect against management wrongdoing and to oversee the audit function (both internal and external). It is responsible for the appointment, compensation, and oversight of the work of the public accounting firm hired by the company for the purposes of preparing or issuing an audit report or related work (i.e., the external audit). The public accounting firm and internal audit director report directly to the audit committee, and the audit committee sets procedures for dealing with audit findings. The audit committee is an extension of the oversight role of the board of directors and, consequently, reports directly to the board.

The Public Company Accounting Oversight Board (PCAOB) requires at least one member of the audit committee to be a "financial expert" (SOX section 407). A financial expert is a person who has an understanding of generally accepted accounting principles and financial statements; has experience in the preparation or auditing of financial statements; has experience in the application of generally accepted accounting principles in connection with the accounting for estimates, accruals, and reserves; has experience with internal accounting controls; and has an understanding of audit committee functions.

IT Governance is an essential ingredient to maintaining a strong control environment. The importance of having an ongoing risk management process for the organization is essential to its long-term success. The emergence of information technology (IT) governance, a discipline that emerged in the early 2000s, is a subset of enterprise governance and includes issues surrounding IT management and security. IT governance focuses on handling transactions, events, and decision-making with regard to IT responsibly; fully disclosing the performance measures used; using independent review and practicing continuous improvement; and adapting to the constantly changing business environment. An organization with effective IT governance would include best practices such as proper asset management to include the oversight and tracking of assets within the organization (e.g., mobile devices and software licenses).

Management's philosophy and operating style are also important in the control environment. Executive management's philosophy and operating style are elements that exert a great deal of influence on the control environment. To establish the vision of the organization, management determines the organization's risk management strategy, establishes the organization's level of acceptable risk, and develops a risk culture. Important in this regard are the following:

- *Behavior toward Other Managers or Personnel.* Do managers work together as a cooperative team? Does a manager listen to his or her subordinates' suggestions or concerns and try to promote a pleasant working environment? Or does the manager regard personnel as expendable commodities?

- *Approach to Business Risk.* Is the organization's risk management philosophy understood by all employees? The risk philosophy reflects the organization's beliefs about risk, as well as how it chooses to deal with those risks in the context of its business activities (sometimes referred to as "risk appetite"; managing risk is discussed in a later section). While most areas of business require managers to take calculated risks, excessive risk-taking may indicate the lack of stability needed for long-term success (Vignette 6.4).

- *Attitude Regarding the Accounting Function.* Because controllers are employees of the organization and ordinarily are expected to take orders from senior managers, management plays a big role in accounting functions. How conscientiously does management make and use accounting estimates? Do managers make responsible budget requests, or do they play budget games? How does management choose among

Audit committee A standing subcommittee of the board of directors whose main objectives are to protect against management wrongdoing and to increase public confidence in the independent auditor's opinion.

IT (information technology) governance A subset of enterprise governance and includes issues surrounding IT management and security.

One Risk Too Many

Elise Minichello built her Wall Street investment brokerage firm almost single-handedly. She had increased annual revenues from $80 million to $600 million over a 10-year period. Minichello had an uncanny knack for knowing when to get into a market and when to get out. An article in a leading business magazine described Minichello as "someone who is really comfortable with risk."

However, her luck ran out in 2008. For years, her controller, Bruce Berlin, had been advising that the control environment needed to be improved. Minichello understood the need for checks on accounting accuracy and control of assets. The accounting information system was first rate and was operated by competent people. Procedures for handling cash and entering transaction data were virtually faultless. Extensive vault facilities had been installed for storing investment instruments, and armed security guards patrolled the building. But Minichello was unwilling to spend money on improving the control environment. Her response to Berlin's recommendation was, "Margins are slim in the finance world. If I bought 'insurance' for everything that could go wrong, I would be out of business. I have to live with risk, and so must the company."

Unfortunately, the control environment was her undoing. Richard Duffy, the corporate treasurer, embezzled $45 million of investors' funds. Over 18 months, he used his knowledge of EFT (electronic funds transfer) codes to shift the money to offshore bank accounts. Unknown to Minichello, he "earned" an additional $12 million in fees for laundering drug money through the brokerage. Three days before his schemes were discovered, he caught a plane to Argentina. Subsequent investigations showed that he had been charged once before with embezzlement but had been acquitted for lack of evidence. When interviewed by CNN at his new home in Buenos Aires, Duffy said that he had learned about effective risk-taking from his former boss. She was fortunate to be able to take risks legally; he had fewer opportunities and had to do it any way he could. He was sorry to have upset Minichello because he liked her and still considered her an important role model.

THOUGHT QUESTIONS

1. What were some of the areas of weakness in the control environment for Minichello's firm?

2. How could the embezzlement scheme have been avoided?

3. What recommendations would you make to Minichello to improve the control environment (assuming the firm survived the embezzlement)?

---

alternative accounting principles? Do they adjust estimates to support preconceived arguments or to justify decisions that are not in the organization's best interest?

■ *Attitude Regarding Information Processing.* What factors are considered in making decisions about information processing (i.e., what is the role of IT governance in these decisions)? For example, would management delay the implementation of a new accounting system if adequate controls were not in place? Are decisions regarding development and implementation of systems part of the enterprise governance process?

Management's philosophy and operating style are reflected throughout the organization. If top management demonstrates its belief that internal control is important, other people in the organization will sense that commitment. As a result, an organizational culture can develop that supports efforts to strengthen the control environment. Such a culture reflects the attitude that risky ventures and corner-cutting should be approached with caution, human beings have dignity and value, organizational plans should be carried out, and high quality accounting data should be regarded as being in everyone's best interest. On the other hand, if management ignores internal control, the organizational culture may reflect a pervasive attitude that internal control is not considered important to the company's success.

Principle 3: *Organization structure* is another principle of the control environment. A formal **organizational structure** provides the framework within which the organization's activities for achieving its objectives are planned, executed, monitored, and controlled. Limits of managerial authority, areas of responsibility, and lines of reporting are defined. Limits of authority define what decisions can be made by which managers. Areas of responsibility define who is expected to do what. Lines of reporting define the relationships that tie together the areas of responsibility. The organizational structure is expressed in and documented by an organizational chart and job descriptions.

Organizational structure The framework within which the organization's activities for achieving its objectives are planned, executed, monitored, and controlled.

The organizational structure may be centralized or decentralized. A centralized organization retains the authority for decision-making at the top level of management while a decentralized organization systematically pushes decision-making authority downward to middle and lower managers. Organizational size or geographical extent does not necessarily imply decentralization. In a decentralized organization, significant authority may be delegated to the managers of business units. Business units may be distinguished by industry or product line, geographical location, functional activity, distribution or marketing network, or a particular project.

Assignment of authority and responsibility is part of the organizational structure. Assignment of authority and responsibility establishes authorization hierarchies and reporting relationships. In many organizations today, delegation of authority to control certain business decisions is being pushed downward to bring decision-making closer to front-line personnel. Delegating authority can often enhance creativity, initiative, and accountability. This delegation of authority increases an organization's capability to react quickly to competitive forces and to customers' needs.

If patterns of authority, responsibility, and reporting are not clear, the control environment usually suffers. Patterns of responsibility can be unclear when an organization has a matrix structure and the manager's responsibilities cross several different divisions or departments, or ambiguities may arise during the transition following a corporate merger or the departure of an authoritarian CEO. Ambiguity is sometimes allowed to become permanent, either deliberately or through negligence. An insecure but power-hungry manager may foster ambiguity as a tool to "divide and conquer," leaving employees in doubt about their decision-making authority or their areas of responsibility. Or a manager may try to convince another manager's employees that he or she controls part of their activities, when in fact no such authority exists. Organizational ambiguity can also persist simply because of management's ineptitude.

Principle 4: *Commitment to competence and development of personnel* contributes to the integrity of the control environment. Competence reflects the knowledge, skills, and abilities required to perform duties appropriately, reliably, and in accordance with applicable laws, regulations, and technical standards. To foster competence, management should establish job requirements and descriptions that specify what knowledge, skills, and abilities are necessary for each position in the organization. Moreover, management should enforce the hiring of only those people who meet these job requirements. To maintain employees' professional competence, development activities must go beyond the initial orientation training and be updated throughout an employee's career. Management can further demonstrate its commitment to competence by letting personnel know it expects high quality performance.

Human resource policies and practices are factors of the control environment. Personnel policies that address hiring, orientation, training, evaluating, counseling, compensating, promoting, and remedial actions help organizations build a team of employees with integrity, ethical values, and competence. An organization should hire the most qualified individuals based on their educational background, prior work experience,

---

Vignette 6.5

Dead-End Job

Following several reports of internal control problems in an insurance company, an internal auditor interviewed several junior managers in the claims department. The remarks of an apparently bright man in his early thirties were as follows:

"I came here 5 years ago believing all the hype about long-term career opportunities and the corporate mission statement about building employee loyalty. But I haven't seen any of it yet. Until recently, I worked hard because I basically like the insurance business. But I get no recognition. Our annual evaluations are a joke. My boss catches me in the hall and asks that I sign the evaluation because it has to be in that afternoon. If I get to see the evaluation at all, it's a glance through the form while he drinks from the water fountain. Apart from one time when we went on a trip together, he has never sat down with me and given me any feedback. Of course, it's not altogether his fault. He has to attend all those meetings and cope with mounds of paperwork.

"Last year we all received an across-the-board 3 percent raise. This year, there were a few merit raises, but they went to the boss's friends. The final blow came when a middle management position opened up in underwriting. I applied for the position because I once worked in an insurance underwriting department, and I really thought I could do a good job. But the company brought in someone from a competing organization. I have nothing against him, but he has less experience than I do. The announcement said that he brought 'refreshing new ideas to the company.' Over the last 3 years, most senior positions have been filled from outside.

"There's no future here. I've had my resume out for 4 months now, and I've already received a couple of tempting offers. When the right offer comes, I'm off. It doesn't surprise me that there have been control problems here. Nobody in the department is happy. Personally, I wouldn't do anything wrong, although I suspect one or two people of deliberate violations. I just goof off when no one is looking—which is most of the time."

THOUGHT QUESTIONS

1. If you were reviewing the results of the internal auditor's interview, how would you address the problems the junior manager points out in this vignette?

2. How can management improve morale and encourage excellence in its employees?

---

past accomplishments, and evidence of integrity and ethical behavior. Management must recognize the importance of effectively orienting and training personnel and should incorporate a variety of training techniques including online or face-to-face courses as well as on-the-job training.

Periodic performance reviews and counseling should focus on helping employees improve performance and add value to the organization. Employees should be properly compensated, and promotion policies should be fair and equitable. Promotions should reinforce outstanding performance, demonstrating the organization's commitment to the advancement of qualified personnel to higher levels of responsibility. Organizations seeking to fill senior positions must balance the advantages of bringing in new personnel from outside against the negative effects on the morale of their internal employees who may aspire to those positions (Vignette 6.5).

An organization should establish written policies and procedures stating the disciplinary actions that will follow violations of expected behavior. Prompt, impersonal disciplinary action sends a message that violations will not be tolerated.

In addition to sound personnel policies and practices, organizations should provide employees with the resources that will enable them to fulfill their job responsibilities. These resources include a supportive working environment, appropriate technology and information, and effective supervisors to whom they can turn for help.

Principle 5: *Accountability* for one's actions with regard to personnel understanding the organization's objectives, knowing how their individual actions interrelate and contribute to those objectives, and recognizing how and for what they will be held accountable.

Risk Assessment

Risk assessment is the systematic identification and analysis of risks that can undermine the achievement of organizational objectives. The COSO 2013 framework describes four principles under this component.

LEARNING OBJECTIVE 10
Understand the importance of risk assessment (to include an evaluation of the potential for fraud), and discuss how changes in the identified risks can change the risk profile of an organization.

> **Principle 6:** An organization's development of its objectives allows it to *identify and assess risks* that prevent the organization from meeting its objectives. Everyone knows that uncertainties exist, and that many of these uncertainties are not predictable. What this component is trying to get management to focus on is the identification of events that could affect the organization's success, both positively (i.e. opportunities) and negatively (i.e. risks to achievement of organizational objectives). These events are affected by both internal (e.g., management's choices with regard to technology) and external (e.g., economic uncertainty) factors. Both past (e.g., payment history) and future (e.g., shifting demographics) events should be considered.

> **Principle 7:** The identification of risk should be considered *across the entire organization* and management should consider *how they will manage these risks.*

The knowledge gained from risk assessment helps management set priorities so it can determine how the organization will manage risk. It is also a first step in developing an audit plan, and in determining how to address the compliance issues required by SOX section 404.

Management has a choice of four responses to risks identified in the risk assessment process: avoid, reduce (or mitigate), share, or accept. *Avoiding* the risk means stopping or quitting the activity so as to get rid of the risk completely. *Reducing or mitigating* the risk means that management takes steps to reduce the likelihood and/or impact of the identified risk, through control activities or other means. *Sharing* the risk means reducing the likelihood or impact of the risk by transferring some of the risk, that is, purchasing insurance to protect an organization from losses due to fire. *Accepting* the risk means taking no action to reduce the likelihood and/or impact of the risk. In some cases, a risk cannot be avoided, but the organization may decide to ignore the risk because it is either impossible to control, it is too expensive to control, or the realization of the risk will have little impact on the achievement of organizational objectives.

Risk assessment The systematic identification and analysis of risks that can undermine the achievement of management objectives. The knowledge gained from risk assessment helps management set priorities so it can determine what control activities to implement.

The risks addressed in the establishment, maintenance, and testing of a company's internal control system are both internal and external, and can undermine the objectives discussed above that relate to the accounting information system activities. The following are some representative types of risks that can threaten accounting information system activities:[13]

- Information security threats
- Computer system failure and/or improper backup of the system
- Accounting system's inability to meet the organization's and users' needs
- Excessive hardware and software acquisition costs
- Excessive operating and maintenance costs
- Inadequate training, development, and supervision of personnel

Information Security Threats

Information security threats include virus infection, "bots," unauthorized access, and theft or destruction of data and computing resources. The stakes in security attacks can be high, and detection rates are relatively low. Understandably, some organizations are reluctant to report security threats because they fear: 1) negative publicity (to shareholders, customers, and suppliers), 2) law enforcement will not be able to help, 3) the amount of loss will be immaterial or 4) competitors will exploit the negative news. Accurately estimating the annual cost of security threats to U.S. companies is difficult. We do know, however, that the total cost of security threats is considerable. The information in **Exhibit 6.3** shows the results of a survey conducted by ISACA and RSA in 2014.

Panel A		Panel B		Panel C	
Who Are the Threats?	Survey Percentage (n=636)	Which Attacks were Successful?	Survey Percentage (n=704)	Motivation for Attacks	Survey Percentage (n=741)
Cybercriminals (e.g., organized crime)	45.6	Phishing (e.g., "we need to have you verify transactions on your Capital One credit card")	68.3	Financial gain	32.8
Nonmalicious insiders (e.g., get into something they shouldn't, or access accidentally)	40.7	Malware (e.g., virus, Trojan horse)	66.5	Disruption of service	24.4
Hackers (e.g., try to break into network to plant malware or overwhelm system with requests)	40.1	Hacking attempts	50.1	Intellectual property theft	19.4
Malicious insiders (e.g., disgruntled employee wanting to "get back" at company)	28.6	Social engineering (e.g., "the Help Desk needs you to reconfirm your password")	46.5	Theft of personally identifiable information (PII)	11.7
Hactivists (e.g., just want to "embarrass" rather than receive financial gain)	19.8	Loss of mobile devices (e.g., mobile phones, tablets)	43.9	Theft of classified data	11.6
State-sponsored cybercriminals (e.g., government pays individuals to try to break into networks in other countries)	17.5	Insider theft (e.g., disgruntled employee)	25.3		
		SQL injections (e.g., SQL execution command that sends database information elsewhere)	21.9		
		Man-in-the-middle attacks (e.g., Stuxnet)	11.1		
		Watering hole (e.g., access a large oil company network by planting malware in a vendor's system)	7.5		

EXHIBIT 6.3 Information from ISACA's *State of Cybersecurity: Implications for 2015*

Source: State of Cybersecurity: Implications for 2015, an ISACA and RSA Conference Survey. ISACA's CSX Cybersecurity Nexus © 2015, data from figures 3, 4, and 9.

In the survey, respondents discussed the types of threats, successful attacks, and motivations for the attacks they experienced in 2014. In general, the largest number of reported exploits (Panel A) came from cybercriminals (45.6%), hackers (40.1%), and non-malicious insiders (40.7%). Note these percentages indicate that many of the respondents to the survey had more than one type of threat during the survey reporting period. The most successful attacks (Panel B) were from malware, phishing, hacking attempts, social engineering, and the loss of mobile devices.

The information security threats noted in the ISACA survey, along with some other common threats are defined below:

- **Malware** is defined as any kind of software meant to disrupt computer operations or secretly collect information (such as password or personal information). Examples of malware include computer viruses, worms, or Trojans. A **computer virus** is a set of executable computer instructions that copies itself into a larger program, modifying that program. In the present environment of shared programs, viruses can spread quickly, typically through infected external media (e.g., flash drives, CDs), networks, or bulletin boards. The Internet and public-domain software are prime sources of viruses. Sometimes a virus activates at a prescribed date in the future—long after being dispatched. Many viruses are simply annoying, but viruses that are more serious destroy programs and data.

- **Phishing** is what looks like a legitimate request for personal information such as passwords or bank account numbers. Typically, these are received via email and may include legitimate-looking logos (e.g., for a bank). Usually, there is a link or file that must be accessed to fulfill the request for personal information.

- **Hackers** are individuals able to gain unauthorized access to data. Hackers can be cybercriminals (e.g., associated with organized crime), state-sponsored (e.g., paid by a government to try to gain unauthorized access to data in another country), or someone who wants to embarrass or call attention to an organization (e.g., "hacktivists" such as Anonymous).

- **Social engineering** is slightly different that phishing in that someone poses as a legitimate individual requesting information. For example, someone posing as a help desk employee calls to "assist" with changing a password (when no request was made). The key is that human interaction is required so as to be able to manipulate or trick someone into providing confidential information.

- **Bots** are software robots that invade an organization's computers [referred to as "zombie computers," since the bots cause the computers to act automatically in response to the "bot-herder's" control inputs through an Internet relay chat (IRC) or other means]. Usually, the bot software is malicious and is installed through **worms** (self-replicating computer programs).

- " **Botnets**," the collection of zombie computers running the bot software, can cause:
  - **Denial of service (DoS)** describes a concerted effort to keep a service or Internet from functioning, either temporarily or indefinitely, by saturating the service with external requests that keep it from responding to legitimate requests.
  - **Spam**, the sending of unsolicited bulk information (usually associated with email spam)
  - Theft of user IDs or other confidential information

- **Trojan horses** (malware that appears to be performing normal functions but is in fact illicitly accessing the host machine to save their files on the user's computer or watch/control the user's computer), or **backdoors** (remotely accessing a computer without having to authenticate and while remaining undetected).

Malware Any kind of software meant to disrupt computer operations or secretly collect information (such as password or personal information).

Computer virus A set of executable computer instructions that copies itself into a larger program, modifying that program.

Phishing An information security breach where a request (an email, for example) for personal information such as passwords or bank account numbers appears to be legitimate.

Hackers Individuals who gain unauthorized access to data.

Social engineering An information security breach where a human being poses as a legitimate individual requesting confidential information such as a password.

Bots Software robots that invade an organization's computers.

Worms Self-replicating computer programs that can wreak havoc on operating systems, applications, file servers, or the entire system.

Botnets The collection of zombie computers running the bot software.

Denial of Service attacks (DoS) A concerted effort to keep a service or Internet from functioning, either temporarily or indefinitely, by saturating the service with external requests that keep it from responding to legitimate requests.

Spam The sending of unsolicited bulk information (usually associated with e-mail spam).

Trojan horses Malware that appears to be performing normal functions but is in fact illicitly accessing the host machine to save its files on the user's computer or to watch and/or control the user's computer.

Backdoors Remotely accessing a computer without having to authenticate all the while remaining undetected.

Unauthorized access may involve people either inside or outside the organization. Among the most common reasons for unauthorized access are industrial espionage, gaining insider information for investment purposes, or gathering information for blackmail or extortion. Perpetrators may alter data in a computer for unauthorized purposes, usually for personal gain. According to the survey respondents, the most common motivations for attacks are financial gain and disruption of service (Panel C of Exhibit 6.3). In another part of the survey, financial services, educational, and transportation industries listed financial gain as the most common motivation for attacks on their organizations. Interestingly, the respondents representing government agencies, telecommunication/utility companies, and retail/wholesale distribution companies listed service disruption as the most common motivation for attack. As you might expect, theft of personally identifiable information was listed as the most common motivation for attacks against health care organizations.

Threats can come from inside or outside the organization. An example of an internal threat includes when an employee creates a fictitious employee or vendor to collect cash payments, creates phony purchase orders to receive deliveries of free goods, or tampers with electronic funds transfer (EFT) messages to divert cash transfers. An example of an external threat is when an outsider gains access to customer credit card or other personal information with the intention to sell or use that information for personal gain.

Theft or deliberate destruction of data and computing resources can be the action of disgruntled employees or ex-employees, frustrated managers, commercial rivals, extremist groups, or terrorists, or can be random acts by computer hackers. Small components, such as cell phones, peripherals (e.g., flashdrives), laptops, and tablets, are frequently stolen. Losses of data on laptops and other mobile devices are a growing security problem, and it is recommended that proprietary data on company laptops, cell phones, and tablets (such as iPads) be encrypted[14] to protect the information if the device is lost or stolen, or that there be an option to remotely wipe the device if it is misplaced or stolen.

Computer System Failure and/or Inadequate Back-Up

Another type of risk in an accounting system is computer system failure and/or inadequate back-up. Most organizations are negatively affected by random computer downtime caused by equipment malfunction or operator error. They may suffer irreparable harm by any large-scale loss of computing capability caused by natural or man-made disasters.[15] The significance of a computer system failure varies considerably among industries. A retail organization that takes thousands of orders each day by telephone must maintain inventory balances and be able to process customer orders at a moment's notice. Commercial airlines are heavily dependent on their reservation systems. Therefore rapid data recovery and business continuity are essential to an organization's survival.

Accounting System's Inability to Meet Organization's and Users' Needs

Yet another type of accounting system risk is the system's inability to meet the organization's and the user's needs. Failure to select a proper accounting information system can be costly for organizations. The implementation team may get so caught up in the excitement of acquiring advanced technology that it fails to research organizational goals and users' needs or ignores needs that have been identified. Alternatively, management may be so concerned about minimizing costs that it implements a system that does not have adequate capacity or that fails to provide essential information. This is why aligning the organization's development and implementation of systems with the organization's strategic plans (i.e., strong IT governance) is so important. Resources allocated to technology can be significant, so it is essential that acquisitions and development be carefully planned to ensure the continued success of the organization.

Excessive Hardware and Software Acquisition Costs

Another accounting system risks relates to excessive hardware and software acquisition costs. Management may acquire computer resources that provide a level of service or types of information that nobody really needs, another example of a weak or non-existent IT governance process. Furthermore, where computer hardware and software acquisition is decentralized, business units may duplicate resources already acquired by other units that could be shared.

Excessive Operating and Maintenance Costs

Another accounting system risk arises from excessive operating and maintenance costs. A related problem arising from decentralized hardware and software acquisition is lack of standardization. With the proliferation of different brands and architectures of computer equipment, mobile devices, and networks, it may be difficult or expensive to provide maintenance support. Excessive ongoing costs may also result from failing to provide systems with adequate capacity or from otherwise cutting corners on implementation costs.

Inadequate Training, Development, and Supervision of Personnel

The final accounting system risk discussed in this chapter is due to inadequate training, development, and supervision of personnel. Failure to provide adequate training, development, and supervision can result in improper or inefficient use of system resources. Data files may be lost or damaged in various ways, including ill-conceived recovery procedures or faulty error correction. Output may not be protected from unauthorized access. Users' lack of control consciousness is compounded by the scarcity of programmed controls in some personal computer software packages.

End users typically work without close supervision by managers or monitoring by internal auditors. Spreadsheets routinely contain errors unrecognized by the users. Few companies maintain inventory lists of the spreadsheets in use or enforce standards for spreadsheet development. Most end users ignore the need for documenting applications and have no consistent training schedules, so the data or reports generated by one user cannot be generated or used by another.

Recognition of the Potential for Fraudulent Activity

The COSO 2013 framework includes a principle directing management to consider where and how potential fraudulent activity could occur.

> **Principle 8:** The organization must consider how the *potential for fraudulent activity* could affect the achievement of organizational objectives. Some of the types of issues that should be considered include:
>
> - Fraudulent financial reporting
> - Errors and inappropriate acts in transaction and master file maintenance authorizations
> - Errors and inappropriate acts in data input, processing, and output
> - Concealment of illegal acts

These issues are discussed in more detail below.

Fraudulent Financial Reporting

Fraudulent financial reporting is a type of management fraud. It is intentional or reckless conduct, whether by act or omission, that results in materially misleading financial reporting. For example, in an effort to overstate reported earnings, management may intentionally violate a generally accepted accounting principle by recognizing revenue before it is earned. Moreover, management may include data in financial statements that are exaggerated or untrue (e.g., recording fictitious sales, setting up "buying companies" to increase sales).

Errors and Inappropriate Acts in Transaction and Master File Maintenance Authorizations

An error is unintentional whereas an inappropriate act (e.g., concealment, fraud) is intentional. Unintentional errors can occur from carelessness, fatigue, poor judgment, incompetence, negligence, or inadequate training. Employees may initiate unauthorized transactions and unauthorized master file maintenance either through negligence or a deliberate act.

Errors and Inappropriate Acts in Data Input, Processing, and Output

A user may make an error when inputting transaction data (as demonstrated in Vignette 6.1). Or an employee may miscount during a physical inventory, causing inventory to be under- or overstated and creating a corresponding misstatement of net income for the period. Transactions may be improperly recorded or processed, or not recorded or processed at all. Data may be lost during summarization and transfer from other subsystems to the general ledger system or may be transferred improperly. Duplicate payments may be made to a vendor or an employee. Wages and benefits may be paid to employees who have been terminated. Errors may be made in payroll calculations and in accruals of sick leave, vacation, pension, or other benefits. Data files may not be backed up, resulting in a loss of data caused by a power outage.

The "black-box syndrome" contributes to errors in data input, processing, and output. Many people do not understand what goes on in the "black box," and they trust all output implicitly. Managers cannot supervise the work of computers, and the review of activities such as electronic authorizations and transactions is often overlooked. In addition poor communication with information system professionals can lead to frustrated operations personnel who cannot get the information they need from the system.

Concealment of Illegal Acts

Illegal acts are violations of laws or government regulations. Theft and the payment of bribes to secure contracts and campaign contributions over the legal limits are examples of illegal activities (and violate the Foreign Corrupt Practices Act). Another example of an illegal act is the intentional understatement of taxable income. The accounting records may be "doctored" to conceal the illegal acts.

Theft may be concealed in a variety of ways. Fictitious items of inventory may be included in the physical count of inventory to conceal theft. Unauthorized purchase orders may be created with the intention of stealing the goods upon receipt. Credit memos may be issued but not sent to customers so that when the amount of the credit is remitted by the customer, the employee can steal it. Accounts that are collectible may be written off without proper authorization and the customer's payment misappropriated. Time cards may be submitted and paychecks issued for fictitious employees. Discounts on payments to vendors may be taken but not recorded and the amounts of the discounts stolen.

Review of Risk Assessment

The COSO 2013 framework reminds management that not only should they review the risk assessment for changes, but also determine any necessary changes to the control system as a result of the review.

Principle 9: The organization should periodically *review the risk assessment to determine if there are any changes to the risks* that might impact the internal control system. The risk assessment can change with any of the following events:

- Changes in the operating environment
- New personnel (especially changes in executive management)
- New or modified accounting systems/new technology
- Rapid growth
- Corporate reengineering
- Expansion into new markets or product lines
- Expanded foreign operations

- New accounting pronouncements
- Government legislation (e.g., Sarbanes-Oxley Act)

Because these events are dynamic, risk assessment needs to be an ongoing process. For example, entering into a new business area where a company has little experience may introduce new risks. Corporate reengineering generally causes staff reductions and changes in supervision and segregation of duties that alter the associated risks. Even the adoption of new accounting principles may affect risks in preparing accurate financial statements. While some of these changes might introduce opportunities for the organization, the effect of these changes on the internal control system should be considered during the risk assessment process.

The effects of risks related to accounting information system activities may create an environment with the following consequences:

- Resources are lost, wasted, or abused.
- Data are not properly organized to provide useful information for decision making.
- Critical information is unavailable when needed.
- Important decisions are based on faulty data.
- Competitors possess critical, confidential information.
- Unfavorable audit opinions are received.
- Public image is tarnished.
- Credit ratings are eroded.
- Investors are reluctant to buy the organization's equity or debt financial instruments.
- Creditors are reluctant to lend money to the organization.
- Fines and other sanctions are levied on the organization.
- Qualified individuals are unwilling to take management or board positions for fear of personal liability.
- Organizational survival is threatened.

Clearly, organizations wish to avoid such adverse consequences.

Cost/Benefit Analysis

Once specific risks are identified and management decides how they want to respond to risk, management must perform a cost/benefit analysis to determine if the benefits of controlling the risk outweigh the costs. The costs include the tangible costs of implementing and maintaining controls and also the intangible costs resulting from the controls' impact on performance. Controls consume resources, time, effort, and computer processing power that otherwise would be available to further organizational objectives. For example, productivity in a plant is slowed because for raw materials to be issued, workers must obtain a requisition signed by the plant supervisor and then sign a receipt for the materials rather than just walk in the warehouse and take what is needed.

The benefit derived from controls is a reduction of losses such as minimizing the unauthorized pilferage of raw materials. Quantifying these losses is difficult but necessary to ensure that resources invested in controls are not wasted. The dollar amount of the loss resulting from a risk should consider both the estimated probable loss associated with each risk and the expected frequency, or likelihood, of occurrence. Obviously, the expected frequency of the theft of cash is much greater than the expected frequency of the theft of land. An infrequent large loss and a frequent small loss might be regarded as equal. The largest dollar amount is associated with losses that are potentially both large and frequent.

A conceptual control cost/benefit model shown in **Exhibit 6.4** illustrates the trade-off between the costs (tangible and intangible) to implement and maintain internal controls and the expected losses (tangible and intangible) resulting from risks.

LEARNING OBJECTIVE 11
Understand how a cost/benefit model is used in risk assessment.

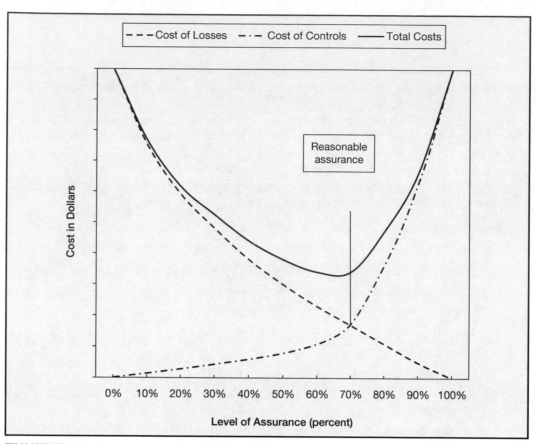

EXHIBIT 6.4 Conceptual Cost/Benefit Model

Reasonable assurance An acceptable level of risk where benefits and costs are equal.

The horizontal axis of the graph represents the level of assurance, ranging from zero to a 100 percent level of assurance of no loss from risks. Actually, no system can be completely secure. The vertical axis represents the costs. Note that as the cost of controls increases, the amount of loss from risk decreases. Also note that to achieve a 100 percent level of assurance, control costs become very high. The total cost curve is the sum of the cost of controls and the amount of loss from risks.

According to the model, the optimum amount to spend on internal controls is determined by the minimum total cost. The minimum total cost is the lowest point on the total cost curve, where one dollar spent on controls equals one dollar saved on loss from risks. The minimum cost point is referred to as the level of **reasonable assurance** and, by inference, is an acceptable level of risk. In Exhibit 6.4, the optimum amount of cost is at the 70 percent level of assurance. To the left of the optimum point (i.e., reading from the 70 percent level of assurance to the left), control costs go down but the cost of the loss from risk goes up, with loss from risk going up faster than control costs go down. Therefore, at any level of assurance to the left of the optimum total cost point, for every dollar spent on controls, more than one dollar is saved on loss. An organization in this situation would spend more on controls up to the point where one dollar spent on controls equals one dollar saved on loss. To the right of the 70 percent level of assurance, control costs go up but loss from risk is going down, with control costs going up faster than loss from risk goes down. Therefore, at any level of assurance to the right of the optimum cost point, for every dollar spent on controls less than one dollar is saved on loss from risk. An organization in this situation would attempt to move back to the point where one dollar spent on controls equals one dollar saved on loss.

Summary

Internal control is a process designed to provide reasonable assurance that organizational objectives related to the reliability of internal and external reporting, the effectiveness and efficiency of operations, and compliance with applicable laws and regulations will be achieved. An organization's board of directors, management, internal auditors, and other personnel are involved in internal control; however, the responsibility for internal control ultimately rests with the chief executive officer.

Because concern for internal control is so strong, a number of public, private, and professional bodies and legislators external to organizations have been vocal in addressing internal control issues. One very significant result of this concern was the passage of the Foreign Corrupt Practices Act. This Act requires companies registered with the Securities and Exchange Commission to keep accurate records and to devise and maintain adequate internal control to protect company assets and to provide reasonable assurance that transactions are executed with management's authorization and financial statements are accurately prepared.

The Sarbanes-Oxley Act (SOX) requires management to provide an assessment of the effectiveness of its internal control, and requires that external auditors express an opinion of management's assessment based on their testing of the system. The Public Company Accounting Oversight Board has issued auditing standards to aid publicly-held companies and auditors in their compliance with sections 302 and 404 of SOX. Another significant result of the concern with internal control were reports issued by the Committee of Sponsoring Organizations of the Treadway Commission (COSO). Two reports (1992 and 2013) developed a common definition and framework for internal control. Another report (ERM 2004) expanded on internal control to include an assessment of all types of risks faced by an organization.

According to the COSO 2013 framework, five components—control environment, risk assessment, control activities, information and communication, and monitoring are necessary for management to meet its operations, reporting, and compliance objectives. In this chapter, we discuss the first two components. Control activities and monitoring are discussed in detail in Chapter 7. Information and communication are not discussed as a separate component of internal control in this chapter because these are topics of the entire textbook, and the relevant principles from the COSO framework are addressed in Chapter 5.

The control environment represents the foundation for the other components of internal control. It establishes the tone of an organization and influences the control consciousness of the organization. The control environment should include IT governance addressing issues surrounding management and decisions regarding IT as part of the organization's overall strategy.

Objective setting is required before risk assessment can occur. Management sets operational, reporting, and compliance objectives that are in line with the organization's mission, as well as its acceptable levels of risk. Management should consider internal and external factors which can affect achievement of their objectives in either a positive (opportunities) or negative (risks) way.

Risk assessment is the systematic identification and analysis of risks that can undermine achievement of organizational objectives. The chapter discusses several types of risks that can affect accounting information systems. After risks are identified, management must determine how they will manage the identified risks—avoid, reduce, share, or accept—based on an analysis of the costs versus benefits of the response. The likelihood and potential impact of risks should also be considered, and then the residual risk should be recalculated. The conceptual cost/benefit model presented in this chapter illustrates the trade-off between the costs to implement and maintain internal control and the expected losses resulting from risks.

Key Terms

Discussion Questions and Problems

1. Who is ultimately responsible for the implementation of cost-effective internal control?
   a. The director of internal auditing
   b. The chief executive officer
   c. The information systems audit manager
   d. The audit and control group in the information systems department
   [CIA adapted]

2. The Foreign Corrupt Practices Act was an important act because it was the first to require that:
   a. SEC-registered companies establish an independent audit committee to oversee the audit function.
   b. the external auditors report any illegal payments to the SEC.
   c. U.S. firms doing business abroad report sizable payments to non-U.S. citizens to the Justice Department.
   d. SEC-registered companies keep records and maintain adequate internal control.

3. The primary objective of an external auditor in obtaining an understanding of a client's internal control is to provide the auditor with:
   a. background information for the publication of audit findings.
   b. knowledge necessary to assess client risk, plan the audit, and determine the nature, timing, and extent of testing.
   c. a basis from which to modify tests of controls.
   d. information necessary to test documentation controls.

4. Which of the following statements about internal control is correct?
   a. Properly maintained internal control reasonably ensures that collusion among employees will never occur.
   b. The internal auditor is responsible for the development and testing of internal control.
   c. With a very strong internal control systems, the auditor has no need to perform substantive tests on significant account balances.
   d. The cost/benefit relationship is a primary criterion that should be considered in designing internal control.

5. Smith, CPA, has been engaged to audit the financial statements of Reed, Inc., a publicly held retailing company. Before assessing control risk Smith is required to obtain an understanding of Reed's control environment.

   Required:
   a. Identify the control environment factors or principles that establish the control environment.
   b. For each control environment factor or principle identified in Part (a), describe what would be of interest to the auditor.

6. Describe the three organization objective categories in the internal control framework. How are they related to the COSO 2013 components of internal control?

7. Below are some situations that occurred in various organizations.
   a. The company president was implicated in a case of high-level fraud, but the matter was hushed up successfully.
   b. An employee expected he would be fired because of a conduct violation, but six months later he was still on the job. Management currently was distracted by the possibility of a hostile takeover.
   c. After a new technical assistant had been on the job for three weeks, it was discovered that she had no relevant qualifications or work experience.
   d. When the internal auditors conducted an inquiry into the high incidence of errors in the accounting department, it emerged that three clerks recently had been transferred there from other departments. Although the clerks had some accounting experience, none was familiar with the company's accounting system.
   e. A customer complained about being overcharged on an invoice, and it turned out the error was deliberate. The billing clerk, who had not benefitted personally in any way, defended himself by saying, "I thought you would appreciate my trying to bring more money into the company."
   f. A colleague explained to a new employee, "It doesn't matter what you do here; just don't get caught."

   Required:
   Discuss the deficiencies that must have existed in the control environment for these situations to have occurred.

8. It is often said that control is achieved through people, and human resource policies and practices certainly make an important contribution to an organization's control environment.

   Required:
   Identify and discuss the main aspects of human resource policies and practices from a control standpoint. Present your answer in the context of a large service organization, such as an insurance company.

9. A corporation is seeking a listing on the New York Stock Exchange, but it does not have an audit committee.

   Required:
   a. Why does it matter whether the corporation has an audit committee?
   b. Discuss the issues the corporation must consider in creating an audit committee.

10. A company has grown from being small to being medium-sized. Top management realizes that its

organizational structure needs to be formalized to strengthen the control environment.

Required:

What must management consider when designing an appropriate organizational structure?

11. Rumors are spreading around an organization that members of top management overstate their travel vouchers. A vice-president is alleged to have submitted a travel claim for a two-week sales trip when he was actually on vacation. Another executive is reported to have told her secretary, "The reimbursement rates for transportation are so low that claiming more miles is the only way to come out even." Several division managers are believed to make regular claims for meals provided at no charge by airlines, conventions, or customers.

Required:

Explain the effect these rumors could have on the control environment.

12. A U.S. construction company paid a bribe to a foreign government official in an effort to land a contract in the official's country. When word leaked out, the U.S. company's CEO said, "Bribery is a standard business practice in the foreign country."

Required:

What is your reaction to the CEO's statement?

13. X has been asked to serve as an outside director on Y Company's board of directors. For this service, X will receive an annual stipend as well as a fee and expense reimbursement for each meeting attended.

Required:

a. What is meant by an outside director and what contribution can an outside director make?

b. What will be some of X's responsibilities as a member of the board of directors?

c. Does the promise of remuneration erode the director's independence on the board?

14. Malcolm Trenton, an ambitious senior manager, routinely took administrative work home in the evening because he spent much of the day in conferences with other managers, subordinates, or clients. He was as surprised as everyone else when a vice-president explained at a hurriedly called meeting that details of an impending merger had been leaked to a corporate raider. The leak had embarrassed the company and undermined merger negotiations. The vice-president announced that he had instructed the internal auditors to conduct a thorough investigation into the source of the leak and that the culprit would be dealt with severely. All company personnel, including executive-level managers, were requested to cooperate fully with the investigation.

Two days later, Trenton's wife left him and filed for divorce. Some time later, Trenton learned that his wife had been seen with one of the corporate raider's staff. She bought a condominium in a fashionable part of town and was last seen driving an expensive automobile.

Required:

a. Discuss the potential dangers of taking work out of the office.

b. Much has been written in recent years about opportunities for people to work at home. Avoiding long commuting times, safety from downtown crime, being able to care for children, and reducing the need for expensive downtown office space have all been cited as advantages to employers as well as employees. Dispersion of the work force is not considered a problem because technology enables people to keep in touch 24 hours a day. Do you think that the internal control implications of working at home might be serious enough to dissuade companies from allowing employees to work remotely?

15. Many organizations have policies regulating the use of controlled substances, and some require all employees to submit to random drug testing. In some cases, safety is the main concern, and vehicle drivers and machinery operators are the main targets of controlled-substance policies. However, education in drug abuse and opportunities to attend rehabilitation programs are being made available to much broader categories of employees. Certain organizations have proposed compulsory drug testing in the accounting and information services areas.

Required:

a. What are the internal control implications of substance abuse in accounting and information services?

b. Do you think that random drug testing of accounting and information services employees is justified?

16. Carcella Company's board of directors instructed its audit committee to investigate an allegation that one of the assertions in the company's interim financial statements was fraudulent.

Required:

If you were a member of the audit committee, how would you suggest the committee proceed with such an investigation? What resources should the audit committee have at its disposal to carry out the charge? What action should the audit committee take if it finds that the allegation is correct? Would the committee's actions be the same if the fraud involved other acts, such as an illegal political contribution?

17. A former employee called a local newspaper and reported that a major company had paid bribes to foreign governments over a period of years to obtain export contracts and had also made large contributions to three members of a U.S. congressional committee to influence legislation leading to the Clean Air Act of

1991. The employee offered to make available to the newspaper copies of internal memos written by senior executives proving that the activities took place.

Required:

What actions do you think this organization could have taken:
  a. to reduce the possibility of involvement in illegal activities by high-level management?
  b. to encourage potential whistle-blowers to reveal their information internally instead of being forced to go outside?

18. Mr. White serves as financial secretary and treasurer of a church in a small town. His responsibilities include maintaining all accounting records, receiving pledge income and plate collections, and making disbursements for all church expenses.

   Mr. White, who is 71 years old, is a lifelong member of the church and is highly respected in the community. He took over the unpaid job 15 years ago after retiring from the military and after his predecessor died. The church officers always have been full of praise for the manner in which Mr. White performed, but lately there has been some concern because of his failing health. No one has been found to help Mr. White with the work.

Required:

Discuss the risks inherent in Mr. White's position in the church.

19. The Arcade Co. of Orlando, Florida, has established a new division that will manage a chain of video-game arcades in forty locations throughout several southern states. The locations will be divided into two regions, each under a regional manager. Each location will be assigned a local manager. As many as sixty machines will be available at certain locations, although the average at each location will be thirty-five machines.

   Management intends to minimize the number of operating and accounting employees to reduce costs. However, it plans to hire sufficient maintenance personnel to minimize downtime of machines. The local manager will be required to collect the coins from the machines and deposit them in a local bank. Access to the game counter and coins in each machine will be by means of a master key. Validated deposit slips are to be mailed to the corporate office by the local manager. Bank statements are to be mailed by the bank directly to the corporate office.

Required:

Identify the specific risks that are inherent in the operations of the new division and the risk responses for each of those risks (avoid, reduce, share, or accept).

20. Define IT governance and describe some "best practices" that would be expected for strong IT governance in an organization.

Spreadsheet Assignment

A type of computer fraud that has been perpetrated at several banks and financial institutions is referred to as the salami technique, so named because it "slices" away tiny pieces of data. All calculated interest amounts are rounded down, and the fraction of a cent shaved from each computation is transferred to an account belonging to the perpetrator (or an accomplice) who is usually an applications developer in the information services department.

   Consider the following account balances from a representative sample of one-tenth of 1 percent of the population of accounts at the Third National Bank:

January Data:

Account	Balance	Monthly Interest	Rounded Interest	Interest Amount Cut Off	Cumulative Amount Transferred
1	35.04				
2	191.66				
3	273.50				
4	301.81				
5	397.15				
6	412.02				
7	688.25				
8	1,517.09				
9	3,242.34				
10	10,083.10				

Your completed table for January should be similar to the following table:

January Data:

Account	Balance	Monthly Interest	Rounded Interest	Interest Amount Cut Off	Cumulative Amount Transferred
1	35.04	0.16060	0.16	0.00060	0.00060
2	191.66	0.87844	0.87	0.00844	0.00904
3	273.50	1.25354	1.25	0.00354	0.01258
4	301.81	1.38330	1.38	0.00330	0.01588
5	397.15	1.82027	1.82	0.00027	0.01615
6	412.02	1.88843	1.88	0.00842	0.02457
7	688.25	3.15448	3.15	0.00448	0.02905
8	1,517.00	6.95292	6.95	0.00292	0.03197
9	3,242.34	14.86073	14.86	0.00073	0.03270
10	10,083.10	46.21421	46.21	0.00421	0.03690

Required:

a. Prepare a spreadsheet to calculate the approximate amount stolen over the course of 1 year if the bank pays 5.5 percent annual interest, compounded monthly. Assume no additional deposits were made to the accounts and no withdrawals of interest or principal were made.

One approach to setting up your spreadsheet is shown below for the month of January. You will need to key in the appropriate formulas or functions to derive the amounts for the last four columns. Use the spreadsheet's round down function for the "Rounded Interest" column.

Account	Balance
1	$ 35.04
2	191.66
3	273.50
4	301.81
5	397.15
6	412.02
7	688.25
8	1,517.09
9	3,242.34
10	10,083.10

To calculate the data for February, copy the rows for January to the blank rows below the data for January and label the copied data "February Data." In the February data, delete the contents of the cells in the "Balance" column. For the balance of account 1, enter a formula to add the January balance of account 1 to the rounded interest amount for account 1 in January. Copy this formula to calculate the balances for accounts 2 through 10. Also, in the February data, modify the "Cumulative Amount Transferred" in the first row to include the total cumulative amount transferred in January.

To calculate the data for March, copy the rows for February to the blank rows below the data for February. No changes need to be made for the March data except for the label, which should be "March Data." Repeat what you did for March for April through December.

b. What changes to the facts stated in the assignment would result in larger profits to the perpetrator? Do the sizes of the account balances influence the profitability of the scheme?

Notes

1. Additional components of internal control are discussed in Chapter 7.
2. Source: Department of Justice: Foreign Corrupt Practices Act (http://www.justice.gov/criminal/fraud/fcpa/)
3. An assertion is a declaration, made by a responsible party, on which others may place reliance.
4. http://www.coso.org/ic.htm
5. www.coso.org/-EMR.htm. Currently, the 2004 framework is being revised.
6. Part of the series of SAS Nos. 104-111 addressing the risk-based nature approach to auditing high-risk areas.
7. The Treadway Commission was sponsored by the American Institute of Certified Public Accountants, American Accounting Association, The Institute of Internal Auditors, Institute of Management Accountants, and Financial Executives Institute.
8. *Public Company Accounting Oversight Board,* https://pcao bus.org/Standards/Auditing/Pages/AS2201.aspx.
9. COBIT 5 (www.ISACA.org), *http://www.isaca.org/COBIT /Pages/Product-Family.aspx*
10. The SAS 70 procedure is essentially an audit of the TPSP's financial reporting controls for the audit period and was required for SOX compliance.
11. Bonding is a type of insurance that compensates organizations for losses occurring from unknown events.
12. For example: "IMA Statement of Ethical Professional Practice," http://www.imanet.org/docs/default-source/press _releases/statement-of-ethical-professional-practice_2 -2-12.pdf?sfvrsn=2, and the "ISACA Code of Professional Ethics" http://www.isaca.org/Certification/Code-of-Profes sional-Ethics/Pages/default.aspx (both retrieved June 23, 2016.)
13. Categorizing risks into mutually exclusive groups is not possible because of their interrelationships and because of the lack of standardization in some terminology. These risks are not intended to be all-inclusive.
14. Encryption is discussed in Chapter 7.
15. The importance of a disaster recovery plan is discussed in Chapter 7.

Control Activities and Monitoring

Source: Tashatuvango/Shutterstock.

Learning Objectives

After studying this chapter, you should be able to:

- Define control activities.
- Explain several fundamental concepts of control activities.
- Discuss how performance reviews serve as an effective control activity.
- Recognize how physical control serves as an effective control activity.
- Understand how segregation of duties serves as an effective control activity.
- Identify the general control activities that are desirable for information processing systems.
- Identify the application control activities that are desirable for information processing systems.
- Explain the purpose of and approaches to monitoring internal control including IT auditing.
- Discuss the importance of protecting information assets.

Source: R. Mackay Photography, LLC/Shutterstock.

Introductory Scenario

A large Southern hospital was grossing more than $250 million a year in patient revenues. Although most amounts due (80 percent) were paid with insurance company checks and other third-party payments, a substantial amount of cash and checks was received each day from emergency room patients and patients paying the portion of their bill not covered by hospitalization insurance.

Cashiers would issue receipts for all cash and checks received on their shifts. The cash and checks for the three daily shifts of cashiers would be combined with the funds received by mail from insurance companies and others. A clerk would total the checks on a calculator to derive the total amount to write on a deposit slip for the checks. She counted the cash and wrote that amount on the deposit slip, and then computed the total deposit amount and wrote it on the deposit slip. This clerk would then give the checks, calculator tape listing the check amounts, cash, and the original deposit slip to a second clerk who would make the deposit in the bank branch across the street. The first clerk would keep a copy of the deposit slip to check the amount against the monthly checking account statement. At least one deposit was made every day. On weekends the deposit was placed in the night depository at the bank. When the second clerk made a deposit, he also picked up any paperwork the bank had for the hospital, such as checking account statements and returned checks. With a daily census of more than 1,500 patients, the hospital had a large number of returned checks. Generally, a returned check was deposited to the hospital's bank account for collection a second time. The clerk delivered the paperwork to the hospital's controller.

The week after a popular street festival, the controller of the hospital received a call from a police officer at the police department's vehicle impoundment lot. A car parked in a location that was restricted during the festival had been towed to the impoundment lot. Following standard procedure, the car's contents had been inventoried. In the glove compartment were several checks, payable to the hospital, marked as "returned for insufficient funds." The car was the property of the hospital clerk who made the deposits at the bank.

The clerk's scheme was simple. He would keep some of the returned checks and turn over only a few of them to the hospital's controller. When making the next deposit, the clerk would add the returned checks to the bottom of the calculator tape that listed the check amounts, thereby increasing the number of checks deposited. To make the amount of the deposit match the total on the original deposit slip, the clerk would take out an amount of cash equal to the amount of checks added. The clerk could not use the original deposit slip so he prepared a new one. On the new deposit slip, the total amount of the deposit was the same, but the amount of cash was less and the amount of checks was more. The bank was never suspicious of the handwritten additions to the calculator tape because they increased the total of the checks, and the deposit slip had no alterations. The hospital was never suspicious because the amount of the deposit on the checking account statement agreed with the hospital's copy of the original deposit slip.

The clerk's scheme was workable. Although the hospital exercised strict control over its blank checks, it was rather careless with its deposit slips. In addition, on two occasions the clerk had asked the bank to encode the hospital's account number on a counter deposit slip, explaining that the desk that held the deposit slips was locked and several slips were needed for additional deposits.

The total loss to the hospital was approximately $250,000.

Introductory Scenario Thought Questions:

1. How could the duties for the clerks be changed to reduce the opportunity for the fraudulent activity described above to occur?
2. What other types of controls could be put in place to ensure that the total deposit reached the bank and was properly recorded?

Nature of Control Activities

In this chapter, we continue with the discussion of the COSO 2013 Framework. Control activities are discussed first followed by monitoring activities. The cube depicting the five components of the COSO 2013 that was presented in Chapter 6 is repeated in **Exhibit 7.1** to put this chapter in context.

As mentioned in Chapter 6, the control environment is the foundation for the other components—risk assessment, control activities, information and communication, and monitoring. If the control environment (or "tone at the top") is favorable, and the risk assessment is evaluated properly, then the operation and monitoring of control activities will be effective.

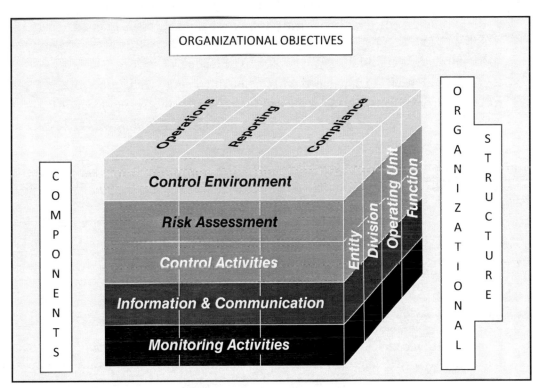

EXHIBIT 7.1 COSO 2013 Framework

Definition of Control Activities

Control activities are the policies and procedures that reduce risks that may undermine the achievement of management objectives. Policies establish what should be done and serve as a basis for the procedures that are needed to comply with the policies. These activities help ensure that management's responses to identified risks are carried out. The COSO 2013 framework includes three principles related to the control activities component: principle 10 requires management to select control activities that will mitigate identified risks, principle 11 states that control activities should include general controls over technology (discussed in a later section of this chapter), and principle 12 requires that management

LEARNING OBJECTIVE 1
Define control activities.

Control activities The policies and procedures that reduce risks which may undermine the achievement of management objectives.

should establish actions to implement those activities. The control activities are carried out with respect to management's operations, reporting, and compliance objectives. Control activities should permeate an organization at all levels and in all functions.

Examples of control activities, often referred to as "controls," are:

- Providing adequate training for new employees
- Requiring proper approvals/authorizations for the issuance of purchase requisitions
- Segregating the duties of handling cash and entering cash transaction data
- Segregating the duties of file maintenance changes from entering transaction data
- Pre-numbering documents to provide a basis for detecting missing or duplicate documents
- Providing locks and other security devices to protect a warehouse
- Requiring identification codes and passwords before access is granted to data files and programs
- Requiring that all disbursements over $50 be made by check
- Recovering from the unplanned termination of computerized processes
- Making backup copies of files and storing the copies in a secure location
- Performing regular reviews and tests of the disaster recovery/business continuity plan
- Requiring monthly reconciliations of the cash account to be performed by someone outside the cash receipts area
- Verifying that user access files are updated promptly to reflect new and terminated employees
- Using a checklist to ensure that tax deposits are made and reports are filed before deadlines

Identification of Control Activities

The COSO 2013 framework includes three principles related to control activities. Two of these relate to the identification of, and actions resulting from, the control activities chosen by management to mitigate identified risks.

Principle 10: recognizes that a major task for an organization is to *identify what control activities are desirable for that particular organization*. There are literally hundreds of control activities. One organization's control activities may not be appropriate for another organization. The methodology for determining control activities is to first establish how management wants to manage the potential risk to the achievement of organizational objectives. Note that management's decision to implement control activities is a "reduce or mitigate" response to the risk. Next, specific control activities can be identified to mitigate specific risks. These controls are built directly into management processes, and should take into consideration the interrelations among the processes—one control could address several risks, and conversely, one risk could require more than one control. **Exhibit 7.2** illustrates this process, encompassing the identification, integration, and implementation of controls.

Principle 12 of the COSO 2013 framework discusses the importance of *developing policies and procedures to ensure control activities are in place and working*. As an example of how to put the process shown in Exhibit 7.2 into practice, suppose that

EXHIBIT 7.2 Process of Identifying Control Activities

Activity: Manage Information Processing Risk		
Identified Objective	**Identified Risk**	**Control Activities (Response)**
Maintain an accounting information system that provides high quality output to those who need it.*	Data files are subject to unauthorized access.	Classify data to isolate confidential data.
		Develop a password system to access files.
		Grant rights to files only to certain users.
	Application modifications (i.e., changes in program code) are implemented incorrectly.	Approve program changes.
		Document program changes.
		Test program changes.
	Compliance with Sarbanes-Oxley documentation requirements are not met.	Have a procedure in place for quarterly review and update of documentation for applications.
		Document reviews and updates.

EXHIBIT 7.3 Results of Identifying Control Activities

*This objective fulfills all three types of organizational objectives: effectiveness and efficiency of operations, reliability of reporting, and compliance with applicable laws and regulations.

management wants to control the organizational objective—manage information processing. **Exhibit 7.3** shows some possible results of the process depicted in Exhibit 7.2, and illustrates how to document the policies and actions that result from the control activities, as directed by principle 12 of the COSO 2013 framework.

As mentioned above, the identified objectives and management of the risks may have one or more vulnerabilities that could prevent the objective from being achieved. Also, an identified vulnerability may require one or more control activities to achieve a targeted level of assurance. For example, a password system may be 90 percent effective in reducing the risk that data files are subject to unauthorized access, thereby allowing a 10 percent error rate. If this error rate is unacceptable, then a complementary control, such as encrypting the data in the files or a biometric system, may be added.[1] Assuming that the biometric control is 80 percent effective (and failure of the two controls is statistically independent), the joint failure rate is only $0.1 \times 0.2 = 0.02$, or 2 percent. Conversely, a single control activity may adequately address more than one risk.

In a real-world situation, there would be more than one objective that relates to the activity of managing information technology. Also, we would go through this same process for every other activity associated with the accounting system (i.e., input, process, store, and output data; manage people; and manage internal control).

Underlying Concepts of Control Activities

LEARNING OBJECTIVE 2
Explain several fundamental concepts of control activities.

Because control activities are so numerous and must be carefully selected and designed to address each risk, it is helpful to realize that all control activities are based on a small number of underlying concepts. The most important of these concepts are:

- *Isolation.* Data, programs, documentation, and information processing facilities should be isolated to protect them from potential hazards (e.g., unauthorized access), and access privileges should be restricted and monitored. In addition, incompatible duties that would enable people to perpetrate and conceal errors or inappropriate activities should be isolated from one another. The more restricted an individual's access to resources and data, the less opportunity that individual has to cause inadvertent or deliberate damage.

- *Redundancy.* Backup copies of programs and data should be made for security reasons. Critical computations should be repeated as a check on accuracy.

- *Comparison.* Comparisons between data provide a check on accuracy and may signal problems to be investigated. For example, comparisons can be made between perpetual inventory records and physical counts, the customer code entered in a computer screen form and the customer codes in the customer master file, and between deposit slips and the cash receipts journal.

- *Assistance.* Control problems often result from the inability to handle a job, inadequate training, and lack of ongoing guidance. Control effectiveness is enhanced by providing help and assistance to employees and, in return, gaining their cooperation in carrying out internal control responsibilities.

- *Oversight.* Supervision of employees, internal audits, and external audits encourage careful work and reduce the likelihood that inappropriate activity will occur. Independent reconciliation and verification activities support this concept.

- *Accountability.* Holding employees accountable for their actions promotes compliance with established control activities (e.g., performance/operating reviews). This also encourages careful work.

Many control activities, such as separating incompatible duties or denying access to certain files, represent the application of a single concept. Others may involve more than one concept.

Placement of Control Activities

The effectiveness of many control activities depends on their existence in both computer software and human operating procedures. For example, an accounting program can print an exception report listing unusual transactions and other events, but the control will be ineffective unless a human reviews the report and investigates/resolves the listed transactions and other events.

The trend with respect to control placement is a movement away from controls in human operating procedures and toward controls programmed into computer software. These are referred to as **automated controls**. For example, a common human procedure is to match an invoice received from a vendor to a purchase order and receiving report to ensure that the goods being billed match the goods that were ordered and received (manual control). A software program, on the other hand, can take the vendor invoice

Automated control Controls programmed into computer software.

data that have been entered in the system and compare them with the purchase order and receiving data in the computer files. The benefit of programmed controls is that a properly written and tested computer program will perform consistently as long as the hardware is reliable. Manual control procedures are weaker in that even in the best control environment, human behavior lacks consistency. However, even with highly computerized controls, at some point there is human interaction in the form of review or oversight of the control function.

Limitations of Control Activities

Control activities, regardless of how well designed and operated, cannot provide *absolute assurance* that all risks associated with the achievement of entity objectives will be eliminated. Two or more people can collude to circumvent control activities, and management has the ability to override control activities. Furthermore, control activities require additional costs to implement and may result in decreases in operational efficiency. Therefore, management assumes some risk at the point where the benefits from control activities do not exceed the cost of the activities, as noted in the description of the cost/benefit model in Chapter 6, Exhibit 6.4.

Categories of Control Activities

Management's ongoing risk assessment determines how the risks should be managed, which in turn influences the types and extent of control activities established. These control activities can affect the risk calculation by reducing the risks management decides to mitigate or eliminate. As mentioned earlier, control activities consist of both the policies in place to help an organization achieve its objectives, and the procedures to enforce that policy.

Control activities can be classified in several different ways, but within any classification scheme the categories overlap. There are three general types of control activities—**preventive controls** (that deal with or stop potential problems through the controls in place), **detective controls** (that provide feedback regarding violations of controls in place) and **corrective controls** (that remedy control violations detected). Some of the control activities discussed below may be a combination of one or more of these types of controls. We will use the classification scheme developed in AU 314 Appendix B.15 to discuss controls, but the important thing to remember is that control activities combine to provide comprehensive protection for an organization regardless of the category into which they fall. The AU 314 Appendix B.15 classification scheme for control activities is as follows:

- Performance reviews
- Physical controls
- Segregation of duties
- Information processing

A map of control activities, broken down into these four categories, is presented in **Exhibit 7.4**. Because of the large number of information processing control activities, and because there are two general areas of focus, the discussion breaks information processing activities into general controls (covering the overall information processing environment, as outlined in Principle 11 of the COSO 2013 framework) and application controls (covering the flow of information through and among applications). Each category is discussed in more detail in the following sections, and examples of these control activities (i.e., performance reviews, physical controls, segregation of duties, and information processing) are discussed for each business process in Chapters 8–11.

Preventive control A control that deals with or stops potential problems through the controls in place.

Detective control A control that provides feedback regarding violations of controls in place.

Corrective control A control that remedies a control violation after it has been detected.

Performance Reviews

Comparison of budgets with actual
Comparison of standard costs with actual
Comparison of return on investment and
  residual income targets with actual
Comparison of various nonfinancial targets with actual
Social media surveys
Feedback reviews

Physical Controls

Smoke and water detectors
Fire suppression devices
Burglar alarms
Survelllance cameras
Individual locks
Security personnel

Segregation of Duties

Segregation of:
  Authorization of transactions, custody of assets,
    modification or creation of data and program files
  Application development and testing
  Application development and use of applications
  Application development and database
    administration
  Rotation of assignments
  Enforced vacation

EXHIBIT 7.4 Map of Control Activities

Performance Reviews

LEARNING OBJECTIVE 3
Discuss how performance reviews serve as an effective control activity.

Control activities in the performance review category are designed to mitigate risks that can have an adverse effect on meeting objectives in the broad category of effectiveness and efficiency of operations. More specific objectives would be, for example, reducing costs, reducing customer complaints, making more deliveries on time, and producing no defective products. Reducing customer complaints by reviewing and responding to feedback on social media, performing satisfaction surveys, and having procedures in place to resolve issues with products or services are all examples of control activities related to the performance review category. Timely performance reviews act as both detective controls (e.g., noting the number of customer complaints about a product) and corrective controls (e.g., following up on the complaints and setting into motion procedures to minimize future complaints). Many organizations today use "big data" to meet objectives related to direct marketing and better serving customers (refer to chapter 14 for a discussion of big data).

Physical Controls

LEARNING OBJECTIVE 4
Recognize how physical controls serve as an effective control activity.

Physical controls Devices and measures that protect computer hardware and other assets, such as cash, inventories, securities, fixed assets, mechanical check signers, and signature plates.

Physical controls mitigate risks that can have an adverse effect on the achievement of entity objectives in the broad categories of effectiveness and efficiency of operations. These are generally classified as preventive/detective controls (e.g., to protect the inventory warehouse from unauthorized access, and set off an alarm with entry violations). More specific objectives would be, for example, minimization of the theft or destruction of assets (both tangible assets and information assets). **Physical controls** include devices and measures that protect computer hardware and other assets, such as cash, inventories, securities, fixed assets, mechanical check signers, and signature plates. Examples of physical controls over information assets (discussed further in section 7.6) include access controls, fire suppression/environmental controls, and encryption of customer credit card information.

Segregation of Duties (SOD)

Another category of control activities is segregation of incompatible duties. These controls mitigate the risks that can adversely affect the achievement of objectives in the broad categories of reliability of external and internal reporting, and effectiveness/efficiency of operations. More specific objectives would be, for example, reduction in the number of errors in data, absence of illegal acts, and reduction in theft of assets. **Segregation of duties (SOD),** a preventive control, ensures that a single individual cannot both perpetrate and conceal an error or an inappropriate act and mandates that the following duties should be segregated:

LEARNING OBJECTIVE 5
Understand how segregation of duties serves as an effective control activity.

- *Authorization* of transactions and other events
- *Custody* of assets
- *Record keeping and modification* of related data and program files (or paper-based records)

Segregation of duties (SOD) A control activity in which authorization of transactions, custody of related assets, and modification or creation of related data and program files (or paper-based records) are segregated so that a single individual cannot both perpetrate and conceal an error or inappropriate activity.

Segregation of duties can be achieved by (1) physical segregation, (2) restriction of access to data, to program files, and to certain functions, or (3) a combination of these means. Access security is discussed in the next section on information processing control activities.

Proper segregation of duties not only prevents a person from both perpetrating and concealing errors and inappropriate acts, but also protects a person from the appearance of being involved in these activities (Vignette 7.1). For example, a procedure requiring that two people open the mail to record payments received from customers protects those employees—if money is missing from a payment envelope, there are two people who witnessed that the envelope was empty. If only one person recorded payments received in the mail, and an envelope was missing cash, that person would not have anyone to verify the envelope was empty, and would most likely be held responsible for the missing cash.

Vignette 7.1

Segregation of Duties Protects People and Organizations

Henry Pleasant was treasurer of his church for 10 years. He received pledge contributions and plate collections, deposited cash, and maintained an accounting system designed specifically for church accounting on his laptop. One day Henry misplaced some pledge checks shortly before setting out to deposit them at the bank. Rather than admit the problem, he made some reversing journal entries in his accounting system to offset the entries for the cash receipts. He also falsified the pledge records to show that the checks had never been received. In fact, the checks had fallen into a trash can. Someone found the checks at the city dump and managed to cash them.

A few months later, a wealthy church member (also a CPA) noticed that her quarterly pledge statement did not reflect a check that had been cashed. After calling the treasurer and receiving a convoluted reply, she contacted the minister who ordered an investigation. An auditor discovered the original and reversing entries. Henry tried to explain that he had made a mistake and attempted to cover it up, but he had no explanation as to how the checks had been cashed. Nobody believed his story, and Henry was accused of theft.

The total amount of the checks was no more than a few hundred dollars, and the church decided not to prosecute. Henry was not bonded. However, he was fired as treasurer and publicly disgraced for "stealing from the Lord."

THOUGHT QUESTIONS

1. How could Henry have protected himself in this situation?
2. What kind of controls should the organization have had in place to ensure that the contributions were all deposited properly?

Closely aligned with segregation of duties is the rotation of assignments within a business unit and "enforced" vacation. Enforced vacation is the requirement that all employees take a certain number of consecutive days off.[2] The intention of assignment rotation is that no one individual always performs the same task; otherwise, the individual may be able to conceal a longstanding pattern of errors or inappropriate actions. Enforced vacations serve the same purpose as rotation of assignments. While segregation of duties is generally thought of as a preventive control, it can also be a detective control in the example of rotation of duties or enforced vacations. Someone who takes over job responsibilities of a person while they are out of the office could detect an irregularity. Many times fraudulent activities have been discovered when employees were on vacation or assignment rotation. In this case, the perception of detection (or realizing someone will check what you are doing) can also work as a preventive control. However, control activities such as enforced vacations and rotation of duties should never be a substitute for proper segregation of duties, because in most cases, fraudulent activities might not have occurred if proper segregation of duties had been in place.

Although not a perfect substitute, the bonding of employees (a type of insurance to pay a specific amount to an employer if an employee causes financial losses) can help to compensate for segregation of duties in small organizations. Employees in sensitive positions, such as those who handle large amounts of cash or negotiable securities, should be bonded regardless of the size of the organization.

Information Processing

Control activities in the information processing category are designed to mitigate risks that have an adverse effect on achieving objectives in all three categories—improving the effectiveness and efficiency of operations, ensuring the quality of external and internal reporting, and complying with applicable laws and regulations. Some of the risks unique to computer processing include:

- Errors are magnified as they proliferate through the system
- Segregation of duties is sometimes difficult (e.g., one program handles the entire purchasing function)
- Changes to programs might be made without regard to the control implications
- Data are more accessible
- Data are invisible, erasable, and compressed—damage can be catastrophic to the business.

Information processing control activities are preventive (e.g., only authorized personnel are permitted to add/delete master file accounts), detective (e.g., an exception report is generated when master file records are added/deleted), and corrective (e.g., management can follow up on unauthorized adjustments to the master file accounts based on information from the exception report).

General controls Control activities that apply to the reliability and consistency of the overall information processing environment. General controls support application controls.

Application controls The control activities that apply to the flow of data in and among individual applications.

Control activities in the information processing category can be separated into two closely related groups. **General controls** relate to the reliability and consistency of the overall information processing environment, and they support application controls. **Application controls** relate to the flow of data in and among individual applications, such as customer billing and cash receipts. Some overlap exists, with information processing controls having characteristics of both general and application controls. Nevertheless, this classification of information processing controls is helpful and is used for the discussion in the next two sections of this chapter.

Information Processing—General Controls

LEARNING OBJECTIVE 6
Identify the general control activities that are desirable for information processing systems.

As principle 11 in the COSO 2013 framework makes clear, IT general controls are the foundation for a solid environment for information processing, which in turn affects the ability of the organization to meet its objectives. As shown in **Exhibit 7.5**, information processing—general controls include:

- Access security
- Network and data service center operation controls
- System software acquisition, implementation, and maintenance controls
- Application software selection (or development), implementation, and maintenance controls[3]

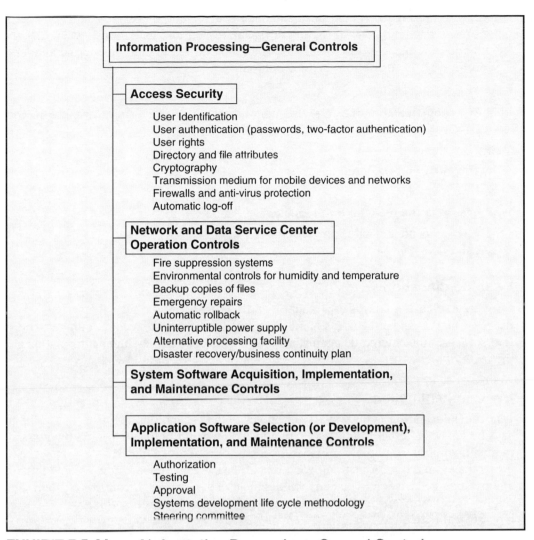

EXHIBIT 7.5 Map of Information Processing—General Controls

Access Security

Access security deals with who can access what. Users should be granted access to the following elements of an accounting system on a need-to-know, or "least-privilege" basis:

- File server or host computer
- Operating systems
- System software
- Database management system
- Application programs
- Data files

Access security may be provided by access security software specifically designed to perform this function or may be included in software designed for other functions, such as operating systems, database management systems, and application programs.

An attempted access violation should cause a warning or error message to appear on the screen and result in either termination of processing or shutdown of a workstation. A log of all access attempts

Access security Control activities that deal with who can access the accounting system and what they can access in the accounting system.

Source: cybrain/Shutterstock.

(successful and failed) should be maintained and include the user identification code, date, time, workstation used, program or data accessed, and data modified. Access security should be subjected periodically to penetration tests designed by internal auditors.

Several ways of restricting access are through:

- User identification
- User authentication (i.e., one or more of these: passwords, smartcards, biometrics, device access table)
- User rights
- Directory and file attributes
- Cryptography
- Transmission medium for mobile devices and networks
- Firewalls and anti-virus protection
- Automatic log off

User Identification

User identification A personal identification code that tells the system who the user is.

User identification (ID) is a personal identification code that tells the system who the user is. The ID can be the user's name, a log-on number, or an account number. The system compares the entered ID against a stored user profile that includes information about the user.

User Authentication

User authentication Verification that the user is who the user claims to be.

User authentication is the way a user proves to the system that the user is who the user says he or she is (either through something you know and/or through something you are). Authentication is commonly provided by a password that is entered by a user when logging on a system (i.e., something you know). The system compares the entered password against the stored user profile that includes the user's password. Ideally, the system should require **two-factor authentication**, which generally combines something you know (e.g., a password) with either:

Two-factor authentication An authentication method that combines something you know (e.g., a password) with either something you have (e.g., an RSA tag inserted into your computer's USB port that generates a random personal identification number every 10 seconds) or something you are (e.g., a biometric, such as a fingerprint).

- "Something you have" (e.g., an RSA tag inserted into your computer's USB port that generates a random personal identification number every 10 seconds which must be entered with your user ID and password) or
- "Something you are" (e.g., a biometric, such as a fingerprint)

Passwords are the most commonly used authentication method. Some access security software randomly generates passwords for users while others allow users to devise their own passwords. Some access security programs provide one-use passwords to prevent brute-force password guessing by unauthorized users.

To prevent unauthorized users from guessing passwords, several rules should be followed in choosing passwords. Do not use your name or family member names, your telephone number, your license plate number, your user identification, any part of your social security number, passwords of all the same letter, or anything that can be discovered through social media (e.g., where you were born or birth dates). Good passwords are at least eight characters long and are composed of a mixture of upper- and lowercase letters, numeric digits, and other keyboard symbols such as @#$%.

Passwords are useful only if they are not shared with others. Better access security systems require that users change their passwords regularly, usually monthly, to stop any undetected use of a stolen or shared password (i.e., a strong organizational password policy that is enforced). Password files should be both read-protected and encrypted.

Although well-designed password systems are a reasonable defense against unauthorized access, they have significant limitations. A poor choice of symbols may enable a person to guess the password. Programs that "crack" stored passwords or "guess" passwords through brute-force attacks can be used to attempt access. As a defense, most security systems lock up a computer or disconnect the user after three incorrect password entries.

Because good passwords must be difficult to guess, they are usually difficult for the user to remember. Nevertheless, to prevent them from falling into the hands of others—users or nonusers—they should never be written down. This rule is hard to follow given that most people have multiple passwords for their computer(s), home security systems, and for accessing information or ordering goods/services over the Internet. With the requirement that passwords be difficult to guess and that they be changed regularly, most of us have difficulty remembering all of them. Mobile apps such as *Keeper* for Android devices, *MyWallet: Password and Credit Card Manager* for iOS (Apple devices), or Dashlane (Android, Windows, and iOS devices) can help you keep track of (and protect) your multiple passwords.

A problem with some password systems is that they are invoked after the operating system has become available to the user. This scheme allows knowledgeable computer users to circumvent the password system. To eliminate this risk, the password system should be integrated into the operating system. Thus, a computer session will not be created for a user until the user has been both identified and authenticated by the system.

An advance over passwords for authenticating users is smartcards. A **smartcard** is a complete portable computer packaged as a plastic, card-sized container that looks like a credit card. The smartcard, which identifies the cardholder, is inserted into a special read/write device connected to the system. Unfortunately, smartcards can be lost or stolen.

The use of biometrics is a significant advance over passwords and smartcards for authenticating users. **Biometrics** is the use of unique functional, behavioral, form, and structural characteristics to provide positive personal identification (i.e., something you are). This technology includes voice pattern recognition, fingerprint scanners, and eye scanners. Voice recognition must perform well in the presence of background noise. Fingerprint scanners are economical and are built into keyboards and mobile devices. The most sophisticated authentication technology is retinal scanners because the structure of eyes is far more unique than are fingerprints. These technologies are used both for physical access to computer equipment and for access to the software.

A way to authenticate a mobile user is through a device access table. A **device access table** ensures that a user is attempting to access the computer system from a specifically authorized device. Read-only-memory (ROM) chips are either built into or installed in computers. When a user attempts to log on, system software reads the device identification embedded in the ROM chip and compares it with data in a stored table to verify that the device is listed in the table. A device access table restricts users to specific devices or sets of devices. Many companies now require employees using mobile devices for remote access to company data or applications (such as cell phones, tablets, or laptops) to agree to a security policy allowing the device to be remotely wiped should that device be lost, stolen, or otherwise compromised to limit unauthorized access to organizational applications and sensitive data.

Smartcard A complete portable computer packaged as a plastic, card-sized container that looks like a credit card and is used to authenticate system users.

Biometrics The use of unique functional, behavioral, form, and structural characteristics to provide positive personal identification.

Device access table A security measure that ensures a user is attempting to access the computer system from a specifically authorized device.

User Rights

Each user, group of users, or application should be granted or denied **user rights**, which are rights to access directories, files/tables, or functions based on specific authorization. Users can be granted or denied rights in a variety of ways. One is through multilevel password systems. For example, many accounting systems have a three-level password system in which the first level permits routine data entry, the second level permits routine processing, and the third level permits non-routine activities, such as master file maintenance.

Another way to limit access to authorized user is through role-based access. Using this approach requires that changes to the role or status of that employee (e.g., termination, transfer) require changes to the access/rights of the employee. The purpose of control activities related to user rights is to make sure the employee has "least-privilege" access—enough accessibility to perform their duties, but not more than they need to effectively fulfill their job responsibilities. Whether employees access the system onsite or from a remote location using a mobile device could also affect user rights.

User rights Rights assigned to each user, group of users, or application to access directories, files/tables, or functions based on a need to know.

User rights are assigned by the system administrator and can be as follows:

Read	Gives the user the right to open files/tables and read their contents.
Write	Gives the user the right to open and change the contents of files/tables.
Execute	Gives the user the right to execute programs.
Erase	Gives the user the right to delete a directory, its files/tables, and subdirectories.
Modify	Gives the user the right to change the attribute or name of files/tables and directories.
File scan	Gives the user the right to see the names of files/tables and directories.

The table in **Exhibit 7.6** gives examples of user rights that are generally acceptable. A table such as this can be used by a system administrator in planning user rights. Once the table is completed, the system administrator sets up user rights in the system.

User	Right	Files
Sales representative	Write	Open sales order file
Sales representative	Read	Shipping transaction file
Shipping clerk	Write	Shipping transaction file
Shipping clerk	Read	Open sales order file
Accounts receivable supervisor	Execute	Open sales order file and shipping transaction file
Billing clerk	Read	Shipping transaction file
Billing clerk	Write	Open invoice file
Cash receipts clerk	Write	Cash receipts transaction file
Accounts receivable supervisor	Execute	Open invoice file and cash receipts transaction file
Purchasing agent	Write	Open purchase order file
Purchasing agent	Read	Receiving transaction file
Receiving clerk	Write	Receiving transaction file
Accounts payable supervisor	Execute	Open purchase order file and receiving transaction file
Cash disbursements clerk	Read	Open purchase order file
Cash disbursements clerk	Read	Receiving transaction file
Cash disbursements clerk	Read	Open invoice file
Cash disbursements clerk	Write	Cash disbursements transaction file
Accounts payable supervisor	Execute	Open invoice file and cash disbursements transaction file
Inventory supervisor	Write	Inventory transaction file

EXHIBIT 7.6 User Rights Table

Directory and File Attributes

Another means of securing access is through **directory and file attributes** that control what can be done to a directory or file. Possible attributes are shown in the following list:

Abbreviation	Attribute
A	Archive Needed (files only)
Ci	Copy Inhibit (files only)
Di	Delete Inhibit (files and directories)
X	Execute Only (files only)
H	Hidden (files and directories)
P	Purge (files and directories)
Ro	Read Only (files only)
Rw	Read Write (files only)
Ri	Rename Inhibit (files and subdirectories)
Sh	Shareable (files only)

These attributes can be used to override user access rights. For example, if a user has been explicitly granted the erase right to a file, but a read-only attribute has been assigned to the file, the user cannot erase the file.

Cryptography

Cryptography is a fairly reliable method of protecting all Internet-related activity (including e-mails) as well as the information that a company physically maintains (databases, programs, etc.). **Cryptography** is the process of transforming, or encrypting, data (usually by scrambling) into a code. When the recipient receives the data, they must be decrypted, or restored, to their original state. This process is illustrated in **Exhibit 7.7**. Much emphasis is placed on the **encryption** side of cryptography because it is this point in the process that determines the ability of a hacker to gain access to data.

Cryptography involves the use of "keys" to manipulate (encrypt) data into code and then to decrypt the code. Frequently, businesses use the same key, called a **private** (or secret) **key**, for both functions, especially if the data will not be transmitted to another location (i.e., "symmetric" encryption, Exhibit 7.7, Panel A). The problem of security arises, however, when data leave their original location. The private key used to encrypt the data is needed by the recipient to decrypt the data. The security of the data will be compromised when the private key is sent between the sender and the receiver. Anyone gaining access to the private key can use it to decrypt the data much in the way someone could use the answer key to figure out the answers on an exam.

This problem of securing data that leave their original location is alleviated by the use of a **public key**, avoiding the necessity of having to maintain and protect pairs of private keys. The combination of a private key and a public key for encryption (asymmetric encryption) can be used to ensure confidentiality of the data and/or to verify the authenticity of the sender.

To ensure confidentiality of the data transmitted, the sending party will use the receiver's public key to encrypt the data before sending it (Exhibit 7.7, Panel B). The receiving party will then use its private key to decode, or decrypt, the data. This "asymmetric encryption" is accomplished without the decrypting (private) key having to be transmitted to the sender. A public key is available to everyone through a publicly accessible repository or directory, so if someone has access to the public key and intercepts an encrypted message, they cannot decrypt the data without the private key. In other words, the **decryption** key (i.e., the private key) never needs to leave its secure location.

Directory and file attributes An access control activity that controls what a user, group of users, or application can do to a directory or file.

Cryptography The process of transforming, or encrypting, data (usually by scrambling) into a "secret code."

Encryption A process, typically involving a mathematical encryption algorithm and an encryption key that scrambles data to prevent unauthorized persons from accessing the data.

Private key A key that performs both encryption and decryption (restoring the encrypted message to clear text) in symmetric encryption, and decryption in asymmetric encryption.

Public key A key that performs encryption, that is, scrambling a clear text message in asymmetric encryption.

Decryption A process that decodes encrypted data (see encryption).

Panel A: Confidentiality of Data Transmitted Using Same Private Key (Symmetric Encryption)

Company A:
Sending an order to Company B

Company B:
Receiving an order from Company A

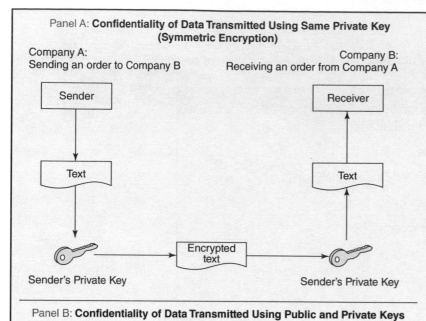

Sender's Private Key

Encrypted text

Sender's Private Key

This panel (A) shows an example of symmetric encryption, whereby the sender (Company A) and the receiver (Company B) use one private key to ensure confidentiality of the data transmitted. The sender's private key is used for both encryption and decryption. The difficulty is maintaining multiple unique private keys if the receiving company, Company B, deals with multiple customers in addition to Company A. Company B would have to maintain and protect several different private keys (one for each "sending" company).

Panel B: Confidentiality of Data Transmitted Using Public and Private Keys (Asymmetric Encryption)

Company A:
Sending an order to Company B

Company B:
Receiving an order from Company A

Sender

Text

Receiver's Public Key

Encrypted text

Receiver's Private Key

Receiver

Text

This panel (B) shows an example of using a combination of public and private keys to verify confidentiality of the data transmitted, whereby the sender (Company A) encrypts its order data using the receiver's (Company B) public key. The receiver (Company B) then decrypts the data using its private key. Using this method, the private key remains private unlike the method in Panel A where the private key has to be transmitted by the sender. One set of public-private keys can be used for dealing with multiple customers. All the customers placing orders with Company B would be sent (or have access to) the receiver's public key to encrypt their order information to ensure the confidentiality of the transmitted data. If Company C accidently received the message Company A sent to Company B, Company C could not decrypt it.

Panel C: Authenticity of Sender

Company A:
Sending an order to Company B

Company B:
Receiving an order from Company A

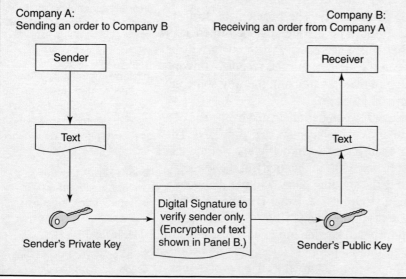

Sender's Private Key

Digital Signature to verify sender only. (Encryption of text shown in Panel B.)

Sender's Public Key

*This panel (C) illustrates how the receiver (Company B) verifies **only** the authenticity of the sender (Company A). In this case, Company A "signs" the message using its private key. This digital signature can be verified by the receiver (Company B) using the sender's (Company A's) public key.*

EXHIBIT 7.7 Cryptography with Public and Private Keys

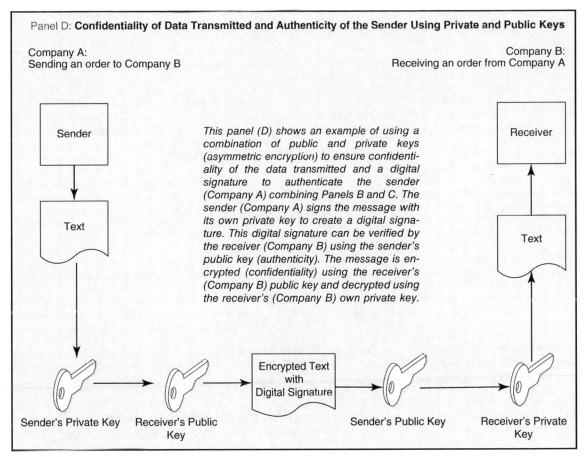

Panel D: **Confidentiality of Data Transmitted and Authenticity of the Sender Using Private and Public Keys**

Company A:
Sending an order to Company B

Company B:
Receiving an order from Company A

Sender

Text

This panel (D) shows an example of using a combination of public and private keys (asymmetric encryption) to ensure confidentiality of the data transmitted and a digital signature to authenticate the sender (Company A) combining Panels B and C. The sender (Company A) signs the message with its own private key to create a digital signature. This digital signature can be verified by the receiver (Company B) using the sender's public key (authenticity). The message is encrypted (confidentiality) using the receiver's (Company B) public key and decrypted using the receiver's (Company B) own private key.

Receiver

Text

Encrypted Text
with
Digital Signature

Sender's Private Key

Receiver's Public Key

Sender's Public Key

Receiver's Private Key

EXHIBIT 7.7 Continued

While Exhibit 7.7, Panel B discusses how to ensure the confidentiality of the data during transmission, the receiving company might want to determine that the sending party is who it claims to be. This is done using a **digital signature**. The sending party uses its private key to create a digital signature (Exhibit 7.7, Panel C). The receiving party (or anyone else) can use the sender's public key to verify the authenticity of the sender (i.e., verify the digital signature has not changed during transmission). Note that Exhibit 7.7, Panel D combines the information in Panels B and C to illustrate both confidentiality of the data during transmission and authentication of the sending party.

> **Digital signature** Extra data appended to an electronic message which identifies and authenticates the sender.

Cryptography is also being applied to databases in an effort to encrypt data "at rest" (e.g., when data are stored in the "cloud" or on servers accessible through a network). Every piece of data is encrypted separately so that a hacker would have to individually break the code of each data element in a database. Some vendors offer database software with varying complexities of encryption codes so customers have some control over how much encryption they want to apply to their records.

Unfortunately, there are some drawbacks to cryptography. Encryption and decryption take time. Asymmetric encryption (Exhibit 7.7, Panel B) algorithms are not as quick to process as are symmetric algorithms (Exhibit 7.7, Panel A). This is due to the length of the encrypted message necessary for a given level of security with public-key encryption. Private key (symmetric) encrypted message lengths are shorter for a given level of security as compared to public key encrypted message lengths. However, public key encryption allows users to send data securely to a company, such as Best Buy, without jeopardizing the security of the private key held by Best Buy to decrypt encrypted information.

Another problem with public key encryption is the potential for "impersonation" of a legitimate public key by someone other than the owner. In other words, just because you think a website is legitimate (i.e., you can safely send them your personal information), you cannot be sure because anyone can create a public/private key pair using someone

Repudiation A customer's denial that an order was placed for goods or services from a vendor.

Digital certificate A form of electronic identification that is issued by a certification authority (CA) after the CA verifies the company participating in e-commerce activities is legitimate.

else's name and bind it to any website. A digital signature (to verify authenticity of the sender, shown in Panel C of Exhibit 7.7) prevents **repudiation**, which is a customer's denial that an order was placed for goods from a vendor. If a vendor shipped goods based on an order received and created an account receivable but the customer repudiates, the vendor may never be able to collect the receivable.

To create a digital signature, software of the sender performs a hashing algorithm on the message. This hashing algorithm reduces the message to a string of digits called a message digest. Regardless of the length of a file, its message digest is always the same length. The message digest is a unique number that can only be calculated from the contents of the message. Sending the message digest with an electronic message guarantees no one has altered the message while in transit, but you still cannot prove who the sender was. The message digest is encrypted with the private key of the sender (as shown in Panel C of Exhibit 7.7). This is the sender's digital signature. It is unique to the sender because it is generated from the contents of the message and the sender's private key.

The digital signature (i.e., the encrypted message digest) and the message are packaged into a digital envelope, which is transmitted to the receiver. The receiver performs two operations—one on the message and one on the digital signature. A hashing algorithm is performed on the clear text message to generate a new message digest. The digital signature is decrypted with the sender's public key resulting in the original message digest. The recipient then compares the new message digest with the original message digest. If they match, the message is authentic. **Exhibit 7.8** depicts the creation and use of a digital signature. To emphasize the explanation of how a digital signature works, this exhibit does not include the encryption and decryption of the message itself—only the encryption and decryption that relate to the digital signature.

Authentication verifies that messages really come from their stated source. In the paper world, a handwritten signature on a document serves as authentication. In the electronic world, a digital signature serves as authentication of the sender. To avoid questions about the authenticity of the source company, a **digital certificate**—a form of electronic identification for doing business on the Internet—is issued by an independent third party called a certification authority (CA). A CA, such as Verisign, will verify the existence and

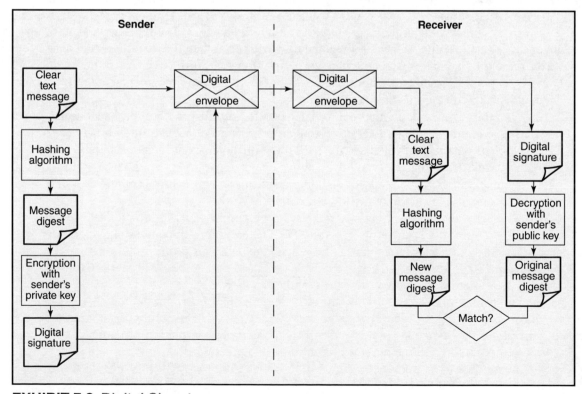

EXHIBIT 7.8 Digital Signature

identity of a company participating in e-commerce activities. Once the CA is satisfied that the company is legitimate, a digital certificate is issued that includes, among other things, the identity of the owner (along with the owner's digital signature), the owner's public key (and expiration date of the key), and the serial number of the digital certificate.[4] The CA binds the digital certificate and the related public key to the secured company website. The Secure Sockets Layer (SSL) protocol, represented by a small lock in the lower right hand corner of a webpage is currently the most commonly accepted protocol used by web browsers to protect sensitive data in transit.

To illustrate how the digital certificate protects an online purchaser, let's use a personal example you can probably relate to (even though the types of transactions we are discussing in this chapter relate to business-to-business transactions). Suppose you want to order the latest tablet from an online electronics retailer. You access the retailer's secured public key through a web browser, such as Firefox or Internet Explorer. The web browser checks to make sure the digital certificate is valid before completing a secured connection to the website. With a valid digital certificate in place, you can feel confident that your order information (such as your credit card number) is being transmitted securely over the Internet to the retailer.[5]

Transmission Medium for Mobile Devices and Networks

Networks present additional concerns over unauthorized access to transmitted data because the transmission medium can be violated. Some results of unauthorized access are eavesdropping on data in transit, alteration of data in transit, and the introduction of unauthorized instructions—particularly viruses—into the network.

Electronic signals may be carried on several types of network media. Because fiber-optic cable carries signals as light waves rather than as electrical impulses, it provides better access security than other types of cable. Eavesdropping on a fiber-optic network is not only difficult but is also readily detectable. Cables carrying electrical impulses, on the other hand, can be tapped more easily with little likelihood of detection. Networks that rely on public dial-up, voice-grade telephone lines offer the least security of all. The advent of mobile devices has become a critical risk exposure area for many businesses, so the importance of restricted access to the network is essential. Limiting activities that can be processed remotely, as well as requirements to use a virtual private network (VPN)—a "tunnel" to the company network that is difficult for an unauthorized person to get into—for remote access can reduce this risk. To prevent eavesdropping any information communicated over insecure networks (such as using the free WiFi at a coffee shop), some form of encryption (shown in Exhibit 7.7) is needed.

Firewalls and Anti-Virus Protection

A popular way of shielding a private network is with a firewall. A **firewall** consists of hardware and software that work together to channel all Internet communications through a control gateway and filter messages coming into the private network. The firewall knows where all messages originate because all have an Internet address. The firewall will allow only messages from addresses that have been approved to pass through it.

Three types of firewalls, in order of the least secure to the most secure, are screening routers, operating system-based firewalls, and application-based firewalls. Screening routers use a set of rules to filter out intruders but do not authenticate users and usually maintain no log of attempted accesses, length of time logged on, and applications accessed. Operating system-based firewalls allow authorized access to the network operating system only. Once accessed, the operating system provides additional security. *Application-based firewalls* are an addition to operating system-based firewalls and restrict access beyond the network operating system to applications, data files, and workstations.

Anti-virus protection software consists of software meant to detect computer viruses that could shut down a system or allow cybercriminals to steal data. While a disadvantage of anti-virus software is that it can only recognize previously identified viruses and malware, it is essential for the network to have some kind of anti-virus detection/protection as part of the organization's cybersecurity toolkit.

Firewall Hardware and software that work together to channel all network communications through a control gateway to filter messages coming into and going out of a private network.

Anti-virus protection software Software designed to detect computer viruses that could shut down a system or allow cybercriminals to steal data.

Automatic Log Off

Automatic log off The disconnection of a workstation from a file server or host computer if there has been no activity for a given period of time.

Procedures can be established for the **automatic log off**, or disconnection, of a workstation from a file server or host computer if there has been no activity for a given period of time. Inactivity could indicate an unattended workstation. Workstations should never be left unattended while programs are being run, and users should be required to return control to a screen menu upstream of any required ID or password entry. Without this control, an unauthorized person with computer experience could retrieve data from main memory or even from a file deleted on a hard drive.

Network and Data Service Center Operation Controls

Network and data service center operation controls address the availability of information processing facilities when needed. Data centers are an artifact of central site management of information technology. While many systems are now set up as client/server and distributed processing systems using networks that require departmental management and support, many of the data center operation controls used with "legacy" mainframe systems are also appropriate for network operations.

Mainframe, client/server, and distributed processing systems all need the protection afforded by the access security discussed in the previous section. In addition, the following network and data service center operation controls need to be implemented:

- Fire suppression systems
- Environmental controls for humidity and temperature
- Backup controls
- Downtime controls
- Recovery controls

Fire Suppression Systems

Computer equipment is subject to damage should there be a fire in the data center. Fire is a major threat to the electrical equipment, so it is essential to protect the data center from this hazard. Fire extinguishers should be available (water-based and gas-based), and easily accessible. There should be equipment to provide early warning of a fire that is heard in an area that has continuous occupation by employees. These systems should be inspected and tested on a regular basis.

Environmental Controls

Computer equipment is also sensitive to temperature and humidity. There should be environmental systems in place to control the temperature and humidity within a certain range. Typically, the range for temperature is between 18 and 21° C (65–70° F) and preferred humidity ranges between 45 and 55%.

Backup Controls

All files should be backed up routinely, and the backup copies should be stored in a secure, off-site location and tested regularly for readability. The backup medium should also minimize cost. The frequency of backup operations should be related to the volatility of the files in question and to the effort in reloading data in the event of data loss or damage. Generally, it is necessary to back up program files only one time. This is done after the programs have been installed and all customization work completed. If additional customization or updating is done at a later time to a program, a new backup of the changed program should be made. Data files, on the other hand, should be backed up frequently. Virtually all transaction files should be backed up at least once a day, and master files in batch systems should be backed up once per posting period. Files in systems with real-time posting may need to be backed up more often than once a day.

Three batch backup strategies and one continuous strategy are as follows:

Batch:	Full	All data, regardless of when or if it has previously been backed up
	Incremental	All data that have been modified since the last incremental backup
	Differential	All data that have been modified since the last full backup
Continuous:		All data are continuously replicated on redundant drives

Incremental and differential backups should not be combined. Use full backups interspersed with incremental backups or with differential backups. Files should be scanned for viruses before being backed up.

Frequent backup and the need to recycle backup media should not be allowed to conflict with the appropriate length of time for retaining backup copies. The retention period should provide an opportunity to correct erroneous or damaged files (Vignette 7.2).

Backups can be performed in-house or by using an online backup service through the Internet (e.g., "cloud" or offsite server farm). The process of backing up data using an online service is similar to that of performing a backup in-house. The first time, you do a complete backup and then smaller incremental or differential backups. However, after the initial backup, backups can be done automatically. Good backup systems compress and encrypt data before transmission. The online service transfers the backup data to a server that is securely stored. Online data and program backup services (e.g., iCloud, Microsoft's Private or Public Cloud services) are becoming more attractive to smaller organizations with small (or non-existent) IT departments to try to save the costs of maintaining data backups on servers in-house Most cloud services only require that the company pay for the services they need.

Vignette 7. 2

The Backup Copy Is Bad, Too!

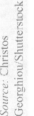

Source: Christos Georghiou/Shutterstock.

When damaged records were detected in an inventory master file, the network administrator retrieved the backup copy made the previous day. However, the same records were damaged in the backup file. In fact, it was soon realized that all four backup files—made the previous four days—were bad.

The company's policy was to make a full backup of the file server at eight o'clock each evening. The backup copies were placed in an off-site fireproof vault. Four backup copies, made on successive evenings, were maintained. After 4 days, a backup disk was recycled.

Unfortunately, the damage to the files occurred a week before it was detected. By that time, file copies containing the undamaged records were no longer available, and all the data had to be rekeyed from paper reports.

With the benefit of hindsight, management changed its backup policies to require retention of backup copies made on Friday evenings for 2 weeks. Backup copies made on the last day of the month were to be kept for 3 months.

THOUGHT QUESTIONS

1. If you were the inventory department manager, would these policies be adequate to protect your data?

2. What other procedures should be added to the backup policies to ensure that lost data can be retrieved or recreated?

Downtime Controls

The repair of computer hardware may take several days and, occasionally, several weeks. Therefore, to reduce the amount of downtime, maintenance schedules should be established for all computer hardware. Conformity with these schedules should be checked routinely. Provision also must be made for emergency repairs to minimize nonproductive downtime.

Recovery Controls

Recovery controls deal with prompt recovery from equipment failure (such as controller failure, electrical failure, or media/head crashes) and natural disasters (such as flood, lightning, fire, earthquake, or hurricane) that could put the information processing facilities out of operation for an extended period.

Automatic Rollback

Automatic rollback The feature of a database management system that is invoked when a program run prematurely terminates. Incomplete transactions are backed out so the database is returned to the state it was in before the transaction began.

When a running program prematurely terminates, it cannot be restarted until associated records and files are returned to their original condition. A database management system has a feature called **automatic rollback** in which incomplete transactions are backed out so the database is returned to the state it was in before the transaction began.

Uninterruptible Power Supply

An uninterruptible power supply that uses batteries is needed for processing to continue during a power outage or power surge. This device will supply power long enough for files to be properly closed and for users to log off.

Alternative Processing Facility

Alternative channels should be identified for use during main channel downtime. Provision must be made for running high-priority programs at an alternative processing facility in the event of extended equipment downtime.

Disaster Recovery Plan

Disaster recovery plan A plan that documents detailed recovery procedures in the event of equipment failure or disasters to quickly and smoothly restore an organization's processing capabilities.

A **disaster recovery plan** documents detailed recovery procedures to quickly and smoothly restore an organization's processing capabilities after a catastrophic incident. Disaster recovery plans are put in place to reduce "business risk" or the risk that in the event of some natural or man-made disaster, the firm will not be able to continue business without significant interruption. Critical resources and services that have highest priority in an emergency situation should be identified. In this context, only about one-third of all information processing qualifies as "essential processing"; this normally includes payroll processing, customer billing, accounts payable, and statutory reporting. A team of key individuals under the direction of a disaster recovery coordinator should be specially trained in recovery situations, and all procedures for dealing with such contingencies should be tested by all company employees regularly in simulation exercises. A disaster recovery plan should address the people involved in recovery as well as the programs, data, and facilities (see Vignette 7.3). The company's contingency plan (sometimes referred to as a "business continuity plan") should include:

■ Ways to minimize the interruption of business (e.g., insurance to replace damaged equipment, alternative sites to conduct business after an emergency).

■ Alternative means to continue processing until the company is at normal capacity (e.g., back-up program and data files). Back-up sites can either be different branches of the same company or other organizations contracted for short-term periods. The sites can be either "cold" sites (where power and space are available to set up processing equipment on short notice) or "hot" sites (a location with a computer system configured in a manner similar to the normal day-to-day processing of the company and available for immediate use).

■ When and how normal operations can be resumed (using simulations to check documentation and effectiveness of plan).

Vignette 7.3

One Stone Unturned

Troy Watson, manager of information services for LA Distributing, received a telephone call at 9:30 Friday night after returning home from dinner. "The fire department just put out a fire at our computer center—it was totally destroyed!" he was told. Putting the company's disaster recovery plan into action, Watson alerted key assistants that information services personnel would be flying to Las Vegas on Sunday morning to resume operations at a contract backup facility. Personnel at the backup facility were also notified.

On Saturday, Watson and his assistants obtained backup program and data records from the secure off-site storage location and made working copies using a local company's computer. Watson returned the backup copies to storage. Early Sunday morning information services personnel boarded a chartered plane and flew to Las Vegas with the working copies of program and

data in tow. Sunday afternoon and evening were spent loading and testing the files.

On Monday morning, data processing resumed as usual, supporting LA Distributing's locations nationwide. While silently congratulating himself, Troy realized that the disaster recovery plan had a serious defect, and that he had taken an unacceptable risk with the company's resources and future.

Everyone had flown on the same airplane.

THOUGHT QUESTIONS

1. Identify any other flaws in the disaster recovery plan.

2. What procedures could LA Distributing set up to ensure this type of disaster is avoided in the future?

- Training personnel in emergency operations (note: continuous updates and reviews of the plan should be part of business continuity plan).

- Plans for taking care of employees who are required to work long shifts to get the company back to normal operation levels. This may include picking up extra clothing or checking on key employees' families for them while they work.

- Keep the business continuity plan simple and practice it regularly so that the procedures become second nature to the employees. Note that during the World Trade Center disaster, Morgan Stanley only lost 7 out of 2,700 employees because everyone knew what they were supposed to do in an emergency.[6]

System Software Acquisition, Implementation, and Maintenance Controls

Control activities also address the acquisition, implementation, and maintenance of system software. System software includes database management systems, communications software, operating systems, utility programs, and security software. These control activities also regulate logging, tracking, and monitoring activities of the information system.

Application Software Selection, Implementation, and Maintenance Controls

Control activities also should address the selection, implementation, and maintenance of application software. Application software, such as accounting systems, may be purchased or developed and customized in-house. New applications and modifications to applications should be properly authorized, tested, approved, and documented. Specifications for new applications should be drawn up jointly by users and information technology personnel. Representatives of user departments, particularly from accounting and internal auditing, should participate in this effort and should also be involved in the selection of application software. External auditors should be consulted to ensure the auditability of the systems. Before implementation, new software should be tested in accordance with a planned test program and the results should be reviewed in light of the system specifications.

To provide further control over application software selection, implementation, and maintenance, every organization of any appreciable size should have an information

Steering committee A committee that establishes or approves information processing policies and operating standards, approves system projects, sets priorities for implementing systems, evaluates the effectiveness of processing operations, and generally monitors and evaluates processing activities.

services steering committee. A **steering committee** establishes or approves information processing policies and operating standards, approves system projects, sets priorities for implementing systems, evaluates the effectiveness of processing operations, and generally monitors and evaluates information processing activities. In many organizations, the steering committee is chaired by the chief information officer and includes representatives from each of the user groups, information specialists, and managers. The committee exercises a control function to ensure that an organization's investment in information processing is in line with the organization's strategies, and that resources are used effectively. Many small companies have no in-house professional information services staff and have to rely on outside consultants, external auditors, and computer vendors as their source of advice. All organizations, regardless of size, need a source of information processing expertise on which they can depend for assistance. The key control activity here is to have an organized, formalized approach to the selection and implementation of system projects.

Information Processing—Application Controls

LEARNING OBJECTIVE 7
Identify the application control activities that are desirable for information processing systems.

As mentioned earlier, whereas information processing general controls relate to the reliability and consistency of the overall information processing environment, application controls apply to the flow of data in and among individual applications. Application controls can be separated into input, processing, output, and master file maintenance controls, a classification scheme that we will use to facilitate our discussion. However, as with many of our other classifications, some overlap exists in which application controls have characteristics of more than one of these categories. The information processing application controls discussed in this section are shown in **Exhibit 7.9**.

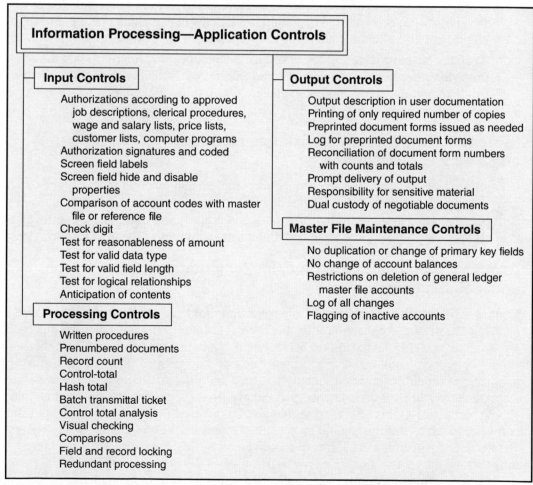

EXHIBIT 7.9 Map of Information Processing—Application Controls

Input Controls

Input controls refer to the authorization, entry, and verification of data entering the system. Most of the errors in an accounting system occur at the data entry point. As a result, many systems now bypass source documents from which data have to be keyed in favor of automated data capture. Regardless of the method of data entry, an accounting system must have numerous data entry and verification controls. Control efforts are greater for the input activity than for any of the other information processing activities.

Input controls Control activities that deal with the authorization, entry, and verification of data entering the system.

Data and Transaction Authorization Controls

Only authorized data should be entered in the system. Authorization is granted by upper management through either general authorizations or specific authorizations. General authorizations cover a whole class of transactions and other events and are communicated in budgets, job descriptions, price lists, credit customers list, and wage or salary lists.

General authorizations also can be built into computer programs that are approved for use in creating such classes of transactions as routine adjusting entries in a general ledger system. Automatically created transactions should be subjected routinely to management review, and exceptions should be identified for investigation. All general authorizations should be reviewed and updated periodically.

A specific authorization applies to a single transaction and is granted on a case-by-case basis. A specific authorization may approve a departure from the provisions of a general authorization. A specific authorization can be evidenced by a handwritten signature on a document or by the entry of an authorization code in the accounting system.

Input Screen Controls

Keyboard entry of data should be made through computer screen forms that are supported with controls. Screens use a block format in which labels (prompts) are placed above or to the left of the empty fields to which they refer. The labels prompt the user for what data should be entered and where it should be entered.

Additional screen controls are properties such as disable and hide. A disabled field is dimmed with background color to indicate it is not available to the user whereas a hidden field cannot be seen. Properties can be set to prevent a user from doing the following:

- Invoking command buttons. An input screen may include a POST button. This button will remain dim until all the appropriate data have been entered in the screen. At that time, the button will become bright and allow the user to invoke the command.

- Accessing certain fields. When a field is disabled on a screen, the user will not be able to tab to the field. Alternatively, the field can be hidden.

- Entering unauthorized information. For example, a user cannot change a field label, such as "Sold to."

All advanced personal computer accounting system packages permit input screens to be completely designed by users and system administrators depending on the appropriate authorization. Users may be authorized to add fields, delete fields from display, move fields, and change fields.

Input Verification Controls

As data are entered in a computer screen form, they are verified for correctness in numerous ways. Input **verification controls** provide programmed edit and validation routines that are done on a point-of-entry basis. Some commonly used checks are as follows:

- Valid codes
- Reasonableness of amounts

Verification controls Programmed edit and validation routines that verify the correctness of entered data. They test for valid codes, reasonableness of amounts, valid data type (numeric, alphanumeric), valid field length, logical relationships, anticipated contents, and valid date.

- Valid data type
- Valid field length
- Logical relationships
- Anticipated contents
- Valid date

Codes, such as a G/L account number from the chart of accounts, customer code, vendor code, and product code, can be validated by comparing the entered code to a master file or a reference file of permissible codes. For example, when the user enters an inventory code to record a sale, the accounting system goes to the inventory master file to see if the entered code matches a code in the master file. If a match is not found, the message "Unknown item number" is displayed on the computer screen.

A common error in the entry of numeric codes is the transposition of numbers. For example, a valid numeric code of 4683 may be entered as 4638. To prevent this type of error, numeric codes can be validated by the use of self-checking digits appended to the number itself. The appended **check digit** or digits are generated from the main number by some arithmetic algorithm. A number and check digit combination that does not satisfy the algorithm indicates an invalid entry. Check digits provide less security than do master file or reference file look-ups but may save retrieval time and may be more economical when many account codes are in use. Reasonableness, or limit, tests are made on amount fields to verify that the data conform to expected characteristics of magnitude or sign. For example, a sales order has a field for quantity sold. When the user enters a number in this field, the accounting system checks that the quantity is a positive amount and then goes to the inventory master file to check the quantity field in the record of the item sold. If the entered quantity exceeds the quantity on hand, the message "Quantity exceeds the available stock on hand" is displayed on the computer screen.

More complicated reasonableness checks compare a number entered with allowable limits contained in a master file or reference file. For example, in a purchasing system, a message querying the user might be displayed if the number entered in the quantity field for computers exceeded 100, whereas a message would not be displayed unless the number entered for screws exceeded 100,000.

An example of a test for valid data type (such as numeric, alphanumeric, date) would be if, for example, the numbers 1441 were entered in a date field, a message such as "invalid month/day" would be displayed on the computer screen. A test for valid data length would result in an error message if, for example, four digits were entered in a zip code field (instead of five digits).

A check for a logical relationship is unique because it looks for an association between two fields, whereas the other checks we have discussed have been on a single field. It may be appropriate to test the value entered for a field by considering another field on the screen to check for a logical association between the two fields. For example, if the value entered for a state field is Texas, then the first digit of the number entered for the zip code must begin with the number 7.

Anticipated contents checks require that a value be entered in a field. For example, when inputting a sales order, the "Quantity" field must be input (i.e., cannot be left blank) before advancing to the next input box.

Provision must be made to override data-entry controls when the transaction data are exceptional but valid. Otherwise, the transaction would be rejected repeatedly. A time card claiming an unusually large (or small) number of hours may simply reflect an unusual situation in the workplace. Usually this contingency is handled by a supervisor who verifies the data and, if appropriate, enters an authorization code to override the control. Such authorization codes must be used cautiously and monitored closely to prevent abuse (Vignette 7.4).

Check digit A single digit appended to a number to validate the number. The digit is computed from the other digits in the number itself.

Vignette 7.4

Think Before You Act!

Source: piskota/Shutterstock.

Nick Hyasi, an ambitious young man, supervised twenty employees in the purchasing department who created purchase orders in the system from authorized purchase requisitions. Extensive controls verified entries for missing, invalid, or incompatible data elements and also included reasonableness checks on quantities and dollar amounts. Occasionally, a valid transaction amount was rejected by the system, and one of Hyasi's responsibilities was to verify the amount on the purchase requisition and then key in an authorization code allowing the purchase order to be processed. The system did not echo the authorization code on the screen, but recorded the code, date, and transaction identification in a log that was routinely reviewed by an internal auditor.

Hyasi had been busy all day when an employee called him to key in his authorization code. "Quick, show me the purchase requisition," he said breathlessly. The clerk showed him a purchase requisition calling for the purchase of fifteen large-screen television sets. The system was programmed to reject quantities greater than ten when the items cost more than $1,000 each. Hyasi knew the requesting manager was outfitting a customer reception area, and the request for televisions seemed reasonable. He quickly keyed in the code and hurried to a meeting.

What Hyasi did not know was that the manager had requested only five televisions and that the employee had added a "1" to make it 15. Also, he did not know that this employee's friend worked in the receiving department. Fortunately for the company, the friend was arrested by a security guard a few weeks later as he was loading televisions into a van. Hyasi was not so fortunate. An investigation showed that he had been negligent in authorizing the doctored purchase requisition.

THOUGHT QUESTIONS

1. List some of the control strengths in the scenario described above.

2. Recommend some control activities that might have kept the situation described above from occurring.

Correction of Data Entry Errors

Error correction follows error detection. It may be possible to simply rekey a transaction to correct it. However, if the entered data have been processed, then correcting or reversing entries must be made. Rekeyed data must be verified to ensure the corrections do not contain errors.

Processing Controls

Processing controls refer to accurate and complete processing of transactions and other events. These controls include written procedures, prenumbered documents, batch controls, control total analysis, visual checking, comparisons, field and record locking, and redundant processing.

> **Processing controls** Control activities that refer to the accurate and complete processing of transactions and other events. Examples are written procedures, prenumbered documents, batch controls, control total analysis, visual checking, and redundant processing.

Written Procedures

All computerized accounting systems include some manual procedures. If these steps are written, they can serve as a guide for employees and ensure consistency of operations. Written procedures are dated and approved by an appropriate manager. Responsibility for maintaining the currency of manual procedures is assigned to specific individuals. Procedure manuals should be available to all relevant personnel and required reading for all new employees. Master copies and/or data files of all procedures should be retained by the controller.

Prenumbered Documents

The prenumbering of internally generated documents, such as sales orders, shipping documents, invoices, purchase orders, receiving documents, and checks, provides a means to ensure that all authorized transactions and other events are processed once and only once. The processing program checks for any missing or duplicate numbers in the sequence and reports them on exception reports for investigation. Prenumbered documents help reduce the risk of insertion of unauthorized transactions and other events.

Batch Controls

A batch consists of a set of records (usually source documents) of related events that have been accumulated for processing at the same time. Batch controls provide assurance that as a batch progresses through the various processing stages it contains the same set of records—no records have been lost or added. These batch controls include the following:

- Record count
- Control total
- Hash total
- Batch transmittal ticket

A **record count** can be made at different points in the system and, if it remains the same, indicates that the same total records are in the batch. This count helps guard against the accidental loss of records. However, by itself the control does not necessarily confirm that the same records are present.

A **control total** is the sum of an amount or quantity field contained in the transaction records. An example is the total, or sum, of the cash disbursements transactions. This total is compared with the total amount that was approved by the treasurer for disbursing, the total amount of the checks signed, and, finally, the total amount of the checks distributed. A **hash total** is a type of control total that is formed from data elements, such as customer numbers, which normally would not be the subject of arithmetic operations. A hash total has no economic, accounting, or arithmetic significance; nevertheless, it should remain the same throughout processing. A change in a control total or a hash total from one processing stage to another is evidence that records have been lost or duplicated or that unauthorized records have been substituted.

To illustrate the use of batch controls, consider the following batch of transactions:

Employee#	Hours Worked	Gross Pay
531	40	$320.00
532	45	405.00
534	40	380.00
545	30	255.00
548	50	462.50

The record count is 5; a hash total of employee numbers yields 2,690; and the control totals of hours worked and gross pay are 205 and $1,822.50, respectively.

A **batch transmittal ticket** is a paper document attached to a batch of source documents in transit from one processing stage to another. An illustration is in **Exhibit 7.10**.

The transmittal ticket records the origin and destination of the batch, the number of documents included, and other information, such as control and hash totals. It serves as a kind of "shipping document" for the batch. It also may serve as a "receipt" to be signed and returned to the sender upon arrival at its destination. Batch tickets often are prenumbered to

---

Record count A count made at different points in the system—if the count remains the same, this indicates the same total records are in the batch. This count helps guard against the accidental loss of records. However, by itself the control does not necessarily confirm that the same records are present.

Control total The sum of an amount or quantity field contained in the transaction records, such as the sum of all the net amounts due in a batch of invoices. Control totals are used to ensure that as a batch progresses through the various processing stages, it contains the same set of records.

Hash total A type of control total to ensure that as a batch of documents progresses through the various processing stages it contains the same set of records. A hash total has no economic, accounting, or arithmetic significance but should remain the same throughout processing. An example is the total of customer numbers.

Batch transmittal ticket A paper document attached to a batch of source documents in transit from one processing stage to another to ensure that as a batch progresses through the various processing stages it contains the same set of records. A transmittal ticket serves as a kind of shipping document and a receipt for the batch.

Batch Transmittal Ticket	
Date: 07/09/2018	Ticket No.: 61067
Point of origin:	Sales
Destination:	Accounts receivable
Transaction type:	Sales orders
Document count:	100
Document numbers (range):	13,667–13,766
Control total: Gross sales =	$48,331
Hash total: Customer numbers =	590,475
Authorized by:	
Received by:	
Processed by:	
Date/time:	
Form #918273	

EXHIBIT 7.10 Batch Transmittal Ticket

protect against the loss of whole batches of records or the insertion of unauthorized ones. The preparation of batch transmittal tickets and the calculation of control and hash totals should be performed independently of processing transactions and other events.

Control Total Analysis

Although **control total analysis** may appear to be appropriate only for batch processing, it can also be suitable for real-time processing by choosing a time frame in which transactions and other events are entered and treating the transactions and other events in that time frame as a batch. A computer program may analyze control totals by comparing them with totals formed earlier in a processing sequence or with totals formed on previous occasions.

Control totals involving previously derived totals may be used to confirm the update of master files. For example, assume that the current balance field in the accounts receivable record of the general ledger master file is $70,000. A sales transaction file contains a total of $8,000 credit sale transactions. After posting the sales transaction file to the general ledger master file, the new balance of accounts receivable should be $78,000. The last record of the sales transaction file could be a control record showing the total debit and credit transactions. The master file update program would compare these control totals to the balance of accounts receivable before and after posting to check the accuracy of its updating process.

Control totals can also be analyzed to check the accuracy of processing by calculating and comparing them for related fields. For example, in payroll processing, control totals can be calculated for gross pay, deductions, and net pay. After processing is completed, net pay should equal gross pay less deductions.

A **batch control report** documents the results of the control total analysis. This report lists the transactions and other events contained in the batch and includes the transaction count and all applicable hash totals and control totals. The report also identifies missing or duplicate transactions and other events.

Control total analysis A control activity that verifies the accuracy of programmed processing. It analyzes control totals by comparing them to totals formed earlier in a processing sequence or to totals formed on previous occasions.

Batch control report A report that documents the results of control total analysis.

Visual Checking

Visual checking of reports and documents for reasonableness can detect errors in processing. Experienced people often have a talent for spotting data that "look wrong."

Occasionally errors are obvious to even the inexperienced, such as accounts that normally have a debit balance reflecting a credit balance.

Comparisons

Comparison of amounts can detect errors in processing. For example, the prices charged for individual items on sales orders should be compared with the selling prices for the items in the inventory master file; or the sum of the individual customer amounts owed in the customer master file should be compared with the amount of the accounts receivable account in the general ledger master file.

Field and Record Locking

Field locking "locks" a field or record that is being updated until that update is complete. This control ensures that two or more users and/or programs do not overwrite each other. For example, if a program is updating the outstanding balances of customers in the customer master file, a user cannot change the address of a customer whose balance is being updated.

Redundant Processing

Redundant processing is another useful processing control. An example is the recording of a quantity and a unit cost. The extended amount can be calculated as required. The same extended amount can be recomputed at different stages in the process to ensure that the initial computation was correct and that the data have not been altered during processing. The emergence of an inconsistency at some point during processing indicates the contamination of the data after their initial entry. Redundancy of all real-time processing is advantageous where the cost of loss of data caused by equipment malfunction is particularly high, such as with an electronic funds transfer (EFT) system.

Output Controls

Output controls Control activities that relate to providing output to the appropriate people and using the output appropriately.

Output controls relate to providing output to the appropriate people and using the output appropriately—to include the proper disposition of the output (e.g., destruction/shredding). The nature of the output produced by each program—target output device, type of stock paper or preprinted forms, expected volume of output, required number of copies, and distribution of the output—is described in user documentation.

Only the required number of copies of printed output should be produced. Any additional or extra copies should be disposed of in accordance with authorized procedures; sensitive material should be shredded. Preprinted document forms, particularly "action document" forms such as checks, sales orders, credit memos, purchase orders, and production orders, should be carefully controlled and issued only for authorized use when needed. A log (indicating the serial numbers of all forms issued and voided) should be kept for each type of preprinted document form, and spoiled forms should be accounted for properly. Ranges of document form numbers used can be reconciled with internally generated transaction numbers, record counts, control totals, and hash totals.

Printed output should be promptly delivered to designated recipients and never left out for just anyone to pick up. Care must be taken to ensure that all paychecks are properly distributed to employees (whether in paper form or through direct deposit) and that all vendor checks are mailed. Responsibility for conveying sensitive material to its proper destination is assigned to specific individuals, and dual custody is required when moving negotiable documents to and from safe storage.

Master File Maintenance Controls

Master file maintenance controls Control activities designed into the master file maintenance function, which is used to add records, change the contents of certain fields in records, and delete records.

Master file maintenance controls are designed into the master file maintenance function, which is used to add records, change the contents of certain fields within records, and delete records. These controls include the following:

- Prohibiting a user from duplicating or changing an existing primary key field.
- Prohibiting a user from directly changing an account balance. Any necessary changes in account balances must be made through the ordinary transaction entry process.

- Restricting deletion of a general ledger master file account unless all the following conditions have been met:
  - The account has a zero balance.
  - No account activity has occurred in the current accounting period.
  - The account is not needed to print documents in the future (W-2s, for example) and is not needed to prepare comparative reports such as comparative balance sheets, income statements, listings of sales by customer.
- Generating a log of all changes to a master file during the current accounting period.
- Flagging accounts as inactive to preclude inappropriate entries, such as entries to accounts for terminated employees.

Monitoring

Internal control needs to be monitored to determine whether it is adequate and effective. Monitoring also includes the modification of existing controls or the design of new ones to minimize those risks where deficiencies in control have been discovered.

LEARNING OBJECTIVE 8
Explain the purpose of and approaches to monitoring internal control including IT auditing.

The COSO 2013 framework discusses two principles related to the monitoring component. **Principle 16** describes how monitoring can be conducted on an ongoing basis, as a separate project, or as a combination of both. Ongoing monitoring includes various comparisons and reconciliations that are inherent in routine supervisory activities. Examples of ongoing monitoring activities are preparing and investigating items on exception reports,[7] reconciling the bank statement with the cash account, reconciling data prepared for operational purposes with data on financial statements, and making other comparisons to ensure that the accounting records correspond to economic reality. The results of Sarbanes-Oxley compliance tests provide a form of monitoring. Section 404 of the Sarbanes-Oxley Act requires that management test the internal controls over financial reporting and report on their assessment of those controls. In many cases, the business process owner is responsible for this activity, and often the internal auditors are involved as well.

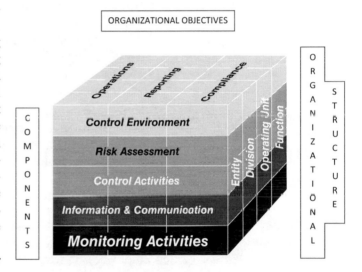

Monitoring conducted as a separate project provides for a more concentrated focus on the adequacy and effectiveness of internal control than does an ongoing monitoring process. An organization also gets help from external parties in monitoring its internal control. Customers will inform management about errors in the billing system if they receive incorrect invoices. On the other hand, customers validate billing data by paying their invoices. When regulatory agencies conduct examinations, such as an FDIC examination of a bank, they will inform the organization of any control deficiencies they discover.

Principle 17 of the COSO 2013 framework directs the organization to report and take corrective action on any internal control violations noted. The resolution of the problems documented in the report should be certified by executive management, and presented to the audit committee of the board of directors. The external auditors also review this information and attest to management's assessment of controls, providing another layer of monitoring.

IT auditing is an important monitoring activity. The COBIT 5 standards discussed in Chapter 6 address the control objectives of IT processes. Statement on Auditing Standards (SAS) No. 94 (first discussed in Chapter 6) directs auditors to perform substantive tests on significant amounts and requires they test controls, based on the complexity

IT (information technology) auditing Auditing methods that include auditing around the computer, auditing with the computer, and auditing through the computer.

Test data A technique for auditing through the computer where the auditor uses hypothetical transactions to audit the programmed controls and logic.

Parallel simulation A technique for auditing through the computer where the auditor attempts to simulate or duplicate the firm's output using another computer program to test actual data and compares the results to those produced by the firm's computer system.

Integrated test facility (ITF) A technique for auditing through the computer where the auditor uses artificial data to test how well the AIS performs its tasks.

Embedded audit module A module that is actually inserted into an application program to monitor and collect data based on transactions.

Cybersecurity How a company protects its information assets (e.g., data, human resource information, financial information, proprietary information). Threats to the security of the assets can come from within the company or from outside the company.

of the IT environment. The methods recommended for conducting IT audits in systems considered "complex" (i.e., any automation in an accounting system):

- *Auditing with the Computer:* Also referred to as computer-assisted audit techniques (CAATs), the auditor uses a computer to perform substantive tests and limited testing of controls. This is the only way to effectively audit a more complex system. Generalized audit software (GAS) is used with this method to extract specific data based on exception conditions (the most common packages are ACL and IDEA). Automated workpaper software is also available for use in generating trial balances (to automate footing, cross-footing, and reconciliation), financial statements, and ratios when a company has many subsidiaries.

- *Auditing through the Computer:* This method involves testing the automated processing steps, program logic, edit routines, and programmed controls. This method is well suited to testing complex IT systems. Techniques for this method include:

- **Test data**: The auditor uses hypothetical transactions (including exception-type transactions) to audit the programmed controls and logic.

- **Parallel simulation**: The auditor attempts to simulate or duplicate the firm's output using another computer program to test actual data and compares the results to those produced by the firm's computer system. Any differences are noted, investigated, and resolved.

- **Integrated test facility (ITF)**: The auditor uses artificial data (e.g., fictitious shipping transactions) to test how well the AIS performs its tasks. These transactions are introduced and processed as the system is being used in normal day-to-day activities, although the data should be removed before the company tries to ship inventory based on a fictitious sales transaction! This method is used when transactions are processed by online systems.

- **Embedded audit module (EAM)**: This module is actually inserted into the application program and allows continuous monitoring of a process. It monitors and collects data based on transactions. The auditor can use this information to test controls and evaluate the control risk.[8]

Cybersecurity

LEARNING OBJECTIVE 9 Discuss the importance of protecting information assets.

Cybersecurity refers to how a company protects its information assets (e.g., data). Threats to the security of the assets can come from within the company (e.g., a disgruntled employee) or from outside the company (e.g., a hacker who tries to steal proprietary information). Information assets include client data, human resources information, health information, financial information, state secrets, and proprietary information (e.g., processes or products unique to the company). Many of these threats were discussed in chapter 6. The risks of not protecting information assets include loss of confidential information, fines or sanctions, and loss of reputation. Several recent system compromises, such as the attacks against Target and Home Depot, raised consumer awareness of the importance of protecting personally identifiable information.

Personally identifiable information (PII) Information, such as credit card information, that can be used to identify a person. Cybercriminals compromise/steal information to impersonate someone else and use that information to open unauthorized accounts and credit cards.

The initial step to develop a cybersecurity program is classifying how sensitive the data is. Next is to determine where the data are stored, and finally determine who "owns" the data. The value of the data is determined by how an unauthorized person could use or abuse the data. For example, **personally identifiable information (PII)** such as credit card information might be sold to cybercriminals who then use the information to make unauthorized purchases. Employee awareness programs and other formalized approaches to protecting the network from various types of attacks such as those discussed in Exhibit 6.4 minimize the potential for losses.

Summary

Control activities are the policies and procedures that reduce risks that may undermine the achievement of objectives in the areas of quality of reported information, effectiveness and efficiency of operations, and compliance with applicable laws and regulations. Hundreds of control activities are available to an organization. Therefore, the challenge is to determine which control activities will reduce an organization's risks to an acceptable level. It is helpful in addressing this challenge to know that control activities are based on a few simple concepts such as isolation, redundancy, comparison, assistance, oversight, and accountability. Control activities categorized as preventive, detective, corrective or a combination of these, can be enforced by performance reviews, physical controls, segregation of duties, and information processing. Performance reviews are conducted by establishing targets for performance measures and then comparing actual outcomes to the targets. Physical security minimizes theft or destruction of assets and promotes accurate reporting of assets. Segregation of duties can prevent employees from being able to both perpetrate and conceal errors and inappropriate activities. A basic tenet is to segregate the duties of the authorization of transactions and other events, the custody of the related assets, and the modification or creation of data and program files (or paper-based records).

Information processing control activities can be separated into two closely related groups—general controls and application controls. General controls apply to the reliability and consistency of the overall information processing environment, and they support application controls. Application controls apply to the flow of data in and among individual applications. General controls include access security, network and data service center operation controls; system software acquisition, implementation, and maintenance controls; and application software selection (or development), implementation, and maintenance controls. Application controls include input, processing, output, and master file maintenance controls.

Internal control needs to be monitored to determine whether it is adequate and effective. Monitoring can be conducted on an ongoing basis, as a separate project, or as a combination of both. IT auditing is an important monitoring activity. Internal IT auditors assist in operational audits and may also assist in the monitoring of controls as required by section 404 of the Sarbanes-Oxley Act. External auditors are also required to have systems auditing knowledge. IT auditors audit with the computer or through the computer.

Information assets are essential the continued growth and success of a company. To be effective, a cybersecurity policy should include identification of threats and vulnerabilities due to attacks from insiders (e.g., disgruntled employee) or by an external hacker (e.g., state-sponsored hacker).

Key Terms

Access security   201
Anti-virus protection   209
Application controls   200
Automated control   196
Automatic log off   210
Automatic rollback   212
Batch control report   219
Batch transmittal ticket   218
Biometrics   203
Check digit   216
Control activities   193
Control total   218
Control total analysis   219
Corrective controls   197
Cryptography   205
Cybersecurity   222
Decryption   205
Detective controls   197
Device access table   203
Digital certificate   208
Digital signature   207
Directory and file attributes   205

Disaster recovery plan   212
Embedded audit module   222
Encryption   205
Firewall   209
General controls   200
Hash total   218
Input controls   215
Integrated test facility (ITF)   222
IT auditing   221
Master file maintenance controls   220
Output controls   220
Parallel simulation   222
Personally identifiable information (PII)   222
Physical controls   198
Preventive controls   197
Private key   205
Processing controls   217
Public key   205
Record count   218
Repudiation   208
Segregation of duties (SOD)   199
Smartcard   203

Discussion Questions, Problems, and Activity

1. Which of the following controls would be most effective in assuring the proper custody of unissued checks?
   a. Direct access to the checks in the safety deposit box is limited to only one corporate officer.
   b. Personnel who post check disbursement transactions to the general ledger master file are not permitted to update the vendor master file.
   c. The ordering of checks is executed on the specific authorization of the board of directors.
   d. The balances in the check disbursements transaction log are periodically compared with the copies of checks issued by independent personnel.

2. If a total were to be computed on each of the following data items, which would best be identified as a hash total for a payroll application?
   a. Hours worked
   b. Overtime hours
   c. Gross pay
   d. Department numbers

3. To access data and program files, what should users be required to enter?
   a. A parity check
   b. A personal identification number
   c. A self-diagnosis test
   d. An echo check

4. Segregation of duties stops which of the following from happening?
   a. One person can add/delete customer accounts and handle the normal data entry of sales.
   b. One person can maintain the cash account and reconcile the cash account.
   c. One person can perpetuate and conceal errors and inappropriate activities.
   d. All of the above.

5. Which of the following is an application control that ensures data are entered correctly?

	Valid Data Type	Anticipated Contents
a.	Yes	Yes
b.	No	No
c.	No	Yes
d.	Yes	No

6. Able Co. inputs purchase transaction data in batches that are subjected to edit checks. What would be a direct output of the edit checks?
   a. Report of all missing purchase orders
   b. Report of all rejected purchase transactions
   c. Printout of all user IDs and passwords
   d. List of all voided receiving documents

7. Which of the following are general controls?
   a. Disaster recovery plan
   b. Validation controls
   c. Output controls
   d. All of the above are general controls

8. Self-checking digits are used to detect which of the following errors?
   a. Assigning a valid code to the wrong vendor
   b. Transposing a vendor code
   c. Losing data between processing functions
   d. Processing data in the wrong sequence

9. Which of the following procedures is most likely to prevent the improper disposition of old computers?
   a. The segregation of duties between those authorized to dispose of old computers and those authorized to enter the disposition transaction
   b. The use of serial numbers to identify old computers that can be sold
   c. Periodic comparison of destruction work orders with authorizing documentation
   d. A periodic analysis of the scrap sales and the repairs and maintenance accounts

10. What should be the role of an information services steering committee?
   a. Initiate all applications development, set priorities for implementing applications, and develop access security.
   b. Assign duties to system personnel, prepare and monitor application implementation plans, and prepare system flowcharts.
   c. Establish or approve information processing policies and operating standards, approve system projects, set priorities for implementing systems, evaluate the effectiveness of processing operations, and generally monitor and evaluate processing activities.
   d. Decide on specific information needs, prepare detailed plans for system evaluations, set priorities for developing applications, and decide what computer hardware will be purchased.
   [CMA adapted]

11. A company updates its accounts receivable master file weekly and retains the master files and corresponding transaction files for the most recent 2-week period. What is the purpose of this practice?
   a. Verify run-to-run control totals for receivables.
   b. Match logical relationships to detect errors in the master file records.
   c. Permit reconstruction of the master file if needed.
   d. Validate groups of updated transactions.
   [CIA adapted]

12. What is a control to ensure that transactions are reconstructed correctly after an unplanned termination of processing?
   a. Automatic rollback
   b. Record count and control total
   c. Anticipation and hash total
   d. Concurrence and sequence number
   [CIA adapted]

13. What is a popular way of shielding an organization's private network from intruders outside of the organization?
   a. Firewall
   b. Uninterruptible power supply
   c. Encryption
   d. File attributes

14. Which of the six underlying control concepts—isolation, redundancy, comparison, oversight, accountability, or assistance—is involved in the following control activities? (Note: some controls may involve more than one concept.)
   a. Locking the warehouse door
   b. Personnel training
   c. Standard cost variance analysis
   d. Having security guards patrol a plant
   e. Segregating the functions of approving purchase requisitions and preparing purchase orders
   f. Storing backup copies of files at a remote location
   g. Checking account numbers against a reference file of authorized numbers
   h. Transmitting an acknowledgment signal following a telecommunications message
   i. Adding a column of figures two times to see if you got the right answer
   j. Having a supervisor check a calculation
   k. Recording an operator's ID number in a stored transaction record
   l. Granting a user a read-only right to a file

15. During processing, a batch of transactions was rejected by a programmed batch control. An examination of the transaction log revealed the following contents in the batch:

Document No.	Date	Account Code	Amount
253	3/1/18	3158	$14,370
254	3/2/18	2096	20,500
255	3/2/18	2437	2,945
255	3/2/18	2437	2,945
257	3/3/18	0972	8,320
258	3/2/18	3660	6,095
259	3/5/18	1491	17,380
260	3/5/18	1491	17,380

The batch control ticket that accompanied the original documents provided the following information:
■ Document count: 8
■ Hash total (formed from account codes): 17,301
■ Control total (of amounts): $103,090

Required:

What might explain the rejection of the batch, and what underlying causes can be inferred from these data?

16. A company accepts sales orders over the telephone and immediately enters the data. The sales data are accumulated in a transaction file and are processed once a day to update master files. At that time, a sales journal is also prepared listing all sales transactions for the day.

Required:

What programmed controls would you recommend to prevent and/or detect errors in transaction data?

17. Lathan Industries, Inc., is a "bottom-line" company that places great emphasis on meeting its budget. Budget proposals are submitted by managers throughout the organization, and the final budget is approved by the CEO only after extensive review and discussion by a budget committee composed of senior executives. Division managers are evaluated on budget conformity, and bonuses are paid for meeting or exceeding sales quotas and keeping costs at or below budgeted levels.

Required:

What internal control issues might arise from Lathan Industries' emphasis on budget conformity? How can an organization balance the need to achieve its strategic and operational plans with the need to promote an effective control environment?

18. Aidbart Company has recently installed a new client/server accounting system. Workstations are located throughout the company. James Lanta, controller, has overall responsibility for the company's accounting information system, but he relies heavily on Sue West, manager of information services, for technical assistance and direction.

Lanta was one of the primary supporters of the new system because he knew it would provide labor savings. However, he is concerned about the security of the new system. Lanta was walking through the purchasing department recently when he observed an Aidbart buyer using a workstation to inquire about the current price for a specific part used by Aidbart. The new system enabled the buyer to view data regarding the part on the screen. In addition to the price of the part, the screen also showed each Aidbart product that used the part and the total manufacturing cost of the products using the part. The buyer told Lanta that, in addition to inquiring about the part, he could also change the costs of parts. Lanta scheduled a meeting with West to review his concerns regarding the new system. Lanta stated, "Sue, I'm concerned about the type and amount of data that can be accessed through the workstations. How can we protect ourselves against unauthorized access to our files? Also, what happens if we have a natural disaster such as a fire, a passive threat such as a power outage, or some active threat resulting in malicious damage? Could we continue to operate? We need to show management that we are on top of these things. Would you please outline the procedures we now have or need to have to protect ourselves?"

West responded by saying, "Jim, there are areas of vulnerability in any accounting information system. The four major points of vulnerability with which we should be concerned are the hardware, the software, the people, and the network."

Required:

For each of the four major points of vulnerability identified above by Sue West, list at least one risk exposure to the system and give your assessment of the degree (low, moderate, high) of possible risk exposure.
[CMA adapted]

19. First National Bank installed personal computers for its tellers at eight local branches. The computers, which are connected to a large computer at the bank's main facility, are used for verifying customer balances and recording all deposits and withdrawals. Real-time posting is performed to ensure that the data in customer files are current.

Required:

List the control activities you would expect to find in this system. Give particular attention to controls that would be advisable as a result of the real-time posting that is used.

20. A small business uses an accounting package that operates on a local area network with four workstations. The master file maintenance program displays the contents of a record so that any desired changes can be made directly to the record. Both character and numeric fields in the master file records can be changed in this manner, and the documentation supplied with the software suggests that errors in account balances can conveniently be corrected by means of the file maintenance program. No listing or other hard copy log is provided of file maintenance activity. The file maintenance program can be accessed from any of the four workstations, but normally only the supervisor makes changes in the master files. The other employees say that they are "scared to touch" these files.

Required:

Discuss the control implications of the master file maintenance procedure just described and suggest ways of reducing the risks involved.

21. One day, a user in the accounting department at Therion Company inadvertently entered an erroneous command and was surprised to see a display of the password file. It contained a complete list of all current passwords, the names and ID numbers of the individuals to whom the passwords were issued, and the tasks, files, and directories to which they had access. The information extended over several screens, with continuation commands allowing the viewer to study each screen in turn. The user recognized the potential value of the information and spent the next hour copying it down. Shortly after this incident, she quit her job and sold the information to MacGregor, Inc., a major competitor of Therion.

Over the next two years, personnel at MacGregor routinely accessed Therion's files via the Internet. The rival firm retrieved sensitive data on production and sales targets. It also made subtle changes to data that misled managers into making faulty decisions on a number of occasions. The penetration went unnoticed until an employee of MacGregor finally placed an anonymous call to Therion's manager of information services.

Upon receipt of the call, all passwords were changed, but fearing adverse publicity and disciplinary action, the manager decided that the matter would be better hushed up. The assistant manager, the only other person to find out about the situation, was given a sizable raise to keep quiet. As a result, neither upper management nor the directors of the company ever learned of the problem.

Required:

Discuss the situation described and identify the control measures that should have been taken (a) to prevent the disclosure of the passwords, (b) to prevent the exploitation of the disclosure, and (c) to ensure that the situation could never have been concealed.

22. Cases of computer fraud are reported in the news almost every day. Indeed, it is estimated that billions of dollars are lost annually through computer fraud. Experts, however, maintain that many crimes are unreported because management is embarrassed to admit its vulnerability and wants to avoid adverse publicity. Management must recognize the severity of the problem and develop and monitor effective control activities to deal with the types of fraud to which computer systems are susceptible on a daily basis. Some types of computer fraud include (a) computer virus, (b) attempted unauthorized access, (c) theft or destruction of computing resources, and (d) destruction of data.

Required:

For each type of fraud named above, identify one or more control activities to mitigate the risk of the fraud occurring. Use the following format.

Type of Fraud	Control Activities
Computer virus	
Attempted unauthorized access	
Theft or destruction of computing resources	
Destruction of data	

23. The headquarters of Gleicken Corporation, a private company with $3.5 million in annual sales, is located in California. For its 150 clients, Gleicken provides an online legal software service that includes data storage and administrative activities for law offices. The company has grown rapidly since its inception three years ago, and its information services department has mushroomed to accommodate this growth. Because Gleicken's president and sales personnel spend a great deal of time out of the office soliciting new clients, the planning of the information services facilities has been left to the information services professionals.

Gleicken recently moved its headquarters facility into a remodeled warehouse on the outskirts of the city. While remodeling the warehouse, the architects retained much of the original structure, including the wood-shingled exterior and exposed wooden beams throughout the interior. The computer hardware is situated in a large open area with high ceilings and skylights. This openness makes the information services area accessible to the rest of the staff and encourages a team approach to problem solving. Before occupying the new facility, city inspectors declared the building safe; that is, it has adequate fire extinguishers, sufficient exits, and the like.

In an effort to provide further protection for its large database of client information, Gleicken has instituted a tape backup procedure on a time-delay mechanism that automatically backs up the database every Sunday evening, avoiding interruption in the daily operations and procedures. All the tapes are then labeled and carefully stored on shelves reserved for this purpose in the information services department. The departmental operator's manual has instructions on how to use these tapes to restore the database should the need arise. In the event of an emergency, there is a home phone list of the individuals in the information services department. Gleicken has recently increased its liability insurance for data loss from $50,000 to the current $100,000.

This past Saturday, the Gleicken headquarters building was completely ruined by fire, and the company must now inform its clients that all their information has been destroyed.

Required:

a. Describe the security weaknesses present at Gleicken Corporation that made it possible for a disastrous data loss to occur.

b. List the components that should have been included in the disaster recovery plan at Gleicken Corporation to ensure computer recovery within 72 hours.

c. What factors, other than those included in the plan itself, should a company consider when formulating a disaster recovery plan?

[CMA adapted]

24. On April 15, Joe Delano, an applications developer employed by Reed Co., was given 2 weeks' notice following some trouble in the information services department. During those 2 weeks, Delano managed to modify the payroll programs so that after entry of a processing date after May 1, no deductions would be made from employee paychecks. He also modified the billing programs to destroy the format of all invoices printed by the computer. He deleted master file records of a number of the organization's largest customers and deleted the back-up copies of the files so the records could not be reconstructed. Delano then deleted the files storing the documentation for most of the applications he had developed and destroyed the hard copies of the documentation as well. He then proceeded to download several expensive software packages.

Not satisfied with his "work," Delano went back to the company one night early in May and damaged several pieces of computer hardware and stole two portable computers. A police investigation, conducted some time later, revealed that Delano had two previous convictions for employment-related crimes.

Required:

List and discuss the control weaknesses that could allow an employee to carry out the acts described.

25. Discuss some of the security issues related to e-business.
26. Why is repudiation an issue in electronic business?
27. Read the *ISACA Journal* article about risks of data breaches by Tommie Singleton (http://www.isaca.org/Journal/archives/2014/Volume-2/Pages/Risk-to-Entities-Regarding-Data-Breaches-Lessons-From-a-Brief-Case-Study.aspx). If you were the CSO (Chief Security Officer) of the state of South Carolina, what recommendations would you make to try to minimize the potential for another data breach?

Student Activity–Play Ball![9]

This in-class activity will be administered and explained in detail by your instructor. The description given here simply gives you an overview of the activity. The purpose of this activity is to give you experience in recognizing the internal control weaknesses and risks in real-world situations and in determining what control activities should be implemented to mitigate the identified risks. The activity is to play a baseball game. In this game, you advance the bases according to the control weaknesses, risks, and activities you identify—not how well you hit a ball. If you do not know how to play baseball, do not be concerned. Your instructor will walk you through the motions, and you will be playing with a team of your classmates.

Notes

1. Encrypting is the process of transforming original data into unintelligible data. This method of protecting data is discussed in more detail in a later section of this chapter.
2. In many banks, for example, tellers are required to take at least 5 consecutive days of vacation, rather than taking their vacation one day at a time.
3. COSO calls this category "Application System Development and Maintenance Controls." Because of the trend away from application development to the implementation of accounting software packages, which COSO also acknowledges, we have adapted the name of this category.
4. For more on digital certificates, refer to http://www.verisign.com.au/repository/tutorial/digital/intro1.shtml
5. For more on the advantages and disadvantages of cryptography, refer to http://www.rsa.com/rsalabs/node.asp?id=2167

6. Mendell, F. "What You Have Not Thought About in Business Continuity Planning," *Presentation at University of Houston-Clear Lake*, April, 2013.
7. To produce an exception report, a program or query language issues instructions to examine the data on file and report items that are out of the normal range or represent an unauthorized activity (refer to Chapter 5).
8. Source: Cerullo, M. V. and M. J. Cerullo (2003). Impact of SAS No. 94 on Computer Audit Techniques. *Information Systems Control Journal*, Volume 1: 53–57.
9. Our gratitude to Ceil M. Pillsbury who wrote the initial versions of these activities, "Systems Softball: An Interactive, Group Game for Teaching Internal Control Evaluation," *Issues in Accounting Education*, Vol 6, No. 1, Spring 1993: 128–138, and to Ed Altemus who helped develop the cases and instructions.

The Financial Process

Source: one photo/Shutterstock.

Chapter Outline

Learning Objectives

After studying this chapter, you should be able to:

- Describe the role of the financial process and list its functions.
- Create analytical financial statements that provide an understanding of the organization's financial status and progress.
- Design coding systems adequate to support the financial process.
- List the types of entries recorded in the financial process and critique the efficiency of data entry.
- Identify risks and understand typical controls found in the financial process.
- Understand conceptual data storage in the financial process.
- Describe common end-of-period functions.
- Describe some of the potential effects of the implementation of International Financial Reporting Standards (IFRS) on financial reporting.

Source: wavebreakmedia/Shutterstock.

Introductory Scenario

Dr. Ajay Raval recently resigned his medical engineering professorship at University School of Medicine to manufacture two recently patented medical devices. AR Enterprises has received US$5 million in funding from a venture capital firm with Dr. Raval retaining a 30 percent interest and an option that, if exercised, can give him 51 percent ownership. He realizes that expected rapid growth will require that he obtain an accounting information system and has listed some factors that may influence the choice of system:

1. Exclusive contracts have been signed with Medical Devices of America in Boston and Equipo Medico in Barcelona for domestic and international distribution, respectively.
2. Present employment is four, with 30 expected within the next six months.
3. Twenty vendors are supplying industry standard parts and manufacturing materials at present; the number is expected to grow to fifty within the year. There are already fifteen additional suppliers for equipment, supplies, and other needs. The new AIS should support electronic data interchange (EDI) to allow for trading partnerships.
4. An audit partner from a large international accounting firm will be coming on board as financial vice-president within 60 days and will be keeping the books until more personnel can be hired.
5. All assembly will be done in-house, with custom parts being contracted out to a machine shop.
6. Of the US$5 million capital, US$4 million is invested in 6-month certificates of deposit.
7. Dr. Raval set up a petty cash fund of $500 to pay for incidental expenses.

Introductory Scenario Thought Questions:

1. Dr. Raval asks for advice concerning the allocation of the US$5 million capital. What would you recommend he do with cash not being used for day-to-day expenses?
2. What are some of the things that should be considered as Dr. Raval sets up his business?
3. What AIS modules would AR Enterprises require to produce financial statements?

An Overview of the Financial Process

The financial process is the core of the AIS. All accounting events sooner or later impact it. This process is comparable to a study of the accounting cycle in principles of accounting. Transactions are recorded in journals (transaction files), these transactions are then posted from the journals to the general ledger (GL master file), and then financial statements are prepared. The most significant conceptual difference is that in the computerized financial process, the vast majority of transactions are first recorded in other processes (e.g., revenue, procurement, inventory) and then transferred to the financial process.

Context of the Financial Process

LEARNING OBJECTIVE 1
Describe the role of the
financial process and list its
functions.

In prior chapters our references to the various business processes (i.e., financial, revenue, procurement, and inventory) included the following elements of the processes that were distinguished only by implication:

- The organization's personnel
- The organization's procedures
- The computerized portions of the processes

In this and immediately succeeding chapters our emphasis will be on the last element, the desired features and functions of the software programs constituting a significant part of the process. AIS software packages are usually composed of modules, with one or more modules composing a part of related AIS processes. For the financial process, we have the general ledger module. Example modules for the other processes include the customer module for the revenue process, the vendor module for the procurement process, and the inventory control module for the inventory process.

Exhibit 8.1 places the financial process in the context of an AIS. Principal data files for each module are shown as is the data transferred (in journal entry form) to the general ledger module from the customer, vendor, and inventory modules. Usually, the cost of sales is accumulated in the customer module by lookups to the inventory control module ("inventory module") as each sale is recorded.

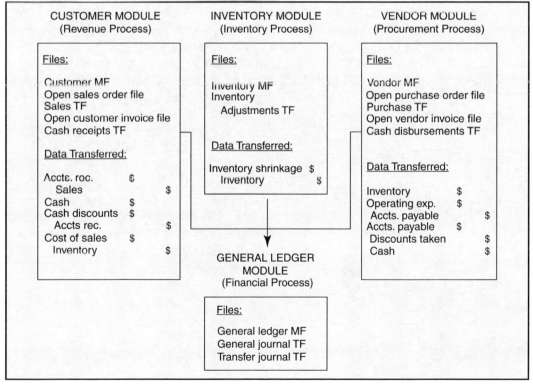

EXHIBIT 8.1 Modular Structure of an AIS Showing Data Flows to the GL Module

MF = Master File; TF = Transaction File

For the sake of brevity we will henceforth refer to modules by the names used in Exhibit 8.1 or by the following commonly used abbreviations:

Module	Abbreviation
General Ledger	GL
Customer/Revenue	Customer (for accounts receivable)
Vendor/Procurement	Vendor (for accounts payable)
Inventory	IC (for inventory control)

Chapters 9, 10, and 11 will cover most of the activities related to the modules listed above as well as other modules in the revenue, procurement and inventory processes.

The financial process (GL module) is distinguished from other processes and modules in one important respect. The other modules in Exhibit 8.1 are directly associated with specific business processes whereas, in a pure sense, the GL module is a financial reporting module. The vendor module, for example, is used to plan, control, and account for the purchase of inventories, supplies, and other purchased resources (such as payroll), and the payment of associated obligations. While some business events are first reflected in the GL, these are usually miscellaneous ones although the amounts involved may be large. Payment of a lawsuit settlement of US$5 million, for example, would likely be recorded in the GL module.

Functions of the Financial Process

Functions included in the financial process are very similar to those found in manual accounting systems, although there are some important differences that significantly improve the efficiency of computerized systems. **Exhibit 8.2** shows an outline of common functions. Our purpose here is to describe the functions in generic terms, as contrasted with specifics of a given software package, although screens from one accounting software package will be used for illustrations. Our discussion of the above functions will begin with the desired result for the GL, that is, financial reports.

LEARNING OBJECTIVE 2
Create analytical financial statements that provide an understanding of the organization's financial status and progress.

Financial Reporting Requirements

Frequently, a distinction is made between the requirements for external reporting and those for internal reporting. Such distinctions are actually matters of degree of detail reported rather than type of data reported. Investors and lenders use the published financial statements to evaluate operations of an entity just as management does. The quantity of detail reported to outsiders is simply less (e.g., external reports do not include proprietary costing data) as compared to that available to management. Therefore, no distinction is made in this chapter between the needs of external and internal users of information.

Conventional Financial Statements

The balance sheet, income statement, and statement of cash flows constitute the basic reporting requirements in the financial process. How these statements are presented is critical. In Chapter 5, we dealt with several general reporting principles. They are:

1. Necessity for concise reports
2. Emphasis on both physical and monetary measures

Source: dizain/Shutterstock.

Major Functions	Maintenance Functions	Daily and Period-End Functions
General ledger module setup	Design account structure Specify journals and names Designate reporting periods	
GL master file maintenance	Add a new account Change data in an account Delete an account Print a log of master file activity	Enter budget data for all accounts
Data entry		Enter normal transactions Create recurring entries Invoke recurring entries Edit transactions Print transaction proof lists Set up automatic distributions
Posting		Provisional posting Permanent posting
Printing		Balance sheet Income statement Cash flow statement Ratio report Print journals Print general ledger Custom reports
End-of-period processing		Import from other modules Close interim period Annual closing: soft closing Hard closing

EXHIBIT 8.2 Functions of the Financial Process

3. Frequency of reporting
4. Responsibility reporting
5. Reporting by function
6. Comparative reporting
7. Exception reporting

With regard to financial statements, comparative reporting and responsibility reporting are the principles requiring further investigation at this point.

Users of a GL module should be able to generate any of the financial statements comparing current balances with prior period balances. As an aid to the reader, these statements should show an analysis of the data as depicted in the Balance Sheet in **Exhibit 8.3**. Data comparisons, absolute changes, and percentage changes shown in the statements facilitate your understanding of the present financial position of the company. A similar analysis of the income statement is equally useful. These presentations that compare data are often called **horizontal analysis** accounting information.

Another desirable type of comparative analysis is called **common-dollar statements** accounting information. In such statements, each item is shown as a percentage of some base amount, which is designated as 100 percent. For balance sheets, the base amount is total assets, while the amount of sales is usually the base amount for income statements. Sometimes these presentations of percentages are called **vertical analysis** of accounting information. The income statement in Exhibit 8.3 is a common dollar analysis, also called vertical analysis of accounting information. A more useful format shows two years with

Horizontal analysis An analysis where balances for the current financial statements are presented along with balances of prior periods for comparison.

Common-dollar statement (vertical analysis) A financial statement where each item is shown as a percentage of some base amount designated as 100%. For the balance sheet, the base amount is total assets. For the income statement, the base amount is sales.

Vertical analysis See common-dollar statement.

SEATON STEEL DOORS
Comparative Balance Sheet

	12/31/18	12/31/17	Incr. (Decr.)	% Change
Current Assets:				
Cash	$ 23,792	$ 21,857	$ 1,935	8.9
Receivables	150,100	103,967	46,133	44.4
Inventory	82,430	94,023	−11,593	−12.3
Total Current Assets	256,322	219,847	36,475	16.6
Long-term Assets:				
Property, Plant, and Equipment	147,320	155,862	−8,542	−5.5
TOTAL ASSETS	$403,642	$375,709	$ 27,933	7.4
Current Liabilities:				
Trade Accounts Payable	$ 12,394	$ 13,857	$−1,463	−10.6
Wages and Payroll Deductions	13,258	8,408	4,850	57.7
Total Current Liabilities	25,652	22,265	3,387	15.2
Long-term Liabilities:				
Bonds Payable	90,000	100,000	−10,000	−10.0
TOTAL LIABILITIES	115,652	122,265	−6,613	−5.4
Shareholders' Equity:				
Common Stock	60,000	50,000	10,000	20.0
Premiums on Stock Issued	12,000	1,000	11,000	1,100.0
Retained Earnings	215,990	202,444	13,546	6.7
TOTAL EQUITY	287,990	253,444	34,546	13.6
TOTAL LIABILITIES, AND EQUITY	$403,642	$375,709	$ 27,933	7.4

SEATON STEEL DOORS
Comparative Income Statement

	For the Year 2018		For the Year 2017	
		Percent		Percent
Sales	$1,473,286	100.0	$1,597,419	100.0
Cost of Sales	949,754	64.5	1,026,071	64.2
Gross Margin	523,532	35.5	571,348	35.8
Expenses				
Selling	354,761	24.1	366,531	22.9
Administrative	138,719	9.4	141,300	8.9
Total Expenses	493,480	33.5	507,831	31.8
Operating Profit	30,052	2.0	63,517	4.0
Interest Expense	6,500	0.4	7,300	0.5
Profit Before Income Taxes	23,552	1.6	56,217	3.5
Federal and State Income Taxes	10,006	0.7	22,486	1.4
Net Income	$ 13,546	0.9	$ 33,731	2.1

EXHIBIT 8.3 Horizontal and Vertical Analysis Compared

vertical analysis of accounting information for each. Vertical analysis income statements and horizontal analysis balance sheets should be available on demand.

A cash flow statement that complies with *Statement of Financial Accounting Standards (SFAS) No. 95: Statement of Cash Flows*[1] is shown in **Exhibit 8.4**. The statement has these parts:

1. Cash flow from operating activities
2. Cash flow from investing activities
3. Cash flow from financing activities

SEATON STEEL DOORS Cash Flow Statement For the Year 2018		
Cash Flows From Operating Activities:		
Net Income		$ 13,546
Add: Depreciation Expense		14,000
Changes in Non-cash Current Accounts:		
Receivables		−46,133
Inventory		11,593
Trade Accounts Payable		−1,463
Wages and Payroll Deductions		4,850
		$ −3,607
Cash Flows from Investing Activities:		
Equipment Sold for Cash	$89,104	
Equipment Acquired for Cash	−94,562	−5,458
Cash Flows from Financing Activities:		
Retirement of 8% Bonds Payable	−100,000	
Issuance of 6.5% Bonds Payable	90,000	
Issuance of Common Stock	21,000	11,000
Net Increase in Cash Balance		$ 1,935

EXHIBIT 8.4 Cash Flow Statement Using the Indirect Method

Details must be shown for each part of the statement. Specifically, all investing and financing activities as well as operating activities must be shown in detail. Notice that while the net amount of cash flow from each activity ranges from about $3,607 (net outflow) for operations to $11,000 (net inflow) for financing, the cash inflows and outflows from investing in equipment are each about $100,000. Cash inflows and outflows from bond financing also are each about $100,000.

Consequently, a cash flow statement omitting these details of equipment sold and acquired and of bond financing activities gives the reader no conception of the magnitudes of cash inflows and outflows. The cash flow statement information in the exhibit is for a single year, although the standard appears to be at least two years of comparative data with many companies showing three years.

While balance sheets and income statements have been used in formats close to the present layout for several centuries, the format of the information in a cash flow statement is of relatively recent origin (1988) and has continually evolved since its predecessor—the statement of changes in financial position—appeared in the 1930s.

Most packaged accounting software is delivered with a predefined set of financial statement formats. The user can (1) adopt these formats as delivered, (2) modify the delivered formats, or (3) totally define a set of financial statement formats. Packaged accounting software usually is delivered with one or more defined charts of accounts. If the user adopts a delivered chart of accounts, then the predefined financial statement formats may be used. But most users need to define their own chart of accounts and must communicate to the system how account data are to be used in the formatted statements. When the user adjusts the chart of accounts to meet the needs of the business, the following information is also required to generate a balance sheet and an income statement:

- Range of account numbers for each statement classification such as current assets, long-term assets, etc.

- The equity account into which net income should be transferred when the books are closed. In the previous chapter we emphasized that no useful informational content can be attached to a datum. Single values convey useful informational content only when placed in a context so that relationships may be judged. Ratios are the common way of expressing these relationships. Consequently, ratios, such as the current ratio, profit on the sales dollar, and asset turnover, convey real information that permits the reader to make tentative judgments regarding an entity's financial position. Inasmuch as the purpose of the AIS is to provide information to users, it seems that ratios should be required rather than imposing the calculation task on the user. A ratio report (**Exhibit 8.5**) fulfills this requirement.

Seaton Steel Doors Comparative Financial Ratio Report			
Ratio Name	Calculation Method	2018	2017
Solvency ratios:			
1. Current	Current assets/current liabilities	10.0	9.9
2. Quick	Cash + marketable securities/ current liabilities	0.9	1.0
3. Current liabilities to net worth	Current liabilities/total equity	0.1	0.1
4. Total liabilities to net worth	Total liabilities/total equity	0.4	0.5
5. Fixed assets to net worth	Fixed assets/total equity	0.5	0.6
Efficiency ratios:			
6. Sales to accounts receivable	Sales/accounts receivable	9.8	15.4
7. Sales to inventory	Sales/inventory	17.9	17.0
8. Sales to assets	Sales/total assets	3.7	4.3
9. Sales to accounts payable	Sales/accounts payable	118.9	115.3
Profitability ratios:			
10. Return on sales	Net income/sales	0.9%	2.1%
11. Return on assets	Net income/assets	3.4%	9.0%
12. Return on equity	Net income/equity	4.7%	13.3%

EXHIBIT 8.5 Comparative Financial Ratio Report

While preferences vary as to which ratios to use, the ratios in Industry Norms and Key Business Ratios published by Dun & Bradstreet Information Services, or the Reuters. com information on publicly-traded stocks (which includes industry and sector ratios), provide a good standard. Only when a user considers ratio trends and compares these with the industry ratios can a tentative judgment be formed regarding the financial status and progress of a company.

For example, in Exhibit 8.5, without considering other environmental or industry-specific information, a user can surmise that the return on equity (ratio 12) is low and that likely causes for the low return include low resource utilization (ratios 6, 8, and 9) plus lax expense control (see comparative income statement percentages in Exhibit 8.3). Moreover, while Seaton is very liquid (ratios 1–5), the negative cash flow from operating activities (see cash flow statement in Exhibit 8.4) cannot persist indefinitely.

Responsibility Reporting

To this point our discussion has been limited to the overall financial statements for an entity. But as duties and responsibilities are allocated within that entity, so must the reporting to managers at various levels be subdivided. In Chapter 5 (Exhibits 5.4 and 5.5) investment centers, profit centers, and cost centers were illustrated. Chart of accounts coding in the GL module must be designed so the AIS can produce statements and reports for individual centers. Remember that the design must not only accommodate various sub-units of the entity, but it must also support functional reporting. Consider the selling and administrative expenses in Exhibit 8.3. If Seaton has various divisions, these expenses will require coding so divisional costs can be reported separately. However, the sales and administrative vice-presidents of Seaton will require detailed statements of expenses for which they are responsible. Thus, the coding scheme adopted must simultaneously support both requirements. Coding schemes are discussed in detail in a later section of this chapter.

Accounting Records—Journals and Ledgers

Most AISs are designed with the assumption that users will desire printed journals and ledgers. Although there is a trend toward screen views of these records rather than "hard-copy" printouts, printed copies will be required on occasion, and the software should accommodate this need.

The appearance of journal and ledger printouts from computerized AISs varies considerably and may be quite different from those traditionally generated by manual systems. A GL trial balance summary from Sage 50 Accounting 2016 is shown in **Exhibit 8.6**. Note by referring to account 10200. Regular Checking Account, the debit balance of $23,386.02 is shown as of March 31, 2018. The details comprising these summary balances can be found in a Detailed Trial Balance.

Account Coding for the Financial Process

The general reporting requirements for the financial process were covered to emphasize their importance in an AIS and to build the foundation for specifying coding requirements for the GL module.

The **chart of accounts** is the listing of account names stored in the financial process along with the codes assigned to the accounts. These accounts are usually referred to as general ledger accounts, and all of them collectively form the general ledger. While a journal (or transaction file) is a chronological listing of transactions, the GL accounts are "boxes" into which transactions appearing in the journal are sorted. In computer parlance, these boxes (accounts) are GL master file records. Because the business activities of organizations differ, and because reporting preferences differ, each organization will have its own unique set of accounts composing the general ledger. For example, a manufacturing company needs work-in-process inventory accounts whereas a merchandising firm does not. An international trading company needs a foreign currency holdings asset account. In

LEARNING OBJECTIVE 3
Design coding systems adequate to support the financial process.

Chart of accounts A listing of all account names along with their numbers, or codes, used by an organization.

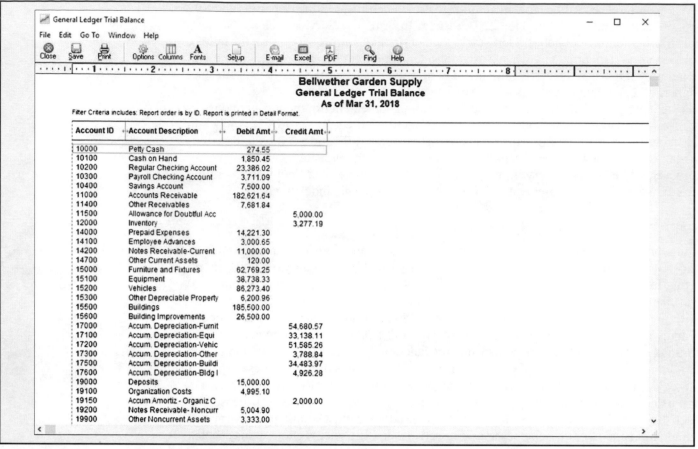

EXHIBIT 8.6 Screen Display of General Ledger Accounts

Source: © 2016 Sage Software, Inc. All rights reserved. Screen shots from Sage 50 Accounting 2016 are reprinted with permission. Sage, the Sage logos, and the Sage product and services names mentioned herein are the registered trademarks of Sage Software, Inc.

addition to the accounts to which transactions will be posted, a computerized GL module requires accounts for financial statement headings, subtotals, and totals.

At the installation of a GL module, certain choices for designing a chart of accounts may be available to the user. Some packages provide account number structures with overall fixed lengths, with a fixed number of fields, and with fixed field lengths. Others are more flexible, permitting the user to specify the length of the account number up to fifty or more characters and a variable number of fields having various user-defined lengths.

Coding Schemes

Coding schemes for GL accounts are well established. The first field of an account identifier (almost always composed solely of numeric symbols in GL) begins with a block code (often the first and second digits of the code) that denotes different parts of the balance sheet and the income statement. A reasonable scheme might be:

10000-Current assets

15000-Tangible long-term assets

19000-Intangible long-term assets

20000-Current liabilities

25000-Long-term liabilities

30000-Equity

40000-Revenue

45000- Other revenues

50000-Cost of goods sold

51000-Selling expenses

52000-Administrative expenses

55000-Other expenses

56000-Income tax expenses

Immediately following the block code in the account identifier is a sequence code that specifies the order of accounts within each group (block) suggested above. Thus, a few selling expense accounts might be coded as:

51011-Sales salaries expense

51012-Sales literature expense

51014-Travel expense

51017-Advertising expense

The above accounts appear in the GL master file in numeric order.

XBRL Coding for SEC Reporting

Another type of coding in the financial process is the coding required for SEC—and FDIC—mandated electronic reporting, the eXtensible Business Reporting Language (XBRL), a new standard for communication of financial information among businesses and through the Internet. XBRL allows financial information to be reported in a context, a sort of "bar code" for financial information. XBRL facilitates the handling of financial data, while reducing the potential for errors, and permits the automatic checking of information. This is done using "tags" which provide information to make the data more readable to the computer. XBRL is covered in more detail in Chapter 5. Please refer to that chapter.

Types of Accounts

For packaged accounting software to have predesigned accounting reports, most packages have different types of GL accounts. Therefore, two new concepts are master accounts and sub-accounts. **Master accounts** are similar to control accounts (as the term is conventionally used in manual accounting systems). **Sub-accounts** are analogous to accounts in a subsidiary ledger. Master and sub-accounts are used when detailed information needs to be maintained in the general ledger because reports are required based on both the detailed and summarized information. Accounts that have no sub-accounts are called **normal accounts**.

Master account An account that is similar to a control account as the term is conventionally used in accounting.

Sub-account An account that is analogous to a subsidiary ledger account.

Normal account An account that has no sub-accounts.

Assume that several cash accounts are to be maintained in the general ledger. This may be accomplished by coding these cash accounts in the following manner.

10100.00-Cash (the master account for cash)

10100.01-Petty cash (sub-account for cash)

10100.02-Checking account (sub-account for cash)

10100.03-Payroll cash account (sub-account for cash)

With this scheme, up to ninety-nine cash accounts can be accommodated in the general ledger accounts for cash because two digits are available to the right of the decimal. No journal entries are made directly to the master account (10100.00). When a detailed financial statement is printed, all accounts (including sub-accounts) appear. In a summary financial statement, the sum of the three subaccounts' information will appear with the label associated with account 10100.00, the master cash account. With this coding scheme, all master accounts have only zeros in the master/sub-account designation field.

Accounts receivable can be used as another example. If a company has only three customers, the chart of accounts accounting information could include the following master and sub-accounts:

11000.00-Accounts receivable

11000.01-Accounts receivable-Customer 1

11000.02-Accounts receivable-Customer 2

11000.03-Accounts receivable-Customer 3

When credit sales are made, entries are made to the accounts ending in 01, 02, or 03. On the other hand, if the organization has many customers, it is preferable to add an entire module for accounts receivable. In this case, the only account in the GL chart of accounts would be 11000.00 Accounts receivable, and entries would be made to this account. The information for each customer's balance would be maintained in the customer master file in the Customer module, which has its own set of codes.

Statistical account An account used to accumulate physical instead of monetary data.

Some AISs have the ability to support **statistical accounts**. These are used to accumulate physical as opposed to monetary data. A natural gas sales revenue account may be followed in the general ledger by "MCF gas sales" with the balance being thousands of cubic feet of gas sold. Various codes, such as the use of "S" or "#" within the account code, may be used to denote statistical accounts.

Coding for the Cash Flow Statement

The preceding coding practices are conventional and are based on practices embodied in popular accounting packages. The previous discussion made no mention of the cash flow statement. This is because the conventional accounting system chart of accounts is not designed to support the creation of this statement. Asset, liability, and equity accounts form the balance sheet, while revenue and expense accounts compose the income statement. All of the monetary data required for preparation of the balance sheet and income statement are found in a traditional accountant's trial balance, but data for the cash flow statement are not. This accounts for the almost total inability of packaged AISs to produce a correct and complete cash flow statement.

Two methods are available for the cash flow statement—direct and indirect. Exhibit 8.4 is the indirect method. Review that exhibit for a moment, thinking of where you can obtain the information required to prepare it. Net income should be in an "income summary" account prior to its being closed to one or more equity accounts. When using the indirect method, nominal accounts, such as depreciation expense and bond premium or discount amortization, are either added to or deducted from net income to calculate cash flow from operations. As a consequence, these accounts must be coded as "cash flow" accounts so they can be processed correctly by the AIS when generating the cash flow statement.

But a more significant problem arises in respect to determining the cash flows from investing and financing activities. The net changes in long-term asset, long-term liability, and equity accounts are not sufficient for the cash flow statement. Rather, the cash impact of all transactions in those long-term accounts must be shown. A fixed asset may have a cost of $500, accumulated depreciation of $300, and be sold for $50 cash, with a loss of $150. The impact on the cash flow is an increase of $50. Therefore, all of these data must be coded in such a way that the AIS can automatically calculate the correct cash flow and reflect it on the statement.

Such coding can be done. Every long-term account (asset, liability, equity) must have subaccounts for beginning balance, increases, and decreases for each regular (nonmaster) account. For property, plant, and equipment, these accounts might be:

15100.00-Property, plant, and equipment (master account)

15100.01-Beginning balance of Property, plant, and equipment

15100.02-Increases in Property, plant, and equipment

15100.03-Decreases in Property, plant, and equipment

15100.04-Corrections to Property, plant, and equipment

Accumulated depreciation accounts and gain/loss on disposition accounts must also be included in the calculation of cash flow.

This process gets very complex if a package is designed to produce a cash flow statement with the users providing the chart of accounts. With this level of complexity and a general level of misunderstanding among designers of accounting packages regarding the details required, it can be difficult with most accounting software packages to produce a correct cash flow statement.

SFAS 95 states a preference for the direct method over the indirect method for creating a cash flow statement, although the majority of SEC-reporting companies publish their cash flow statements using the indirect method. Direct and indirect methods relate to how the operating activities (first section of the cash flow statement) are presented. In other words, the net cash flows from operating activities (a total of −$3,607 shown in Exhibits 8.4 and 8.7) are the same for both methods. Cash flows from investing and financing activities are reported in the same way whether using the direct or indirect method. The direct method shows all flows in and out of all cash accounts as a group. **Exhibit 8.7** is a cash flow statement prepared using the direct method. Note that this statement is an analysis of the cash account. That is, all data in the statement can be gleaned from the cash accounts. Therefore, if sub-accounts for cash are created that reflect each cash flow statement category, then a statement can easily be prepared from these sub-accounts. For other purposes, the accounts roll up to report by cash account type (checking, payroll, and petty cash). Account identifiers applying this concept for Seaton Steel Doors might be as follows:

Cash Flows from Operating Activities:

10100.02.01-checking, customer collections

10100.02.02-checking, payments to vendors

10100.02.03-checking, operating expenses

10100.02.04-checking, interest payments

10100.02.05-checking, income taxes

SEATON STEEL DOORS Cash Flow Statement For the Year 2018		
Cash flow from Operations:		
Collections from customers		$1,427,153
Payments to vendors		−939,624
Operating expenses		−474,630
Interest expense		−6,500
Income taxes		−10,006
		$ −3,607
Cash flow from Investing:		
Equipment sold for cash	$ 89,104	
Equipment acquired for cash	−94,562	−5,458
Cash flow from Financing:		
Retirement of 8% Bonds Payable	−100,000	
Issuance of 6.5% Bonds Payable	90,000	
Issuance of Common Stock	21,000	11,000
Net increase in cash balance		$ 1,935

EXHIBIT 8.7 Cash Flow Statement Using the Direct Method

Cash Flows from Investing Activities:

10100.02.06-checking, receipts-fixed asset dispositions

10100.02.07-checking, payments-fixed asset acquisitions

Cash Flows from Financing Activities:

10100.02.08-checking, proceeds from bond issuances

10100.02.09-checking, payments for bond retirements

10100.02.10-checking, proceeds from stock issuances

10100.02.11-checking, payments for stock retirements

Because all cash transfers to the payroll account are classified in the checking account as expense payments, no cash flow coding is required in the payroll checking account. Petty cash can usually be assumed to represent expenses; therefore, the petty cash reimbursements from the checking account are so classified.

The direct method is easier to implement in the system, and has the added advantage that the real magnitude of cash flow through the entity is revealed because essentially you are restating the results of operations on a cash basis, rather than on an accrual basis. Notice that with the indirect method (Exhibit 8.4) you have no idea of the magnitude of cash flows related to operations, although the net income and changes to the current asset and current liability accounts can be easily tracked by the external report reader from the income statement and balance sheet. The magnitude of the cash flows from operations could be less than or more than those from investing or financing. But the direct method (Exhibit 8.7) reveals that cash inflows from operations are almost fifteen times that of either investing or financing activities (e.g., customer collections of $1,427,153 and securities issuances of $111,000).

Coding for Ad-Hoc Reporting

Selections of GL account balances and budget amounts are frequently required for reports to mid- and low-level managers. With appropriate design of the reporting programs and adequate foresight in the chart of accounts design, much can be accomplished based on menu prompts. Of course, if a report generator is available, even more reporting combinations are possible.

A simple example will illustrate how coding may occur. Home Builders, Inc., (HBI) wishes to accumulate job costs within the GL module. The GL construction-in-progress account is 3000.0000. The four digits to the right of the decimal are used to code and accumulate cost information as shown in **Exhibit 8.8**. Each construction job is assigned a two-digit identifier. All materials, labor, and overhead costs relate to one of the eight construction stages. A single foreman supervises each job for all construction stages.

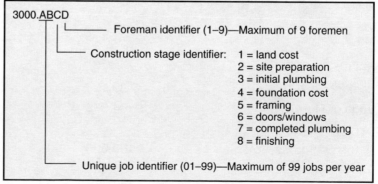

EXHIBIT 8.8 Use of Sub-Accounts to Maintain Detailed Data in the GL Module

To record the purchase of doors for job 21, which is supervised by foreman 8, a debit is made to account 3000.2168. To produce reports, the user is prompted to input the report title, the range of accounts to be included in the report and, if multiple categories are to be included, how to sort, subtotal, and total the report. If all accounts within a specified category (e.g., job, construction stage, and foreman) are to be included, a question mark (?) is to be used rather than a number. The question mark is a wild card for a single character, indicating that all accounts for that position are to be included in the report.

Some illustrative report specifications are:

Beginning Account	Ending Account	Report Contents
3000.??3?	3000.??3?	Initial plumbing costs for all jobs and foremen
3000.??17	3000.??17	Land costs for all jobs supervised by foreman 7
3000.231?	3000.234?	Total cost of job 23 at construction stages 1 through 4

The program must also inquire as to the primary and secondary sort fields and request the total and subtotal for the report. For example, the first report, which is initial plumbing costs for all jobs and foremen, can be sorted first by job and secondarily by foreman. By changing report specifications, a variety of reports can be obtained on an ad-hoc basis; thus, a user is not confined to fixed content reports. A desirable attribute is the ability to "catalog" and name reports once they are designed so the user need not repeat the design process each time.

This system, by accommodating 99 jobs, 8 construction steps and 9 foremen, yields a potential of over 8,000 general ledger accounts for job costs alone. Long before this limit is approached, most companies will find that using a separate job cost module as opposed to using the GL module for job costing is a more efficient accounting method.

The chart of accounts flexibility designed into commercial accounting packages varies widely. At the low end, some packages do not support master/sub-accounts whereas at the high end one may create as many fields within the numbering system as desired. Some packages in the mid-range market permit account numbers up to fifty digits in length. Public utility companies and defense contractors commonly require from thirty-five to fifty digit account identifiers, although most companies will find a limit of ten digits quite adequate.

Transaction Entry

When, as is usually the case, the GL module is supplemented by other modules, most of the input data for the financial process are captured by the other modules and transferred to the GL module. Transactions that do not fall within the scope of other modules are entered directly into the GL module. Three types of transaction entries are in the financial process and include:

LEARNING OBJECTIVE 4
List the types of entries recorded in the financial process and critique the efficiency of data entry.

1. Data captured in and transferred from other processes to the financial process
2. Transactions originally recorded in the financial process
3. End-of-period adjustments required in the financial process

Imported Data

If the system includes a full complement of modules, the volume of original entries in the GL module is minimal. Only those transactions that do not fit in other modules in use are recorded in the GL module. Sales and most cash receipt transactions are recorded in the Customer module. Merchandise purchases and most cash payments are recorded in the Vendor module. Employee transactions are handled in the Payroll module. These data are subsequently transferred to the GL.

Transactions Recorded in the GL Module

Generally speaking, transactions that are not categorized as sales, purchases, cash payments or receipts, or payroll are initially recorded in the GL module. A couple of transaction types are noteworthy. In manual systems, accountants have long embraced a rule that "all cash receipts should be recorded in the cash receipts journal," and that "all cash payments should be recorded in the cash payments journal." In a computerized system, most cash payments are recorded in the Vendor module and most cash receipts are recorded in the Customer module. But issuance or retirement of bonds and stock are not related to either customers or vendors. Therefore, such financing transactions are recorded in the GL module unless there is a module for bonds payable. Likewise, disposals of long-term assets are usually recorded in the GL module, although acquisitions of fixed assets may be recorded in the Vendor module because the supplier is a vendor to us, albeit not a "trade" vendor.

Exhibit 8.9 shows an example of the journal entry screen in the GL module of Sage 50 Accounting 2016 software. The transaction is the journal entry to record the addition of a computer to the inventory for computers/schools. In this entry, we have debited Inventory-Computers/Schools (GL account 12000-00) and credited the Membership Contributions account (GL account 39002-00).

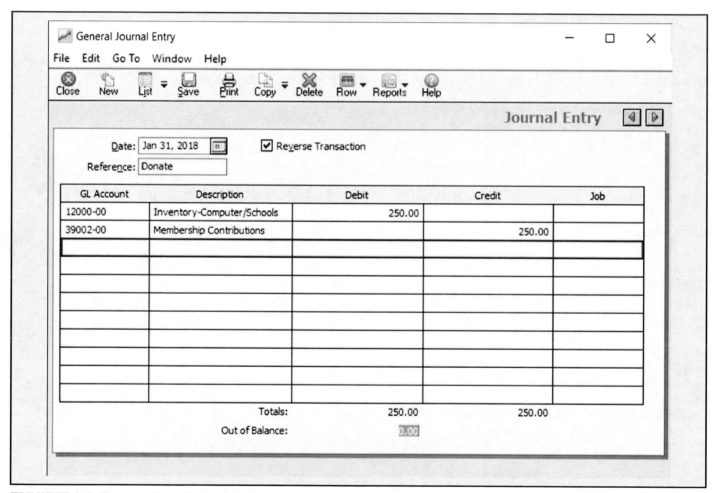

EXHIBIT 8.9 Transaction Entry Screen

Source: © 2016 Sage Software, Inc. All rights reserved. Screen shots from Sage 50 Accounting 2016 are reprinted with permission. Sage, the Sage logos, and the Sage product and services names mentioned herein are the registered trademarks of Sage Software, Inc.

Some accounting software allows the user to enter out-of-balance entries, although a warning is given to the user before they are accepted. Although some may believe this is a defect, others view it as a desirable feature. Suppose, for example, you are entering a batch of fifty transactions with debits to be made to various accounts and all offsetting credits to the same account. One-half hour remains in the business day, and you cannot finish the task during that period. Company security policy forbids a user from leaving a computer workstation without exiting from the AIS. If the AIS requires completed and balanced entries, you must work overtime. But if out-of-balance entries are permitted, then you can stop at the end of the business day and complete the batch the following business day. Also, a user may occasionally know the accounts to be debited, but cannot determine the credit account. With an out-of-balance entry, the debits can be entered one day, and the entry completed when the information is available. Notice the field "Out of Balance" on the data-entry screen to show the amount by which an entry is out of balance.

At any point, the user can print a proof list of a batch to scan for reasonableness or to determine which transactions are not balanced. Additions or changes may be made to entries and batches before they are posted.

Adjusting and Reversing Entries

Other events recorded in GL include end-of-period adjustments to match expenses with revenues, and reversing entries. Adjusting entries are made for the following events:

- Prepaid revenues not yet earned, such as rent revenue and the related unearned rent liability accounts.

- Prepaid expenses not yet incurred, such as insurance expense and the related prepaid insurance asset account.

- Uncollected revenues that have been earned, such as revenue from a partially-completed contract that has not yet been received, and the related accounts receivable.

- Unpaid expenses that have been incurred, such as interest expense, and the related interest payable account.

- Noncash expenses, such as depreciation expense, necessary for the income statement.

Those adjustments requiring reversal are so designated, and the AIS automatically keys in the reversing entry so it refers to the related adjusting entry. Conventional closing entries are not normally made in computerized systems. The closing process sums the balances of all the nominal accounts, zeros out those balances, and transfers the net amount to the profit and loss (income) summary or directly to the appropriate equity account(s).

A software package may have one or many journals in the GL module. When the user has an option of creating one or more journals for the GL module, this is done through the "GL Setup" function (Exhibit 8.2).

Budgeting

Comprehensive Model

Some of the more sophisticated AIS packages include a comprehensive budgeting module that encompasses sales, production, procurement, and human resources as well as the financial process. Such a budgeting model permits you to project sales based either on individual products and/or aggregate sales. Advertising and product promotion are budgeted simultaneously with the sales budget. Finished goods budgets are then derived followed by production budgets, as well as procurement and human resource budgets. Finally, the financial budget includes cash flows, financing requirements, and pro forma financial statements.

An integrated comprehensive budget model represents a third dimension of the AIS. To this point, our depictions of the AIS have been two-dimensional. The budget module introduces a third dimension because it overlays the entire previously described AIS. The portion of the AIS previously described is distinguished from the budget module overlay by being called the transaction (or event) processing system (TPS).

Most comprehensive budget modules rely heavily on actual data maintained in master files used in the TPS rather than being stand-alone systems. The budget module extracts ending balances (physical and financial) from the TPS. Completed budgets that meet the objectives and goals of management are accepted. The budget system may insert detailed budget amounts into TPS master files, thereby permitting budget versus actual reporting.

These integrated and comprehensive budget modules are extremely useful in planning operations because they permit management to rapidly test various scenarios. Moreover, because the module is an integral part of the entire AIS, performance reporting is greatly enhanced.

Piecemeal Budgeting

The manual entry of budget data in the TPS is far more common than the use of comprehensive budget modules. Master file fields are provided to hold monthly or even weekly budget data. For example, an inventory master file account may contain budgeted unit and dollar sales for that product by month for all company locations, just as an expense account may contain monthly budget data for all departments.

Thus, for most AISs, budget data are entered into the GL accounts at the beginning of each fiscal year. Ordinarily these entries are made directly in the master file rather than being journalized in any manner. In most cases, budgeted asset, liability, equity, revenue, and expense balances are entered for all months of the entire year. As the year progresses and with appropriate authorization, modifications are made to the budget amounts.

Efficiency Features in Data Entry

Several possible features increase significantly the efficiency of data entry in the GL module. Such features discussed here are recurring entries, automatic distribution entries, dollar and cents entries, and auto-enter.

Recurring Entries

Recurring entry A feature that automates recurring journal entries, such as entries for depreciation, amortization, and accrued liabilities.

Most businesses record transactions and adjustments that are encountered repeatedly. Rather than making the entry each time, most AISs have a feature known as **recurring entries** that automates the process. First, the user sets up and stores the journal entry for an event that will be repeated. When the entry is needed, the user invokes the recurring entry, a process that is far easier than rekeying it each time. Often, a batch of recurring entries is stored and invoked all together. In some cases, the software automatically makes (invokes) the recurring entry with a fixed frequency. An interest accrual and a standard monthly depreciation charge are examples of such events for which recurring entries can be used in a general ledger module.

While most packages provide for recurring entries on a monthly basis only, other software solutions provide considerable variety. When setting up the recurring entry, some possible parameters are:

- Starting period and final period for the entry
- Number of times the entry should be made
- Frequency of the entry—weekly, monthly, or quarterly

In highly automated systems, the program may invoke scheduled recurring entries by reference to the computer system's internal clock. This is particularly useful when periodic payments are due; the system can automatically generate checks for payments at appropriate times. Some possibilities for making an entry are:

- The last day of each month
- The third Wednesday of each month
- The 5th of each month
- Every Thursday
- Five times per year
- Monthly through, but not beyond, October 31, 2018.

When a recurring entry is composed, you may specify that it be made each Tuesday at 12:01 a.m. As soon as the internal computer clock reaches this time, the AIS automatically invokes the entry by placing a copy in the general journal transaction file.

Recurring entries can be further categorized into those of fixed amounts and those of varying amounts. At the beginning of the fiscal year, the accounting department will usually budget a fixed amount of depreciation for each month of that year. In contrast, recurring entries for items such as interest accruals and utility bills will vary from month to month. While fixed amount entries can be made once for the entire year, varying amount entries must be modified each month.

Adjusting entries that must be reversed at the beginning of each accounting period represent another application of recurring entries. Most commercial systems permit the user to designate those adjusting entries (entered as recurring entries) that need to be reversed at the beginning of the following period. This reversal then occurs automatically, often as the final step in the "closing" process. That is, when a user instructs the system to close the books, the closing occurs, and then reversing entries are made to begin the new accounting period.

Automatic Distribution Entries

Often the amount of a transaction must be allocated over several accounts in some standard manner. Property insurance and taxes may be allocated to departments based on square feet occupied. In this case, the recognition of insurance and tax expenses may require not a simple debit and credit, but rather many debits and one credit.

The **automatic distribution entry** feature automates this process. To set up an automatic distribution entry, the user specifies to which sub-accounts entries should be distributed and how the allocation should be made. Entries are then made to a master account, but the AIS computes and places amounts in the related sub-accounts.

Automatic distribution entries (also called "allocation entries") are essential to efficient data entry in many companies, particularly those in regulated industries that may be required by law to allocate many expenses to many different accounts.

Automatic distribution entry A feature that automates the distribution of the amount of a transaction to several accounts.

Dollar versus Cents Entry

When entering monetary values, the manner in which the entry occurs can impact the number of keystrokes required. For other computer applications this is not as important as it is for AISs, which require a large volume of data entry. Two methods for entering monetary values are illustrated in **Exhibit 8.10**.

Data to Be Entered	Dollar Entry		Cents Entry	
	Keystrokes	Displayed and Recorded	Keystrokes	Displayed and Recorded
$53.59	53.59	53.59	5359	53.59
$72.00	72	72.00	7200	72.00

EXHIBIT 8.10 Comparison of Dollar and Cents Entry

Note that **dollar entry** saves three keystrokes for data comprised of even dollars. **Cents entry** saves one keystroke (no decimal) for fractional dollar values. Inasmuch as most accounting data contain fractional dollar amounts, cents entry is usually the more efficient choice. If a data-entry clerk records three thousand debits and credits daily, then three thousand keystrokes are saved. Most accounting packages, because they are designed for large transaction volumes, almost universally support cents entry, but can also support dollar entry or provide an option to the user. In Exhibit 8.10, dollar entry for the first item is fifty-three and fifty-nine one hundredths dollars, while the cents entry is five thousand three hundred fifty-nine cents.

Dollar entry A way to enter monetary data into an accounting information system that saves three keystrokes for data composed of even dollars. The keystrokes to enter $72.00 would be 72.

Cents entry A way to enter monetary data into an accounting information system that saves one keystroke (no decimal) for fractional dollar values.

Auto-enter

Auto-enter A feature that saves keystrokes when entering data that are always represented by a fixed number of characters. After the user enters the characters, the program automatically moves to the next field so the user does not have to press the enter key after entering the field contents.

A final method of saving keystrokes is called **auto-enter**. This method is used only in conjunction with data that are always represented by a fixed number of characters. In AISs, the most common data are account numbers and dates. If the data-entry screen requires a date entry of MMDDYYYY, such as 04192018 for April 19, 2018, then nine keystrokes are normally required, eight keystrokes to enter the date digits and one to press the enter key. With a fixed length field, the program can be designed to automatically move to the following field when an item has been completed. Most data-entry screens are a mixture of fixed and variable length fields, and a new user at first finds auto-entry confusing because the "Enter" key must be used with some fields but not with others. Only after a user becomes accustomed to using a particular screen is a rhythm developed that makes efficient use of auto-entry. Therefore, auto-entry is highly desirable for accounting input programs that are used frequently and for sustained periods.

Recurring entries, automatic distribution entries, dollar versus cents entry, and auto-enter are applicable, not only to the GL module, but to all modules composing an AIS.

Reporting Periods and Time-sensitive Entries

Most organizations desire twelve monthly reporting periods per year. Banks, on the other hand, report daily and need 366 periods (to cover leap years). A few organizations, especially department stores, use a 13-month year. Each month is 4 weeks long and includes four weekends, thereby permitting comparison of monthly data from one year to the next. Consider the month of May 2019 (four weekends) versus May 2020 (five weekends). If a comparison of May 2020 department store sales showed an increase of 20 percent over May 2019, you could easily, but mistakenly, conclude that May 2020 was significantly better than the preceding May when, in reality, sales were down. Some businesses try to make interim data comparable by having two months of four weeks followed by a third month of five weeks because a quarter has 13 weeks.

Many organizations like to have a final reporting/closing period at the end of the year that covers no time, sometimes known as the audit period. After the normal 12 months are closed, some annual adjustments are made in what is usually the thirteenth period. Often, adjustments suggested by outside auditors are made in this period. If the organization uses thirteen operating periods, then the audit period is the fourteenth.

Accounting packages frequently give the user a choice regarding the number of reporting periods (interim periods) for each fiscal year. But that choice is often restricted to either twelve or thirteen, rather than being user-specified. When the user can select the number of interim periods, this is done using the GL setup process function (Exhibit 8.2).

Time-sensitive entries A feature that permits you to make entries in the current period, in past periods and, in some cases, in future periods.

A rather important feature for GL packages is **time-sensitive entries**. This feature permits you to make entries in the current period, in past periods and, in some cases, in future periods. Before time-sensitive entries became commonly available, a user had to close the books for an old reporting period before making any entries in a new period. In some cases, this meant that all adjusting entries for the year-end had to be made in the GL before a user could record payroll time worked in the new year, or that all end-of-year bad debt adjustments had to be completed before customers could be billed for new orders. Most packages now allow entries to prior periods but only until those periods are closed.

The ability to make entries for future periods is a convenience rather than a necessity. It is often easier to make all future entries related to a series of transactions at one time rather than over the next several weeks or months.

Posting in the GL Module

Because the data entered in the financial process has different sources, you might think the posting process varies according to the data source. However, this is not the case. Rather, the desirability for a "clean" set of records (thereby providing an effective audit trail) and for accuracy in reporting seem to be the most significant motivators in selecting the posting processes.

Detail or Summary Transfers

The transfer of data to the GL module from other modules can be made in summary or in detail, depending on the software design and the available user options. Such a summary data transfer from the procurement process to the GL module might be as follows:

Merchandise Inventory	543,000	
Accounts Payable		543,000
Accounts Payable	610,000	
Cash in Bank		603,000
Cash Discounts on Purchases		7,000

This example is realistic in assuming that the merchandise purchased during a month is typically different from the amount paid for merchandise previously acquired. In contrast to the entry above, a detailed transfer of data would include every individual entry recording either a merchandise purchase or a payment on accounts payable.

An advantage of detail data transfers is that a complete audit trail is available in the GL module. This assumes particular importance when the other modules are deficient in audit trails. Disadvantages of detailed transfers are as follows:

- Increased processing time to transfer detailed data
- Additional storage space required for detailed data
- Difficulty locating unusual entries due to large amounts of data in the GL master files

Another design choice is between transferring data from other modules directly to GL master file records (the ledger) or to transaction files (journals) in the GL module. When detailed data are transferred, the storage and processing time is doubled if the transfers are to transaction files because the data must be handled again when posted to the GL master file. Transaction files (journals) for data coming from each module are common for detailed transfers. A separate transaction file (general journal) is used for entries that originate in the GL module.

Batch Posting versus Real-Time Posting

As discussed in Chapter 3, transactions may be posted throughout the system (all modules) simultaneously with their entry (real-time posting) or in batches (batch posting). As a general rule, posting must occur frequently enough that data are current when required for reporting or for making inquiries. Because most organizations prepare financial reports monthly, a monthly posting in the financial process is sufficient in most cases.

Provisional Posting

A processing feature unique to GL modules is **provisional posting**, sometimes called "pencil posting." This feature applies only when batch posting is used. An important control that is built into most packages permits a user to change recorded transactions only so long as they have not been permanently posted. If the provisional posting feature is present, a user pencil-posts, prints (provisional) financial statements, scans the statements for possible errors, makes any necessary corrections to transaction files, provisional posts again, prints, scans for errors, and so on until satisfied that the statements are correct. Only then does "ink posting" occur. Any errors discovered after "ink" posting occurs must be remedied with correcting or reversing entries.

Provisional posting is far more useful than is often realized. By scanning provisionally posted financial statements, obvious errors may be found, such as a credit to inventory rather than to bonds payable, resulting in a negative inventory balance. Regular users of

Provisional posting (pencil posting) A feature that applies only when batch posting is used. Transaction files are posted to the general ledger accounts so that provisional financial statements can be printed. If errors are noted, corrections can be made to the transaction files, which are posted again.

an organization's financial statements usually have an idea what reasonable amounts are for an account and may discover errors by scanning provisional statements. To avoid being confused with final financial statements, provisional statements should bear a prominent message that emphasizes their tentative nature.

Status of Accounts

Inactive account An account that can no longer receive entries or be adjusted.

As financial and business processes of an organization change, entries may no longer be made to certain accounts. Assume that Seaton Steel Doors has been advertising in trade journals and, upon evaluation, decides that the expense is no longer justifiable. The account "Trade Journal Advertising Expense" will no longer be needed. When the decision is made and all anticipated entries have been made to the account, it should be designated as an **inactive account**. The AIS will prevent further entries from being made to that account identifier, but the account will be maintained (i.e., not deleted) in the GL because it is needed for the remainder of the present year for current reporting and is needed during next year for comparative reporting. The change to inactive status is accomplished through the Master File Maintenance menu option (Exhibit 8.2).

Risks and Controls in the Financial Process

LEARNING OBJECTIVE 5
Identify risks and understand typical controls found in the financial process.

The reporting function for any company is essential to its continued success. Investors, creditors, suppliers, auditors, regulators, and management rely on the relevance and accuracy of the reports generated from the financial process. For a firm to receive an unqualified audit opinion and be compliant with section 302 of the Sarbanes-Oxley (SOX) Act (requiring CEO and CFO attestation of responsibility for financial statements), a company must have good controls over the financial process (to be in compliance with section 404 of SOX). Several risks inherent to this process include the following:

Transaction Risks

- *Unauthorized transactions*: for example, transactions approved/created by unauthorized persons, transactions for unauthorized amounts, transactions created at unauthorized times (e.g., when the company is closed).

- *Incorrect/nonrecorded/fictitious transactions*: for example, transactions that are not recorded (e.g., payments to vendors), or are fictitious (e.g., recording credit sales that never happened) to give false impressions of the company's activity, leading to misstated financial statements.

- *Unauthorized or incorrect adjusting entries*: for example, duplicated entries or improper entries can misrepresent the underlying economics of the company.

- *Incomplete information*: for example, obstruction in the flow of information can lead to decision makers not having complete information for critical decisions.

- *Incorrect transfer of information*: for example, when the summary control account balances do not agree with the detailed data in subsidiary ledger master files.

- *Information processing errors*: for example, exposure of assets to unauthorized use, loss, or misappropriation.

- *Improper allocation*: for example, incorrect intracompany allocations that distort responsibility reports.

- Problems with *transaction activity not being reported in the proper accounting period*: for example, not adjusting unearned revenue or prepaid expense accounts properly.

- *Incorrect reported account balances*: for example, not recording impairment of fixed or intangible assets.

- *Improper tax calculations*: for example, penalties assessed for late filing of, or failure to file, government tax or regulatory reports because of computation based on erroneous data.

Following the control activity categories from Chapter 7, examples of controls in the financial process are discussed next.

Performance Reviews

Budget Tracking and Performance Evaluation

Procedures must be established and authorized for tracking the budget and for preparing responsibility reports. Care must be taken to distribute revenues and direct costs properly and to allocate indirect costs fairly. Where difficult allocation problems arise, it is possible that the items themselves are not controllable by responsibility center managers and should be omitted from the reports or segregated and labeled noncontrollable. Reports should be prepared according to authorized schedules.

Internal Audit

Internal audit procedures should be established to verify that budget preparation/ tracking and transaction authorization, recording, and processing are all handled in accordance with management's written policies and procedures. Provision should be made for independent confirmation, on an appropriate sample basis, of data appearing in management reports. All computer-created transactions should be subject to management review. The utility of internal management reports should routinely be reviewed.

External Reporting

The financial statements, tax returns, and regulatory reports should be independently reviewed for content, format, and compliance with statutory regulations before issuance or filing. Ratio analysis and analysis of trends and variances provide some assurance that reported amounts are correct. Checklists should be used to verify compliance with filing deadlines.

Physical Controls

The financial reporting function should be separated from the day-to-day recording of routine accounting transactions, and file maintenance functions, with proper oversight by management.

Segregation of Duties

File maintenance and recording of adjusting and closing entries should be separated from the routine transaction processing. Review of the financial statements should be done by the CEO and CFO (per SOX section 302). The distribution of internal reports containing proprietary information should be carefully controlled and recorded.

Information Processing

Authorization Controls

Only authorized personnel should have access to the reporting function. Access can be controlled through user identification and passwords.

The chart of accounts and associated coding schemes should be properly authorized, and a method of uniquely identifying transactions should be established. General and specific authorizations should be defined for recording, processing, and reporting transactions. These authorizations should extend to procedures for handling adjusting and closing entries and for end-of-period cutoff. Similar authorizations are required for access to the accounting information system and for such sensitive activities as file maintenance.

Special authorization should be required for the disposal of capital resources. Authority to write down or write off assets and authority to initiate the disposal of assets should be separated from responsibility for actual disposal.

Data Verification Controls

Input data should be verified as accurate in the various processes. Data input directly into the GL module, such as depreciation calculations, should be reviewed periodically and checked for reasonableness.

Processing Controls

For data input directly into the GL module, there should be documentation and independent checks of transactions. Summarized information received from other processes for the purpose of preparing financial statements should be periodically reviewed to determine that the financial statements are accurately stated. Output controls limiting who has access to generated reports should be enforced, so that for example, competitors do not receive reports that include proprietary costing information.

Conceptual File Structures

LEARNING OBJECTIVE 6
Understand conceptual data storage in the financial process.

The outputs that are required for any AIS (reports and documents) determine the events to be captured and recorded. In like manner, master file contents in which data are summarized are a consequence of output needs.

Master File Design

The GL master file must accumulate and retain all data required for financial statements and detailed responsibility reporting as well as codes required for operation of the GL module. **Exhibit 8.11** depicts for Seaton Steel Doors the fields that are found in each GL master file record for normal accounts and subaccounts, and there is a record for each such account. The first column describes the contents of the field; the second describes the nature of the data; and the third describes the field length.

Description	Data Type	Field Length
Account number (X.YY.)	A/N	7
Account name	A/N	25
Account status (A = active, I = inactive)	A/N	1
Automatic allocation account (sub-accounts)	A/N	1
Current account balance	N	10
End month 1 balance	N	10
End month 2 balance	N	10
End month 3 balance (continues through month 12)	N	10
Prior year month 1 balance	N	10
Prior year month 2 balance	N	10
Prior year month 3 balance (continues through month 12)	N	10
Budget for month 1	N	10
Budget for month 2	N	10
Budget for month 3 (continues through month 12)	N	10

EXHIBIT 8.11 GL Master File Record Layout—Normal and Sub-Accounts

Notice that, in addition to the current account balance, normal and sub-accounts contain monthly historical balances for the current and prior years. Retention of this data is necessary to produce analytical financial statements that compare current performance to prior performance (both last month and the same month last year) and with budget data. Account status indicates whether the account is active, thus permitting or denying the ability to make entries to the account.

As mentioned in Chapter 3 and illustrated in Chapter 4, for audit evidence a second GL master file may be used to maintain a record of each change in the current balance. An alternative that requires more processing time but less storage space is to use the master file, as depicted in Exhibit 8.11, along with a copy of transaction files sorted by account number. Programs that either display or print the general ledger must then refer to the master file for beginning balances and to relevant parts of the transaction file to obtain a list of transactions for each account.

Master accounts need not contain monetary values because monetary values are stored in the sub-accounts supporting each master account. Master accounts are integrated into the same table as the normal and sub-accounts, but several fields are unnecessary and are therefore blank. Remember that entries are not normally made to master accounts. The exception is the "on screen" entries that are made to master accounts when automatic distribution allocations have been set up. Thus, master account records need to indicate whether "on screen" entries are permitted to a master account. **Exhibit 8.12** shows the fields necessary for a master account.

Description	Data Type	Field Length
Account number (X.YY.)	A/N	7
Account name	A/N	25
Account status (A = active, I = inactive)	A/N	1
Automatic allocation account = Y, otherwise = N	A/N	1

EXHIBIT 8.12 GL Master File Record Layout—Master Accounts

Transaction File Design

It is assumed that Seaton Steel Doors has one transaction file (journal) in the GL module in which all original entries, recurring entries, and transferred entries are recorded (see **Exhibit 8.13**). Each record is a debit or a credit. Credits are negative amounts. New entries have a default value of U (unposted) in field 7 that is changed to a P when posting occurs.

Description	Data Type	Field Length
Sequential numeric entry ID	N	4
Date of transaction	N	8
Account number debited or credited	A/N	7
Amount of entry (credits are negative)	N	10
Source document ID	A/N	10
Comment	A/N	50
Posting status (P = posted, U = unposted)	A/N	1

EXHIBIT 8.13 GL Transaction File Layout

End-of-Period Processing

LEARNING OBJECTIVE 7
Describe common end-of-period functions.

The first step in this process is to transfer transaction data from other processes. In some designs, the GL module "pulls" the data from the other modules. A more common approach is for the other modules to "push," or post, the data into the GL module.

At the end of each interim fiscal period—week, month, or quarter—selected for reporting purposes, an interim closing will occur. In the past, it was common for this closing to erase all transaction details and to carry balances forward to the new period. With the rapid decline in the cost of storing data, and the desire for electronic access and manipulation of detailed data for ad-hoc reporting purposes, the more popular designs now retain transaction detail for the entire year or even longer. In these more recent designs, the principal purpose of interim closings is to update monthly summary fields in the account records, such as those shown in Exhibit 8.11 (end-of-month and prior-year-month balances).

Soft closing A closing for interim accounting periods in which entries can still be made in the earlier interim periods.

Most closings for interim periods are known as **"soft" closings**, meaning that, subject to proper controls, entries can still be made in the earlier interim periods. Annual closings usually support both soft and **"hard" closings**. These concepts are similar to the concepts of provisional and permanent posting discussed earlier in this chapter. However, while soft closings permit additional entries to be made, provisional posting permits existing entries to be changed. Permanently posted entries (ink posting) cannot be modified even though a soft closing has occurred.

Hard closing Closing for annual accounting periods after which no entries can be made in the period closed.

A company may go through several soft closings of all interim periods composing the year. If the company does not have a separate "audit" period, then a hard closing will be made when all adjustments proposed by the auditors have been recorded. If desired, hard closings may be made each month.

The Effects of the Implementation of International Financial Reporting Standards (IFRS)

LEARNING OBJECTIVE 8
Describe some of the potential effects of the implementation of international financial reporting standards (IFRS) on systems.

The potential implications resulting from changing reporting standards from U.S. Generally Accepted Accounting Principles (GAAP) to **International Financial Reporting Standards (IFRS)** are currently being considered among standard-setting and regulatory agencies in the U.S. Currently, the U.S. FASB is working to "converge" the U.S. GAAP with IFRS. Over 120 countries have adopted IFRS already, with more planned in the next few years, so it is just a matter of time before the U.S. will also adopt the IFRS standards. Many of the higher-end enterprise resource planning packages such as SAP provide companies with the ability to generate both U.S. GAAP-compliant and IFRS-compliant financial reports. As recently as 2014 the SEC encouraged companies to voluntarily provide IFRS-based supplemental financial information (along with the required GAAP information) as an alternative to incorporation of IFRS.[2]

International Financial Reporting Standards (IFRS) Accounting standards issued by the International Accounting Standards Board.

The move toward compliance with IFRS could have significant impact on financial reporting and the systems that generate those reports. Under current regulations, the requirement to reconcile U.S. GAAP and IFRS net assets and net earnings (required for non-U.S. companies' financial reports presented under IFRS standards) basically requires a company to maintain two sets of books, which can be onerous to say the least.[3] Significant differences in areas such as revenue recognition, consolidated entity reporting, expense recognition, and exchange gains/losses are encouraging the shift of some U.S. GAAP principles to align more closely with IFRS principles—for example, the consideration of what constitutes an entity that should be consolidated.

Examples of the differences between IFRS and U.S. GAAP financial reporting include:

- *Differences in revenue recognition*: Under IFRS, there are four categories of revenue: sale of goods, services, others' use of entity assets (e.g., royalties), and construction; some of the allowable methods for revenue recognition differ from U.S. GAAP.

- *Differences in impairment adjustments*: Under IFRS, adjustments can be reversed, and the impairment testing model differs from U.S. GAAP models.

- *Differences in the treatment of some expenses:* Under U.S. GAAP, all research and development costs must be expensed, under IFRS, development costs meeting specific criterion can be capitalized.

- *Differences in depreciation:* Under IFRS, component depreciation is allowable—e.g., the depreciation of a corporate jet would include different depreciation methods/lives for the fuselage and the engine(s)—while under U.S. GAAP, the entire asset (in this case, the entire plane) is depreciated using one method/economic useful life value.

- *Differences in the treatment of expenses related to inventory and leased assets:* Under IFRS, the LIFO costing assumption is prohibited, and IFRS does not recognize the operating v. capital lease classification characteristic of U.S. GAAP (operating leases are a form of off-balance sheet financing under U.S. GAAP).

- *Differences in the classification of some financial instruments:* For example, under IFRS, convertible instruments must be split between liability and equity classifications, which could cause changes to an organization's U.S. GAAP-calculated debt ratio and affect related debt covenants.

- *Differences in how entities are consolidated:* Under IFRS, whether or not an entity is consolidated is determined by how much power one company has to govern financial and operating policies of another.

These issues could have significant effects on the financial processes of an organization. Proper coding is essential to creating the necessary reports. One of the most important considerations in the decision to purchase or develop a new system is whether or not the new system can accommodate IFRS.

Summary

The financial process is the locus of the AIS. All data processed by the AIS eventually are reflected either directly (transaction dollars) or indirectly (employee attendance) in the financial process. It provides structure and discipline to the entire AIS as well as business processes and culminates in the production of financial statements. This process results in reports used by both external and internal users. Proper controls and accurate information must be attested to by executive management for purposes of the audit report and SOX compliance (specifically, sections 302 and 404).

Extensive and flexible coding schemes enable the financial process to gather and process data necessary for the organization to meet its reporting and operating objectives. The financial process accommodates both transaction processing and budgeting. Features may be designed into these so the AIS can be operated efficiently. Posting methods must be selected based on a balancing of operational efficiency and data integrity on the one hand versus timely reporting on the other. Coding for the financial process also includes determining the "tags" for financial information using XBRL required for electronic SEC reporting.

Changes in reporting requirements under the impending International Financial Reporting Standards (IFRS) are an important consideration in the development or purchase of a new accounting system. Differences in revenue recognition, expense recognition, impairment models, consolidation issues, and financial instrument classifications will have a significant impact on the financial reporting of the future.

Key Terms

Auto-enter   248
Automatic distribution entry   247
Cents entry   247
Chart of accounts   237
Common-dollar statements   233
Dollar entry   247
Hard closing   254
Horizontal analysis   233
Inactive account   250
International Financial Reporting Standards (IFRS)   254

Master account   239
Normal account   239
Provisional posting (pencil posting)   249
Recurring entry   246
Soft closing   254
Statistical account   240
Sub-account   239
Time-sensitive entries   248
Vertical analysis   233

Discussion Questions and Problems

1. **Required:**

   a. Prepare a comparative balance sheet with vertical analysis accounting information for December 31 and January 31 using the data in Exhibit 4.23 in Chapter 4 and using the following data for December:

Cash in bank	$ 4,100
Accounts receivable	10,300
Equipment	15,000
Accumulated depreciation	1,800
Accounts payable	2,800
Owner's equity	24,800

   b. Prepare an actual versus budget income statement with horizontal analysis accounting information using the data in Exhibit 4.23 in Chapter 4 and the following budget data for January:

Sales of services	18,300
Salary expense	6,200
Depreciation expense	375
Repair expense	2,150
Rent expense	3,150

2. Two large publicly held companies in the computer industry had net income in 2018 of approximately $8 billion. Therefore, the two companies performed equally.

   Required:

   a. Evaluate the fairness of the conclusion above, based upon the facts given.
   b. What additional facts would you like to have to compare the performance of the two companies?

3. **Required:**

   Prepare a ratio report using the data in Exhibit 4.23 in Chapter 4. To the extent that actual (as contrasted with budget) data are available, make your report comparative. (Note that because the data assumes a service organization, not all of the ratios presented in the chapter are relevant.)

4. The following accounts and balances appear on the records of Fiberboard Processing, Inc. (see below): Both the petty cash and payroll cash accounts are operated as imprest accounts. That is, their balances never change because all payments from them are reimbursed from the general checking account.

   a. Characterize the nature of each account above as normal, master, or sub-account.
   b. Calculate the total cash balance.
   c. If the company printed a summary balance sheet, what accounts and amounts would appear on the statement?
   d. Prepare a direct method cash flow statement.

Account No.	Description	Account Balance Debit	Account Balance Credit
100.PET.00	Petty Cash	$ 500	
101.CHK.00	General checking—cash		
101.CHK.01	Collections from sales	367,200	
101.CHK.02	Payments to merchandise suppliers		$215,400
101.CHK.03	Payments for operating expenses		73,700
101.CHK.05	Payments for corporate income taxes		3,900
101.CHK.10	Proceeds—fixed asset dispositions	5,800	
101.CHK.11	Payments for fixed assets acquired		6,300
101.CHK.20	Proceeds from bond issuances	130,000	
101.CHK.21	Proceeds for bond retirements		80,000
101.CHK.30	Proceeds from stock issuances	47,000	
101.CHK.31	Payments for stock acquisitions		13,000
102.PAY.00	Payroll cash account	1,000	

5. Describe the three categories of data recorded in the GL module.
6. From a historical perspective, accountants have insisted that certain types of transactions be recorded in specific journals. Conversion to computerized systems has impacted some of these "rules."

   Required:

   a. What are the assignments of transactions to various journals using manual systems?
   b. What is the basis for such assignments?
   c. How do these assignments differ in a computerized system?

7. Respond to the following questions:

   a. Should accounting data-entry programs require that journal entries be balanced?
   b. If the answer to the above is YES, when should the requirement be imposed?

8. Most organizations have a number of adjustments required at the end of each interim period, such as a month.

   Required:

   What technique exists for automating these adjustments and what are the steps involved in using the technique?

9. NNH&V Cable TV operates cable TV systems in larger cities in the northern two-thirds of New Hampshire and Vermont. The franchise agreement with the cities requires an annual reporting to each city council of operating profit in that city. Thirty-three company expense categories, such as cable system repairs, repair truck depreciation, truck repairs, truck operating cost, as well as repair personnel costs, must be allocated to city-level income statements based on population calculated to a percentage that includes one decimal place. Cities currently served by NNH&V and their populations are:

Berlin, NH	13,084
Conway, NH	8,939
Hanover, VT	15,980
Laconia, NH	15,575
Lebanon, VT	11,134

   Depreciation on the repair trucks is $8,000 per month. To record the monthly depreciation, five accounts are debited and a single credit is made to Accumulated Depreciation–Trucks.

   Required:

   a. Calculate the amount of depreciation to be allocated to the respective city-level income statements.

b. How might entries made to the thirty-three accounts of NNH&V be automated to save on data-entry costs?
c. Assuming that the number of transactions and monthly adjustments that must be allocated is fifty-five, how many debits or credits can be saved by the solution you recommended in b?

10. Seven thousand customers of Merchants Retailing Company have credit cards issued by the department store chain. Charges to accounts are made by bar code input. After receiving monthly statements of account, customers remit by check to the company's central accounting office. Payment statistics on these accounts for July are:

Active accounts	5,700
Total number of payments received in July	5,321
Number of account balances paid in full	978
Number of minimum payments (even dollar amounts)	4,229
Number of other even dollar amount payments	85
Number of other odd dollar amount payments	29

Checks received on account are recorded in the company AIS by keyboard entry. Payments for even dollar amounts may be recorded by entering the dollar digits only. To save on keystrokes, data-entry personnel can use the key combination of CTRL-B to enter a payment for the full account balance and the combination of CTRL-M when the minimum payment is remitted. Other remittances require the entry of the dollar digits and the decimal followed by the cents digits.

Required:

a. Using July remittances as a representative month, how many keystrokes can be saved by changing to cents entry?
b. Assume that Lodestone Mining Company receives 5,321 payments a month based on invoiced amounts, of which 1 percent are even amounts. How many keystrokes a month will be saved by converting from dollar entry to cents entry?

11. Provide your responses to the following questions:

a. What factors may suggest the number of interim periods in a year?
b. If one wishes to obtain data that are comparable from one calendar quarter to the same quarter in the preceding year, what are two solutions?

12. Respond to the following questions:

a. Describe the concept of time-sensitive entries.
b. What are some problems that are ameliorated by the ability to make time-sensitive entries?

13. Describe provisional posting and its benefits.
14. Describe/discuss the following:
    a. Describe "inactive" accounts.
    b. Why is the capability of retaining inactive accounts in the general ledger a desirable feature?
15. Describe/discuss the following:
    a. How do monthly closings compare with annual closings?
    b. Distinguish between "soft" and "hard" closings.
    c. How do soft closings differ from provisional posting?
16. Develop a coding system for recording expense items in a multi-segment organization. The intention is to provide for the retrieval of data in the following configurations:

    Company-wide total of an individual expense
    Divisional total of an individual expense
    Departmental total of an individual expense
    Divisional total expenses
    Departmental total expenses

    The company has four divisions, and the maximum number of departments in any one division is fifteen. The company has 500 different expense items.
17. Dolly and Madison Ford is a partnership that sells automobiles. The company has two dealerships—Baytown Ford and Liberty Ford. Each dealership sells two makes of automobiles—Mustang and Taurus.
    Additional information:
    ■ Neither dealership maintains a parts inventory.
    ■ Each dealership owns its equipment, furniture and fixtures, but rents its location.
    ■ Each dealership has a manager, a bookkeeper, and four salespeople, all of whom are paid a salary.
    ■ Each dealership collects state sales tax on automobile sales.
    ■ The accounting system uses accrual-basis accounting.
    ■ The accounting system uses a perpetual inventory system for automobiles.

Required:

Prepare an appropriate chart of accounts for the company's computerized accounting system using either a spreadsheet or word processing program. The chart of accounts should enable the accounting system to report the following:
  a. For both dealerships combined:
     1. Report operating profit.
     2. Report automobile inventory accounts for each make of automobile and for both makes combined.
  b. For each dealership:
     1. Report operating profit.
     2. Report sales and cost of sales for each make of automobile.
     3. Report inventory accounts for each make of automobile.

Use the appropriate block codes given in the chapter in the "Coding Schemes" section. Include not only the accounts needed to accomplish the above reporting requirements, but all other accounts that are needed for recording typical day-to-day transactions involved in operating an automobile dealership (except for parts inventory, as noted above).

Notes

1. SFAS is the abbreviation for Statement of Financial Accounting Standards, the statements issued by the Financial Accounting Standards Board.
2. *Comparability in International Accounting Standards—An Overview.* Retrieved from the FASB website at: http://www .fasb.org/jsp/FASB/Page/SectionPage&cid=11761562 45663&pf=true
3. More discussion on this topic can be found at: http:// finance.yahoo.com/news/gaap-ifrs-standards-convergence -efforts-174331863.html (March 17, 2013).

The Revenue Process

Source: Rawpixel/Shutterstock.

Learning Objectives

After studying this chapter, you should be able to:

- Explain the various activities of the revenue process.
- Describe the flow of data through the revenue process.
- Illustrate the balance forward and open item methods of accounting for receivables.
- Explain the revenue accounting modules and their functions.
- Describe typical reports required for effective management of the revenue process.
- Identify risks and understand typical controls found in the revenue process.
- Set forth data entry aspects that are peculiar to the revenue process.
- Explain the nature of cycle billing and the advent of e-invoicing.
- Recognize the relationship between monthly closings and statements of account.

Source: Aysezgicmeli/Shutterstock.

Introductory Scenario

Grace worked as a secretary at the U.S. Embassy in Bangkok for five years, after which she returned to her hometown of Santa Monica to live. While in Thailand, her mail was often lost or delayed. She had difficulty paying bills on time, and experienced problems in conducting personal business in the States from such a great distance. Upon investigation, she found that U.S. expatriates working overseas for governmental agencies or U.S. companies often experienced these problems. Especially affected were those consultants who had short-term engagements of a few months in one country and then moved to another foreign location. Thus, Grace had resolved that upon returning to the States she would start a business to assist U.S. expatriates with such problems.

Naming her business Expat Services, Inc. (ESI), Grace solicited customers whose mail is directed to her business address. Customers notify Grace by telephone, fax, and e-mail where and when to forward their mail. She combines all of a customer's mail in one container and forwards it to the customer by FedEx, DHL, or International mail. Grace also offers a bill-paying service whereby she opens customer bills, such as Visa and MasterCard, pays them, and includes the paid bills in customer mailings. Grace realized there is both a fixed and variable cost of providing these services. Therefore, the customers pay a flat annual fee plus charges based on the type and level of services performed. Customers are required to maintain a deposit with ESI to cover any charges. At any given time, most customers have a credit balance.

For general accounting and taxes, Grace has retained an accounting service that recommended a cash-basis accounting system. For all customer collections, CASH is debited and SERVICE INCOME is credited. Grace just received the following income statement for the first six months of operations from the accounting service:

ESI Statement of Income		
Six Months Ending September 30, 2018		
Service income		$155,349
Salaries and wages	$34,000	
Postage and shipping	65,800	
Mailing and office supplies	3,000	
Phone and Internet costs	2,200	
Depreciation of equipment	5,000	
Other expenses	12,000	122,000
NET INCOME		$ 33,349

Grace is pleased that her business is profitable so early. However, she is concerned about having sufficient funds to pay corporate income taxes at the end of the year. Also, Grace observes an advertisement in *Expatriate News* by a new competitor who is charging only a fixed monthly rate for services that is 7% higher than Grace's fixed charge.

Introductory Scenario Thought Questions:

1. Because Grace has a small business, what are the merits of cash basis versus accrual basis for the business?
2. Which type of accounting method would you recommend for ESI (i.e., balance forward or open item billing) and why?
3. Would her competitor be more likely to attract customers with high activity volume or low activity volume?

Overview of the Revenue Process

Whereas the primary purpose of the financial process is to summarize data and report on the overall financial progress and status of the organization, purposes of the revenue process include not only reporting but also, to a significant degree, the facilitation and control of certain business activities of the organization. Alternative names for the revenue process are the sales process or the selling and collection process.

In a merchandising organization, the relevant business activities are depicted in sequence in **Exhibit 9.1**. The initial step is the creation of demand through various advertising media, promotional events, and direct solicitation of orders either by phone or by an outside sales force. Receipt and acceptance of orders is the next step. A customer order is an offer to purchase merchandise or services from our company, and the acknowledgment is an acceptance of that offer, thus completing a binding contract for a sale.

LEARNING OBJECTIVE 1
Explain the various activities of the revenue process.

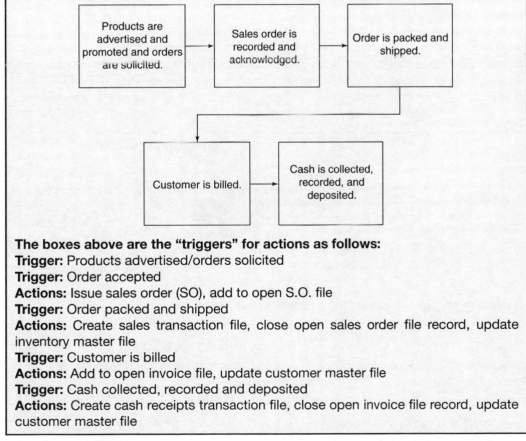

The boxes above are the "triggers" for actions as follows:
Trigger: Products advertised/orders solicited
Trigger: Order accepted
Actions: Issue sales order (SO), add to open S.O. file
Trigger: Order packed and shipped
Actions: Create sales transaction file, close open sales order file record, update inventory master file
Trigger: Customer is billed
Actions: Add to open invoice file, update customer master file
Trigger: Cash collected, recorded and deposited
Actions: Create cash receipts transaction file, close open invoice file record, update customer master file

EXHIBIT 9.1 Revenue Activities for Merchandising Organization

On the agreed-upon date for filling the order, it is packaged and shipped to the customer. The customer is billed, either concurrently with the shipment or immediately thereafter. The customer subsequently pays our company, and the receipt is deposited in the company bank account, completing the revenue process.

If the entity for which we are accounting is a service organization (rather than a merchandising organization), the "order is packed and shipped" function in Exhibit 9.1 is replaced by one that reads "service is rendered." After the service is rendered, the client is billed and cash is collected. The revenue process for tax-supported (governmental bodies) and contribution-supported organizations (charities) is shown in **Exhibit 9.2** and is discussed below. The situation depicted in Exhibit 9.2 is simplified because most governmental units and charities also receive funds from services rendered and products sold. For example, a city government will furnish water to the populace and bill based on usage. Likewise, public television may sell promotional items to their subscribers.

Tax- and Contribution-Supported Organizations

Tax-supported organizations raise revenue through various types of taxes. The federal government raises most of its revenue through personal and corporate income taxes. It also imposes excise taxes on fuel, automobile tires, liquor, cigarettes, and other commodities, and it charges for certain types of services, such as the use of national parks. Most state governments also raise revenue through income taxes, but some rely largely or solely on sales taxes. City and county governments impose property taxes on businesses, residences, and personal property and charge fees for recording property titles. City and county governments may also impose income or sales taxes. Some municipalities raise revenues from taxes on restaurants and lodging facilities, and from the sale of fishing, hunting, marriage, and other licenses. The revenue process in tax-supported organizations consists of property valuation and tax assessment and tax collection applications, as shown in Exhibit 9.2.

Contribution-supported organizations generate all or most of their revenue from contributions by members, by the general public, or by corporate donors. Examples are churches, fraternal organizations, relief agencies, public radio and television stations, and museums. Such organizations often try to encourage regular giving in the form of pledges, or they may have periodic fund-raising campaigns. Pledges are recorded as a receivable

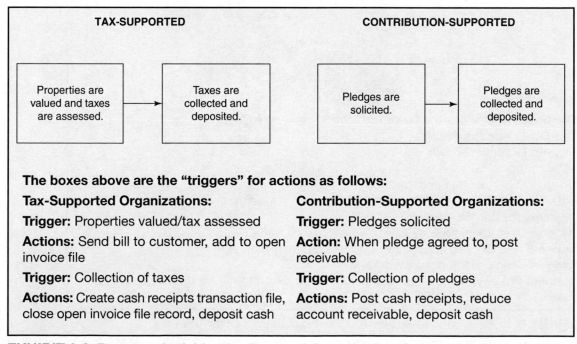

EXHIBIT 9.2 Revenue Activities for Tax- and Contribution-Supported Organizations

(as required by SFAS 116). Virtually all nongovernmental not-for-profit organizations establish endowment funds and encourage supporters to remember them in their wills. Finally, many not-for-profit organizations receive financial support in the form of grants from government agencies, foundations, and corporate sponsors. The revenue process in contribution-supported organizations consists of applications related to fund-raising and cash receipts, as shown in Exhibit 9.2.

Even some primarily sales-supported organizations, such as private schools and symphony orchestras, augment revenue by contributions and use various kinds of fund-raising. They do so because market prices for their products are too low to provide adequate levels of revenue for survival.

The sections that follow focus on sales-supported organizations, but occasional references are made to accounting system features for tax- and contribution-supported organizations.

Sales-Supported Organizations

Sales-supported organizations derive revenue by selling goods and services. Examples of goods include food, clothing, fuel, appliances, vehicles, and machinery. Examples of services include transportation, entertainment, health care, and security and fire protection. The revenue process in sales-supported organizations typically include modules to record the creation/completion of sales orders, shipping, and accounts receivable/cash collections. A sales analysis module may also be included.

Sales are initiated in a variety of ways, for example:

- A customer walks into a store and buys something using cash, check, or credit/debit card.
- A customer places an order for goods or services to be provided later.
- A customer buys goods previously sent on approval or consignment.
- A fan buys a ticket to watch a sporting event.
- A company contracts with an accounting firm for a consulting engagement.
- A passenger buys an airline ticket.

Source: iQoncept/Shutterstock.

Because accounting theory defines a sale as the exchange of goods or services for revenue, revenue may be earned at a single point in time, when title to a shipment of goods passes to a customer, or over a period when goods or services are provided.[1]

Organizations treat credit sales differently from cash sales. A seller offering credit terms wants assurance that the customer will pay when required to do so. This assurance is provided by credit screening to determine whether the customer has or will have the resources to pay and whether previous experience bears out the customer's willingness to pay. A credit check may be made by the organization itself or by a credit agency that sells such services for a fee.

When a sale occurs, goods are carried away by the customer or the goods are shipped to the customer. Ownership of intangibles may be conveyed by oral or written agreement. Services may be provided personally to customers, as in the case of consultations or haircuts, or may be provided by working on the customer's property, as in landscaping or automobile repair.

Data Flows in the Revenue Process

The simplest type of sale is completed in a single transaction. Many sales between businesses are in response to orders received earlier. Rather than collecting payment immediately, credit may be extended, with the organization collecting the payment later. Credit sales give

LEARNING OBJECTIVE 2
Describe the flow of data through the revenue process.

rise to accounts receivable on the books of either the selling organization or a financial intermediary such as a credit card company. When payment (either cash or check) is collected for credit sales, customers' accounts must be credited and the payment itself must be safeguarded and deposited promptly. For purposes of our discussion, any payment type will be termed a "cash receipt" whether the payment is cash, check, or credit card.

Collection efforts are not always successful, and organizations extending credit suffer some level of bad debts as part of doing business. Sales returns reverse the sales transaction: revenue is lost, goods are returned, and any payment collected is refunded to the customer. Sales allowances reduce revenue and receivables and may require a partial refund of payment, but the goods are not returned.

Sales Order Processing

A sale can be complicated by a timing difference between the receipt of an order and the shipment of goods or the provision of services. The information related to the order for a good or service is called a sales order. You may want to refer back to Chapter 3, Exhibit 3.9, for an illustration of a sales order. Orders may originate from various sources. A representative from a business may walk into an office supply store or sales office and order a product. A business customer may submit a purchase order by mail, telephone, fax, electronic data interchange (EDI), or through a web site. In response, the organization may send an acknowledgment for the order. An outside sales representative may call in an order or return from a sales trip with a number of orders. An independent broker or agent may close a sale and forward the order to a client company. A **standing order** may be in effect for goods or services to be supplied at a regular frequency.

Sales orders typically list the goods or services to be delivered, their prices, and the terms and conditions of the sale. Preparation of a sales order is not recognized as an accounting transaction, and no monetary amounts are posted to master files. Nevertheless, sales orders are stored in an open sales order file and are tracked by the sales-order processing application until they are filled by the shipment of the goods or provision of the requested services. (See **Exhibit 9.3**.) This information is important to sales managers for analyzing the productivity of the sales representatives, as well for analyzing the time it

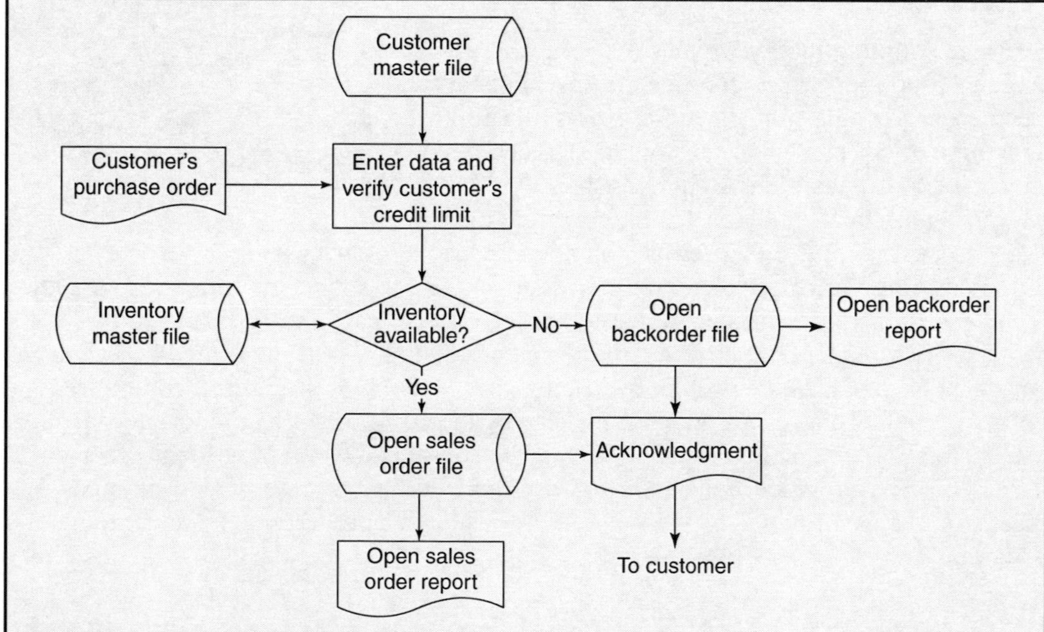

Standing order A purchase order from a customer to a supplier specifying a series of dates and quantities for shipment of goods until notified by the customer to stop.

Trigger: Receipt of customer purchase order

Actions: If order accepted, issue sales order (if inventory available), add to open sales order file; otherwise issue backorder and send acknowledgment to customer

EXHIBIT 9.3 Sales Order Processing

takes to fill orders. The purpose of the sales-order processing application is to ensure that orders are filled promptly and accurately.

The shipment of goods and determination of cost of goods sold form interfaces between the revenue process and the inventory process. The shipment of goods may be promised immediately or scheduled for a future time or over some future period. The order may be filled from inventory. However, inventories may temporarily be depleted and the items backordered. **Backorders** may be recorded in the open sales order file or in a separate open backorder file until the inventory is replenished and the goods can be shipped. If it appears that an abnormally long delay will ensue, the customer may be offered a substitute product.

In some cases, no inventories are maintained at all, and goods are acquired from suppliers or the factory only as needed to fill orders in hand. Some catalog or mail order companies operate in this manner. As customers submit orders for products, the firm submits matching orders to its suppliers. The organization acts like a broker, although the goods may be routed through its facility. A pure broker arranges for goods to be shipped directly from a supplier to the customer.

Sales orders for services should define the services to be provided, the period over which they will be provided, and the date on which they are to begin. The services may begin immediately or may be scheduled for some time in the future.

In some industries and professions, the sales order takes a different form. If custom goods or services are involved, a negotiated contract may accompany the sales order or replace it. In public accounting firms, an **engagement letter** replaces the conventional sales order. The letter lists the accounting services to be provided, the responsibilities of the accounting firm and the client, the expected deliverable(s), and the fees to be charged.

Trade Credit Sales

Organizations selling to business customers extend commercial or **trade credit** on whatever credit terms they choose to offer. An organization tries to establish a credit policy that strikes a balance between excessive bad debts on the one hand (because the credit policy is too relaxed), and the potential loss of sales and profits on the other (because the credit policy is too strict). A loose credit policy could result in unacceptable losses from uncollectible accounts, while a tight policy may drive away prospective customers who cannot meet the more strict credit standards.

Within the framework of the overall credit policy, decisions are made to extend credit to particular customers. An organization's willingness to extend credit depends on a customer's reputation, financial stability, and previous payment record. Credit references obtained from banks or suppliers doing business with the prospective customer may provide evidence of creditworthiness, or a credit check may be required. In the past, organizations conducted their own credit checks. But the expense and delays involved have now persuaded most organizations—as well as credit card institutions—to purchase credit information from commercial agencies. The best known agency providing information on corporations is Dun & Bradstreet, Inc. A credit decision also depends on the organization's eagerness to do business with that customer.

Upon completion of the credit screening, the organization may close an impending sale or assign the customer a credit limit or rating to facilitate future credit sales. A **credit limit** sets a maximum on the amount of credit that will be extended to a customer. A **credit rating** is a classification of customers by creditworthiness. The highest rating may authorize virtually unlimited credit, while the lowest may deny credit altogether. After credit has been established for a customer, the decision to sell on credit is essentially reduced to a programmed decision, although borderline cases may arise that need to be handled on a case-by-case basis by a specific authorization.

Customers' credit limits or ratings can be stored in the organization's customer master file (Exhibit 9.3) or a separate credit file. Sales representatives may be required to query the file to verify the customer's credit limit before accepting a sale. Alternatively, sales order

Backorders Sales orders that cannot be filled because the inventory is depleted.

Engagement letter A letter used by public accounting firms that lists the accounting services to be provided, the responsibilities of the accounting firm and the client, the expected end product, and the fees to be charged.

Trade credit Credit extended to an organization's commercial customers.

Credit limit A dollar ceiling up to which credit will automatically be extended without the need for further credit screening.

Credit rating A classification of customers by creditworthiness.

processing software can do this automatically. If a credit limit is used, the customer's outstanding balance must be subtracted from the credit limit to determine the available credit for future sales. A real-time system may be needed to update customer balance information. Credit arrangements should be reviewed periodically and may be restructured to recognize changes in the customer's payment history. A delinquent customer should be placed on a **credit hold**, which restricts the extension of additional credit to a customer until payments are received.

Shipping Goods to Customers

Goods are retrieved from inventory, packed, and shipped to customers to fill sales orders. A flowchart of this activity is in **Exhibit 9.4**. A **picking list** may be prepared to facilitate retrieval. This document identifies the products and quantity ordered and gives the warehouse location, aisle number, shelf position, bin number, or other reference to the location of the goods. The information is particularly helpful if inventories are spread throughout a large warehouse or among several buildings. If the inventories are smaller and are confined to a small area, information on the location of the items may not be needed, and a copy of the sales order may be used in place of a picking list.

A **shipping document** or **packing slip** should accompany the goods in transit. Instead of a shipping document, a copy of the sales order or a copy of the sales invoice (possibly with price data omitted) may be used. If the goods are shipped by a common carrier, a bill of lading provides a contract between the shipper and the carrier. You may want to turn back to Chapter 3, Exhibit 3.2, for an illustration of a bill of lading.

The **FOB point** is the location at which title to the goods changes from the shipper to the customer. It may be the shipper's loading dock (FOB shipping point), the customer's receiving dock (FOB destination), or some intermediate point, such as a common carrier's terminal, a state line, or a national border. US GAAP financial accounting rules specify that when the goods cross the FOB point, a sale is recognized and the transaction can be recorded in the sales or shipment transaction file. Also, the shipper is responsible for loss of or damage to the goods up to the FOB point, and insurance coverage may be necessary. The FOB point should be specified on the sales order and on the shipping document.

Credit hold A restriction of additional credit to a customer who has a delinquent balance.

Picking list A list that identifies the products and quantities ordered and gives the warehouse location, aisle number, shelf position, bin number, or other reference to the location of the goods.

Shipping document See packing slip.

Packing slip (also known as shipping document) A document that accompanies goods in transit.

FOB point The location at which title to the goods changes from the shipper organization to the customer.

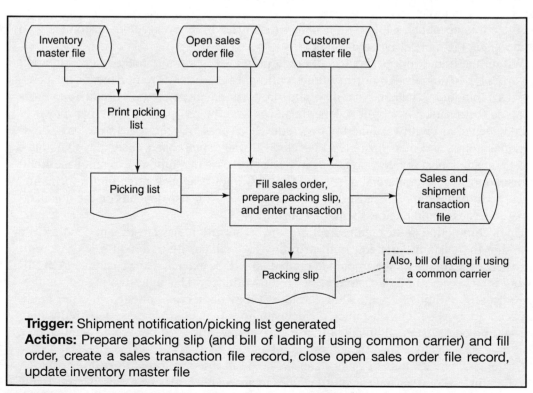

Trigger: Shipment notification/picking list generated
Actions: Prepare packing slip (and bill of lading if using common carrier) and fill order, create a sales transaction file record, close open sales order file record, update inventory master file

EXHIBIT 9.4 Shipment of Goods

Customer Invoicing

An invoice requests payment from the customer for a credit sale. The invoice is normally a paper document listing the goods or services provided and specifying the amount, due date, and credit terms. You may want to refer back to Chapter 3, Exhibit 3.10, for an illustration of a sales (customer) invoice. An invoice for the sale of goods is normally prepared when the goods are shipped. If goods are supplied or services are provided over a period of time, invoices for progress payments may be submitted during the period and a final invoice submitted at the end. The pattern of progress payments, if any, must be agreed to when the sales contract is drawn up. In some situations, payment is not expected until a monthly statement is sent to customers, but more commonly the invoices represent the request for payment.

A **cash discount** may be offered for prompt payment, or a service charge may be imposed if payment is made beyond the due date. An example of a cash discount are the terms "2/10, n/30," which means that the customer can earn a 2 percent discount by paying within 10 days of the invoice date. Otherwise the net amount is due at the end of 30 days. A typical service charge for delinquent payment is 1 percent or 1.5 percent per month. Prompt collection from customers is always important, but it becomes vital in times of high interest rates; organizations cannot afford to finance a high level of accounts receivable that represent "free credit" to their customers.

Cash discount A discount provided to a customer for prompt payment.

When preparing the invoice, the organization should record the account receivable by maintaining an open invoice file containing a record of each invoice. The invoice data should also be posted— periodically or in real time—to the customer master file to update the customer's balance. (See **Exhibit 9.5**.)

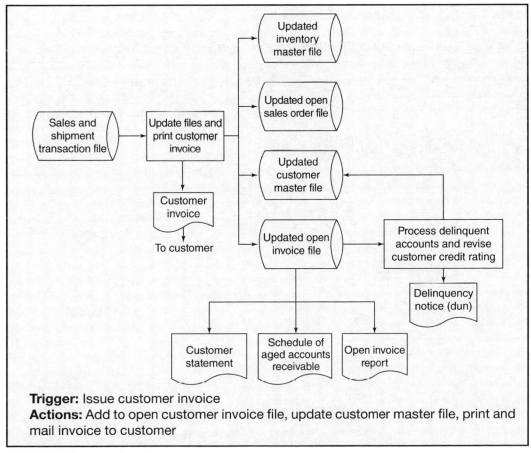

Trigger: Issue customer invoice
Actions: Add to open customer invoice file, update customer master file, print and mail invoice to customer

EXHIBIT 9.5 Customer Invoicing

Customer statement A statement sent to a customer, usually once a month. The statement lists the invoices issued during the month just ended and the amounts received.

Dun Delinquency notice sent to past due customer.

A statement is sent to each active customer, usually once a month. The **customer statement** lists the invoices issued during the month just ended and any payments received during the statement period. Most organizations send statements only when the customer has current activity or an outstanding balance; some send them only if the balance is overdue. The statement is prepared from data in either the customer master file or the open invoice file. Statements provide the normal means of notifying the customer that a balance is outstanding. But if payment is delayed for an excessive period of time, a delinquency notice, or **dun**, may be sent. The delinquency notice may be a preprinted business form, or it may consist of a letter from the credit manager or some other individual. The letter often spells out what action the organization proposes to take to secure payment and may also notify the customer that further credit sales will not be approved until the amounts are paid.

Accounting Methods for Customer Accounts

LEARNING OBJECTIVE 3
Illustrate the balance forward and open item methods of accounting for receivables.

Balance forward A method of accounting for accounts receivable where receipts are applied to the outstanding balance rather than against particular invoices.

Open item A method of accounting for accounts receivable where receipts are correlated with individual invoices, and invoice records remain in the open invoice file until payment is received.

Balance Forward and Open Item Accounting Methods

The two approaches to accounting for accounts receivable are **balance forward** and **open item** methods. The balance forward method applies receipts to the outstanding balance rather than against particular invoices; no attempt is made to match individual payments and invoices. Invoices are regarded as "open" only during the current period, and the open invoice file is archived at the end of the period. On the customer statement, amounts associated with invoices, receipts, and credits from the previous and earlier periods are collapsed into a balance forward (similar to the credit card statements issued for consumer accounts). Under the open item method, receipts are correlated with individual invoices, and invoice records remain in the open invoice file until payment is received.

Exhibit 9.6 illustrates the two methods. Each account is shown for the month of May and after the "closing" process at the end of May. The balance forward account begins in May with a balance carried forward from April of $400. Three sales are made to the customer in May, represented by the invoices for $100, $75, and $200. The customer pays $350 on the account in May and receives a credit of $40. At the end of May, the account balance of $385 is carried forward to June. All activity prior to June 1 is either erased or archived. With the open item method, all items still open (not matched yet with receipts or credits) at the end of April are carried forward to May. The beginning balance consists of a March invoice for $250 and an April invoice for $150. May activity is the same as for the balance forward account with the exception that the customer remittance of $350 specified that it was for the March $250 invoice and the May $100 invoice.

A Balance Forward Account				An Open Item Account				
May 1 Bal.	400			Mar invoice	250			Appearance of accounts on May 31
				Apr invoice	150			
May invoice	100			May invoice	100			
May invoice	75			May invoice	75			
May invoice	200			May invoice	200			
		Receipt	350			Receipt	350	
		May credit	40			May credit	40	
June 1 Bal.	385			Apr invoice	150	May credit	40	Appearance of accounts on June 1
				May invoice	75			
				May invoice	200			

EXHIBIT 9.6 Illustration of Balance Forward and Open Item Accounting Methods

Thus, when the receipt for $350 is posted, it is matched with these two invoices. Because the customer has not "taken" the $40 credit (and told us which item to apply it to), it is an open item. When the "books are closed" at the end of May, all matched items are either erased or archived, and the open items are carried forward to June.

A significant disadvantage of the balance forward method is the difficulty in resolving specific items disputed by a customer because the items no longer appear in the active files (recall the last time you disputed a charge listed on your credit card statement!) Suppose, for example, that the balance forward customer represented in Exhibit 9.6 is dissatisfied with the April sale of $150 and does not intend to pay the invoice. Notification was received along with the $350 payment. At this point the information in the customer account does not have sufficient detail to explain the problem and access must be made to any available archived data. In contrast, the disputed invoice remains in the account until settled with the open item method.

You might wonder why all accounts are not maintained on an open item basis. Remember that with balance forward, receipts are applied to the balance and, by implication, to the oldest invoices. Balance forward customers either pay the month-end account balance or they make payments against that balance.

The statement of account sent to the customer at month-end is the primary document in the balance forward method. The customer pays upon receipt of the statement. In contrast, open item customers pay on invoice, making that the primary document for open item customers. As a practical matter, many open item customers prefer not to receive a monthly statement of account, because the invoice is the only document they use to authenticate the transaction.

Most accounting software packages permit each customer to be set up as either a balance forward account or an open item account. As a general rule, the customer determines whether the account will be balance forward or open item by the mode of payment selected. If the customer pays on the statement, then the only practical way to handle the account is balance forward. If account is paid on invoice(s), the account must be set up as open item. In most instances, accounts with business organizations are open item. Occasionally, a business such as an office supply store might have business customers who prefer to pay monthly, so the office supply store might use both the invoices and the statement of account to document the payment.

Sales Taxes

Sales tax is payable by consumers in most states on certain goods and services. The tax rate and the goods and services to which it applies vary between states, counties, cities, and other local jurisdictions. Profit-seeking enterprises may be exempt from paying sales tax on purchases of materials or supplies that they resell but are required to collect the tax from their customers. Not-for-profit organizations are frequently exempt. Sales tax collections create current liabilities until the amounts are deposited with the state and/or local revenue authorities. Sales taxes form another interface with the procurement cycle. The laws of some states permit companies to remit the sales tax either when the sale is closed or when payment is received. Many companies choose the latter option because it has more favorable cash-flow implications. However, care must be taken to match properly the amount of the sales tax liability with the amount of the original sales. Whichever approach is adopted, provision must be made for handling sales to organizations that are exempted from paying sales tax.

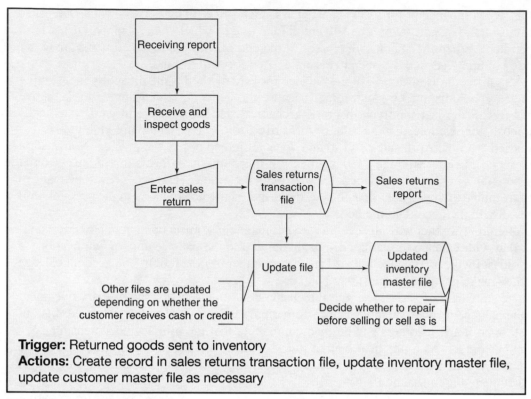

Trigger: Returned goods sent to inventory
Actions: Create record in sales returns transaction file, update inventory master file, update customer master file as necessary

EXHIBIT 9.7 Sales Return

Sales Returns and Allowances

Goods may be returned to the seller for a variety of reasons. For example, the goods may never have been ordered, orders may have been duplicated, excess quantities may have been shipped, prices may be higher than were originally agreed to, customers may have changed their minds, the seller may have repossessed the goods because customers did not pay for them, or the goods may have been damaged in transit or were defective in some other respect.

In the case of damaged or defective goods, the customer may keep the goods and seek an allowance or adjustment of the invoice amount instead of returning the goods. The seller organization can either approve the allowance or insist on the original amount. Organizations may set policies governing returns and allowances and try to discourage abuses, but few organizations can eliminate returns and allowances altogether.

A **sales return** requires the reduction of sales revenue by the full amount of the sale. The selling organization must take several actions (**Exhibit 9.7**). The first action is to return the goods to inventory. Then, the organization will have to decide whether to repair the goods before selling them or selling them "as is" at less than their normal sales price. Another action is to adjust the customer's account or refund cash already received by the selling organization. The organization may refund the entire sales amount and applicable sales tax, or it may give a partial refund, retaining a restocking charge.

A **sales allowance** involves a partial reduction of sales revenue (**Exhibit 9.8**). If the sale was a credit sale and the customer has already paid, the customer may be issued a **credit memo** to be used as an offset against future sales. The account balance of a business customer with trade credit may be reduced. The organization prepares and processes a credit memo or its electronic equivalent to initiate a transaction entry in the Customer (accounts receivable) module. If the sale was a credit card sale, a refund slip is sent to the issuing financial institution. The associated credit will appear on the customer's credit card statement—possibly on a later statement than the one listing the sale. If the company has a "cash refund" policy, a voucher is prepared and processed through the accounts payable system, resulting in a check being issued to the customer. Such a transaction bridges the revenue and procurement processes.

Sales return A reduction of sales revenue by the full amount of the sale because the customer returns the goods to the seller.

Sales allowance A partial reduction of sales revenue because the goods sold to the customer are damaged or defective but the customer chooses to keep the goods.

Credit memo A document issued to a customer indicating a reduction of the amount owed.

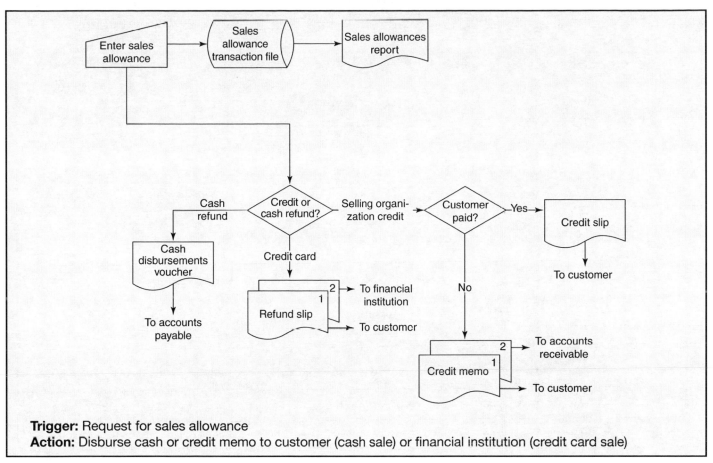

Trigger: Request for sales allowance
Action: Disburse cash or credit memo to customer (cash sale) or financial institution (credit card sale)

EXHIBIT 9.8 Sales Allowance

Cash Receipts

Cash receipts (i.e., payment remitted) from customers complete the revenue cycle
(**Exhibit 9.9**). Customers remitting payment in settlement of accounts receivable normally enclose a copy of the invoice or a **remittance advice** that is provided with the
invoice along with their check.

The remittance advice indicates the amount of the check and, if the customer is paying for specific items (an open item customer), indicates which invoices are being paid
and which credits—if any—are being taken. The remittance advice serves as a source
document. When incoming mail is opened in the organization's mailroom and logged in,
the remittance advice total is compared with the amount of the payment received, and
any discrepancies are investigated. Checks and remittance advices are then segregated
for separate processing with the check promptly deposited in the bank and data from
the remittance slips keyed into the cash receipts transaction file. A day's receipts may
be segregated into one or more batches before entry and the batches are so identifiable
in the accounting software. Copies of deposit slips should be retained for comparison to
on-screen or hard-copy batch details and totals and with bank statements.

> **Remittance advice**
> A document that shows the
> invoice or invoices to which
> a customer's payment will be
> applied.

Sales Analysis

Many organizations analyze historical sales data to provide planning and control information for managers. Sales may be analyzed by customer, by customer type, by region
or territory, by product type, or by sales representative. Frequently, some subset of the
data is isolated for analysis, such as all sales that exceed a specified dollar threshold. It
is possible for management, for instance, to obtain information on the breakdown, by

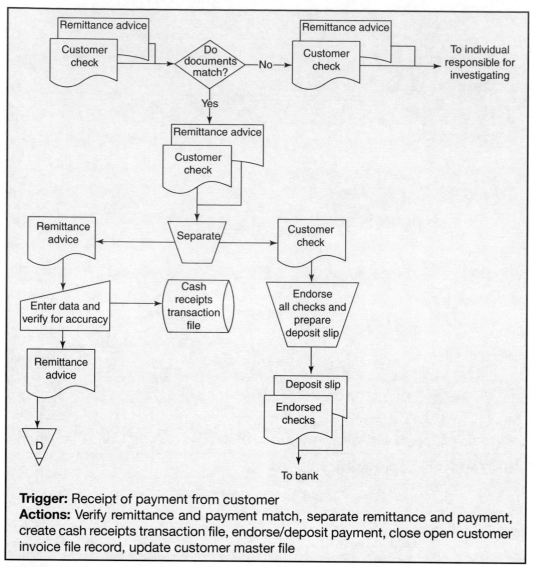

EXHIBIT 9.9 Cash Receipts

customer, of all individual sales exceeding $5,000 that were made in the southwestern United States.

Although less commonly used, gross profit analyses are more useful than sales analyses. **Gross profit analysis** may reveal that a customer whom management considers excellent is, in reality, not providing a profit to the company. Gross profit is sales revenue minus cost of sales.

In all cases, the key to successful sales and gross profit analysis is the use of a comprehensive system of transaction coding that permits the identification and association of transaction data with the required characteristics to meet a particular request. In the example report mentioned above, the sales transactions would have to be coded with the customer identification, the sales amount, and the territory in which the sale occurred.

AIS Structure for the Revenue Process

LEARNING OBJECTIVE 4
Explain the revenue accounting modules and their functions.

In most AISs, the revenue process is represented by two modules—sales order processing and accounts receivable. The information needed to record and track sales orders is controlled by the former while the accounts receivable/cash receipts (or customer) module is used to record sales and payment collections, to manage receivables, and to report on both customer activity and status as well as on sales.

Gross profit analysis
An analysis by customer of sales revenue minus cost of goods sold.

Sales Order Functions

The typical functions for a sales order (SO) processing module are shown in **Exhibit 9.10**. The first section contains those actions required to set up the SO module for use. These include various default values to be automatically used in data entry screens, the design of forms used in the module, and setup of tables of values that are used for data lookup purposes. Data entry is the second function, which is principally composed of the recording of sales orders, the completion or release of an order (including the printing of the shipping document), and the recording of merchandise returns. These entries might be done daily. The third principal function is printing various sales order reports. Note that operation of the sales order module relies heavily on data stored in the customer (accounts receivable) module, and the SO module contains an open file (open sales order file) but no master file. Thus, the end-of-period processes are simple.

Major Functions	Maintenance Functions	Daily and Period-End Functions
Sales order module setup	General defaults (e.g., decimal places, customer terms code, sales tax codes) Design forms (e.g., order acknowledgment, sales order, shipping label) Rate table maintenance (e.g., UPS, freight lines)	
Date entry		**Sales order entry:** Enter new sales order Modify an existing sales order Cancel an existing sales order **Order completion:** Issue a shipping order Bill a shipped order **Sales returns:** Authorize a sales return Issue credit for a sales return
Printing		**New orders:** By customer By salesperson **Aging reports:** By promised ship date By customer **Billed sales:** By customer By salesperson Promised/delivered performance
End-of-period processing		Transfer closed orders to history file Delete canceled sales orders Reconcile open sales orders with inventory reserved stock

EXHIBIT 9.10 Functions in Sales Order Module

Canceled sales orders should be erased from the file. Completed (or closed) sales orders should be transferred to a history file, and finally, products required for open sales orders should be reconciled with the reserved stock noted in the inventory module.

Accounts Receivable Functions

In contrast to the sales order module, the customer (accounts receivable) module contains several transaction files and a master file that contains a record for each customer. **Exhibit 9.11** depicts the typical functions in the customer (accounts receivable) module.

Major Functions	Maintenance Functions	Daily and Period-End Functions
Customer (accounts receivable) module setup	Specify GL posting accounts Specify data tables Specify customer type Design forms	Cash/accounts receivable/inventory/ sales/cost of sales/cash discounts Credit terms/sales taxes Open item/balance forward Invoice/account statement
Customer account maintenance	Add new customer Change customer data Deactivate customer Delete customer account 1099 Tasks	Print 1099s Reset 1099 balances
Data entry	Write off customer balances	**Record sales and print invoices:** Enter normal sale transactions Invoke recurring transactions Create recurring transactions Record customer payments Record customer credits Print data entry proof lists Sales/receipts/credits/adjustments
Posting		Customer invoices Customer payments Other credits Finance charges
Printing		**Accounting records:** Journals (e.g., sales, cash receipts, adjustments, finance charges) Customer ledger Statements of account Dunning notices Sales tax report(s) **Management reports:** Aging of accounts Customer credit analysis Discounts taken report Gross profit by customer Projected cash receipts
End-of-period processing		Post transactions to GL module Close customer accounts

EXHIBIT 9.11 Functions in Customer (Accounts Receivable) Module

These functions, as is the case with the sales order module illustration discussed previously in this chapter, are intended to demonstrate the principal activities rather than to be an exhaustive list of all functions and activities that might be found in the customer (accounts receivable) module.

In module setup, the first requirement is to specify the account numbers of those accounts in the general ledger module to which data will be transferred from the customer (accounts receivable) module. As a minimum, this will permit entries for sales, cost of goods sold, and cash collections on customer accounts. A second setup function is to set up table files for such items as credit terms and sales taxes. Various other defaults may be established that speed data entry, such as specifying the customer type (e.g., open item). Finally, most packages permit you to specify the size of forms and where various items of data should be printed on those forms.

Customer account maintenance permits the user to set up new customer accounts, to modify data recorded in previously established accounts, to place customers on an inactive status, and to delete customers from the customer master file. The customer accounting module is used to record sales and to produce the related invoices. Regular billings, for example, service contracts or retainers, are usually set up as recurring entries and invoices are produced automatically. Customer payments are also recorded in this module. The "posting" function presumes that the accounts receivable function is set up for batch posting. In the event of real-time posting, posting occurs simultaneously with data entry.

In our example of customer module functions, printing is divided into "accounting records" and "management reports." In many packages, no such distinction is made. Reports available in different packages vary widely, as does their quality. Those listed here are considered to be among the most basic, although others may be required depending on particular business operations and management needs.

Data are usually transferred to the general ledger at the end of each period, most often monthly. This transfer may be in summary or complete transaction details may be transferred. Account balances will be brought forward and cleared transactions will be either erased or moved to archival files, depending on whether the customer is set up as a balance forward or open item account.

Reporting for the Revenue Process

When considering reporting requirements for the revenue process, we must remember the activities encompassed by the process. Again these are:

LEARNING OBJECTIVE 5
Describe typical reports required for effective management of the revenue process.

- Advertising, promotion, and sales order solicitation (either through receipt of a customer's purchase order, or through a sales representative contacting a customer)
- Sales order processing
- Shipping
- Billing (i.e., issuing a customer invoice)
- Payment collection, recording, and depositing payment

Reporting requirements for each of the above activities will be covered in the following section.

Reporting for Advertising and Order Solicitation

While advertising, promotion, and sales solicitations are functions in the business revenue process, the costs of these activities are accounted for in the procurement and financial processes. In Chapter 8—The Financial Process—we illustrated coding of advertising accounts for a department store, with multiple categories for classifying the costs. Thus, further treatment of this topic will be deferred to Chapter 10—The Procurement Process.

Reporting for Sales Orders

The management of sales orders is a critical factor in the success of any business. It is important that you be able to promise delivery dates to customers and to perform in accordance with your promises. Orders received are recorded in the sales order module and reports are generated from it showing the status of unfilled sales orders.

One logical file resides in the sales order module (hereinafter abbreviated as SO)—an open file containing the sales orders. As orders are filled, the accounting program may immediately move an SO to an archive file, or may simply mark it as filled, with the archiving occurring at month-end closing.

Most sales order reports are partial or complete SO listings with the sequence of the listing varied for different purposes. **Exhibit 9.12** shows SOs with a primary sequence by required shipment date and secondary sequence by customer ID. This particular report can be used to monitor SOs to ensure that shipments are timely.

Detailed Sales Order Report by Date Required
October 18, 2018—10:31 A.M.

Item	Description	Unit of Measure	Order Quantity	Order Value	Shipped Quantity	Shipped Value
Require Date:	10/19/18					
SO#	10-147					
Customer:	DFWS1 Salesperson: BRJ					
Customer PO:	K451					
FUS4120	Fujitsu Scanpartner FI-4120C	ea	20	$ 16,000.00		
SO2600	Sony RS320MT P4/2600	ea	10	$ 12,000.00	5	$ 6,000.00
HP5700	HPT5700 Thin Client	ea	8	$ 4,000.00		
ASW-12	Antistatic wipes -12 pack	gross	3	$ 30.00		
			Subtotal	$ 32,030.00		$ 6,000.00
SO#	10-139					
Customer	RGVD Salesperson: MP					
Customer PO:	99-271					
DELXPS	Dell Dimension XPS P4	ea	7	$ 9,600.00		
EP1280	Epson Stylus Photo 1280	ea	4	$ 1,340.00		
			Subtotal	$ 10,940.00		
			Required: 10/19/18	$ 42,970.00		$ 6,000.00
Required Date:	10/21/18					
SO#	10-151					
Customer	2BRO Salesperson: RRS					
Customer PO:	3872					
PL1400	PowerLeap 1400C Upgrade	ea	28	$ 3,500.00		
AOPCD	Aopen CDRW Drive	ea	35	$ 1,575.00		
			Subtotal	$ 5,075.00		
			Required: 10/21/18	$ 5,075.00		
			Report total	$ 48,045.00		$ 6,000.00

EXHIBIT 9.12 Open Sales Order Report

A secondary use of the report is to complement cash budgeting by indicating when orders may be shipped and the ensuing payment will be collected. A listing of SOs with the primary sequence by product and secondary sequence by date required can be used to plan production. A listing of SOs received last week by salesperson can be used to judge the effectiveness of sales employees (this requires selecting SOs between two dates and then sequencing the selected SOs by salesperson).

Please notice the following aspects of the Open Sales Order Report in Exhibit 9.12. Sales orders may be completely filled in one shipment or may be spread over multiple shipments, depending on product availability and customer request. The report does not include all open sales orders, but only those selected by specifying a beginning and ending date.

To illustrate another aspect of sales orders, sales order numbers in the reports to management are our numbers issued in the sequence in which orders are recorded. Thus, we might set up the sequence as follows: the first SO listed in the report (10–147, representing the 147th order recorded in October, the 10th month) is the oldest of the SOs listed because they are listed in order by the date the company promised to ship goods to the customer.

Reports for Shipping

The most critical report for shipping activities is the picking list. A picking list identifies the products and quantity of each item ordered and gives the warehouse location, aisle number, shelf position, bin number, or other reference to the location of the goods. Products are stored in warehouses by categories so they can be easily found. When orders must be filled, shipping personnel assemble orders by locating and pulling each item for each order. Orders may be filled one by one, or a worker may pull a flat up and down aisles, pulling several orders at once. So that orders can be pulled efficiently, picking lists are sequenced so that as the shipping clerk moves in an orderly fashion up and down the aisles, the products can be pulled in that order.

As a personal example, when purchasing groceries on a weekly basis, you probably review the entire shopping list at least once on each aisle to avoid retracing your steps. A picking list would order your grocery list so that you could go straight down the list as you proceed through the store. **Exhibit 9.13** is a picking list for SO# 10–139 and

PICKING LIST
10/19/18   09:00 A.M.

Location		Order No.	Cust	Item ID	Description	Unit	
Aisle	Bin #	Order No.	Cust	Item ID	Description	Meas.	Quan.
2	7	10-147	DFWS1	FUS4120	Fujitsu Scanpartner FI-4120C	ea	20
2	12	10-147	DFWS1	SO2600	Sony RS320MT P4/2600	ea	10
2	12	10-139	RGVD	SO2600	Dell Dimension XPS P4	ea	7
3	9	10-147	DFWS1	HP5700	HPT5700 Thin Client	ea	8
4	3	10-139	RGVD	EP1280	Epson Stylus Photo 1280	ea	4
6	7	10-147	DFWS1	ASW-12	Antistatic wipes – 12 pack	gross	3

Packing Proof

Order#	Items
10-139	2
10-147	4

Orders pulled by: John Smith

Orders verified by: Susan Johnson

EXHIBIT 9.13 Picking List

SO# 10–147, shown in Exhibit 9.12. The product items are listed by aisle and bin number, permitting the order-filler to make one pass through the warehouse to fill two orders. When the orders have been pulled, a product count provides a verification of their accuracy.

In automated warehouses, machines and conveyor belts assemble orders automatically using electronic picking lists. The AIS would typically transfer the picking list to a net-worked computer dedicated to control of these order assembly processes.

Billing and Reporting

A type of aging of receivables report that indicates when cash is expected to be collected from billed shipments is used for cash budgeting. Similar information is obtained from open SOs, but both the amounts to be received and the timing of receipts are more predictable once the sale has been consummated. **Exhibit 9.14** shows an aging report that includes both. Predicting when customers will remit payment is somewhat speculative. However, based on past payment patterns of specific customers, useful information can be obtained. For example, notice that invoice number I-201 is scheduled for collection in December even though it is due in October. Because a customer will usually be extended the same credit terms consistently, the AIS can contain an algorithm that will maintain a payment code for each customer based on his or her payment history. That code is then used to predict payment on any invoice or order.

The cash collection budget in Exhibit 9.14 contains amounts for open sales orders and billed receivables. This estimate must be supplemented with an estimate of SOs not yet received as of October 19 that will result in collections during the cash budget period. With that addition, estimated collections can be combined with estimated payments for the period.

CASH COLLECTIONS BUDGET as of October 19, 2018							
				Estimated Collections			
Cust #	SO# or Invoice #	Shipping or Billed	Terms	Oct	Nov	Dec	Jan
Completed Sales:							
JMB2	I-199	7/20/2018	n90	$ 12,500			
URL1	I-201	8/28/2018	1/10,n/60			$ 930	
ACM1	I-223	9/15/2018	n30	$ 2,100			
CWC2	I-227	9/17/2018	2/10,n30		$ 8,700		
GEM1	I-228	10/02/2018	n15	$ 3,200			
DFWS	I-229	10/19/2018	2/10,n30		$ 32,030		
RGVD	I-230	10/19/2018	n/60			$ 10,940	
				$ 17,800	**$ 40,730**	**$ 11,870**	**$ -**
Open Sales Orders:							
2BRO	10-151	10/21/2018	2/10,n45		$ 5,075		
AAA7	10-152	11/12/2018	2/10,n30			$ 3,000	
ORP2	10-153	11/14/2018	n60				$ 23,200
PRR1	10-154	11/21/2018	2/10,n30			$ 12,000	
				$ -	$ 5,075	$ 15,000	$ 23,200
Est. collection of SOs & Invoices				**$ 17,800**	**$ 45,805**	**$ 26,870**	**$ 23,200**

EXHIBIT 9.14 Estimated Cash Collections

Collection Reports

For the revenue process, the most commonly mentioned report is a Schedule of Aged Accounts Receivable. The content and format of the report depends on the task for which the report is used. While this is not necessarily an exhaustive list, aging reports are commonly used for the following purposes:

- As a tool for contacting customers regarding overdue amounts
- As a tool for monitoring customers who are habitually delinquent in their payments
- As a basis for calculating the bad debt provision
- As a tool for writing off small, miscellaneous, delinquent amounts

As discussed earlier in this chapter, customer accounts may be treated as open item or balance forward.

Open Item Aging

A **detailed aging report** of open item accounts lists individual invoices by customer, whereas a **summary aging report** requires only one line for each customer with all invoices for a single customer combined. In most accounting packages, the aging report is comprehensive, meaning that every account is included in the report. As a result, collection personnel looking for overdue accounts must review the entire report to find those that are overdue. An exception report is a better alternative. The software should permit the user to specify both a minimum dollar amount and an overdue status (perhaps at least 60 days overdue) as criteria for inclusion of accounts on the report. With such a report, all accounts listed will require some management attention.

Exhibit 9.15 is a detailed aging of open item accounts with a requirement that the listed invoices be at least $100 and over 60 days delinquent.

Detailed aging report
A detailed aging report is prepared for open item accounts and lists each unpaid invoice by customer.

Summary aging report
An aging report that presents information about amounts owed by customers and includes only one line for each customer with all invoices for a single customer combined.

				Invoice		Total Acct.Bal.	Days Delinquent		
Customer ID	Customer Name	Cust. Contact	Cust.Phone #	Invoice	Due Date		61–90	91–120	over 120+
AAA2	Austin Auto Appraisal	Joe Wiley	512-444-3333	I-220	10/28/2018	$ 4,000	$ 1,300		
Notes:									
CWC2	Cal's Worth Cleaners	Eileen Black	512-333-4444			$ 3,100			$ 615
Notes				I-173	8/12/2018				$ 2,485
				I-181	8/25/2018				
LTB1	Lake Travis Boating	Bubba Smith	512-111-5555			$ 8,000		$ 5,400	
Notes				I-208	9/23/2018		$ 700		
				I-215	10/7/2018				
ZAP1	Zack's Auto Polishing	Jay Deno	512-777-8888			$ 110		$ 110	
Notes				I-206	9/12/2018				

AGING OF ACCOUNTS RECEIVABLE — December 31, 2018 — Invoices over $100 and more than 60 days delinquent

EXHIBIT 9.15 Schedule of Aged Accounts Receivable

Note that the aging report is only a worksheet to aid the collection officer in collecting amounts overdue. Consequently, totals are not necessary on the report. It contains the departmental contact in the customer's accounts payable or procurement department, along with the contact person's telephone number. A space is provided for notes indicating action promised by the customer's personnel. Most AIS software permits collection personnel to browse details of delinquent customer accounts on-screen while contacting the customer. Often electronic notes may be attached to the customer accounts.

If the organization provides for bad debts by analyzing accounts receivable (as opposed to calculating the provision as a percent of net sales), then an all-inclusive account aging is required with totals. For purposes of calculating the bad debt adjustment, a summary rather than a detailed aging report is preferred because the details are unimportant.

Customers frequently take discounts they have not earned and take allowances promised by salespeople that are not yet recognized when billing occurs. These amounts are seldom collectible. Therefore, from time to time the organization will write off old, small amounts that appear in customer accounts. This can most easily be accomplished if an aging of accounts is prepared that selects amounts less than perhaps $20 that are over 90 days old. A clerical employee can then review the aging and propose adjustments to the customer accounts.

Balance Forward Aging

Preparing an aging report for balance forward accounts is not straightforward because no detail may be available before the current period. In some balance forward systems, detail is retained in customer accounts for a given number of months (in some systems this may be specified when the software is installed), but statements are prepared on a balance forward basis. In these systems, a reasonably good aging can be prepared because details of recent charges are available. Because the balance forward system implicitly applies any receipts to the oldest items, a disputed item may be buried in the account for a long time if the account is active.

For those balance forward systems that do not maintain details before the current month, the aging must be calculated by reference to other data. Suppose that a balance forward account is as follows:

A Balance Forward Customer Account			
Beg. bal., April 1	12,000	April 5 receipt	700
April 10 invoice	3,000		
April 26 invoice	1,000		

With this information, at the end of April the account can be aged as $4,000 current and $11,300 prior to April ($12,000—$700). We have no idea of the age of the $11,300. But if we have retained a summary of sales to that customer by month, an aging can be calculated. Suppose the master file record for the customer contains the following data:

Sales for prior month	4,000
Sales for 2nd prior month	2,000
Sales for 3rd prior rnonth	4,500

The account can now be aged as follows:

Account balance 4/30	15,300	
Less April charges	4,000	Current
	11,300	
Less sales for prior month (March)	2,000	31–60 days old
	9,300	
Less sales for 2nd prior month (February)	4,500	61–90 days old
	4,800	More than 90 days old

The above system is commonly used for aging balance forward accounts when no prior-month detail is maintained (and because receipts are always applied to the oldest amounts) and provides an identical aging to that available when details are retained for several months. The advantage of maintaining several months' detail is that the data are readily available when a customer inquires about a prior month's activity.

Discounts Taken Report

Organizations extending credit often extend a cash discount (e.g., 2/10, n/30) to those customers who pay within the discount period (e.g., within 10 days). The purpose of the discount is to encourage early payment. However, if virtually all customers take the discount, the discount may be too costly to the organization because many of the customers taking the discount would likely pay early even if the discount were smaller (such as 1/10, n/30). If few customers take the discount, it is too small to be an effective motivator for early payment. For example, suppose a company has credit sales of $100,000 monthly. With terms of 2/10, n/30, if 98 percent of the customers take the discount, the total discount taken will be $1,960 ($100,000 × .98 × .02). Alternatively, with terms of 1/10, n/30, if 80 percent of the customers take the discount, the total discount taken will be $800 ($100,000 × .80 × .01). Collecting the marginal $18,000 [$100,000 × (.98 − .80)] early has a cost of $1,160 ($1,960 − $800). Our company has the additional funds ($18,000) 20 days early. This is an effective interest rate of about 36 percent annually.[2] Thus, our discount rate is very costly and should be lowered to 1 percent.

Market interest rates fluctuate constantly, and the desirability of taking certain discounts changes with these rates. If the early payment incentive is to be effective, but not too costly, credit terms must be adjusted along with significant changes in the market interest rate. Any organization offering cash discounts should monitor customer behavior regularly. This can be done by periodically calculating the percent of dollar sales on which discounts were taken. **Exhibit 9.16** shows such a calculation.

In the example shown in the exhibit above, note that market interest rates, as indicated by the 3-month U.S. Treasury bill rate, have been increasing steadily during the year. The company has been offering a 1 percent discount, with the result that the number of customers taking the discount and paying early declined until the fourth quarter, when the rate was increased to 2 percent.

Although payment behavior in customers will change rather slowly, they do respond to changes in the interest rate. You may wish to produce this report on a quarterly basis, showing several quarters' information so as to spot trends in payment patterns. The report should be part of a planned, regular review of discount policy.

CASH DISCOUNTS TAKEN Most Recent Four Quarters December 31, 2018					
		Discounts			
Calendar Quarter	Credit Terms	Taken	Offered	Percent Taken/Offered	Beginning of Quarter 3-Mo. T-Bill Rate
1	1/10,n/30	$ 14,820	$ 17,000	87%	4.92%
2	1/10,n/30	$ 15,700	$ 21,000	75%	5.13%
3	1/10,n/30	$ 17,300	$ 25,000	69%	5.50%
4	2/10,n/30	$ 12,900	$ 17,000	76%	6.11%

EXHIBIT 9.16 Reporting for Discounts Taken

Sales Analysis Reporting

Effective use of fields in customer master files to accumulate data such as sales and gross profit can significantly enhance and facilitate the reporting of a variety of sales information. In Chapter 5, Exhibits 5.7, 5.8, and 5.9 illustrate reporting of sales by customer. Another, perhaps even more valuable analysis, is a report of gross profit by customer. An organization that has been reporting sales, but not gross profit by customer may be surprised by such a report. As an illustration, consider **Exhibit 9.17** and compare it with Exhibit 5.7.

Although Calloway Bros. appears to be an important customer in Exhibit 5.7, the gross profit earned is quite disappointing, as is the rate of gross profit on the sales dollar. When the cost of sales efforts is associated with Calloway Bros., it may be decided that serving this customer is a losing proposition; the customer can now be recognized as a problem that requires management attention.

Another valuable sales analysis is a listing of sales and/or gross profits by salesperson. If the report compares current with past and budget performance levels, you can make a tentative judgment of the performance of individual sales personnel. A few of the other ways in which sales can be reported include:

- by geographic area
- by customer category (wholesale versus retail)
- by product line

NORTHWEST SALES REPS, INC Gross Profits by Customer Fourth Quarter, 2018					
		This Year		Last Year	
Customer		Amount	Percent	Amount	Percent
Able Company		$ 6,000	18.75%	$ 4,000	15.38%
Baker, Inc.		8,000	18.60%	8,400	19.40%
Calloway Bros.		7,500	9.04%	9,000	9.47%
Dunn Partnership		3,000	17.65%	2,500	15.15%
Page 1					

EXHIBIT 9.17 Gross Profit Reporting

Coding for Customer Accounts

In most cases, codes for customer accounts are rather straightforward and simple. Often a sequential number with a fixed number of characters will be assigned as new customers are acquired. If, for example, company personnel believe that the number of customers is very unlikely to exceed 10,000 for the near future, then the numbers from 1000 through 9999 may be used sequentially to identify customers. A best practice is to exclude those numbers between 0001 and 0999 because users are prone to omit the leading zeros causing the account specification to be incomplete. Some companies use alpha characters to abbreviate the customer's name as a part of the account number. Because of the possibility of duplicate abbreviations, these are often followed by a sequential number to complete the identification. Texas Instruments might, for example, be TI01 whereas Texas International can be assigned TI02.

In some cases, you may want to distinguish between sales to different locations or divisions of a single company. Hewlett-Packard locations might be distinguished by HP-PA and HP-COR for the Palo Alto, California, and Corvallis, Oregon, locations. If reports by company as well as location are desired, then these "location" accounts can be designated as sub-accounts and a master account created simply called HP-00.

Audit Trails for the Revenue Process

Audit trail requirements for the revenue process are modest. You should be able to trace from source documents to the sales and cash receipts transaction files (journals), from the transaction files to the customer accounts in the customer master file, to the inventory accounts in the inventory master file (in the inventory module), to the invoice records in the open customer invoice file, and to data transferred at month-end to the general ledger (GL transaction file and GL master file). Exhibits 9.3, 9.4, 9.5, and 9.9 show these transaction data flows in more detail except for the month-end transfers to the GL module.

The audit trail also works in reverse to enable tracing from accounts back through the system to the source documents.

An analysis of each customer account should be available to permit you to trace from the beginning balance to the ending balance. For open-item customers, the beginning and ending balances will be all of those items (invoices, credit memos, unapplied credits, and unidentified remittances) that are open at the beginning and end of the period in question. Finally, you should be able to trace backwards from reports to accounts to journals to source documents.

Risks and Controls in the Revenue Process

Section 404 of the Sarbanes-Oxley Act requires that executive management attest to the establishment, maintenance, and assessment of the control system of the company. The revenue process is essential to the longevity and success of the company. Controls over the billing and cash collection processes must be in place to mitigate risks associated with generating revenue. Cash and inventory represent the most liquid assets in a company and are easily misappropriated without proper controls. Some of the typical risks that one might find in the revenue process include:

LEARNING OBJECTIVE 6
Identify risks and understand typical controls found in the revenue process.

Sales and Billing Risks

- *Customer credit risks*: for example, extending credit to poor credit risk individuals or businesses, granting credit to customers in excess of the authorized amount, or failing to perform credit checks on new customers.
- *Discounts and allowances risks*: for example, offering excessive discounts or allowances, ignoring credit terms, or facilitating kickbacks.
- *Billing risks*: for example, errors or misstatements of billing amounts, failure to record sales, or failure to bill customers.
- *Pricing risks*: for example, giving "favorable pricing" arrangements not in compliance with stated policies, failing to update prices as costs change, or arbitrarily assigning prices to products.

- *Recording risks*: for example, recording sales at less than the amount billed, recording receivables for sales never made, improperly classifying or not recording returns/allowances, or misappropriated credit memos.

Cash Handling Risks

- *Payment receipts risks*: for example, failure to record payment receipts, misappropriation of payment receipts, improper/incorrect journal entries, improper/incorrect recording of receipts to customer accounts, or failure to properly reconcile the cash account.
- *Posting risks*: for example, improper posting of payment receipts (e.g., to expense accounts), delaying of receipt posting to conceal the misappropriation of payments, or uncollectible accounts written off without proper authorization.
- *Asset risks*: for example, improper safeguarding of cash/checks or improper handling procedures.

Following the control activity categories from Chapter 7, examples of controls in the revenue process are reviewed next.

Performance Reviews

Periodic reviews should be made of the written policies in place to authorize the activities listed and should be updated as necessary. Only predetermined, properly authorized individuals should be allowed to set credit policies, prices, and credit limits. Only approved customers should be extended credit, and reviews of past due accounts receivable should be done regularly, with problem customers noted and contacted. Regular review of sales representative performance, including sales returns and allowances for that representative, and aging of orders should also be performed by sales managers.

Physical Controls

Controls over cash and inventory are essential to protecting the company's operations. Cash and checks received should be properly safeguarded (e.g., locked in a vault), with deposits of customer receipts made daily (if possible). Access to cash should be limited to a few individuals, with regular surprise audits of cash on hand, and independent verification of proper deposits. Inventory should be carefully controlled with limited access to the inventory control function.

Segregation of Duties

Segregation of duties is essential in the revenue process. The sales order function should be separate from the credit decision, shipping, billing, and collection functions. The inventory control and shipping functions should be separate. Incoming mail should be opened by personnel who are independent of the treasury and accounts receivable functions. Approval for accounts receivables write-offs should be separate from the accounts receivables function. Bank reconciliations should be done regularly and should be performed by someone other than the person responsible for recording receipts or making the deposits. Much of the required segregation can be achieved through levels of passwords, limiting access to those authorized to perform a function. For example, with proper password controls, a sales representative might be able to check on a shipment of goods, but would be unable to directly update any information on the shipment.

Information Processing

Authorization Controls

Using levels of passwords, access to information can be limited to authorized personnel. Access can also be limited to both data and program files. Proper authorization of transactions, an input control, is required for the approval of credit terms, the setting of prices, the shipment of goods or provision of services, the granting of credit for returns and allowances, the determination of discounts, and the write-off of uncollectible receivables.

Pricing controls should be maintained to ensure that prices are updated when required, and that any discounts (e.g., volume discounts) are properly authorized by written policies and procedures. Deviations from standard prices, or credit extended to unapproved customers should result in an exception report distributed to management for review and follow up. Delinquent accounts should be promptly identified and followed up. This activity should be independent from the routine servicing of accounts receivable and payment receipts. Formal policies should be in place for investigating and following up on backorders, returns, credit memos, and write-offs of uncollectible accounts.

Data Verification Controls

The input must be validated to determine that data are accurate. Reasonableness checks can be programmed into the accounting systems. An example of a data verification control is that sales quantities and shipment quantities must be positive. Data that fail the verification tests should be rejected and reported. Any exceptions should be investigated by a supervisor.

Processing Controls

The use of prenumbered documents helps to control and restrict access to sales order forms, shipping documents, and invoices. Transactions should be entered in numerical sequence, with gaps or duplications reported on exception reports and investigated promptly. Gaps or duplication issues should be resolved quickly. No goods should be shipped without a formal shipping document, and bills of lading or other contracts should be evidenced in writing.

To ensure that all processing is accurate, independent checks should be made to ascertain that the correct prices are being charged to preapproved customers. Invoice quantities and amounts should be verified against the sales order and shipping records, with discrepancies reported and investigated promptly. The open customer invoice file is beneficial because of the routine matching of payments with specific invoices, allowing the system to easily generate exception reports of delinquent invoices.

Output controls must be in place to determine that all invoices and properly authorized credit memos are mailed to the customers. Receipts must be recorded and deposited properly, with independent reconciliation of the cash account performed regularly.

Data Entry in the Revenue Process

The principal events to be recorded in the revenue process are the recording of:

LEARNING OBJECTIVE 7
Set forth data entry aspects that are peculiar to the revenue process.

- Sales orders in the sales order module
- Shipping orders—usually the picking lists
- Billing of the customer
- Receipt of cash from customers

Sales Order Entry

All data regarding the sales order must be entered. **Exhibit 9.18** shows a sales order screen from Sage 50 Accounting 2016. To enter a purchase order received from Snowden Interior Design, the user enters the customer ID, using the magnifying glass. You can click on the magnifying glass icon to view input choices and then select from the choices. Having chosen the customer ID, the software program fills in default information from the customer master file.

After selecting the item number, the description and unit sales price appear in the sales order entry. After entering the quantity of an item ordered (Line 1:6 units), the program fills in the default information from the inventory master file and totals the sales order.

In most AIS software packages the inventory records are updated (posted) in real time. If batch posting is used, sales orders may be accepted for which stock is not available.

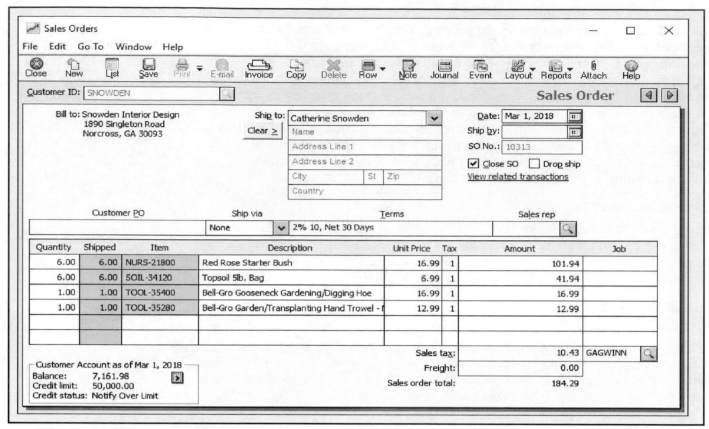

EXHIBIT 9.18 Sales Order Entry Screen

Source: © 2016 Sage Software, Inc. All rights reserved. Screen shots from Sage 50 Accounting 2016 are reprinted with permission. Sage, the Sage logos, and the Sage product and services names mentioned herein are the registered trademarks of Sage Software, Inc.

When the sales order entry is completed, the quantities of product ordered are usually noted as committed to customers in the inventory records. Also, the customer's open credit balance is reduced immediately upon acceptance of the order (note that Snowden Interior Design has exceeded their credit limit and should be notified). This is done either by reducing a field for open credit in the customer account or adding to a dollar field for the open order amount.

We have been assuming that the organization sells physical product and, as a consequence, needs to enter sales orders. But some service organizations use sales orders as well. Services being sold are limited, and the SO system may be connected to an "inventory" of billable hours that is also a personnel scheduling module. When an advertising agency secures a contract to develop and place advertisements in certain magazines, several services are involved with different bill rates. Therefore, a SO may be recorded for each ad and/or magazine outlet selected by the advertising agency. As the work is done, billings may be made against the open SO.

Invoice Entry

If a customer's order has been entered into the SO module, the sales order information can be automatically transferred to a sales invoice. In Sage 50 Accounting 2016 you enter the Sales/Invoicing task at which time a sales invoice form appears. After selecting the customer ID and one of the customer's sales orders, the data from the sales order are automatically duplicated in the sales invoice.

Notice in Exhibit 9.18, a column labeled "shipped." When this field is populated, the invoice dollar amounts are automatically generated. When the sales invoice is printed, an invoice number is automatically assigned, and the sale is recorded in the sales transaction file. If the SO module is not used, a sale is recorded by completing the sales invoice.

Recording Receipts

Prelists and Proof Lists

Under a manual system of accounting, a cash receipts prelist (refer to Chapter 3, Exhibit 3.3) is prepared as the mail is opened. The prelist and the remittance advices are used to record the customer payments in the cash receipts journal. The checks along with either a copy of the prelist or its total are used to prepare a deposit slip. Any errors made on the prelist or in the cash receipts journal entries are located and corrected subsequently.

An automated AIS provides a more effective way to avoid these types of clerical errors. Customer remittances are immediately entered into the AIS, and a proof list for a batch of checks is generated. This list will often include only the batch number and date in the heading with the lines being the customer ID, name, and the total paid. The list is summed to show the total dollar amount of the batch and serves as a listing of checks for the bank deposit.

Recording Balance-forward Receipts

Recording cash receipts for balance forward customers is trivial. At a minimum, you need to enter the customer ID and the amount received in the cash receipts entry screen.

Recording Open Item Receipts

Entry of cash receipts for open item customers can be relatively complex as compared to balance forward customers. Receipts are applied to open item accounts using one of the three methods listed below:

- Pre-identification
- Post-identification
- Automatic identification

Pre-identification

This method is illustrated in **Exhibit 9.19**, a cash receipts screen from Sage 50 Accounting 2016. Pre-identification is the most commonly used method and is the most direct. With **pre-identification (pre-ID)**, you are required to identify the open invoices being paid. In most cases, a remittance advice listing those items to which the customer payment should be applied accompanies the customer's check.

In our example, Armstrong Landscaping invoice #10122 for $10,790.42 is being paid. When Armstrong sends a check and a remittance advice, the customer ID is selected, and the amount(s) received are selected under the "Apply to Invoices" column. Note that all the open invoices for Armstrong Landscaping are displayed in the upper half of the screen (invoice numbers 10122 to 10336). This information is retrieved from the open invoice file. Because the amount received from Armstrong Landscaping is $10,790.42, you can check the pay field for invoice number 10122, and the amount is filled in automatically. This transaction is recorded in the cash receipts transaction file. Note that this invoice payment was submitted after the due date. A report such as the schedule of Aged Accounts Receivable report (Exhibit 9.15) can help management more effectively manage payments to avoid having cash inflow problems from overdue accounts.

Post-identification

With **post-identification (post-ID)**, recording of open item receipts on account is identical to that of entering receipts on balance forward accounts. You simply enter the customer ID and the remittance total. The accounting system records the entry as an **open receipt**, and it is identified as such in the customer account. After the receipt entries are proofed, corrected, and posted, accounting employees browse the customer accounts and, using the remittance advices, match open receipts with open invoices.

Post-ID expedites the printing of a proof list and the deposit of funds because (1) a check may be entered even though the customer has not specified how to apply it and (2) data entry is simplified. An added and not insignificant advantage is that workloads in the accounts receivable accounting function can be more efficiently allocated by having accounting

Pre-identification (Pre-ID) A method of recording open item receipts on account. You are required to identify the open invoices to which the receipt applies before entering the receipt.

Post-identification (Post-ID) A method of recording open item receipts on account. The customer ID and remittance total are entered, then matched with specific open invoices after posting.

Open receipt A customer's payment that has not been designated as being for any particular invoice; therefore, it can be applied to any of the customer's outstanding invoices.

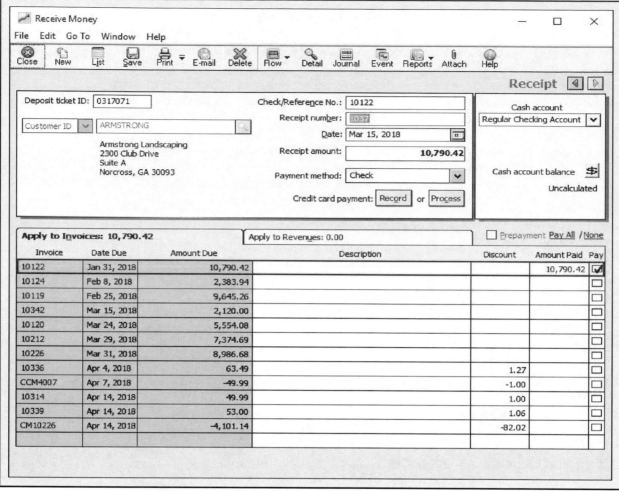

EXHIBIT 9.19 Cash Receipts Entry Screen

Source: © 2016 Sage Software, Inc. All rights reserved. Sage, the Sage logos, and the Sage product and services names mentioned herein are the registered trademarks of Sage Software, Inc.

personnel match open items during slack work times. But for those open item customers who receive a monthly statement, matching should occur before statements are printed.

Although it has significant advantages, post-ID is not common. This is likely due to the complexity in creating programs that permit you to easily tag open items to be matched. Additional complexities include:

- Discounts for early payment
- Interest charges on late payments
- Partial payment of invoices

Automatic Identification

automatic invoice identification A method for recording open item receipts where payment remittances are entered and the AIS software program matches the remittances with specific open items.

Using **automatic invoice identification**, total cash remittances are entered, and the AIS matches the remittances with specific open items. A type of artificial intelligence program uses repetitive calculations to associate the bulk of cash receipts. For a simple illustration consider the following open items in a customer account:

A Customer Account			
Invoice	420	Credit memo	75
Invoice	290	Receipt	1055
Invoice	710		

The receipt application program attempts to match the receipt to the open items by trying the various combinations of these items as follows:

Matching Attempt	Combination of Open Items	Matches Receipt
1	420	No
2	290	No
3	710	No
4	420 + 290 = 710	No
5	420 + 710 = 1,110	No
6	290 + 710 = 1000	No
7	420 − 75 = 345	No
and so on until		
11	420 + 710 − 75 = 1055	Yes

We get a match on the eleventh try, but because there may be other combinations of invoices and credit memos that equal the receipt, the program must calculate all possibilities. If there are two or more possibilities, the computer must tentatively mark both data sets so that a human operator can scan the accounts and make the final decision using remittance advices. For example, if the receipt had been $710, the program would be unable to ascertain whether it was in payment of the $710 invoice or the two invoices for $420 plus $290.

The above example is trivial compared to the reality of most businesses. Most accounts will have many more open items. In addition, cash and other discounts and interest on delinquent accounts must be considered. Because even the most sophisticated auto ID programs are unable to resolve all matches, post-ID must be used to resolve the remainder.

Only a handful of AIS packages at the highest end of the market support automatic invoice ID. The method is rare because the up-front programming cost is so high. But the cost is rapidly recovered in high volume operations.

Posting

The frequency of posting of sales and cash receipts depends on the circumstances. Monitoring credit limits is probably the most time-critical activity that is related to receivables. If multiple orders may be accepted from a customer in a single day, and if it is essential that credit limits be strictly observed, real-time posting may be required. However, posting of sales and cash receipts is usually by batch. Batches of transactions are entered, proof lists are printed and scanned for accuracy, any errors are corrected, and then the transaction batch is posted. On a single day in a large company, each data-entry clerk may enter multiple batches, with each batch being posted on the same day as soon as the proof list is verified. In other situations, posting may be only daily or even weekly. At the extreme, posting must be completed before statements of account are printed for customers.

Cycle Billing and E-Invoicing

When an organization's customer accounts are predominantly open item, the billing and customer remittances are normally distributed rather evenly throughout the month. But if most accounts are recorded using the balance forward method, billing may occur at the end of each month. This arrangement may cause the workload in the accounts receivable department to be extremely high just prior to issuance of statements and about two weeks after the receipt of the statements by the customers. A procedure for alleviating the problem of uneven workload is called **cycle billing**. Instead of billing at one time each month,

LEARNING OBJECTIVE 8
Explain the nature of cycle billing and the advent of e-invoicing.

Cycle billing A procedure for billing customers throughout the month by dividing customer accounts into groups and billing each group at a different time during the month.

customer billing is spread throughout the month by dividing customer accounts into groups and billing each group at a different time during the month. One-fourth of the customers might be billed on each of the first four Wednesdays in the month, or 20 groups could be created with billing occurring on the first 20 working days of each month. Not only would the billing be spread over the month, but so would the processing of customer receipts. The savings from cycle billing are such that its use is nearly universal in many different industries.

E-invoicing A system where a sales-supported company uses a web-based application to bill its customers as items are shipped to customers.

A practice that is becoming popular for billing is **e-invoicing**, which is carried out between trading partners to facilitate billing and payment between suppliers and customers. With e-invoicing, a sales-supported company uses a web-based application to bill its customers as items are shipped to customers. For example, Microsoft has a web-based system—MS Invoice—that allows their suppliers to submit their invoices electronically to Microsoft.

Here's a simple example of how two companies might take advantage of an e-invoicing system: Jones Company might use an EDI system (discussed in Chapter 10) to order goods from their supplier, Smithers Pipeline Supply. Smithers Pipeline then uses its e-invoicing web application to invoice Jones Company. In turn, Jones Company would use the e-invoicing application to accept or reject the invoice after matching it with the order and receiving report (also done electronically). Once the invoice is approved, payment can then be transferred to Smithers Pipeline. For both parties to the transaction, e-invoicing is a more efficient way to monitor and manage cash. In addition, Smithers Pipeline can review a history of invoices sent to their customers, such as Jones Company, without having direct access to customer data. The transactional information is stored in the web application provider's cloud or other storage medium, and the customer controls how much data Smithers Pipeline can see.

Benefits of e-invoicing include:

- Reduction of costs in the accounts receivable function (reductions in collection costs, processing costs, storage costs, and system development and training costs).

- Improved account reconciliation: the e-invoicing system allows for electronic remittance advices that specify invoices paid, credits applied, and other adjustments (such as discounts taken). This reduces the need for a phone call to the customer when a consolidated payment is made to ask which invoices were paid.

- Better cash management (more efficient invoicing and faster payment from customers).

The shortcomings of e-invoicing include:

- Lack of standardization,[3]

- Differences in laws regarding legal and administrative terms (if the supplier and customer are in different countries), and

- Security of e-invoicing systems (particularly if web-based) to minimize the potential for fraudulent activity.

Monthly Closings and Statements of Account

LEARNING OBJECTIVE 9
Recognize the relationship between monthly closings and statements of account.

If an organization uses four monthly cycle billings, it "closes the books" four times in a month in the receivables module, albeit for only one-fourth of the accounts in each closing. Statements of account show the beginning account balance, charges on the account during that billing cycle, payments on the account, and the ending balance. Then the accounts are closed and the balance is brought forward to a new period. If you close the accounts and then print statements, the only information available to place on a statement is the ending balance.

For open item accounts, the order of operations is reversed. That is, monthly closing should occur, and then statements should be printed. The statements will then contain all open items and nothing else. Remember that under the open item method, matched items appear in the account until closing occurs, at which time they are deleted from the active files. Statements printed before closing would contain these matched items. We wish to call our customers' attention to unpaid invoices; other data on the statements distract from this purpose.

Inter-Module Data Transfers

If the entire AIS uses real-time posting, then each time a revenue event is recorded, related data flow throughout the system. For a sale this includes entries in (1) the sales transaction file and the customer master file, (2) the inventory master file, (3) the accounts receivable and sales accounts, in the GL master file, and perhaps a journal in the GL module. If commission sales are involved, entries are also made in the sales commissions earned master file and transaction file in the payroll module. If the sale represents the completion of a job, there may also be an interaction with a job cost module. When an error occurs in recording the sale—perhaps an error in the quantity of an inventory item sold—that error is instantly propagated throughout the system.

For these and other reasons covered in the earlier chapters on control, most AIS software updates other modules on an "as needed" basis. The GL module is usually updated monthly. The inventory master file may be updated in real time or, if merchandise has already been committed to customers, batch posting on a daily basis would suffice in most cases.

Summary

The revenue function in an organization is monitored and controlled using a sales order module and a customer (accounts receivable) module. An order (an accounting event) is recorded in the sales order module and monitored through that module until the order is shipped. Usually this consummation of the transaction is recorded in the SO module, although in some systems the billing may occur in the customer module. Subsequent to the sale, the customer module is used to monitor and report on the transaction, and when payment is received from the customer, it is recorded in the customer module.

These revenue process modules produce invoices, statements of account, and reports, such as sales tax information necessary to comply with tax and regulatory requirements. In addition, hard copies (printed output) should be available for all transaction and master files. Proper controls should be in place to assure the accurate, timely, and relevant processing of sales orders, invoices, and cash receipts. The AIS should be able to produce all reports required to manage the revenue process of the organization.

The chapter also discusses billing cycles and e-invoicing. To be successful, a company must be able to monitor and manage its cash flows. New web-based e-invoicing applications allow a company to invoice its customers in a less costly, more efficient manner that, in turn, should result in a shorter timetable for receiving payment.

Key Terms

1. In the following section of a flowchart for a credit sales and cash receipts system, what could symbol ✕ represent?
   a. separating checks and remittances.
   b. enter data.
   c. issue transaction file.
   d. create credit memo.

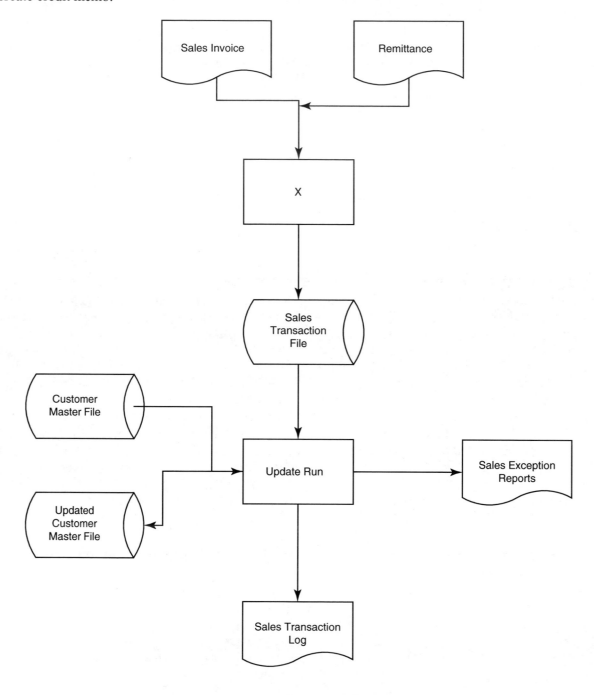

Use the following flowchart of the sales and cash receipts subsystems for questions 2 and 3.

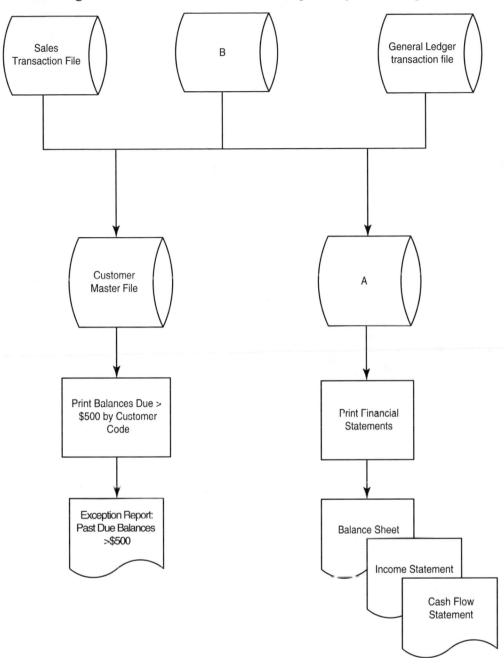

2. Symbol A most likely represents:
   a. remittance advice file.
   b. customer master file.
   c. general ledger master file.
   d. cash disbursements transactions file.

3. Symbol B most likely represents:
   a. remittance advices.
   b. cash disbursement advices.
   c. customer checks.
   d. cash receipts transaction file.

Use the following flowchart of the cash receipts subsystem for Rockmart Manufacturing for questions 4-8.

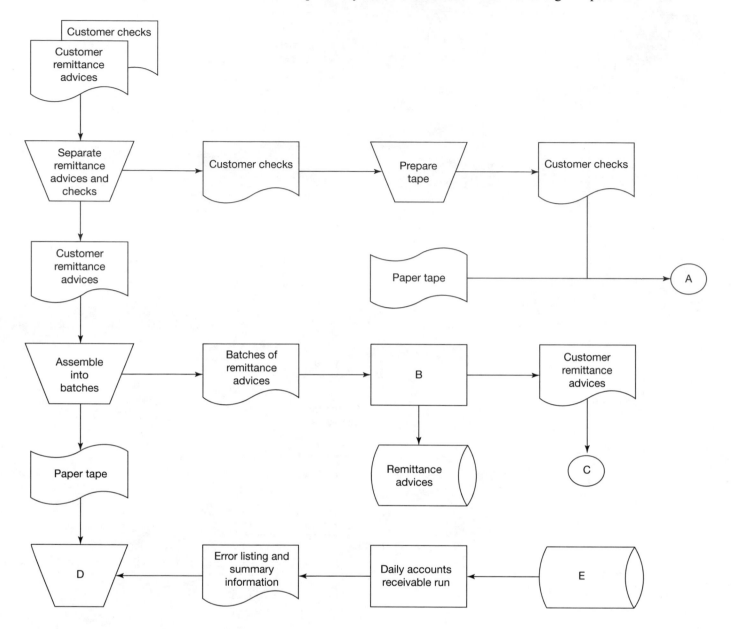

4. The customer checks accompanied by the control tape (refer to symbol A) would be:
   a. forwarded daily to the billing department for deposit.
   b. taken by the mail clerk to the bank for deposit daily.
   c. forwarded to the treasurer for deposit daily.
   d. accumulated for a week and then forwarded to the treasurer for deposit weekly.
   [CMA adapted]
5. The appropriate description that should be placed in symbol B would be:
   a. keying and verifying.
   b. collate remittance advices.
   c. batch processing.
   [CMA adapted]

6. The next action to take with the customer remittance advices (refer to symbol C) would be to:
   a. discard them immediately.
   b. file them daily by batch number.
   c. forward them to the internal audit department for internal review.
   d. forward them to the treasurer to compare with the monthly bank statement.
   [CMA adapted]
7. The appropriate description that should be placed in symbol D would be:
   a. attach batch total to report and file.
   b. reconcile cash balances.
   c. compare batch total and correct as necessary.
   d. proof report.
   [CMA adapted]

8. The appropriate description that should be placed in symbol E would be:
   a. accounts receivable (customer) master file.
   b. bad debts master file.
   c. remittance advice master file.
   d. cash projection file.
   [CMA adapted]

9. A bank credit card department uses a point system to assign credit limits to new applicants for revolving credit plans. Applicants scoring more than 100 points are assigned a credit limit of $5,000; those scoring 51 through 100 points are given a limit of $3,000; those scoring 31 through 50 are given a limit of $1,000; and those scoring 21 through 30 are given a limit of $500. Those applicants scoring 20 and less are refused a credit card. Points contribute to the total score according to various attributes taken from the applicant's questionnaire as shown on the right:

Attribute	Points
Has regular employment	20
Earns between $40,000 and $60,000 per year	10
Earns more than $75,000 per year	20
Is a professional	20
Has lived at the present address for at least 6 months	10
Is married	5
Owns a home	10
Subscribes to a telephone or cell phone in own name	5
Owns an automobile	5
Has bank checking account	10
Has bank savings account	5
Has at least one major credit card	10
Has more than two credit cards	–10
Has previously declared bankruptcy	–30

Required:

Determine the credit limit to be assigned to Miss Rosalind Baker, a registered architect, who has just moved to a new community. She has earned about $100,000 annually for the past 5 years, owns a car, recently established checking and saving accounts at a local bank, and has a Shell Oil Company credit card (on which she charges gasoline for her automobile) and a MasterCard. Currently she rents an apartment in which she has both a business and a personal telephone. She has a clean credit record.

10. Cistern Company is a wholesaler of plumbing fixtures and related products. The company's large inventory extends throughout three warehouse buildings designated A-Shed, B-Shed, and C-Shed. Inventory records include a 15-digit item number and a 30-character product description.

One of the buildings (C-Shed) is divided into bays, numbered 1 to 50 for the storage of large items, such as bathtubs, prefabricated shower stalls, sinks, toilets, and lengths of pipe. The other two buildings (A and B) are lined with four-tier shelves for the storage of small items, such as faucets, elbow joints, ball cocks, and cans of jointing compound. These two building have aisles (as opposed to bays), which are numbered 1 to 20. The position of each item in building A and B is designated by a location code consisting of the shelf (A–D) and the shelf compartment (1–50). For example, "B-25" corresponds to the B-shelf and compartment #25.

Required:

Design a picking list to be used by the company for assisting in the filling of sales orders. Fill in the form with some items, creating descriptions, locations, etc. to illustrate how data would appear on the form.

11. During August, the following invoices were issued by "One Company" to its customer, "Another Company":

Date	Invoice #	Amount
8/03	9508	$ 350
8/10	9583	1,750
8/13	9665	800
8/21	9697	1,230

Invoice #9267, dated 7/13 for $500, was outstanding as of August 1. On August 28, Another sent a check for $2,250, in payment of invoices #9267 and #9583. Invoice #9508 had been returned earlier because of a dispute regarding the items listed. The invoices dated 8/13 and 8/21 were not due until some time in September.

Required:

a. Show the records that will be maintained by One Company as of August 31 and as of September 1 if Another Company's accounts were maintained using (1) balance forward and (2) open item methods.

b. Late in September (before any further sales or payments were made involving Another), the controller of Another Company telephoned to report that part of his company's payables records had been deleted by an inexperienced computer operator. To help him reconstruct Another's records, he needed to know which invoices had been paid during the period from August 1 onward and which remained open. What information could be provided to the controller, assuming that One's receivables systems was of each type mentioned in Part a?

c. Given the facts provided above, which method would you recommend that One Company use to account for the Another Company account? Why?

d. If no payment was received during August from Another Company and a payment for $4,280 is received on September 10 that did not identify what was being paid, would this affect your answer to Part c?

12. Which files do you usually find in a sales order module versus an accounts receivable (customer) module? Why does this difference exist?

13. Richards Book Locator (RBL) in Manhattan, Kansas, uses the balance forward method for receivables. The records for Ted Dodge, a collector of old and rare accounting books, show the following for the month of November:

Ted Dodge			
10/31 Balance forward	1,225	11/13 Receipt	300
11/03 Invoice 3289	45		
11/20 Invoice 3312	130		

The records contain the following data regarding sales to Ted for the past few months:

October	$400
September	150
August	-0-
July	620
June	800

Required:

Perform an aging of Ted Dodge's account as of November 30 assuming the aging periods are 0–30 days, 31–60 days, 61–90 days, 91–120 days, and over 120 days. Assume all receipts are applied to the oldest invoices. You do not need to prepare a formal report.

14. Answer the following questions:
a. Describe the system known as "cycle billing."
b. Why is cycle billing used?
c. Is cycle billing equally applicable to both the open item and balance forward methods of accounting for receivables?

15. Name and describe three methods of identifying payments on account in an open item accounts receivable system.

16. Ace Cleaning Company provides janitorial services to industrial clients. Most of Ace's work is done under ongoing contracts in which the same amount is billed each month. But one-time cleaning jobs are also undertaken, both for regular clients and for others; these are billed according to the number of labor hours expended on the particular job. Ace does not offer discounts for prompt payment (i.e., the terms for basic invoices are "net 30"), but it does impose a penalty of 1½ percent per month on accounts more than 30 days overdue. The invoices must show the name of the crew leader.

Required:

Design an invoice form for Ace Cleaning Company.

17. What is the sequence of printing monthly statements and closing customer accounts? Does the choice of open item or balance forward have any implication for the sequence chosen?

18. Value Clothing is a large distributor of all types of clothing acquired from buy-outs, overstocks, and factory seconds. All sales are on account with terms of net 30 days from date of the monthly statement. The number of delinquent accounts and uncollectible accounts has increased significantly during the last 12 months. Management has determined that the information generated from the present accounts receivable system is inadequate and is not timely. Top management has requested a new system to satisfy the following objectives:
1. Produce current and timely reports regarding customers that would provide useful information to:
   a. aid in controlling bad debts.
   b. notify the Sales Department of customer accounts that are delinquent (accounts that should lose charging privileges).
   c. notify the Sales Department of customers whose accounts are considered uncollectible (accounts that should be closed and written off).
2. Produce timely notices to customers regarding:
   a. amounts owed to Value Clothing.
   b. a change of status of their accounts (for example, loss of charge privileges, account closed).
3. Incorporate the necessary procedures and controls to minimize the chance for errors in customers' accounts.

A project team you've been working with has selected a new accounting system with, what you believe, is a good customer (accounts receivable) module. A brief description of the reports and other output generated by the new system is given below:

1. Accounts Receivable Register—a daily alphabetical listing of all customers' accounts that shows balance as of the last statement, activity since the last statement, and account balance.
2. Customer Statements—monthly statements for each customer showing activity since the last statement and account balance; the top portion of the statement is returned with the payment and serves as the cash payment remittance advice.
3. Aging Schedule—All Customers—a monthly schedule of all customers with outstanding balances displaying the total amount owed with the total classified into age groups: 0–30 days, 31–60 days, 61–90 days, over 91 days; the schedule includes totals and percentages for each age category.
4. Aging Schedule—Past Due Customers—a schedule prepared monthly that includes only those customers whose accounts are past due, that is over 30 days outstanding classified by age. The credit manager uses this schedule to decide which customers will receive delinquent notices, temporary suspension of charge privileges, or have their accounts closed.
5. Activity Reports—monthly reports that show:
   a. Customers who have not purchased any merchandise for 90 days
   b. Customers whose account balance exceeds their credit limit
   c. Customers whose accounts are delinquent, yet they have current sales on account.
6. Delinquency and Write-off Register—a monthly alphabetical listing of customers' accounts that are:
   a. delinquent
   b. closed
   These listings show name, account number, and balance. Related notices are prepared and sent to these customers.
7. Summary Journal Entries—entries are prepared monthly to record write-offs to the accounts receivable file.

Required:

a. Identify the data that should be captured and stored for each customer.
b. Review the proposed reports to be generated by the new accounts receivable system.
   1. Discuss whether the proposed reports should be adequate to satisfy the objectives enumerated.
   2. Recommend changes, if any, which should be made in the descriptions of the proposed reports and other output generated by the new accounts receivable system.
   [CMA adapted]
19. What are some of the advantages and disadvantages of e-invoicing?

Notes

1. Refer to the discussion in chapter 8 regarding potential differences in revenue recognition because of IFRS.
2. The discount of 2 percent is given for paying 20 days early (i.e., by day 10). Because there are eighteen 20-day periods (360/20) in a year, the annual interest rate is 36 percent (18 periods $\times$ 2%).
3. The EU (European Union) has been working to standardize e-invoicing so as to facilitate the "seamless" flow of invoices across the EU. For updates on the progress of this project, refer to:
http://ec.europa.eu/growth/single-market/public-procurement/e-procurement/e-invoicing/index_en.htm

The Procurement Process

CHAPTER 10

Source: pixel.com/Shutterstock.

Chapter Outline

Overview of the Procurement Process

Data Flows in the Procurement process

AIS Structure for the Procurement Process

Reporting for the Procurement Process

Coding for Vendor Accounts

Audit Trails for the Procurement Process

Risks and Controls in the Procurement Process

Data Entry in the Procurement Process

Posting

Retainages

Learning Objectives

After studying this chapter, you should be able to:

- Explain the various activities in the procurement process.
- Describe the flow of data through the procurement process.
- Describe the purpose of various functions in the purchase order and vendor modules.
- Identify and describe the principal reports required for effective management of the procurement process.
- Identify risks and understand typical controls found in the procurement process.
- Set forth data-entry aspects that are unique to the procurement process.
- Explain the nature and purpose of retainages and how they are automated.

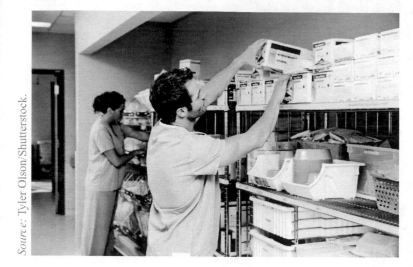

Source: Tyler Olson/Shutterstock.

Introductory Scenario

Polk Memorial Children's Hospital operates a centralized procurement system for drugs, medical and administrative supplies, food, and other consumables. Departmental, laboratory, and office managers submit purchase requisitions, and the central procurement department issues purchase orders to vendors. Some purchase orders request one-time deliveries while others, typically for routinely needed items, call for regular deliveries over a period of time. The centralized system enables the hospital to shop around among vendors and negotiate larger volume discounts. It also facilitates internal control by separating the authorization of purchases from the function of dealing with particular vendors.

Until recently, the hospital's procurement system functioned along traditional lines. Purchase orders were prepared and mailed to vendors. When supplies were urgently needed, procurement clerks would phone in orders to vendors and later confirm them in writing. However, 9 months ago, the hospital administrator announced conversion to an electronic data interchange (EDI) system* for procurement. The goal was to have at least 90 percent of purchases handled by electronic purchase orders within one calendar year of the announcement date.

Some problems had to be overcome. Polk Memorial Children's Hospital and the twenty to thirty largest vendors already had the necessary computer hardware resources to implement the EDI system, and proven commercial software was available for immediate installation. But many smaller vendors had inadequate computer facilities. Although these vendors had a strong incentive to come on board, their ability to do so within the 12-month time window was doubtful. The hospital had to choose between helping these vendors acquire the necessary resources to receive and process electronic purchase orders, or simply eliminating the vendors from the active vendor list. A task force was appointed to find ways of smoothing the transition to the new EDI environment.

Other things that had to be addressed as the EDI system approached the implementation deadline related to other conversion issues. For example, the procurement clerks had to adapt to the greatly increased speed of purchase order processing. On several occasions, errors in purchase requisitions could not be corrected before unwanted goods were delivered. Fortunately, the items were nonperishable and were returned to the vendor.

Introductory Scenario Thought Questions:

1. If you were a member of this task force, what would your recommendations be to encourage smaller vendors to join the EDI environment?
2. If you were one of the smaller vendors, what would you request or require from the hospital to join the EDI environment?
3. If you were the head of the procurement department at the hospital, what types of reports would you request to monitor vendor performance (e.g., to determine whether to keep a vendor on your preferred list, or to minimize the shipment of erroneous goods due to requisition errors)?

*A system involving the exchange of documents for procurement through a computer system.

Overview of the Procurement Process

The procurement process handles the buying of tangible and intangible resources needed by an organization. It is alternatively referred to as the expenditure, purchasing, or acquisition process. "Resources" in this context include both goods and services. Acquired goods may consist of raw materials, parts or components, supplies, merchandise, fixed assets, or intangibles such as patents or computer programs. Acquired services included those provided by contractors, catering companies, janitorial companies, consultants, law firms, and accounting firms.

Of the three business processes—revenue, procurement, and inventory—procurement varies least from one type of organization to another. The procurement process normally includes purchase order processing, receiving, and accounts payable/cash disbursements. You may want to refer back to Chapter 4, Exhibit 4.26, and review the block diagram. The relevant business activities in the procurement process are depicted in sequence in **Exhibit 10.1.**

Acquired services also include those provided by the organization's employees. While the procurement of goods and services from vendors and the procurement of services from employees share many characteristics, the procurement of employee services has some unique features that distinguish it from the procurement of goods and services from vendors. For example, the payment for employee services includes withholding of various taxes and the provision for health care and other benefits. These unique features associated with payroll and human resource management have resulted in separate software for that function. Because of space limitations, the human resource/payroll process is not covered in this textbook, but can be thought of as a module in the procurement process.

LEARNING OBJECTIVE 1
Explain the various activities in the procurement process.

Procuring Goods and Vendor Services

Goods and services are purchased to meet an organization's needs. Examples of activities involved in procuring goods and services are:

- Purchasing raw materials needed for current production.
- Ordering long lead-time materials needed to support future production.
- Replenishing inventories of raw materials, supplies, or merchandise.
- Taking advantage of an attractive volume discount on frequently purchased goods.
- Contracting with a shipping company to deliver goods the organization sells to customers.
- Hiring a consultant to advise on production problems or to recommend a new marketing strategy.
- Hiring a software vendor to write a computer program.
- Hiring an accounting firm to perform the annual audit.
- Retaining a law firm to defend the company against lawsuits.

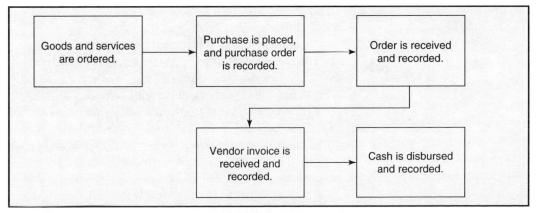

EXHIBIT 10.1 Procurement-related Business Activities

An organization normally purchases goods and services in a market of competing vendors. Criteria for selecting vendors include prospective vendors' stability and reliability, reputation for quality, promised delivery schedules, and prices and terms offered. On the other hand, company policy may restrict outsourcing.[1] A corporation may force division managers to buy from other divisions rather than from outside vendors. On a larger scale, companies in some countries are obliged to purchase specified classes of goods from domestic producers and are prohibited from importing those goods from abroad.

With the advent of electronic data interchange (EDI), considerable debate continues over how much competition organizations should foster among their vendors. While organizations commonly keep the same accounting firms and law firms for many years, they have traditionally dealt with large numbers of raw materials and merchandise vendors, with the objective of driving prices down. Current practices find many organizations concentrating their purchasing on relatively few vendors and demanding, in exchange for the increased business, lower prices and tighter delivery schedules. The surviving vendors are called **trading partners** because the relationship between the businesses is specified by detailed procurement contracts. In addition, considerable planning and operations data are shared by both the purchasing and selling organizations. Setting up relationships with a limited number of suppliers can also allow the company to minimize its inventory holdings by setting up a "just-in-time" inventory system with its trading partners. This practice may require the supplier to ship smaller (albeit more costly) shipments to the company more often, but provides a more secure relationship for both parties. The trading partner relationship is discussed further in the next section.

Trading partners A relationship between two businesses wherein their association is specified by detailed procurement contracts.

Paying for Procured Goods and Vendor Services

Vendors must be paid for the goods and services they provide. Payment for goods and services (especially if those payments include payroll) typically makes the largest demand on an organization's cash.

Data Flows in the Procurement Process

Ordering Goods and Vendor Services

LEARNING OBJECTIVE 2
Describe the flow of data through the procurement process.

Exhibit 10.2 shows the major data flows involved in the procurement of goods and vendor services by an organization. Managers throughout an organization are authorized to purchase goods and services within the constraints of their responsibilities and budgets, subject to any limitations imposed by company policy. Providing managers with budgets confers authority to managers to spend up to a prescribed ceiling on goods and services related to their assigned responsibilities. For example, a transportation manager may have budget coverage to acquire a new delivery truck. However, corporate-level approval would probably be needed if the manager wanted to purchase an entire fleet of trucks. In some cases, a manager requiring goods or services is permitted to deal directly with vendors. More commonly, orders are channeled through a central procurement, buying, or purchasing department, which purchases goods and services from "approved" vendors. This separation of duties has important internal control implications.

Procurement is initiated when a departmental manager authorizes a purchase requisition and forwards it to the procurement department. Before placing the order, the procurement department is normally required to validate the authorization and verify that the requesting manager has budget availability; the procurement department may also be required to review the request for reasonableness. In the event of a

Source: Dreamstudios/Shutterstock.

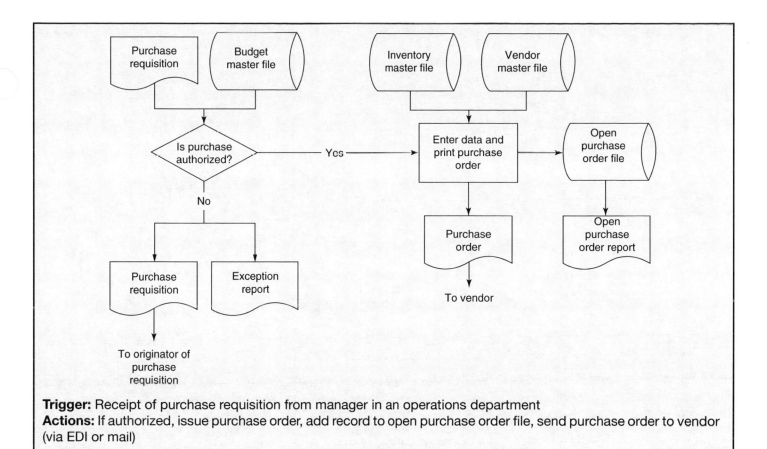

Trigger: Receipt of purchase requisition from manager in an operations department
Actions: If authorized, issue purchase order, add record to open purchase order file, send purchase order to vendor (via EDI or mail)

EXHIBIT 10.2 Purchase Order Processing

problem, the procurement agent may call the manager or return the requisition for clarification. Otherwise, the procurement agent places an order with a vendor for the requested goods or services.

The order for goods or services has traditionally been in the form of a paper purchase order that is mailed to a vendor. The vendor address and other data, such as the name and telephone number of the contact person and the availability of credit terms, may be retrieved from the vendor master file.

Electronic Data Interchange

In **electronic data interchange (EDI)** systems (**Exhibit 10.3**) the traditional paper purchase order is replaced by an electronic message transmitted from the purchasing organization's computer to the vendor's computer. EDI links the accounting information systems of the purchasing organization and its vendors, greatly speeding up the procurement process, reducing the costs of paperwork, and eliminating data entry errors, a major source of purchasing errors.

With EDI, documents are transmitted from one computer to another in machine-readable form. The sending organization formats a business document, such as a purchase order, into a standard format that the receiving organization's computer can read. In the initial stages of EDI, the data exchanges are usually purchase orders, order acknowledgments, and invoices, all in electronic rather than paper form, as illustrated in Exhibit 10.3.

As mentioned earlier, the trading partner relationship (i.e., between buyer and seller in an EDI relationship) denotes a special association between vendor and customer. Most companies, upon implementing EDI, reduce the number of vendors while simultaneously

Electronic data interchange (EDI) The transmission of business documents in machine-readable form between two organizations known as "trading partners."

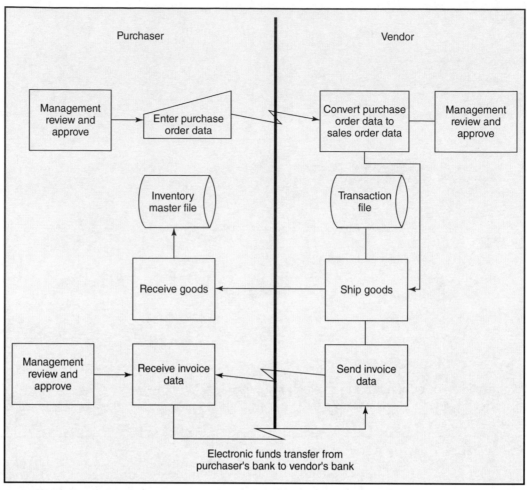

EXHIBIT 10.3 Use of Electronic Data Interchange (EDI) and Electronic Funds Transfer (EFT) for Procuring Goods and Services

cementing a closer relationship between the remaining ones. The volume of purchases from continuing vendors is normally increased because the vendors are now fewer. Often prices are negotiated and fixed for longer periods than before. Information previously considered confidential (such as planned products and product volumes) is provided to vendors so they can plan their activities to fulfill order requirements more promptly and efficiently. Appendix A to this chapter discusses EDI protocols and EDI architectures. In all cases, the purchase order information is stored in an **open purchase order file**. Procurement personnel are responsible for periodically reviewing the file records and following up on unfilled orders. After a prescribed period, an unfilled order may be canceled.

Open purchase order file A file that contains data on all purchase orders that remain "open" because the order has not yet been filled.

Upon receipt of the order, the vendor may ship the goods immediately or send an acknowledgment or confirmation indicating a future shipment date. In an EDI system, a confirmation message can be returned electronically. The vendor should also confirm that the goods can be supplied at the stated price. Alternatively, the vendor may notify the procurement department that prices have changed or that the goods are unavailable. Sometimes substitutes are suggested, and the procurement department (usually in consultation with the requesting department) must ascertain whether substitutes are acceptable. A similar procedure is followed for the routine procurement of outside services.

Ordering Custom Goods and Vendor Services

Routinely purchased goods may be ordered from suppliers' catalogs or price lists. But price lists may not be available for large, nonroutine purchases, and competitive bids may be solicited. In a typical bidding situation, a **request for quotation (RFQ)** or **request for proposal (RFP)** is prepared and sent to prospective vendors. Vendors then respond with a description of the goods or services they are willing to provide and a bid price. In addition to ranking the responses by bid price, the procurement agent must screen the responses to determine the ability of the vendors to meet quality standards and to supply the goods or provide the services within the required period. The requesting manager may be called in to help evaluate quality. If all responses seem equally competent, the lowest bid will generally be accepted. In fact, a procurement agent normally is required to justify accepting a bid that is higher than the lowest bid.

Several factors may complicate competitive bidding. First, only one or two vendors may choose to respond to the solicitation. The other vendors may feel the order would not be worthwhile, or they may have low expectations of winning. Second, several vendors may respond, but the procurement department may decide to look elsewhere for the required goods or services and not to accept any of the bids. Third, where complex goods or services are involved, the vendors' proposals may vary so much that the procurement agent and requesting managers find it difficult to appropriately compare such dissimilar proposals.

When the vendor selection has been made, a formal contract may be drawn up specifying precisely what the vendor is expected to do. The contract then becomes a supplement to the purchase order. Contracts of this type frequently identify **deliverables**, such as manufactured products, subassemblies, computer programs, or reports (e.g., a network vulnerability assessment report).

> **Request for quotation (RFQ)** A solicitation sent to prospective vendors to submit a bid price for supplying a required good or service.
>
> **Request for proposal (RFP)** A solicitation sent to prospective vendors to submit proposals on how specifications relating to a required good or service can best be met and to submit a bid price for supplying the proposed good or service.
>
> **Deliverables** The goods or other items that a vendor must deliver to a customer to meet contractual obligations.

Receiving

The purchased goods may be delivered all at once or over a specified period. Organizations with just-in-time inventory systems may require vendors to deliver materials and parts as they are needed for production. For example, an automobile tire vendor may be required to make daily deliveries of the tires needed for that day's production. Daily delivery of relatively small quantities of goods obviously increases the vendor's costs, and the vendor is likely to agree to such terms only in exchange for higher prices, favored treatment by the purchasing organization, or both. Typical favors include membership in a select group of vendors, a declaration of intent to buy from the vendor for an extended period, and access to information about the organization's long-term procurement requirements.

When the goods are received from the vendor, the receiving department should check them, possibly with the assistance of quality assurance personnel, to verify that their identity, quantity, and quality conform to the purchase order. Often the quantity is left blank on the receiving department's copy of the purchase order, or the quantity field in a record is not accessible by the receiving department, to ensure an independent physical count of the goods received. This physical count and the quantity ordered should be compared for a match. The receiving information is keyed directly into a computer or may be captured electronically by a bar code reader. The data are stored in a purchases or receiving transaction file. A paper **receiving report**, or **ticket**, may be prepared documenting the receipt of the goods.

> **Receiving report** A report that documents the receipt of goods that were purchased.
>
> **Ticket** Another name for a receiving report.

If the goods do not conform to applicable specifications or were never ordered, they should be returned promptly to the vendor. If the goods are deficient but generally acceptable, they may be retained; but an allowance claim should be submitted to the vendor requesting a reduction in the invoice price. Alternatively, an insurance claim may be filed for compensation for damage in transit. If the shipment is complete and the goods are acceptable, the associated record in the open purchase order record is retrieved and flagged "closed." Partial shipments are recorded in an appropriate manner without closing the open purchase order record. A flowchart of the receiving subsystem is in **Exhibit 10.4**.

Services are usually rendered over a period of time. For example, a vendor may contract to cut the grass and trim the shrubbery once a week during the summer months. Another vendor may contract to install and test a new computer system during a three-month

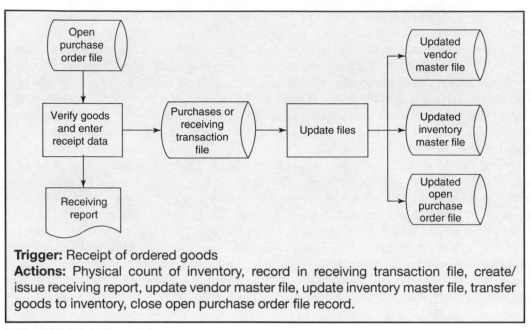

Trigger: Receipt of ordered goods
Actions: Physical count of inventory, record in receiving transaction file, create/ issue receiving report, update vendor master file, update inventory master file, transfer goods to inventory, close open purchase order file record.

EXHIBIT 10.4 Receiving

Acceptance report A report that documents that the provision of services has been completed.

time window. Contracts to provide services may or may not have definite termination dates. When they do not, the purchasing organization should confirm that the provision of services has been completed. For instance, an **acceptance report** should be signed when a new computer system has been installed and tested.

Vendor Invoicing

A flowchart of the vendor invoicing subsystem is in **Exhibit 10.5**. The receipt of goods or provision of contracted services places the organization under an obligation to pay the vendor. If no credit arrangements have been reached between the vendor and the buyer organization, cash terms (i.e., immediate payment) may be insisted on, or payment may even have to be made in advance. When credit is extended, the goods are usually delivered in anticipation of payment at some later date. Issuance of a valid purchase order is cus- tomarily understood to imply a promise to pay in accordance with the applicable terms as long as the goods or services conform to the specifications.

Even when credit has been extended, contracts for custom goods or services may require advance payments before work begins, progress payments during the course of the work, or both. Commonly, the progress payments are scheduled to coincide with the attainment of recognizable milestones in the work. For example, if a computer system has been ordered, a progress payment may be due when the hardware has been installed and tested. In this way, the organization has some assurance that the work is progressing at the rate claimed by the vendor. The vendor signals its expectation that the goods or services will be paid for by sending an invoice. At month-end, the vendor may also send a statement listing all outstanding invoices and the total amount owed. In some cases, the amount owed is broken down into age categories: current, 1–30 days overdue, and so forth.

The organization should compare the vendor's invoice with (1) the purchase order data (which should reconcile with the original purchase requisition) and (2) the receiving data. The purchase order data provide assurance the goods or services were ordered and also show the agreed-upon prices. The receiving data provide assurance the goods arrived or the services were indeed provided. In an e-invoicing system, the comparison of purchase order data, receiving data, and invoice data may be performed by the e-invoicing app. Dis- crepancies can be printed out or displayed on a screen for human review and resolution.

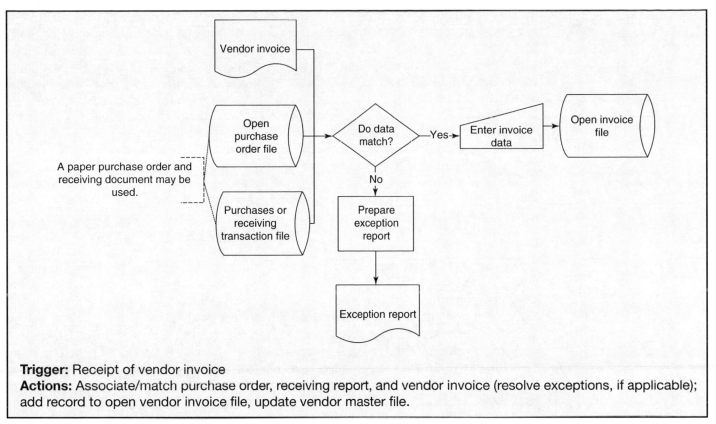

Trigger: Receipt of vendor invoice
Actions: Associate/match purchase order, receiving report, and vendor invoice (resolve exceptions, if applicable); add record to open vendor invoice file, update vendor master file.

EXHIBIT 10.5 Vendor Invoicing

When any discrepancies or uncertainties have been resolved, the invoice data are keyed into an **open vendor invoice file**. Approval of the invoice establishes the account payable (which is added to the related vendor master file field), and disbursement activities begin. Invoice approval is normally a formality as long as the goods or services have been provided as ordered, and the quantities and prices stated on the invoice are correct. If the data are not correct, the invoice may be returned to the vendor. Also, as already mentioned, an allowance claim may be sent to the vendor requesting an adjustment of the invoice amount to reflect deficiencies in the goods or damage sustained during shipment.

Open vendor invoice file A file that contains data on all invoices from vendors that remain "open" because the invoice has not yet been paid.

Disbursing Payment

Disbursement to vendors may be made immediately upon approval of the invoice or may be delayed. The payment schedule adopted depends on the availability of any favorable cash discounts for prompt payment and on the organization's current cash position. The **cash requirements forecast** may be prepared at regular intervals, such as once a week or twice a month, showing the amount of cash needed to pay certain categories of invoices. Also, a **schedule of aged accounts payable** may be prepared to determine outstanding invoices by vendor and by age (refer to Chapter 3, Exhibit 3.12, for an example of an aged accounts payable report). After reviewing the cash requirements forecast and the aging schedule, management selects invoices for payment and decides on payment dates.

Organizations are naturally interested in conserving cash and normally delay payment so long as it is favorable for them to do so. If a sufficiently large discount is offered, payment will be made by the discount date. Otherwise, payment is likely to be delayed until the invoice becomes due. If the organization is currently short of cash, it may ignore the due date; but doing so risks loss of credit rating. Sometimes an organization pays invoices selectively. The organization may pay an invoice to a vendor to maintain or improve a good credit standing, while delaying other invoices from less critical vendors. The more

Cash requirements forecast A report that is prepared at regular intervals listing all outstanding invoices, usually broken down into categories, and the amount of cash needed to pay the outstanding invoices. This report helps management select invoices for payment and decide on payment dates.

Schedule of aged accounts payable (also known as vendor aged detail) A report that lists the unpaid vendor invoices by whether they are current, which is typically 0–30 days from the date of the invoice, or whether they are delinquent and, if so, by the number of days.

pressure a vendor can exert, the more quickly that vendor's invoices will be paid. However, these considerations may be modified by a company policy providing for cash disbursements only at prescribed intervals. Many organizations have regular payment dates each month, such as the first and the fifteenth, and payment on other dates may require special approval. The periodic-payment pattern lends itself to batch processing of large numbers of disbursements. The actual disbursement of payment is the responsibility of the treasurer or, in very small organizations, a vice-president or the president.

Payment may take any of several forms. Very small amounts can be paid in currency from a petty cash fund. To maintain proper control over cash disbursements, organizations should set strict limits (e.g., $50 or less) on petty cash disbursements.

Electronic funds transfer (EFT) A method to electronically transfer funds to pay an invoice.

Vendors are commonly paid by check although **electronic funds transfer** or **EFT** may be used. When EFT is used for payment, a manufacturer using EDI may elect to pay outstanding purchase obligations by electronically directing its bank to transfer funds to the supplier. This process uses the same technology as EDI, but is different in that an electronic document is ordering monetary resources to be transferred rather than ordering merchandise or some other trading function. Another way to handle payments is through e-invoicing, discussed in Chapter 9. As the purchaser of items, we would use the e-invoicing app to match the purchase order, receiving report, and vendor's invoice. If they match, we could authorize payment through the e-invoicing app.

When checks are used for payment, check signing may be performed manually, but in large organizations, check-writing machines using signature blocks or facsimile plates perform this function. Check-writing machines contain counters that record the number of checks signed providing an important control over cash disbursements. Alternatively, checks can be written and signed by laser printers. Signatures are stored in a machine-readable medium, and control counts can be made by associated software. In some cases, checks over a certain amount may require a second signature. This requires review of the checks prior to mailing to make sure that the proper signatures are in place. Checks to vendors are usually placed in the mail immediately after being signed.

Cash disbursements transaction file A file that stores the data relating to a cash disbursements transaction.

Cash disbursements journal (also known as check register) A printout, or listing, of the cash disbursements transaction file.

Check register See cash disbursements journal.

Cash disbursements to vendors are recorded in a **cash disbursements transaction file**. Listings of this file are referred to as the **cash disbursements journal**, or **check register**. Disbursement records should include the date, the name and number of the payee, the amount of the check, and—in the case of a disbursement to a vendor—the vendor's invoice number.

In most cases, all the checks payable to vendors will be cashed. Nevertheless, canceled checks should be compared with entries in the cash disbursements journal to identify any uncashed checks as well as any fraudulent checks that may be charged against the organization's bank account. A flowchart of the cash disbursements subsystem is in **Exhibit 10.6**.

AIS Structure for the Procurement Process

LEARNING OBJECTIVE 3
Describe the purpose of various functions in the purchase order and vendor modules.

In most AISs, the procurement function is represented by two modules—purchase order and accounts payable (or vendor module). The issuance of purchase orders (POs), the monitoring of outstanding POs, and the reporting on outstanding purchase orders are effected through the PO module, while the vendor module is used to record, manage, and pay purchase obligations.

Purchase Order Module Functions

Exhibit 10.7 shows the typical functions in the purchase order module.

The module setup is similar to that of the sales order module considered in Chapter 9. This module has two major data-entry processes—the creation and issuance of purchase orders and recording of merchandise received or services rendered. There is, however, one significant difference between the operation of the sales order and purchase order modules. When a sale occurs and goods are shipped, we have all the data available to document the transaction. The timing of events for the procurement process is not as easily

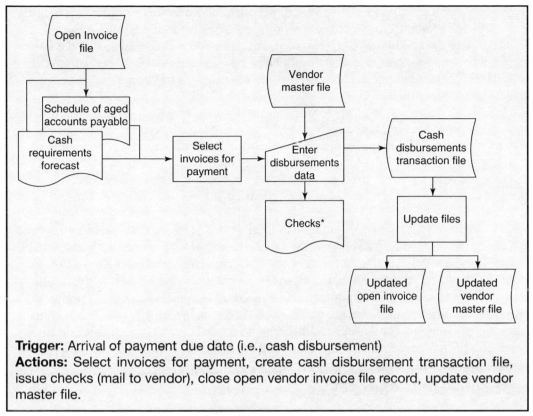

Trigger: Arrival of payment due date (i.e., cash disbursement)

Actions: Select invoices for payment, create cash disbursement transaction file, issue checks (mail to vendor), close open vendor invoice file record, update vendor master file.

EXHIBIT 10.6 Payment Disbursements

*Note that an electronic fund transfer might be used in lieu of a check for disbursements.

Major Functions	Maintenance Functions	Daily and Period-End Functions
Purchase order module setup	General defaults (e.g., ship via FOB, GL inventory account)	
	Design forms (e.g., purchase order, return request, receiving report)	
Data entry		**Create purchase orders:** Enter purchase order data Print purchase orders Transmit purchase orders via EDI **Record receipt of:** Merchandise Services rendered
Printing		**Open purchase orders:** By vendor By expected date of receipt By product ID Cash requirements projection
End-of-period processing		Archive filled purchase orders Delete canceled purchase orders Update GL for deliveries Reconcile unfilled purchase orders with inventory on order

EXHIBIT 10.7 Functions in Purchase Order Module

determined. For a purchase to be recorded, we must have a purchase order, a receiving report, and an invoice from the vendor. A problem arises when the purchased goods are received before the vendor invoice is received. We cannot "book" the payable or the inventory because the vendor invoice is not available. Consequently, we have merchandise that is available for sale, but because it has not been recorded on the books, sales personnel are unaware of its availability.

Often, the AIS allows you to record the inventory availability by debiting the inventory account upon receipt, and crediting a type of suspense account that might be called "unbilled payables." When the invoice is received and matched with the PO and receiving report, an entry is made debiting unbilled payables and crediting accounts payable. This procedure increases the required accounting somewhat but permits merchandise to be placed in inventory immediately upon receipt and updates the inventory records so sales orders can be filled.

Our illustrative purchase order function in Exhibit 10.7 assumes that inventory receipts are recorded in this module and posted on a real-time basis to the inventory module. The GL inventory control account and the unbilled payables are updated at the end of each month. It should be recognized that some AISs do not have this feature, and that others may place the receiving function in the vendor (accounts payable) module. At month-end, some POs are unfilled, and some are partially unfilled. The inventory module will contain data on items on order. The system should compare the unfilled POs with these inventory records and print an exception report so any differences can be resolved.

Vendor (Accounts Payable) Module Functions

The typical functions in an accounts payable module are shown in **Exhibit 10.8**.

The first setup step is to indicate the default account identifiers for GL data, which have been recorded in the vendor module. In the financial process (Chapter 8), automatic distribution entries were introduced. This feature is probably most useful in the vendor (accounts payable) module because some invoices should be allocated to various responsibility centers. The auto-distributions option permits you to specify a master account (perhaps property taxes or insurance) to which entries will be made, with the transaction total being allocated among sub-accounts based on percentages specified with this option.

The 1099 tasks are a unique aspect of vendor account maintenance. For the company's vendors whose activities require the reporting of this information (e.g., contractors), a field in the vendor master file is used to accumulate payments for an entire year, and the form 1099 is used to report the payments to the IRS and the payee.

With the assumptions that: (1) purchases are recorded when the goods arrive, (2) invoices are booked when they are received and matched with the purchase order and the receiving report, the "Data entry" function is used to record the invoice data. This entry will debit "unbilled payables" and credit "accounts payable" This removes the unbilled payable for items that have been received prior to receipt of a vendor invoice. The posting reference to the unbilled payables account should contain both a sequential entry identifier and the PO number. Including the PO number on both debits and credits to the unbilled payables account facilitates a month-end analysis and reconciliation of the account to the list of receiving reports for which invoices have not yet been received. The usual data-entry process is to enter batches of invoices or credit memos, print a proof list of each batch entered, scan the list for errors, correct the errors, and print a new proof list, repeating this process until the entries are deemed correct. Then the batch of entries can be posted to vendor accounts.

The process for paying vendor invoices is more involved. Usually a company will have a regular schedule for making payments, perhaps daily or even weekly. When a payment day arrives, open invoices will be selected for payment. The quality of design in creating this program option can radically affect your ability to manage accounts payable effectively. The simplest design permits the user to browse through the open invoices, look at each on the screen and either select it for payment or skip over it. Thus, if a firm makes

Major Functions	Maintenance Functions	Daily and Period-End Functions
Vendor (accounts payable) module setup	Specify GL posting accounts Specify auto-distributions Specify accounts payable aging periods Format forms	Cash/accounts payable/inventory/ cash discounts/unbilled payables 1099 tax forms Checks
Vendor account maintenance	Add new vendor Change vendor data Deactivate vendor Delete vendor account Perform 1099 tasks	Print 1099 tax forms Reset 1099 balances
Data entry		Enter/edit invoice entries Enter/edit credit memo entries Record invoices/credit memos entered Select open items for payment Print data entry proof lists Print list of selected items Pay invoices/print checks Enter manual checks
Posting		Vendor invoices/credit memos Payments to vendors
Printing		**Accounting records:** Transaction files Open purchase order file Vendor master file **Management reports:** Accounts payable cash budget Discounts lost Vendor performance Vendor volume
End-of-period processing		Post transactions to GL module Archive and reset journals Delete paid invoices from file

EXHIBIT 10.8 Functions in Vendor (Accounts Payable) Module

payments weekly and usually has 100 open invoices, someone must examine each invoice record individually each week. This can be a time-consuming and expensive process.

A more effective design permits the setting of criteria for selection of invoices. The criteria should include:

- Select all invoices coming due on or before a specified date.
- Select all invoices with discount expiration on or before a specified date.
- Select all invoices with a specified vendor.
- Select all invoices over a specified monetary amount.
- Select all invoices under a specified monetary amount.

You should be able to select one or more of the above options to automatically select invoices for possible payment. For example, if today is February 7 and checks will not be issued again for another week, you might select all invoices with the discount date expiring from the 8th through the 14th to avoid losing discounts. You may also want to include all invoices that have or will come due on or before the 14th.

Suppose that the preceding selections are made, a "List of Items Selected to Pay" is printed, and the total of the list exceeds the available cash balance. At this point, the responsible manager may (1) deselect some items individually or (2) execute the selection process again using more restrictive selection criteria. After taking one of these actions, the "List of Items Selected to Pay" should be run again to ensure an appropriate amount of cash will be disbursed. Once an acceptable list is compiled, checks can be printed or EFT invoked.

Printing batches of checks is an efficient way to issue checks, but a company will find it necessary from time to time to issue single checks on short notice. Any such check must be entered into the accounting system before another batch is printed so the checks will appear in the Cash Payments (Disbursements) Transaction File (check register) in numeric order.

After each batch of entries has been printed (the proof list) and corrected, the batch may be posted. Therefore, posting may be invoked several times a day, daily, or just before the periodic payment of open invoices. It is essential that the records be updated before selection of items for payment so the open invoice file is current.

All accounting records must be printed just before end-of-period processing, although they also may be printed at other times if desired. The following section of this chapter describes the management reports in some detail.

At the end of the accounting period (usually monthly), a summary or the full detail of transactions (invoices booked and payments made) is transferred to the GL module. The journals in the Accounts Payable module are cleared for a new period and their contents transferred to archival files. All paid invoices are transferred from the open invoice file to a history file.

Reporting for the Procurement Process

LEARNING OBJECTIVE 4
Identify and describe the principal reports required for effective management of the procurement process.

The modules composing the procurement process have two uses: (1) to support the business activities of the procurement process, and (2) to report on the procurement process so management can judge the effectiveness with which the process is operating and can remedy any deficiencies. When considering these reporting requirements, we must recall the related activities:

- Initial selection and continuing review of vendors (vendor performance)
- Ordering of merchandise and services and monitoring delivery
- Receipt of merchandise and services
- Recording of liabilities from purchases
- Timely payment of purchase-related liabilities

Reporting requirements for each of the above activities are covered in the following section.

Reporting for Vendor Performance

The effectiveness of vendors in achieving price, quality, and delivery promises is critical to the success of most organizations. Activities that are not continually monitored will eventually get "out of control" and will often result in large losses before being discovered. Continually monitoring the performance of vendors is essential.

Exhibit 10.9 is an example of a vendor performance report. Because it is impossible to eliminate late deliveries and defective goods, the report must cover some reasonable length of time, which can be expected to vary from one organization to another and may even be affected by the nature of the merchandise. In this case, we have assumed that quarterly is an appropriate time period.

Various conclusions can be made about the vendors shown in the report. AutoMax seems to be an adequate vendor, as far as on-time deliveries and quality of merchandise.

		Deliveries, No. of and $			Late Deliveries, No. of and $			Defective Merchandise, $		
		Vendor Performance Report								
		Quarter Ending April 30, 2018								
		Page 1 of 7								
ID	Vendor Name	This Quarter	Last Quarter	Prior Yr. Quarter	This Quarter	Last Quarter	Prior Yr. Quarter	This Quarter	Last Quarter	Prior Yr. Quarter
AZ1	Auto Max	5	6	3	0	1	2			
		$25,000	$22,050	$18,000	$–	$1,200	$1,000	$100	$–	$500
BK1	Baku Paint	10	11	4	3	1	0			
		$12,000	$13,000	$8,000	$8,000	$1,500		$–	$75	$–
D31	D3 Company	7	9	6	0	0	1			
		$4,500	$3,700	$3,950	$–	$–	$140	$1,243	$780	$–
FR2	Fred Body Co.	1	2	5	0	0	0			
		$80	$177	$4,721	$–	$–	$–	$–	$27	$–

EXHIBIT 10.9 Vendor Performance Report

Baku Paint exhibits a severe problem with late deliveries (16 percent). Defective merchandise is an increasing problem with D3 Company. Fred Body does not exhibit issues with deliveries or quality of merchandise. If merchandise purchased from them can be easily acquired from another vendor, we might consider eliminating Fred Body as a vendor for this reason—maintenance of relationships with vendors has a fixed cost, and our purchases from Fred Body have fallen to a very low volume. This suggests that purchasing from another existing vendor might be more efficient.

Reporting for Outstanding Purchase Orders

Several management problems can be addressed with unfilled purchase order reports. Different problems require aging based on different data items on the PO. Financial planners want a report forecasting future PO cash requirements. Procurement officers desire a report to monitor the expected deliveries because they are responsible for having merchandise available when required. With such a report, procurement officers can maintain contact with suppliers to obtain assurance that merchandise will arrive by the scheduled dates. Whereas this report for procurement officers will include all purchase orders, another PO report will include only those POs related to shipments expected to arrive in the immediate future. This report can be used to anticipate these arrivals at the receiving dock and to schedule personnel and equipment to expedite the unloading and transfer of merchandise in stock.

Because these PO reports will be used for different purposes, they will be arranged differently and will include different data. Some examples of the differences include:

- The PO records that are included in reports
- The order in which the PO records appear
- The data from each PO record that appears in the report
- The order in which the same data appear in different reports (layout)

For example, the PO cash requirements forecast does not require detailed information about what was ordered; the report only lists the expected cash payments on each PO. On the other hand, the expected deliveries report must contain details on both the inventory items coming in and the quantities expected.

Reporting for Vendor Invoices

The PO cash requirements forecast shows the expected cash payments of open invoices (usually by day or week, depending on the frequency with which invoices are paid) and is integrated along with the SO cash receipts forecast into an overall cash budget. The frequency with which this cash budget is printed usually ranges from daily to weekly.

The discounts lost report is used to judge the efficiency of the cash payments operation. Historically, the effective interest rate on cash discounts has been higher than other sources of credit. Discount terms of 2/10, n/30 translate to an effective interest rate of about 36 percent annually as explained in Chapter 9. Consequently, our aspiration is to take all discounts so the Discounts Lost account has a zero balance. As a practical matter, some discounts are lost. But a report should be produced at least monthly that shows the detail of all discounts lost, with appropriate personnel given the task of determining why they were lost. Only then can a judgment be rendered as to whether the loss was justifiable, and actions taken to ensure that, in the future, the unjustified losses are avoided. **Exhibit 10.10** contains a few lines of such a report.

In Exhibit 10.10, the first item has been investigated by "URM" who found the vendor invoice had been misfiled, thus delaying the payment. If such an event happens frequently, a procedural change in the filing process should be implemented to minimize this type of error. Of course, the remaining items on the report should be investigated. Note that this is an exception report, because only those items requiring management attention appear on it.

Discounts Lost January 2018								
Invoice No.	Vendor Name	Date of		Invoice Amount	Discount Terms	Discount Lost	Reason for Loss	Invoice by
		Discount	Payment					
286-3	Jones Co.	12/25/18	01/12/19	$8,349.97	2/10, n30	$167.00	*Misfiled*	*URM*
BZ497	Acton, Inc.	12/15/18	01/12/19	9,730.61	1/15, EOM	97.31		
843928	Ray's Shop	01/22/18	02/29/19	4,781.00	2/10. n45	95.62		

EXHIBIT 10.10 Reporting for Discounts Lost

Coding for Vendor Accounts

Coding for vendor accounts was illustrated in the first column of the Vendor Performance Report in Exhibit 10.9 using a combination of alphabetic and numeric symbols. While some organizations use initials or other abbreviations from the vendor name plus one or more numeric symbols as an identifier, others use numeric identifiers exclusively. An advantage in the use of only numeric identifiers is that if bar codes are in use, a more compact bar code symbology can be used than if the ID includes alphabetic characters.

Audit Trails for the Procurement Process

Audit trails for the procurement process can be somewhat more complicated than those of the revenue process because, unlike the revenue process, two journal entries may be made at different times for a purchase. For example, in the case of when the invoice is sent separately from the shipment of the goods resulting in the first entry being made when goods are received and the second entry being made when the payable is recorded upon receipt of the invoice. These purchase entries are:

For recording the receipt of goods:		
Inventory	$x	
Unbilled payables		$x
For the payable after the invoice is matched with other documents:		
Unbilled payables	$x	
Accounts payable		$x

An adequate audit trail in the procurement process permits tracing from:

- Source documents to the purchases and cash disbursements transaction files,
- From the transaction files to the vendor accounts in the vendor master file,
- From the vendor master file to the related inventory accounts in the inventory master file (in the inventory module),
- From the inventory master file to the invoice records in the open vendor invoice file, and finally,
- From the open vendor invoice file to data transferred at month-end to the general ledger (GL transaction file and GL master file).

Exhibits 10.4 and 10.6 show these transaction data flows in more detail except for the month-end transfers to the GL module. The audit trail also works in reverse to enable tracing from accounts back through the system to the source documents.

The most common deficiency in audit trails is in postings from the purchases transaction file. Posting references from the purchases transaction file to the inventory accounts should include both the sequential receiving report ID number and the PO number. Posting references from the purchases transaction file to the vendor accounts and invoice records should include a sequentially assigned AP voucher number.[2] Posting references from the purchases transaction file to the unbilled payables account in the GL master file should include the PO number and the AP voucher number. Rarely does the audit trail between the cash disbursements transaction file and vendor accounts in the vendor master file have a deficiency because the check number is ordinarily used as a posting reference.

Risks and Controls in the Procurement Process

LEARNING OBJECTIVE 5
Identify risks and understand typical controls found in the procurement process.

Strong internal controls over the procurement process are essential to the successful operations of a business. Section 404 of the Sarbanes-Oxley Act requires that management attest to the establishment, maintenance, and assessment of the control system. Because the procurement process represents another aspect of cash and inventory handling, controls over the payables and cash disbursement functions must be in place to mitigate risks associated with maintaining inventory and paying vendors. The approval and issuance of purchase orders should also be carefully controlled. Some of the typical risks one might find in the procurement process include:

Source: Photick/Shutterstock.

Procurement of Goods and Vendor/Employee Services Risks

- Risks related to improper purchases: for example, purchases made for individual (as opposed to organizational) use, purchases of supplies not needed, purchases recorded incorrectly (or not at all), purchases made to unauthorized vendors, or purchases made with unfavorable payment terms.

■ Risks related to the payment of wages: for example, wages paid for unauthorized or incomplete work, wages paid to fictitious employees, wages paid based on erroneous wage rates or total hours, incorrect classification of payroll expenses/taxes, or incorrect deductions/withholding.

Disbursement of Cash/Payment Risks

■ Payment risks: for example, payment made for goods/services that are not authorized or have not been received, discounts lost because of late payments, misappropriation of discounts taken, duplicate payments, forged signatures/endorsements, or alterations to the vendor invoice or payee on a disbursement.

■ Recording risks: for example, disbursements incorrectly recorded/not recorded at all, gaps in the sequence of prenumbered checks, checks issued without proper backup documentation, disbursement and distribution of checks in different accounting periods, or manipulation of the bank reconciliation.

Following the control activity categories from Chapter 7, examples of controls in the procurement process might include:

Performance Reviews

Review of vendor performance as to (1) how long it takes to receive an order, (2) the quality of the orders received (e.g., rejected shipment report), and (3) how often items are backordered all aid management in determining whether a vendor is meeting the company's expectations. Reviews of procurement agent performance to determine productivity and compliance with set procedures also help management monitor the procurement process. Performance reviews of the personnel who inspect shipments received should also be done regularly to make sure inspectors are not receiving kickbacks or unnecessarily rejecting too many shipments.

Physical Controls

Physical controls over inventory, shipping, and cash disbursement functions are necessary to ensure smooth operations for the company. Access to cash and prenumbered checks should be restricted to authorized personnel. Access to inventory should also be limited to authorized inventory control personnel, and warehouses should have controlled access. Prenumbered purchase orders should also be locked up and accessible to a limited number of authorized individuals.[3]

Segregation of Duties

Adequate segregation of duties should be maintained between the procurement, receiving, and disbursement functions. The authority to approve disbursement vouchers should be separate from the authority to sign checks. The need for segregation of duties also extends to the payroll area, to include separation between the functions of hiring of employees, collecting/approving time cards, and preparing and distributing paychecks. In computerized systems, segregation of duties can be attained through the use of passwords, file/record locks, and designated terminal access. These types of controls, for example, allow a receiving clerk to read, but not write to, an open purchase order.

Information Processing

Authorization Controls

Proper authorization is needed to initiate a purchase order, to receive goods and services, to capture/approve employee data, and to disburse payment. Authority to initiate the procurement process generally resides with the departmental manager. Purchases are generally handled by a procurement agent (after proper authorization and budget availability of the order has been verified). Authorized vendors and/or purchase approval limits should be reviewed and updated as necessary. Rejected purchase orders should be captured by the system in an exception report.

The receipt of goods should be verified by a receiving clerk, with the quantities received verified against the original order. The goods received should also be compared to the vendor's shipping document. The clerk can verify this information through the open purchase order file.

The use of electronic time cards aids in the capture of employee time data, allowing supervisors to verify employee time (especially overtime or special-time rates). Limits can be set so that, for example, an employee cannot input time in excess of 50 hours per week without a supervisor's authorization.

The accounts payable department has the authority to disburse payment to vendors. The treasurer has the final responsibility to determine that proper supporting data have been entered into the system to substantiate the claim for payment. The software program can compare the purchase order data and the receiving report with the vendor invoice data before a voucher is prepared. Checks in excess of a pre-set amount should require a second signature. The meter readings on the automatic check-signing equipment and all prenumbered checks should be properly accounted for (i.e., either issued, voided, or unused).

Data Verification Controls

Data verification and error controls are input controls to ensure data accuracy. Reasonableness checks should be made to validate data entries for purchases, receipts, employee time, and disbursements. All quantities ordered or received should be positive (unless returns are treated as negative receipts). All employee time should be positive and bear a reasonable relationship to the standard 40-hour work week. Claims for large hours or excessive wage rates should result in an exception report that is promptly investigated and resolved by a supervisor.

Processing Controls

Prenumbered documents are an important control in the procurement process. Purchase orders, receiving documents, accounts payable vouchers, and checks should be serially prenumbered to ensure all transactions are processed. All numbers in the series should be accounted for (i.e., either issued, voided, or unused)—gaps in the sequence should be reported in an exception report and investigated promptly. Access to the inventory of prenumbered documents should be carefully controlled, or the numbers can be sequentially generated by the computer as orders, vouchers, or checks are prepared.

In a batch system, the processing of accounts payable vouchers or payroll checks lend themselves well to batch controls, such as record counts, control totals, and hash totals. For example, a control total may be entered in the computer along with the accounts payable vouchers. The application program accumulates the batch total and compares it with the amount entered. When automatic check-signing equipment is used, the meter readings on the machine provide another batch total that should be reconciled with earlier totals.

File maintenance activities should be carefully recorded on a log and monitored, with access limited to those not involved in posting routine transactions.

Output controls include the preparation of reports such as the cash disbursements report (i.e., check register). The listing of check numbers can be compared to the number of checks issued/printed and the number of vouchers processed. The bank reconciliation should be performed by an individual who is independent of check printing and signing. Care must be taken to ensure that all paychecks are properly distributed to employees (or electronically distributed through direct deposit) and that all vendor checks are mailed.

Data Entry in the Procurement Process

LEARNING OBJECTIVE 6
Set forth data-entry aspects that are unique to the procurement process.

While there are a variety of data-entry points for the procurement process, attention must be focused on (1) purchase order entry and (2) data entry related to selecting and making payments on account.

Purchase Order Entry

Data entry for purchase orders is the most voluminous task in the procurement process. All the detail of what you wish to order must be entered in the system. A completed purchase order entry screen from the Sage 50 Accounting 2016 accounting package appears in **Exhibit 10.11**. You must first enter the vendor ID, which you can also access by choosing the magnifying glass. If you are buying from a new vendor, a record for this vendor must first be set up in the vendor master file. Having chosen the vendor ID, the software program then retrieves additional information about this vendor from the vendor master file to fill in other fields on the purchase order.

Once the vendor information is verified, the purchase order information can be entered. The program fills in the default information regarding the product description and unit cost from the inventory master file. The quantity to be ordered is then entered. The unit cost, extended cost, and PO total are automatically generated. When the purchase order is printed, it is posted to the open purchase order file.

Accounts Payable Data Entry

Purchase Transactions

Data entry is less complicated when orders are received that conform exactly to their purchase orders. A simple screen allows you to convert the PO to a vendor invoice that

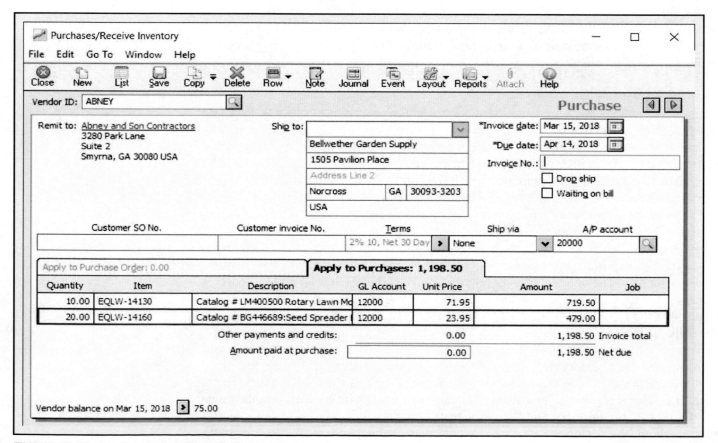

EXHIBIT 10.11 Purchase Order Entry Screen

© 2016 Sage Software, Inc. All rights reserved. Screen shots from Sage 50 Accounting 2016 are reprinted with permission. Sage, the Sage logos, and the Sage product and services names mentioned herein are the registered trademarks of Sage Software, Inc.

is now payable. If there are discrepancies from the PO, then these changes must be entered.

While the majority of accounts payable will arise from merchandise purchases that are supported by formal purchase orders, other expenditures—especially those for services—may first appear in the vendor system as a vendor invoice being recorded. These data-entry screens are more complex.

Payments Disbursements Transactions

Data entry for payment disbursements requires you to select invoices to pay, as discussed earlier in the chapter. The process is to select items for payment individually or by criteria, to print or view a screen report of selected items, make any desired modifications, and then direct the system to print the checks. While both open item and balance forward are relatively standard accounting methods used in accounts receivable, accounts payable modules usually support only open item because companies usually pay according to individual invoices rather than monthly statements.

To pay a vendor invoice, you select the Purchases task in Sage 50 Accounting 2016. A Payments (i.e., cash disbursements) screen appears. When the user enters a vendor ID a list of unpaid invoices for that vendor appears as shown in **Exhibit 10.12**.

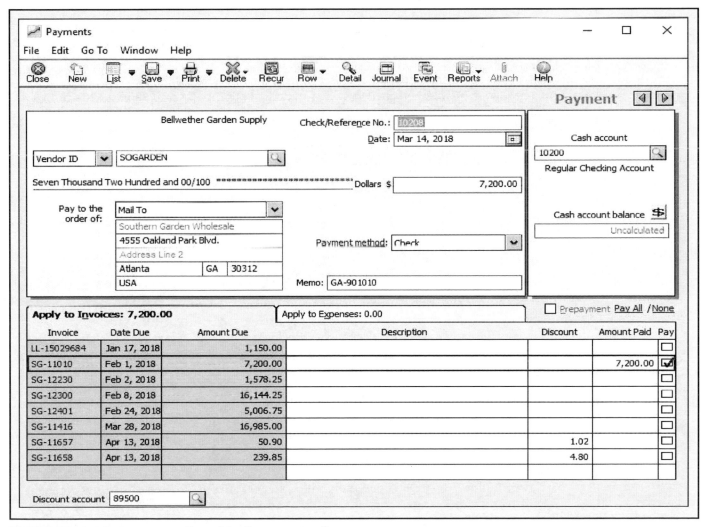

EXHIBIT 10.12 Accounts Payable Data-entry Screen

© 2016 Sage Software, Inc. All rights reserved. Screen shots from Sage 50 Accounting 2016 are reprinted with permission. Sage, the Sage logos, and the Sage product and services names mentioned herein are the registered trademarks of Sage Software, Inc.

The user then selects the invoice and enters the amount to be paid. When the "Payment" button in the upper right-hand corner of the screen is clicked, a check is printed and a transaction is recorded to decrease Cash ($7200.00 in this case) and to decrease Accounts Payable by the same amount. Note that this payment is being made well after the due date. This could be due to discrepancies in the vendor's invoice (e.g., the quantity does not match the receiving report), or cash flow problems (e.g., there is not enough money in the company's account to pay the invoice). Management can use reports such as the PO Cash Requirements Forecast, along with the Estimated Cash Collections report (Exhibit 9.14) to monitor which invoices are due to be paid and how much money will be available to pay invoices. This avoids having a reduction in credit rating due to tardy payments.

Posting

Payables are usually posted less frequently than receivables unless payments are made daily. All transactions (both purchases and cash disbursements) should be posted before selection of invoices to pay. As a result, all new purchases will be reflected in the open invoice file and all invoices paid will be so marked.

Retainages

LEARNING OBJECTIVE 7
Explain the nature and purpose of retainages and how they are automated.

While most organizations do not need this feature in payables, it is sufficiently common to justify a brief treatment here. Retainages are commonly required for construction contractors. Many large construction contracts require progress payments as certain milestones in the project are reached. Assume a school district awards a $1 million construction contract. As each one-fourth of the contract is completed, one-fourth of the contract amount is to be paid, with a 10 percent deduction (or retainage) to assure completion of the contract. The payments are calculated as follows:

Percent Complete	Gross Payment	Retainage	Net Payment
25%	$250,000	$25,000	$225,000
50%	$250,000	$25,000	$225,000
75%	$250,000	$25,000	$225,000
100%	$250,000	($75,000)	$325,000

For the first three payments, the retainage is deducted. When the contract is complete and the building is accepted, then the final payment is due plus the earlier amounts retained. The purpose of retainages is to provide additional assurance the contractor will complete the agreed-upon task to the satisfaction of the school district.

A majority of mid- and high-end accounting packages support retainages so that, once the vendor is set up, a specified amount or percent is withheld from each payment to the vendor and these retainages are automatically added to the final payment. Note that the construction contractor has an accounting problem also, but on the receivables side. The first contractor bill will be for $250,000, but a remittance of only $225,000 is expected. Thus, the contractor's receivables module needs to accommodate retainages.

General contractor A contracting company that subcontracts part of the work.

The building contractor is usually called a **general contractor** because that company will likely subcontract some parts of the building process. Consequently, the general contractor needs the ability to account for retainages in both the receivables module and the payables module because payments to subcontractors will likely be subject to retainage.

Summary

The procurement process in an organization is monitored and controlled using a purchase order module and a vendor (accounts payable) module. An order (an accounting event) is recorded in the purchase order (PO) module and monitored through that module until the goods or services are received. Usually, this activity is recorded in the PO module, although in some systems the receiving may be recorded in the accounts payable module. Subsequent to the receipt of the goods or services, the accounts payable module is used to monitor receipt and recording of the vendor invoice. This module is also used for selecting which invoices to pay and when. When payment is made to a vendor, it is recorded in the accounts payable module. These procurement process modules produce reports such as a vendor performance report, PO cash requirements report, AP cash budget, and a discounts lost report. In addition, hard copies (printed output) of all transaction files (journals) and master files (ledgers) should be available. The AIS should be able to produce all reports required to manage the procurement process of the organization.

Segregation of duties is probably the most important control activity in the procurement process. The purchase authorization, ordering, receiving, and cash disbursements functions should be separated. Much of the required segregation can be built into the AIS itself through user identification and passwords. In addition, physical controls are essential in the cash disbursement and inventory control areas.

Key Terms

Acceptance report   306
Cash disbursements journal   308
Cash disbursements transaction file   308
Cash requirements forecast   307
Check register   308
Deliverables   305
Electronic data interchange (EDI)   303
Electronic funds transfer (EFT)   308
General contractor   320

Open vendor invoice file   307
Open purchase order file   304
Receiving report   305
Request for proposal (RFP)   305
Request for quotation (RFQ)   305
Schedule of aged accounts payable   307
Ticket   305
Trading partners   302

Appendix A: EDI Protocols and EDI Architectures

In an EDI system, two businesses communicate via their computers to place and receive orders. If the two businesses have different systems, transferring information between the businesses must be in a standard format that is readable by both systems.

EDI Standards and Protocols

When paper documents are used, personnel processing them easily adapt to different document shapes, fonts, and layouts. Computers do not have this ability. Therefore, standards are necessary for electronic document transfers. The computer must know the order of data received and where each data element begins and ends. These standard messages can be viewed as the electronic equivalents of preprinted paper forms. EDI standards are set under the supervision of the American National Standards Institute (ANSI) domestically and the United Nations internationally. The basic ANSI standard for EDI that is used by most domestic companies is called X.12. EDIFACT (EDI For Administration, Commerce, and Transportation) is the international standard more commonly used overseas. In addition to these basic standards, many variations have been adopted by standards committees for specific industries. In fact, most major industries have specific standards that are necessary because of the unique aspects of the industry. For example, documents relating to crude oil must indicate the specific gravity of the oil, whereas most industries have no use for that information.

You can gain an idea of the format of electronic documents by looking at the electronic purchase order shown in **Exhibit A.1**. The upper part of Exhibit A.1 describes the data shown in the bottom part.

The interchange control header's function is to direct the transmission to the intended recipient. Because a single EDI transmission may include a variety of documents, the functional group header encloses all documents of a particular type (invoice, sales order, acknowledgment, etc.). Each document has a description, in this case an invoice. Invoice header data are then followed by the line item detail. The trailer fields complement the header fields, thereby enclosing the data. The complete format specifications for any EDI document are known as a **transaction set**. A few of the hundreds of transaction sets that have been developed are:

Purchase Order	Purchase Order Change	Price Change
Invoice	Statement	Receiving Advice
Sales Tax Return	Credit/Debit Adjustment	PO Acknowledgment
Ship Notice/Manifest	PO Change	Order Status Inquiry
Request for Quotation	Response to Quotation Request	Price Sales Catalog

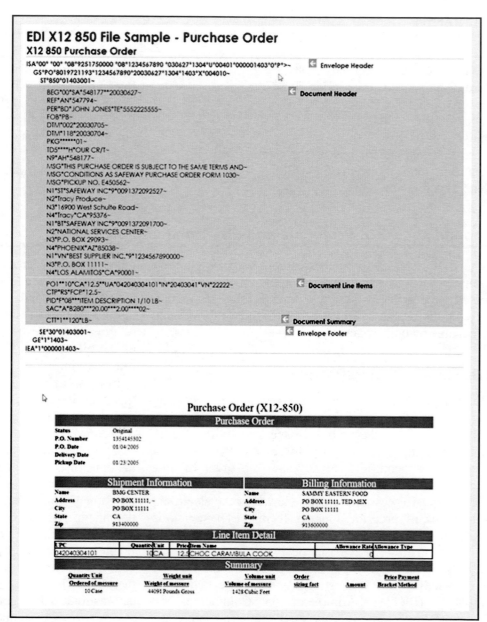

EXHIBIT A.1 Paper Document Mapped to X.12 Purchase Order Standard

Source: www.amosoft.com (Visited June 16, 2013).

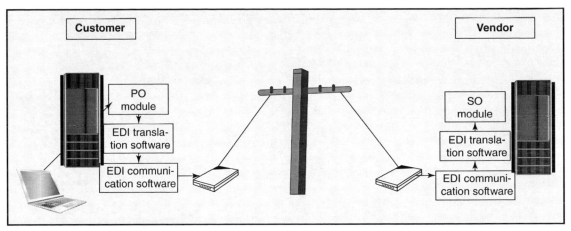

EXHIBIT A.2 Point-to-Point EDI

While Exhibit A.1 illustrates the basic X.12 format, it must be emphasized that most companies use a customized industry standard instead.

A few of the industries that have adopted variations of X.12 include:

Aircraft Manufacture	Grocery	Printed Office Product
Airline	Health	Care Publishing
Automobile Manufacture	Insurance	Railroads
Chemical	Law Firms	Utilities
Electronics Manufacture	Petroleum Refining	Warehousing

The early development of EDI standards provided efficient means of processing transactions within an industry. Ford Motor Company could process transactions with its dealers and with its materials suppliers. Automating its transactions with architects, insurance companies, and labor unions was another matter, however. Thus, the most recent developments have included the development of some standards for data exchange among industries.

EDI Architectures

EDI architectures can be point-to-point, using a value-added network, or Internet-based. These architectures are explained in this section.

Point-to-Point Transmission

The simplest EDI installation would be a personal computer running EDI software. Customer personnel might initiate a transaction by entering conventional purchase order (PO) data into a screen on a company PC. The EDI software then translates the data to an appropriate transmittable format, dials the designated vendor's computer and, upon establishing a connection, transmits the PO data to the vendor's EDI system. Upon receipt of the document in the EDI standard format, the vendor's software translates the data to the format appropriate for its accounting system. Such a system is known as **point-to-point** and is illustrated in **Exhibit A.2**. A customer's computer is connected directly via a dedicated line to a vendor's computer so electronic documents can be exchanged.

The point-to-point system may perform satisfactorily, but it has certain limitations. When the customer tries to transmit EDI documents, all data lines may be busy at the vendor's location. Also, a vendor who uses X.12 may acquire a new customer who uses EDIFACT and, consequently, cannot send transmissions in an acceptable format.

Value-Added Network for EDI

The way to eliminate these limitations is to use a third-party **value-added network** (VAN). A VAN is a service provider that expedites the delivery of electronic documents over a private network. Many VANs are available including large U.S. companies, such as GE Global eXchange Services, EDS, and IBM. The functions of a VAN are to:

- Provide implementation and continuing support for new EDI users
- Accept EDI transmissions to outside parties and store them
- Deliver EDI transmissions when requested by intended recipients
- Translate the transmissions from the sender's format to that of the recipient, if necessary
- Guarantee security and reliability

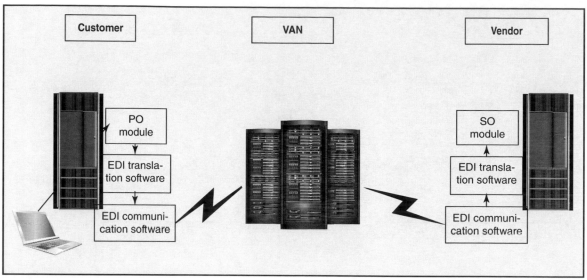

EXHIBIT A.3 EDI Using a VAN

Exhibit A.3 illustrates the role of a VAN in EDI.

Trading partners may have different VANs. In this case, the EDI documents are transmitted by one VAN to the other. With the use of a VAN for EDI, a single transmission delivery to the VAN may include order acknowledgments and invoices for several different customers as well as purchase orders and other documents for suppliers. In picking up (receiving) your EDI, mail would include a variety of documents from a variety of parties. While the delivery and receipt of EDI is greatly expedited by using VANs, software is necessary to sort and store incoming documents efficiently.

While most use of a VAN is in batch mode, some applications are interactive EDI. When real time is used, both the purchaser and seller must be connected simultaneously to the VAN. A purchaser may maintain a connection from the placing of an order until an order acceptance has been received from the seller, with the lapsed time being less than 10 minutes. In contrast, an order acceptance may not be received until the next day with batch processing.

Internet-Based EDI

EDI is very expensive and time-consuming to implement. Costs can be very high for a mainframe installation plus fees of 70 cents per transaction. Therefore, many small and mid-size entities (SMEs) have not been able to justify the high cost of EDI.

Progress has been made in merging EDI and Internet technologies to create a low-cost option for companies of all sizes. Three approaches to support EDI over the Internet are:

1. Internet EDI
2. Web-EDI
3. XML/EDI

While these appear to be an attractive alternative, these approaches lack the security, reliability, and audit trails of traditional EDI, certainly a concern to accountants and auditors. As a result some companies are reluctant to move EDI to the Internet. The risks are discussed later in this appendix.

Internet EDI

A much cheaper way to transport messages using EDI standards is to replace VANs with Internet service providers. However, the Internet mail protocol (SMTP) cannot guarantee privacy, authenticity of the sender, or delivery. To overcome some of these weaknesses, a subgroup of the Internet Engineering Task Force, a large open international community of network designers, operators, vendors, and researchers concerned with the evolution and operation of the Internet, has issued standards for using encryption and digital certificates in an effort to secure EDI messages over the Internet. This subgroup is called EDIINT for Electronic Data Interchange-Internet Integration. The trading partners purchase connectivity software that supports EDIINT. Encryption helps with the privacy issue domestically. But a problem with multinational EDI partners is that U.S. software vendors cannot export strong encryption software for legal reasons. See **Vignette A.1** for an example of the use of Internet EDI.

Web-EDI

With Web-EDI, a small business can participate in an EDI exchange with only a browser and an Internet connection. One of the trading partners, usually the larger company, provides its own Web-based EDI hosting service or hires a third-party hosting service. If the company provides its own hosting service, it develops or purchases web-based forms for every EDI message it accepts and stores them on a web server (or uses a VAN). The forms become an interface to that company's EDI system. The smaller trading partners can log onto the web site and complete a form

Vignette A.1

Walmart and EDI

Walmart requires its suppliers with more than 3,500 invoices per year to do EDIIMT (EDI over the Internet) using AS2, a specification that allows the safe delivery of EDI documents over the Internet. For suppliers with fewer than 3,500 invoices per year, they may choose to do Web-EDI, which is a free, web-based solution that allows suppliers to receive purchase orders and send invoices without the expense of an EDI package. However, Walmart does not require suppliers to have specific software for EDI translation as long as the suppliers connect to the Walmart's network using an interoperable-tested AS2 communication package. The cost of the EDI translation packages varies depends on a supplier's needs and by individual software package.

(for example, an invoice). The form is submitted to the web server where it is validated and packaged as an EDI message. From this point on, the message is routed in the larger company's system as a normal EDI message. When messages go from the web site to the smaller partners, they are either converted to clear-text e-mail or to a web form. The entire cost is borne by the owner of the web site, that is, the larger company, which has a sufficiently large volume to justify the cost. The EDI translation from web-based forms is handled by packages such as Harbinger's Harbinger Express. Harbinger also offers a repository of web-based forms that can be used by trading partners.

XML/EDI

XML stands for eXtensible Markup Language. XML is a web-oriented standard that, like EDI, allows companies to exchange information and conduct transactions with partners.

XML/EDI uses templates, or a formal definition of the structure of messages. These templates describe the structure of the message, not the data, and how to interpret the message. They enable mapping of the EDI messages from the way the data are stored in a database to the EDI standard message. Unlike Web-EDI, XML/EDI processes the message on the client's side. For example, suppose McConnell Co. is a small vendor that wants to send an invoice to giant, Neimans. Neimans has upgraded its WEB-EDI to XML/EDI, and McConnell Co. has upgraded its accounting package to one that supports XML/EDI. The Neimans accountant downloads the XML/EDI template for an invoice. The accounting package software agent helps the accountant create the invoice and ensures integration of the data with McConnell's accounting software. A **software agent** is software that can perform routine tasks that require intelligence.

Key Terms for Appendix A

Point-to-point   A transmission system wherein a customer's computer is connected directly via a dedicated line to a vendor's computer so electronic documents can be exchanged.

Software agent   Software that can perform routine tasks that require intelligence.

Transaction set   The complete format specifications for any EDI document.

Value-added network (VAN)   Value-added network (VAN) A service provider that expedites the delivery of electronic documents over a private network. A reseller of mid- to low-end accounting software.

Discussion Questions and Problems

1. Which activity would be most effective in providing reasonable assurance that recorded purchases are free of material errors?
   a. The clerk on the loading dock compares quantities listed on the purchase orders versus the receiving reports.
   b. An internal auditor compares a sample of vendor invoices with purchase orders.
   c. The department manager who authorized the purchase must sign the receiving reports.
   d. The accounts payable clerk matches the purchase orders, receiving reports, and vendors' invoices.

2. Your task is to determine that purchases, which are initiated in various departments, have been properly authorized. If the procurement department makes all purchases, to which of the following documents would you vouch purchases?
   a. Purchase requisitions
   b. Purchase orders
   c. Invoices
   d. Receiving reports

3. In an electronic data interchange system, which of the following statements about a purchase order is correct?
   a. The vendor electronically retrieves the purchaser's purchase order from the purchaser's open purchase order file.
   b. The purchaser's purchase order is mailed or faxed to the vendor.
   c. The purchaser does not need to store purchase order data in an open purchase order file.
   d. The purchaser's purchase order is in the form of a message that is transmitted electronically to the vendor.

4. To determine whether accounts payables are complete, you want to perform a test to verify that all merchandise received has been recorded. What documents would be best for this test?
   a. Purchase orders
   b. Receiving reports
   c. Purchase requisitions
   d. Vendors' invoices

5. Which of the following documents should the receiving clerk use to verify his/her physical count matches what was received?
   a. Purchase requisition and purchase order
   b. Receiving document and vendor invoice
   c. Vendor's packing slip and purchase order
   d. Receiving report and vendor's packing slip

6. Describe the flow of data in the procurement process that is initiated when the purchasing organization issues a check to a vendor in payment of an invoice for merchandise purchased.

7. The vendor performance report in Exhibit 10.9 includes all vendor records.

   Required:

   Review the report and list the ways in which the report might be improved to meet standards of good reporting discussed in Chapter 5.

8. In the revenue process a sale is normally recorded when the goods are shipped by debiting Accounts Receivable and Cost of Goods Sold, and crediting Sales and Inventory.

   Required:

   a. Explain why the procurement process is not a mirror image of the revenue process.
   b. Explain what accommodation is required in the procurement process.

9. In the Grand Manufacturing Company's AIS, each PO record includes the following data fields:

Purchase order number	Manufacturer's item number
Date of order	In-house item number
Purchase requisition number	Description
Name of originating department	Quantity ordered
Vendor ID	S.K.U. (each, pair, dozen, quart, feet, lbs, etc.)
Vendor name	Unit price
Requested delivery date	Extended price
Gross dollar amount	

Required:

a. An open purchase order report is needed that will be used by the procurement agent to monitor outstanding orders and assure goods will be received when required. Prepare the layout for such a report selecting the fields to be included, the arrangement of the fields, and the order of the records in the report.
b. Critique the necessity for maintaining all of the fields in Requirement a in the PO module.

10. The records in the open vendor invoice file for Poor Company as of May 15, 2014, are as follows:

Vendor	Voucher #	Due Date	Gross Amount	Discount Date	Discount
Helium Co.	332	5/03	$ 250	4/13	2.0%
	346	5/10	1,300	4/20	2.0%
	391	6/15	875	5/25	2.0%
Neon Co.	318	4/20	700	4/01	1.0%
	329	5/01	550	4/10	1.0%
	358	6/11	2,400	5/20	1.0%
	373	5/21	160	5/06	1.0%
Xenon Co.	325	4/23	300	4/03	1.5%
	347	6/11	1,900	5/20	1.5%
	386	6/01	2,500	5/17	1.5%

Required:

a. Make a list of the vouchers and amounts that should be paid on May 15 if checks are cut on a weekly basis. Our priority is to pay all past due invoices, keep our accounts current, and take all discounts, in that order. Discounts are taken if we write the check on or before the discount date.

b. After making the list, we discover that our cash balance is only $7,723. Which items should be paid given this constraint?

11. Assuming that batch posting is used for vendor accounts, how frequently should the accounts be posted?

12. Sharon's Electrical Service has signed a contract with Dekalb School District for electrical work. The contract is for $1.4 million to be paid in five installments as each 1/5 of the work is completed with a 5 percent retainage. Sharon expects these five milestones to be reached in the months of July, August, October, November, and January.

Required:

Calculate the amount of cash Sharon can expect to receive and the month in which it will be received if she bills in the month of the milestone and collects in the following month.

13. Answer the following questions:
a. What is the purpose of the 1099 tax form?
b. What parties receive a copy or original of the 1099?

14. Toys-R-Y'all has asked your firm to install a computerized accounting system at its Baytown warehouse. The management wants you to flowchart how the computerized system will work from the point of receipt of the goods, to the creation of the purchases transaction file, to the update of the related master and open files.

When the goods arrive, the receiving clerk will count the goods and enter the transaction data through a keyboard. The input prompt and the open purchase order file will display the details of the goods ordered so the clerk can compare the purchase order and the actual goods received. The entered data will go into the purchases transaction file. At the end of the day, the purchases transaction file will be posted to the:
1. Open purchase order file
2. Inventory master file
3. Vendor master file

Required:

Prepare a systems flowchart for the receiving subsystem as it is described above

At the beginning of your class, please turn in (1) a printout of your flowchart and (2) the electronic file for your flowchart (which can be submitted electronically, if available).

Independent work: You are encouraged to discuss this assignment and to share insights and experiences with other students. However, you are expected to complete work independently on this assignment.[4]

Notes

1. Issues and risks related to outsourcing of components are discussed in Chapter 11; audit requirements for outsourcing are discussed in Chapter 6 (SSAE No.16).

2. Because each open invoice requires a unique identifier, the accounting system assigns sequential numbers that are called "voucher" numbers.

3. Limited access to documents can also be controlled through the electronic issuance of purchase orders and/or checks generated sequentially using sequence coding that can be reviewed/audited for sequence gaps. Gap reports can then be generated and resolved by authorized personnel.

4. We are grateful to Ed Altemus, who wrote this problem.

The Inventory Process

Source: Rawpixel.com/Shutterstock.

Learning Objectives

After studying this chapter, you should be able to:

- Explain the various activities in the inventory process.
- Differentiate between periodic and perpetual inventory methods.
- Summarize the concept of supply chain management (SCM) systems, including how electronic data interchange (EDI) can facilitate SCM and how inventory is tracked.
- Describe the concept of outsourcing and the costs/benefits associated with outsourcing components or activities.
- Describe the flow of data through the inventory process.
- Describe the functions in the inventory module and explain what each accomplishes.
- Describe the challenges associated with maintaining proper inventory levels.
- Identify and describe the principal reports required for effective management of the inventory process.
- Identify risks and understand typical controls found in the inventory process.

Source: El Nariz/Shutterstock.

Introductory Scenario

Connor Hendrix had grown up working for his father's company. The elder Hendrix had started a meat packing company when Connor was in junior high school. The company specializes in premium quality bacon, sausage, and ham and sells to both regional and local grocery companies in the Kansas City area. The company has grown considerably under the senior Hendrix's leadership having reached sales of $15 million in the most recent year.

Connor was concerned because the company still used an antiquated paper-based accounting system. The accountants had to work a lot of overtime at the end of reporting periods. However, Connor's main concern was with the lack of control over inventory. The meat products were highly perishable, and Connor had observed losses caused by slow handling and employee theft occurring more and more frequently. In addition, the reports that managers needed to control inventory were usually too late to be useful and often did not always include information helpful for monitoring inventory levels.

When Connor talked to his father about considering an automated alternative to handling and accounting for inventory, the elder Hendrix discarded the idea as an idealistic, unnecessary notion. The truth of the matter was that Mr. Hendrix was intimidated by technology and did not feel comfortable tackling something he knew nothing about.

Connor had to walk on eggshells when it came to working at his father's company and suggesting new business ideas. The elder Hendrix was very sensitive to the perception by other employees in the company that Connor might be getting special treatment. So he made every attempt to make Connor prove he earned his pay and promotions. Connor had worked up from the lowest position to a junior manager. Now, Connor was earning a master's degree at a local university because his father wanted him to have at least the same or even more education than others in the company.

When Connor took his accounting information systems course, he was surprised that the course included a topic that was very important to him personally. Connor felt even more driven to do something about the inventory system at the company and realized the AIS course could be just the ammunition he needed to persuade his father to automate the inventory system. Under his AIS professor's direction, Connor undertook a special class project to investigate inventory systems that would be appropriate for the meat company. Connor felt that if he went to his father with a well-researched proposal, he would have a better chance of persuading the elder Hendrix.

Introductory Scenario Thought Questions:

1. What would be some of the advantages of having an automated inventory system that Connor could present to his father?
2. To portray a balanced presentation, what would be some of the disadvantages of having an automated inventory system that Connor should tell his father?
3. Discuss reports would be helpful to inventory managers and the executive management team that would reduce inventory theft, spoilage, and other aspects of poor inventory management.

Overview of the Inventory Process

The inventory process sits between the revenue (Chapter 9) and the procurement (Chapter 10) processes. The subject matter of the inventory process is both products and services that are sold by an organization. Thus, some details of the inventory process have already been covered. This chapter reiterates some of the material previously discussed about inventory and adds information specific to the inventory process.

The Inventory Process in Mercantile Organizations

Inventory processes in manufacturing organizations are varied. For example, manufacturing processes in paper mills and automotive plants are both complex but are very different. Accordingly, any textbook treatment of inventory problems encountered by paper manufacturers would not necessarily be applicable to automobile manufacturers. Because a consideration of manufacturing inventory processes would greatly expand this text and because they are ordinarily covered in cost accounting courses, this chapter is confined to a discussion of mercantile and service organizations.

LEARNING OBJECTIVE 1
Explain the various activities in the inventory process.

The inventory process of mercantile organizations, although not as complex as that of manufacturers, is one of the most complex processes in an organization. The receiving, storing, and shipping merchandise activities are depicted in **Exhibit 11.1**. When merchandise is received, personnel with appropriate skill and knowledge levels are assigned to verify and inspect the merchandise for quality standards. For diamonds, a gemologist may be required; for petroleum fuel, a chemical engineer; and for bulk wine, a professional taster. While tests may be required for some products, for others a simple visual observation is adequate. Because receiving personnel sign for merchandise received, thereby acknowledging receipt of the specified quantities, physical counts or verifications are required upon delivery. When discrete objects such as boxes of soft drinks are received, a simple physical count is made. In contrast, bulk delivery of wheat or alcohol may require a volume or weight count.

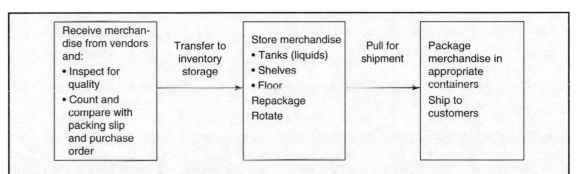

Trigger: Receipt of goods from vendor/physical verification of shipment
Actions: Create inventory adjustments transaction file (if needed), create purchases and receiving transaction file, close record in open purchase order file, update inventory master file, transfer to warehouse for storage.

Trigger: Transfer of inventory to warehouse/storage
Actions: Repackage (if necessary), store, rotate stock (so oldest perishable items sold first)

Trigger: Receipt of information for shipment of goods to customer
Actions: Match items packaged for shipment to the sales order, create sales and shipment transactions file, update inventory master file, update customer master file

EXHIBIT 11.1 Inventory-Related Business Activities

Most of the time, the merchandise is stored in structures. These structures vary from large tanks storing thousands of barrels of chemicals to warehouses with shelves, bins, or movable flats. Product is often purchased and sold in different units with the requirement that it be repackaged. Perishable goods must be stored and moved (rotated) so the oldest is sold first.

Based on customer orders, merchandise is pulled, packed, and delivered to customers. This process may involve pumping fuel oil into a tanker truck, sending software over the Internet, or filling a prescription at a pharmacy. In the first two cases, no physical packaging is required. In the latter case, repackaging occurs at the time of the sale.

Periodic and Perpetual Inventory Systems

LEARNING OBJECTIVE 2
Differentiate between periodic and perpetual inventory methods.

The two inventory control (IC) methods to account for inventory that are presented in the first accounting course are periodic and perpetual.[1] With periodic inventory, you rely on periodic physical inventory counts to calculate an overall cost of goods sold amount. Cost of goods sold is calculated as follows:

> Merchandise Inventory, beginning balance
> Plus Merchandise Purchases (net of returns, allowances, and/or discounts)
> Less Merchandise Inventory, ending balance
> Equals Cost of Goods Sold

Inventory control is achieved through these periodic counts and visual observation of the inventory. Usually no records are maintained by product or sales units, or of dollar sales, or of the cost of goods sold. Occasionally, an AIS is designed to support the collection of sales data by product line. If the periodic inventory is then tabulated by product line, a hardware store, for example, can calculate cost of goods sold and gross profit by tools, building materials, and so forth.

When an accounting system does not have an IC module, inventory records must be kept manually, or the periodic method must be used. On the other hand, all accounting system IC modules should use a perpetual inventory method in which the details of both units and inventory values are automatically maintained on a continuous basis. For many companies, controlling inventory is a major contributor to the success of the business; the next section discusses newer approaches to maintaining inventory records and monitoring costs associated with inventory.

Supply Chain Management Systems

LEARNING OBJECTIVE 3
Summarize the concept of supply chain management (SCM) systems, including how EDI can facilitate SCM and how inventory is tracked.

Accounting information systems may range in scope from what is referred to as financial modules (GL, customer, and vendor) to systems that comprise an enterprise-wide system, tying all internal processes in a company, including manufacturing, into one system. These latter systems are called **enterprise resource planning (ERP)** systems. While packages such as SAP (e.g., Business by Design), Oracle E-Business Suite, and Sage ERP X3 certainly qualify as ERP packages, the concept can be applied to midrange software as well. As long as the software encompasses all *internal operations,* it can be appropriately characterized as ERP software.

Enterprise resource planning (ERP) software A software package that comprises an enterprise-wide system, tying all internal processes in a company, including manufacturing, into one system.

Companies such as Walmart and General Motors have pioneered the development of new systems that extend beyond the reach of these packages that cover internal operations. By using electronic data interchange and other technologies, these systems manage the purchase and receipt of merchandise in a manner that allows an organization to minimize inventory on hand. This objective of minimizing inventory is sometimes known as **just-in-time inventory**.

Just-in-time inventory A system to manage the purchase and receipt of merchandise or parts in a manner that allows an organization to minimize inventory on hand.

Software systems that extend an organization's reach outside to suppliers and customers, managing the planning and flow of merchandise inventory, are known as **supply chain management (SCM)** systems. SCM systems permit companies to respond to changes in global supply and demand by connecting manufacturers, distributors, and retailers—that is, the entire supply chain. ERP vendors have begun adding modules to their software to enable SCM. A leading product is ProcureWare (which offers inventory management and controls through various database platforms, including a cloud-based platform). Examples of other highly-rated SCM systems include Procurify, PathGuide Latitude WMS, Freightview, and Oracle E-Business Suite. Mid-sized businesses can also benefit from third-party add-on SCM modules with products such as U Route, which has features to support inventory activities from ordering to tracking and reporting for mid-sized businesses. Many SCM system vendors are offering a cloud-based option for their clients.[2] Most vendors of small business and mid-market accounting systems packages have electronic commerce capabilities, a significant element in SCM.

Supply chain management system (SCM) A system that allows an organization to connect the chain of manufacturers, distributors, and retailers in managing inventory planning and flow throughout the supply chain.

To illustrate how an SCM benefits an organization, let's look at an example. If an oil refinery on the Gulf coast were to be put out of service due to a fire, the SCM package of the refining company might, upon being given that information, automatically redirect deliveries of crude oil to refineries and of gasoline to wholesalers and retail outlets. This planning would include scheduling tanker ships and tanker trucks. Some of the tasks that SCM software can perform include:

- Systematize the location and production capabilities of factories and distribution centers
- Unify worldwide inventory management and order fulfillment
- Optimize the global supply chain
- Integrate tax efficiency into the global planning process

EDI and Supply Chain Management

Two contributions of EDI to supply chain management should be obvious at this point—(1) the elimination of the expense of purchasing, handling, and mailing paper documents and (2) efficiencies gained by avoiding data entry of incoming documents. For large companies that exchange a lot of documents, these two benefits easily pay for the high cost of EDI. According to http://www.edibasics.com/benefits-of-edi/, a major electronics manufacturer was able to reduce its costs to process a purchase order to $1.35 by adopting EDI (prior to that, the cost was $38 to process a purchase order). The most significant gains ensue from efficiencies arising from closely integrating operations between suppliers and customers. Inventory levels can be reduced, allowing for just-in-time inventory systems, because the time to place an order is reduced from days to minutes. Because the supplier often has budget data of the purchaser, inventory can be replenished immediately.

Trading partners are frequently granted limited access to each other's AIS or SCM. A vendor could monitor a customer's inventory and might in some instances, be responsible for maintaining that inventory without the necessity of receiving a purchase order. Experienced EDI users often eliminate other steps in the procurement process. Many companies are using the e-invoicing system discussed earlier. Orders received are compared with the related purchase order and vendor invoice to isolate any discrepancies, which are then addressed. Payment is made when ordered goods are received.

Tracking Inventory

An advance in the technology of tracking inventory is **radio frequency identification (RFID)**. RFID goes beyond the tracking ability of Universal Product Codes (UPC) because its code can identify not only a class or type of product, but can also identify an *individual* product as it moves along the supply chain and ends up in the possession of an individual. Other advantages of RFID over UPC technology include the ability to scan the code from farther away (in some cases, up to 90 feet away), better tracking of inventory movement (making it easier to track theft), and efficiencies in product recall and detection of counterfeit items. The RFID tag is quite small, and its transponder contains a memory chip that allows for the unique product code. The tag is detected as it passes through the electromagnetic zone by an antenna in the transceiver. This eliminates the need for a laser reader, which is required to read a UPC code. In December of 2004, EPCglobal Inc. developed standards for RFID technology. This standard allows the interaction of RFID technology, the Internet (for use in e-commerce), and related electronic product codes. The second generation of these tags incorporates 1) the ability to make use of the technology internationally and 2) an increase in the speed of data transmission. Examples of RFID currently in use include the embedded computer chips used to help track lost pets, airline baggage handling tags, identification badges (used instead of magnetic strips), and EZ tag passes for toll roads in Texas.[3]

Radio frequency identification (RFID) Considered the "next generation of barcodes," RFID is a code that identifies not only a class or type of product but also an individual product as it moves along the supply chain and ends up in the possession of an individual.

Source: Trueffelpix/Shutterstock.

While this technology is extremely valuable for tracking inventory and replacing cashiers with point-of-sale checkout stands, there are privacy issues that should be considered. For example, if the RFID tag is not erased at checkout, it could be easily read without the consumer's knowledge and provide unauthorized readers information about credit cards or other personal consumer information. Auditors and accounting professionals involved with the development and implementation of RFID technology in their organization should be aware of these and any other security concerns to ensure that these issues are addressed.[4] Companies ranging from Golf Club Car (a maker of golf carts) to NYK Logistics (container shipment company) to Paramount Harvests (a major supplier of pistachios) are taking advantage of RFID techonology.[5] Walmart has instituted a scheduled implementation of RFID for its supply chain.[6]

Outsourcing

LEARNING OBJECTIVE 4
Describe the concept of outsourcing and the costs/benefits associated with outsourcing components or activities.

Outsourcing Transferring a non-core activity (or activities) to a third-party service provider.

Service level agreement (SLA) A document that is key to protecting an organization who outsources a good or service. The SLA can include things like specifications of deliverables required from the third-party service provider.

Outsourcing is described as having a third party perform non-core activities (such as payroll, computer processing, or customer service) or provide/produce specific components necessary for production. The outsourced function or component may come from a third-party service provider that is either in the same country as the organization contracting for an outsourced product or service, or the third-party service provider may be located overseas.

The most common reason to outsource is to save money. This can mean savings in labor and/or component costs. In addition, some outsourced services such as customer technical support services can provide 24/7 support for worldwide operations. Sometimes, the technology is more advanced at another organization so that the outsourced component is produced more cheaply and with higher quality.

There are, however, many risks to outsourcing. The more obvious risks are those related to geopolitical issues (e.g., wars, embargos) and currency fluctuations. In addition, jobs in the contracting organization's home country can be lost due to the outsourcing of the activity or component. Other risks have to do with security, in the sense that laws in the third-party service provider's country might differ from those of the lead organization's country. For example, laws regarding information privacy, patents, and copyrights in countries such as India and Thailand differ significantly from the laws in the U.S. Another often overlooked risk is renegotiation risk. This has to do with the resulting transfer of intellectual property when outsourcing an activity or component. When renegotiating an outsourcing contract, the lead organization no longer has the advantage of having exclusive knowledge of the product or service, and may be at a disadvantage during the negotiation of a new or renewed contract with the third-party service provider (who now also has that proprietary knowledge). Other issues that need to be addressed in the decision to outsource have to do with whether or not there will be decreases in the quality of the product or service outsourced. The key to protecting an organization interested in outsourcing a good or service lies in the strength of its **service level agreement (SLA)**. These SLAs can require due-diligence reviews, AICPA Statement on Standards for Attestation Engagements (SSAE) No. 16 and AICPA Service Organization Control (SOC) reports (discussed in Chapter 6), and specific definitions of deliverables by the third-party service provider. For example, the SLA might require that background checks be performed on employees in sensitive areas or with access to confidential/private customer information, or the SLA might specify requirements with regard to the protection of sensitive or proprietary information (e.g., signing a nondisclosure agreement).

Source: Fabrik Bilder/Shutterstock.

AIS Structure for the Inventory Process

While in most accounting systems the IC module composes the entire inventory record-keeping process, most data entry relating to inventory occurs in the revenue process (customer and sales order modules) and in the purchasing process (vendor and purchase order modules).

Inventory Data Flows

Data flows in inventory systems vary considerably depending on the AIS design. While batch posting is most common with other modules, the majority of inventory modules use real-time posting. This mode of processing permits sales personnel to make commitments on a real-time basis to those customers desiring to place orders. **Exhibit 11.2** is a conceptual representation of data flows in an inventory system and depicts the reality of a batch posting system. An understanding of the steps required in the batch mode provides a foundation for an understanding of what occurs in real time. We will now describe the data flows in batch mode and then mention those aspects in which a real-time system differs.

Inventory adjustments are common to both batch and real-time IC systems. When a physical inventory is taken and compared with the perpetual records, discrepancies are often discovered. After you ensure the physical count is correct, an entry should be made in the inventory adjustments transaction file that corrects the book balances. The Sales and Shipment Transaction File is created by programs in the customer (account receivable) module, and the Purchases and Receiving File is created by a program in the vendor (accounts payable) module. These three transaction files are used to update the inventory master file from which various reports are derived (two examples are shown in Exhibit 11.2.)

LEARNING OBJECTIVE 5
Describe the flow of data through the inventory process.

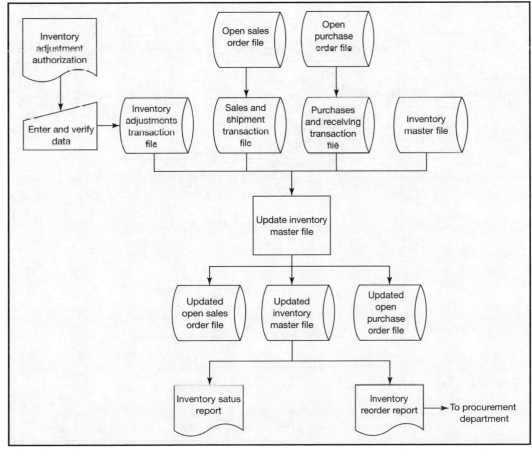

EXHIBIT 11.2 Merchandise Inventory Data Flows—Batch Posting

Real-time posting to the Inventory Master File is accomplished simultaneously with data entry. The only transaction file in the IC module is for adjustments. In Chapter 10—the procurement process—we discussed a separation of the recording of merchandise receipts and the booking of the related accounts payable. In such cases, receipts are recorded in the AP/vendor module when the merchandise arrives, and liabilities are recorded when the invoice arrives.

Inventory Control Functions

LEARNING OBJECTIVE 6
Describe the functions in the inventory module and explain what each accomplishes.

Exhibit 11.3 shows a typical structure for the inventory module. Probably the most significant difference between the inventory module and other parts of the AIS is the amount of detail required for each inventory item and the large number of ways that inventory can be classified. Thus, even though direct entry of data into the inventory module may be minimal, the module is quite complex. In fact, Exhibit 11.3 could contain far more aspects of inventory management, but it has been simplified to point out some of the most common issues. This exhibit assumes real-time posting of all changes to the inventory master file. In addition, it is assumed that merchandise is recorded in inventory when received rather than waiting until all documents have been assembled to permit the booking of a payable.

Major Functions	Maintenance Functions	Daily and Period-End Functions
Inventory module setup	Design product identifiers Defaults: number of decimal places, inventory method, pricing formulas Specify location codes Select warehouse method Specify GL posting accounts	
Inventory item maintenance	Add inventory item Change inventory data Mark inventory item for hold or deletion Update price lists	
Data entry	Enter inventory adjustments	Record warehouse transfers
Printing		Accounting records: Bin labels Price tags Journals (receipts and adjustments) Inventory ledger (units and value) Inventory trial balance Management reports: Order recommendations Excess inventory Inventory turnover Sales by inventory item Gross profit by inventory item Returns and allowances Inventory and PO aging
End-of-period processing		Post transactions to G/L archive Reset journal Delete unneeded accounts

EXHIBIT 11.3 Inventory Module Functions

Inventory Module Setup

The first major function in the inventory module, which is shown in Exhibit 11.3, is "Inventory Module Setup."

Design Product Identifiers

The first maintenance function in the "Inventory Module Setup" is "Design Product Identifiers." The design requirements of product identifiers are somewhat different from those for all other modules for two related reasons. First, often numerous identifiers are required. Second, while the principal users of customer, vendor, and GL account numbers are accountants, warehouse personnel make extensive use of inventory account numbers. Accordingly, it is usually essential that account numbers have a mnemonic association with the physical attributes of the product. For example, a sheet of grade A, 1/2-inch plywood might be identified as PW-5-A. If all products are so identified, employees in receiving, warehousing, and shipping can easily learn and use the product numbers.

The design requirements, then, include the ability to:

- Define the number and length of fields in the identifier.
- Use alphabetic as well as numeric symbols.

Some software packages permit you to design the identifier, while others specify the number of fields and their lengths. Almost all packages permit the use of alphanumeric identifiers.

Set Defaults for Operation of the Module

Another function in the "Inventory Module Setup" is "Defaults." Each inventory record will be composed of a large number of data fields. Very often one value for a data field is frequently used. When this is the case, the software is usually designed so you can press Enter when the cursor moves to that field, and the **default value** is automatically inserted. This use of default values can speed up the data entry of inventory records significantly.

> **Default value** A frequently used value for a field that is filled in by the user. The software program stores this default value for the field so the user has to fill in the field only if the default value is not correct.

The data fields for quantity and prices can have a default number of decimal places. Barrels of alcohol in the inventory of a patent-medicine drug manufacturer might require information to the 100ths of a barrel (i.e., necessitating two decimal places in the quantity field). In contrast, the quantity field for window air conditioners would require no decimal places. Similarly, cost and sales prices might vary from amounts with three decimal places to even dollars (with no decimal places). Because most of a given organization's entire inventory will use the same inventory method, a user-specified default is desirable to specify methods, such as specific identification, FIFO, or LIFO, or average cost. Therefore, such a default expedites entry of new products.

Automatic pricing is a feature that saves countless personnel hours. When the cost of inventory items changes, selling prices are often adjusted accordingly. Often, different pricing levels are used for different customers. In more sophisticated IC systems, different selling prices are calculated at the time of sale by applying formulas to the cost of merchandise. Some formulas that might be used and their meanings are:

> **Automatic pricing** A feature in the inventory module in which pricing formulas are stored so that when the cost of an item changes, the selling price is automatically recalculated.

Formula	Interpretation
C+.2	Cost plus 20 percent
C/.8	Cost divided by 0.8 (20 percent profit based on selling price)[7]
C+$10	Cost plus $ 10

If an IC module does not support automatic pricing and a supplier's new price list of 100 items is received, not only must the new cost be entered, but each selling price must also be manually changed. Therefore, to update the inventory records of a company that has three selling prices, 100 entries will be required if automatic pricing is supported, but 400 entries will be required without the feature. Automatic pricing formulas are usually stored in each inventory record, permitting the use of default formulas for each specific product.

Specify Location Codes

Location code A code used to designate where inventory is stored.

Another maintenance task in the "Inventory Module Setup" is "Specify Location Codes." **Location codes** are used to designate where inventory is stored, allowing a picking list to be created for warehouse employees to locate items for shipment to customers. The location codes may identify shelves, bins, floors, and/ or even buildings in different countries. Codes required for all locations are entered into a locations table in the IC module.

Select Warehouse Method

Warehouse method When an organization has inventory stored in multiple locations, they choose to either maintain a different inventory record for each part at every location or to maintain one record for each part.

Another critical task in the module setup is to select a warehouse method. You have two ways (sometimes called **warehouse methods**) of accounting for inventory that is stored in multiple locations. These will be called methods one and two. With method one, there is a different inventory record for each part at every location. If we stock 1,200 items and have three warehouses in which each item is stocked, then the IC module will contain 3,600 master file records. For method two, there is only one record for every part, with the quantities for each warehouse being maintained in a separate table related to each inventory record. Consequently, with method two, we will have only 1,200 master file records. The significance of these two methods is discussed later in this chapter.

Specify General Ledger Posting Accounts

Another task in the inventory module setup is to specify the GL accounts to which inventory data will be posted. Adjustments to inventory for scrap, spoilage, and other shrinkage are recorded in the inventory module. However, all other entries affecting inventory are made in other modules. For example, receipts of inventory are recorded in the vendor (accounts payable) module with a debit to an inventory account and a credit to a suspense account—"unbilled payables."[8] Sales of inventory are made in the customer (accounts receivable) module with a debit to cost of goods sold and a credit to an inventory account. The GL account numbers for all accounts used in making entries in the inventory module must be specified during setup.

Inventory Item Maintenance

The second major function for the inventory module shown in Exhibit 11.3 is "Inventory item maintenance."

Add and Change Inventory Records

You can add new inventory items (one record for each item) and make changes to an existing record, such as sales price, location, and preferred vendor ID. **Exhibit 11.4** is an example data-entry screen from the Sage 50 Accounting 2016 program for adding and changing an inventory master file record.

The first field on this screen is for the item (Item ID) number. This ID is a unique identifier that fits the company's product numbering system. Clicking on the magnifying glass retrieves records from the inventory master file so you can see what product numbers are used. If you are making a change to an existing inventory record, you can select the inventory item. If you are adding a new record, you must enter the new item number. For a new record, you must also enter a short, generic description of the product and the item class. The program tracks descriptions ("Prefabricated Birdhouse"), unit prices ($59.99), item type (SUPPLY), location information (Row 9), preferred vendor ID ("ABNEY") and the cost of sales account (50000).

The "cost method" (e.g., FIFO, LIFO) can also be chosen from the pull-down menu on the screen. Other information, such as stock quantity, is also tracked through the program.

Set Inventory Item for Hold or Deletion

A task that might be desirable is to set certain inventory items for hold or deletion. You may wish to change the status of an inventory item to "hold" for several reasons. Items received may be of poor quality, and the buyer may be negotiating with the vendor for a price reduction.

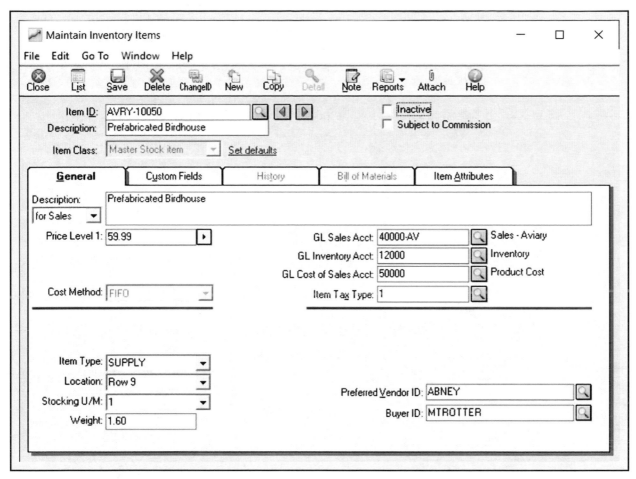

EXHIBIT 11.4 Master File Data-entry Screen

Source: © 2016 Sage Software, Inc. All rights reserved. Screen shots from Sage 50 Accounting 2016 are reprinted with permission. Sage, the Sage logos, and the Sage product and services names mentioned herein are the registered trademarks of Sage Software, Inc.

After negotiations are completed, the items may be placed on sale. Alternatively, a food or drug company may have reports of spoiled product and needs to refuse orders until necessary inspections or other actions are taken to ensure the inventory is safe for sale.

Occasionally inventory master file records for inventory accounts need to be deleted. In Chapters 8, 9, and 10 we assumed master file records are deleted one at a time. Although individual account deletion is common, this method is inefficient. When you decide a given product will be discontinued and not replenished, the product's master file record can be marked for deletion. Before deletion occurs, the following conditions must be met:

- The account has a zero balance.
- The account has no activity in the current period.
- The account will not be needed in the future for comparative reporting purposes.

Once the inventory account has been marked, no additional action is required by you except to invoke a "mass delete" at the end of the accounting period. The program should automatically check for the above conditions and delete the appropriate accounts. This process as described allows you to delete superannuated (i.e., unused or unneeded) accounts.

Update Price Lists

Another maintenance task that the IC module might perform is to update the price lists. From time to time our suppliers send us new price lists. Our costs must then be updated by individually looking up each master file record and making the change. If our part numbers are different from the vendor's part numbers, this is even more laborious. A well-designed IC module will expedite this process in several respects. First, it will permit lookups by vendor part number as well as by our identifier. Second, the program can be designed to bring up the cost field for every part purchased from a given supplier, sorted by supplier's part number order, so we can update costs by proceeding directly down the new price list.

Electronic updates are even more efficient. If we have a system designed to be compatible with our vendor's system, the vendor may furnish us with an automated price list to be transferred to our files under program control. The ultimate system would permit our vendors to update relevant prices on our computers from their location—a feature available in some SCM packages.

Data Entry

The third major function in Exhibit 11.3 for the inventory module is "Data Entry." This is where we record transactions in the inventory adjustments transaction file.

Enter Inventory Adjustments

In many IC modules, the only data entry is for inventory spoilage and other shrinkage. The journal entry would be a debit to the Loss from Spoilage account and a credit to the Merchandise Inventory account. If the causes for inventory losses can be ascertained with reasonable accuracy, separate expense accounts should be debited for the respective causes. This permits management to monitor the type and magnitude of losses and take action when appropriate.

Exhibit 11.5 shows the data entry screen for an inventory adjustment in Sage 50 Accounting 2016. Using this screen, the user can record adjustments due to damage

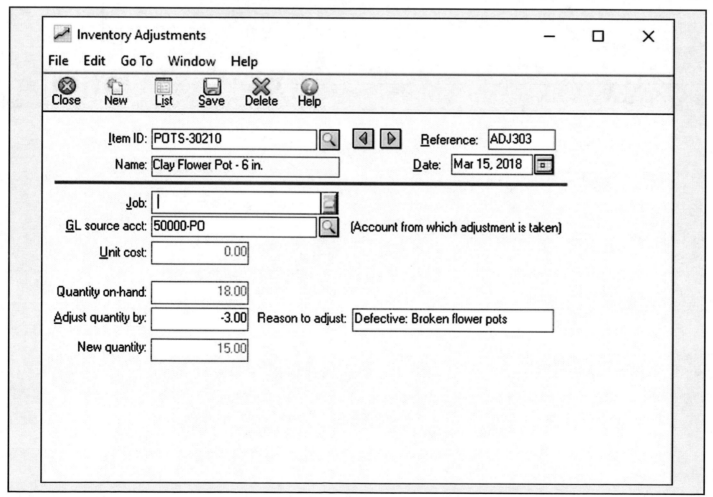

EXHIBIT 11.5 Data-entry Screen for Inventory Adjustment Transaction

Source: © 2016 Sage Software, Inc. All rights reserved. Screen shots from Sage 50 Accounting 2016 are reprinted with permission. Sage, the Sage logos, and the Sage product and services names mentioned herein are the registered trademarks of Sage Software, Inc.

or pilferage. The adjustment in the exhibit is for some damaged flower pots. The adjustment reduces the quantity on hand by three damaged flower pots (item number POTS-30210). Once the item number is entered (by clicking on the magnifying glass and choosing the item), the item description is automatically generated. Note that the sequence number of the adjustment transaction (ADJ303) is automatically generated, as is the date. When the adjustment is "saved," the inventory quantity on hand is reduced by three units.

Record Warehouse Transfers

It is also possible to identify a location for a particular inventory item. If inventory items are dispersed geographically rather than concentrated at one location, it may occasionally be advisable to transfer product between warehouses rather than reorder. Thus, the ability to record these transfers is necessary. If our warehouses are geographically dispersed, we probably want to use warehouse method one described earlier in this chapter. With widely dispersed warehouses, it is usually more economical to reorder merchandise even though excess inventory exists in other warehouses.

Printing Accounting Records

The fourth major function in the IC module in Exhibit 11.3 for the inventory module is "Printing." IC modules commonly support the printing of bin labels that describe the inventory item. These labels are then affixed to the bin or shelf where the item is stored. Some modules still print price tags, although the prevalence of bar code and RFID tag use today is making price tags less common.

You can also print the journal and the inventory ledger in the IC module. A unique aspect of the inventory ledger compared with those in the GL, customer, and vendor modules is that any printout should include beginning balances, activity, and ending balances *both in units of the product and the cost valuation.*

Another useful printout is an inventory trial balance, which is a simple listing of each inventory ID, description, units on hand, unit cost, and total cost value of each item. This trial balance is most often used to compare the quantities in the accounting records with physical counts of the inventory. Most companies perform inventory cycle counts, such that perhaps one-twelfth of the total inventory is counted each month using count tags.[9] Count tags are then compared with the inventory trial balance. Any discrepancies are investigated and, if a recount finds the physical counts to be correct, the inventory records are updated. We will discuss some other useful reports for managing inventory in the section under learning objective 8.

Managing Inventory Levels

The most common inventory problems for mercantile organizations are as follows:

LEARNING OBJECTIVE 7
Describe the challenges associated with maintaining proper inventory levels.

- Maintaining an economic level of inventory on hand
- Avoiding obsolete inventory
- Managing the selection of products to achieve satisfactory profitability and customer satisfaction

Exhibit 11.6–Graph A shows the quantity of an inventory item on hand through two cycles of ordering. The vertical axis shows the inventory quantity and the horizontal axis represents time. The first cycle begins with the product fully stocked (at the maximum stocking level). As time passes, sales occur, and the inventory level declines until it reaches the lead-time stock level. **Lead time** is the period of time between the ordering of product and its receipt from a vendor. If you sell three items a day and the time lapse between the date merchandise is ordered and the date it is received is 8 days, then the **lead-time stock** required is 24 units (3 units x 8 days). When the quantity available for sale declines to the lead-time stock level, an order is placed for additional product.

Lead time The period of time between the ordering of inventory and its receipt from a vendor.

Lead-time stock The number of units of inventory that covers sales of inventory during lead time without encroaching on the safety stock.

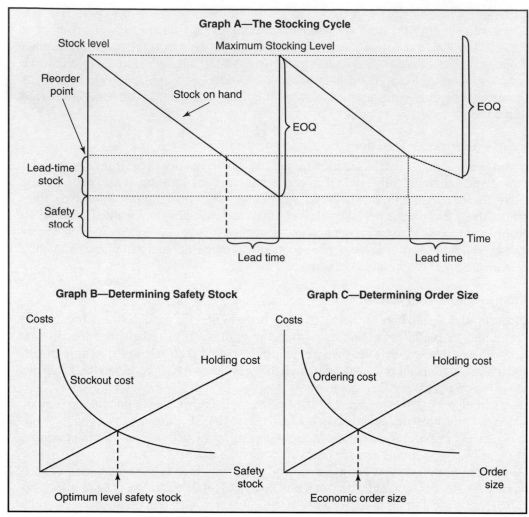

EXHIBIT 11.6 Inventory Cycles and Inventory Management

Safety stock The quantity of inventory that is necessary to avoid the loss of sales due to stockouts.

If sales continue at the normal rate, a shipment of the product will be received as the quantity on hand reaches the safety stock level. **Safety stock** is that quantity of inventory deemed necessary to avoid the loss of sales due to not having the merchandise available to sell to customers. Addition of the inventory received to the safety stock brings the stock level back up to the maximum stocking level.

We have explained conceptually how the lead-time stock and the safety-stock levels depicted in Exhibit 11.6–Graph A are determined. The sum of the safety stock and the lead-time stock defines the **reorder point**. The decline of inventory to the reorder point triggers the issuance of a purchase order to replenish the item.

Reorder point The sum of the safety stock and the lead time stock.

Holding costs (or carrying costs) Costs associated with maintaining and storing inventory.

Stockout cost The contribution margin lost on sales due to stockouts.

Two categories of cost are associated with calculation of safety stock—holding costs and stockout costs. **Holding costs** (or **carrying costs**) are the costs of holding inventory, such as interest on funds invested in the inventory, warehousing, property taxes, and insurance. The larger the amount of safety stock, the larger the holding costs. **Stockout cost** is the contribution margin lost on sales due to the inability to fill customer orders because the requested items are not available in inventory. The larger the quantity of safety stock, the smaller the stockout cost. Whereas holding costs are usually linearly and positively related to safety stock, stockout cost declines with an increase in the size of safety stock, but at a declining rate. Thus, these two costs must be balanced to arrive at an optimal level of safety stock. **Exhibit 11.6–Graph B** depicts these relationships among holding cost, stockout cost, and safety stock, and shows that the optimum safety stock is where the two cost functions intersect.

The optimum order size is commonly known as the **economic order quantity (EOQ)**. EOQ is the result of balancing the cost of holding merchandise against the cost of ordering merchandise. **Ordering costs** include the creation of a purchase order, sending it to the vendor, handling the merchandise when received, and paying the resulting invoice. As indicated in **Exhibit 11.6–Graph C**, if the order size is small you will have many orders at a high ordering cost, but as the order size increases the ordering cost declines at a declining rate. As the order size increases, the holding costs increase because inventories are larger. Thus, the EOQ is the order size that minimizes the total cost, which is at the point where holding and ordering costs are equal.

Refer again to Exhibit 11.6–Graph A. At the bottom of the graph, we have the safety stock and right above that the lead-time stock. The sum of the EOQ and the safety stock equals the **maximum stocking level**. Therefore, these three amounts—safety stock, lead-time stock, and EOQ—must be derived to manage merchandise inventory at appropriate levels. The first inventory cycle in Graph A depicts an ideal situation. Sales of the product are at a constant and predictable rate; purchase orders are made at the precise time and in the exact amount; and deliveries of orders are on time. Such is rarely the case as is suggested by the second cycle depicted. For some reason, the rate of sales in the second cycle declines during the lead time, with the result that when the replenishment order arrives, we are overstocked (above the maximum stocking level) on inventory. If in the second cycle the rate of sales increases, rather than decreases, we will use some safety stock and will be below the maximum stocking level when the new order arrives. If in the first inventory cycle we place an order after some of the lead-time stock is used, the appropriate size of an order is such that when the order is received the quantity on hand will be at the maximum stocking level. Therefore, the order size will be greater than EOQ. This situation points out the fact that EOQ is the minimum order size. A simplifying assumption made in the graph is no seasonal factor in sales. Even with these limitations, we have a conceptual model of inventory management that permits us to design reports for management that represent a significant improvement over those commonly found in IC modules.

Reports to Assist Management in Managing Inventory

A large number of management reports may be required in a mercantile organization depending on the nature of operations as well as the preferences of management. We will confine our attention to those that are required by most organizations.

Order Recommendations Report

The most popular IC report is the **Order Recommendations Report**. This report includes only those inventory items that are at or below the reorder point. A well-designed report will also suggest the appropriate order size. Many discussions of inventory management assume this amount will be equal to EOQ, but this is not necessarily the case. EOQ is the minimum order quantity. If the current inventory balance is below the reorder point, a quantity should be ordered that will bring the balance on hand when the order is received up to the maximum stocking level. Such a report is shown in **Exhibit 11.7**.

Note the various columns of data in the report. Inventory units on hand less units committed (promised to customers) equals **free stock**. The sum of free stock plus units on order (labeled "available" in the report) is compared with the reorder point. If the amount available is less than the reorder point, then an order size is suggested. Only those inventory records that suggest that a PO be issued are included on this report. This is an exception report because only items requiring management attention are included.

Economic order quantity (EOQ) The optimum size for an order of inventory where holding and ordering costs are equal.

Ordering cost Includes the creation of a PO, sending it to the vendor, handling the merchandise when received, and paying the resulting invoice.

Maximum stocking level The level at which an item is fully-stocked—the safety stock plus the economic order quantity.

LEARNING OBJECTIVE 8
Identify and describe the principal reports required for effective management of the inventory process.

Order recommendations report A report of inventory items that are at or below the reorder point.

Free stock The stock available for sale after consideration of stock committed to customers.

Item ID	Description	Unit	On Hand	Committed	Free Stock	On Order	Available	Reorder Point	EOQ	Order Size
H102	Locking Handle	Ea.	300	150	150	200	350	350	200	200
H202	Door Hinge	Ea.	70	25	45		45	100	90	145
H702	Brown Stain	Pint	37	10	27	50	77	80	60	63
H802	Turpentine	Gal.	230	100	130		130	140	300	310
L102	½" Plywood	Ea.	5	120	−115	200	85	150	200	265
R100	Asphalt Tile	Doz.	324	500	−176	330	154	200	600	646

PORTLAND HARDWARE
Order Recommendations
October 12, 2018

Potential Purchase Commitment $5,729.64

EXHIBIT 11.7 Order Recommendations Report

Notice in Exhibit 11.7 that available locking handles exactly equals the reorder point; therefore, the suggested order size is equal to EOQ. The amount available for all of the other items is less than the reorder point and the recommended order size is equal to that difference plus the EOQ. Assuming that either this difference is due to a delay in running this report or a random aberration in sales, the order sizes should result in maximum stocking levels upon receipt of these orders. The total dollars that would be committed to purchases if everything recommended were purchased will be compared with expected cash availability. Some factors that may cause management to deviate from these order size recommendations include:

- Expected cash shortages
- Changes expected in the rate of sales
- Expected shortages of the product

Excess Inventory Report

Excess inventory report A report of overstocked inventory items.

While the purpose of the order recommendations report is to assure that sufficient inventory is on hand to meet sales demand, the **excess inventory report** serves to call management's attention to significantly overstocked items. Recall that our graph of inventory replenishment cycles in Exhibit 11.6 Graph A shows overstocked merchandise at the end of the second cycle. Such overstocked items should appear on the excess inventory report only if they are important in dollar value. Being overstocked in pencils by 10 percent is not nearly as important as being overstocked by 10 percent in industrial diamonds, which have a far greater value. As a consequence, you should set a threshold level so only excess inventory of a material dollar value is included on the excess inventory report. Unfortunately, most excess inventory reports include all overstocked items whether the value is material or not. Given the randomness of inventory fluctuations, many items will usually be slightly overstocked resulting in a report that includes more irrelevant items than relevant items.

Exhibit 11.8 is an excess inventory report. In running the report, only excess inventory items having a cost of greater than $50 are selected for inclusion. Actions that might be taken by the management of Portland Hardware to address the listed products include

					Free	On		Maximum		
Item ID	Description	Unit	On Hand	Committed	Stock	Order	Available	Level	Excess	Cost
H201	Cabinet Hinges	Ea.	832	30	802		802	500	302	$151
H283	Wood Screws	Lb.	130	4	126		126	70	56	84
H401	Padlocks	Ea.	90	10	80		80	50	30	360
H801	Paint Stripper	Gal.	300	6	294	50	344	100	244	1,230

PORTLAND HARDWARE
Excess Inventory of Greater Than $50
October 12, 2018

Total Excess Inventory $1,825

EXHIBIT 11.8 Excess Inventory Report

attempting to cancel the purchase order for 50 gallons of paint stripper and placing any or all of the overstocked items on sale. Excluding items only slightly overstocked shortens this report because there are likely to be many such items.

A Combination Order Recommendations and Excess Inventory Report

Earlier in the chapter, we introduced two methods of accounting for inventory stored in multiple locations (warehouses). Method one, with a record for each item at every location, will result in order recommendations based on the quantity at each location. Consequently, while one location may be short of merchandise with the Order Recommendations Report suggesting an order, another location may be overstocked, but trans-shipment may not be economical.

In contrast, method two that supports one record for merchandise at multiple locations, will result in order recommendations based on the total quantity available at all locations. If transfer of inventory between locations is ordinarily not feasible, then method one is a good choice. At the other extreme is when the multiple "warehouses" are adjacent or close to one another, then method two works the best. Neither method works well when the proper choice would be to place orders a significant part of the time and also to transfer inventory often. In these cases, you must make a judgment as to the most economical course of action. While mathematical models are possible to solve such problems, they do not exist in typical accounting packages, but may be found in SCM packages. A good reporting solution in an accounting package is to *merge* the Order Recommendations Report and the Excess Inventory Report, so when there is a shortage of an item at one location and an excess at another, both records appear adjacent in the report. Then, with a general knowledge of shipping costs, the manager can scan the report and decide whether to order or transfer merchandise.

Inventory Turnover Report

While the excess inventory report may include obsolete stock, it cannot be relied upon to do so. Often sales of a stock item will cease when the stocking level is between the maximum stocking level and the reorder point. An **inventory turnover report** can be relied on to indicate such dormant stock items. **Exhibit 11.9** shows an inventory turnover report including all items with a turnover of less than 0.5 times a month.

Inventory turnover report Indicates dormant inventory items that have not meant a minimum "turnover" or sales expectation.

Sales and Gross Profit Report

A final category of reports is used to determine which products are marginally desirable and might be given additional advertising and/or promotional emphasis to improve their performance. Those products that hold no promise of improvement should be dropped.

PORTLAND HARDWARE
Products Turning Over Less Than 0.5 Times Monthly
October 12, 2018

Item ID	Description	Unit	3-Mo. Sale Average	Available Units	Turnover Rate	Total Cost
R102	Roofing Shakes	Sq.	850	3,200	0.27	$29,750
G281	Garden Hose	Ea.	24	130	0.18	2,600
G300	Sprinkler	Ea.	40	90	0.44	180
						Total Cost $32,530

EXHIBIT 11.9 Inventory Turnover Report

Gross profit by product report Shows the physical volume and the dollar amount so volume and pricing effects can be distinguished.

Exhibit 11.10 shows a **sales and gross profit by product report** that can be used for these purposes.

The report shows the physical volume as well as the dollar amount so volume and pricing effects can be distinguished. For example, lawn mower volume is up compared to last month, but the gross profit is down, probably due to seasonal pricing. On the other hand, door hinges volume is up, and the gross profit is up as well. A product sales report assumes the same form as the product gross profit report except the last three columns are sales rather than gross profit.

PORTLAND HARDWARE
Sales and Product Gross Profit
October 12, 2018

Item ID	Description	Units Sold			Gross Profit		
		This Month	Last Month	Incr. (Decr.)	This Month	Last Month	Incr. (Decr.)
G281	Garden Hose	870	900	(30)	$2,700	$2,500	$200
G300	Sprinkler	21	23	(2)	50	55	(5)
G400	Lawn Mower	30	28	2	1,200	1,400	(200)
H102	Locking Handle	424	200	224	8,480	4,000	4,480
H201	Cabinet Hinges	92	103	(11)	37	45	(8)
H202	Door Hinge	397	350	47	340	325	15

EXHIBIT 11.10 Gross Profit by Product Report

Returns and Allowances Report and Inventory and PO Aging Report

Returns and allowances report A report of merchandise returns and allowances for each product that have been given to customers due to shipment errors and/or defective merchandise.

Another report that may be necessary is the **Returns and Allowances Report** showing the merchandise returns and allowances for each product that have been granted to customers due to shipment errors and defective merchandise. This report must be monitored closely because of customer dissatisfaction and the expense of processing such returns.

To monitor the status of inventory receipts, the purchasing department needs a report that shows inventory on hand and committed along with open purchase orders and the dates on which the related merchandise is expected to be received. This report might be called the **Inventory and PO Aging Report**. By reviewing this report, purchasing managers can anticipate shortages in merchandise and, if the added expense can be justified, expedite vendor shipments. This report is essential if the organization is attempting to maintain just-in-time (i.e., minimal) inventory levels.

Inventory and PO aging report A status report showing inventory on hand and committed along with open purchase orders and expected delivery dates.

End-of-Period Processing

The last major function in Exhibit 11.3 for the inventory module is "End-of-Period Processing."

Post Transactions to General Ledger

At the end of each period, usually a month, transactions that have been recorded in the IC module must be posted (transferred) to the GL module in either summary form or in detail. This transfer may be either to a transaction file in the GL module or directly to the GL accounts affected. We believe that a better audit trail is maintained if a transaction file in the GL module receives this data.

Archive and Reset Journal

The inventory adjustments transaction file should be transferred to an archival (history) file at the end of each period. Simultaneously, all data should be cleared from the file so it is ready to receive entries for the next period.

Delete Unneeded Inventory Items

In the discussion of inventory item maintenance, we explained "marking" inventory items for deletion. At the end of each period, a mass deletion of these marked items should be invoked.

Risks and Controls in the Inventory Process

Inventory represents one of the organization's most liquid assets (cash and accounts receivable are generally the most liquid). Consequently, inventory management is a "key" control. In other words, losses in this area characterize one of the largest risk exposures for a company. As part of a company's compliance with section 404 of the Sarbanes-Oxley Act, management is responsible for the establishment, maintenance, and assessment of the controls critical to the inventory process. Some of the typical risks one might find in the inventory process pertain primarily to the management of inventories and include:

LEARNING OBJECTIVE 9
Identify risks and understand typical controls in the inventory process.

- Material misstatement of inventory valuation
- Improper classification or determination of inventory costs
- Errors in cost allocations
- Improper application of cost flow models (e.g., FIFO, LIFO, average cost)
- Errors in the perpetual inventory records resulting in overstocking or obsolescence of items in inventory
- Improper evaluation of carrying costs versus stockout costs
- Failure to identify low turnover inventory items
- Improper evaluation of the market value of inventory
- Excessive losses due to shrinkage or theft of inventory
- Misappropriation of materials or goods due to manipulation of inventory adjustments or valuations
- Unauthorized shipments of inventory
- Fictitious physical counts of inventory to conceal pilferage
- Errors due to the improper classification of goods held on consignment

Following the control activity categories from Chapter 7, examples of controls in the inventory process might include:

Performance Reviews

Review of inventory turnover, spoilage, and losses should be performed regularly. This includes review of adjustments made due to returns or allowances granted for damaged inventory. Exception reports listing low-turnover items and spoilage should be generated regularly, with listed exceptions investigated and resolved promptly. Reports on the quality of items received into inventory should also be reviewed, and vendors who ship inconsistent or poor quality items and/or who ship behind schedule should be replaced. Access logs should be reviewed periodically to determine that transaction input is properly entered by authorized individuals.

Physical Controls

Much of the burden of safeguarding inventories falls on physical security measures. Limited access to storerooms or warehouses, security fences, electronic sensing and monitoring devices, surveillance cameras, fire/smoke detectors, and security patrols all play an important role. Access to inventory and inventory records should be controlled by badges, biometrics, user identification, and passwords. Locks and security codes should be changed periodically to further limit unauthorized access. Employees in sensitive areas should be bonded to minimize loss to the company in the case of fraud. Other physical controls include quality control procedures (with regard to acceptance of shipments from vendors) and regular physical counts of inventory on hand. The results of the physical count should be compared to the computer-generated inventory on hand listing.

Segregation of Duties

The functions of custody of inventory and the responsibility for the maintenance of the inventory master file records should be separated. If the procurement and revenue processes have proper segregation over the ordering and receiving functions, respectively, this aids in the segregation of duties as well. In addition, the shipping and receiving functions (discussed in Chapters 9 and 10) should be separate from the inventory control function. Responsibility for reviewing inventory evaluations and approving changes to inventory valuations (e.g., write-downs or write-offs) should be separated from the maintenance of perpetual inventory records and the authority to dispose of obsolete or scrap items.

Information Processing

Authorization Controls

Although authority to accept raw materials into inventory lies with the receiving department and authority to transport finished goods lies with the shipping department, controls should ensure that all input data are properly authorized. Orders of inventory should be properly authorized (perhaps even done automatically, based on the order recommendations report) at the economic order quantity. Any one-time or special orders to manage seasonal fluctuations in demand should be properly authorized and documented. Actual inventory levels should be compared with reorder points and maximum levels established by management. The choice to maintain a just-in-time inventory should be periodically evaluated to determine that it is still cost-effective in terms of holding vs. stockout costs.

Overhead application rates and cost standards should be approved by upper management; any exceptions or intended deviations from established rates or standards should be approved in writing.

Written authorization should be required before any item of equipment, materials, goods, or scrap can be removed from the plant facilities. These activities should be promptly reported and independently reviewed.

Data Verification Controls

Real-time inventory systems require point-of-entry controls because of the immediate update of master file records. Inventory part or product numbers should be validated by check digits or by table/ file look-up. Retrieval of the associated master file record allows the data-entry clerk to compare the inventory description on the computer with the inventory description on the source document. Limit and reasonableness checks should be made of quantity and dollar amounts of inventory ordered.

Processing Controls

Prenumbered documents are useful controls for inventory adjustments, for the disposition of inventory or scrap, and for work orders and requisitions. Batch controls, such as comparing control totals formed from quantities in the receiving and materials issuance transaction files to changes in the control total of on-hand quantities in the raw materials inventory master file, can be useful to control materials requisitions.

Weekly or daily posting is needed for virtually all inventories and, in many cases, real-time processing is necessary. File maintenance activities must be carefully controlled, particularly when adjusting cost or sales price fields. Edit logs should be independently compared with file maintenance authorizations. Inventory adjustments should be entered as transactions to create a proper audit trail.

Strong output controls should be in place when setting up the programmed criteria to initiate a purchase order transaction (e.g., when setting up automatic reorder points). Changes to the master file records should be strictly controlled. Reports regarding reorders, spoilage, and obsolescence of inventory should be distributed to the appropriate managers for review.

Summary

Inventory management is usually one of the most complex accounting system processes. To make the topic manageable within one chapter, we confined our attention to mercantile organizations. The two methods to account for inventory are periodic and perpetual. All AIS inventory modules use a perpetual inventory system. The various activities in the inventory process include receiving merchandise inventory from vendors, inspecting the goods for quality, counting the goods received, and comparing the goods with the packing slip and purchase order. The goods are then transferred into storage. When the goods are sold, they are pulled, packed, and shipped to the customers. Physical controls over inventory and proper inventory management are essential to customer satisfaction (i.e., inventory availability) and success of the company.

A very sophisticated software system can extend an organization's reach outside to suppliers and customers, managing the planning and flow of merchandise inventory.

This system, known as a supply chain management (SCM) system, permits companies to respond to changes in global supply and demand by connecting manufacturers, distributors, and retailers, that is, the entire supply chain.

Outsourcing of a product or service has gained in popularity over the last 20 years. Outsourcing a product or service can be done to a third-party service provider either located in the home country of the organization or can be located overseas. Prior to deciding whether or not to outsource an activity or product, a company should consider not only the benefits (e.g., cost savings), but also the risks (e.g., currency fluctuations, renegotiation risk) associated with outsourcing.

The biggest challenges to managing inventory are to maintain an economic level of inventory on hand, to avoid obsolete inventory, and to manage the selection of products to achieve satisfactory profitability. An understanding of such concepts as lead-time stock, safety stock, economic order quantity, maximum stocking level, reorder point, and the relationship among stockout, holding, and ordering costs can provide ways to solve these inventory problems.

Many reports can help with managing proper levels of inventory. The ones described in this chapter are Order Recommendations Report, Excess Inventory Report, Inventory Turnover Report, Sales and Gross Profit Report, Returns and Allowances Report, and Inventory and PO Aging Report.

Key Terms

Automatic pricing   337
Default value   337
Economic order quantity (EOQ)   343
Enterprise resource planning (ERP)   332
Excess inventory report   344
Free stock   343
Gross profit by product report   346
Holding costs (or carrying costs)   342
Inventory and PO aging report   347
Inventory turnover report   345
Just-in-time inventory   332
Lead time   341
Lead-time stock   341

Location codes   338
Maximum stocking level   343
Order recommendations report   343
Ordering cost   343
Outsourcing   334
Radio frequency identification (RFID)   333
Reorder point   342
Returns and allowances report   346
Safety stock   342
Service level agreement (SLA)   334
Stockout cost   342
Supply chain management (SCM)   332
Warehouse methods   338

Discussion Questions and Problems

1. The economic order quantity is equal to the maximum stocking level less:
   a. safety stock.
   b. lead-time stock.
   c. the sum of safety and lead-time stock.
   d. holding cost.
2. Lead-time stock is:
   a. the number of days between the placement of an order and its fulfillment.
   b. the balance between stock out cost and holding cost.
   c. lead time in days multiplied times the sales rate per day.
   d. related to EOQ.
3. The type of entry you always expect to find in the inventory transaction file is one recording:
   a. sales.
   b. adjustments to inventory balances.
   c. purchases.
   d. returns.
4. The purpose of the excess inventory report is to call management's attention to:
   a. obsolete inventory.
   b. all inventory items for which the on hand plus on order less committed stock is greater than the maximum stocking level.

   c. all inventory items for which the on hand plus on order less committed stock is greater than the safety stock plus the EOQ by a material dollar value.
   d. poor control over purchase orders.
5. The purpose of the inventory turnover report is to:
   a. reveal obsolete inventory.
   b. measure sales efficiency.
   c. show overstocked items.
   d. measure the effectiveness of the purchasing function.
6. Peachtree Distribution of Atlanta has just taken a physical inventory of frozen food on hand. Included in the inventory listing are the following counts:

Item	Unit of Measure	Count
Cut green beans	carton of 1 dozen	125
Spinach	carton of 1 dozen	55
NY strip steaks	package of 5	77

A listing from the inventory records in the AIS shows the following:

Item	Free stock*	Committed	On Order	EOQ	Safety Stock
Cut green beans	73	60	85	85	30
Spinach	10	45	17	25	15
NY strip steaks	55	20	-0-	30	15

*On hand less committed

Required:

Calculate the number of units by which the inventory records should be adjusted for each of the products.

7. Refer to the data in problem 6. If the lead-time stock is 30, 12, and 40 for beans, spinach, and steaks, respectively, what quantities need to be ordered?

8. Alaskan Outfitters has 3 warehouses and stocks 1,285 products.

Required:

a. How many inventory records will Alaskan have if it uses warehouse method one?

b. How many will it have using method two?

c. If its warehouses are widely distributed (Juneau, Anchorage, and Fairbanks), what impact will this have on its choice of warehouse method chosen?

9. Pensacola Grocery Wholesalers, which is open 5 days a week, purchases groceries and other items in bulk and sells in small quantities to bait shops, marinas, and small food stores. Several stock items are listed below along with the unit of purchase, stocking unit, and unit of sale.

Inventory Item	Purchase Unit	Stocking Unit	Sales Unit
Pasta Roni, 144g box	Case of 30 boxes	Box	Box
Heinz Dill Relish, 296ml jar	Case of 24 jars	Case	Jar
Van Camp's Pork & Beans, 425g can	Case of 24 cans	Can	Can

Other information related to the items is:

Inventory Item	Weekly Sale Rate	On Order	On Hand	Committed	Reorder Pt.	EOQ
Pasta Roni	400	110	0	5	300	12
Heinz Dill Relish	300	10	15	0	10	15
VC's Pork & Beans	500	200	0	0	120	20

Weekly sale rate and committed are expressed in sales units; on hand and reorder point are in stocking units; and on order and EOQ are in purchase units.

Required:

a. Calculate the number of business days the inventory on hand will likely last for each item.
b. Calculate the number of units (cases) that should be ordered for each item.

10. Review the gross profit report in Exhibit 11.10.

Required:

a. For what purposes is the report used?
b. What improvements could be made in this report based upon the reporting principles discussed in Chapter 5?

11. An inventory application calls for the weekly updating, or posting, of the merchandise inventory master file from the purchases transaction file and the sale transaction file. This updating process is performed every Friday just before the close of business. Sales of Item No. #12345 are stable at a rate of 5 units a day, 5 days a week. Purchases are made every 3 weeks in quantities of 75 units, and the purchased goods are received first thing Monday morning. On Friday evening, January 28, the inventory level of Item No. 12345 in the warehouse was 10 units, and the balance for the item in the inventory master file was verified as being correct. The receipt of purchased goods was scheduled for the following Monday.

Required:

Perform a simulation for the month of February to determine the maximum discrepancy between the actual quantity of Item No. 12345 on hand and the balance shown in the inventory master file. Set up a table with a line for each day in the month and calculate the quantity on hand corresponding to the stated pattern of purchases and sales. Also calculate the net transaction activity used to update the inventory master file on each updating date and the resulting balance in the inventory master file.

Notes

1. You will recall in Chapter 8 we mentioned the module in the AIS for inventory would be referred to as the IC (inventory control) module.
2. For more information about popular ERP and SCM systems, refer to: http://www.top10erp.org/ (which rates ERP systems) and http://www.softwareadvice.com/scm/ (which rates SCM products)
3. Source: Serepca, B. and B. Moody (2005), "Radio Frequency Identification: What Does It Mean for Auditors?" *Information Systems Control Journal,* 2005 (Volume 4): 33-35.
4. *Ibid.*
5. http://www.rfidjournal.com/faq/show?55.
6. Source: Silwa, C. (2004), "Walmart Updates RFID Road Map, Revises Expectations for '05 Deadline," *Computerworld,* May 19, 2004.
7. For example, a $10.00 cost divided by 0.8 yields a selling price of $12.50. The $2.50 profit ($12.50 − $10.00) is 20 percent of the $12.50 selling price.
8. This concept is described in Chapter 10.
9. Count tags are sequentially number tags that give the inventory ID and the quantity at a particular location. These tags are attached to inventory items when they are counted.

Database Structure of Accounting Systems

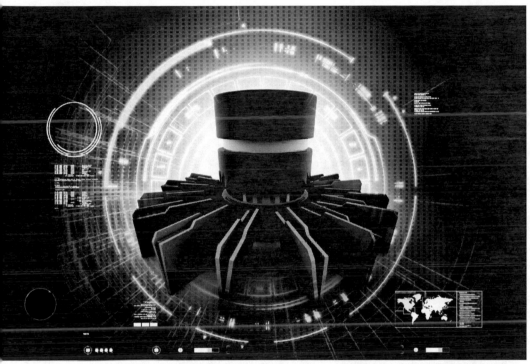

Source: deepadesigns/Shutterstock.

Learning Objectives

After studying this chapter, you should be able to:

- Explain the general structure of an accounting system that uses conventional files.

- Explain the general structure of an accounting system that uses a database.

- Explain the advantages and disadvantages of an accounting system that uses a database.

- Describe how a database management system works.

- Distinguish among the three levels of the database architecture.

- Determine the different forms of relationships in a database.

- Define a database schema and subschema.

- Summarize the functions of a data dictionary.

- Explain the functions of a database administrator.

- Define the components of a relational database.

- Explain how relational operations display new tables.

- Explain how queries are used to generate output from a relational database.

- Explain the association between database tables and files.

Source: S_Photo/Shutterstock.

Introductory Scenario

Fancy Footwork, Inc. owns and operates sports footwear outlets in five northwestern states. A few years ago, the company introduced a bar coding system that allowed checkout clerks to retrieve product price information. When a customer reached the checkout counter, the clerk scanned the bar code on the product, and the computerized cash register looked up the price, figured the sales tax, and displayed the total. The computer also printed out a sales invoice and, if necessary, a credit card slip for the customer to sign. The bar coding system improved efficiency because clerks no longer had to key in prices from printed tags; it cut down on errors; and it enabled stores to offer short-term discounts on selected products without the hassle of disseminating detailed information to sales associates.

Initially, each store's cash registers were connected to one computer in the store that housed all the program and data files. One of the responsibilities of the assistant store manager was to maintain the sales price reference file. A typical large store offered about 100 different products, and sales prices rarely changed more than once a month. However, special discounts might be offered for a few days or even for part of a day. The assistant manager would spend about 10 minutes a day on reference file maintenance.

After the bar coding system had been in operation for a while, a few enterprising store managers learned that, because the sales system used a database management system, additional information could be stored. Not only could the system generate all the information needed for financial reporting purposes, but it also could generate reports that managers needed for managing operations and making decisions. As a result, managers started adding more information, such as cost, purchase date, and product classification, to the sales price file. Cost data were useful in calculating markups and gross margin, and purchase dates were helpful in determining how long products remained in stock. Other data helped managers in their marketing efforts. Analyzing sales by product classification alerted managers to which products were "hot" and which were lagging. Seasonality is important in the sports equipment industry, and the seasonal patterns for different types of sports footwear had been documented for many years. But managers noticed more subtle patterns that enabled them to adjust purchasing levels to local demand. Managers gained more detailed insights into their local markets than they had ever had and managed inventory more effectively.

Introductory Scenario Thought Questions:

1. If Fancy Footwork were a dance club, what types of nonaccounting information might be useful for management to have?
2. If Fancy Footwork were a grocery store, what types of nonaccounting information might be useful for management to have?
3. Based on the experience of the store managers, how did a sales system built on a database management system help the managers?

General Structure of Accounting Systems

An accounting system must be able to support an organization's operations, mandatory external reporting requirements, and management decision making. Because a large part of the reporting required to support day-to-day operations and mandatory external reporting requirements is known in advance, most accounting systems are structured so that data can be processed and extracted as needed. But retrieving nonroutine, unplanned information needed for decision making can be problematic. Have you ever been frustrated by the fact that desired data were stored in the accounting system but could not be accessed and combined in a manner that would satisfy an immediate need?

As the business environment becomes more complex and better information is needed for making good decisions, management is becoming keenly aware of the need to structure accounting systems so data about all important business activities can be captured, processed, and stored in a way that more useful information can be provided. For example, an accounting system can report what sales in dollars were for a particular time period, and the accounting system can report who the organization's salespeople are. But is the accounting system able to combine and filter this data and produce a report, on the spur of the moment, of which salesperson sold the most units of the organization's two highest selling products during a specific time period? Managers need to be able to get *what* information they need *when* they need it—not weeks later. Fortunately, technology has advanced to the point that we can structure accounting systems to provide routine information *and* respond to spontaneous requests for information by using what is called a database. Not only is the database technology available, but also the cost of the technology is affordable. For you to become proficient users, auditors, or implementers of computerized accounting systems, it is imperative that you have knowledge of database fundamentals.

To establish an appreciation of the significance of a database, we will first examine how accounting systems were structured before we had database technology. This inspection will expose the weaknesses that databases have overcome. (In addition, you may encounter accounting systems with the older structure in your accounting career.)

General Structure of an Accounting System Using Conventional Files

The earliest computerized accounting systems used conventional files that separated accounting data into independent files that mimicked the journals and ledgers in traditional manual systems. **Exhibit 12.1** shows the general structure of these accounting systems.

The files of accounting data were "owned" by the application programs. For example, the accounts receivable application owned the open customer invoice file, the customer master file, and the cash receipts transaction file. The accounts payable application owned the open vendor invoice file, the vendor master file, and the cash disbursements transaction file. The application programs accessed their data files directly.

Conventional file processing systems, also called **legacy systems**, were easily understood and operated, and many control problems were amenable to simple solutions. However, these systems were inflexible and, for the most part, generated only the information that met an organization's needs for routine operational and external financial reporting.

Conventional files had the following disadvantages:

- ■ *Programming Complexity*. Application developers who wrote the programs for the applications had to write computer code for storing and retrieving records, maintaining index files and pointers, and, in some cases, for sorting and merging files. Much of the same code was repeated from one application program to the next.

- ■ *Application Program and Data Dependency*. Application programs were dependent on the physical structure of the data they processed. If a new field was added to a record in a file or an existing field was changed or deleted to meet the needs of one application program, all the other application programs accessing the same file also had to be modified. An initially insignificant change caused a domino effect possibly extending over several programs.

margin notes:

LEARNING OBJECTIVE 1
Explain the general structure of an accounting system that uses conventional files.

Legacy systems Conventional file processing systems.

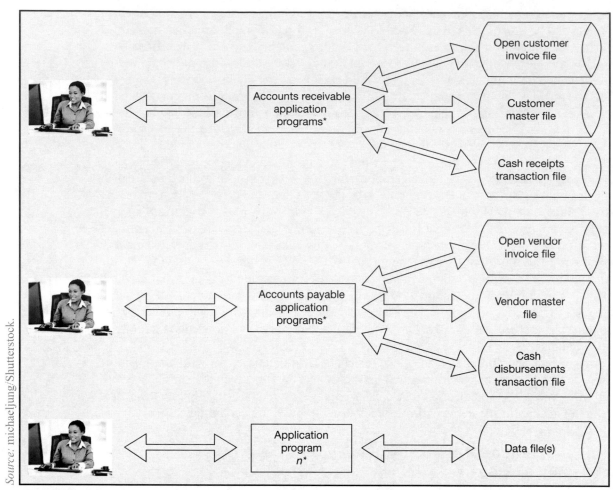

EXHIBIT 12.1 An Accounting System Using Conventional Files

Source: michaeljung/Shutterstock.

*Each application program contains a description of the data in the file(s).

- **Poor Data Integration**. Although accounting programs could be written to access one another's data files, users were not be able to retrieve data stored in different files for ad hoc, that is, unplanned, spur of the moment, requests. If a request was made for a nonroutine report, the organization's application developers had to write a new program to retrieve the data from the appropriate files. This process was expensive and time-consuming and, in many cases, produced the information much too late to be useful.

- **Data Redundancy**. The same data, such as a customer's name and address, were stored in several separate files.

  This last problem, data redundancy, caused additional problems:

- **Lack of Data Quality**. When the same data were stored in more than one location, a change to the data might not be made in all locations. Have you ever tried to change your address with an organization only to find that some of the mailings you receive are sent to the new address but some are still mailed to your old address? Data had a high risk of being neither accurate nor current.

- **Data Inconsistency**. Data stored in more than one location were often stored in different formats. For example, a social security number could be stored in one file with a nine-digit numeric format but with a packed decimal format in another file. Application developers had to wrestle with such inconsistencies when writing programs that accessed multiple files.

- **Inefficient Use of Resources.** Secondary storage was wasted by storing the same data in multiple locations. Also, it was costly to input the same data in storage more than one time. As an organization grew and its informational needs became more complex, file ownership by individual application programs caused difficulties. In fact, the incentive for developing database systems originally came from frustration with large accounting systems using conventional files.

General Structure of an Accounting System Using a Database

Database systems were first used in the 1960s by large organizations and were installed on mainframe computers to process transactions. During the 1980s, database systems were developed for midrange computers and personal computers, so they were within the reach of small firms, departments of large organizations, and individuals. With the growth of networks, database technology migrated to the client-server and distributed processing environments. However, whether database systems are used on mainframes, midrange computers, networks, personal computers, or "in the cloud," the theory, structure, design, and management issues remain substantially the same. Therefore, in this discussion, system platforms are distinguished only when the issues differ significantly.

LEARNING OBJECTIVE 2
Explain the general structure of an accounting system that uses a database.

The more recently developed accounting systems are based on database technology because they offer many advantages. In the illustration of data flows in an accounting system in Chapter 4, it was not obvious whether the system used conventional files or a database because both types of systems perform basic transaction processing in much the same way. The difference in the two types is, however, very obvious when you try to retrieve data on the spur of the moment for decision making. If you can interactively query the data in the accounting system, then you know you are working with a database. In some prepackaged accounting systems, the accounting software and the database software are combined into one package. But with others, the database software is purchased separately from the accounting software.

A database system consists of two major components:

- A database
- A database management system.

Database

A **database** is an organization's total collection of data on computer storage devices. It is an electronic store of data that can be accessed as needed by all accounting applications and by users. In a database, the data are pooled and are "owned" by the entire accounting system.

A database contains tables that contain records. Records contain fields, or data elements, which contain bytes, or characters. Bytes contain bits. **Exhibit 12.2** compares the data hierarchy of a conventional file to that of a database.

The hierarchy from the file and table level to the bit level is similar for a database and a conventional file. The difference in the hierarchy is that a database goes one step further to pool all the tables into one reservoir. The fact that tables are pooled gives a database its remarkable ability to *relate data elements even though they are stored in different tables.* This is the important feature that makes it possible for users to filter and retrieve data in many different combinations.

In addition to the tables, a database contains the following:

- Index files
- Metadata about data elements
- Metadata about application programs.

An **index file** is an auxiliary file to a data file and is used to increase the speed at which records in the related data file are sorted and accessed. An index file contains only two fields—an index key and a record address. The file is always maintained in order of the index key.

Database A database is an organization's total collection of data on computer storage devices. It is an electronic store of data that can be accessed as needed by all accounting applications and by users.

Index file An auxiliary file to a data file and is used to increase the speed at which records in the related data file are sorted and accessed.

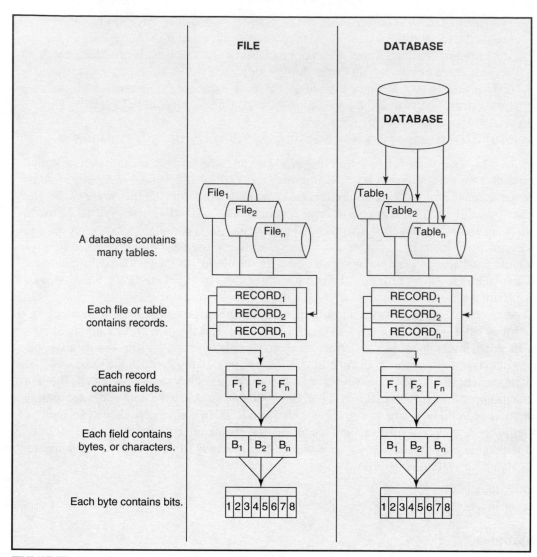

FILE	DATABASE

A database contains many tables.

File₁ File₂ Fileₙ

Table₁ Table₂ Tableₙ

Each file or table contains records.

| RECORD₁ |
| RECORD₂ |
| RECORDₙ |

| RECORD₁ |
| RECORD₂ |
| RECORDₙ |

Each record contains fields.

| F₁ | F₂ | Fₙ |

| F₁ | F₂ | Fₙ |

Each field contains bytes, or characters.

| B₁ | B₂ | Bₙ |

| B₁ | B₂ | Bₙ |

Each byte contains bits.

| 1 | 2 | 3 | 4 | 5 | 6 | 7 | 8 |

| 1 | 2 | 3 | 4 | 5 | 6 | 7 | 8 |

EXHIBIT 12.2 Hierarchy of Data Elements in a Conventional File and a Database

When creating a new table of data, the user opens the database management system and keys in information about each field that will be in the new table. Suppose, for example, that we need to create a table for all the employees in our organization. We specify that the employee table will have four fields—EmpNo, FName, LName, Dept. In addition, we mark each field as to whether or not it will be an index field. The database management system software then takes care of creating one index file for each field that we designate as an index field. If sorting employees by last name is a frequent activity, then we would want to have an index file with its records maintained in alphabetical order of last name. If the employee table is also frequently sorted by department, then another index file would be maintained in department order. **Exhibit 12.3** shows an employee table and two index files—one for the employees' last names and one for the employees' departments.

If we issue a command to sort the employee table in Exhibit 12.3 in alphabetical order of last name, the sorting program will print the table in alphabetical order. The records in the table are not actually rearranged. The sorting program goes to the index file for last name and reads the first record—Campbell, employee 160. Then the program retrieves the entire record for employee number 160 from the employee table. Then the sorting program reads the next record in the index file, which is Chen. The sorting program then retrieves the entire record for employee number 110 from the employee table. The sorting

EMPLOYEE TABLE			
EmpNo	FName	LName	Dept
100	Somnath	Gosh	MIS
110	Jiangping	Chen	Accounting
120	Mark	Muir	Finance
130	Pat	Jackson	Marketing
140	Sandra	Garcia	MIS
150	Joseph	Gilmore	Engineering
160	Michael	Campbell	Accounting
170	Fernando	Gomez	Accounting

INDEX FILE (LAST NAME)	
LName (index key)	EmpNo (record address)
Campbell	160
Chen	110
Garcia	140
Gilmore	150
Gomez	170
Gosh	100
Jackson	130
Muir	120

INDEX FILE (DEPARTMENT)	
Dept (index key)	EmpNo (record address)
Accounting	110
Accounting	160
Accounting	170
Engineering	150
Finance	120
Marketing	130
MIS	100
MIS	140

EXHIBIT 12.3 Example of Index Files to Supplement a Table of Data

program continues in the same fashion until all the records in the employee table have been retrieved in alphabetical order of last name. The table would be printed as shown below.

Employee Table			
LName	FName	EmpNo	Dept
Campbell	Michael	160	Accounting
Chen	Jiangping	110	Accounting
Garcia	Sandra	140	MIS
Gilmore	Joseph	150	Engineering
Gomez	Fernando	170	Accounting
Gosh	Somnath	100	MIS
Jackson	Pat	130	Marketing
Muir	Mark	120	Finance

We used a small table to demonstrate the use of index files. In a real business situation, the table would be very large with hundreds or thousands of records, and each record would have many more fields than the four in our example. Reading the records for the purpose of sorting and retrieving data without the help of an index file could take a very long time.

A database also contains **metadata**, which are data about data. Metadata about elements contain essential information about the data elements in the database. These metadata are in a special file that is called a data dictionary. This dictionary is defined and illustrated later in this chapter. The final item in a database is metadata about application programs. These data are about the structure and format of forms, reports, and queries.

Database Management System

Metadata Data about data. Metadata about elements contain essential information about the data elements in a database.

Database management system (DBMS) A collection of software specially designed to manage the data in a database in response to instructions issued by application programs or requests made by users.

A **database management system (DBMS)** is a collection of software specially designed to manage the data in a database in response to instructions issued by application programs or requests made by users. An overview of an accounting system that uses a database and its companion database management system is depicted in **Exhibit 12.4**.

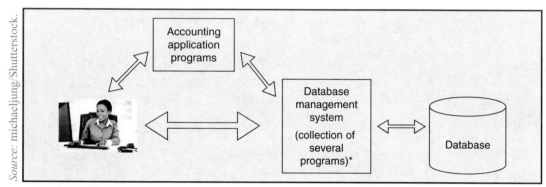

EXHIBIT 12.4 Overview of an Accounting System that Uses a Database

*The DBMS includes a description of the data in the database.

As in an accounting system using conventional files (Exhibit 12.1), users can also interact with accounting application programs but this is where the similarities stop. In an accounting system using a database, the application programs interact with the database management system, and the database management system, in turn, interfaces with the data stored in a database. Note that a user can also interact directly with the database management system.

The development of database management system software requires highly skilled information technology specialists. Therefore, this software is purchased commercially rather than developed in-house.

Advantages and Disadvantages of a Database

LEARNING OBJECTIVE 3
Explain the advantages and disadvantages of an accounting system that uses a database.

A database offers several advantages over conventional files. At this time, these advantages are simply listed and explained. The underlying reasons of why a database is able to provide these advantages will become apparent as you study the rest of the chapter.

■ *Data Integration.* Data elements can be combined in virtually limitless ways, providing the illusion of files of varying content and format. Different application programs and interactive queries can perceive the same data in different configurations as needed. With a database, it is much easier to bring data together to help in making business decisions (Vignette 12.1). Data integration is the one feature of a database that makes it far superior to conventional files.

■ *Program and Data Independence.* Application programs are independent of the physical structure of the data they process. As is shown in Exhibit 12.4, application programs communicate with the database management system rather than with the data. The physical storage details are hidden from the programs. Therefore, the

Vignette 12.1

Conventional Files or a Database?

You recently implemented for your client an accounting system that uses a database. Your client's major competitor uses conventional files. Your client is trying to decide whether she should continue carrying a particular inventory item. To make this decision, she needs data produced by the accounting system, such as the total number of units sold over the last 12 months, seasonal variability, the average price at which the units sold, which customer bought the most units, and at what average price the largest customer bought. Your client wants to make sure the sale of large quantities was not the result of deep price cuts. Because the data are in a database, your client can quickly get a report with the requested information. For the competitor to get a report with the same information, a special program would have to be written.

THOUGHT QUESTION

1. Which company has a competitive edge?

physical structure of the data in the database can be changed without necessitating a change in the application programs that access the data. This data independence feature also makes it easy for users to retrieve data.

■ *Programming Simplification.* When conventional files were used, most of the responsibility for designing data storage and retrieval methods and file-related processes was borne by the application developers. Database management systems, on the other hand, are normally supplied with all storage, retrieval, and similar processes already in place. All that remains for application developers is interfacing their programs with the database management system. Access to data is provided by standardized languages available in the database management system. These statements can easily be embedded in the program code, thereby simplifying the writing of application programs. The database management system, not the application program, contains the description of the data in the database.

■ *Data Quality and Efficiency.* Each data element is stored only once, and multiple programs can access every data element as needed.

■ *Data Security.* Security features can be written into a database management system to prevent unauthorized access or inadvertent contamination of data. Users who do not have a legitimate need for specific data are prohibited from accessing that data. Moreover, of the data that can be accessed, only specific operations on the data may be authorized. For example, one program or user may be allowed to view data but not change it. Another program or user may be permitted to add records but not delete them. You will recall "user rights" as an information processing general control discussed in Chapter 7. Regular backup policies and procedures can easily be enforced in a database.

Set against these substantial advantages of using a database are some significant disadvantages:

■ *Increased Hardware Requirements.* A database management system requires more processing power than a system using conventional files because of the greater number of instructions. The software itself may be large, and secondary storage may need to be increased to accommodate access linkages such as index files.

■ *Required Technical Skills.* The successful implementation and operation of a database management system require that application developers and other information systems personnel have database technical skills. On the other hand, it is relatively easy to implement and operate a personal computer database management system. As a matter of fact, one reason for the proliferation of personal computer database management systems is their ease of use. Novices can learn quickly to use the basic functions of a database management system and can perform more sophisticated functions as their knowledge of the system increases.

- **Difficult Conversion from Conventional Files.** Converting existing application programs to work with a database management system requires the modification of program code relating to the storage and structure of the existing files. Moreover, data that formerly resided in independent data files must be restructured for inclusion in the database.

- **Vulnerability to System Failure.** Every application depends on the database management system. The failure of any component of the system can bring operations to a standstill. Therefore, elaborate measures have to be taken to protect the data from a system crash or malfunction and to provide for speedy recovery if the database is damaged or destroyed.

- **Potential for Error Contamination.** The immediate availability of data to many different users precludes easy isolation and correction of erroneous data. Procedures for careful screening and editing of data before they enter the database are essential.

How a Database Management System Works

LEARNING OBJECTIVE 4
Describe how a database management system works.

Database management system products make it possible for users to interface with a database in three ways:

- Through application programs
- Through a query language
- Through the forms and reports facilities of the database management system.

Query language A high-level, English-like language that enables users to make ad hoc, spur of the moment, requests from a computer.

Application developers embed query language statements within application programs to help in the processing of data. A **query language** is a high-level, English-like language. Because it is peculiar to database processing, it is not part of any standard programming language. A query language includes commands for opening files, inserting records, deleting records, or changing the value of data elements. Structured Query Language, or SQL (pronounced SE′-quel), is the most important query language used in the database management system products that are widely used today. SQL has been endorsed by the American National Standards Institute (ANSI) as the preferred language for manipulating databases.

A second way that users can interface with a database is by using the query language of the database management system. This method enables users to make ad hoc, spur-of-the-moment requests from a computer.

The third way that users can interface with a database is through the forms and reports facilities of a database management system product. Forms are generally used to input data into the database whereas reports are used to display data stored in the database. Users can create their own forms and reports or accept the default ones created automatically by the database management system product.

Exhibit 12.5 provides a general overview of how a data request is handled by a typical database management system product. The details vary from product to product, but the principles are essentially the same.

The numbers that appear in Exhibit 12.5 correspond to the numbers of the following steps:

1. The data request goes to the database management system through the communication facility of the computer's operating system. Application programs go to a run time routine. Query language commands go to a query language processor. Forms and reports go to the forms processor or report writer.
2. The requests are then forwarded to the database management system engine.
3. The database management system engine determines the exact physical location of the data required for the request and forwards this information to the data management facility of the computer's operating system. Then, the operating system locates the data.

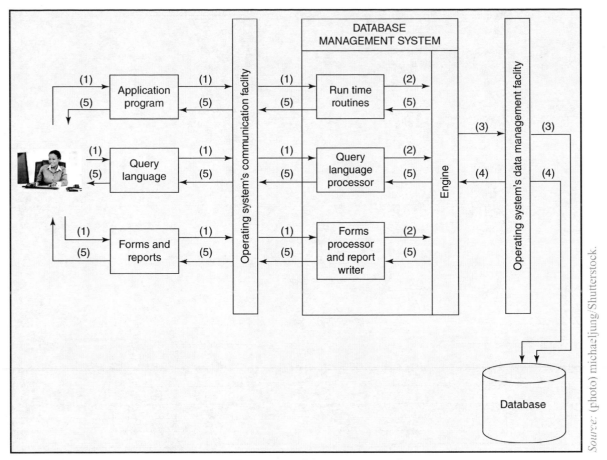

EXHIBIT 12.5 Data Request in a Database Management System

4. The operating system brings the data into the computer's random access memory where the database management system engine processes the data request according to the instructions from the application programs, query language, forms, or reports. Then, the database management system engine again works with the computer's operating system to store the data back in a physical location in the database.

5. The database management system engine sends the requested data to the user through the communication facility of the computer's operating system.

Database Architecture

A framework that is helpful for discussing different aspects of a database is its architecture. The literal meaning of architecture is the style of a building, the qualities that distinguish a building of one time, region, or group from that of another. We use the word architecture figuratively in the sense of the architecture of a symphony, the architecture of a molecule, or the architecture of a system. Database architecture, then, is the collection of large-scale qualities that give the database its unique style.

LEARNING OBJECTIVE 5
Distinguish among the three levels of the database architecture.

Logical and Physical Data Structures

The database architecture differentiates between the logical structure and the physical structure of a database. The **logical structure** is the way the data are thought about, or "viewed," by users. Accountants are concerned almost exclusively with the logical structure. The **physical structure** is the way the data are physically stored on storage devices. The physical structure of the database is of concern to information technology specialists. These two structures can be better understood in the context of the three levels of the database architecture: the external level, the conceptual level, and the internal level. The

Logical structure The way data are thought about, or "viewed," by users.

Physical structure The way the data are physically stored on storage devices.

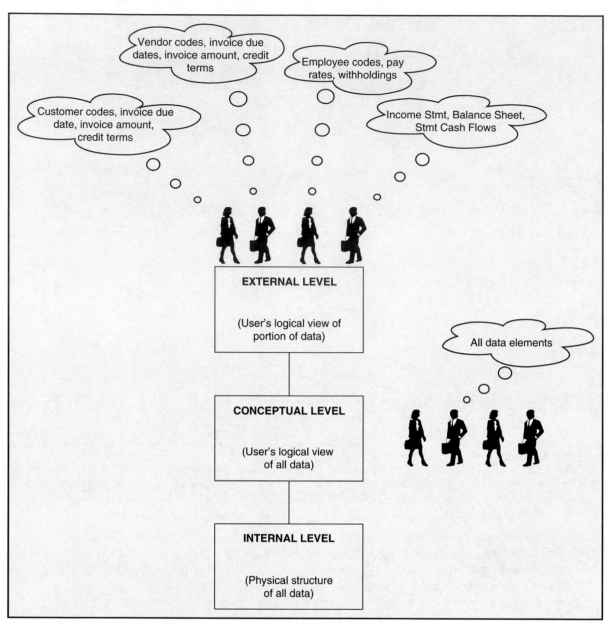

EXHIBIT 12.6 Three-Level Architecture of a Database

external and conceptual levels in the architecture correspond to the logical view, or logical structure, of the data. The internal level represents the physical view, or physical structure, of the data. These levels are depicted in **Exhibit 12.6** and explained below.

External Level

The external level is the way the data elements are viewed logically by individual users. A user generally is interested in only a portion of the entire database. For example, a user in the cash receipts department views the database as a collection of customer codes, customer invoice due dates, customer invoice amounts, and customer credit terms. An employee in cash disbursements views the database as a collection of vendor codes, vendor invoice due dates, vendor invoice amounts, and vendor credit terms. An employee in the payroll department views the database as a collection of employee codes, pay rates, and withholdings. Users of financial statements view the database as a collection of account balances presented in the financial statement formats.

Conceptual Level

The conceptual level is the way all the data in the entire database are viewed logically. The conceptual level supports the external level in that any data available to any user exists in the conceptual level. The conceptual level is the hub for both the external and the internal levels.

Internal Level

The internal level is the physical implementation of the conceptual level. It includes the file organizations used to store data on the physical storage devices. The database management system determines what file organizations are available and then works with the operating system to arrange the data on storage devices and to establish techniques for data retrieval.

Data Relationships

The logical structure of a database consists not only of data elements but also the complex relationships among data elements. A **relationship** is a connection, or interaction, between tables.

These relationships give additional meaning to the data. For example, not only can the typical requests, such as processing transactions and other events, be made, but a special request can be made for the names of all customers who purchased a given inventory item during a specified time period. This special request could be very helpful to a marketing manager who wants to target a marketing campaign for a new inventory item that complements the old inventory item the customer is already buying. As we mentioned earlier in this chapter, data integration is the primary feature of a database that makes it superior to conventional files.

Relationships may exist because of the nature of the data elements themselves, for example, the relationship between customer code and name. Or they may exist because of the need to relate information in the database in some prescribed manner, for example, the need to relate customers to their invoices. The possibilities depend on how one record in one table can relate to another record, or records, in another table and are as follows:

- One-to-one relationship
- One-to-many relationship (and the reverse—many-to-one)
- Many-to-many relationship.

LEARNING OBJECTIVE 6
Determine the different forms of relationships in a database.

Relationship A connection, or interaction, between tables in a database. These relationships give additional meaning to the data.

One-to-One Relationship

In a **one-to-one relationship** one record in the first table matches only one record in the second table, and one record in the second table matches only one record in the first table. A one-to-one relationship is written as 1:1 and exists, for example, between manager and department, because a manager can manage only one department, and one department can be managed by only one manager. This relationship would be implemented as shown in the tables below.[1]

One-to-one relationship A relationship in a database in which one record in the first table matches only one record in the second table, and one record in the second table matches only one record in the first table.

Manager Table

Mgr. Code	Last Name
E400	Lanier
E410	Temple
E420	Gonzales
E430	Hodge

Department Table

Dept. Code	Name	Mgr. Code
D03	Marketing	E410
D04	Accounting	E430
D08	Manufacturing	E400
D11	Finance	E420

One record in the manager table matches only one record in the department table, and one record in the department table matches only one record in the manager table.

Consider, for example, the record for manager code E400 in the manager table. This record matches only one record in the department table. If you look at all the records in the department table, you will find manager code E400 in only one record. Now, look at the record in the department table for department code D03 and manager E410. This record matches only one record in the manager table. If you look at all the records in the manager table, you will find manager code E410 in only one record.

You may wonder at this point why we would not simply combine all the data into one table and store the one table. The reason is that the ability to disaggregate data and then combine it in various ways is the characteristic that gives a database management system its flexibility to meet the needs of different users.

One-to-Many Relationship

One-to-many relationship A relationship in a database in which one record in the first table matches many records in the second table, but one record in the second table matches only one record in the first table.

In a **one-to-many relationship**, one record in the first table matches many records in the second table, *but* one record in the second table matches only one record in the first table. A one-to-many relationship is written as 1:* and exists, for example, between customers and invoices. One customer can have many invoices, and many invoices can belong to one customer. This relationship would be implemented as shown in the tables below.

Customer Table

Customer Code	Name	City
C100	Aberdeen Park	San Antonio
C200	Allen	Dallas

Invoice Table

Invoice Number	Invoice Date	Customer Code
I00022	6/30/18	C100
I00023	6/30/18	C200
I00024	7/01/18	C100
I00025	7/01/18	C200

One record in the customer table matches many records in the invoice table, but one record in the invoice table matches only one record in the customer table. Consider, for example, the record for customer code C100 in the customer table. This record matches two records in the invoice table. If you consider the record for invoice number I00022 with customer code C100 in the invoice table, you will see that it matches only one record in the customer table.

A one-to-many relationship has a distinction that is not present in a one-to-one or many-to-many relationship (defined in the next section). A one-to-many relationship is asymmetrical, so to speak, whereas the other two types of relationships are symmetrical. When we look at the relationship from the first table (customer table in this example) to the second table (invoice table), *one record* in the first table matches *many records* in the second table. However, when we view the relationship from the second table to the first table, *one record* in the second table matches only *one record* in the first table. You will recall that we do not have a difference in the relationship from the first table to the second table versus the second table to the first table in a one-to-one relationship. In that case, *one record* in the first table matches *one record* in the second table *and one record* in the second table matches *one record* in the first table. You will notice as you study a many-to-many relationship that we have the same relationship from the first table to the second table and from the second table to the first table. It is only in the one-to-many relationship that a difference occurs.

Many-to-many relationship A relationship in a database in which one record in the first table can match many records in the second table, and one record in the second table can match many records in the first table.

Many-to-Many Relationship

In a **many-to-many relationship**, one record in the first table can match many records in the second table, *and* one record in the second table can match many records in the first table. A many-to-many relationship is written as *:* and exists, for example, between customers and merchandise inventory. One customer can purchase many products, and one product can be purchased by many customers. For example, the customer Aberdeen Park could purchase both pool treatment and rope-20´, and so could the customer Allen. In the same way, pool treatment could be purchased by both Aberdeen Park and Allen, and so could rope-20´. One record in the customer table can match many records in the inventory table, *and* one record in the inventory table can match many records in the customer table.

In database implementation, a many-to-many relationship is broken down into two one-to-many relationships. Therefore, to implement the many-to-many relationship between customer and inventory, a connecting, or bridge, table called the customer-inventory table is created so that customer and customer-inventory have a one-to-many relationship, and inventory and customer-inventory have a one-to-many relationship.

Customer-Inventory Table

Customer Code	Product No.	Quantity Sold
C100	P1050	600
C100	P1080	12
C200	P1050	400
C200	P1080	6

Customer Table

Customer Code	Name	City
C100	Aberdeen Park	San Antonio
C200	Allen	Dallas

Inventory Table

Product No.	Description	Sales Price
P1050	Pool Trtmnt	$ 1.60
P1080	Rope—20´	60.00

The record for customer code C100 in the customer table matches two records in the customer-inventory table. One record in the customer-inventory table, for example, the first record for C100, matches only one record in the customer table. The same one-to-many relationships exist in the inventory table and the customer-inventory table.

Schemas and Subschemas

Schemas exist at all three levels in the database architecture: the external, conceptual, and internal levels. A **schema** defines:

- The logical view of the data if the schema is at the external level or the conceptual level and the physical view of the data if the schema is at the internal level
- The relationships among the data
- The domains for the data elements
- The business rules that apply to the data.

The **conceptual schema** is for the entire database and is at the conceptual level of the database architecture. The **external subschema** is a subset of the conceptual schema that is required by a particular application program or user and is at the external level of the database architecture. The **internal schema** describes how the conceptual schema is implemented physically. It specifies how data are stored at the level of stored records, stored record formats, indexes, hashing algorithms, pointers, block sizes, and storage media. The internal schema depicts the internal level of the database architecture.

Schema A definition of the logical view of the data in a database if the schema is at the external level or the conceptual level, or the physical view of the data if the schema is at the internal level, the relationships among the data, the domains for the data elements, and the business rules that apply to the data.

Conceptual schema The schema for the entire database and is at the conceptual level of the database architecture.

External subschema A subset of the conceptual schema that is required by a particular application program or user and is at the external level of the database architecture.

LEARNING OBJECTIVE 7
Define a database schema and subschema.

Internal schema A description of how the conceptual schema of a database is implemented physically. It specifies how data are stored at the level of stored records, stored record formats, indexes, hashing algorithms, pointers, block sizes, and storage media. The internal schema depicts the internal level of the database architecture.

Mapping The process of making a data element in one schema correspond to an element in another schema. Mapping is done at two levels. (1) between the external and conceptual levels and (2) between the conceptual and internal levels.

Data definition language (DDL) Software subroutines in a database management system that are used to define the external and conceptual schema.

Domain A set of all possible values a data element can have.

Business rules Constraints on business activities that can be enforced by the database or application programs.

Data dictionary A special file, stored in the database itself, that provides metadata on the name, description, length, type, source, use, and location of each data element stored in the database. The data dictionary also discloses whether a data element is the primary key of a record.

LEARNING OBJECTIVE 8
Summarize the functions of a data dictionary.

The database management system is responsible for mapping among the conceptual, external, and internal schemas. **Mapping** is the process of making a data element in one schema correspond to an element in another schema. Mapping is done at two levels: (1) between the external and conceptual levels and (2) between the conceptual and internal levels. You may want to review Exhibit 12.6. The conceptual/internal mapping defines the correspondence between the conceptual view and the stored database. If a change is made to the storage structure, then the conceptual/internal mapping also must be changed. This isolates the effects of such changes to below the conceptual level to maintain program and data independence, that is, the independence of the application programs from the physical structure of the data. The external/conceptual mapping defines the correspondence between a particular external view and the conceptual view.

When implementing a database, the external and conceptual schemas are defined using software subroutines of the database management system product. Although terminology differs among various database management system programs, these subroutines are called **data definition language (DDL)**. Some database management system products provide a graphical interface for this task.

Domain is a set of all possible values a data element can have. For example, it could be specified that quantity sold can be between 1 and 9999. Date hired can be from January 1, 2015, through December 31, 2019. **Business rules** are constraints on business activities that can be enforced by the database or application programs. A constraint that can be enforced by a database would be the value of the data elements. For example, an edit rule would enforce that one particular data element must have four digits and begin with the number 1 if for department one or begin with the number 2 if for department two.

Data Dictionary

A **data dictionary** is a special file, stored in the database itself, which provides metadata on the data elements stored in the database. The data dictionary documents the design of the database. **Exhibit 12.7** illustrates a portion of a sample data dictionary describing the data element named CustCode.

The dictionary shows the data element's name, description, length, type, the source of the data element's value, the application programs that use the data element, the records where the data element is found, and whether or not the data element is a primary key, which is defined later in this chapter. If a data element is calculated from other data elements, for example, extended amount is calculated by multiplying quantity sold by unit sales price, the calculation would be given as the source. The data type for customer code

Data Element Name	Description	Length	Type	Source	
CustCode	Code that uniquely identifies each customer	5	Alphanumeric	Customer code listing	(*record continues*)

Application Programs That Use	Records Where Found (Relationships)	Primary Key
Update open sales order file	Open sales order	
Record sale transactions	Sale transaction	
Update open sales invoice	Open sales invoice	
Update customer master file	Customer	Yes
Record cash receipt transactions	Cash receipt transaction	

EXHIBIT 12.7 Portion of a Sample Data Dictionary

is alphanumeric meaning a combination of letters of the alphabet and numbers. Other data types are currency, number, text, and date. Currency and number data types should also indicate the number of decimal places in the number, for example, currency (2) or number (0). Other information that may be in a data dictionary includes outputs in which the data element appears, frequency of use, and which users are authorized to change the data elements. The same information would be provided for every data element in the database.

The database management system checks the data dictionary to enforce standard data element definitions every time the database is accessed and is involved in information processing. For example, the data dictionary would not allow a customer code to be entered if it exceeded its specified field length. A data dictionary may be queried like any other table to ascertain, for example, the effects of a change in the database structure. The data dictionary may provide security information by recording each access to the database. This feature allows usage statistics to be collected and attempted security violations to be identified.

In an active data dictionary, changes to the information about data elements are made automatically by the software whenever changes are made in the database structure. For example, the data dictionary would examine the statements entered to create schema and subschema definitions. It would extract the data and data relationships defined and store these relationships. A passive data dictionary, on the other hand, has to be updated separately to keep it current.

Database Administrator

When a database is used, the data reside in one or a few locations within an organization and are used simultaneously by many people. The centralization of data and the complexity of the database environment create the need for specialized management. Therefore, most medium and large organizations have established the position of **database administrator (DBA)** who is responsible for planning, organizing, and maintaining the database to satisfy users' needs. The DBA typically is supported by a staff.

The preferred position of the DBA in the organizational structure is a staff position to the director of information services. A staff position for the DBA provides a global perspective of all the information systems in an organization and gives the DBA the authority to enforce the standards developed for the database. The recommended position of the DBA is shown in the example of a functional organizational chart in **Exhibit 12.8**.[2]

Planning and organizing a database combines the DBA's knowledge of the organization's goals with technical knowledge of database systems. The DBA participates in the

LEARNING OBJECTIVE 9
Explain the functions of a database administrator.

Database administrator (DBA) An employee who is responsible for planning, organizing, and maintaining the database to satisfy users' needs.

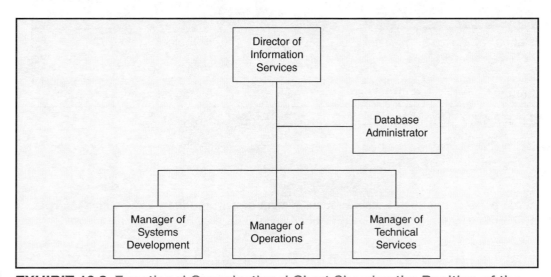

EXHIBIT 12.8 Functional Organizational Chart Showing the Position of the Database Administrator

preliminary planning for a database, selects the database management system product, creates the structure of the database, and loads the data into the database. To implement the database, the DBA defines the schemas and mappings using the database management system product's data definition language or a graphical interface provided for this purpose. Loading the data into the database generally is done with the assistance of a database management system utility program.

The DBA creates the data dictionary and develops standards for the database. Users who enter data must make certain the data conform to a standard format. A standard for telephone number, for example, could be ten characters (##########). Therefore, a twelve-character (###.###.####) or other format would not be accepted. Standardized naming conventions are designed to ensure that one name is not given to more than one data element. For example, the customer's code would always be CustCode; CustNo would not be accepted. The DBA is responsible for developing application program standards so the instructions conform to database access restrictions and to names for data elements.

The DBA develops operating procedures for efficient running of the database, such as establishing procedures for logging transactions and other events, making backups, recovering data in the event of loss or damage, and maintaining data security.[3] Also, the DBA monitors performance of the database by collecting and analyzing statistics, such as run time for applications and makes adjustments to the database when necessary.

Relational Database Model

Most contemporary databases are based on the relational model. The relational model is easy to build and permits data relationships to be defined on an ad hoc basis, making it very flexible. Its operational power and simplicity enable nontechnical users to retrieve data without the help of an application developer, and users can build and implement relational databases.

The relational model is an application of the mathematical framework of set theory and has emerged largely as the result of the work of the mathematician E. F. Codd. It is supported by relational algebra and calculus. Fortunately, an understanding of the mathematics involved is not required to use the model. Codd's formal model uses the terms relation, tuple (which rhymes with "couple"), and attribute, but in practice other words are often used to mean the same things. **Exhibit 12.9** shows how the terms are used:

Codd's Formal Model	Information Technology Specialists	Users
Relation*	File	Table
Tuple	Record	Row
Attribute	Field	Data element or column

EXHIBIT 12.9 Interchangeable Relational Model Terms

*Do not confuse relation with relationship. A relation is a table. A relationship is an association among tables, rows, and data elements.

Some popular relational database management system products are Oracle, MySQL, Microsoft SQL Server, and Microsoft Access.

Components of a Relational Database

LEARNING OBJECTIVE 10
Define the components of a relational database.

As mentioned earlier in this chapter, recently developed accounting systems use database technology. At this point, we can expand this statement to say that the model used for these accounting systems is the relational model. In this section, we discuss some important components of a relational database.

Tables

In the relational model, data are perceived by the user to be arranged in simple tables with rows and columns. An important feature of the tables in a relational database is that the tables can be related to one another. The tables give users the illusion of distinct files.

Primary Keys

Each table in a relational database consists of records comprised of a primary key and related (nonkey) data elements. A **primary key** is one or a group of data elements that uniquely identifies a record. The primary key may be a single data element, in which case it is called a **simple key**. Alternatively, the key may be the combination of two or more data elements, in which case it is called a **composite key, compound key,** or **concatenated key**. To assign the primary key, we need to determine which data element or group of data elements would make each individual record in a table different from all the other records in the table. No other record in the table would have the same value for that particular data element, or in the case of a composite key the same values for the data elements. The convention we use in this book is to denote the name of the primary key for a table with capital letters. In the following table we have two customers:

Primary key One or a group of data elements that uniquely identify a record.

Simple key A primary key that is a single data element.

Composite key (compound key, concatenated key) A primary key that is the combination of two or more data elements.

Compound key See composite key.

Concatenated key See composite key.

Customer Table

CUSTCODE	Name	City
C100	Aberdeen Park	San Antonio
C200	Allen	Dallas

We use only two customers to simplify the example. An organization would have many more, perhaps thousands, and the file would store more data about each customer, such as current balance, credit limit, credit terms, type of customer (wholesale or retail), and tax code (taxable or nontaxable). Also, the customer's address would be broken down into separate data elements for street, city, state, and zip code. The data element CustCode, which is an internally assigned sequential number, uniquely identifies each record in the table so it would serve as the primary key. Although Name or City would also uniquely identify these records as the table stands now, the table of customers may grow, and it would be possible to have more than one customer with the same name or in the same city.

An example of when a composite key would be necessary can be shown with this table:

Invoice Line Table

INVNO	PRODNO	Qty
I00022	P1050	600
I00022	P1080	12
I00023	P1100	1
I00023	P1130	2
I00023	P1050	400
I00024	P1130	3

INVNO alone will not uniquely identify a record in this table because frequently more than one record has the same invoice number due to the fact that one invoice can have multiple lines. The same can be said for PRODNO because one product can appear on many invoices. Although Qty (quantity sold) happens to be unique in our small table, in reality this would not be the case. Therefore, it is necessary to use the combination of INVNO and PRODNO to uniquely identify each record. For example, consider the composite key of the first record, which is I00022/P1050. No other record in the table has these same values for the composite key.

Index Keys

A word of caution needs to be said regarding confusion that arises in the use of the word "key." We have explained the use of a key as a unique identifier that must be assigned when tables are designed. This particular key is called a primary key. However, when a database is implemented, another type of key, called an index key, comes into play. An **index key** is a data element on which the database management system builds an index file, which was explained earlier in this chapter (see Exhibit 12.3) to improve the performance of the database. Whereas primary keys are unique, index keys may or may not be unique. Consider the Customer Table with the three data elements—customer code, customer name, and city. When implementing a database, we could designate customer name and city as index keys. The result would be that our customer data file would have two auxiliary index files. One index file would be maintained in alphabetical order of customer name and one in alphabetical order of city. For clarity, either primary key or logical key is used to refer to the data element that is a unique identifier, and either index key or physical key is used to refer to the data element on which an index is built.

> **Index key** A data element on which the database management system builds an index file to improve the performance of the database.

You may wonder why every data element should not be an index key. The reason is that this practice would overly burden the system. Because index files are maintained in order, every time a record is added or deleted in the data file, the system has to also update the index files that are affected. And remember, you can always sort on any data element; it will just be quicker if an index file has been established. Therefore, it is best to reserve indexes for only frequently recurring sorting and retrieving tasks.

Foreign Keys

As mentioned earlier, tables in a database can have 1:1, 1:*, or *:* relationships. These relationships are built by joining, or connecting, tables using a single, common data element that appears in the tables being joined. This characteristic of a database brings up another new term—foreign key. A **foreign key** is the primary key of a table that is placed in another table so the tables can be joined. The rules for placing foreign keys in tables are as follows:

> **Foreign key** The primary key of a table that is placed in another table so the tables can be joined.

- In a one-to-one relationship, it generally does not matter in which table the foreign key is placed.
- In a one-to-many relationship, the foreign key must be placed in the table of the many side of the relationship.
- In a many-to-many relationship, a connecting table must be created to break the relationship into two one-to-many relationships so the above rule for that relationship applies.

Earlier in this chapter we used manager and department tables in a relational database to demonstrate data relationships. The tables for that one-to-one relationship are repeated here.

Manager Table

MGRCODE	LName
E400	Lanier
E410	Temple
E420	Gonzales
E430	Hodge

Department Table

DEPTCODE	Name	*MgrCode*
D03	Marketing	E410
D04	Accounting	E430
D08	Manufacturing	E400
D11	Finance	E420

MGRCODE is the primary key of the manager table, and DEPTCODE is the primary key of the department table. The relationship between the two tables is created by placing the primary key of the manager table as a foreign key in the department table. The convention we use in this book is to denote the foreign key in a table with italicized print. It would have worked just as well to place the primary key of the department table (DEPTCODE) as a foreign key in the manager table.

A one-to-many relationship is shown in the customer and invoice tables below. In this relationship, the primary key of the customer table CUSTCODE, is placed as a foreign key in the invoice table, the many side of the relationship.

Customer Table

CUSTCODE	Name	City
C100	Aberdeen Park	San Antonio
C200	Allen	Dallas

Invoice Table

INVNO	InvDate	*CustCode*
I00022	6/30/18	C100
I00023	6/30/18	C200
I00024	7/01/18	C100
I00025	7/01/18	C200

Note that the one-to-many relationship will not work as efficiently if we place the primary key of the invoice table as a foreign key in the customer table. If we were to add a column to the customer table for invoice number, we could, for example, put in I00022 for C100. But where would we put I00024, which also belongs to C100? Any means we devise to add I00024 to the customer table will not be as efficient as placing the primary key of the customer table as a foreign key in the invoice table.

Relational Operations

To understand how the relational operations work, imagine yourself with several tables of data printed on sheets of paper, a pair of scissors, and a glue stick. First, you make copies of the tables, called the source tables, so you can leave the original tables intact. Using the copies, you "cut and paste" rows and columns of data to create a new table that contains only the data you are interested in. This is the way that operations work. They display (not store) new tables containing only the information you want. The common operations performed on tables in an accounting system include the following:

LEARNING OBJECTIVE 12
Explain how relational operations display new tables.

- Selection
- Projection

- Join
- Union
- Intersection
- Difference

Selection and projection are used on one source table whereas the last four operations are used on two source tables. Illustrations of using selection and projection individually and in combination are based on the following source table, which is a customer table. For simplicity, we will assume our table has only three columns, or data elements.

Customer Table

CUSTCODE	Name	CurrentBal
C200	Leeds Hotel	4,500
C210	Franklin Resorts	0
C220	Lee	6,200
C230	Manchester Camp	2,900

Selection

Selection displays a new table with only the desired rows from a single source table whose columns meet prescribed conditions. The new table will have fewer rows than the source table but the same number of columns. A request for customers whose current balance is more than $4,000 will produce the following new table:

CUSTCODE	Name	CurrentBal
C200	Leeds Hotel	4,500
C220	Lee	6,200

Projection

Projection displays a new table with only the desired columns from a single source table. The new table will have fewer columns than the source table but the same number of rows. A request for the names of all customers and their current balances will produce the following new table:

Name	CurrentBal
Leeds Hotel	4,500
Franklin Resorts	0
Lee	6.200
Manchester Camp	2,900

Selection and Projection

Selection and projection used in combination display a new table with only the desired columns of the desired rows from a single source table. The new table will have both fewer columns and rows than are in the single source table. A request for the name of the customer and the customer's current balance if the current balance is more than $4,000 will display the following new table:

Name	CurrentBal
Leeds Hotel	4,500
Lee	6,200

Join

Join is the operation that materializes the 1:1, 1:*, or *:* relationships between tables. Join displays a new table from two source tables that have different columns except for one column that is the same. This same column is the primary key in one table and the foreign key in another table. The new table is based on a match of the common column in the two source tables. The new table is wider than either of the two source tables because it contains all the columns from both source tables. Join is probably the most frequently used operation in accounting systems. Suppose we have the two following source tables (invoice and customer) and we want to join every customer name with the customer's outstanding invoice or invoices:

Invoice Table

INVOICENO	CustCode
I00050	C220
I00051	C230
I00052	C200

Customer Table

CUSTCODE	Name
C200	Leeds Hotel
C210	Franklin Resorts
C220	Lee
C230	Manchester Camp

The program will take the first record in the invoice table and look for a match on Cust-Code C220 in the customer table. When a match is found, the rows of the invoice table and the customer table are combined to create a new record in a new table. Then, the program takes the second record in the invoice table and looks for a match on CustCode C230 in the customer table, and so forth. The new table is below:

INVOICENO	CustCode	Name
I00050	C220	Lee
I00051	C230	Manchester Camp
I00052	C200	Leeds Hotel

Union

For the next three operations—union, intersection, and difference—to work, the tables must be "union" compatible. This means that each table must have the same number of columns, and the corresponding columns must come from the same domain. The illustrations for these three operations will be performed on the following two source tables (credit card customer and savings account customer tables):

Credit Card Customer Table

CUSTCODE	CustName
C200	East Bank
C210	St. Agnes Hospital
C220	Spark Manufacturing
C230	National Petroleum

Savings Account Customer Table

CUSTCODE	CustName
C190	West Bank
C202	St. William Hospital
C220	Spark Manufacturing
C230	National Petroleum

Union displays a new table from two source tables that have the same columns. The new table most likely will be longer than either of the two source tables because it will contain all the rows from both source tables; however, duplicate rows will be eliminated. The new table will contain the same columns. A request for all customers, whether credit card, savings account, or both, will display the following new table:

CUSTCODE	CustName
C200	East Bank
C210	St. Agnes Hospital
C220	Spark Manufacturing
C230	National Petroleum
C190	West Bank
C202	St. William Hospital

Intersection

Intersection also displays a new table from two source tables that have the same columns. The new table most likely will be shorter than either of the two source tables because it will contain only those rows that exist in exactly the same way in both source tables. The new table will have the same columns as are in the two source tables. A request for customers who are both credit card and savings account customers will display the following new table:

CUSTCODE	CustName
C220	Spark Manufacturing
C230	National Petroleum

Difference

Difference also displays a new table from two source tables that have the same columns. The new table most likely is shorter than either of the two source tables because it contains only rows occurring in the first source table but not in the second source table.

A request for customers who are credit card customers but are not also savings account customers will display the following new table:

CUSTCODE	CustName
C200	East Bank
C210	St. Agnes Hospital

Imagine how helpful this new table would be for a bank that wants to develop new savings account customers!

Queries and Outputs

The tables in a relational database, if designed properly, will provide all the information needed to create and print documents, such as a sales (customer) invoice, financial statements, and all other types of output needed by the users of the accounting system whether planned in advance or requested on the spur of the moment. For example, assume that we want to create and print the invoice in **Exhibit 12.10**:

LEARNING OBJECTIVE 12
Explain how queries are used to generate output from a relational database.

Invoice

Aca Pool Co.
2700 Bay Area Blvd.
Clear Lake City, TX 77058-1098
Tel: (713) 555-1234
Fax: (713) 555-1235

Invoice Number: I00022

Date: 6/30/18

Customer Code: C100

Customer Name and Address:
Aberdeen Pk
San Antonio

Sales Representative: Ted Marks

PRODUCT NO.	QUANTITY	DESCRIPTION	UNIT PRICE	EXTENDED AMOUNT
P1050	600	Pool Trtmnt	$1.60	$960.00
P1080	12	Rope-20'	$60.00	$720.00
			TOTAL DUE	$1,680.00

THANK YOU FOR YOUR ORDER!

EXHIBIT 12.10 Sales (Customer) Invoice

Also assume that our database contains the tables in **Exhibit 12.11**.[4] The sales invoice can be printed from these tables. Please take a few minutes to look at the first record in the invoice table to see that the invoice number and the invoice date from that table appear on the sales invoice in Exhibit 12.10. Next, note that employee code and customer code in the

INVOICE TABLE

INVNO	InvDate	EmpCode	CustCode
I00022	6/30/18	E021	C100
I00023	6/30/18	E021	C200
I00024	7/01/18	E022	C100
I00025	7/01/18	E023	C300
I00026	7/01/18	E023	C400

INVOICE LINE TABLE

INVNO	PRODNO	Qty
I00022	P1050	600
I00022	P1080	12
I00023	P1050	400
I00023	P1100	1
I00023	P1130	2
I00024	P1130	3
I00025	P1080	10
I00025	P1130	5
I00026	P1100	3

INVENTORY TABLE

PRODNO	Desc	Price
P1050	Pool Trtmnt	1.60
P1080	Rope-20'	60.00
P1100	Table/Umb	1,050.00
P1130	Lounger	80.00

EMPLOYEE TABLE

EMPCODE	EmpName	CommRate
E021	Ted Marks	.06
E022	Reji Geer	.06
E023	Judy Clark	.06

CUSTOMER TABLE

CUSTCODE	Name	City
C100	Aberdeen Park	San Antonio
C200	Allen	Dallas
C300	Scamell	Orlando
C400	Allen	Aubum

EXHIBIT 12.11 Tables in Relational Database

Virtual data element A data element that is not stored in a database but instead is calculated on demand from other data elements that are stored in the database.

invoice table are foreign keys (denoted by italicized print) so are used to connect to other tables to retrieve information for the sales invoice. The lines on the invoice come from the invoice line table and the connection from the invoice line table to the inventory table. You may note, however, that the two extended amounts that are on the sales invoice are not in the tables. The reason is that extended amount can be derived from quantity sold and unit sales price, which are stored in the database tables. Data elements that are not stored in a database but instead are calculated on demand from other data elements that are stored in the database are called **virtual data elements**.

To be able to print the invoice we would first need to create and run a query that joins the tables in Exhibit 12.11 and then multiplies the quantity of each product sold by its selling price. In these queries we use the relational operations, such as selection, projection, and join. Next, we would use the report facility of the database management system to design an invoice that looks like the one in Exhibit 12.10. The invoice would be populated with the result of the query and data elements from the various tables that should appear on the invoice. The invoice design would take care of totaling the amounts for total due.

We can also generate the financial statements by designing queries and reports. For example, to calculate the amount of sales to go on the income statement, a query would multiply the quantity of each product sold in the invoice line table by its selling price in the inventory table and sum the amounts for a particular time period. A report would be created for the income statement and would include the result of this query. To calculate the accounts receivable amount for the balance sheet, some of the tables in Exhibit 12.11 plus other tables in the database would have to be queried. Specifically, cash receipts transactions, or events, would be recorded in tables in such a way that cash receipts could be matched with invoices. The total of the invoices for which no cash receipts were matched would equal the accounts receivable amount. A report would be created for the balance sheet and would include this amount.

An important feature of a relational database management system is that it not only can perform the typical accounting system functions such as recording and processing transactions and other events and producing output, such as invoices and financial statements, but the data stored in the database can be retrieved in any combination that we need, when we need it. For example, if we need to know which customers were sold which products in June, we could query the database tables in Exhibit 12.11 by using SQL. The fundamental structure of SQL statements is SELECT, FROM, WHERE. Do not confuse SELECT with the relational operation selection. SELECT is a SQL verb used to perform projection, selection, and other actions. Selection, on the other hand, is the operation of obtaining a subset of rows from a table. The query, that is, which customers were sold which products, would be written in SQL as follows:

SELECT	Name, Desc
FROM	Invoice, InvoiceLine, Inventory, Customer
WHERE	InvDate BETWEEN 06/01/18 and 06/30/18
	AND Invoice.InvNo¼InvoiceLine.InvNo
	AND Invoice.CustCode¼Customer.CustCode
	AND InvoiceLine.ProdNo¼Inventory.ProdNo
ORDER BY	Name

SELECT specifies the table columns—a projection operation. In our above query, we specify that we want to retrieve the name (which is in the customer table) and the description (which is in the inventory table). FROM specifies the tables that need to be searched to satisfy this query. In our query we need the four tables—Invoice, InvoiceLine, Inventory, and Customer. WHERE specifies the conditions of the query. Several conditions can be expressed in a WHERE clause. In our query we have four conditions. The first condition is that the invoice dates should fall between June 1, 2018, and June 30, 2018 (a selection operation). Another condition is that the invoice and invoice line tables need to be joined on invoice number (a join operation). The third condition is that the invoice and customer tables need to be joined on customer code (another join operation). The fourth condition is that the invoice line and inventory tables need to be joined on product number (another join operation). In the lines that begin with AND, the word before the period is the name of the table, and the word after the period is the name of the data element. ORDER BY will order the query's result by the customers' names.

Assume that the five invoices in our invoice table are the only sales for the months of June and July. The result of our query for which customers were sold which products in June is:

Name	Description
Aberdeen Park	Pool trtmnt
Aberdeen Park	Rope-20'
Allen	Table/Umb
Allen	Lounger
Allen	Pool trtmnt

In our example, we had only two sale transactions in June so we could have easily retrieved this information manually. But imagine how helpful this query function would be for a business with hundreds, thousands, or millions of transactions and other events!

The result of every query is a new table even if the result is a single number. In this case, the table would have one row and one column.

A second way (other than using SQL) that a user can query a database is to use a database management system feature called query by example. This is a graphical interface that allows users to enter what information they are looking for. The database management system's query facility constructs the appropriate SQL statements to send to the database engine.

Association Between Tables and Files

LEARNING OBJECTIVE 13
Explain the association between database tables and files.

Accountants often speak of files instead of database tables because a file is our logical view of the data in the database. We visualize the data in terms of the four types of files mentioned in Chapter 3—reference file, open file, transaction file, and master file. Sometimes one database table comprises one file, and sometimes it takes more than one database table to comprise the logical file. For example, in Chapter 3 we illustrated several files. We said the sale transaction file was actually made up of two files as follows:

Sale Transaction File 1:

Invoice No.	Invoice Date	Customer Code	Cash/Credit Sales	Sale Order No.
I00022	6/30/18	C100	2	S0585

Sale Transaction File 2:

Invoice No.	Product No.	Quantity Shipped/ Delivered
I00022	P1050	600
I00022	P1080	12

The first *file* corresponds to the invoice *table* in Exhibit 12.11. The second *file* corresponds to the invoice line *table* in Exhibit 12.11. Any differences in the file and the tables are caused by omitting or including certain data elements to keep the illustrations simple yet make points that are important to each chapter's topics.

Another file that was illustrated in Chapter 3 was the following customer master file:

Customer Code	Name	Address	Credit Limit	Credit Terms	Tax Code	Amount Owing
C100	Aberdeen Park	San Antonio, TX	50,000	2/10, net 30	E	1,680
C200	G. H. Allen	Dallas, TX	50,000	2/10, net 30	T1	1,134

This customer master *file* corresponds to the customer *table* in Exhibit 12.11. In the file from Chapter 3, we show the amount owing as being a stored data element rather than a virtual data element. Because this is an amount that is frequently accessed, storing the amount improves response time as opposed to a database query that would have to match the invoices for a desired customer code to the cash receipts for the desired customer code and then total the amounts (which are also virtual data elements) of invoices for which no matches were found.

Assuming that no calculated amounts are stored, the number of on-demand calculations that will have to be made in an accounting system are immense. Therefore, for the sake of fast response, many amounts in accounting systems that could be calculated are, in fact, stored. To illustrate the advantage of storing data elements, consider the preparation of the financial statements. In the previous section of this chapter, we explained how the accounts receivable balance would be calculated by performing several operations on tables. A process similar to this would be involved in determining the current balance of every account that appears on the financial statements. A way to increase response time for retrieving general ledger account balances for the preparation of the financial statements (or for ad hoc queries) is to store all the chart of account balances in the tables that comprise a general ledger master file. These totals would be stored and updated periodically to avoid having to make calculations every time a financial statement is printed or an account balance is retrieved for any other purpose. In Chapter 3, we described the general ledger master file. The file shows only the record for account number 1230, which is accounts receivable.

General Ledger Master File 1:

Account No.	Beginning Balance	Current Balance*
1230	0	2,814

* A positive number denotes a debit balance, and a negative number denotes a credit balance.

General Ledger Master File 2:

Account No.	Debit/Credit Activity*	Date	Explanation
1230	1,680	6/30/18	Credit Sales
1230	1,134	6/30/18	Credit Sales

* Positive numbers are debits, and negative numbers are credits.

File 1 and file 2 are separate tables in a database so the logical general ledger master file is comprised of two tables.

Summary

As the business environment becomes more complex and better information is needed for making good decisions, management is becoming keenly aware of the need to store data for all important business activities and to structure their data so it will be more useful to them. The data in an accounting system must be able to support an organization's operations, mandatory external reporting requirements, and management decision making. Sophisticated computer technology, in general, and databases, in particular, make it possible for accounting systems to achieve this goal. Accounting systems that use a database have several advantages over accounting systems that use conventional files. These advantages include application program and data independence, data quality and security, and programming simplification. With a database the data reside in one or a few locations within an organization and are used simultaneously by many people; therefore, centralized management is required.

The database's architecture has three levels: the external level, the conceptual level, and the internal level. The architecture differentiates between the way users think about, or logically view, the data within a database and the way the data are stored physically. The external level is the way the data are logically viewed by users. A user generally is interested in only a portion of the entire database.

The conceptual level is the way the entire database is logically viewed, and the internal level is the physical storage of the data. Relationships are established among data elements to facilitate data retrieval. Data relationships take the forms of one-to-one, one-to-many, or many-to-many. These relationships are depicted by the database schema and subschemas. The relational database has become very popular and is the foundation for recently developed accounting systems.

Key Terms

Business rules   368
Composite key   371
Compound key   371
Concatenated key   371
Conceptual schema   367
Data definition language (DDL)   368
Data dictionary   368
Database   357
Database administrator (DBA)   369
Database management system (DBMS)   360
Domain   368
External subschema   367
Foreign key   372
Index file   357
Index key   372

Internal schema   367
Legacy systems   355
Logical structure   363
Many-to-many relationship   366
Mapping   368
Metadata   360
One-to-many relationship   366
One-to-one relationship   365
Physical structure   363
Primary key   371
Query language   362
Relationship   365
Schema   367
Simple key   371
Virtual data element   378

Discussion Questions, Problems, and Activity

1. What is an integrated set of computer programs that facilitate the creation, manipulation, and querying of integrated files called?
   a. Compiler
   b. Operating system
   c. Assembly language
   d. Database management system
   [CIA adapted]

2. In the inventory module of an accounting system that uses a database, one stored record contains part number, part name, part color, and part weight. What are these individual items called?
   a. Fields
   b. Stored files
   c. Bytes
   d. Occurrences
   [CIA adapted]

3. A major advantage of using a database management system is the separation of file management tasks from what or whom?
   a. Users
   b. Databases
   c. Job entry subsystems
   d. d. Application programs
   [CIA adapted]

4. The database approach to accounting systems and the resulting concept of database management systems have several unique characteristics not found in

conventional file systems. Which one of the following statements does NOT apply to database systems?

  a. Database systems have data independence, the concept that the data and the programs are maintained separately except during processing.

  b. Database systems contain a data definition language that helps describe each schema and subschema.

  c. The database administrator is the part of the software package that instructs the operating aspects of the program when data are retrieved.

  d. A primary goal of database systems is to minimize data redundancy

[CIA adapted]

5. Which of the following should **not** be the responsibility of a database administrator?

  a. Designing the content and organization of the database.

  b. Developing applications to access the database.

  c. Protecting the database and its software.

  d. Monitoring and improving the efficiency of the database.

[CIA adapted]

6. Describe how a data request is handled by a database management system product. Use Exhibit 12.5 to guide your explanation.

7. Suppose we have the following table for the customer master file in a relational database. Frequently, it is necessary to sort the file in alphabetical order of the customer's name. What can be done to speed up the sorting process? Explain in detail how to implement your solution and how it would work.

Customer Master File

CUSTCODE	CustName	Other Data	CurrentBal
C200	Leeds Hotel		4,500
C210	Franklin Resorts		0
C220	Lee		6,200
C230	Manchester Camp		2,900

8. Morgan Electrical Supplies distributes electrical components to the construction industry. Morgan began as a local supplier 15 years ago and has grown rapidly to become a major competitor in the north central U.S. As the business grew and the variety of components to be stocked expanded, Morgan implemented a computerized inventory system. Other applications, such as accounts receivable, accounts payable, payroll, and sales analysis were gradually computerized as each function expanded. The inventory system, due to its operational importance, has been upgraded to a real-time posting system while all the other applications use batch posting. Over the years, Morgan has developed or acquired more than 100 application programs and maintained 150 files.

Morgan faces stiff competition from local suppliers throughout its marketing area. At a management meeting, the sales manager complained about the difficulty in obtaining immediate, current information to respond to customer inquiries. Other managers stated that they also had difficulty obtaining timely data from the system. As a result, the controller engaged a consulting firm to explore the situation. The consultant recommended installing an accounting system that uses a database, and Morgan proceeded on this course, employing Jack Gibbons as the database administrator.

At a recent management meeting, Gibbons presented an overview of the new accounting system using Exhibit 12.4. Gibbons explained that the database approach assumes an organizational, data-oriented viewpoint, as it recognizes that a centralized database represents a vital resource. Instead of being assigned to applications, data are more appropriately used and managed for the entire organization. The operating system physically moves data to and from storage. The database management system software has a data definition language with which the data structures and characteristics can be specified. As a result, the roles of the application programs and query software and the tasks of the application programmers and users are simplified. Under the database approach, the data are available to all users subject to security restrictions.

Required:

  a. If you were Gibbons and making the presentation to management, how would you describe the basic difference between the old accounting system that uses conventional files and the new one that uses a database?

  b. If you were Gibbons and making the presentation to management, how would you describe at least three advantages and three disadvantages of the new accounting system that uses a database?

  c. Describe the duties and responsibilities of Jack Gibbons, the data administrator.

[CMA adapted]

9. The purchasing process at Beltaine Company includes purchasing goods, receiving the goods, and paying for the goods. Purchase requisitions are submitted by various user departments, indicating the items needed, the quantities needed, and the required delivery schedule. The purchasing department enters the purchase data (including prices taken from the vendor price lists), prints purchase orders, and mails the purchase orders to the respective

vendors. Upon receipt of the goods, the receiving department enters data about quantities of items received and their condition upon arrival and prints a receiving report. After receiving the vendor's invoice, the accounts payable department prepares a check payable to the vendor.

Required:

Construct a data dictionary with fifteen of the required data elements for the purchasing process. Provide an appropriate name, description, length, and data type for each data element.

10. A construction company is creating a database for its job costing and general ledger applications.

Required:

Construct a data dictionary with twenty of the required data elements for the job costing and general ledger applications. Provide an appropriate name, description, length, and data type for each data element.

11. Consider the following two tables:

CUSTOMER CODE (primary key)	Customer Name	Other Data	Current Balance
C200	Leeds Hotel	...	4,500
C210	Franklin Resorts	...	0

SALES ORDER NO. (primary key)	Sales Order Date
SO661	03/15/18
SO662	03/15/18
SO663	03/16/18

Required:

a. What type of relationship do the tables have, that is, a one-to-one, one-to-many, many-to-one, or many-to-many?
b. What do you need to add to one of the tables so the tables can be joined?
c. Where would you place your answer to part b?

12. Consider the following two tables:

DEPARTMENT CODE (primary key)	Department Name	Building	Other Data
D01	Engineering	Delta	...
D02	Accounting	Bayou	...

EQUIPMENT (primary key)	Description	Other Data
EQ100	CopierK36	...
EQ110	FileServer16	...

Required:

a. What type of relationship do the tables have, that is, a one-to-one, one-to-many, many-to-one, or many-to-many?
b. What do you need to add to one of the tables so the tables can be joined?
c. Where would you place your answer to part b?

13. Consider the following vendor master file in a relational database:

Vendor Master File

Vendor Code	Vendor Name	Zip Code	Other Data	Current Balance
V200	Major Pool Supplies	37044	...	9,000
V210	Deakin Pool Supplies	37068	...	600
V220	Coventry Auto Co.	37084	...	4,200
V230	Fennell Chemical Co.	37044	...	3,500

Required:

a. What database operation(s) would you perform on the table if you want to create a new table with just the name of the vendors and their outstanding balances? Draw the new table.
b. What database operation(s) would you perform on the table if you want to create a new table with the name and current balance of the vendors whose current balances are more than $4,000? Draw the new table.

14. Richards Company's accounting system uses a relational database management system. The system includes a customer master file. If a customer has not made a purchase in over 18 months, the customer's record is moved from the active customer master file to the inactive master file. Below are the tables for the customer master files.

Active Customer Master File

Customer Code	Customer Name	Address	Other Data	Current Balance
C20	Baynes	San Francisco	...	2,500
C50	Nash	London	...	5,000
C60	Geoffrey	London	...	3,200

Inactive Customer Master File

Customer Code	Customer Name	Address	Other Data	Current Balance
C10	De Joria	New York	. . .	0
C30	Sangster	London	. . .	0
C40	Wyatt	Milan	. . .	3,000

Required:

Suppose that next week you are going to be in London, England, and want to call on all your company's customers, whether active or inactive, who are located there. What database operations would you perform on the two tables to produce one table with the names of the customers who are located in London? Draw your new table.

15. What is the first word of each line in an SQL query? What do the words specify?

Activity

Create a table for a customer master file in Microsoft Access (refer to Chapter 3 and Chapter 9). Create three fields for your table—customer code, customer name, and customer city. Make up five records. Submit a printout and your Access electronic file.

Notes

1. The way that the relationships are implemented will vary depending on the type of database. For this explanation, we use tables based on the relational data model. The fact that this model is not covered until later in this chapter should not distract from the explanation.
2. A functional organizational chart depicts groupings based on the specific specialties of the units instead of groupings based on, for example, products, projects, or geographic locations. Organizational charts naturally differ according to the size and structure of the organization.
3. A log file is a record of system activity. This file stores information such as the date, time, and user identification codes for all failed and successful attempts to log onto a system; what tables/files, if any, were affected; and what activity occurred, for example, invoked a program or renamed a file. Log files differ widely from system to system depending on the nature of the system.
4. The steps that are taken to develop the tables in a relational database are covered in Chapter 13.

Developing a Relational Database for an Accounting Information System

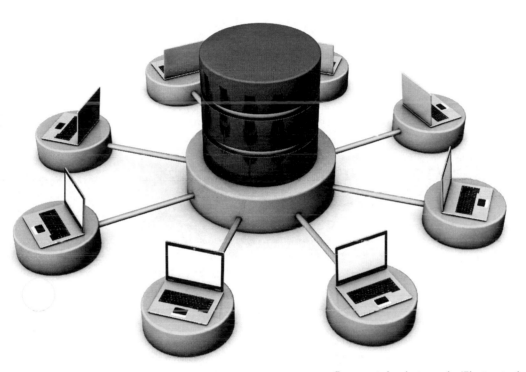

Source: style-photography/Shutterstock.

Chapter Outline

Why Accountants Need to Know About Database Development and Implementation

System Output Approach

REA Framework Approach

Comparison of REA Framework and System Output

Implementing a Database Approach

Learning Objectives

After studying this chapter, you should be able to:

- Perform the steps required to develop a relational database for an accounting system using the system output approach.
- Define events, resources, and agents.
- Define the symbols used in an entity-relationship diagram.
- Perform the steps required to develop a relational database for an accounting system using the REA framework approach.
- Compare the REA framework and system output approaches to developing a database.
- Summarize how a database is implemented.

Source: Pressmaster/Shutterstock.

Introductory Scenario

Chris Hampton, chief information officer of Sabrina Industries, was charged with organizing a task force to develop a new database management system for the company's accounting system. In her master's degree program several years earlier, Hampton had written a thesis on the resource, event, and agent (REA) framework approach to database development. With this background, it was only natural that she would favor this approach when challenged to develop Sabrina's new system. The existing system had been in use for several years and was based on conventional files. Both the hardware and software platforms were becoming costly to maintain. Furthermore, over time the company had grown in size and complexity to the point where information processing was seriously impaired by the present system's limitations.

Hampton always welcomed opportunities to educate her colleagues about developments in information systems technology. At a meeting of the executive committee, she explained to senior managers what the REA framework approach was and how it would result in a database management system that would finally "bring the company into the twenty-first century." In her presentation, Hampton did an excellent job of explaining REA, walking the necessary fine line between talking over people's heads and talking down to them. When she sat down, several senior managers complimented her on the quality of the presentation. Then they asked her to share details of the task force she planned to create.

Hampton explained that because the REA framework focused on business events, her strategy was to organize a task force made up of at least one representative user from each functional area of the company. In addition, accountants, auditors, and information specialists would be on the task force. The accountants and auditors would be instrumental in ensuring that internal and external reporting requirements would be satisfied, that proper internal controls would be designed into the system, and that the system would be auditable.

Introductory Scenario Thought Questions:

1. What does REA stand for and what are the definitions of each term?
2. What are some examples of relationships between entities?
3. What was Chris Hampton's mission, and what was her strategy for fulfilling this mission?

Why Accountants Need to Know about Database Development and Implementation

The details of developing a relational database for an accounting system go far beyond the scope of an accounting information systems course. However, as accountants, whether you become users, auditors, system implementers, or designers, it will be helpful for you to understand some of the issues involved in developing a database even though the primary responsibility for developing it is borne by the system designers. Knowledge of some major issues of database development and familiarity with some of the tools used in developing a database will give you a depth of knowledge that will enable you to perform your duties more effectively and efficiently. For example, you will be able to:

- Locate the data required.
- Filter and extract the data in the combinations required.
- Recognize why the database is or is not providing the data as required.
- Determine what changes need to be made to the database to get the data required.
- Understand why particular data elements are arranged in particular tables.

For an accounting system to be successful, all users, not only accountants but other decision makers throughout the organization, must actively participate in developing the database. For example, marketing managers would need to participate in developing the portion of the database that relates to sales to ensure that the managers will get the data they require. Strong participation of accountants in database development will ensure that accountants will be able to locate and extract data for themselves and for other managers of the organization. Furthermore, this participation will ensure that the system will produce all necessary financial statements, reports, and documents.

The end product of the development process is a set of "normalized" tables that will store the data in the accounting system. These tables comprise the transaction files, master files, open files, and reference files in the accounting system. You saw some normalized tables in the previous chapter in Exhibit 12.11. **Normalized tables** are free of data redundancy and anomalies and, thus, ensure the stability of the database over time. Anomalies are unexpected results that occur during operation of the database. **Insertion anomalies** occur when we attempt to store a value for one data element but cannot because the value of another data element is unknown. **Deletion anomalies** occur when a value for one data element we wish to keep is unexpectedly deleted at the same time that a value of another data element is deleted. Illustrations of these anomalies are presented later in this chapter.

When developing a relational database for an accounting system, one of two approaches can be used:

1. Begin by identifying the contents of the desired system output, such as a report or a document.
2. Begin by identifying the entities (resources, events, and agents) in the organization and their relationships.

The first approach is the one that has traditionally been used and is still widely accepted. The second approach also has many advocates. To establish a frame of reference, we will refer to the first approach as the system output approach and the second as the REA (resources, events, and agents) framework approach.

System Output Approach

The steps required to develop a database using the system output approach are to:

1. Identify and document the system outputs and the contents of the outputs that are required by users. Mockups of the reports and documents serve as documentation of the outputs.[1]
2. Identify and document what data elements need to be stored to produce the output. A list serves as documentation of the necessary data elements.
3. Determine what tables to create and what data elements to put in which tables by using a process called data normalization.
4. Evaluate the tables to determine if additional tables need to be created.
5. Document the tables with a data access diagram.

Normalized tables Database tables that are free of data redundancy and anomalies and, thus, ensure the stability of the database over time.

Insertion anomalies An unexpected result during operation of a database in which a value for one data element cannot be stored because the value of another data element is unknown.

Deletion anomalies An unexpected result during operation of a database in which a value for one data element you wish to keep is unexpectedly deleted at the same time that a value of another data element is deleted.

LEARNING OBJECTIVE 1
Perform the steps required to develop a relational database for an accounting system using the system output approach.

Step 1. Identify and document the system outputs and the contents of the outputs that are required by users.

To demonstrate the system output approach to developing a database, we will assume that an in-depth study of users' needs has revealed that our accounting system needs to produce a sales (customer) invoice for each sale. An example of a sales invoice was shown in Exhibit 3.10 in Chapter 3. (You may want to turn back now and review the contents of the invoice.) Many data elements must be captured about a sale transaction so they can appear on the sales invoice. To simplify this example, we will work with an invoice that contains a minimum amount of information. We will assume that our company is Aca Pool Co. The invoice that we want to be able to produce from our accounting system appears in **Exhibit 13.1**.

Step 2. Identify and document what data elements need to be stored to produce the output.

The following data elements need to be available for each sale transaction so they will appear on the sales invoice:

Invoice number	Product number
Invoice date	Quantity sold
Customer code	Product description
Customer name	Unit sales price
Customer address	Extended amount
Sales representative name	Total due

Invoice	Aca Pool Co.
Invoice Number: Date: Customer Code:	2700 Bay Area Blvd. Clear Lake City, TX 77058-1098 Tel: (713) 555-1234 Fax: (713) 555-1235

Customer Name and Address:	Sales Representative:

PRODUCT NO.	QUANTITY	DESCRIPTION	UNIT PRICE	EXTENDED AMOUNT
			TOTAL DUE	

EXHIBIT 13.1 Sales (Customer) Invoice

The permanent elements of the sales invoice are the title of the document (Invoice), company name (Aca Pool Co.), address, telephone number, fax number, and labels for the various data elements.

Step 3. Determine what tables to create and what data elements to put in which tables by using a process called data normalization.

Conceivably, we could store all of these data elements in one table because we would have recorded all the necessary information about the sale and would have the data we need to produce a sales invoice. However, we will explain why one table would not be appropriate.

Suppose that we have four customers—Aberdeen Park, Allen, Scamell, and Allen. The second Allen customer is a different one from the first Allen customer; they just happen to have the same last names. We make one sale to Aberdeen Park on 6/30/18 for two different products, one sale to the first Allen customer on 6/30/18 for three products, another sale to Aberdeen Park on 7/1/18 for one product, one sale to Scamell on 7/01/18 for two products, and one sale to the second Allen customer on 7/01/18 for one product. If we were to store all of the data elements about the five sales in one table, the table would appear as follows:

Invoice Table (Sale Transaction)—Unnormalized

InvNo	InvDate	Cust Code	Name	City	EmpName	ProdNo	Desc	Price	Qty
I00022	6/30/18	C100	Aberdeen Pk	San Antonio	Ted Marks	P1050	Pool Trtmnt	1.60	600
						P1080	Rope-20'	60.00	12
I00023	6/30/18	C200	Allen	Dallas	Ted Marks	P1050	Pool Trtmnt	1.60	400
						P1100	Table/Umb	1050.00	1
						P1130	Lounger	80.00	
I00024	7/01/18	C100	Aberdeen Pk	San Antonio	Reji Greer	P1130	Lounger	80.00	3
I00025	7/01/18	C300	Scamell	Oriando	Judy Clark	P1080	Rope-20'	60.00	10
						P1130	Lounger	80.00	5
I00026	7/01/18	C400	Allen	Auburn	Judy Clark	P1100	Table/Umb	1050.00	3

Note that it is not necessary to store extended amount and total due because these are virtual data elements (i.e., calculated from other stored data elements). Also note that instead of having a column heading of sales representative name, we use employee name because sales representatives are employees of Aca Pool Co.

The previous table is unnormalized. Some of the data elements (namely, product number, product description, unit sales price, and quantity sold) have multiple values. Invoice number I00022 has two values for product number, two for product description, two for unit sales price, and two for quantity sold. Invoice number I00023 has three values for each of these data elements. Invoice number I00024 has only one value for these data elements, and so forth. Because product number, product description, unit sales price, and quantity sold have multiple values, they are called repeating data elements. On the other hand, invoice number, invoice date, customer code, customer name, customer city, and employee name appear only one time (are not repeating) on each invoice regardless of the number of different products sold to a customer in one sale transaction.

A table in a relational database cannot have multiple values for one cell. To remedy this problem, we could store each repeating value in its own row. If we did this, our table would appear as shown in **Exhibit 13.2**.

InvNo	InvDate	Cust Code	Name	City	EmpName	ProdNo	Desc	Price	Qty
I00022	6/30/18	C100	Aberdeen Pk	San Antonio	Ted Marks	P1050	Pool Trtmnt	1.60	600
I00022	6/30/18	C100	Aberdeen Pk	San Antonio	Ted Marks	P1080	Rope-20'	60.00	12
I00023	6/30/18	C200	Allen	Dallas	Ted Marks	P1050	Pool Trtmnt	1.60	400
I00023	6/30/18	C200	Allen	Dallas	Ted Marks	P1100	Table/Umb	1050.00	1
I00023	6/30/18	C200	Allen	Dallas	Ted Marks	P1130	Lounger	80.00	2
I00024	7/01/18	C100	Aberdeen Pk	San Antonio	Reji Greer	P1130	Lounger	80.00	3
I00025	7/01/18	C300	Scamell	Orlando	Judy Clark	P1080	Rope-20'	60.00	10
I00025	7/01/18	C300	Scamell	Orlando	Judy Clark	P1130	Lounger	80.00	5
I00026	7/01/18	C400	Allen	Auburn	Judy Clark	P1100	Table/Umb	1050.00	3

EXHIBIT 13.2 Invoice Table (Sale Transaction)—Unnormalized

We have eliminated the multiple values for a single cell, but our table exhibits a great deal of data redundancy and this causes several undesirable consequences. For example, if we need to change the description of product number P1050, P1080, or P1100 we would need to change each description two times in this table. A change in the description of product number P1130 would require three changes. Also, if we need to change the city for Aberdeen Park or for Allen (C200), we would need to change each city three times. A change in the city for Scamell would require two changes. In addition to having to make the same change multiple times, there is the risk that the changes will not be made consistently. If you wanted to produce a report about some aspect of pool treatment and in one place it was spelled "Pool Trtmnt" but spelled "Pool Trtmnt" in another, you probably would not get the correct information.

In addition to data redundancy, our table has some anomalies, which are illustrated later. To eliminate the problems of redundancy and anomalies, we need to take the appropriate steps to get the table of data into the proper normal form. Seven normal forms exist; however, normalization beyond the third normal form is necessary only for very specialized applications. Generally, the third normal form is sufficient for accounting applications. Each normal form reduces data redundancy and/or anomalies to a greater extent. In other words, data in the second normal form (2NF) have fewer instances of data redundancy and/or anomalies than data in the first normal form (1NF). Data in the third normal form (3NF) have fewer instances of data redundancy and/or anomalies than data in the second normal form.

The three steps that will normalize data with respect to the third normal form are listed below. Each step converts a table into a higher normal form.

1. Move all repeating data elements to a new table and assign primary keys to the original and new tables. This step converts the data into 1NF.
2. Move all non-key data elements to a new table if they do not depend on, or are not determined by, the entire primary key and assign primary keys to the original and new tables. This step converts the data into 2NF.
3. Move any transitive dependencies to new tables and assign primary keys to the original and new tables. A **transitive dependency** exists when a non-key data element depends on, or is determined by, another non-key data element. In other words, a data element depends on, or is determined by, a data element other than the primary key. This step converts the data into 3NF.

Transitive dependency A situation in a relational database table in which a nonkey data element depends on, or is determined by, another nonkey data element. In other words, an attribute depends on, or is determined by, an attribute other than the primary key.

We will now apply these steps to the data that are in Exhibit 13.2 to get the data into 3NF. As we complete each of these three steps, note we will do the following five substeps:

A. Break tables apart.
B. Determine the type of relationship between the tables, i.e., one-to-one, one-to-many. (These are described in Chapter 12.)

C. Determine the primary key on the "one" side of the relationship.
D. Place the primary key of the "one" side of the relationship as the foreign key on the "many" side of the relationship.
E. Determine the primary key of the "many" side of the relationship.

First Normal Form

A table is in 1NF if the table has no multivalued, or repeating, data elements. If we move the repeating data elements, which we identified earlier, to a new table, the two tables will appear as follows. Because the new table stores those data elements that are found on the *lines* of an invoice, we will name the new table "Invoice Line Table."

Invoice Line Table

ProdNo	Desc	Price	Qty
P1080	Pool Trtmnt	1.60	600
P1030	Rope-20'	60.00	12
P1050	Pool Trtmnt	1.60	400
P1100	Table/Umb	1050.00	1
P1130	Lounger	80.00	2
P1130	Lounger	80.00	3
P1080	Rope-20'	60.00	10
P1130	Lounger	80.00	5
P1100	Table/Umb	1050.00	3

Invoice Table

InvNo	InvDate	Cust Code	Name	City	EmpName
I00022	6/30/18	C100	Aberdeen Pk	San Antonio	Ted Marks
I00023	6/30/18	C200	Allen	Dallas	Ted Marks
I00024	7/01/18	C100	Aberdeen Pk	San Antonio	Reji Greer
I00025	7/01/18	C300	Scamell	Orlando	Judy Clark
I00026	7/01/18	C400	Allen	Auburn	Judy Clark

Both tables are in 1NF. A database table cannot have duplicate rows because they would be counterproductive to the goal of reducing data redundancy. Therefore, the above invoice table has only five rows as contrasted with the nine rows in Exhibit 13.2. The invoice line table, on the other hand, has nine rows.

The invoice table and the invoice line table have a one-to-many (1:*) relationship. One record in the invoice table can match many records in the invoice line table. Invoice I00022 is related to two lines in the invoice line table; I00023 is related to three lines; I00024 is related to one line; I00025 is related to two lines; I00026 is related to one line. However, one record in the invoice line table matches only one record in the invoice table. The first record in the invoice line table goes with I00022 only. The second record goes with I00022 only; the third record goes with I00023 only, and so forth. Because we have not assigned primary and foreign keys yet, you cannot clearly see these relationships. However, if you review the table in Exhibit 13.2, these relationships will be obvious.

Now we need to assign a primary key to the invoice table. You will recall from Chapter 12 that a primary key is one or a group of data elements that uniquely identifies a record. The invoice number serves this purpose for the invoice table and is denoted by capital letters in the table in **Exhibit 13.3**.

INVNO	InvDate	CustCode	Name	City	EmpName
I00022	6/30/18	C100	Aberdeen Pk	San Antonio	Ted Marks
I00023	6/30/18	C200	Allen	Dallas	Ted Marks
I00024	7/01/18	C100	Aberdeen Pk	San Antonio	Reji Greer
I00025	7/01/18	C300	Scamell	Orlando	Judy Clark
I00026	7/01/18	C400	Allen	Auburn	Judy Clark

EXHIBIT 13.3 Invoice Table in First Normal Form[2]

To associate an invoice with its lines, we will add "InvNo," the primary key of the invoice table, to the invoice line table. You will recall from Chapter 12 that in a 1:* relationship, the foreign key goes in the many side of the relationship. To uniquely identify each record in the invoice line table, the primary key needs to be a composite key—the combination of InvNo and ProdNo. Only one record in the invoice line table has the primary key of I00022/P1050, or I00022/P1080, or I00023/P1050, and so forth. A key that is both a primary and a foreign key, as is invoice number, is capitalized and italicized. The invoice line table in 1NF is shown in **Exhibit 13.4**.

INVNO	PRODNO	Desc	Price	Qty
I00022	P1050	Pool Trtmnt	1.60	600
I00022	P1080	Rope-20'	60.00	12
I00023	P1050	Pool Trtmnt	1.60	400
I00023	P1100	Table/Umb	1050.00	1
I00023	P1130	Lounger	80.00	2
I00024	P1130	Lounger	80.00	3
I00025	P1080	Rope-20'	60.00	10
I00025	P1130	Lounger	80.00	5
I00026	P1100	Table/Umb	1050.00	3

EXHIBIT 13.4 Invoice Line Table in First Normal Form

By converting our tables into 1NF, we have reduced (although not yet eliminated) data redundancy. Thus, we have minimized the risk of errors in our data. However, we have anomalies in our tables. We can now illustrate an insertion anomaly with the invoice table in Exhibit 13.3. As previously noted in this chapter, an insertion anomaly occurs when you attempt to store a value for one data element but cannot because the value of another data element is unknown. Suppose our company has approved a new customer, J. T. Wong, who needs to be added to the database. Because we have not made a sale to Wong, there is no invoice number. Invoice number is the primary key for the invoice table, and the contents of a primary key cannot be empty; that is, the primary key cannot have a null value. Therefore, we would not be able to add Wong to the database until a sale had been made to him.

A deletion anomaly occurs when a value for one data element we wish to keep is unexpectedly deleted at the same time that a value of another data element is deleted. Suppose Aca Pool Co. receives payment in full from Aberdeen Park for its two invoices (I00022 and I00024). When we remove Aberdeen Park's invoices from the invoice table because they are no longer outstanding, Aberdeen Park's customer code, name, and city are also deleted.

Second Normal Form

Converting a table into 2NF only applies to a table that has a composite key. If a table has a single primary key, it is already in 2NF. Therefore, the invoice table in Exhibit 13.3 not only is in 1NF but also is in 2NF. The invoice line table in Exhibit 13.4 above, however, has a composite key and needs to be converted to 2NF. To reach 2NF, a table must be in 1NF and every non-key data element must depend on, or be determined by, the *entire* primary key. If any non-key data elements do not depend on the entire primary key, those non-key data elements and the part of the composite key they depend on are moved to other tables. As we work through the process of converting the invoice line table to 2NF, you will notice that we are decomposing the tables into single themes.

You may want to review the invoice line table in Exhibit 13.4. Product number, description, and unit sales price in the invoice line table need to be moved to a separate table because these fields are determined by product number only and not by the table's entire primary key (invoice number and product number). The quantity sold needs to stay in the invoice line table because it is determined by a particular invoice number. The invoice line table and the new inventory table, which are in 2NF, are shown in **Exhibit 13.5**.

Invoice Line Table

INVNO	PRODNO	Qty
I00022	P1050	600
I00022	P1080	12
I00023	P1050	400
I00023	P1100	1
I00023	P1130	2
I00024	P1130	3
I00025	P1080	10
I00025	P1130	5
I00026	P1100	3

Inventory Table

PRODNO	Desc	Price
P1050	Pool Trtmnt	1.60
P1080	Rope-20'	60.00
P1100	Table-Umb	1050.00
P1130	Lounger	80.00

EXHIBIT 13.5 Invoice Line and Inventory Tables in Second Normal Form

These tables have a many-to-one (*:1) relationship because one record in the invoice line table can match only one record in the inventory table, but one record in the inventory table can match many records in the invoice line table. Therefore, the primary key of the one side of the relationship (product number in the inventory table) needs to be a foreign key in the many side of the relationship (invoice line table) to join the two tables.

The invoice line table still needs the composite primary key of invoice number and product number to uniquely identify each record and to determine the quantity sold. You will recall that invoice number I00022 includes two different products—600 units of one and 12 units of the other. You may want to look at Exhibit 13.2 and review the invoice table. Without the product number in the invoice line table, we would know only that we sold 600 units and 12 units; we would not know which products were actually sold.

We now have the following three tables in our database, all in 2NF:

1. Invoice table (Exhibit 13.3)
2. Invoice line table (Exhibit 13.5)
3. Inventory table (Exhibit 13.5)

Third Normal Form

A table is in 3NF if it is in 2NF and has no transitive dependencies. You will recall that a transitive dependency exists when a non-key data element is dependent on, or determined by, another non-key data element. One of our three tables has a transitive dependency—the invoice table. This table, which is in 2NF, is repeated below for your consideration:

Invoice Table

INVNO	InvDate	CustCode	Name	City	EmpName
I00022	6/30/18	C100	Aberdeen Pk	San Antonio	Ted Marks
I00023	6/30/18	C200	Allen	Dallas	Ted Marks
I00024	7/01/18	C100	Aberdeen Pk	San Antonio	Reji Greer
I00025	7/01/18	C300	Scamell	Orlando	Judy Clark
I00026	7/01/18	C400	Allen	Auburn	Judy Clark

In this table, invoice number (the primary key) determines customer code (a non-key data element). Customer code (a non-key data element) determines the customer's name and city. In other words, name and city are not determined by the primary key invoice number. A short-hand version of this situation is as follows:

INVNO determines CustCode determines Name and City.

To eliminate the transitive dependency, customer code, name, and city should be moved to another table as follows:

Customer Table

CustCode	Name	City
C100	Aberdeen Pk	San Antonio
C200	Allen	Dallas
C300	Scamell	Orlando
C400	Allen	Auburn

The remaining invoice table contains invoice number, invoice date, and employee name because invoice date and employee name are determined by the primary key invoice number. Note that we have separated the invoice table into a customer theme and an invoice theme. The remaining invoice table is as follows:

Invoice Table

INVNO	InvDate	EmpName
I00022	6/30/18	Ted Marks
I00023	6/30/18	Ted Marks
I00024	7/01/18	Reji Greer
I00025	7/01/18	Judy Clark
I00026	7/01/18	Judy Clark

The customer and invoice tables have a one-to-many relationship because one record in the customer table can match many records in the invoice table. However, one record in the invoice table can match only one record in the customer table.

The primary key of the customer table is customer code because it uniquely identifies each record. Customer code also needs to be a foreign key in the invoice table, the many side of the relationship, to join the two tables to create our invoices. The customer and invoice tables are now in 3NF as shown in **Exhibit 13.6**.

Customer Table

CUSTCODE	Name	City
C100	Aberdeen Pk	San Antonio
C200	Allen	Dallas
C300	Scamell	Orlando
C400	Allen	Auburn

Invoice Table

INVNO	InvDate	EmpName	CustCode
I00022	6/30/18	Ted Marks	C100
I00023	6/30/18	Ted Marks	C200
I00024	7/01/18	Reji Greer	C100
I00025	7/01/18	Judy Clark	C300
I00026	7/01/18	Judy Clark	C400

EXHIBIT 13.6 Customer and Invoice Tables in Third Normal Form

The two tables in Exhibit 13.6 can be used to illustrate another important database property—referential integrity. **Referential integrity** prohibits undesired actions from occurring. For example, referential integrity ensures that sales will be made only to approved and existing customers. If we try to enter a sale in the invoice table to customer J. T. Wong, the system will not accept the sale because we do not have a customer code for Wong. We need to create a record for Wong in the customer table before we can record a sale to him. Referential integrity would also ensure that if we try to delete the record for customer code C100 in the customer table, we will not be able to because two records in the invoice table point to customer code C100. The two records in the invoice table that point to C100 have to be deleted before we can delete C100 from the customer table.

Because the invoice table, invoice line table, and inventory table had no transitive dependencies, the procedure we used to convert them into 2NF also converted them into 3NF. We now have four tables in our database, all in 3NF, which are shown in **Exhibit 13.7**. Primary keys are in capital letters and foreign keys are in italics. Elements that are both primary and foreign keys are in capitalized italics.

Referential integrity A database property that prohibits undesired actions from occurring. For example, referential integrity ensures that sales will be made only to approved and existing customers.

Invoice Line Table

INVNO	PRODNO	Qty
I00022	P1050	600
I00022	P1080	12
I00023	P1050	400
I00023	P1100	1
I00023	P1130	2
I00024	P1130	3
I00025	P1080	10
I00025	P1130	5
I00026	P1100	3

Invoice Table

INVNO	InvDate	EmpName	CustCode
I00022	6/30/18	Ted Marks	C100
I00023	6/30/18	Ted Marks	C200
I00024	7/01/18	Reji Greer	C100
I00025	7/01/18	Judy Clark	C300
I00026	7/01/18	Judy Clark	C400

Customer Table

CUSTCODE	Name	City
C100	Aberdeen Pk	San Antonio
C200	Allen	Dallas
C300	Scamell	Orlando
C400	Allen	Auburn

Inventory Table

PRODNO	Desc	Price
P1050	Pool Trtmnt	1.60
P1080	Rope-20'	60.00
P1100	Table-Umb	1050.00
P1130	Lounger	80.00

EXHIBIT 13.7 Tables in Third Normal Form Before Considering Additional Tables

Step 4. Evaluate the tables to determine if additional tables need to be created.

In evaluating the tables in Exhibit 13.7, we notice that the flexibility of our database could be improved by the addition of an employee table because several items of data are needed for each employee. Suppose the study of users' needs revealed that the employees who are sales representatives are paid on commission. As the tables stand now, there is no appropriate place to add a column for commission rate. If we were to add commission rate to the invoice table where we now have employee name, we would create anomalies in the tables. Therefore, we will create the following employee table:

Employee Table

EMPCODE	EmpName	CommRate
E021	Ted Marks	.06
E022	Reji Greer	.06
E023	Judy Clark	.06

The employee table and the invoice table have a one-to-many relationship. One record in the employee table matches many records in the invoice table, but one record in the invoice table matches only one record in the employee table. The primary key for the employee table is employee code. The employee table can be linked to the invoice table by replacing the employee name data element in the invoice table with employee code and making employee code a foreign key. The complete set of tables is in **Exhibit 13.8**.

Invoice Line Table

INVNO	PRODNO	Qty
I00022	P1050	600
I00022	P1080	12
I00023	P1050	400
I00023	P1100	1
I00023	P1130	2
I00024	P1130	3
I00025	P1080	10
I00025	P1130	5
I00026	P1100	3

Invoice Table

INVNO	InvDate	EmpCode	CustCode
I00022	6/30/18	E021	C100
I00023	6/30/18	E021	C200
I00024	7/01/18	E022	C100
I00025	7/01/18	E023	C300
I00026	7/01/18	E023	C400

Customer Table

CUSTCODE	Name	City
C100	Aberdeen Pk	San Antonio
C200	Allen	Dallas
C300	Scamell	Orlando
C400	Allen	Auburn

Inventory Table

PRODNO	Desc	Price
P1050	Pool Trtmnt	1.60
P1080	Rope-20'	60.00
P1100	Table-Umb	1050.00
P1130	Lounger	80.00

Employee Table

EMPCODE	EmpName	CommRate
E021	Ted Marks	.06
E022	Reji Greer	.06
E023	Judy Clark	.06

EXHIBIT 13.8 Complete Set of Tables in Third Normal Form Using System Output Approach

Our tables are now free from anomalies. If we want to add J. T. Wong as a new customer, we can do so regardless of whether a sale has been made to him. Also, if Aberdeen Park pays for its two outstanding invoices (I00022 and I00024), we will not delete Aberdeen Park from the database.

The tables we have created are the logical structure of the data, that is, the way the data are thought about or "viewed" by users. Single tables or combinations of tables comprise logical files. For example, the invoice table and the invoice line table comprise the sale transaction file. The inventory, employee, and customer tables each are master files. As other required outputs are identified, additional data elements would be added to the tables. For example, the warehouse supervisor would need a report that shows for each inventory item the quantity on hand, the reorder point, and the reorder quantity. Therefore, these data elements would be added to the inventory table. Payroll would need to know the social security number, pay rate, insurance code, deduction code, and withholding code for each employee so these data elements would be added to the employee table. The customer table would need to include state, zip code, type (wholesale or retail), credit limit, and credit terms to name a few data elements.

The data are not stored electronically as tables. Because the database management system software takes care of the physical details, accountants do not need to be concerned with this aspect. When we create and use tables in a database management system, the appearance of the data is just as you see on these printed pages. For data input purposes, a form is sometimes created so that the user sees only the form instead of the table with its rows and columns. However, the input form is simply a user interface between the user and the table.

One final point in designing the tables is that in practice we would not have live data in them at this stage. Data are added after the tables are constructed. Data were included to help you see more clearly how to normalize tables.

Step 5. Document the tables with a data access diagram.

Now that we know what tables we need to have and how the data elements should be arranged, we can document the tables with a data access diagram. The diagram is in **Exhibit 13.9**.

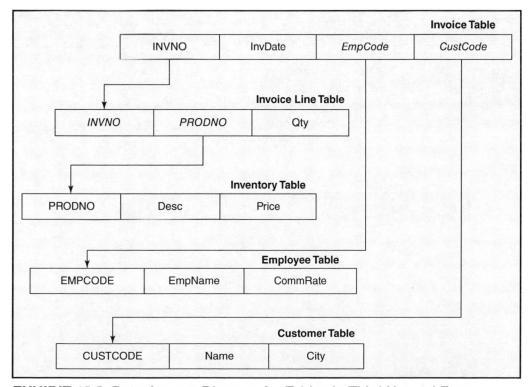

EXHIBIT 13.9 Data Access Diagram for Tables in Third Normal Form

By reviewing the data access diagram, you will see that we are able to produce the sales (customer) invoice that was shown in Exhibit 13.1 because each of the data elements needed for the invoice are in tables in the database, and the tables are joined. Also keep in mind how helpful this diagram would be to you as a user, auditor, or implementer of the system to help you locate, filter, and extract data.

REA Framework Approach[3]

A second approach to developing a relational database for an accounting system is the REA (resource, event, and agent) framework approach. This approach uses some terms that may at first seem new to you; however, you will soon find that they are familiar aspects of a business and its accounting system. Even though the initials that describe the framework are always in the order REA, we describe and discuss the "E" (event) first because the events must be identified before the events' resources and agents can be determined.

REA Terminology

LEARNING OBJECTIVE 2
Define events, resources, and agents.

Event A business activity. Business events, or activities, comprise business processes.

Resource In the context of database design, that which is involved in a business activity (event). Generally, a resource is an asset, such as inventory, cash, or whatever is acquired, used, or disposed of in an event.

Agent The individual or group of individuals who are involved in an event. An agent can be internal to the organization, such as a sales representative or an accounts receivables clerk, or external to the organization, such as a vendor or a customer. An agent is generally a legal entity, such as a person, corporation, or partnership.

Entity A collective term for resources, events, and agents in database design.

A business **event** is a business activity. Business events, or activities, comprise business processes. For example, a business process is making a sale. The events, or activities, that comprise the process are call on a customer, receive a customer's order, deliver/ship the goods ordered, or render the service ordered. A transaction is always an event. A transaction occurs in the example of making a sale when the goods are essentially delivered or the services are rendered. However, an event extends beyond transactions to also include other activities, such as calling on a customer or receiving a customer's order, which may lead to a transaction. When identifying an event, it is important to differentiate between a business activity and an accounting information system activity. Accounting information system activities are necessary to input, process, store, and output data about a business event. However, accounting information system activities are not the events according to the REA framework.

A **resource** is what is involved in the event. Generally, a resource is an asset, such as inventory, cash, or whatever is acquired, used, or disposed of in an event.

An **agent** is the individual or group of individuals who are involved in an event. An agent can be internal to the organization, such as a sales representative or an accounts receivables clerk, or external to the organization, such as a vendor or a customer. An agent is generally a legal entity, such as a person, corporation, or partnership. Events, resources, and agents are collectively referred to as **entities**.

Relationships are, as we defined them in Chapter 12, connections, or interactions. Relationships between entities can be any of the types discussed in Chapter 12, that is, one-to-one, one-to-many (many-to-one), and many-to-many. Examples of relationships between entities are:

Entity	Relationship	Entiy
Sale	is made by	Sales Representative
Sale	is made to	Customer
Sale	consists of	Inventory
Sale	results in	Cash receipt
Cash receipt	comes from	Customer
Cash receipt	is collected by	Cashier
Cash receipt	is deposited to	Cash (bank account)

Entities or Relationships	Attributes
Customer	Code, name, street, city, state, zip code, type, credit limit, credit terms
Vendor	Code, name, address, credit limit, credit terms
Employee	Code, name, address, spouse/dependent(s), job skill, pay rate, birth date, insurance code, deductions code, withholding code
Inventory	Product number, description, warehouse location, unit cost, unit sales price, reorder point, reorder quantity, quantity on order, quantity on hand
Shareholder	Code, name, number of shares owned, purchase date, cost
Sale	Invoice number, date, customer code, product number, extended amount, total amount
Purchase	Purchase order number, date, vendor code, product number, extended amount, total amount
Cash receipt	Cash receipt number, date, amount
Cash disbursement	Check number, date, amount
Cash	Bank account code, bank name, bank account balance, date of deposit
Sale/inventory*	Quantity sold

*This is the only relationship in the list. The others are entities.

EXHIBIT 13.10 Entities or Relationships and Their Attributes

Attributes are the same as the data elements that we discussed in the example of the system output approach to developing a database. In the REA framework we refer to **attributes** as the properties, or characteristics, of entities and relationships. Some examples of entities and their attributes are shown in **Exhibit 13.10.**

Attribute A property, or characteristic, of entities and relationships.

Entity-Relationship Diagram

An **entity-relationship (E-R) diagram** is prepared to document the entities (resources, events, and agents), relationships, and perhaps attributes. The following symbols represent the various components of an E-R diagram:

LEARNING OBJECTIVE 3
Define the symbols used in an entity-relationship diagram.

Entity-relationship (E-R) diagram Documentation of the entities (resources, events, and agents), relationships, and perhaps attributes in a database.

- A *rectangle* represents an entity (a resource, event, or agent) and contains the name of the entity. An entity's name is a noun that is singular in number and is written in capital letters.
- An *ellipse* represents an attribute.
- A *diamond* represents a relationship between entities. A relationship's name begins with a verb, such as consists or made, and is written in lowercase letters. The type of relationship (1:1, 1:*, *:*) is printed next to each entity.
- A *line* links (1) entity to relationship, (2) attribute to entity, and (3) attribute to relationship.

Entity-relationship diagrams are only loosely standardized. As a result, you will often see variations in the use of these symbols.

Developing the Database

We will now illustrate how to develop a relational database for an accounting system using the REA framework approach. To keep the illustration straightforward and to make it possible for you to compare this approach with the system output approach, we will restrict our focus to the sales activities of an organization. We will simplify the event by assuming that our organization makes over-the-counter sales where the customer walks in, an employee (sales representative) sells products to the customer and turns over the products to the customer, and the customer walks out. All sales are on credit, and employees are paid commissions on their sales. The steps required to develop a database using the REA framework approach are to:

1. Identify and document the business events, or activities, that are of interest to users and the resources and agents that are related to the events.
2. Identify and document the relationships among the events, resources, and agents that are of interest to users.
3. Identify and document the attributes that are related to the resources, events, agents, and relationships that are of interest to users.
4. Determine what tables to create and what data elements to put in which tables by referring to the E-R diagram.
5. Evaluate the tables to be sure they are in the third normal form.
6. Document the tables with a data access diagram.

Step 1. Identify and document the business events, or activities, that are of interest to users and the resources and agents that are related to the events.

To demonstrate the REA framework approach, we will assume that an in-depth study of the business processes in the organization to be served by the accounting system has identified one event, or activity, that needs to be included in the database. For simplicity, we are limiting the events to only one. The event that has been identified is a sale to a customer. This event is a transaction, although, as mentioned earlier, this does not have to be the case.

The resource involved in the sale event is inventory, which is an asset. The agents involved in the sale event are employee and customer. The table on the right can help us keep track of the entities.

Entities		
Resources	**Events**	**Agents**
Inventory	Sale	Employee Customer

We begin our E-R diagram by drawing symbols to represent the above entities and arranging the entities in the same positions as they are in the table. Our E-R diagram is shown in **Exhibit 13.11**.

Step 2. Identify and document the relationships among the events, resources, and agents that are of interest to users.

A study of the business processes would uncover the relationships among the events, resources, and agents. The typical relationships are that events are directly related to resources that are acquired, used, and disposed of; events are directly related to agents who participate

EXHIBIT 13.11 Entities in Entity-Relationship Diagram

in the events; and events are directly related to each other. In our example, we have a relationship between sale and inventory, between sale and employee, and between sale and customer.

We also need to figure out the type of relationship. The most accurate way to do this is to think in terms of tables even though we are not ready to actually create them yet, because we will have one table for each entity. We can determine whether the relationship between two entity tables is 1:1, 1:* (*:1), or *:* using the same analysis that we introduced in Chapter 12 when we defined the types of relationships. We will proceed with our analysis of each relationship.

- **Sale and inventory.** If we examine this sale/inventory relationship from the viewpoint of the sale, we know that one sale can consist of many products. Another way of saying this is that one record in the sale table can be matched with many records in the inventory table. If we examine the sale/inventory relationship from the viewpoint of the inventory, we know that one product can be included in many sales. Another way of stating this is that one record in the inventory table can be matched with many records in the sale table. The relationship between the sale and inventory tables, therefore, is many-to-many (*:*).

- **Sale and employee.** If we examine this sale/employee relationship from the viewpoint of the sale, we know that one sale can be matched with one employee. From the viewpoint of the employee, one employee can be matched with many sales. Therefore, the relationship between sale and employee is many-to-one (*:1).

- **Sale and customer.** From the viewpoint of the sale, one sale can be matched with one customer. From the viewpoint of the customer, one customer can be matched with many sales. Therefore, the relationship between sale and customer is many-to-one (*:1).

To recap, the relationships are:

Relationship	Type of Relationship
Sale consists of inventory	*:*
Sale is made by an employee	*:1
Sale is made to a customer	*:1

The relationships are added to the E-R diagram in **Exhibit 13.12**.

A relationship is denoted by a diamond between the sale event and its related inventory resource and between the sale event and its related employee and customer agents. Lines are drawn from the diamonds to the entities. A description of the relationship is written inside the diamond so that the E-R diagram reads as a series of simple sentences. The relationships can be interpreted in both directions, that is, left to right or right to left. However, the wording describing the relationship changes slightly when you change directions. For example, we have designed our E-R diagram in Exhibit 13.12 by starting each relationship with the sale event entity in the center and then stating how the event is related to its resource and its agents. Therefore, a sale consists of inventory. However, if we choose to read from the resource to the event (left to right), the interpretation is that inventory comprises a sale. If our diagram had more than one event, you would also be able to see that an E-R diagram can be read from top to bottom or from bottom to top.

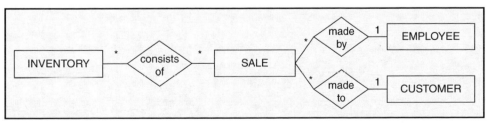

EXHIBIT 13.12 Entities and Relationships in Entity-Relationship Diagram

Step 3. Identify and document the attributes that are related to the resources, events, agents, and relationships that are of interest to users.

Suppose the study of business processes indicated that the attributes of the entities and relationships that are of interest are:

Entities*	Attributes
Sale	Invoice number, date, employee code, customer code
Inventory	Product number, description, unit sales price
Employee	Employee code, name, commission rate
Customer	Code, name, city
Sale-Inventory	Invoice number, product number, quantity sold
*The sale-employee and the sale-customer relationships have no attributes.	

The attributes must be sufficient to make it possible for the accounting system to store or generate sales data that are required for sales documents, financial reports, and operational reports and to provide sales data needed by marketing managers. To simplify this illustration, only a minimum number of attributes are used. In reality, many more attributes for some of these entities would need to be stored to accommodate the reporting for other business activities in the organization. For example, an attribute defining a customer as either a wholesale or retail customer could be required by a marketing manager who would want a report of sales by customer type. Payroll would need to know an employee's social security number and withholdings and deductions information. Those attributes would be added when developing the portion of the database that relates to those business activities.

In **Exhibit 13.13**, the attributes are shown for only the inventory and sale entities. As you can see, adding the attributes to all of our entities would clutter the diagram. Therefore, documenting the attributes in a list would be preferable.

Step 4. Determine what tables to create and what data elements to put in which tables by referring to the E-R diagram.

We can now construct the tables for the relational database to correspond with the E-R diagram in Exhibit 13.12 and the list of attributes.[4] We prepare one table for each entity and one for each many-to-many relationship. Therefore, we will have the following five tables:

- Sale table
- Sale-Inventory table
- Inventory table
- Employee table
- Customer table

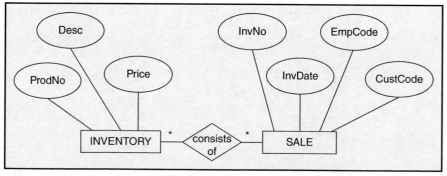

EXHIBIT 13.13 Partial Entity-Relationship Diagram with Attributes

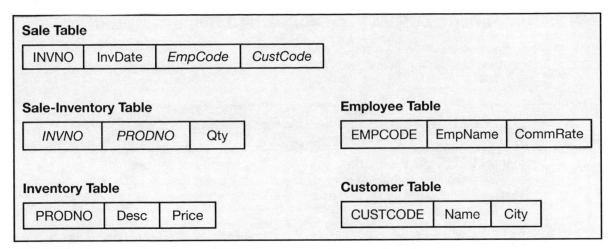

Sale Table

INVNO	InvDate	EmpCode	CustCode

Sale-Inventory Table

INVNO	PRODNO	Qty

Employee Table

EMPCODE	EmpName	CommRate

Inventory Table

PRODNO	Desc	Price

Customer Table

CUSTCODE	Name	City

EXHIBIT 13.14 Tables Using REA Framework Approach

The attributes that are included in the tables are from the list prepared in step 3. When constructing the tables, we need to assign primary keys to uniquely identify records in each table and foreign keys to relate the tables. Because these issues were discussed in Chapter 12, we will not repeat them here. Primary keys are in capital letters and foreign keys are in italics. Data elements that are both primary and foreign keys are in capitalized italics. Our tables are shown in **Exhibit 13.14**.

By preparing a table for a *:* relationship, we actually took the *:* relationship between the sale and the inventory entities and broke it down into two 1:* relationships. The sale table and the sale-inventory table have a 1:* relationship because one record in the sale table can match many records in the sale-inventory table, but one record in the sale-inventory table can match only one record in the sale table. Assuming the same data we used in the system output approach, the invoice number I00022, for example, could match I00022/P1050 and I00022/ P1080 in the sale-inventory table. However, I00022/P1050 in the sale-inventory table matches only I00022 in the sale table.

The inventory table and the sale-inventory table also have a 1:* relationship. One record in the inventory table can match many records in the sale-inventory table, but one record in the sale-inventory table can match only one record in the inventory table. Again, assuming the same data used in the system output approach, product number P1050 could match I00022/P1050 and I00023/P1050 in the sale-inventory table.

Step 5. Evaluate the tables to be sure they are in the third normal form.
Preparing the tables from the E-R diagram helps to ensure that the tables are normalized. However, the tables may still have some data redundancy and anomaly problems. Therefore, the tables should always be analyzed to make certain the data meet the same three criteria we had for normalizing the tables in the system output approach, which are:

1. All repeating data elements are in separate tables.
2. All non-key data elements depend on, or are determined by, the entire primary key.
3. No transitive dependencies are in the tables.

Step 6. Document the tables with a data access diagram.
At this point, you can prepare a data access diagram for the tables as we did when we used the system output approach.

Comparison of REA Framework and System Output

LEARNING OBJECTIVE 5
Compare the REA framework and system output approaches to developing a database.

To recap what has been involved in developing a database and to help you compare the two approaches, the following table compares the steps required for both approaches.

Steps for Developing a Relational Database for an Accounting System	
REA Framework Approach	**Systems Output Approach**
• Identify and document the business events, or activities, that are of interest to users and the resources and agents that are related to the events.	• Identify and document the system outputs and the contents of the outputs that are of interest to users.
• Identify and document the relationships among the events, resources, and agents that are of interest to users.	• Identify and document what data elements need to be stored to produce the output.
• Identify and document the attributes that are related to the resources, events, agents, and relationships that are of interest to users.	
• Determine what tables to create and what data elements to put in which tables by referring to the E-R diagram.	• Determine what tables to create and what data elements to put in which tables by using a process called data normalization.
• Evaluate the tables to be sure they are in the third normal form.	• Evaluate the tables to determine if additional tables need to be created.
• Document the tables with a data access diagram.	• Document the tables with a data access diagram.

One distinct difference in the system output approach and the REA framework approach is that the system output approach focuses on identifying the desired system outputs. The REA framework approach focuses on identifying business events, or activities, in the organization.

If you compare the tables that resulted from the system output approach in Exhibit 13.8 with those prepared under the REA framework approach in Exhibit 13.14, you will see that the tables are very similar. The tables are compared in **Exhibit 13.15**.

What is named the sale table in the REA framework approach is named the invoice table in the system output approach. What is named the sale/inventory table in the REA framework approach is named the invoice line table in the system output approach.

Although it may not be obvious from our simple illustrations, advocates of the REA framework approach believe that this approach results in tables that classify data in ways that will support more views of the data. Therefore, the tables and relationships generated from this approach will provide an organization with a greater ability to manage data for both transaction processing and decision making and to respond better to changing information needs.

Implementing a Database Approach

LEARNING OBJECTIVE 6
Summarize how a database is implemented.

After the tables have been designed, the database can be implemented. Implementation begins by defining the schema (i.e., the tables, the relationships among the data, the domains for data elements, and the business rules that apply to the data) using the

REA FRAMEWORK APPROACH

Sale Table

INVNO	InvDate	*EmpCode*	*CustCode*

Sale-Inventory Table

INVNO	*PRODNO*	Qty

Inventory Table

PRODNO	Desc	Price

Employee Table

EMPCODE	EmpName	CommRate

Customer Table

CUSTCODE	Name	City

SYSTEM OUTPUT APPROACH

Invoice Table

INVNO	InvDate	*EmpCode*	*CustCode*

Invoice Line Table

INVNO	*PRODNO*	Qty

Inventory Table

PRODNO	Desc	Price

Employee Table

EMPCODE	EmpName	CommRate

Customer Table

CUSTCODE	Name	City

EXHIBIT 13.15 Comparison of Tables Using REA Framework Approach and System Output Approach

database management system's data definition language or graphical interface. This process is called the logical database design and, in terms of the three-level architecture described in Chapter 12, corresponds to the conceptual and external levels. Next, the physical database is designed for the stored database in terms of physical storage structures, record placement, and access paths. The particular database management system determines the storage options available. This phase corresponds to the internal level in the three-level architecture. Finally, the data can be entered in the tables, a process that is called populating the tables. Implementation is generally performed by a database administrator.

Summary

Whether you become users, auditors, implementers, or designers of accounting information systems, it will be extremely helpful for you to understand some of the issues involved in developing a database even though the primary responsibility for developing it is borne by system designers. Knowledge of some major issues of database development and familiarity with some of the tools used in developing a database will give you a depth of knowledge that will enable you to function more effectively and efficiently.

The end product of developing a database is a set of "normalized" tables that will store the data in the accounting system. The tables comprise the transaction files, master files, open files, and reference files in the accounting system. Each table has a unique key and an accompanying set of relationships among the keys. When developing a relational database for an accounting system, one of two approaches can be used:

1. Begin by identifying the contents of the desired system output, such as a report or a document. We refer to this as the system output approach.
2. Begin by identifying the entities (resources, events, and agents) in the organization and their relationships. We refer to this as the REA framework approach.

The system output approach has traditionally been used and is still widely accepted. The REA framework approach also has many advocates. The steps required to develop a database using the system output approach and the REA framework approach are covered in this chapter.

One distinct difference in the system output approach and the REA framework approach is that the system output approach focuses on identifying the desired system outputs. The REA framework approach focuses on identifying business events, or activities, in the organization. When you compare the tables that result from the system output approach with those prepared under the REA framework approach, you will see that the tables are very similar.

Although it may not be obvious from our simple illustrations, advocates of the REA framework approach believe that this approach results in tables that classify data in ways that will support more views of the data. Therefore, the tables and relationships generated from this approach will provide an organization with a greater ability to manage data for both transaction processing and decision making and to respond better to changing information needs.

Key Terms

Agent   400
Attribute   401
Deletion anomalies   389
Entity   400
Entity-relationship (E-R) diagram   401
Event   400

Insertion anomalies   389
Normalized tables   389
Referential integrity   397
Resource   400
Transitive dependency   392

Discussion Questions, Problems, and Activity

1. Using a system output approach to developing a database, you have determined that the accounting system needs to produce a purchase order for each purchase the organization places. The desired format of the purchase order is as follows:

Purchase Order	Aca Pool Co.
P. O. Number: Date: Vendor Code:	2700 Bay Area Blvd. Clear Lake City, TX 77058-1098 Tel: (713) 555-1234 Fax: (713) 555-1235

Vendor Name and Address:

PRODUCT NO.	QUANTITY	DESCRIPTION	UNIT COST	EXTENDED AMOUNT
			TOTAL DUE	

Required:

    a. What data elements need to be stored to produce the purchase order?

    b. What are the three steps that should be taken to normalize the data you identified in Part a with respect to 3NF?

    c. What tables should be in the database so the accounting system can produce a purchase order? Use data normalization to develop your tables.

2. Refer to the tables you created for the purchase order in the previous question.

Required:

Draw a data access diagram and discuss briefly how the tables and relationships would be involved in printing a purchase order.

3. A new sales order processing system is being designed for a corporate client. During the initial design process, the specifications shown here have been proposed for the sales transaction file and the open sales order file.

Sales Transaction File	Open Sales Order File
Invoice number	Sales order number
Data-entry clerk number	Customer purchase order number
Invoice date	Date of sales order
Sales representative number	Promised shipment date
Sales order number	Customer number
Customer purchase order number	Customer name
Customer number	Customer shipping address
Customer shipping address	Customer billing address
Product number	Product number
S.K.U.	Product description
Quantity sold	S.K.U.
Unit sales price	Quantity ordered
	Unit sales price
	Extended price

Transaction records are to be retrieved by invoice number, whereas open sales order records are to be retrieved by sales order number. The transaction file is to be purged once a month. The open sales order file is permanent although individual records will be purged after the order has been filled. Customer billing addresses are more or less permanent, but shipping addresses can vary from sale to sale because customers may request shipment to branch offices or field sites.

Required:

    a. Analyze these file specifications to provide a normalized logical data structure defining the schema of a relational database management system. Provide tables of data elements describing your final normalized form.

    b. Provide a data access diagram showing how the data records would be retrieved.

4. A new purchase order processing system is being designed for a corporate client. The specifications shown below have been proposed for the purchases transaction file and the open purchase order file.

Purchases Transaction File	Open Purchase Order File
Transaction number	Purchase order number
Data-entry clerk number	Purchase requisition number
Date received	Date of purchase order
Purchase order number	Expected receipt date
Vendor code	Vendor code
Product number	Vendor name
S.K.U.	Product description
Quantity received	S.K.U.
Unit purchase price	Quantity ordered
	Unit purchase price
	Extended price

Transaction records are to be retrieved by transaction number, whereas open purchase order records are to be retrieved by purchase order number. The transaction file is to be purged once a month. The open purchase order file is permanent although individual records will be purged after the order has been filled.

Required:

    a. Analyze these file specifications to provide a normalized logical data structure defining the schema of a relational database management system. Provide tables of data elements describing your final normalized form.

    b. Provide a data access diagram showing how the data records would be retrieved.

5. A project manager in the organization where you are the controller wants to get a weekly report on each project she supervises. After spending some time with the manager to determine what data need to be on the report, you and the manager have agreed on the this format for the report:

Project Report

Project Number:

Project Description:

Date Started:

Date Completed:

EMP. NO.	NAME	SPECIALTY	EST. HOURS	ACTUAL HOURS	VARIANCE
TOTAL HOURS AND VARIANCE:					

Required:

a. What data elements need to be stored to produce each project report?

b. What are the three steps that should be taken to normalize the data you identified in Part a with respect to 3NF?

c. What tables should be in the database so the accounting system can produce a project report? Use data normalization to develop your tables.

6. Refer to the tables you created for the project report in the previous question.

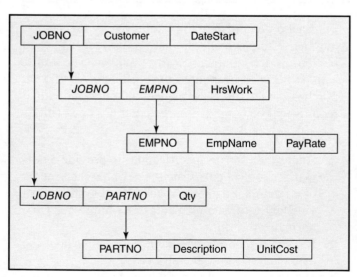

Required:

Draw a data access diagram and discuss briefly how the tables and relationships would be involved in printing a project report.

7. The data access diagram and corresponding tables for part of a job cost system are shown below.

Primary keys are shown in capital letters, and foreign keys are shown in italicized letters.

The tables for this problem 7 are on the following page.

Tables for Problem 7:

Table 1		
JOBNO	Customer	DateStart
100	Red Company	01/01/18
101	Blue Company	02/02/18
102	Gray Company	03/03/18

Table 2		
JOBNO	EMPNO	HrsWork
100	800	40
100	801	40
100	802	30
101	802	10
101	803	40
102	804	40
102	805	40

Table 3

EMPNO	EmpName	PayRate
800	M. Mercury	8.50
801	V. Venus	9.00
802	E. Earth	7.00
803	M. Mars	8.00
804	J. Jupiter	10.00
805	S. Saturn	9.00

Table 4

JOBNO	PARTNO	Qty
100	300	2
100	301	5
100	302	10
100	303	6
101	300	4
101	302	5
102	300	20
102	303	1

Table 5

PARTNO	Description	UnitCost
300	10-in. widget	100
301	12-in. widget	120
302	14-in. widget	140
303	16-in. widget	160

Required:

a. Determine the materials and labor costs of each of the active jobs.

b. Comment on the mechanism of retrieving records from Tables 2 through 5.

8. Using the REA approach to developing a database for an accounting system, you have identified one event, or activity, that needs to be included in the database. The event is a purchase from a vendor. The organization makes over-the-counter purchases in which the purchasing agent makes a purchase and immediately receives the goods purchased. All purchases are on account, and the company uses a voucher number to uniquely identify all purchases.

Required:

a. Identify any resources and agents that are related to the purchase event. Document the event and any resources and agents with an E-R diagram.

b. Identify the relationship among the events, resources, and agents. Add these relationships to your E-R diagram. Indicate on your E-R diagram the type of each relationship, that is, 1:1, 1:*, *:1, or *:*.

c. Identify and list the attributes that are related to the resources, events, agents, and relationships.

d. Create the appropriate database tables by referring to the E-R diagram.

9. Document the tables you developed in the previous question with a data access diagram.

10. The steering committee of the organization you work for has decided to develop a relational database for a new accounting system. The committee has asked you to explain the different approaches to developing the database. How would you compare the system output approach and the REA approach to the committee?

Student Activity

1. Create two tables for a sales transaction file in the Microsoft Access database (refer to Exhibits 13.3 and 13.4). Populate the tables to show data for one invoice (i.e., one sale) with three products sold on the one invoice. Make up your own data. Submit your Microsoft Access files to your instructor electronically.

2. The purpose of this assignment is to build a customer invoicing accounting application in the Microsoft Access database. This assignment will help you understand and put into practice the concepts you learned about in the database management system chapters.

Required:

1. Create five relational tables (the ones in Exhibit 13.8).
2. Populate the five tables.
3. Establish relationships among the tables.
4. Create a query using the query-by-example (QBE) method.
5. Create an invoice document to display the results of the query.
6. Print customer invoices.

Your instructor will give you help in completing the first few requirements above and will provide detailed instructions for completing the remaining requirements. Submit your Microsoft Access files to your instructor electronically.

Notes

1. You will recall from Chapter 2 that documentation can be in the form of graphical and/or narrative descriptions.

2. The procedure we used to convert this table to 1NF also converted it to 2NF. Second normal form is discussed in the next section of this chapter.

3. The REA framework was introduced by William E. McCarthy in his definitive work, "*The REA Model: A Generalized Framework for Accounting in a Shared Data Environment*," The Accounting Review, July 1982: 554–578.

4. Do not be concerned that you did not see an invoice in the E-R diagram. You will recall that we do not include accounting information system activities in the REA framework approach, only business process activities. When constructing the tables from the E-R diagram, you will see that the table for the sale event is the same as what was called an invoice table when we used the system output approach for developing the database.

Big Data and Data Analytics

COLLECTION

STORAGE

RESEARCH

BIG DATA

SHARED

ANALYSIS

EXABYTE

VISUALIZATION

VOLUME

Source: Trueffelpix/Shutterstock.

Learning Objectives

After studying this chapter, you should be able to:

- Understand the concept of big data.
- Recognize how big data can be used to predict behavior.
- Recognize the impacts and benefits of big data for organizations.
- Discuss the risks and the control challenges of big data.
- Discuss tools used to perform data analytics.
- Explain the role of cloud computing in big data.

Source: Everett Historical/Shutterstock.

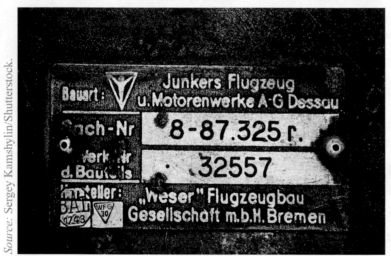

Source: Sergey Kamshylin/Shutterstock.

Introductory Scenario

You work for an aviation history magazine controlled by the two owners, Emily and John. The magazine started as a quarterly newsletter which focused on interviewing U.S. WWII veterans, especially Army Air Corps aviators (pilots and crew). The first newsletter was released in 2004. Since its beginnings, the popularity of the newsletter has grown exponentially with subscribers numbering in the thousands. The owners decided to make the newsletter a magazine with photos and other history about WWII included in each issue. Since many of the veterans are now in their 90s, Emily and John have recently hired five journalists to help collect as much information from the remaining veterans as they can.

Some of the new hires have suggested creating an online version of the magazine. They also would like to interview former Luftwaffe and RAF aviators, based on suggestions from some U.S. veteran interviewees who thought the magazine should include aviators from both sides of the conflict. The new hire journalists want to travel to Germany, Canada, France, and other countries where many of these veterans live to conduct face-to-face interviews. They are requesting mobile devices such as tablets, scanners, and smart phones to help record interviews and store other historical information they plan to collect to "flesh out" the interviews with the veterans. Emily and John do not know much about the security concerns of the latest "smart" technology. The company has strong brand recognition for quality interviews and historically sound articles, reasonable per issue pricing, and consistency from issue to issue.

The company has a limited Internet presence and uses its website only for marketing to potential subscribers. No online purchasing functions are available. While the company is very profitable, it has made limited use of the Internet to expand the exposure of the magazine. The CEO has asked you to recommend immediate and long-term actions to take related to the corporate stance on social media and mobile devices for the journalists and other employees.

Introductory Scenario Thought Questions:

1. Describe for the two owners what immediate steps they should take regarding the development and use of social media (e.g., Facebook, Twitter, etc.) to "spread the word" about the magazine.
2. What risks does the expansion in use of social media and mobile devices create for the organization?

Introduction to Big Data

What Is Big Data?

Big data refers to the voluminous amounts of data that are generated every day by all of us whether on Twitter, Facebook, LinkedIn, or through our browsing history and online purchases. Organizations are looking to make use of the data that are available to identify customers' likes and dislikes, their buying habits, and other behaviors. Big data can be collected via our activity on the Internet or through other surveillance methods. Big data has three attributes: velocity, variety, and volume. The analysis of big data defies traditional methods of analysis because data are changing rapidly (*velocity*), the data are so varied (*variety*), and individuals are producing incredible amounts of data (*volume*) about themselves every day from visits to websites; this includes purchases, and social media postings of texts, photos, and videos. So what does an organization do with all this data?

Organizations can use these huge data sets to create bigger and more useful information that allows them to serve their current customers and to attract new customers. Making use of big data is not without its challenges (more on this in a later section). In essence, the trick is to be able to sift through all the data collected (much of which can probably be ignored) and find the data that are most useful to fulfill the strategy of the organization by identifying patterns, trends, or other relationships useful for decision making.

Types of Data Available for Analysis

ISACA's white paper "Big Data Impacts and Benefits" (March 2013) discusses data in terms of types of data that are:

- Volunteered
- Observed
- Inferred (e.g., analysis of a credit score)

Volunteered data are data provided by individuals on platforms such as social media. You might provide information about your interests, relationship status, or employment to perhaps attract employers (e.g., LinkedIn) or friends (e.g., Facebook). The data you provide is what you choose to provide and can be as detailed as you wish it to be. **Observed data** are data captured through recording geo-location or activity on websites. Your browser history or records of the ads or links in a website you click on are recorded as you shop, research, or play Internet games. **Inferred data** are data gathered based on combinations of volunteered or observed data. An example of inferred data would be a calculated credit score or an overall rating of a restaurant on Yelp. Additionally, data can be categorized as structured (e.g., numbers or text), unstructured (e.g., surveillance video), or semi-structured (e.g., Twitter feeds). **Structured data** refers to data that most of us are familiar with from our accounting courses: numbers and text that are formatted for use in relational databases and spreadsheet analysis (e.g., graphs). **Unstructured data** refers to data such as videos, audio recordings, and photos, which cannot be easily formatted for use with traditional analysis tools such as spreadsheets. **Semi-structured data** are somewhere in between; for example, data that have been tagged with XML for reporting purposes. As discussed earlier in this text, XML provides context for financial information provided on a company's 10-K and other SEC reports.

Source: Rawpixel.com/Shutterstock.

LEARNING OBJECTIVE 1
Understand the concept of big data.

Big data The voluminous amount of data that is generated every day by all of us through Internet access, mobile device use, and other means.

Volunteered data Data individuals choose to provide on platforms such as social media.

Observed data Data captured through recording geo-location or activity on websites.

Inferred data Data gathered based on combinations of volunteered or observed data (e.g., a credit rating).

Structured data refers to data such as numbers and text that are formatted for use in relational databases and spreadsheet analysis.

Unstructured data Data such as videos, audio recordings, and photos, which cannot be easily formatted for use with traditional analysis tools such as spreadsheets.

Semi-structured data Data that are somewhat unstructured but provide context for analysis; for example, data that have been tagged with XML for reporting purposes.

Using Big Data to Predict Behavior

Types of Big Data Analysis

LEARNING OBJECTIVE 2
Recognize how big data can be used to predict behavior.

Predictive analysis The process of harnessing the power of big data to predict trends and behavior such as buying patterns or potential insider threats.

Prescriptive analytics Using big data to prescribe solutions to issues noted by predictive analysis.

Many organizations are trying to harness the power of big data to predict trends and, ultimately, consumer or employee behavior. This process is known as **predictive analysis**. For example, big data can be used to predict buying patterns of individuals or identify potential insider threats from employees. On a smaller scale, you could probably evaluate several Twitter feeds related to a topic and perhaps identify characteristics of the person(s) on the feed. On a larger scale, the analysis of big data such as preferences, click traffic (identifying web sites visited, which ads are viewed, etc.), recent purchases and the like can assist companies in the identification of trends and help with targeted marketing of new products and services. With advanced levels of big data analysis, optimization models can provide **prescriptive analytics** to prescribe solutions to issues noted by predictive analysis. For purposes of the discussion here, we will focus on predictive analysis.

How Big Data Can Be Used to Predict Behavior

The use of big data to predict consumer behavior resulting from a new product or marketing campaign is fairly obvious. Based on consumer feedback on social media, surveys, and demographic information, a marketing campaign can be directed at specific groups of people. Companies can use the information to develop targeted services or products to meet the needs of current customers or to try to attract new customers.

Another way to use big data is to predict or analyze behavior of dissatisfied employees. As auditors and security professionals, the potential for losses due to an insider threat is a significant concern. When identifying insider threats, big data can help identify behaviors that are inconsistent with the job responsibilities of an individual. Often these insider threats are not caught by typical access controls because the employee has access to files and data as part of their job. Sometimes, the inconsistent behavior might be triggered from the outside—for example, a disgruntled employee is "encouraged" by an outsider to pass proprietary information. What big data provides is a way to analyze and predict behavior by identifying anomalies. Evaluating the volume of data accessed, the speed of machine traffic, the variety of social indicators of dissatisfaction, and the trustworthiness (or reputation) of the data allow some tools—often using a type of "machine learning" or "artificial intelligence—to model behavior and look for anomalies in behavior or activity."

Consider the following scenario: John Doe is a mid-level clerk at ABC Company. He has access to proprietary data about upcoming contracts and bids in his position in the procurement department. ABC management is concerned that information about the bid process is being leaked to give certain vendors an advantage over others when competing for large construction contracts. The data analysts begin to collect data on the procurement department's activity. Data collection of Mr. Doe's downloading activity shows his activity is higher than the other clerks in the same job function, is higher than his activity over the previous 90-day period, and is taking place primarily in the middle of the night and on weekends. Additionally, activity records show that much of the data were downloaded onto insecure USB drives. Mr. Doe's email activity has recently increased by over 500% to DEF Company, one of the more successful bidders for contracts with ABC Company. The combination of these activities could suggest that Mr. Doe is passing confidential/proprietary information about contracts and competitor bids to this third party, giving DEF Company an unfair advantage in the bidding process. If it is further discovered that Mr. Doe was recently passed over for a promotion, this might indicate he has the potential to pose a significant threat to the security of data and the bidding process maintained by ABC Company.

Impacts and Benefits of Big Data

Impacts of Big Data

There are many impacts related to big data collection and use that can affect the company's ability utilize big data. Many of these impacts have to do with deciding what data to collect, where/how to store it, and what to do with the data once collected. Some major impacts include:

LEARNING OBJECTIVE 3
Recognize the impacts and benefits of big data for organizations.

- Privacy concerns: this is probably the area of greatest concern to accountants and auditors, as data (even if its authenticity is questionable) must be protected from unauthorized users and weak privacy laws.

- Governance effects: the organization needs to determine the data to be gathered and how it should be maintained and delivered.

- Impacts on planning: this includes justification of the collection process and organization of outcomes to address particular goals related to collecting the data, for example, supporting a just-in-time inventory system or managing the IT support function.

- Utilization impacts: the increase in the use of data for prediction and development of strategy have led to companies such as NetFlix and Amazon.com (normally competitors in the sales of movies, for example) to cooperate by having Amazon.com provide the cloud infrastructure to allow individuals to stream NetFlix to their computers, mobile devices, or TVs.

- Impact on the assurance function: the company collecting the data must develop a framework for the protection/control of data, with a focus on ensuring the quality of data (so as to reach the proper conclusions about the data).

Of the impacts listed above, privacy of the information collected is, as you can probably imagine, is one of the biggest concerns. The variety of laws among countries with regard to privacy, coupled with the number of laws within a country (whether general or related to a sector, such as health information in the U.S.), makes data privacy a significant challenge. Because the data sets are so large and so complex, the combination of advanced persistent threats (APTs) against data security and vulnerabilities in data storage (e.g., cloud) can keep security professionals awake at night trying to figure out how to balance availability and protection of data. With proper data policies and procedures in place, an organization should be able to identify sensitive data (ensuring proper security), demonstrate compliance with applicable laws/regulations, monitor the data and IT environment, and react/respond to incidents promptly.

Benefits of Utilizing Big Data

There are many benefits to leveraging big data. Some benefits that can improve competitive advantage and market appeal include:

- Better planning and prediction results.
- Ability to target the marketing of products to their current and potential customers.
- Increased customer loyalty and customer satisfaction from being able to respond quickly to customer feedback and suggestions.
- Operational efficiency improvements that encourage innovation and lead to better-informed business decisions.
- Agility in responding to changes in the market because of a company's ability to act on market demand predictions in near real-time.

Source: Rawpixel.com/Shutterstock.

The key to gaining the most benefits from big data is to plan and strategize about what information is needed and how to harvest it to help the organization move forward with its plans.

Challenges to Employing Big Data for Decision-Making

Organizations face several challenges to consider when taking advantage of the availability of big data. Much of the data is without the "structure" accountants and management are accustomed to. "Scrubbing" the data so it can be used in analysis can be at once frustrating and rewarding. Vulnerable data sources need to be protected with limited access (which includes limiting/restricting the ability to manipulate data), and proper data classification allows better control of the data. Ensuring data quality is probably the biggest and most important challenge to users of big data. This includes identifying the accuracy, objectivity, believability, and reputation of the data.

Consider an example: Think of a Twitter feed. Many times the accuracy, objectivity, believability and reputation of the data in the feed could be questionable. This will in turn affect the relevancy of the data, and whether or not it can be relied upon by the user. The quality of the data has to do with the relevancy of the information presented, its completeness, how current the information is, and how much information is included. Other quality issues include the representation, interpretability, understandability, and ability to manipulate the data. Again, think of a Twitter feed. It is most likely relevant to someone, but whether or not it is complete and representative of the participants is questionable. Perhaps manipulation of data is limited and the interpretability might be difficult especially when someone uses their own "shorthand." The quality issues related to security and accessibility have to do with the availability/timeliness of and type of access to the data. For the Twitter feed, the availability and timeliness are—sometimes unfortunately— almost instantaneous. Do we really want to know every thought every minute from the latest Hollywood megastar? Access in the Twitter example is restricted to those who have a Twitter account, but the security is far from perfect. Recall that Twitter has been down for extended periods; Keith Wagstaff of NBC News reported that research suggests that one in 10 Twitter accounts—many attributed to celebrities and politicians—are bogus (November 25, 2013).

Risks and Controls Associated with Big Data

Risks Related to Big Data

LEARNING OBJECTIVE 4
Discuss the risks and the control challenges of big data.

In our discussion of the impacts, benefits, and challenges of big data, we alluded to some of the risks related to the collection and use of big data. We focus here on several significant risks associated with the availability and use of this data. These risks include:

- Compromise of confidential information. Personally identifiable information (PII), or personal health information (PHI), are examples of types of information that are protected by law in the U.S. When collecting data outside the U.S., it is important to be aware that accessing and using private data is strictly regulated in some countries (such as Europe), but could be loosely regulated in other countries.

- Security of proprietary information of the company. Companies generally wish to protect pricing, order details, other financial information from access by competitors.

- Risk related to data destruction after the data is used. Organizations might be tempted to keep everything, especially since data storage prices keep decreasing; however, there should be a policy on how and when data are disposed of. The reality is that keeping everything is risky in terms of data protection (particularly if the data resides in the cloud).

- Risk of inadequate data use due to data coming from external and possibly unreliable sources. Personnel need the expertise to know what data an organization has and how to interpret the data to avoid legal trouble or misinterpretation of information. What is important is to determine what data to keep/look at and what data to ignore.

- Risks of unexpected costs as a company tries to move from simply using big data for exploration and discovery to using big data to develop business intelligence. Other costs such as those associated with processing or getting the data in a format useful for analysis should be considered. The decision to involve a third party to obtain or analyze the data can also affect risk.

- Risk related to interpreting a parameter incorrectly, leading to an incorrect conclusion about an individual, for example, using health data parameters to identify someone with an "unhealthy lifestyle" to predict health care needs. Remember that correlation does not imply causation so if you are trying to predict potentially fraudulent activity, be careful how you interpret your findings. Say you discover several duplicate payments related to lease payments for an office. Further investigation would then show that these "duplicate" payments are legitimate based on a review of the lease agreement and how the payments were set up.

- Risk related to storage of the data. Who owns the data? How is it stored so as to be in compliance with local and international regulatory/privacy requirements? If big data sets are stored in the cloud, is there a strong service level agreement that addresses the risk of a compromise of confidential or private information? Are there proper safeguards in place to reduce business risk?

- Reputation risk affected by the breach or loss of private information.

- Other risks associated with maintaining large quantities of data. Examples include operational risks (e.g., geopolitical) or technology-based risks (e.g., risk associated with bypassing IT safeguards).

Recommended Controls for Big Data

What kind of controls would be useful to reduce the risks associated with big data? ISACA (March 2013) groups recommended controls in four categories:

- Strong "tone at the top." This includes establishing and implementing a data policy (i.e., governance). Creating an inventory of the data is an important step so that data can be classified with regard to its sensitivity and relevance to the organization. Vulnerabilities identified should be analyzed for impact and probability, and a process should be in place for escalation when data is compromised (that is, who is responsible). Materiality limits should also be developed to identify relevant/valuable/vulnerable data sets.

- Assurance of data quality. This includes assigning ownership and responsibility for material data sets.

- Confidentiality and privacy of personal information and proprietary information. This requires identifying all sensitive data and determining how the data will be secured in transit and at rest, that is, in storage. Logical and physical controls such as requiring passwords for access, masking sensitive data (for example, credit card information), screen saver lock out, and physical controls such as server room security should be in place. Sensitive data should be encrypted.

- Availability of data. This includes having a disaster recovery program (DRP) in place to protect the restoration of data. This DRP must be tested to ensure data can be recovered and protected in the event of an incident.

These recommendations show the role that governance, that is, data policies and monitoring/oversight, plays in mitigating the risks identified above. A recommendation to protect the privacy of data suggested by the Software and Information Industry Association

De-identify Eliminating personal identifiers in data to protect the individual or business.

(SIIA) is to **de-identify** the data as soon as possible to eliminate personal identifiers in the data and minimize the opportunity for personal data to be compromised. This allows an organization to analyze trends in the data, but still support individual privacy. COBIT 5.0 places accountability for governance of big data at the board level. The C-suite executives are responsible for the process practices.

Tools for Data Analytics

Current Trends and Tools for Data Analytics

Data collection is now measured in **petabytes** (approximately 1000 terabytes or 2^{50th} bytes), which means that large quantities of data (much of which is not structured in the traditional sense of the word) need to be stored somewhere. Before any analysis can be performed on big data, the data have to be stored and set up for access and security. Open source products such as Apache Hadoop (http://hortonworks.com/apache/hadoop/) provide such ser-

LEARNING OBJECTIVE 5
Discuss tools used to perform data analytics.

Petabytes Approximately 1000 terabytes or 2^{50th} bytes.

vices allowing companies who use these products the ability to handle data processing (e.g., MapReduce), data warehousing (Apache Hive), data extraction/transformation/loading (e.g., Apache Pig), data analytics (e.g, Apache Spark and Apache Impala), and resource scheduling (Yet Another Resource Negotiator or YARN). Hadoop's data processing system provides a distributed file system (Hadoop Distributed File System or HDFS) to allow companies to make use of large quantities of data through parallel processing and scaling "out" by adding servers, rather adding than larger/faster/expensive hardware (as would be needed in relational data warehousing), to handle the parallel processing.

In the past, companies have made use of the traditional spreadsheet and database software tools for analyzing structured data that work with relational databases. Dealing with semi-structured (such as emails) or unstructured data (such as videos or photos) presents a challenge as the traditional tools may not be the most effective tools to analyze these types of data. In addition, traditional analytic tools cannot accommodate the volume of data and the speed with which the data are generated and collected. Developing and making use of big data analytics opens up new risk frontiers related to technology and operations. Obviously, organizations cannot afford to lag their competitors in the use of business intelligence and predictive analytics, but there is still a risk associated with these analytics. For IT professionals, maintaining and operating large volumes of non-structured data is a new frontier. ISACA's January 2014 white paper on big data analytics suggests some best practices. Because the adoption of a big data program involves capital investment in both personnel that have analytic skills and the technology to exploit the analytics, companies need to weigh the decision of adopting a program (i.e., technological risk) versus not adopting a program (i.e., business risk). Essential to success in exploiting big data includes developing a convincing case to justify the program. The justification would discuss

- Expected returns to the organization,
- Impact the analytics will have on the business model,
- Opportunity costs associated with choosing to pursue big data analytics, rather than something else, and
- Effects on investments already made by the organization.

Many organizations are considering harnessing the power of big data to explore ways to expand/change their business and gain a competitive advantage. The nice thing for many businesses is that the data already exist and are usually accessible, for example, data related to previous purchases by customers, health information collected by doctors on patients, or the results of marketing campaigns. Once the analysis is completed, the organization can evaluate the success or failure of the effort using relevant performance measures. To make the most of big data analytics, it is important to have individuals with the necessary skill sets to work with the data. Ideally, there should be a willingness to share information among the various business units, the ability to identify data sources, and the computational resources necessary to take full advantage of data available for analysis.

Tool that are not open source like Apache's tools, but available to perform analytics and data visualization include analytic packages such as IDEA and ACL, and data visualization software packages such as Tableau. These can be used to analyze and protect data by providing system use logs and other security information collectors to reduce risk of unauthorized access or modification of data.

Source: staticnak/Shutterstock.

Cloud Computing in Big Data

Many companies store some or much of their data in the cloud. We will begin our discussion by explaining the concept of cloud computing and then discuss the role of the cloud in big data storage and analytics.

LEARNING OBJECTIVE 6
Explain the role of cloud computing in big data.

Definition of Cloud Computing

Cloud computing is a general term that refers to large-scale computing resources being provided over the Internet. These computing resources are more related to enterprise-level information technology (IT) in business use rather than to a consumer's home computing needs. Since these computing resources do not reside physically on site but are available over the Internet, they are considered to be "in the cloud."

Cloud computing provides computing resources in three broad categories, or layers: infrastructure-as-a-service (IaaS), platform-as-a-service (PaaS), and application software-as-a-service (SaaS). **Infrastructure-as-a-service (IaaS)** is a cloud service that offers the hosting of virtual machines and servers for clients, as well as client application support, data back up, and disaster recovery planning. In essence, the cloud provider offers usage of infrastructure (i.e., computing hardware) to the client while the client maintains control over the operating systems and applications. **Platform-as-a-service (PaaS)** is a cloud service that provides tools, which includes the operating system, for the client to configure its data storage and develop applications on the cloud provider's servers. This service is usually scalable across multiple servers. **Software-as-a-service (SaaS)** is the most inclusive cloud service that comprises infrastructure, platforms, and applications (i.e., software) from the cloud service provider. The cloud provider handles all levels of computing for the client. This includes the infrastructure (e.g., hardware), the platform (e.g., operating systems), and the software (e.g., installation, updates to the software, and licensing) for the client. A client can obtain whichever services needed from the cloud providers over the Internet without physically maintaining its own computer hardware, database, and/or application software.

Exhibit 14.1 illustrates the cloud service categories, or layers, described above and indicates the level of management by the cloud provider for each layer. The client company manages anything that is not included in the services of the cloud provider. For example, with SaaS, the cloud provider manages the infrastructure, the platform, and the software applications. The client company manages only the company's devices and its people. This arrangement is similar to the "thin client" concept in the client/server

Cloud computing A general term that refers to large-scale computing resources being provided over the Internet.

Infrastructure-as-a-service (IaaS) A cloud service offering the hosting of virtual machines and servers for clients, as well as client application support, data back up, and disaster recovery planning.

Platform-as-a-service (PaaS) A cloud service that offers tools, which includes the operating system, for the client to configure their data storage and develop applications on the cloud provider's servers.

Software-as-a-service (SaaS) The most inclusive cloud service that comprises infrastructure, platforms, and applications (i.e., software) from the cloud service provider. The cloud provider handles all levels of computing for the client.

Chapter 14 Big Data and Data Analytics   **421**

network architecture wherein the client devices house very few local programs but are part of a network with one or more servers that handle most of the processing activities, file storage, etc. This thin-client arrangement allows a reduction in network traffic because the client device handles only instructions that are sent to the server for processing. Similarly, SaaS allows for the client company (the "thin" part of the arrangement) to avoid the cost of maintaining software, hardware, and data center operations by paying the cloud provider based on usage, effectively eliminating the fixed costs associated with maintaining a data center and the requisite hardware (both virtual and physical) and related software.

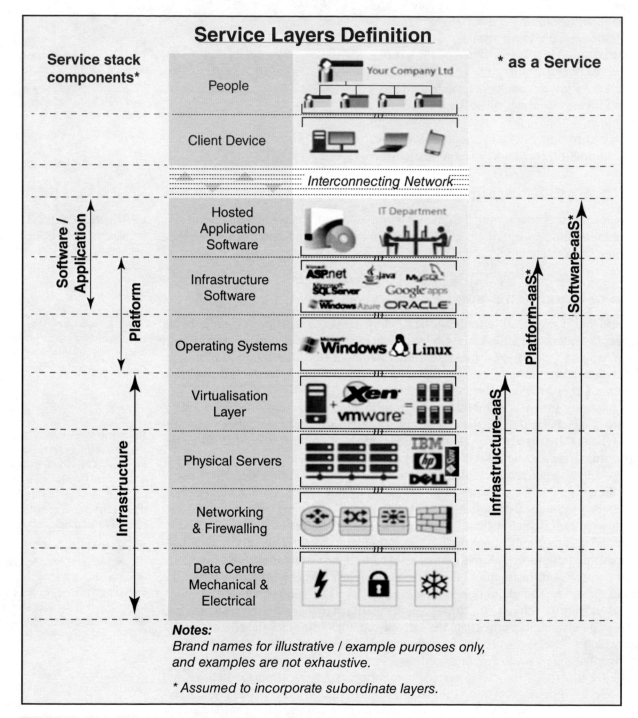

EXHIBIT 14.1 Service Layers for Cloud Services

Source: https://www.katescomment.com/iaas-paas-saas-definition/comment-page-1/#comment-1412145, by Kate Craig-Wood, Managing Director of Memset LTD.

In the case of IaaS, the cloud provider manages the hardware, such as data center functions related to networking and security (e.g., firewalls), servers, and virtual machines. The client company manages everything else (i.e., operating systems, software, the client devices, and the people). PaaS falls in between SaaS and IaaS in terms of what is managed by the client company and what is managed by the cloud provider. In PaaS, the client company manages the hosted application software, the client company devices, and the people.

Users typically purchase the IT functions and services they need from cloud service providers, and costs are based on usage. Cloud service providers such as Amazon Web Services LLC (aws.amazon.com), Google, and Microsoft all offer comprehensive cloud computing services to enterprise clients. For example, Google App Engine allows users to run their applications on Google's infrastructure.

The Role of Cloud Computing in Big Data

Cloud computing has become a major player in the storage and processing of big data. Commercially available products allow companies to take advantage the platform-as-a-service (PaaS) and infrastructure-as-a-service (IaaS) products to store and analyze their big data. PaaS products allow businesses to manage the configuration of the data storage, while the IaaS products allow virtual machines and clusters to be built so the business can configure the tools installed with the data storage to accommodate adjustments in resources needed as a client's workload and usage change. The biggest challenge is to get the data to the cloud provider. This generally requires the transfer of hard drives to the provider. The provider then uploads the data to their servers. The benefit of using the cloud to support big data functions includes flexibility and low capital investment since the company does not have to purchase hardware to store data. Cloud providers can provide storage at a lower cost than maintaining the data on site. Some drawbacks of using the cloud for big data include the expense (which is ongoing and based on space and outbound data traffic), slower performance (i.e., cloud provider does not provide dedicated hardware like you would have with on-site hardware), and issues with data security (e.g., how access to data is controlled if multiple clients share a server). The key is to pick the right solution (on-site versus cloud) for the company's big data projects.

Summary

"Big data" refers to the data all of us generate as we access the Internet, use our mobile devices, purchase products and services, and navigate using GPS. As individuals and organizations continue to produce more data through web browsing, location tracking of mobile devices, social media postings, as well as traditional data generation (through purchases of goods and services, for example), the use and protection of data will become more important. In order to maintain a competitive advantage, organizations will have to make use of big data to direct their efforts in attracting and maintaining customers. Analysis and interpretation of the volumes of data available will require new skill sets that are in short supply in the current job market.

Organizations must weigh the risks associated with collecting, analyzing, storing, and destroying big data against the risks associated with facing competitors who utilize their big data to efficiently expand their customer and product/service bases. Auditors and IT security professionals must help in the governance of big data by providing assurance services related to privacy, storage, and protection of sensitive data (whether personal data or data related to a competitive advantage, such as intellectual property).

Some companies consider using cloud service providers for data storage and processing. Cloud computing is a general term that refers to large-scale computing resources being provided over the Internet, whether the computing resources are infrastructure-as-a-service (IaaS), platform-as-a-service (PaaS), or software-as-a-service (SaaS). Companies now can obtain some or all of these computing capacities from the "cloud" without worrying about maintaining their own computer hardware, database, and application software. Interest in utilizing the cloud for storage of large data sets has increased. Although practical and cost-effective, dependence on cloud providers for data storage requires attention to security concerns related to the protection of private information from unauthorized access and use.

Key Terms

Big data   415
Cloud computing   421
De-identify   420
Inferred data   415
Infrastructure-as-a-service (IaaS)   421
Observed data   415
Petabytes   420
Platform-as-a-service (PaaS)   421

Predictive analysis   416
Prescriptive analytics   416
Semi-structured data   415
Software-as-a-service (SaaS)   421
Structured data   415
Unstructured data   415
Volunteered data   415

Discussion Questions and Problems

1. You work for a company that produces shoes for adults and children. Your CEO has come to you requesting information about this "big data" he's been hearing about at his CEO monthly breakfast meetings. He asks for a definition of big data and how it can be used for the company. The company has a website and currently 20% of the sales come from online customers.

   Requirements:

   a. Provide a definition of big data.
   b. Explain to the CEO how data collected can be used to improve marketing of the company's products.

2. Your CEO from question 1 asks about utilizing social media to improve the company's reputation online. However, he has some concerns about the way data are collected.

   Requirement:

   Discuss the types of data that can be collected from social media and other online sources.

3. You are the CIO (Chief Information Officer) of a financial institution that is getting ready to offer a new type of savings account that pays interest at a competitive market rate.

   Requirement:

   How could you use predictive analysis to try to develop a larger customer base for the new product?

4. You work in the marketing department of an online bookstore.

   Requirement:

   What information might you analyze to target a new book release to your existing customers?

5. Discuss potential privacy issues related to collecting data from Internet traffic and social media.

6. Research Apache Hadoop at http://hortonworks.com/.

   Requirement:

   Discuss some traits of their products that make them unique.

7. Discuss some of the topics that should be covered in a business case that would convince executive management of the need to take advantage of big data opportunities.

8. Discuss some of the advantages and disadvantages of cloud computing. Assume the data that are being considered for the cloud are the email server and the HR server. Make a recommendation as to whether to move the email server and/or the HR server to the cloud.

9. Discuss the three common "as-a-service" products available for cloud computing. Which of these allows a company to maintain the most control over its data functions?

10. Which of the "as-a-service" products discussed in question 9 available from cloud computing companies is most beneficial from a cost standpoint for a small, but growing manufacturing company that does not have the resources (or the personnel) to maintain an on-site data center? What are some of the risks of this level of service? How can a company protect itself?

References

Blanchard, R. and K. O'Sullivan. 2015. Big data risk and opportunity. *Internal Auditor (IA)*, October: 65–67.

ISACA.org. 2014. Generating value from big data analytics. http://www.isaca.org/Knowledge-Center/Research/Documents/Generating-Value-from-Big-Data-Analytics_whp_Eng_0114.pdf, January.

ISACA.org. 2013. Big data impacts and benefits. www.isaca.org/Big-Data-WP, March.

ISACA.org. 2013. Privacy and big data. http://www.isaca.org/Knowledge-Center/Research/ResearchDeliverables/Pages/Privacy-and-Big-Data.aspx, August.

ISACA.org. 2012. Security considerations for cloud computing. http://www.isaca.org/Knowledge-Center/Research/ResearchDeliverables/Pages/Security-Considerations-for-Cloud-Computing.aspx, September.

Jackson, R.A. 2013. Big data. *Internal Auditor*, February: 35–38.

Lopez, K. and J. D'Antoni. 2014. The modern data warehouse—How big data impacts analytics architecture. *Business Intelligence Journal*, 19(3): 8–15.

Moffitt, K.C. and M.A. Visarhelyi. 2013. AIS in an age of big data. *Journal of Information Systems*, 27 (2): 1–19.

Riffat, M. 2014. Big data—Not a panacea. *ISACA Journal*, 2014(3): 1–3.

Wagstaff, K. 2013. 1 in 10 twitter accounts is fake, say researchers. http://www.nbcnews.com/technology/1-10-twitter-accounts-fake-say-researchers-2D11655362 (November 25).

Willhite, J. 2014. Getting started in "Big Data". CFO Journal located at: http://blogs.wsj.com/cfo/2014/02/04/getting-started-in-big-data/

Glossary

Acceptance report A report that documents that the provision of services has been completed.

Access security Control activities that deal with who can access the accounting system and what they can access in the accounting system.

Account An element in an accounting system that is used to classify and summarize monetary measurements of business activity of a similar nature. An account is established whenever it is necessary to provide useful information about a particular type of economic event.

Accounting events Economic events that have or may become accounting transactions. For example, a completed sale is an accounting event that has become an accounting transaction; a sales order is an accounting event that may or may not become an accounting transaction.

Accounting information Information that meets the legitimate needs of external users, communicates among parties transacting business with one another, and provides a basis for informed management decisions. It can be expressed in monetary terms as well as ratios, percentages, or units and includes any data that are either directly or indirectly reflected in the financial statements whether in this or in future periods.

Accounting information system A system that delivers accounting information. Its purposes are: to meet an organization's statutory reporting requirements; to provide relevant and accurate accounting information to those who need it and when they need it; to conduct or at least enable most business processes ranging from the recording of sales orders to the reconciliation of bank accounts after liabilities have been paid; and to protect the organization from possible risks stemming from abuse of accounting data or of the system itself.

Accounting software Sets of instructions that tell hardware what to do in order to process data. Such software includes general ledger, customer, and human resource accounting.

Accounting systems implementation An area of high growth within public accounting involving, particularly, the installation and support of prepackaged accounting systems software.

Accounting transaction Economic events that affect an organization's accounting equation.

Accounts payable subsystem A subsystem in the procurement process that is concerned with paying for goods and services purchased from vendors. It may be further divided into the vendor invoicing subsystem and the cash disbursements subsystem. The accounts payable subsystem involves processing invoices received from vendors, maintaining records of vendor balances and total liabilities, and disbursing cash.

Accounts receivable subsystem A subsystem in the revenue process that is concerned with receiving payment for goods and services sold to customers. It may be further divided into the customer invoicing subsystem and the cash receipts subsystem. The accounts receivable subsystem involves preparing customer invoices and periodic customer statements, maintaining records of customer balances and total receivables, and collecting cash.

Activity report A listing of the transaction file showing the transaction activities that have occurred over a period of time.

Agent The individual or group of individuals who are involved in an event. An agent can be internal to the organization, such as a sales representative or an accounts receivables clerk, or external to the organization, such as a vendor or a customer. An agent is generally a legal entity, such as a person, corporation, or partnership.

Anti-virus protection software Software designed to detect computer viruses that could shut down a system or allow cybercriminals to steal data.

Application controls The control activities that apply to the flow of data in and among individual applications.

Archive file A file, or copy of a file, that provides a permanent record.

Attribute A property, or characteristic, of entities and relationships.

Audit committee A standing subcommittee of the board of directors whose main objectives are to protect against management wrongdoing and to increase public confidence in the independent auditor's opinion.

Audit trail A set of processing references that enables the tracing of an event from its source to its designation or, alternatively, from its designation back to its source. It consists of codes (or references) attached to data as they flow through the accounting system so they can be traced from originating documents, to transaction and open files, and to their inclusion in output reports and documents and vice versa.

Auto-enter A feature that saves keystrokes when entering data that are always represented by a fixed number of characters. After the user enters the characters, the program automatically moves to the next field so the user does not have to press the enter key after entering the field contents.

Automated control Controls programmed into computer software.

Automatic distribution entry A feature that automates the distribution of the amount of a transaction to several accounts. The user specifies to which sub-accounts entries should be distributed and how the allocation should be made. Entries are then made to a master account, but the accounting information system computes and places amounts in the related sub accounts.

Automatic invoice identification A method for recording open item receipts where total cash remittances are entered with no remittance advice data, and the AIS includes a software program that matches the remittances with specific open items.

Automatic log off The disconnection of a workstation from a file server or host computer if there has been no activity for a given period of time.

Automatic pricing A feature in the inventory module in which pricing formulas are stored so that when the cost of an item changes, the selling price is automatically calculated.

Automatic rollback The feature of a database management system that is invoked when a program run prematurely terminates. Incomplete transactions are backed out so the database is returned to the state it was in before the transaction began.

Backdoors Remotely accessing a computer without having to authenticate all the while remaining undetected.

Backorders Sales orders that cannot be filled because the inventory is depleted.

Backup file A duplicate copy of a file that is made for security reasons in case the original file becomes damaged or lost.

Balance forward A method of accounting for accounts receivable where receipts are applied to the outstanding balance rather than against particular invoices. This method contrasts with the open item method.

Balance sheet The financial statement that presents the overall financial position of an organization at a given moment.

Batch code A sequential identifying number for a specific batch of data which can be used for tracing between journals and the ledger accounts.

Batch control report A report that documents the results of control total analysis.

Batch transmittal ticket A paper document attached to a batch of source documents in transit from one processing stage to another to ensure that as a batch progresses through the various processing stages it contains the same set of records. A transmittal ticket serves as a kind of shipping document and a receipt for the batch.

Big data The voluminous amount of data that is generated every day by all of us through Internet access, mobile device use, and other means.

Bill of lading A written contract between the shipper (also known as consignor) of goods and a carrier engaged in the business of transporting goods. This document evidences receipt of the goods for shipment.

Biometrics The use of unique functional, behavioral, form, and structural characteristics to provide positive personal identification.

Block coding A complex coding system that assigns meaning to various positions within a code.

Block diagram A type of graphical systems documentation that provides an overview of an accounting system in terms of its major subsystems. Two varieties are commonly used– horizontal and hierarchical. A horizontal block diagram shows the subsystems of an accounting system and the direction of

the information flows among the subsystems. A hierarchical block diagram shows the analysis of an accounting system into successive levels of subsystems or, alternatively, the synthesis of subsystems into a complete system. The connecting lines show the associations among the levels.

Board of directors A committee that primarily represents stockholders but may also represent employees, communities, and environmental interests. The board is responsible for overseeing operations, evaluating management's performance, and assuring that the organization is in compliance with applicable laws and regulations.

Botnets The collection of zombie computers running the bot software.

Bots Software robots that invade an organization's computers. The organization's computers are referred to as "zombie computers" since the bots cause them to act automatically in response to the "bot-herder's" control inputs through an Internet relay chat (IRC) or other means.

Business process A group of interrelated business events. The business processes comprise the first, or most general, level of subsystems in an accounting information system and are defined according to the types of events they capture, process, store, and communicate. Four business processes are revenue, purchasing, inventory, and financial.

Business process mapping A form of business process modeling that can be described as an enhanced flowchart—a graphical representation of a business process that includes (1) descriptions of exactly what the process does to promote the organization's strategy, (2) who is responsible for what, (3) standards to be maintained in the process, and (4) performance indicator s or other measures of process success.

Business process modeling Another form of graphical representation. Common languages used to illustrate the business process include the Business Process Modeling Notation (BPMN) and the Unified Modeling Language (UML). Business process modeling has the advantage of allowing communication to stakeholders and others regarding how the process operates.

Business rules Constraints on business activities that can be enforced by the database or application programs.

Calculation (computation) A processing activity in which data are manipulated mathematically. Examples are determination of extended amounts, payroll withholdings, purchase or sales discounts, and sales commissions.

CASE (Computer-Aided Software Engineering) Software that consists of a number of tools that assist in the development of information systems. Among these tools are aids for the preparation of various types of systems documentation, including block diagrams, data flow diagrams, and systems and program flowcharts.

Cash disbursements journal (also known as check register) A printout, or listing, of the cash disbursements transaction file.

Cash disbursements transaction file A file that stores the data relating to a cash disbursements transaction.

Cash discount A discount provided to a customer for prompt payment. Typical cash discount terms are 2/10, n/30 which means the customer can earn a 2% discount by paying within

10 days of the invoice date. Otherwise, the net amount is due at the end of 30 days.

Cash receipts prelist A record, maintained by date, of each cash receipt.

Cash requirements forecast A report that is prepared at regular intervals listing all outstanding invoices, usually broken down into categories, and the amount of cash needed to pay the outstanding invoices. This report helps management select invoices for payment and decide on payment dates.

Cents entry A way to enter monetary data into an accounting information system that saves one keystroke (no decimal) for fractional dollar values. The user enters only cents. The keystrokes to enter $53.59 would be 5359.

Chart of accounts A listing of all account names along with their numbers, or codes, used by an organization.

Check digit A single digit appended to a number to validate the number. The digit is computed from the other digits in the number itself.

Check register See cash disbursements journal.

Classification A processing activity in which data are classified, or divided, into categories. For example, inventory transactions data may be classified into receipts, issuances, and backorders. General ledger accounts are classified into balance sheet and income statement accounts.

Click fraud The creation of false web traffic without the user's knowledge.

Cloud computing A general term that refers to large-scale computing resources being provided over the Internet.

Common-dollar statement (vertical analysis) A financial statement where each item is shown as a percentage of some base amount designated as 100%. For the balance sheet, the base amount is total assets. For the income statement, the base amount is sales.

Comparative reporting The arranging together of actual data for a current period with either budget data for the current period or actual data for the prior period, thereby facilitating comparison of the data.

Comparison A processing activity in which data are compared to determine whether they are similar. For example, a comparison is made when the name of a customer is checked against a list of individuals or organizations to whom credit terms have been extended.

Components of internal control The elements that enable an organization to achieve management objectives. The internal control components are the control environment, risk assessment, control activities, information and communication, and monitoring.

Composite key (compound key, concatenated key) A primary key that is the combination of two or more data elements.

Compound key See composite key.

Computer hardware The most visible component of computerized accounting systems. It performs the essential functions of input, processing, storage, transmission, and output of data.

Computer virus A set of executable computer instructions that copies itself into a larger program, modifying that program. In the present environment of shared programs, viruses can spread quickly, typically through infected files, networks, or bulletin boards.

Concatenated key See composite key.

Conceptual schema The schema for the entire database and is at the conceptual level of the database architecture.

Concise reports Reports that contain only the data that are essential to the performance of the recipient's duties.

Consulting services A wide range of services, such as systems implementation, business valuations, litigation support, estate planning, employee benefits, strategic planning, health care, forensics (fraud) and financing arrangements.

Context diagram A type of graphical system documentation that shows a high-level overview of the system. Only the system being diagramed and its relevant environment are displayed.

Control account One master general ledger account that represents several related subsidiary ledger accounts. The amount in the control account equals the sum of the control account's subsidiary ledger account balances.

Control activities The policies and procedures that reduce risks which may undermine the achievement of management objectives.

Control environment The foundation for the other components of internal control. It establishes the tone of an organization and influences the control consciousness of the organization.

Control total The sum of an amount or quantity field contained in the transaction records, such as the sum of all the net amounts due in a batch of invoices. Control totals are used to ensure that as a batch progresses through the various processing stages, it contains the same set of records.

Control total analysis A control activity that verifies the accuracy of programmed processing. It analyzes control totals by comparing them to totals formed earlier in a processing sequence or to totals formed on previous occasions.

Corrective control A control that remedies a control violation after it has been detected.

COSO 2013 An internal control framework developed by The Committee of Sponsoring Organizations that is required for publicly-traded companies in the U.S.

Cost accounting subsystem A subsystem in the inventory process that is concerned with the accumulation of product costs in manufacturing and merchandising organizations or with the accumulation of the costs of providing services.

Credit hold A restriction of additional credit to a customer who has a delinquent balance.

Credit limit A dollar ceiling up to which credit will automatically be extended without the need for further credit screening.

Credit memo A document issued to a customer indicating a reduction of the amount owed.

Credit rating A classification of customers by creditworthiness. The highest rating may authorize virtually unlimited credit, while the lowest may deny credit altogether.

Cryptography The process of transforming, or encrypting, data (usually by scrambling) into a "secret code."

Customer statement A statement sent to a customer, usually once a month. The statement lists the invoices issued during the month just ended and the amounts received.

Cybersecurity How a company protects its information assets (e.g., data, human resource information, financial information, proprietary information). Threats to the security of the assets can come from within the company or from outside the company.

Cycle billing A procedure for billing customers throughout the month by dividing customer accounts into groups and billing each group at a different time during the month. This procedure eliminates the problem of a heavy work load that results from billing all customers at the same time each month.

Data definition language (DDL) Software subroutines in a database management system that are used to define the external and conceptual schema.

Data dictionary A special file, stored in the database itself, that provides metadata on the name, description, length, type, source, use, and location of each data element stored in the database. The data dictionary also discloses whether a data element is the primary key of a record.

Data flow diagram A type of graphical system documentation that provides a more detailed representation of an accounting system than a block diagram, but fewer technical details than a system flowchart. It shows only what an accounting system is doing, not how the system is doing it.

Database A database is an organization's total collection of data on computer storage devices. It is an electronic store of data that can be accessed as needed by all accounting applications and by users.

Database administrator (DBA) An employee who is responsible for planning, organizing, and maintaining the database to satisfy users' needs.

Database management system (DBMS) A collection of software specially designed to manage the data in a database in response to instructions issued by application programs or requests made by users.

Decryption A process that decodes encrypted data (see encryption).

Default value A frequently used value for a field that is filled in by the user. The software program stores this default value for the field so the user has to fill in the field only if the default value is not correct.

De-identify Eliminating personal identifiers in data to protect the individual or business.

Deletion anomalies An unexpected result during operation of a database in which a value for one data element you wish to keep is unexpectedly deleted at the same time that a value of another data element is deleted.

Deliverables The goods or other items that a vendor must deliver to a customer to meet contractual obligations, such as manufactured products, subassemblies, computer programs, or reports.

Demonstration script Scripts that are used to guide demonstrations of AIS packages.

Denial of Service attacks (DoS) A concerted effort to keep a service or Internet from functioning, either temporarily or indefinitely, by saturating the service with external requests that keep it from responding to legitimate requests.

Detailed aging report An aging report that presents information about amounts owed by customers. A detailed aging report is prepared for open item accounts and lists each unpaid invoice by customer.

Detective control A control that provides feedback regarding violations of controls in place.

Device access table A security measure that ensures a user is attempting to access the computer system from a specifically authorized device.

Digital certificate A form of electronic identification that is issued by a certification authority (CA) after the CA verifies the company participating in e-commerce activities is legitimate.

Digital signature Extra data appended to an electronic message which identifies and authenticates the sender.

Directory and file attributes An access control activity that controls what a user, group of users, or application can do to a directory or file.

Disaster recovery plan A plan that documents detailed recovery procedures in the event of equipment failure or disasters to quickly and smoothly restore an organization's processing capabilities.

Documentation standards Written policies and procedures that govern the preparation, use, and maintenance of documentation.

Dollar entry A way to enter monetary data into an accounting information system that saves three keystrokes for data composed of even dollars. The keystrokes to enter $72.00 would be 72. However, if the number has cents, the decimal and the number of cents must be entered. The keystrokes to enter $53.59 would be 53.59.

Domain A set of all possible values a data element can have.

Dun Delinquency notice sent to past due customer.

Economic events Events of an organization that may not necessarily affect its accounting equation.

Economic order quantity (EOQ) The optimum size for an order of inventory items.

E-invoicing A system where a sales-supported company uses a web-based application to bill its customers as items are shipped to customers.

Electronic data interchange (EDI) The transmission of business documents in machine-readable form between two organizations known as "trading partners."

Electronic funds transfer (EFT) A method to electronically transfer funds to pay an invoice.

Embedded audit module A module that is actually inserted into an application program to monitor and collect data based on transactions.

Encryption A process, typically involving a mathematical encryption algorithm and an encryption key that scrambles data to prevent unauthorized persons from accessing the data.

Engagement letter A letter used by public accounting firms that lists the accounting services to be provided, the responsibilities of the accounting firm and the client, the expected end product, and the fees to be charged.

Enterprise resource planning (ERP) software Software that groups an organization's accounting function with finance, sales, manufacturing, and human resources into a coherent, integrated system making financial and operational data available to personnel throughout the organization.

Enterprise risk management (ERM) A comprehensive and integrated framework for managing credit risk, market risk, operational risk, economic capital and risk transfer in order to maximize firm value.

Entity A collective term for resources, events, and agents in data base design.

Entity coding Coding that identifies master file records (such as general ledger, customer, vendor, employee, and inventory) using account numbers or alphabetic characters.

Entity-relationship (E-R) diagram Documentation of the entities (resources, events, and agents), relationships, and perhaps attributes in a database.

Event A business activity. Business events, or activities, comprise business processes.

Event coding Coding that is used to uniquely identify events recorded in an accounting information system. An event may be a transaction event, such as a sale, or a non-transaction event, such as the receipt and acceptance of a sales order.

Events accounting An accounting system that captures accounting events, which are economic events that have or may become accounting transactions, and other events that are relevant to the operating of the organization.

Exception reporting The reporting of data reflecting a significant deviance from expected, budged, or normal that should be reported to managers.

Excess inventory report A report of overstocked inventory items.

External auditor An auditor who performs a public service by expressing an opinion about the "fairness" of a client's financial statements. The auditor's opinion gives stockholders, creditors, and others confidence that an organization's financial statements provide a basis for investment decisions.

External reporting Reporting by an organization to parties outside of the organization.

External subschema A subset of the conceptual schema that is required by a particular application program or user and is at the external level of the database architecture.

External transaction A transaction that arises from an exchange with an outsider, such as the purchase or sale of goods and services.

File maintenance A nonroutine process in which changes are made to a master file through direct intervention by a user. Examples are adding new records to a file, deleting unwanted ones, and changing the content of existing records.

Financial process One of the business processes in an accounting system. It provides for the following types of transactions. (1) data captured in and transferred from other processes to the financial process, (2) transactions originally recorded in the financial process, and (3) end-of-period adjustments required in the financial process.

Firewall Hardware and software that work together to channel all network communications through a control gateway to filter messages coming in and going out of a private network.

FOB point The location at which title to the goods changes from the shipper organization to the customer.

Foreign Corrupt Practices Act (FCPA) An act that (1) established criminal liability for bribery of foreign officials by any U.S. company and (2) established provisions for record keeping and internal control for all companies registered with the Securities and Exchange Commission.

Foreign key The primary key of a table that is placed in another table so the tables can be joined.

Free stock The stock available for sale after consideration of stock committed to customers.

General contractor A contracting company that subcontracts part of the work.

General controls Control activities that apply to the reliability and consistency of the overall information processing environment. General controls support application controls.

General ledger A collection of all the asset, liability, ownership equity, revenue, and expense accounts used by an organization. Each account in the general ledger has an account number, an account name, and the amounts (debits and credits) of the transactions that affect the account's balance.

General ledger master file A file that stores detailed data about the general ledger accounts in an accounting system.

Governmental auditor An auditor who is employed by a government agency to report to government officials and the public.

Gross profit analysis An analysis by customer of sales revenue minus cost of goods sold.

Gross profit by product report Shows the physical volume and the dollar amount so volume and pricing effects can be distinguished.

Group code A code that can be used to express significant amounts of information. Most often it is used in a hierarchical structure so that the largest category is identified by the first symbols, followed by increasingly detailed subcategories as you move to the right.

Hackers Individuals who gain unauthorized access to data. They may be cybercriminals, state-sponsored, or someone who wants to embarrass or call attention to an organization.

Hard closing Closing for annual accounting periods after which no entries can be made in the period closed.

Hash total A type of control total to ensure that as a batch of documents progresses through the various processing stages it contains the same set of records. A hash total has no economic, accounting, or arithmetic significance but should remain the same throughout processing. An example is the total of customer numbers.

Holding costs (or carrying costs) Costs associated with maintaining and storing inventory.

Horizontal analysis An analysis where balances for the current financial statements are presented along with balances of prior periods for comparison.

HTML HyperText Markup Language is a markup language that is used to create Web pages.

Implementation of AIS See AIS implementation.

Inactive account An account that can no longer receive entries or be adjusted.

Index file An auxiliary file to a data file and is used to increase the speed at which records in the related data file are sorted and accessed.

Index key A data element on which the database management system builds an index file to improve the performance of the database.

Inferred data Data gathered based on combinations of volunteered or observed data (e.g., a credit rating).

Infrastructure-as-a-service (IaaS) A cloud service offering the hosting of virtual machines and servers for clients, as well as client application support, data back up, and disaster recovery planning. In essence, the cloud provider offers usage of infrastructure (i.e., computing hardware) to the client, while the client maintains control over operating systems and applications.

Input controls Control activities that deal with the authorization, entry, and verification of data entering the system.

Input data An information processing activity that captures and feeds transaction and other data into the accounting system for processing. Input is an interface between the users and the accounting system.

Insertion anomalies An unexpected result during operation of a database in which a value for one data element cannot be stored because the value of another data element is unknown.

Installation of AIS See AIS implementation.

Instance document An XBRL document that has been tagged according to the rules of XBRL making it available for analysis and processing.

Integrated test facility (ITF) A technique for auditing through the computer where the auditor uses artificial data to test how well the AIS performs its tasks.

Interactive EDI A real-time system in which both the purchaser and the seller are connected simultaneously to a value-added network.

Internal auditor An auditor who is employed by a business firm to perform auditing for corporate management. An internal auditor lacks the necessary independence to express opinions about the financial statements of the organization for which he/she works, but is nevertheless part of the same quality assurance program.

Internal control A process designed to provide reasonable assurance that management objectives related to the quality of data, the effectiveness and efficiency of operations, and compliance with applicable laws and regulations will be achieved.

Internal control flowchart A system flowchart that also shows the functional areas to permit identification of the authorization of transactions, the custody of assets, and the recording functions. In addition, an internal control flowchart identifies all existing control procedures for preventing or detecting errors and irregularities.

Internal schema A description of how the conceptual schema of a database is implemented physically. It specifies how data are stored at the level of stored records, stored record formats, indexes, hashing algorithms, pointers, block sizes, and storage media. The internal schema depicts the internal level of the database architecture.

Internal transaction A transaction that arises largely from the accumulation of cost data and the assignment of costs to products, business units, or activities.

International Financial Reporting Standards (IFRS) Accounting standards issued by the International Accounting Standards Board.

Inventory and PO aging report A report used to monitor the status of inventory receipts. The report shows inventory on hand and committed along with open purchase orders and the dates on which the related merchandise is expected to arrive.

Inventory management subsystem A subsystem in the inventory process that is concerned with accounting for raw materials, finished goods, merchandise, and supplies inventories. Inventory management extends to the regulation of inventory levels to satisfy demand while avoiding the extremes of stockouts or excessive inventory levels.

Inventory process One of the business processes in an accounting system. The scope of the inventory process depends on the nature of an organization. In manufacturing and construction organizations, the inventory process encompasses events related to the transformation of raw materials into finished goods, the accumulation of product costs, and the management of inventories. In a merchandising organization, the inventory process encompasses events related to the accumulation of product costs and the management of merchandise inventories. In a service organization, the inventory process encompasses events related to the accumulation of the cost of services and the management of parts and supplies inventory.

Inventory turnover report Indicates dormant inventory items that have not meant a minimum "turnover" or sales expectation.

IT (information technology) auditing Auditing methods that include auditing around the computer, auditing with the computer, and auditing through the computer.

IT (information technology) governance A subset of corporate governance and includes issues surrounding IT management and security.

Journal A listing of transactions in chronological order that is considered the "book of original entry." A special journal is created to record a particular type of transaction such as sale transactions. The general journal is used to record all transactions that are not recorded in special journals.

Just-in-time inventory An inventory system that strives to minimize inventory levels.

Lead time The period of time between the ordering of inventory and its receipt from a vendor.

Lead-time stock The number of units of inventory that covers sales of inventory during lead time without encroaching on the safety stock.

Legacy systems Conventional file processing systems.

Level 0 data flow diagram A type of graphical systems documentation that describes the entire accounting system on a single sheet of paper. All major processes, data stores, data flows, and external entities are shown.

Location code A code used to designate where inventory is stored. It may include shelves, bins, floors, and/or even buildings in different countries.

Logical structure The way data are thought about, or "viewed," by users.

Malware Any kind of software meant to disrupt computer operations or secretly collect information (such as password or personal information). Examples of malware include computer viruses, worms, or Trojans.

Many-to-many relationship A relationship in a database in which one record in the first table can match many records in the second table, and one record in the second table can match many records in the first table.

Mapping The process of making a data element in one schema correspond to an element in another schema. Mapping is done at two levels. (1) between the external and conceptual levels and (2) between the conceptual and internal levels.

Master account An account that is similar to a control account as the term is conventionally used in accounting.

Master file maintenance controls Control activities designed into the master file maintenance function, which is used to add records, change the contents of certain fields in records, and delete records.

Maximum stocking level The level at which an item is fully-stocked; the safety stock plus the economic order quantity.

Merging A file processing activity that consists of combining two or more files into a single composite file.

Metadata Data about data. Metadata about elements contain essential information about the data elements in a database.

Mnemonic code A code that expresses some logical association between the characters forming the code and the item being identified.

Module A subdivision of the accounting information system in which transactions of a particular type are recorded, processed, and then transferred to the general ledger module.

Normal account An account that has no sub-accounts.

Normalized tables Database tables that are free of data redundancy and anomalies and, thus, ensure the stability of the database over time.

Observed data Data captured through recording geo-location or activity on websites.

One-to-many relationship A relationship in a database in which one record in the first table matches many records in the second table, but one record in the second table matches only one record in the first table.

One-to-one relationship A relationship in a database in which one record in the first table matches only one record in the second table, and one record in the second table matches only one record in the first table.

Open file A file that stores the data about transactions that have been started but cannot be fully processed until a subsequent event occurs. An example is a sales order open file pending shipment of ordered goods or completion of services.

Open invoice file A file that contains data on all invoices from vendors that remain "open" because the invoice has not yet been paid. A record is written to the open invoice file when a vendor invoice is received, and the record is purged after the invoice is paid.

Open item A method of accounting for accounts receivable where receipts are correlated with individual invoices, and invoice records remain in the open invoice file until payment is received. This method contrasts with the balance forward method.

Open purchase order file A file that contains data on all purchase orders that remain "open" because the order has not yet been filled. A record is written to the open purchase order file when a purchase order is issued, and the record is purged after the goods or services are received.

Open receipt A customer's payment that has not been designated as being for any particular invoice; therefore, it can be applied to any of the customer's outstanding invoices.

Order recommendations report A report of inventory items that are at or below the reorder point.

Ordering cost Includes the creation of a PO, sending it to the vendor, handling the merchandise when received, and paying the resulting invoice.

Organizational objectives The critical results that management must achieve to increase the organization's probability of being successful. The three categories of organizational objectives are effectiveness and efficiency of operations, reliability of both internal and external reporting, and compliance with applicable laws and regulations.

Organizational structure The framework within which the organization's activities for achieving its objectives are planned, executed, monitored, and controlled. Limits of managerial authority, areas of responsibility, and lines of reporting are defined. Areas of responsibility define who is expected to do what. Limits of authority define what decisions which managers can make. Lines of reporting determine the relationships that tie together the areas of responsibility.

Output Various documents and reports needed by managers and employees within an organization to facilitate day-to-day operations and decision making, as well as documents and reports needed by people outside the organization. Examples of output are a sales journal, sales order, general journal, tax return, and budget variance report.

Output controls Control activities that relate to providing output to the appropriate people and using the output appropriately.

Output data An information processing activity that retrieves, formats, and distributes data to users. Output is an interface between the users and the accounting system.

Outsourcing Transferring a function (or functions) to a third party service provider. Examples include having an outside company process payroll or transferring the tech support function overseas.

Packing slip (also known as shipping document) A document that accompanies goods in transit.

Parallel simulation A technique for auditing through the computer where the auditor attempts to simulate or duplicate the firm's output using another computer program to test actual data and compares the results to those produced by the firm's computer system.

Payroll subsystem The business process that is concerned with the payment of wages, salaries, and sales commissions to employees and the related withholding of taxes and other deductions. It includes the custody and disposition of liabilities arising from amounts withheld from employee earnings. It also includes depositing tax withholdings and reporting withholding data to the appropriate federal, state, and local taxing authorities.

Personally identifiable information (PII) Information, such as credit card information, that can be used to identify a person. Cybercriminals compromise/steal information to impersonate someone else and use that information to open unauthorized accounts and credit cards.

Petabytes Approximately 1000 terabytes or 2 to the 50th power bytes.

Phishing An information security breach where a request (an email, for example) for personal information such as passwords or bank account numbers appears to be legitimate.

Physical controls Devices and measures that protect computer hardware and other assets, such as cash, inventories, securities, fixed assets, mechanical check signers, and signature plates.

Physical structure The way the data are physically stored on storage devices.

Picking list A list that identifies the products and quantities ordered and gives the warehouse location, aisle number, shelf position, bin number, or other reference to the location of the goods. The list is used to facilitate the filling of orders for shipment.

Platform-as-a-service (PaaS) A cloud service that offers tools, which includes the operating system, for the client to configure their data storage and develop applications on the cloud provider's servers. This service is usually scalable across multiple servers.

Point-to-point A transmission system wherein a customer's computer is connected directly via a dedicated line to a vendor's computer so electronic documents can be exchanged.

Post-identification (Post-ID) A method of recording open item receipts on account. You simply enter the customer ID and the remittance total. The AIS records the entry as an open receipt and it is identified as such in the customer account. After the receipt entries are proofed, corrected, and posted, clerical employees browse the customer accounts and, using the remittance advices, match open receipts with open invoices.

Predictive analysis The process of harnessing the power of big data to predict trends and behavior such as buying patterns or potential insider threats.

Pre-identification (Pre-ID) A method of recording open item receipts on account. You are required to identify the open invoices to which the receipt applies before entering the receipt.

Prescriptive analytics Using big data to prescribe solutions to issues noted by predictive analysis.

Preventive control A control that deals with or stops potential problems through the controls in place.

Primary key One or a group of data elements that uniquely identify a record.

Private key A key that performs both encryption and decryption (restoring the encrypted message to clear text) in symmetric encryption and decryption in asymmetric encryption.

Process data An information processing activity that transforms data according to a prescribed set of instructions. Some of the basic types of processing are classification, comparison, summarization, and calculation.

Process owner The individual responsible for the application software for a business process.

Processing controls Control activities that refer to the accurate and complete processing of transactions and other events. Examples are written procedures, pre-numbered documents, batch controls, control total analysis, visual checking, and redundant processing.

Procurement process (purchasing, expenditure, or acquisition process) A business process that encompasses activities related to the acquisition of goods and services and the disbursement of money in exchange for these goods and services.

Production control subsystem A subsystem in the inventory process of a manufacturing organization. It handles the initiation of production orders in the factory and the tracking and control of production operations. It also includes the preparation of bills of materials, preparation of labor and machine schedules, and the routing of products through the factory.

Program file A file that contains instructions to tell the computer how to process the data stored in the accounting system.

Provisional posting (pencil posting) A feature that applies only when batch posting is used. Transaction files are posted to the general ledger accounts so that provisional financial statements can be printed. If errors are noted, corrections can be made to the transaction files, which are posted again. When the user is satisfied that the statements are correct, "ink posting" occurs. Errors discovered after "ink" posting occurs must be remedied with correcting or reversing entries.

Proxy server A server that acts as a go-between between a user and the Internet for security purposes. The proxy server receives the request for the Internet service; evaluates the request; makes the request from the Internet; receives the response; and then forwards the response to the user.

Public Company Accounting Oversight Board (PCAOB) An organization created by the Sarbanes-Oxley Act of 2002 to issue auditing standards, oversee quality control, and set independence standards for auditors of public companies.

Public key A key that performs encryption, that is, scrambling a clear text message in asymmetric encryption.

Purchase order A document that a customer issues to request goods or services. The essential data elements in a purchase order are the customer's and vendor's names and addresses, the goods or services being ordered, and the expected delivery or performance date.

Purchase order processing subsystem A subsystem in the procurement process that is concerned with the issuance and tracking of purchase orders to vendors, or suppliers. The purchase order processing subsystem may extend to the negotiation and monitoring of agreements with subcontractors.

Purchasing process See procurement process.

Query language A high-level, English-like language that enables users to make ad hoc, spur of the moment, requests from a computer.

Radio frequency identification (RFID) Considered the "next generation of barcodes," RFID is a code that identifies not only a class or type of product but also an individual product as it moves along the supply chain and ends up in the possession of a n individual.

Reasonable assurance An acceptable level of risk where benefits and costs are equal.

Receiving report A report that documents the receipt of goods that were purchased. The essential data elements are a description of the goods, the quantity received, the quality, or condition, of the goods, and the date received.

Receiving subsystem A subsystem in the procurement process that is concerned with the receipt, inspection, and acceptance of goods and the distribution of the goods within the organization.

Record count A count made at different points in the system. If the count remains the same, this indicates the same total records are in the batch. This count helps guard against the accidental loss of records. However, by itself the control does not necessarily confirm that the same records are present.

Record sequencing The process of placing data in a specified order.

Recurring entry A feature that automates recurring journal entries, such as entries for depreciation, amortization, and accrued liabilities. The user sets up and stores recurring entries. They may be set up to run in a batch mode and invoked with a fixed frequency.

Reference file A file that stores data that are used repeatedly for processing transactions. An example is a tax table reference file that is used for processing payroll transactions.

Reference identifier An identifier that leads an accountant or auditor from a data item's specific location in the accounting information system to its preceding or successor location.

Referential integrity A database property that prohibits undesired actions from occurring. For example, referential integrity ensures that sales will be made only to approved and existing customers.

Relationship A connection, or interaction, between tables in a database. These relationships give additional meaning to the data.

Remittance advice A document that shows the invoice or invoices to which a customer's payment will be applied. A remittance advice is usually provided with the invoice so it can be detached and included with the customer's payment.

Reorder point The sum of the safety stock and the lead time stock.

Repudiation A customer's denial that an order was placed for goods or services from a vendor.

Request for proposal (RFP) A solicitation sent to prospective vendors to submit proposals on how specifications relating to a required good or service can best be met and to submit a bid price for supplying the proposed good or service.

Request for quotation (RFQ) A solicitation sent to prospective vendors to submit a bid price for supplying a required good or service.

Resource In the context of database design, that which is involved in a business activity (event). Generally, a resource is an asset, such as inventory, cash, or whatever is acquired, used, or disposed of in an event.

Responsibility reporting The process of reporting to a manager data that measure activities over which the manager has some authority and for which activities the manager is held responsible.

Returns and allowances report A report of merchandise returns and allowances for each product that have been given to customers due to shipment errors and/or defective merchandise.

Revenue process (also selling or selling and collection process) One of the business processes in an accounting system. It pertains to the distribution of resources to customers and others and the collection of earned revenues. The revenue process typically includes the functions of sales, sales order processing, shipping, and accounts receivable.

Risk assessment The systematic identification and analysis of risks that can undermine the achievement of management objectives. The knowledge gained from risk assessment helps management set priorities so it can determine what control activities to implement.

Safety stock The quantity of inventory that is necessary to avoid the loss of sales due to stockouts.

Sales allowance A partial reduction of sales revenue because the goods sold to the customer are damaged or defective but the customer chooses to keep the goods.

Sales analysis subsystem A subsystem in the revenue process. It is a decision support activity that is concerned with the analysis of historical sales data to provide management with information for marketing and similar purposes.

Sales invoice A document used to bill a customer that indicates the dollar amount of a sale and the date the amount is due.

Sales order A document created internally to facilitate the delivery of goods or services. The essential data elements in a sales order are the customer's name and address, the goods or services being ordered, and the expected delivery or performance date.

Sales order processing subsystem A subsystem in the revenue process that is concerned with processing orders received from customers for the subsequent delivery of goods or provision of services.

Sales return A reduction of sales revenue by the full amount of the sale because the customer returns the goods to the seller.

Sales subsystem A subsystem in the revenue process that is concerned with the sale of goods or the provision of services for immediate delivery.

Sarbanes-Oxley Act of 2002 (SOX) Passed in 2002 to protect investors by improving the "transparency" (i.e., accuracy and reliability) of corporate disclosures issued by publicly-held companies after financial disasters such as the Enron debacle.

Schedule of aged accounts payable (also known as vendor aged detail) A report that lists the unpaid vendor invoices by whether they are current, which is typically 0–30 days from the date of the invoice, or whether they are delinquent and, if so, by the number of days.

Schedule of aged accounts receivable (also known as customer aged detail) A report that lists the unpaid sales (customer) invoices by whether they are current, which is typically 0–30 days from the date of the invoice, or whether they are delinquent and, if so, by the number of days.

Schema A definition of the logical view of the data in a database if the schema is at the external level or the conceptual level, or the physical view of the data if the schema is at the internal level; the relationships among the data; the domains for the data elements; and the business rules that apply to the data.

Scratch file A file that is set up during a processing operation to aid in the processing and is purged when the operation is completed.

Segregation of duties (SOD) A control activity in which authorization of transactions, custody of related assets, and modification or creation of related data and program files (or paper-based records) are segregated so that a single individual cannot both perpetrate and conceal an error or inappropriate activity.

Semi-structured data Data that are somewhat unstructured but provide context for analysis; for example, data that have been tagged with XML for reporting purposes.

Sequence code Typically, the most simple coding system used by accountants; a numerical code.

Service level agreement (SLA) A document that is key to protecting an organization interested in outsourcing a good or service. An SLA can require due-diligence reviews, Statement on Standards for Attestation Engagements (SSAE) No. 16 and Service Organization Control (SOC) reports, and specific definitions of deliverables by the third-party service provider.

Shipping document See packing slip.

Shipping subsystem A subsystem in the revenue process that is concerned with the retrieval of goods from the warehouse, the preparation of goods for shipment, the preparation of the paperwork to accompany shipped goods, and the recording of the shipments.

Simple key A primary key that is a single data element.

Smartcard A complete portable computer packaged as a plastic, card-sized container that looks like a credit card and is used to authenticate system users.

SMB A small to medium-size business.

SME A small to midsize enterprise business.

SOC Service Organization Control.

Social engineering An information security breach where a human being poses as a legitimate individual requesting confidential information such as a password.

Soft closing A closing for interim accounting periods in which entries can still be made in the earlier interim periods.

Software agent Software that can perform routine tasks that require intelligence.

Software-as-a-service (SaaS) The most inclusive cloud service that comprises infrastructure, platforms, and applications (i.e., software) from the cloud service provider. The cloud provider handles all levels of computing for the client. This includes the infrastructure (e.g., hardware), the platform (e.g., operating systems), and the software (e.g., installation, updates to the software, and licensing) for the client.

Sorting A file processing activity that consists of rearranging the records in a file into some meaningful sequence, usually in either ascending or descending order of an appropriate data attribute, or key. For example, a vendor master file may be sorted in alphabetical order of the vendor names.

Source document A document that captures data about transactions and other events and about file maintenance for entry into an accounting system. Examples of internally generated source documents are employee time cards, purchase requisitions, receiving reports, and production orders. Externally generated source documents include purchase orders from customers, remittance advices and checks from customers, and debit or credit memos from banks.

Source document automation The electronic capture of data.

Spam The sending of unsolicited bulk information (usually associated with e-mail spam).

SSAE Statement on Standards for Attestation Engagements.

Standing order A purchase order from a customer to a supplier specifying a series of dates and quantities for shipment of goods until notified by the customer to stop.

Statement of cash flows The financial statement that reports the cash receipts and cash payments of an organization during a stated period of time.

Statement of changes in ownership equity The financial statement that summarizes the transactions affecting the accounts in the Ownership Equity section of the Balance Sheet for a stated period of time.

Statement of income The financial statement that reports the profitability of an organization for a stated period of time such as a month or a year.

Statistical account An account used to accumulate physical instead of monetary data. For example, a natural gas revenue account may be followed in the general ledger by an "MCF Gas Sales" account with the balance being in the thousands of cubic feet of gas sold.

Status report A listing of the balances in the master and open files as of a specific point in time. Examples are a balance sheet, an income statement, and an inventory reorder report.

Steering committee A committee that establishes or approves information processing policies and operating standards, approves system projects, sets priorities for implementing systems, evaluates the effectiveness of processing operations, and generally monitors and evaluates processing activities.

Stockout cost The contribution margin lost on sales due to the inability to fill customer orders because the requested items are not available in inventory.

Store data An information processing activity that provides for the storage of data to accommodate the timing differences between the input, process, and output of the data. Stored data should be able to support an organization's operations, mandatory external reporting requirements, and management decision making.

Structured data Data such as numbers and text that are formatted for use in relational databases and spreadsheet analysis.

Sub-account An account that is analogous to a subsidiary ledger account.

Subsidiary ledger A collection of individual accounts that comprise the details for a related control account in the general ledger. The sum of the individual account balances equals the amount of the related control account.

Subsidiary ledger master file A file that stores detailed data about the subsidiary ledger accounts in an accounting system.

Summarization (aggregation) A processing activity in which data are added to produce a summary total. For example, the dollar amounts in the cash disbursements transaction file may be added to produce a daily cash disbursements summary total.

Summary aging report An aging report that presents information about amounts owed by customers and includes only one line for each customer with all invoices for a single customer combined.

Supply chain management system (SCM) A system that extends an organizations' reach outside to suppliers and customers, managing the planning and flow of merchandise inventory.

System documentation Documentation that provides an inside view of the accounting system and is written in precise technical language.

System flowchart A type of graphical system documentation that shows what a system does and how the system does it. It documents complex activities and details the sources of information, the processes involved, and the disposition of the information.

System narrative description The highest level and broadest form of systems documentation. This description is the basic source of information regarding the system's goals and objectives and helps accountants quickly understand the system without being involved with the details of each file or database table and each program.

Systems implementation Systems installation, conversion planning, resolution of operational and software incompatibilities, data transfer to the new system, training of client personnel, testing the new system, and monitoring operations for an initial period.

Tag (or label) In XRL, a unique identifier applied to an item of financial data, such as "net profit." However, a tag is more than a simple identifier. It provides a range of information about the item.

Taxonomy In X RL, a dictionary of element names that represent financial reporting concepts (e.g., cash and cash equivalents, accounts receivable, net income) and are established by the X RL consortium. These taxonomies are used to tag data.

Test data A technique for auditing through the computer where the auditor uses hypothetical transactions to audit the programmed controls and logic.

The Software Alliance (BSA) An association of global software companies that serves as the world's leading antipiracy organization.

Ticket Another name for a receiving report.

Time card A document for recording the time an employee started and stopped working each day and the number of hours worked.

Time-sensitive entries A feature that permits you to make entries in the current period, in past periods and, in some cases, in future periods.

Trade credit Credit extended to an organization's commercial customers.

Trading partners A relationship between two businesses wherein their association is specified by detailed procurement contracts.

Transaction file A file that stores records pertaining to a group of like transactions occurring during a short period of time. Examples are sales, cash receipts, and purchases transaction files A transaction file corresponds to a paper journal.

Transaction set The complete format specifications for any EDI document.

Transitive dependency A situation in a relational database table in which a nonkey data element depends on, or is determined by, another nonkey data element. In other words, an attribute depends on, or is determined by, an attribute other than the primary key.

Trojan horses Malware that appears to be performing normal functions but is in fact illicitly accessing the host machine to save its files on the user's computer or to watch and/or control the user's computer.

Two-factor authentication An authentication method that combines something you know (e.g., a password) with either something you have (e.g., an RSA tag inserted into your computer's USB port that generates a random personal identifica-

tion number every 10 seconds) or something you are (e.g., a biometric, such as a fingerprint).

Universal Product Code (UPC) The bar code symbology and coding system used by the grocery and other industries.

Unstructured data Data such as videos, audio recordings, and photos, which cannot be easily formatted for use with traditional analysis tools such as spreadsheets.

Updating/Posting An information processing activity that updates the balances in master files to reflect transaction activity. For example, cash receipt and cash disbursement amounts are posted to the cash account in the general ledger master file to produce an updated cash balance.

User authentication Verification that the user is who the user claims to be.

User documentation Documentation that describes a system "from the outside, looking in."

User identification A personal identification code that tells the system who the user is.

User rights Rights assigned to each user, group of users, or application to access directories, files/tables, or functions based on a need to know.

Value-added network (VAN) A service provider that expedites the delivery of electronic documents over a private network.

Verification controls Programmed edit and validation routines that verify the correctness of entered data. They test for valid codes, reasonableness of amounts, valid data type (numeric, alphanumeric), valid field length, logical relationships, anticipated contents, and valid date.

Vertical analysis See common-dollar statement.

Virtual data element A data element that is not stored in a database but instead is calculated on demand from other data elements that are stored in the database.

Virtual private network (VPN) An Internet with tunneling (i.e., tunnels of secured data flows using cryptography and authorization algorithms) technology.

Volunteered data Data individuals choose to provide on platforms such as social media.

Warehouse method A method of accounting for inventory stored in multiple locations.

Worms Self-replicating computer programs that can wreak havoc on operating systems, applications, file servers, or the entire system.

XBRL (eXtensible Business Reporting Language) A markup language derived from XML used for the electronic communication of specifically business and financial data. XBRL attaches an identity to words and numbers.

XML (eXtensible Markup Language) A markup language used specifically for Web applications. Extensible simply means users can extend the basic language by defining markup elements themselves.

Index

Instructor Supplements

- Solutions Manual
- PowerPoint™ Lecture Slides
- Test Item File/Test Bank

Student Supplements

- Lecture Guide

⠿ *Textbook Media Press*

The Quality Instructors Expect
At Prices Students Can Afford

Replacing Oligarch Textbooks Since 2004

Cynthia D. Heagy
University of Houston - Clear Lake

Constance M. Lehmann
University of Houston - Clear Lake

Accounting Information Systems 9e:
A Practitioner Emphasis

www.textbookmedia.com

info@textbookmedia.com

Instructor Supplements

- Solutions Manual
- PowerPoint™ Lecture Slides
- Test Item File/Test Bank

Student Supplements

- Lecture Guide

Textbook Media Press

The Quality Instructors Expect
At Prices Students Can Afford

Replacing Oligarch Textbooks Since 2004

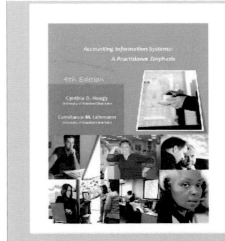

Cynthia D. Heagy
University of Houston - Clear Lake

Constance M. Lehmann
University of Houston - Clear Lake

Accounting Information Systems 9e:
A Practitioner Emphasis

www.textbookmedia.com

info@textbookmedia.com